DOGMAS
AND DREAMS

DOGMAS
AND DREAMS
A READER IN MODERN POLITICAL IDEOLOGIES

Third Edition

edited by

Nancy S. Love
Pennsylvania State University

A Division of Congressional Quarterly Inc.
Washington, D.C.

CQ Press
1255 22nd Street, NW, Suite 400
Washington, DC 20037

Phone, 202-729-1900; toll-free, 1-866-427-7737 (1-866-4CQ-PRESS)

Web: www.cqpress.com

Text credits can be found on page 739.

Cover design by Naylor Design Inc.

Composition by Circle Graphics

♾ The paper used in this publication exceeds the requirements of the American National
Standard for Information Sciences—Permanence of Paper for Printed Library Materials,
ANSI Z39.48-1992.

Printed and bound in the United States of America

09   08   07   06   05   1   2   3   4   5

Library of Congress Cataloging-in-Publication Data

Dogmas and dreams / edited by Nancy S. Love.— 3rd ed.
        p. cm.
    Includes bibliographical references.
    ISBN 1-56802-998-5 (alk. paper)
    1. Political science. 2. Ideology. 3. Right and left (Political science) I. Love,
Nancy Sue. II. Title.

    JA66.D64 2005
    320.5—dc22

                                                            2005015155

To my teachers
and
my students

CONTENTS

Preface   xiii

Introduction: Ideology and Democracy   1

Part One—Liberalism   11

1. John Locke
   Treatise of Civil Government   17

2. John Stuart Mill
   On Liberty   29

3. James Madison, Alexander Hamilton, and John Jay
   The Federalist Papers, nos. 10 and 51   57

4. Thomas Hill Green
   "Lecture on Liberal Legislation and Freedom of Contract"   67

5. Franklin D. Roosevelt
   "The Continuing Struggle for Liberalism"   76

6. Milton Friedman
   Capitalism and Freedom   86

7. Isaac Kramnick
   "Equal Opportunity and the 'Race of Life'"   109

Part Two—Conservatism   123

8. Michael Oakeshott
   "On Being Conservative"   129

9. Edmund Burke
   Reflections on the Revolution in France   152

10. Irving Kristol
    "The Neoconservative Persuasion:
    What it was, and what it is"   165

11. Phyllis Schlafly
    The Power of the Positive Woman   170

12. Allan Bloom
    "The Democratization of the University"   185

Part Three—Socialism   207

13. Charles Fourier
    "Utopian Socialism"   213

14. Karl Marx
    "Estranged Labor"   236

15. Karl Marx and Friedrich Engels
    The Communist Manifesto   249

16. Karl Marx
    "Value, Price, and Profit"   276

17. V. I. Lenin
    State and Revolution   293

18. V. I. Lenin
    Imperialism, the Highest Stage of Capitalism:
    A Popular Outline   308

19. Eduard Bernstein
    Evolutionary Socialism   314

20. Tom Hayden and Dick Flacks
    "The Port Huron Statement at 40"   333

Part Four—Anarchism   347

21. Emma Goldman
    "Anarchism: What It Really Stands For"   353

22. Henry David Thoreau
    "Essay on Civil Disobedience"   365

23. Petyr Kropotkin
    Mutual Aid   373

24. Mikhail Bakunin
    "Scientific Anarchism"   385

Part Five—Fascism   401

25. Benito Mussolini
    Fascism: Doctrine and Institutions   409

26. Adolf Hitler
    Mein Kampf   419

27. Andrew Macdonald
    The Turner Diaries   453

28. Bob Moser
    "Age of Rage: Young Extremists Find New Targets—
    and New Recruits"   467

Part Six—Feminism   471

29. Mary Wollstonecraft
    Vindication of the Rights of Woman   481

30. Betty Friedan
    "Our Revolution Is Unique"   489

31. Heidi Hartmann
    "The Unhappy Marriage of Marxism and Feminism:
    Towards a More Progressive Union"   497

32. Monique Wittig
    "One Is Not Born a Woman"   517

33. Audre Lorde
    "Age, Race, Class, and Sex: Women Redefining
    Difference"   522

34. Gloria Anzaldúa

   "*La Conciencia de la Mestiza*: Towards a
      New Consciousness"   531

35. Chandra Talpade Mohanty

   "'Under Western Eyes' Revisited: Feminist Solidarity through
      Anticapitalist Struggles"   544

Part Seven—Environmentalism and Ecology   569

36. Ralph Waldo Emerson

   Nature   575

37. Rachel Carson

   Silent Spring   585

38. Al Gore

   Earth in the Balance: Ecology and the Human Spirit   592

39. Petra Kelly

   "Thinking Green!"   605

40. Murray Bookchin and Dave Foreman

   *Defending the Earth: A Dialogue Between Murray Bookchin and
      Dave Foreman*   610

41. Vandana Shiva

   Stolen Harvest: The Hijacking of the Global Food Supply   628

Part Eight—Nationalism and Globalization   641

42. Joseph Mazzini

   The Duties of Man   647

43. Benedict Anderson

   *Imagined Communities: Reflections on the Origin and Spread of
      Nationalism*   654

44. Kenichi Ohmae

   The End of the Nation State: The Rise of Regional Economies   663

45. Sulayman Nyang
"Religion and the Maintenance of Boundaries:
An Islamic View"   673

46. Edward W. Said
"Origins of Terrorism"   683

47. Samuel P. Huntington
"The Clash of Civilizations?"   696

48. Benjamin R. Barber
"Jihad Vs. McWorld"   710

49. Fred R. Dallmayr
"Globalization: Curse or Promise?"   722

Credits   739

PREFACE

THE EVENTS OF 9/11 and the "war on terror" have dramatically changed global politics and, with it, the meaning of political ideologies. The power of global capitalism, the rise of new fundamentalisms, the erosion of national sovereignty, the decline in electoral participation, and the increasing prominence of cultural politics and social movements—these developments and many others challenge the traditional left/right ideological spectrum. It is, then, no surprise that some scholars anticipate the "end of ideology." They need only point to the proliferation of prefixes—the *neos* and *posts*—to support their position.

Similar predictions were common when this reader first appeared in 1991, shortly after the demise of the former Soviet Union. Yet the traditional ideologies of left and right—liberalism and conservatism, socialism and fascism—have persisted. They have continued to evolve in response to events, and they still inform our political discourse. However, today they are increasingly accompanied by new variants, by ideologies that are redefining the political spectrum and challenging concepts of politics-as-usual. This process had already begun in 1998 when the second edition of this reader appeared, and so it included an updated feminism section, with selections from black and postcolonial feminists, and a new section on environmentalism and ecology. Both heralded a politics "beyond left and right," an alternative politics now moving, in bell hooks's famous phrase, "from margin to center."

The continuation of this tendency, combined with recent political events, has prompted more significant changes in the third edition. To address the changing nature of political ideologies post-9/11, I have added a section on nationalism and globalization, which provides multiple perspectives on the "new" fundamentalisms and the politics of global capital and culture, including selections from Sulayman Nyang, Edward Said, Samuel Huntington, Benjamin Barber, and Fred Dallmayr. I have also further expanded the feminism and environmentalism and ecology sections to emphasize the increasing role these ideologies now play in the transformation of mainstream politics. Finally, I have updated the selections from traditional left/right ideologies to illustrate how they continue to respond to new political challenges. Their persistence alongside the newer alternatives, I argue, reaffirms the importance of ideologies in contemporary politics. Given their close association with the politics of nation-states, traditional ideologies may be increasingly supplanted by fresh conceptual approaches that better reflect our changing political future. Nevertheless, there is ample evidence that political ideologies continue to set the terms of public discourse for democratic citizens in our ever expanding global world.

I would like to thank individually some of the teachers and students to whom I dedicate this book. Isaac Kramnick introduced me to the study of ideologies when I assisted in his course "Liberalism and Its Critics" at Cornell University. He is a superb teacher, and his influence on me was profound. My thanks here for its subtler forms, which could not be cited and included in the text itself. I also want to thank my students at Pennsylvania State University. Those enrolled in my ideologies course tested the selections for earlier editions and evaluated my introductions to them. Rochelle Quiggle and Lisa Leipold provided valuable research assistance and helped, along with Tracey Dolan, Ellen Foley, Eric Georgette, and Regina Moore, to prepare the manuscript.

For a project such as this, staff support is especially important. Barbara Ayalla typed much of the initial text. Jo Ann Harris and Debbie Price took over at critical points when it seemed it would never be completed. Darlene Irby-Adesalu supervised the whole process with grace and good humor.

At Chatham House, the original publishers, my thanks to Nancy Benson, Chris Kelaher, Melissa Martin, and Katharine Miller for seeing the first two editions successfully through the production process and to the late Edward Artinian for his confidence in the project itself.

Thanks for more recent backing by CQ Press, especially to Brenda Carter, whose support has made this third edition possible. Thanks as well to Charisse Kiino for soliciting and providing excellent suggestions for revisions, to Colleen Ganey for her assistance with the editorial process, to Joan Gossett for supervising the production process, and, once again, to Katharine Miller for copyediting the revised manuscript. Last, I could not have asked for a better research assistant than Sushmita Chatterjee for the new nationalism and globalization section.

Nancy S. Love
July 2005

DOGMAS
AND DREAMS

INTRODUCTION
IDEOLOGY AND DEMOCRACY

IDEOLOGY AND DEMOCRACY. These terms share a long history. What do they mean? How are they related? Etymologically, *democracy* means rule by the people, or *demos*. Although this seems relatively clear, controversy continues over who the people are and how they should rule. *Ideology* is an even more confusing word. The *Oxford English Dictionary* provides two standard definitions. The first is descriptive or neutral: ideology is the "science of ideas." This definition—indeed, the word itself—originated with Antoine Destutt de Tracy, an eighteenth-century French philosopher. Contemporary social scientists who study ideologies as "belief systems" follow this usage. The second definition is critical or deprecatory: ideology is "ideal or abstract speculation" and "unpractical or visionary theorizing."[1] This better fits popular usage, which includes pejorative references to ideologues as advocates, even dogmatists. Both definitions are common today, but there is some historical distance between them. As John Thompson points out, few now proudly proclaim themselves ideologues.[2] Yet Tracy and his followers once did just that. Why were they proud to be Ideologues? How did ideology become a pejorative term? In answering these questions, I also address another: Why study ideologies? The answers to all these questions concern the relationship between ideology and democracy.

The History of Ideology

The history of ideology begins with Tracy's notion that ideas originate in sensory experience and that their origins can be studied scientifically. Tracy contrasted ideology with metaphysics: "Ideology was very sensible since it supposes nothing doubtful or unknown; does not call to mind any [supernatural] idea of cause. . . . Its meaning is very clear to everyone."[3] For Tracy, the professed science of ideas had positive political connotations. Ideology constituted a challenge to existing authorities, for philosophers and priests were superfluous if ideas were "very clear to everyone." And if everyone could understand ideas, then everyone should discuss them and decide among them. Tracy explicitly associated his sensationalist psychology with democratic politics. He was a French revolutionary, a defender of individual freedom and representative government. A friend attested to Tracy's (and his compatriots') political aspirations: "*Ideology* they told me would change the face of the earth, and that is exactly why those who wish the world to always remain stupid (and with good cause) detest ideology and the ideologues."[4]

This history further complicates the definition of ideology by adding a third forgotten meaning. According to Tracy, ideology was a democratic philosophy, a defense of popular intelligence. The "science of ideas," today a neutral definition, originally had positive connotations and only later developed pejorative ones. Napoleon, Tracy's contemporary, first used the term pejoratively, referring to the Ideologues as a "metaphysical faction" and, less flatteringly, as "dangerous dreamers" and "windbags . . . who have always fought the existing authorities."[5] Here, too, the term had political connotations. In his famous denunciation of ideology, Napoleon says:

> We must lay the blame for the ills that our fair France has suffered on ideology, that shadowy metaphysics. . . . Indeed, who was it that proclaimed the principle of insurrection to be a duty? Who adulated the people and attributed to it a sovereignty which it was incapable of exercising? Who destroyed respect for and the sanctity of laws by describing them, not as sacred principles of justice, but only as the will of an assembly composed of men ignorant of civil, criminal, administrative, political, and military law?[6]

Like Tracy, Napoleon links ideology and democracy, but his linkage is a negative one: with their democratic dreams, the Ideologues destroyed the illusions necessary for social order and human happiness.

Were Tracy's Ideologues a "metaphysical faction"? Was democracy a "shadowy metaphysics"? Perhaps. Tracy did regard "ideas as the only things that exist for us, the only means we have to know things."[7] He also spoke of ideology "changing the face of the earth." But this is not our concern here. History has vindicated democracy; today it is a reality. Yet history has also preserved the negative connotations of ideology. Today, Tracy would no doubt agree that democrats should not be ideologues—at least not in Napoleon's pejorative sense. The continuing history of ideology reveals its incompatibility with democracy.

Karl Marx, a nineteenth-century German philosopher, took the next significant step in that history. Marx knew Tracy's work and probably adopted the term from him. Like Napoleon, Marx criticized the Ideologues' idealism; he too associated ideology with metaphysics. But Marx disagreed with Napoleon about the origins of such metaphysical illusions: he traced them to class conflict, not to democratic politics. His significant step was this socioeconomic explanation of ideology. According to Marx, ideologies have three general characteristics: they are social, functional, and illusory forms of consciousness. Marx argues that societies develop forms of consciousness suited to their historical circumstances. Class relations are the most important influences on social consciousness. Marx says, "The ideas of the ruling class are in every epoch the ruling ideas, i.e., the class which is the ruling material force of society, is at the same time its ruling intellectual force."[8] Ideologies function for the ruling class as illusions, helping to legitimate that class by making its rule seem natural and its interests seem general.

In fact, every ruling class protects its own interests, and history involves conflict between classes. For Marx, then, ideology is an obstacle to democracy. It prevents the oppressed class from understanding and challenging the sources of its oppression. Indeed, Marx fears that democracy itself may become an ideology. As you see in the selections by him in this book, Marx distinguishes between political emancipation and human emancipation. Political emancipation grants individual rights but without eliminating economic oppression; freedom remains illusory because economic circumstances prevent people from exercising it. For example, we are not "free to choose" where we work or the conditions under which we work if we must work to live and we live in a company town. In contrast, human emancipation involves a genuine—that is, economic and political—democracy. It involves providing people with the economic security they require to choose freely. Only after people see through the ideological illusion of rights, Marx argues, will they organize truly to emancipate themselves.

The question that arises here is: Why would people believe ideological illusions? Sigmund Freud, the next major figure in the history of ideology, offers an answer. Freud's focus is religion, not ideology, but he suggests that the two belief systems have a common origin: "Having recognized religious doctrines to be illusions, we are at once confronted with the further question: may not all cultural possessions, which we esteem highly and by which we let our life be ruled, be of a similar nature? Should not the assumptions that regulate our political institutions likewise be called illusions?"[9] To understand this need for illusions, it is necessary to look briefly at Freud's psychological theory.

According to Freud, the psyche has three parts: id, ego, and superego. The id contains the basic instincts, eros (libido), and thanatos (aggression). The ego mediates between those instincts and reality, balancing internal desires and external demands. The superego is the conscience, the site of internalized social values, which helps the ego control the id. For Freud, social life requires that individuals repress and/or redirect their instincts. Needless to say, this is a painful process. However, along with its many prohibitions, society provides substitute gratifications. Ideologies, the locus of social values, help to discipline individuals, but they also provide a sense of security and identity—they give life meaning. Such shared meanings, Freud argues, are fundamental for psychological well-being. According to Freud, most individuals do not really want to be free; freedom can be frightening. Indeed, later Freudians have explained the appeal of fascism as an "escape from freedom." Freud's concept of ideology is, then, also in some tension with democracy: ideologies allow individuals simply to accept existing values, sparing them the responsibility of creating their own.

Of the many other figures in the history of ideology, I discuss only one: Karl Mannheim.[10] His work is important because he states what Marx and Freud imply: ideology is often a conservative force in history. Mannheim's basic distinction is between ideology and utopia. In his usage, an ideological perspective values the status quo and reinforces it by obscuring other alternatives. In contrast, a utopian perspective values what does not yet exist and promotes the changes necessary to create it. Utopias also obscure; they neglect ideological (and other) barriers to change. But, whereas ideologies restrict political activity, utopias encourage it. Again, democracy, which requires an active citizenry, is incompatible with ideology.

Popular intelligence to popular illusions—that summarizes the history of ideology. Tracy's democratic philosophy is followed by Napoleon's shadowy metaphysics, Marx's false consciousness, Freud's wish fulfillment, and Mannheim's social conformity. In each of these later philosophies Napoleon's pejorative usage persists but assumes a new meaning. Their recurring theme is not the association of ideology and democracy, but the opposition between them. Today, it seems, democrats should not be ideologues. So, why study ideology?

Why Study Ideology?

Ideologies are important in modern politics, and that is the standard reason for studying them. Political scientists identify several functions of ideologies. The most important is political legitimation: ideologies outline basic values by which politics should proceed. Another, related function is that ideologies help to socialize individuals, giving them a shared identity. Language is a major component of this identity: ideologies provide shared meanings that facilitate communication between individuals. Ideologies also mobilize people, whether by class, group, nation, party, race, or sex. Unlike Mannheim, political scientists argue that, in performing these functions, ideologies can be sources of both stability and instability, concord and conflict. According to Roy Macridis, "The dynamics of politics . . . lie in the ideas people develop."[11] Leon Baradat concludes, "A clear understanding of current ideologies is essential to anyone who hopes to grasp the political realities of our time."[12]

This is true. We live, for better or worse, in an ideological age. Ideologies are a crucial part of the study of modern politics. But there is another, more important, reason for studying ideologies: democracy. Political scientists' standard definitions of ideology include "a set of closely related beliefs, or ideas, or even attitudes, *characteristic of* a group or community" and "a value or belief system *accepted as* fact or truth by some group."[13] These definitions parallel the neutral—and neutralized—usage offered in the *Oxford English Dictionary*. They also suggest that everyone has an ideology. That *you* have an ideology. But what is it? And why do you have it? Because it is "characteristic" or "accepted"? In a democracy, this answer is inadequate. What such definitions ignore is the political problem, the problem of democracy, raised by Tracy. Ideologies not only perform certain functions; they also raise claims to truth that require justification. In a democracy, these claims should not be ascribed to you or imposed on you. They can be justified only through discussion. By studying ideologies, you can discuss their various claims and decide among them.

Even democracy—to be true to itself—must be a topic of discussion. It is not enough to be a democrat. Democracy, as John Stuart Mill tells us, does not thrive on dogma. Instead, democrats must learn to think democratically. This means resurrecting ideology as Tracy's democratic philosophy, as the demonstration of ideas. Such demonstrations are more difficult today, for most people no longer share Tracy's confidence in sensory experience. Empiricism, along with metaphysics, has lost its power. Our evaluative standards come from ourselves—from our considered, collective judgment. Nevertheless, since ideas should not be ascribed to us or imposed on us, we can specify conditions for exercising that judgment.

Jürgen Habermas has attempted to do just that. As part of his theory of democratic discourse, he describes an ideal speech situation, which fulfills three conditions. First, anyone should be able to raise any issue for discussion. Second, during discussions, everyone should speak sincerely and seek understanding. Third, any decisions reached should apply equally to all. Habermas describes these conditions as "symmetrical relations in the distribution of assertion and dispute, revelation and concealment, prescription and conformity among the partners of communication."[14] They are, he argues, linguistic approximations of truth, freedom, and justice. Of course, there are many obstacles to overcome before actual democracies could even approximate these ideal conditions. Without equal educational opportunities and some economic security, many individuals will have neither the ability nor the energy to debate basic political values. Still, Habermas's ideal speech situation illustrates the challenges involved in thinking democratically and in recovering a positive sense of ideology.

One of these challenges is thinking about the meaning of democracy itself. By associating ideology with science, Tracy presents democracy as a neutral, even objective, process. This was probably an effective strategy when the Ideologues needed to mobilize support for the French Revolution. However, the continuing history of democratic revolutions suggests that the meaning of democracy is far from obvious. Although many ideologies included here claim to be democratic, they define democracy in profoundly different ways. Liberal democracy, democratic socialism, anarchist direct action, feminist consciousness-raising, environmental justice, global cosmopolitanism, to mention a few—all involve different concepts of democratic politics. Such variety suggests that democracy is not itself an ideology, but is better understood as an "essentially contestable concept" or an "inherently debatable and changeable idea."[15] Even ideologies that reject democratic institutions—such as fascism—offer critiques that contribute to the debate. Writing in the wake of German fascism, Habermas recognized the need for a public discourse about democratic politics. He insisted that the procedures for his ideal speech situation also be a topic of ongoing democratic discussion.

Political Ideology and Political Theory

Unfortunately, political theorists often denigrate the study of political ideology, making it difficult to regain a positive sense of the concept. It has become customary to distinguish political ideologies from political theories. According to Roy Macridis, "What separates theory or philosophy from ideology is that while the first two involve contemplation, organization of ideas, and whenever possible, demonstration, ideology incites people to action."[16] He adds that because of their collective, active nature "ideologies are inevitably highly simplified, and even distorted, versions of the original [philosophical] doctrines."[17]

David Ingersoll and Donald Matthews agree that "ideology is rather easily distinguished from traditional philosophy." They also suggest that "what is often called the Age of Ideology came about as a reaction to classical philosophic thought and its apparent lack of concern with processes by which change could be effected."[18] Again, the distinction from theory rests on the simplification and the action orientation associated with ideology. Lyman Tower Sargent further distinguishes between political ideology (group beliefs), political theory (scientific generalizations), and political philosophy (normative theory). He admonishes students that the first term, political ideology, "should never be used in place of either of the other two terms."[19]

With the theory/ideology distinction, these authors raise an important issue: the relationship between theory and practice. They suggest that ideologies play a mediating role between theory and practice; ideologies help translate ideas into action. To explain this translation process, Macridis examines the debt political ideologies owe to political theories. How, he asks, do ideas become ideologies? He answers that history involves a dialectic between ideas and needs. Only when the two forces converge is an ideology created. Otherwise, "heartfelt demands arising from the social body may fail for the lack of ideas; and ideas may go begging for a long time for the lack of relevance to social needs."[20] He concludes that a philosophy becomes an ideology when it provides a framework for political action to meet social needs.

Still, too much can be made of the theory/ideology distinction. Some scholars recognize that political theory is seldom above the political fray. Often the best way to understand a theory is to see it in historical context. According to Richard Ashcraft, the dominance of philosophical methods in political theory has led to the denigration of political ideologies. Ashcraft notes that these methods divorce theory from history and politics. Political theorists "link historically-rooted political theory with ideology, and great political theory with trans-historical philosophy."[21] This, he argues, is a difficult distinction to sustain. It is also a self-serving one, for it allows theorists to ignore the relationship between their ideas and their context. Their work, it implies, is above politics or outside history. For this reason, political theorists do not need to be self-critical. The distinction between political theory and political ideology can, then, be undemocratic, when it allows theorists to avoid thinking democratically about their assumptions, indeed about the very distinction between great philosophical and minor ideological texts. This suggests another reason to study ideologies. Reading texts historically, for their political implications, promotes a democratic political theory. It encourages theorists to consider whose interests certain ideas serve.

How to Study Ideology

I have suggested three reasons for studying political ideologies: to understand modern politics, to think democratically, and to democratize political theory. But how should ideologies be studied? What should you look for? How should you look for it?

Regarding the first question—what to look for—you already know to explore the historical context for these political ideologies. You should also examine three aspects of the ideologies themselves. Ideologies generally include these elements: (1) a critique of existing society, (2) a vision of a better future, and (3) a strategy for getting from here to there. All three are usually informed by an underlying concept of human nature. Try to organize your reading of these texts around these components.[22]

To understand ideologies, you also need to look at them in a particular way. You should practice "connected knowing."[23] Most of us are (or have learned to be) "separate knowers." Knowledge for us involves separation from the subject—here, an ideology—and mastery over it. Our epistemological stance is to doubt, to criticize. As my students tell me, they read Karl Marx to understand how he is different and why he is wrong. Genuine understanding, however, involves intimacy and equality between self and subject. A "connected knower" cares about how others understand themselves and tries to see them in their own terms. Connected knowers are, for the purposes of understanding, believers. To study ideologies effectively, you need to approach them this way, to enter into their different world views. Does she mean, you ask, that I should become a Marxist? Yes. And a liberal, a conservative, a fascist, an anarchist, a feminist, and an environmentalist. At least temporarily. Separate knowing is extremely important; you need to develop your critical capacities. But it is an inappropriate way to begin studying an ideology because you need to understand a subject—and that means suspending disbelief—before you can criticize it effectively. In the process, you may also find that it has something to offer.

Studying ideologies this way is risky business. It changes people. You become aware of your own assumptions and begin to assess them. But you should demand no less of yourself. Ignorance may be bliss—but an unexamined life is not worth living. Again, democracy does not thrive on dogma.

What Ideologies to Study

The ideologies represented here were chosen for two reasons. First, all are important in modern politics. The selections for each ideology cover both its historical origins and its contemporary manifestations. Second, these ideologies represent a range of political beliefs. As you read, disagreements will emerge. For example, conservatives and socialists will attack liberals' concept of individual freedom. Anarchists will question liberal democracy and proletarian dictatorship because both legitimate state power. Fascists will accuse liberals and socialists of denigrating the state. Feminists will suggest that the other ideologies, with the possible exception of anarchism, exclude the concerns of women and minorities. Ecologists who claim "we are neither left nor right, we are in front" will challenge existing approaches to ideology. The impact of globalization on the nation-state, the standard context for ideological politics, will also suggest the need to redefine the meaning of ideology. These are only a few of the differences you will discover. By studying these ideologies, by exploring their assumptions and comparing their positions, you will begin to understand political alternatives and be able to choose among them. You will learn to think democratically, even about democracy itself.

NOTES

1. *Oxford English Dictionary*, 1933, s.v. "Ideology."

2. John B. Thompson, *Studies in the Theory of Ideology* (Berkeley: University of California Press, 1984), 1.

3. Antoine Destutt de Tracy, "Mémoire sur la Faculté de penser," MIN (*Mémoires de l'Institut national. Classe des Sciences morales et politiques*, 5 vols. [Paris: 1798–1804]), 1:323, quoted in Emmet Kennedy, " 'Ideology' from Destutt de Tracy to Marx," *Journal of the History of Ideas* 40 (July–September 1979): 353–368, quote on 354–355. For a more extensive discussion of Tracy, see Emmet Kennedy, *A Philosophe in the Age of Revolution: Destutt de Tracy and the Origins of Ideology* (Philadelphia: American Philosophical Society, 1978).

4. Biran to Abbe Feletz, 11 thermidor X [30 July 1802], *Œuvres de Maine de Biran*, VI, 140, quoted in Kennedy, " 'Ideology,' " 357–358.

5. Quoted in Kennedy, " 'Ideology,' " 358.

6. Napoleon, "Reponse a l'adresse du Conseil d'État," in *Moniteur* (21 decembre 1812), 1408, quoted in Kennedy, " 'Ideology,' " 360.

7. Kennedy, " 'Ideology,' " 364.

8. Karl Marx and Friedrich Engels, *The German Ideology*, ed. C. J. Arthur (New York: International Publishers, 1977), 64.

9. Sigmund Freud, *The Future of an Illusion*, trans. W. D. Robson-Scott (New York: Liveright, 1955), 59. My remarks here parallel those of Mostafa Rejai, s.v. "Ideology," in the *Dictionary of the History of Ideas*, vol. 2, 1973.

10. Karl Mannheim, *Ideology and Utopia*, trans. Louis Wirth and Edward Shils (London: Routledge and Kegan Paul, 1948).

11. Roy Macridis, *Contemporary Political Ideologies*, 4th ed. (Glenview, Ill.: Scott, Foresman, 1989), 12.

12. Leon P. Baradat, *Political Ideologies: Their Origins and Impact*, 3rd ed. (Englewood Cliffs, N.J.: Prentice Hall, 1994), x.

13. John Petrov Plamenatz, *Ideology* (New York: Praeger, 1970), 15; and Lyman Tower Sargent, *Contemporary Political Ideologies: A Comparative Analysis*, 10th ed. (Belmont, Calif.: Wadsworth, 1996), 3. Italics mine.

14. Jürgen Habermas, "Towards a Theory of Communicative Competence," *Inquiry* 13 (1970): 371.

15. Anthony Arblaster, *Democracy* (Minneapolis: University of Minnesota Press, 1987), 5.

16. Macridis, *Contemporary Political Ideologies*, 3.

17. Ibid.

18. David Ingersoll and Donald Matthews, *The Philosophic Roots of Modern Ideology: Liberalism, Communism, Fascism* (Englewood Cliffs, N.J.: Prentice Hall, 1986), 7.

19. Sargent, *Contemporary Political Ideologies*, 11. Sargent also acknowledges that many use the latter two terms interchangeably, as I do.

20. Macridis, *Contemporary Political Ideologies*, 3.

21. Richard Ashcraft, "Political Theory and the Problem of Ideology," *Journal of Politics* 42 (August 1980): 687–705.

22. Alison M. Jaggar, *Feminist Politics and Human Nature* (Totowa, N.J.: Rowman and Allenheld, 1983), 16.

23. For this distinction, see Mary Field Belenky et al., *Women's Ways of Knowing* (New York: Basic Books, 1986), chap. 6. These authors argue that "connected knowing" is more common among women.

PART ONE

Liberalism

LIBERAL DEMOCRACY. Liberalism *and* democracy; liberalism *or* democracy. How, if at all, do liberalism and democracy fit together? In an American setting this is a difficult question, since variations on liberal themes dominate the political spectrum. It helps to consider liberalism in historical context as Isaac Kramnick, the last author included in this part, does. Kramnick distinguishes between two faces of liberalism. The first is progressive: liberalism as a democratic transformation from an old aristocratic and monarchical order. The second is regressive: liberalism as the consolidation of a new status quo, now presumably based on merit. Liberal principles—individual freedom, competitive markets, and limited government—remain the same. Depending on the context, however, their political implications are dramatically different.

John Locke's *Treatise of Civil Government* represents progressive liberalism. In the Glorious Revolution of 1688, the English Parliament deposed James II and replaced him with William of Orange; in exchange for the crown, William accepted parliamentary government and a bill of rights. Although parts of it may have been written earlier, scholars agree that Locke's *Treatise of Civil Government* is a defense of that political transformation.[1] In it he rejects hierarchical notions of society and argues that individuals are born free and equal in a state of nature. That is, "a state of liberty, yet it is not a state of license." Individuals are free, but not to do whatever they please. A law of nature exists that "being all equal and independent, no one ought to harm another in his life, health, liberty, or possessions." But not everyone obeys this law. Conflicts frequently arise, and life is very insecure. Ultimately, the state of nature is indistinguishable from a state of war. For this reason, people form governments to protect their rights to life, liberty, and, especially, property.

Because Lockean government is limited to protecting those rights, it fits well with certain economic relations—for example, the free exchange of private property. Locke's individuals own themselves and hence their labor and its products. In the state of nature, everyone is free to accumulate property, but everyone does not accumulate an equal amount. In chapter 5, "Of Property," from his *Treatise,* Locke explains how accumulation eventually re-creates a hierarchy in which some labor for others.[2] This hierarchy, however, is a meritocracy, not an aristocracy or monarchy: here, status is achieved, not ascribed. According to Locke, equal opportunity justifies unequal outcomes. As he put it, God gave the world "to the use of the industrious and rational . . . not to the fancy or covetousness of the quarrelsome and contentious." Locke concludes that those with more property have proven themselves more rational and so they should also possess more rights. Women, slaves, and nonpropertied men (laborers) have an equal right to life, but are generally less free economically and politically. Locke's sovereign people, those who expressly consent to government, are educated, white, men with substantial property. In other words, liberalism was far from democratic at its origins. Yet the principle of individual freedom articulated by Locke required later liberals eventually to extend rights to anyone who demanded them.

Gradually, liberalism has been democratized.[3] The English Reform Acts of 1832 and 1867 expanded the suffrage, although only to more white males. Writing in the wake of these acts, John Stuart Mill reveals the regressive face of liberalism, its tensions with democratic participation. His *On Liberty* is a classic statement of liberal rights to freedom of assembly, opinion, and speech. However, unlike Locke, who argued that freedom was an individual right, Mill supports liberty on utilitarian grounds: freedom serves a useful function for society. Fearing the tendency of democracy to majority tyranny, Mill defends liberty because it improves individuals and ultimately humanity. Indeed, Mill thinks, "the only unfailing and permanent source of improvement is liberty." His basic principle, that "the sole end for which mankind are warranted, individually or collectively, in interfering with the liberty of action of any of their number, is self-protection," is meant to protect exceptional individuals from the democratic masses.

According to Mill, democratic societies are prone to collective mediocrity and class conflict, since the majority who rule are inevitably the less educated and less wealthy. Representative institutions can improve the quality of democratic politics only when the people choose their leaders wisely. Mill fears that elections alone will not guarantee good public officials. He proposes a system of proportional representation, to guarantee minorities some seats in Parliament, and plural voting, to give the more qualified voters greater influence in elections. For Mill, however, the tensions between liberalism and democracy are temporary. In his autobiography, written with Harriet Taylor, he describes himself as a short-term conservative, and a long-term socialist: "We were now much less democrats than I had been because so long as education continues to be so wretchedly imperfect, we dreaded the ignorance and especially the selfishness and brutality of the masses; but our ideal of ultimate improvement went far beyond Democracy, and would class us decidedly under the designation of Socialist."[4] When the people are ready, they should rule.

America's founding fathers were also acutely aware of the tensions between liberalism and democracy. Jeremy Belknap, a New England clergyman, expressed their sentiments well: "Let it stand as a principle that government originates from the people; but let the people be taught . . . that they are not able to govern themselves."[5] *The Federalist Papers,* published in New York during the ratification debates, present the Constitution as a liberal solution to democratic problems. According to Madison, two difficulties arise in framing a government: "You must first enable the government to control the governed; and in the next place oblige it to control itself." *Federalist* no. 10 addresses the first difficulty: the vulnerability of democracy to the violence of factions. Minority factions pose little problem, since they are easily outvoted. Majority factions are a different story: pure democracies have no cure for them, but representation allows a larger territory, making it unlikely that a majority will exist and organize. Federalism also provides the appropriate distance between representatives and constituents: state legislatures are tied to local issues; national government is freed from them. Together, representation and federalism ensure that "a coalition of a majority of the whole society could seldom take place on any other principles than those of justice and the general good." The second difficulty that Madison identifies—"to oblige the government to control itself"—remains, according to Madison, for the populace cannot be counted on to restrain government. The auxiliary precautions discussed in *Federalist* no. 51—separation of powers, checks and balances—are thus required to limit government by pitting "ambition against ambition," thereby "supplying, by opposite and rival interests, the defect of better motives."

The Federalist Papers uphold the new Constitution's balance between liberalism and democracy: government is limited by minority rights and legitimated by majority rule. Has the balance worked? Some critics of liberal-democratic institutions argue that it has worked too well, creating an inefficient government and an apathetic citizenry. More progressive liberals also question the claim that competing interests can produce the common good. In his "Lecture on Liberal Legislation and Freedom of Contract," T. H. Green argues that freedom involves more than the removal of restraints. Freedom is better understood "in the positive sense: in other words, the liberation of the powers of all men equally for contributions to a common good." Freedom of contract is, at best, a means to this higher end and can be restricted to prevent practices that "injure individuals" because such actions also injure society. For example, Green argues that government should regulate working conditions, hours, and wages; provide decent housing and public schools; and prohibit destructive pursuits, such as alcohol consumption. These regulations do not constitute "overlegislation" or "grandmotherly government," he claims, because it is the purpose of government "to maintain the conditions without which a free exercise of the human faculties is impossible."

Franklin Delano Roosevelt's response to the Great Depression was partly based on Green's radical liberalism. Roosevelt's New Deal was intended "not only to save the system, but also to remove from it the abuses, evils, and widespread maladjustments which had brought it to the very brink of destruction." According to Roosevelt, the increased concentration of economic power in a few hands was a major cause of the depression. He argues that liberals believe "the Government has the definite duty to use all its power and resources to meet new social problems with new social controls—to insure to the average person the right to his own economic and political life, liberty, and the pursuit of happiness." His program of progressive reforms—minimum wages and maximum hours, public works projects, farm subsidies, monopoly controls, judicial reforms, cheap housing, etc.—was designed to achieve this goal.

Of course, other liberals have argued that these very reforms undermined economic and political freedoms. Advocating a return to an earlier free-market or classical liberalism, Milton Friedman asserts that a common logic links liberalism and capitalism: "The kind of economic organization that provides economic freedom directly, namely, competitive capitalism, also promotes political freedom because it separates economic power from political power and in this way enables the one to offset the other."[6] Friedman praises markets for coordinating the economy and minimizing government control. Government still must enforce the rules of the game, prevent nontechnical monopolies, guard against neighborhood effects, and protect the helpless—but that is all it needs to do. Friedman contends that government should abolish programs that support business and labor, rich and poor. His list of unjustifiable government interventions ranges from paying agricultural subsidies to establishing minimum wages to creating national parks. What he does not discuss are the disadvantages of markets—such as economic instability and insecurity—which prompted these programs in the first place. He generally assumes that everyone has an equal opportunity to succeed, and, when circumstances suggest otherwise, he concludes that life is simply unfair.

Does each of us have an equal opportunity—and, if not, should government try to equalize our chances? In the final selection, "Equal Opportunity and the 'Race of Life,' " Isaac Kramnick addresses this question in the context of debates over affirmative action and reverse discrimination. According to Kramnick, the freedom to compete economically parallels the freedom to participate politically.

Here, too, a once-progressive liberalism has now become regressive: whereas Locke attacked an old aristocratic elite, Friedman defends a new meritocratic one. Kramnick characterizes the transformation: "A doctrine originally designed to serve the class interests of the talented 'have-nots' against the talented 'haves' now pits the talented 'haves' against the allegedly untalented 'have-nots.'" For liberals, this poses a problem. They see life as a race in which some win, and some lose. But some never start. Or they start late. Or they carry extra weight. Individuals are not born free and equal in a state of nature. They are born with particular advantages or disadvantages—among them, class, race, and gender identities. Yet only equal opportunity can justify unequal outcomes; if the race is rigged, it is unfair. Liberal principles require government action to make it fair. But they also require limited government. In short, welfare-state liberalism conflicts with laissez-faire liberalism. Both are right, and both are wrong. Each, Kramnick argues, articulates a face of liberalism.

What is to be done? Liberals may insist on striving for equality of opportunity, or they may simply conclude that life is unfair. Perhaps liberalism, despite its internal tensions, is the best option. You may ultimately reach that conclusion. Right now, however, it is premature. What if life is not a race? Kramnick asks, "What would a new world view look like?" The other ideologies presented in later parts of this book offer diverse answers to that question.

NOTES

1. John Locke, *Two Treatises of Government*, ed. Peter Laslett (New York: Cambridge University Press, 1988), introduction.

2. For a detailed discussion of this interpretation of Locke, see Crawford Brough MacPherson, *The Political Theory of Possessive Individualism: Hobbes to Locke* (Oxford: Clarendon Press, 1962).

3. Crawford Brough MacPherson, *The Real World of Democracy* (Oxford: Clarendon Press, 1966), chap. 1.

4. Quoted in Sanford A. Lakoff, *Equality in Political Philosophy* (Cambridge, Mass.: Harvard University Press, 1964), 130.

5. Quoted in Richard Hofstadter, *The American Political Tradition and the Men Who Made It* (New York: Knopf, 1948), 7.

6. Friedman also notes the historical connection, i.e., all liberal-democratic countries have capitalist economies. (The obverse is not true.)

1

John Locke

———◆———

Treatise of Civil Government (1690)

John Locke (1632–1704) lived during the Glorious Revolution of 1688, by which the English Parliament deposed King James II and replaced him with William of Orange. In the Treatise of Civil Government *Locke defends the Glorious Revolution and the principles of individual rights and limited government it established.*

Chapter 1
Of Civil-Government

3. POLITICAL POWER, then, I take to be a right of making laws, with penalties of death, and consequently all less penalties for the regulating and preserving of property, and of employing the force of the community in the execution of such laws, and in the defence of the commonwealth from foreign injury, and all this only for the public good.

Chapter 2
Of the State of Nature

4. To understand political power aright, and derive it from its original, we must consider what estate all men are naturally in, and that is, a state of perfect freedom to order their actions, and dispose of their possessions and persons as they think fit, within the bounds of the law of Nature, without asking leave or depending upon the will of any other man.

A state also of equality, wherein all the power and jurisdiction is reciprocal, no one having more than another, there being nothing more evident than that creatures of the same species and rank, promiscuously born to all the same advantages of Nature, and the use of the same facilities, should also be equal one amongst another, without subordination or subjection, unless the lord and master of them all should, by any manifest declaration of his will, set one above another, and confer on him, by an evident and clear appointment, an undoubted right to dominion and sovereignty.

5. This equality of men by Nature, the judicious Hooker looks upon as so evident in itself, and beyond all question, that he makes it the foundation of that obligation to mutual love amongst men on which he builds the duties they owe one another, and from whence he derives the great maxims of justice and charity. His words are:

"The like natural inducement hath brought men to know that it is no less their duty to love others than themselves, for seeing those things which are equal, must needs all have one measure; if I cannot but wish to receive good, even as much at every man's hands, as any man can wish unto his own soul, how should I look to have any part of my desire herein satisfied, unless myself be careful to satisfy the like desire, which is undoubtedly in other men weak, being of one and the same nature: to have anything offered them repugnant to this desire must needs, in all respects, grieve them as much as me; so that if I do harm, I must look to suffer, there being no reason that others should show greater measure of love to me than they have by me showed unto them; my desire, therefore, to be loved of my equals in Nature, as much as possible may be, imposeth upon me a natural duty of bearing to themward fully the like affection. From which relation of equality between ourselves and them that are as ourselves, what several rules and canons natural reason hath drawn for direction of life no man is ignorant." (*Eccl. Pol.* i.)

6. But though this be a state of liberty, yet it is not a state of licence; though man in that state have an uncontrollable liberty to dispose of his person or possessions, yet he has not liberty to destroy himself, or so much as any creature in his possession, but where some nobler use than its bare preservation calls for it. The state of Nature has a law of Nature to govern it, which obliges every one, and reason, which is that law, teaches all mankind who will but consult it, that being all equal and independent, no one ought to harm another in his life, health, liberty or possessions; for men being all the workmanship of one omnipotent and infinitely wise Maker; all the servants of one sovereign Master, sent into the world by His order and about His business; they are His property, whose workmanship they are made to last during His, not one another's pleasure. And, being furnished with like faculties, sharing all in one community of Nature, there can-

not be supposed any such subordination among us that may authorise us to destroy one another, as if we were made for one another's uses, as the inferior ranks of creatures are for ours. Every one as he is bound to preserve himself, and not to quit his station wilfully, so by the like reason, when his own preservation comes not in competition, ought he as much as he can to preserve the rest of mankind, and not unless it be to do justice on an offender, take away or impair the life, or what tends to the preservation of the life, the liberty, health, limb, or goods of another.

7. And that all men may be restrained from invading others' rights, and from doing hurt to one another, and the law of Nature be observed, which willeth the peace and preservation of all mankind, the execution of the law of Nature is in that state put into every man's hands, whereby every one has a right to punish the transgressors of that law to such a degree as may hinder its violation. For the law of Nature would, as all other laws that concern men in this world, be in vain if there were nobody that in the state of Nature had a power to execute that law, and thereby preserve the innocent and restrain offenders; and if any one in the state of Nature may punish another for any evil he has done, every one may do so. For in that state of perfect equality, where naturally there is no superiority or jurisdiction of one over another, what any may do in prosecution of that law, every one must needs have a right to do. . . .

Chapter 3
Of the State of War

16. The state of war is a state of enmity and destruction; and therefore declaring by word or action, not a passionate and hasty, but sedate, settled design upon another man's life puts him in a state of war with him against whom he has declared such an intention, and so has exposed his life to the other's power to be taken away by him, or any one that joins with him in his defence, and espouses his quarrel; it being reasonable and just I should have a right to destroy that which threatens me with destruction; for by the fundamental law of Nature, man being to be preserved as much as possible, when all cannot be preserved, the safety of the innocent is to be preferred, and one may destroy a man who makes war upon him, or has discovered an enmity to his being, for the same reason that he may kill a wolf or a lion, because they are not under the ties of the common law of reason, have no other rule but that of force and violence, and so may be treated as a beast of prey, those dangerous and noxious creatures that will be sure to destroy him whenever he falls into their power.

17. And hence it is that he who attempts to get another man into his absolute power does thereby put himself into a state of war with him; it being to be understood as a declaration of a design upon his life. For I have reason to conclude that he who would get me into his power without my consent would use me as he pleased when he had got me there, and destroy me too when he had a fancy to it; for nobody can desire to have me in his absolute power unless it be to compel me by force to that which is against the right of my freedom—i.e., make me a slave. To be free from such force is the only security of my preservation, and reason bids me look on him as an enemy to my preservation who would take away that freedom which is the fence to it; so that he who makes an attempt to enslave me thereby puts himself into a state of war with me. He that in the state of Nature would take away the freedom that belongs to any one in that state must necessarily be supposed to have a design to take away everything else, that freedom being the foundation of all the rest; as he that in the state of society would take away the freedom belonging to those of that society or commonwealth must be supposed to design to take away from them everything else, and so be looked on as in a state of war.

18. This makes it lawful for a man to kill a thief who has not in the least hurt him, nor declared any design upon his life, any farther than by the use of force, so to get him in his power as to take away his money, or what he pleases, from him; because using force, where he has no right to get me into his power, let his pretence be what it will, I have no reason to suppose that he who would take away my liberty would not, when he had me in his power, take away everything else. And, therefore, it is lawful for me to treat him as one who has put himself into a state of war with me—i.e., kill him if I can; for to that hazard does he justly expose himself whoever introduces a state of war, and is aggressor in it.

19. And here we have the plain difference between the state of Nature and the state of war, which however some men have confounded,[i] are as far distant as a state of peace, goodwill, mutual assistance, and preservation; and a state of enmity, malice, violence, and mutual destruction are one from another. Men living together according to reason without a common superior on earth, with authority to judge between them, is properly the state of Nature. But force, or a declared design of force upon the person of another, where there is no common superior on earth to appeal to for relief, is the state of war; and it is the want of such an appeal gives a man the right of war even against an aggressor, though he be in society and a fellow-subject. Thus, a thief whom I cannot harm, but by appeal to the law, for having stolen all that I am worth, I may kill when he sets on

i Locke's reference here is probably to Hobbes' concept of the state of nature as being identical with the state of war.—Ed.

me to rob me but of my horse or coat, because the law, which was made for my preservation, where it cannot interpose to secure my life from present force, which if lost is capable of no reparation, permits me my own defence and the right of war, a liberty to kill the aggressor, because the aggressor allows not time to appeal to our common judge, nor the decision of the law, for remedy in a case where the mischief may be irreparable. Want of a common judge with authority puts all men in a state of Nature; force without right upon a man's person makes a state of war both where there is, and is not, a common judge.

20. But when the actual force is over, the state of war ceases between those that are in society and are equally on both sides subject to the judge; and, therefore, in such controversies, where the question is put, "Who shall be judge?" it cannot be meant who shall decide the controversy; every one knows what Jephtha here tells us, that "the Lord the Judge" shall judge. Where there is no judge on earth the appeal lies to God in Heaven. That question then cannot mean who shall judge, whether another hath put himself in a state of war with me, and whether I may, as Jephtha did, appeal to Heaven in it? Of that I myself can only judge in my own conscience, as I will answer it at the great day to the Supreme Judge of all men.

Chapter 5
Of Property

26. God, who hath given the world to men in common, hath also given them reason to make use of it to the best advantage of life and convenience. The earth and all that is therein is given to men for the support and comfort of their being. And though all the fruits it naturally produces, and beasts it feeds, belong to mankind in common, as they are produced by the spontaneous hand of Nature, and nobody has originally a private dominion exclusive of the rest of mankind in any of them, as they are thus in their natural state, yet being given for the use of men, there must of necessity be a means to appropriate them some way or other before they can be of any use, or at all beneficial, to any particular men. The fruit or venison which nourishes the wild Indian, who knows no enclosure, and is still a tenant in common, must be his, and so his—i.e., a part of him, that another can no longer have any right to it before it can do him any good for the support of his life.

27. Though the earth and all inferior creatures be common to all men, yet every man has a "property" in his own "person." This nobody has any right to but himself. The "labour" of his body and the "work" of his hands, we may say, are properly his. Whatsoever, then, he removes out of the state that Nature hath

provided and left it in, he hath mixed his labour with it, and joined to it something that is his own, and thereby makes it his property. It being by him removed from the common state Nature placed it in, it hath by this labour something annexed to it that excludes the common right of other men. For this "labour" being the unquestionable property of the labourer, no man but he can have a right to what that is once joined to, at least where there is enough, and as good left in common for others.

28. He that is nourished by the acorns he picked up under an oak, or the apples he gathered from the trees in the wood, has certainly appropriated them to himself. Nobody can deny but the nourishment is his. I ask, then, when did they begin to be his? when he digested? or when he ate? or when he boiled? or when he brought them home? or when he picked them up? And it is plain, if the first gathering made them not his, nothing else could. That labour put a distinction between them and common. That added something to them more than Nature, the common mother of all, had done, and so they became his private right. And will any one say he had no right to those acorns or apples he thus appropriated because he had not the consent of all mankind to make them his? Was it a robbery thus to assume to himself what belonged to all in common? If such a consent as that was necessary, man had starved, notwithstanding the plenty God had given him. We see in commons, which remain so by compact, that it is the taking any part of what is common, and removing it out of the state Nature leaves it in, which begins the property, without which the common is of no use. And the taking of this or that part does not depend on the express consent of all the commoners. Thus, the grass my horse has bit, the turfs my servant has cut, and the ore I have digged in any place, where I have a right to them in common with others, become my property without the assignation or consent of anybody. The labour that was mine, removing them out of that common state they were in, hath fixed my property in them.

29. By making an explicit consent of every commoner necessary to any one's appropriating to himself any part of what is given in common, children or servants could not cut the meat which their father or master had provided for them in common without assigning to every one his peculiar part. Though the water running in the fountain be every one's yet who can doubt but that in the pitcher is his only who drew it out? His labour hath taken it out of the hands of Nature where it was common, and belonged equally to all her children, and hath thereby appropriated it to himself. . . .

31. It will, perhaps, be objected to this, that if gathering the acorns or other fruits of the earth, etc., makes a right to them, then any one may engross as much as he will. To which I answer, Not so. The same law of Nature that does by this means give us property, does also bound that property too. "God has

given us all things richly." Is the voice of reason confirmed by inspiration? But how far has He given it us—"to enjoy"? As much as any one can make use of to any advantage of life before it spoils, so much he may by his labor fix a property in. Whatever is beyond this is more than his share, and belongs to others. Nothing was made by God for man to spoil or destroy. And thus considering the plenty of natural provisions there was a long time in the world, and the few spenders, and to how small a part of that provision the industry of one man could extend itself and engross it to the prejudice of others, especially keeping within the bounds set by reason of what might serve for his use, there could be then little room for quarrels or contentions about property so established.

32. But the chief matter of property being now not the fruits of the earth and the beasts that subsist on it, but the earth itself, as that which takes in and carries with it all the rest, I think it is plain that property in that too is acquired as the former. As much land as a man tills, plants, improves, cultivates, and can use the product of, so much is his property. He by his labour does, as it were, enclose it from the common. Nor will it invalidate his right to say everybody else has an equal title to it, and therefore he cannot appropriate, he cannot enclose, without the consent of all his fellow-commoners, all mankind. God, when He gave the world in common to all mankind, commanded man also to labor, and the penury of his condition required it of him. God and his reason commanded him to subdue the earth—i.e., improve it for the benefit of life and therein lay out something upon it that was his own, his labour. He that, in obedience to this command of God, subdued, tilled, and sowed any part of it, thereby annexed to it something that was his property, which another had no title to, nor could without injury take from him.

33. Nor was this appropriation of any parcel of land, by improving it, any prejudice to any other man, since there was still enough and as good left, and more than the yet unprovided could use. So that, in effect, there was never the less left for others because of his enclosure for himself. For he that leaves as much as another can make use of does as good as take nothing at all. Nobody could think himself injured by the drinking of another man, though he took a good draught, who had a whole river of the same water left him to quench his thirst. And the case of land and water, where there is enough of both, is perfectly the same.

34. God gave the world to men in common, but since He gave it them for their benefit and the greatest conveniencies of life they were capable to draw from it, it cannot be supposed He meant it should always remain common and uncultivated. He gave it to the use of the industrious and rational (and labour was to be his title to it); not to the fancy or covetousness of the quarrelsome and contentious. He that had as good left for his improvement as was already taken up needed not complain, ought not to meddle with what was already improved

by another's labour; if he did it is plain he desired the benefit of another's pains, which he had no right to, and not the ground which God had given him, in common with others, to labour on, and whereof there was as good left as that already possessed, and more than he knew what to do with, or his industry could reach to. . . .

36. The measure of property Nature well set, by the extent of men's labour and the conveniency of life. No man's labour could subdue or appropriate all, nor could his enjoyment consume more than a small part; so that it was impossible for any man, this way, to entrench upon the right of another or acquire to himself a property to the prejudice of his neighbour, who would still have room for as good and as large a possession (after the other had taken out his) as before it was appropriated. Which measure did confine every man's possession to a very moderate proportion, and such as he might appropriate to himself without injury to anybody in the first ages of the world, when men were more in danger to be lost, by wandering from their company, in the then vast wilderness of the earth than to be straitened for want of room to plant in. And the same measure may be allowed still, without prejudice to anybody, full as the world seems. For, supposing a man or family, in the state they were at first, peopling the world by the children of Adam or Noah, let him plant in some inland vacant places of America. We shall find that the possessions he could make himself, upon the measures we have given, would not be very large, nor, even to this day, prejudice the rest of mankind or give them reason to complain or think themselves injured by this man's encroachment, though the race of men have now spread themselves to all the corners of the world, and do infinitely exceed the small number was at the beginning. Nay, the extent of ground is of so little value without labour that I have heard it affirmed that in Spain itself a man may be permitted to plough, sow, and reap, without being disturbed, upon land he has no other title to, but only his making use of it. But, on the contrary, the inhabitants think themselves beholden to him who, by his industry on neglected, and consequently waste land, has increased the stock of corn, which they wanted. But be this as it will, which I lay no stress on, this I dare boldly affirm, that the same rule of propriety—viz., that every man should have as much as he could make use of, would hold still in the world, without straitening anybody, since there is land enough in the world to suffice double the inhabitants, had not the invention of money, and the tacit agreement of men to put a value on it, introduced (by consent) larger possession and aright to them; which, how it has done, I shall by and by show more at large.

37. This is certain, that in the beginning, before the desire of having more than men needed had altered the intrinsic value of things, which depends only on their usefulness to the life of man, or had agreed that a little piece of yellow

metal, which would keep without wasting or decay, should be worth a great piece of flesh or a whole heap of corn, though men had a right to appropriate by their labour, each one to himself, as much of the things of Nature as he could use, yet this could not be much, nor to the prejudice of others, where the same plenty was still left, to those who would use the same industry.

Before the appropriation of land, he who gathered as much of the wild fruit, killed, caught, or tamed as many of the beasts as he could—he that so employed his pains about any of the spontaneous products of Nature as any way to alter them from the state Nature put them in, by placing any of his labour on them, did thereby acquire a property in them; but if they perished in his possession without their due use—if the fruits rotted or the venison putrefied before he could spend it, he offended against the common law of Nature, and was liable to be punished: he invaded his neighbour's share, for he had no right farther than his use called for any of them, and they might serve to afford him conveniencies of life.

38. The same measures governed the possession of land, too. Whatsoever he tilled and reaped, laid up and made use of before it spoiled, that was his peculiar right; whatsoever he enclosed, and could feed and make use of, the cattle and product was also his. But if either the grass of his enclosure rotted on the ground, or the fruit of his planting perished without gathering and laying up, this part of the earth, notwithstanding his enclosure, was still to be looked on as waste, and might be the possession of any other. Thus, at the beginning, Cain might take as much ground as he could till and make it his own land, and yet leave enough to Abel's sheep to feed on: a few acres would serve for both their possessions. But as families increased and industry enlarged their stocks, their possessions enlarged with the need of them; but yet it was commonly without any fixed property in the ground they made use of till they incorporated, settled themselves together, and built cities, and then, by consent, they came in time to set out the bounds of their distinct territories and agree on limits between them and their neighbours, and by laws within themselves settled the properties of those of the same society. For we see that in that part of the world which was first inhabited, and therefore like to be best peopled, even as low down as Abraham's time, they wandered with their flocks and their herds, which was their substance, freely up and down—and this Abraham did in a country where he was a stranger; whence it is plain that, at least, a great part of the land lay in common, that the inhabitants valued it not, nor claimed property in any more than they made use of; but when there was not room enough in the same place for their herds to feed together, they, by consent, as Abraham and Lot did (Gen. xiii. 5), separated and enlarged their pasture where it best liked them. And for the same reason, Esau went from his father and his brother, and planted in Mount Seir (Gen. xxxvi. 6). . . .

40. Nor is it so strange as, perhaps, before consideration, it may appear, that the property of labour should be able to overbalance the community of land, for it is labour indeed that puts the difference of value on everything; and let any one consider what the difference is between an acre of land planted with tobacco or sugar, sown with wheat or barley, and an acre of the same land lying in common without any husbandry upon it, and he will find that the improvement of labour makes the far greater part of the value. I think it will be but a very modest computation to say, that of the products of the earth useful to the life of man, nine-tenths are the effects of labour. Nay, if we will rightly estimate things as they come to our use, and cast up the several expenses about them—what in them is purely owing to Nature and what to labour—we shall find that in most of them ninety-nine hundredths are wholly to be put on the account of labour.

41. There cannot be a clearer demonstration of anything than several nations of the Americans are of this, who are rich in land and poor in all the comforts of life; whom Nature, having furnished as liberally as any other people with the materials of plenty—i.e., a fruitful soil, apt to produce in abundance what might serve for food, raiment, and delight; yet, for want of improving it by labour, have not one hundredth part of the conveniencies we enjoy, and a king of a large and fruitful territory there feeds, lodges, and is clad worse than a day labourer in England. . . .

43. An acre of land that bears here twenty bushels of wheat, and another in America, which, with the same husbandry, would do the like, are, without doubt, of the same natural, intrinsic value. But yet the benefit mankind receives from one in a year is worth five pounds, and the other possibly not worth a penny; if all the profit an Indian received from it were to be valued and sold here, at least I may truly say, not one thousandth. It is labour, then, which puts the greatest part of value upon land, without which it would scarcely be worth anything; it is to that we owe the greatest part of all its useful products; for all that the straw, bran, bread, of that acre of wheat, is more worth than the product of an acre of as good land which lies waste is all the effect of labour. For it is not barely the ploughman's pains, the reaper's and thresher's toil, and the baker's sweat, is to be counted into the bread we eat; the labour of those who broke the oxen, who digged and wrought the iron and stones, who felled and framed the timber employed about the plough, mill, oven, or any other utensils, which are a vast number, requisite to this corn, from its sowing to its being made bread, must all be charged on the account of labour, and received as an effect of that; Nature and the earth furnished only the almost worthless materials as in themselves. It would be a strange catalogue of things that industry provided and made use of about every loaf of bread before it came to our use if we could trace them; iron, wood, leather, bark, timber, stone, bricks, coals, lime, cloth, dyeing-drugs, pitch, tar, masts, ropes, and all the materials made use of in the ship that brought any of the commodities

made use of by any of the workmen, to any part of the work, all which it would be almost impossible, at least too long, to reckon up. . . .

46. The greatest part of things really useful to the life of man, and such as the necessity of substituting made the first commoners of the world look after—as it doth the Americans now—are generally things of short duration, such as—if they are not consumed by use—will decay and perish of themselves. Gold, silver, and diamonds are things that fancy or agreement hath put the value on, more than real use and the necessary support of life. Now of those good things which Nature hath provided in common, every one hath a right (as hath been said) to as much as he could use, and had a property in all he could effect with his labour; all that his industry could extend to, to alter from the state Nature had put it in, was his. He that gathered a hundred bushels of acorns or apples had thereby a property in them; they were his goods as soon as gathered. He was only to look that he used them before they spoiled, else he took more than his share, and robbed others. And, indeed, it was a foolish thing, as well as dishonest, to hoard up more than he could make use of. If he gave away a part to anybody else, so that it perished not uselessly in his possession, these he also made use of. And if he also bartered away plums that would have rotted in a week, for nuts that would last good for his eating a whole year, he did no injury; he wasted not the common stock; destroyed no part of the portion of goods that belonged to others, so long as nothing perished uselessly in his hands. Again, if he would give his nuts for a piece of metal, pleased with its colour, or exchange his sheep for shells, or wool for a sparkling pebble or a diamond, and keep those by him all his life, he invaded not the right of others; he might heap up as much of these durable things as he pleased; the exceeding of the bounds of his just property not lying in the largeness of his possessions, but the perishing of anything uselessly in it.

47. And thus came in the use of money; some lasting thing that men might keep without spoiling, and that, by mutual consent, men would take in exchange for the truly useful but perishable supports of life.

48. And as different degrees of industry were apt to give men possessions in different proportions, so this invention of money gave them the opportunity to continue and enlarge them. For supposing an island, separate from all possible commerce with the rest of the world, wherein there were but a hundred families, but there were sheep, horses, and cows, with other useful animals, wholesome fruits, and land enough for corn for a hundred thousand times as many, but nothing in the island, either because of its commonness or perishableness, fit to supply the place of money. What reason could any one have there to enlarge his possessions beyond the use of his family, and a plentiful supply to its consumption, either in what their own industry produced, or they could barter for like perishable, useful commodities with others? Where there is not something both

lasting and scarce, and so valuable to be hoarded up, there men will not be apt to enlarge their possessions of land, were it never so rich, never so free for them to take. For I ask, what would a man value ten thousand or an hundred thousand acres of excellent land, ready cultivated and well stocked, too, with cattle, in the middle of the inland parts of America, where he had no hopes of commerce with other part of the world, to draw money to him by the sale of the product? It would not be worth the enclosing, and we should see him give up again to the wild common of Nature whatever was more than would supply the conveniences of life, to be had there for him and his family.

49. Thus, in the beginning, all the world was America, and more so than that is now; for no such thing as money was anywhere known. Find out something that hath the use and value of money amongst his neighbours, you shall see the same man will begin presently to enlarge his possessions.

50. But since gold and silver, being little useful to the life of man, in proportion to food, raiment, and carriage, has its value only from the consent of men—whereof labour yet makes in great part the measure—it is plain that the consent of men have agreed to a disproportionate and unequal possession of the earth—I mean out of the bounds of society and compact; for in governments the laws regulate it; they having, by consent, found out and agreed in a way how a man may, rightfully and without injury, possess more than he himself can make use of by receiving gold and silver, which may continue long in a man's possession without decaying for the overplus, and agreeing those metals should have a value.

51. And thus, I think, it is very easy to conceive, without any difficulty, how labour could at first begin a title of property in the common things of Nature, and how the spending it upon our uses bounded it; so that there could then be no reason of quarrelling about title, nor any doubt about the largeness of possession it gave. Right and conveniency went together. For as a man had a right to all he could employ his labour upon, so he had no temptation to labour for more than he could make use of. This left no room for controversy about the title, nor for encroachment on the right of others. What portion a man carved to himself was easily seen; and it was useless, as well as dishonest, to carve himself too much, or take more than he needed.

2

John Stuart Mill

———•••———

On Liberty (1859)

John Stuart Mill (1806–1873), the son of the utilitarian philosopher James Mill, grapples in this selection with the dangers of democracy. Writing in the wake of the English Reform Acts of 1832 and 1867, which expanded suffrage, he reveals liberals' fears of majority tyranny and collective mediocrity. His major works, in addition to On Liberty, *were* Principles of Political Economy *(1848),* Considerations on Representative Government *(1861),* Utilitarianism *(1863), and* The Subjection of Women *(1869).*

Chapter 1
Introductory

THE SUBJECT of this Essay is not the so-called Liberty of the Will, so unfortunately opposed to the misnamed doctrine of Philosophical Necessity; but Civil, or Social Liberty: the nature and limits of the power which can be legitimately exercised by society over the individual. A question seldom stated, and hardly ever discussed, in general terms, but which profoundly influences the practical controversies of the age by its latent presence, and is likely soon to make itself recognised as the vital question of the future. It is so far from being new, that, in a certain sense, it has divided mankind, almost from the remotest ages; but in the stage of progress into which the more civilized portions of the species have now entered, it presents itself under new conditions, and requires a different and more fundamental treatment.

The struggle between Liberty and Authority is the most conspicuous feature in the portions of history with which we are earliest familiar, particularly in that

29

of Greece, Rome, and England. But in old times this contest was between subject, or some classes of subject, and the Government. By liberty, was meant protection against the tyranny of the political rulers. The rulers were conceived
(except in some of the popular governments of Greece) as in a necessarily antagonistic position to the people whom they ruled. They consisted of a governing
One, or a governing tribe or caste, who derived their authority from inheritance
or conquest, who, at all events, did not hold it at the pleasure of the governed,
and whose supremacy men did not venture, perhaps did not desire, to contest,
whatever precautions might be taken against its oppressive exercise. Their power
was regarded as necessary, but also as highly dangerous; as a weapon which they
would attempt to use against their subjects, no less than against external enemies. To prevent the weaker members of the community from being preyed
upon by innumerable vultures, it was needful that there should be an animal of
prey stronger than the rest, commissioned to keep them down. But as the king
of the vultures would be no less bent upon preying on the flock than any of the
minor harpies, it was indispensable to be in a perpetual attitude of defence
against his beak and claws. The aim, therefore, of patriots was to set limits to
power which the ruler should be suffered to exercise over the community; and
this limitation was what they meant by liberty. It was attempted in two ways.
First, by obtaining a recognition of certain immunities, called political liberties
or rights, which it was to be regarded as a breach of duty in the ruler to infringe,
and which if he did infringe, specific resistance, or general rebellion, was held to
be justifiable. A second, and generally a later expedient, was the establishment of
constitutional checks, by which the consent of the community, or of a body of
some sort, supposed to represent its interests, was made a necessary condition to
some of the more important acts of the governing power. To the first of these
modes of limitation, the ruling power, in most European countries, was compelled, more or less, to submit. It was not so with the second; and, to attain this,
or when already in some degree possessed, to attain it more completely, became
everywhere the principal object of the lovers of liberty. And so long as mankind
were content to combat one enemy by another, and to be ruled by a master, on
condition of being guaranteed more or less efficaciously against his tyranny, they
did not carry their aspirations beyond this point.

A time, however, came, in the progress of human affairs, when men ceased to
think it a necessity of nature that their governors should be an independent
power, opposed in interest to themselves. It appeared to them much better that
the various magistrates of the State should be their tenants or delegates, revoca-
ble at their pleasure. In that way alone, it seemed, could they have complete
security that the powers of government would never be abused to their disadvan-

tage. By degrees this new demand for elective and temporary rulers became the prominent object of the exertions of the popular party, wherever any such party existed; and superseded, to a considerable extent, the previous efforts to limit the power of rulers. As the struggle proceeded for making the ruling power emanate from the periodical choice of the ruled, some persons began to think that too much importance had been attached to the limitation of the power itself. *That* (it might seem) was a resource against rulers whose interests were habitually opposed to those of the people. What was now wanted was, that the rulers should be identified with the people; that their interest and will should be the interest and will of the nation. The nation did not need to be protected against its own will. There was no fear of its tyrannizing over itself. Let the rulers be effectually responsible to it, promptly removable by it, and it could afford to trust them with power of which it could itself dictate the use to be made. Their power was but the nation's own power, concentrated, and in a form convenient for exercise. This mode of thought, or rather perhaps of feeling, was common among the last generation of European liberalism, in the Continental section of which it still apparently predominates. Those who admit any limit to what a government may do, except in the case of such governments as they think ought not to exist, stand out as brilliant exceptions among the political thinkers of the Continent. A similar tone of sentiment might by this time have been prevalent in our own country, if the circumstances which for a time encouraged it, had continued unaltered.

But, in political and philosophical theories, as well as in persons, success discloses faults and infirmities which failure might have concealed from observation. The notion, that the people have no need to limit their power over themselves, might seem axiomatic, when popular government was a thing only dreamed about, or read of as having existed at some distant period of the past. Neither was that notion necessarily disturbed by such temporary aberrations as those of the French Revolution, the worst of which were the work of an usurping few, and which, in any case, belonged, not to the permanent working of popular institutions, but to a sudden and convulsive outbreak against monarchical and aristocratic despotism. In time, however, a democratic republic came to occupy a large portion of the earth's surface, and made itself felt as one of the most powerful members of the community of nations; and elective and responsible government became subject to the observations and criticisms which wait upon a great existing fact. It was now perceived that such phrases as "self-government," and "the power of the people over themselves," do not express the true state of the case. The "people" who exercise the power are not always the same people with those over whom it is exercised; and the "self-government" spoken of is not the government of each by himself, but of each by all the rest. The will of the people, moreover, practically means the will of the most numerous or the most active *part* of the people; the majority, or those who succeed in making themselves accepted as the majority; the people, consequently, *may* desire to oppress a part of their number; and precautions are as much needed against this as against any other abuse of power. The limitation, therefore, of the power of government over individuals loses none of its importance when the holders of power are regularly accountable to the community, that is, to the strongest party therein. This view of things, recommending itself equally to the intelligence of thinkers and to the inclination of those important classes in European society to whose real or supposed interests democracy is adverse, has had no difficulty in establishing itself; and in political speculations "the tyranny of the majority" is now generally included among the evils against which society requires to be on its guard.

Like other tyrannies, the tyranny of the majority was at first, and is still vulgarly, held in dread, chiefly as operating through the acts of the public authorities. But reflecting persons perceived that when society is itself the tyrant—society collectively over the separate individuals who compose it—its means of tyrannising are not restricted to the acts which it may do by the hands of its political functionaries. Society can and does execute its own mandates: and if it issues wrong mandates instead of right, or any mandates at all in things with which it ought not to meddle, it practises a social tyranny more formidable than many kinds of political oppression, since, though not usually upheld by such extreme penalties, it leaves fewer means of escape, penetrating much more deeply into the details of life, and enslaving the soul itself. Protection, therefore, against the tyranny of the magistrate is not enough: there needs protection also against the tyranny of the prevailing opinion and feeling; against the tendency of society to impose, by other means than civil penalties, its own ideas and practices as rules of conduct on those who dissent from them; to fetter the development, and, if possible, prevent the formation, of any individuality not in harmony with its ways, and compel all characters to fashion themselves upon the model of its own. There is a limit to the legitimate interference of collective opinion with individual independence: and to find that limit, and maintain it against encroachment, is as indispensable to a good condition of human affairs, as protection against political despotism.

But though this proposition is not likely to be contested in general terms, the practical question, where to place the limit—how to make the fitting adjustment between individual independence and social control—is a subject on which nearly everything remains to be done. All that makes existence valuable to any one, depends on the enforcement of restraints upon the actions of other people. Some rules of conduct, therefore, must be imposed, by law in the first place, and by opinion on many things which are not fit subjects for the operation of law.

What these rules should be is the principal question in human affairs; but if we except a few of the most obvious cases, it is one of those which least progress has been made in resolving. No two ages, and scarcely any two countries, have decided it alike; and the decision of one age or country is a wonder to another. Yet the people of any given age and country no more suspect any difficulty in it, than if it were a subject on which mankind had always been agreed. The rules which obtain among themselves appear to them self-evident and self-justifying. This all but universal illusion is one of the examples of the magical influence of custom, which is not only, as the proverb says, a second nature, but is continually mistaken for the first. The effect of custom, in preventing any misgiving respecting the rules of conduct which mankind impose on one another, is all the more complete because the subject is one on which it is not generally considered necessary that reasons should be given, either by one person to others or by each to himself. People are accustomed to believe, and have been encouraged in the belief by some who aspire to the character of philosophers, that their feelings, on subjects of this nature, are better than reasons, and render reasons unnecessary. The practical principle which guides them to their opinions on the regulation of human conduct, is the feeling in each person's mind that everybody should be required to act as he, and those with whom he sympathizes, would like them to act. No one, indeed, acknowledges to himself that his standard of judgment is his own liking; but an opinion on a point of conduct, not supported by reasons, can only count as one person's preference; and if the reasons, when given, are a mere appeal to similar preference felt by other people, it is still only many people's liking instead of one. To an ordinary man, however, his own preference, thus supported, is not only a perfectly satisfactory reason, but the only one he generally has for any of his notions of morality, taste, or propriety, which are not expressly written in his religious creed; and his chief guide in the interpretation even of that. Men's opinions, accordingly, on what is laudable or blamable, are affected by all the multifarious causes which influence their wishes in regard to the conduct of others, and which are as numerous as those which determine their wishes on any other subject. Sometimes their reason—at other times their prejudices or superstitions: often their social affections, not seldom their antisocial ones, their envy or jealousy, their arrogance or contemptuousness: but most commonly their desires or fears for themselves—their legitimate or illegitimate self-interest. Wherever there is an ascendant class, a large portion of the morality of the country emanates from its class interests, and its feelings of class superiority. The morality between Spartans and Helots, between planters and negroes, between princes and subjects, between nobles and roturiers [plebeians], between men and women, has been for the most part the creation of these class interests and feelings: and the sentiments thus generated react in turn upon the moral feelings of the members of the ascendant class, in their relations among themselves. Where, on the other hand, a class, formerly ascendant, has lost its ascendancy, or where its ascendancy is unpopular, the prevailing moral sentiments frequently bear the impress of an impatient dislike of superiority. Another grand determining principle of the rules of conduct, both in act and forbearance, which have been enforced by law or opinion, has been the servility of mankind towards the supposed preferences or aversions of their temporal masters or of their gods. This servility, though essentially selfish, is not hypocrisy; it gives rise to perfectly genuine sentiments of abhorrence; it made men burn magicians and heretics. Among so many baser influences, the general and obvious interests of society have of course had a share, and a large one, in the direction of the moral sentiments: less, however, as a matter of reason, and on their own account, than as a consequence of the sympathies and antipathies which grew out of them: and sympathies and antipathies which had little or nothing to do with the interests of society, have made themselves felt in the establishment of moralities with quite as great force.

The likings and dislikings of society, or of some powerful portion of it, are thus the main thing which has practically determined the rules laid down for general observance, under the penalties of law or opinion. And in general, those who have been in advance of society in thought and feeling, have left this condition of things unassailed in principle, however they may have come into conflict with it in some of its details. They have occupied themselves rather in inquiring what things society ought to like or dislike, than in questions whether its likings or dislikings should be a law to individuals. They preferred endeavoring to alter the feelings of mankind on the particular points on which they were themselves heretical, rather than make common cause in defence of freedom, with heretics generally. The only case in which the higher ground has been taken on principle and maintained with consistency, by any but an individual here and there, is that of religious belief: a case instructive in many ways, and not least so as forming a most striking instance of the fallibility of what is called the moral sense: for the *odium theologicum*, in a sincere bigot, is one of the most unequivocal cases of moral feelings. Those who first broke the yoke of what called itself the Universal Church, were in general as little willing to permit difference of religious opinion as that church itself. But when the heat of the conflict was over, without giving a complete victory to any party, and each church or sect was reduced to limit its hopes to retaining possession of the ground it already occupied; minorities, seeing that they had no chance of becoming majorities, were under the necessity of pleading to those whom they could not convert, for permission to differ. It is accordingly on this battle-field, almost solely, that the rights of the individual against society have been asserted on broad grounds of principle, and the claim of society to exercise authority over dissentients openly controverted. The great writers to whom the world owes what religious liberty it possesses, have mostly asserted freedom of conscience as an indefeasible right, and denied absolutely that a human being is accountable to others for his religious belief. Yet so natural to mankind is intolerance in whatever they really care about, that religious freedom has hardly anywhere been practically realised, except where religious indifference, which dislikes to have its peace disturbed by theological quarrels, has added its weight to the scale. In the minds of almost all religious persons, even in the most tolerant countries, the duty of toleration is admitted with tacit reserves. One person will bear with dissent in matters of church government, but not of dogma; another can tolerate everybody, short of a Papist or a Unitarian; another, every one who believes in revealed religion; a few extend their charity a little further, but stop at the belief in a God and in a future state. Wherever the sentiment of the majority is still genuine and intense, it is found to have abated little of its claim to be obeyed.

In England, from the peculiar circumstances of our political history, though the yoke of opinion is perhaps heavier, that of law is lighter, than in most other countries of Europe; and there is considerable jealousy of direct interference, by the legislative or the executive power, with private conduct; not so much from any just regard for the independence of the individual, as from the still subsisting habit of looking on the government as representing an opposite interest to the public. The majority have not yet learnt to feel the power of the government their power, or its opinions their opinions. When they do so, individual liberty will probably be as much exposed to invasion from the government, as it already is from public opinion. But, as yet, there is a considerable amount of feeling ready to be called forth against any attempt of the law to control individuals in things in which they have not hitherto been accustomed to be controlled by it; and this with very little discrimination as to whether the matter is, or is not, within the legitimate sphere of legal control; insomuch that the feeling, highly salutary on the whole, is perhaps quite as often misplaced as well grounded in the particular instances of its application. There is, in fact, no recognised principle by which the propriety or impropriety of government interference is customarily tested. People decide according to their personal preferences. Some, whenever they see any good to be done, or evil to be remedied, would willingly instigate the government to undertake the business; while others prefer to bear almost any amount of social evil, rather than add one to the departments of human interests amenable to governmental control. And men range themselves on one or the other side in any particular case, according to this general direction of their sentiments; or according to the degree of interest which they feel in the particular thing which it is proposed that the government should do, or according to the belief they entertain that the government would, or would not, do it in the manner they prefer; but very rarely on account of any opinion to which they consistently adhere, as to what things are fit to be done by a government. And it seems to me that in consequence of this absence of rule or principle, one side is at present as often wrong as the other; the interference of government is, with about equal frequency, improperly invoked and improperly condemned.

The object of this Essay is to assert one very simple principle, as entitled to govern absolutely the dealings of society with the individual in the way of compulsion and control, whether the means used be physical force in the form of legal penalties, or the moral coercion of public opinion. That principle is, that the sole end for which mankind are warranted, individually or collectively, in interfering with the liberty of action of any of their number, is self-protection. That the only purpose for which power can be rightfully exercised over any member of a civilized community, against his will, is to prevent harm to others. His own good, either physical or moral, is not a sufficient warrant. He cannot rightfully be compelled to do or forbear because it will be better for him to do so, because it will make him happier, because, in the opinions of others, to do so would be wise, or even right. These are good reasons for remonstrating with him, or reasoning with him, or persuading him, or entreating him, but not for compelling him, or visiting him with any evil in case he do otherwise. To justify that, the conduct from which it is desired to deter him, must be calculated to produce evil to some one else. The only part of the conduct of any one, for which he is amenable to society, is that which concerns others. In the part which merely concerns himself, his independence is, of right, absolute. Over himself, over his own body and mind, the individual is sovereign.

It is, perhaps, hardly necessary to say that this doctrine is meant to apply only to human beings in the maturity of their faculties. We are not speaking of children, or of young persons below the age which the law may fix as that of manhood or womanhood. Those who are still in a state to require being taken care of by others, must be protected against their own actions as well as against external injury. For the same reason, we may leave out of consideration those backward states of society in which the race itself may be considered as in its nonage. The early difficulties in the way of spontaneous progress are so great, that there is seldom any choice of means for overcoming them; and a ruler full of the spirit of improvement is warranted in the use of any expedients that will attain an end, perhaps otherwise unattainable. Despotism is a legitimate mode of government in dealing with barbarians, provided the end be their improvement, and the means justified by actually effecting that end. Liberty, as a principle, has no application to any state of things anterior to the time when mankind have become capable of being improved by free and equal discussion. Until then, there is nothing for them but implicit obedience to an Akbar or a Charlemagne, if they are so fortunate as to find one. But as soon as mankind have attained the capacity for being guided to their own improvement by conviction or persuasion (a period long since reached in all nations with whom we need here concern ourselves), compulsion, either in the direct form or in that of pains and penalties for non-compliance, is no longer admissible as a means to their own good, and justifiable only for the security of others.

It is proper to state that I forgo any advantage which could be derived to my argument from the idea of abstract right, as a thing independent of utility. I regard utility as the ultimate appeal on all ethical questions; but it must be utility in the largest sense, grounded on the permanent interests of man as a progressive being. Those interests, I contend, authorise the subjection of individual spontaneity to external control, only in respect to those actions of each, which concern the interest of other people. If any one does an act hurtful to others, there is a *prima facie* case for punishing him, by law, or, where legal penalties are not safely applicable, by general disapprobation. There are also many positive acts for the benefit of others, which he may rightfully be compelled to perform; such as to give evidence in a court of justice; to bear his fair share in the common defence, or in any other joint work necessary to the interest of the society of which he enjoys the protection; and to perform certain acts of individual beneficence, such as saving a fellow-creature's life, or interposing to protect the defenceless against ill-usage, things which whenever it is obviously a man's duty to do, he may rightfully be made responsible to society for not doing. A person may cause evil to others not only by his actions but by his inaction, and in either case he is justly accountable to them for the injury. The latter case, it is true, requires a much more cautious exercise of compulsion than the former. To make any one answerable for doing evil to others, is the rule; to make him answerable for not preventing evil, is, comparatively speaking, the exception. Yet there are many cases clear enough and grave enough to justify that exception. In all things which regard the external relations of the individual, he is *de jure* amenable to those whose interests are concerned, and, if need be, to society as their protector. There are often good reasons for not holding him to the responsibility; but these reasons must arise from the special expediencies of the case: either because it is a kind of case in which he is on the whole likely to act better, when left to his own discretion, than when controlled in any way in which society have it in their power to control him; or because the attempt to exercise control would produce other evils, greater than those which it would prevent. When such reasons as these preclude the enforcement of responsibility, the conscience of the agent himself should step into the vacant judgment seat, and protect those interests of others which have no external protection; judging himself all the more rigidly, because the case does not admit of his being made accountable to the judgment of his fellow-creatures.

But there is a sphere of action in which society, as distinguished from the individual, has, if any, only an indirect interest; comprehending all that portion of a person's life and conduct which affects only himself, or if it also affects others, only with their free, voluntary, and undeceived consent and participation. When I say only himself, I mean directly, and in the first instance; for whatever affects himself, may affect others through himself; and the objection which may be grounded on this contingency, will receive consideration in the sequel. This, then, is the appropriate region of human liberty. It comprises, first, the inward domain of consciousness; demanding liberty of conscience in the most comprehensive sense; liberty of thought and feeling; absolute freedom of opinion and sentiment on all subjects, practical or speculative, scientific, moral, or theological. The liberty of expressing and publishing opinions may seem to fall under a different principle, since it belongs to that part of the conduct of an individual which concerns other people; but, being almost of as much importance as the liberty of thought itself, and resting in great part on the same reasons, is practically inseparable from it. Secondly, the principle requires liberty of tastes and pursuits; of framing the plan of our life to suit our own character; of doing as we like, subject to such consequences as may follow: without impediment from our fellow creatures, so long as what we do does not harm them, even though they should think our conduct foolish, perverse, or wrong. Thirdly, from this liberty of each individual, follows the liberty, within the same limits, of combination among individuals; freedom to unite, for any purpose not involving harm to others: the persons combining being supposed to be of full age, and not forced or deceived.

No society in which these liberties are not, on the whole, respected, is free, whatever may be its form of government; and none is completely free in which they do not exist absolute and unqualified. The only freedom which deserves the name, is that of pursuing our own good in our own way, so long as we do not attempt to deprive others of theirs, or impede their efforts to obtain it. Each is the proper guardian of his own health, whether bodily, *or* mental and spiritual. Mankind are greater gainers by suffering each other to live as seems good to themselves, than by compelling each to live as seems good to the rest.

Though this doctrine is anything but new, and to some persons, may have the air of a truism, there is no doctrine which stands more directly opposed to the general tendency of existing opinion and practice. Society has expended fully as much effort in the attempt (according to its lights) to compel people to conform to its notions of personal as of social excellence. The ancient commonwealths thought themselves entitled to practise, and the ancient philosophers countenanced, the regulation of every part of private conduct by public authority, on the ground that the State had a deep interest in the whole bodily and mental discipline of every one of its citizens; a mode of thinking which may have been admissible in small republics surrounded by powerful enemies, in constant peril of being subverted by foreign attack or internal commotion, to which even a short interval of relaxed energy and self-command might so easily be fatal, that they could not afford to wait for the salutary permanent effects of freedom. In the modern world, the greater size of political communities, and, above all, the separation between spiritual and temporal authority (which placed the direction of men's consciences in other hands than those which controlled their worldly affairs), prevented so great an interference by law in the details of private life; but the engines of moral repression have been wielded more strenuously against divergence from the reigning opinion in self-regarding, than even in social matters; religion, the most powerful of the elements which have entered into the formation of moral feeling, having almost always been governed either by the ambition of a hierarchy, seeking control over every department of human conduct, or by the spirit of Puritanism. And some of those modern reformers who have placed themselves in strongest opposition to the religions of the past, have been no way behind either churches or sects in their assertion of the right of spiritual domination: M. Comte, in particular, whose social system, as unfolded in his *Système de Politique Positive,* aims at establishing (though by moral more than by legal appliances) a despotism of society over the individual, surpassing anything contemplated in the political ideal of the most rigid disciplinarian among the ancient philosophers.

Apart from the peculiar tenets of individual thinkers, there is also in the world at large an increasing inclination to stretch unduly the powers of society over the individual, both by the force of opinion and even by that of legislation; and as the tendency of all the changes taking place in the world is to strengthen society, and diminish the power of the individual, this encroachment is not one of the evils which tend spontaneously to disappear, but, on the contrary, to grow more and more formidable. The disposition of mankind, whether as rulers or as fellow citizens, to impose their own opinions and inclinations as a rule of conduct on others, is so energetically supported by some of the best and by some of the worst feelings incident to human nature, that it is hardly ever kept under restraint by anything but want of power; and as the power is not declining, but growing, unless a strong barrier of moral conviction can be raised against the mischief, we must expect, in the present circumstances of the world, to see it increase.

It will be convenient for the argument, if, instead of at once entering upon the general thesis, we confine ourselves in the first instance to a single branch of it, on which the principle here stated is, if not fully, yet to a certain point, recognized by the current opinions. This one branch is the Liberty of Thought: from which it is impossible to separate the cognate liberty of speaking and of writing. Although these liberties, to some considerable amount, form part of the political morality of all countries which profess religious toleration and free institutions, the grounds, both philosophical and practical, on which they rest, are perhaps not so familiar to the general mind, nor so thoroughly appreciated by many even of the leaders of opinion, as might have been expected. Those grounds, when rightly understood, are of much wider application than to only one division of the subject, and a thorough consideration of this part of the question will be found the best introduction to the remainder. Those to whom nothing which I am about to say will be new, may therefore, I hope, excuse me, if on a subject which for now three centuries has been so often discussed, I venture on one discussion more.

Chapter 2
Of the Liberty of Thought and Discussion

The time, it is to be hoped, is gone by, when any defence would be necessary of the "liberty of the press" as one of the securities against corrupt or tyrannical government. No argument, we may suppose, can now be needed, against permitting a legislature or an executive, not identified in interest with the people, to prescribe opinions to them, and determine what doctrines or what arguments they shall be allowed to hear. This aspect of the question, besides, has been so often and so triumphantly enforced by preceding writers, that it needs not be specially insisted on in this place. Though the law of England, on the subject of the press, is as servile to this day as it was in the time of the Tudors, there is little danger of its being actually put in force against political discussion, except during some temporary panic, when fear of insurrection drives ministers and judges from their propriety; and, speaking generally, it is not, in constitutional countries, to be apprehended, that the government, whether completely responsible to the people or not, will often attempt to control the expression of the opinion, except when in doing so it makes itself the organ of the general intolerance of the public. Let us suppose, therefore, that the government is entirely at one with the people, and never thinks of exerting any power of coercion unless in agreement with what it conceives to be their voice. But I deny the right of the people to exercise such coercion, either by themselves or by their government. The power itself is illegitimate. The best government has no more title to it than the worst. It is as noxious, or more noxious, when exerted in accordance with public opinion, than when in opposition to it. If all mankind minus one were of one opinion, mankind would be no more justified in silencing that one person, than he, if he had the power, would be justified in silencing mankind. Were an opinion a personal possession of no value except to the owner, if to be obstructed in the enjoyment of it were simply a private injury, it would make some difference whether the injury was inflicted only on a few persons or on many. But the peculiar evil of silencing the expression of an opinion, is that it is robbing the human race, posterity as well as the existing generation; those who dissent from the opinion, still more than those who hold it. If the opinion is right, they are deprived of the opportunity of exchanging error for truth: if wrong, they lose, what is almost as great a benefit, the clearer perception and livelier impression of truth, produced by its collision with error.

It is necessary to consider separately these two hypotheses, each of which has a distinct branch of the argument corresponding to it. We can never be sure that the opinion that we are endeavoring to stifle is a false opinion; and if we were sure, stifling it would be an evil still.

First: the opinion which it is attempted to suppress by authority may possibly be true. Those who desire to suppress it, of course, deny its truth; but they are not infallible. They have no authority to decide the question for all mankind, and exclude every other person from the means of judging. To refuse a hearing to an opinion, because they are sure that it is false, is to assume that *their* certainty is the same thing as *absolute* certainty. All silencing of discussion is an assumption of infallibility. Its condemnation may be allowed to rest on this common argument, not the worse for being common.

Unfortunately for the good sense of mankind, the fact of their fallibility is far from carrying the weight in their practical judgment which is always allowed to it in theory; for while every one well knows himself to be fallible, few think it necessary to take any precautions against their own fallibility, or admit the supposition that any opinion, of which they feel very certain, may be one of the examples of the error to which they acknowledge themselves to be liable. Absolute princes, or others who are accustomed to unlimited deference, usually feel this complete confidence in their own opinions on nearly all subjects. People more happily situated, who sometimes hear their opinions disputed, and are not wholly unused to be set right when they are wrong, place the same unbounded reliance only on such of their opinions as are shared by all who surround them, or to whom they habitually defer; for in proportion to a man's want of confidence in his own solitary judgment, does he usually repose, with implicit trust, on the infallibility of "the world" in general. And the world, to each individual, means the part of it with which he comes in contact; his party, his sect, his church, his class of society; the man may be called, by comparison, almost liberal and large-minded to whom it means anything so comprehensive as his own country or his own age. Nor is his faith in this collective authority at all shaken by his being aware that other ages, countries, sects, churches, classes, and parties have thought, and even now think, the exact reverse. He devolves upon his own world the responsibility of being in the right against the dissentient worlds of other people; and it never troubles him that the mere accident has decided which of these numerous worlds is the object of his reliance, and that the same causes which make him a churchman in London, would have made him a Buddhist or a Confucian in Peking. Yet it is as evident in itself, as any amount of argument can make it, that ages are no more infallible than individuals; every age having held many opinions which subsequent ages have deemed not only false but absurd; and it is as certain that many opinions now general, will be rejected by future ages, as it is that many, once general, are rejected by the present.

The objection likely to be made to this argument would probably take some such form as the following. There is no greater assumption of infallibility in forbidding the propagation of error, than in any other thing which is done by public authority on its own judgment and responsibility. Judgment is given to men that they may use it. Because it may be used erroneously, are men to be told that they ought not to use it at all? To prohibit what they think pernicious, is not claiming exemption from error, but fulfilling the duty incumbent on them, although fallible, of acting on their conscientious conviction. If we were never to act on our opinions, because those opinions may be wrong, we should leave all our interests uncared for, and all our duties unperformed. An objection which applies to all conduct can be no valid objection to any conduct in particular. It is the duty of governments, and of individuals, to form the truest opinions they can; to form them carefully, and never impose them upon others unless they are quite sure of being right. But when they are sure (such reasoners may say), it is not conscientiousness but cowardice to shrink from acting on their opinions, and allow doctrines which they honestly think dangerous to the welfare of mankind, either in this life or in another, to be scattered abroad without restraint, because other people, in less enlightened times, have persecuted opinions now believed to be true. Let us take care, it may be said, not to make the same mistake: but governments and nations have made mistakes in other things, which are not denied to be fit subjects for the exercise of authority: they have laid on bad taxes, made unjust wars. Ought we therefore to lay on no taxes, and, under whatever provocation, make no wars? Men, and governments, must act to the best of their ability. There is no such thing as absolute certainty, but there is assurance sufficient for the purposes of human life. We may, and must, assume our opinion to be true for the guidance of our own conduct: and it is assuming no more when we forbid bad men to pervert society by the propagation of opinions which we regard as false and pernicious.

I answer, that it is assuming very much more. There is the greatest difference between presuming an opinion to be true, because, with every opportunity for contesting it, it has not been refuted, and assuming its truth for the purpose of not permitting its refutation. Complete liberty of contradicting and disproving our opinion is the very condition which justifies us in assuming its truth for purposes of action; and on no other terms can a being with human faculties have any rational assurance of being right.

When we consider either the history of opinion, or the ordinary conduct of human life, to what is it to be ascribed that the one and the other are no worse than they are? Not certainly to the inherent force of the human understanding; for, on any matter not self-evident, there are ninety-nine persons totally incapable of judging of it for one who is capable; and the capacity of the hundredth person is only comparative; for the majority of the eminent men of every past generation held many opinions now known to be erroneous, and did or approved numerous things which no one will now justify. Why is it, then, that there is on the whole a preponderance among mankind of rational opinions and rational conduct? If there really is this preponderance—which there must be unless human affairs are, and have always been, in an almost desperate state—it is owing to a quality of the human mind, the source of everything respectable in man either as an intellectual or as a moral being, namely, that his errors are corrigible. He is capable of rectifying his mistakes, by discussion and experience. Not by experience alone. There must be discussion, to show how experience is to be interpreted. Wrong opinions and practices gradually yield to fact and argument; but facts and arguments, to produce any effect on the mind, must be brought before it. Very few facts are able to tell their own story, without comments to bring out their meaning. The whole strength and value, then, of human judgment, depending on the one property, that it can be set right when it is wrong, reliance can be placed on it only when the means of setting it right are kept constantly at hand. In the case of any person whose judgment is really deserving of confidence, how has it become so? Because he has kept his mind open to criticism of his opinions and conduct. Because it has been his practice to listen to all that could be said against him; to profit by as much of it as was just, and to expound to himself, and upon occasion to others, the fallacy of what was fallacious. Because he has felt, that the only way in which a human being can make some approach to knowing the whole of a subject, is by hearing what can be said about it by persons of every variety of opinion, and studying all modes in which it can be looked at by every character of mind. No wise man ever acquired his wisdom in any mode but this; nor is it in the nature of human intellect to become wise in any other manner. The steady habit of correcting and completing his own opinion by collating it with those of others, so far from causing doubt and hesitation in carrying it into practice, is the only stable foundation for a just reliance on it; for, being cognisant of all that can, at least obviously, be said against him, and having taken up his position against all gainsayers—knowing that he has sought for objections and difficulties, instead of avoiding them, and has shut out no light which can be thrown upon the subject from any quarter—he has a right to think his judgment better than that of any person, or any multitude, who have not gone through a similar process.

It is not too much to require that what the wisest of mankind, those who are best entitled to trust their own judgment, find necessary to warrant their relying on it, should be submitted to by that miscellaneous collection of a few wise and many foolish individuals, called the public. The most intolerant of churches, the Roman Catholic Church, even at the canonisation of a saint, admits, and listens patiently to, a "devil's advocate." The holiest of men, it appears, cannot be admitted to posthumous honors until all that the devil could say against him is known and weighed. If even the Newtonian philosophy were not permitted to be questioned, mankind could not feel as complete assurance of its truth as they now do. The beliefs which we have most warrant for have no safeguard to rest on, but a standing invitation to the whole world to prove them unfounded. If the challenge is not accepted, or is accepted and the attempt fails, we are far enough from certainty still; but we have done the best that the existing state of human reason admits of; we have neglected nothing that could give the truth a chance of reaching us: if the lists are kept open, we may hope that if there be a better truth, it will be found when the human mind is capable of receiving it; and in the meantime we may rely on having attained such approach to truth as is possible in our own day. This is the amount of certainty attainable by a fallible being, and this the sole way of attaining it.

Strange it is, that men should admit the validity of the arguments for free discussion, but object to their being "pushed to an extreme," not seeing that unless the reasons are good for an extreme case, they are not good for any case. Strange that they should imagine that they are not assuming infallibility, when they acknowledge that there should be free discussion on all subjects which can possibly be *doubtful,* but think that some particular principle or doctrine should be forbidden to be questioned because it is so *certain,* that is, because *they are certain* that it is certain. To call any proposition certain, while there is anyone who would deny its certainty if permitted, but who is not permitted, is to assume that we ourselves, and those who agree with us, are the judges of certainty, and judges without hearing the other side.

In the present age—which has been described as "destitute of faith but terrified at skepticism"—in which people feel sure, not so much that their opinions are true, as that they should not know what to do without them—the claims of an opinion to be protected from public attack are rested not so much on its truth, as on its importance to society. There are, it is alleged, certain beliefs so useful, not to say indispensable, to well-being that it is as much the duty of governments to uphold those beliefs, as to protect any other of the interests of society. In a case of such necessity, and so directly in the line of their duty, something less than infallibility may, it is maintained, warrant, and even bind, governments to act on their own opinion, confirmed by the general opinion of mankind. It is also often argued, and still oftener thought, that none but bad men would desire to weaken these salutary beliefs; and there can be nothing wrong, it is thought, in restraining bad men, and prohibiting what only such men would wish to practise. This mode of thinking makes the justification of restraints on discussion not a question of the truth of doctrines, but of their usefulness; and flatters itself by that means to escape the responsibility of claiming to be an infallible judge of opinions. But those who thus satisfy themselves, do not perceive that the assumption of infallibility is merely shifted from one point to another. The usefulness of an opinion is itself matter of opinion: as disputable, as open to discussion, and requiring discussion as much as the opinion itself. There is the same need of an infallible judge of opinions to decide an opinion to be noxious, as to decide it to be false, unless the opinion condemned has full opportunity of defending itself. And it will not do to say that the heretic may be allowed to maintain the utility or harmlessness of his opinion, though forbidden to maintain its truth. The truth of an opinion is part of its utility. If we would know whether or not it is desirable that a proposition should be believed, is it possible to exclude the consideration of whether or not it is true? In the opinion, not of bad men, but of the best men, no belief which is contrary to truth can be really useful: and can you prevent such men from urging that plea when they are charged with culpability for denying some doctrine which they are told is useful, but which they believe to be false? Those who are on the side of received opinions never fail to take all possible advantage of this plea; you do not find *them* handling the question of utility as if it could be completely abstracted from that of truth: on the contrary, it is, above all, because their doctrine is "the truth," that the knowledge or the belief of it is held to be so indispensable. There can be no fair discussion of the question of usefulness when an argument so vital may be employed on one side, but not on the other. And in point of fact, when law or public feeling do not permit the truth of an opinion to be disputed, they are just as little tolerant of a denial of its usefulness. The utmost they allow is an extenuation of its absolute necessity, or of the positive guilt of rejecting it.

In order more fully to illustrate the mischief of denying a hearing to opinions because we, in our own judgment, have condemned them, it will be desirable to fix down the discussion to a concrete case; and I choose, by preference, the cases which are least favourable to me—in which the argument against freedom of opinion, both on the score of truth and on that of utility, is considered the strongest.

Let the opinions impugned be the belief in a God and in a future state, or any of the commonly received doctrines of morality. To fight the battle on such ground gives a great advantage to an unfair antagonist; since he will be sure to say (and many who have no desire to be unfair will say it internally), Are these the doctrines which you do not deem sufficiently certain to be taken under the protection of law? Is the belief in a God one of the opinions to feel sure of which you hold to be assuming infallibility? But I must be permitted to observe, that it is not the feeling sure of a doctrine (be it what it may) which I call an assumption of infallibility. It is the undertaking to decide that question *for others* without allowing them to hear what can be said on the contrary side. And I denounce and reprobate this pretension not the less, if put forth on the side of my most solemn convictions. However positive anyone's persuasion may be, not only of the falsity but of the pernicious consequences—not only of the pernicious consequences, but (to adopt expressions which I altogether condemn) the immorality and impiety of an opinion, yet if, in pursuance of that private judgment, though backed by the public judgment of his country or his contemporaries, he prevents the opinion from being heard in its defence, he assumes infallibility. And so far from the assumption being less objectionable or less dangerous because the opinion is called immoral or impious, this is the case of all others in which it is most fatal. There [*sic*] are exactly the occasions on which the men of one generation commit those dreadful mistakes which excite the astonishment and horror of posterity. It is among such that we find the instances memorable in history, when the arm of the law has been employed to root out the best men and the noblest doctrine; with deplorable success as to the men, though some of the doctrines have survived to be (as if in mockery) invoked in defence of similar conduct toward those who dissent from *them,* or from their received interpretation.

Mankind can hardly be too often reminded that there was once a man called Socrates, between whom and the legal authorities and public opinion of his time there took place a memorable collision. Born in an age and country abounding in individual greatness, this man has been handed down to us by those who best knew both him and the age, as the most virtuous man in it; while *we* know him as the head and prototype of all subsequent teachers of virtue, the source equally of the lofty inspiration of Plato and the judicious utilitarianism of Aristotle, *"i maestri di color che sanno,"* the two headsprings of ethical as of all other philosophy. This acknowledged master of all the eminent thinkers who have since lived—whose fame, still growing after more than two thousand years, all but outweighs the whole remainder of the names which make his native city illustrious— was put to death by his countrymen, after a judicial conviction, for impiety and immorality. Impiety, in denying the gods recognized by the State; indeed, his accuser asserted (see the "Apologia") that he believed in no gods at all. Immorality, in being, by his doctrines and instructions, a "corruptor of youth." Of these charges the tribunal, there is every ground for believing, honestly found him guilty, and condemned the man who probably of all then born had deserved best of mankind to be put to death as a criminal.

To pass from this to the only other instance of judicial iniquity, the mention of which, after the condemnation of Socrates, would not be an anticlimax: the event which took place on Calvary rather more than eighteen hundred years ago. The man who left on the memory of those who witnessed his life and conversation such an impression of his moral grandeur that eighteen subsequent centuries have done homage to him as the Almighty in person, was ignominiously put to death, as what? As a blasphemer. Men did not merely mistake their benefactor, they mistook him for the exact contrary of what he was, and treated him as that prodigy of impiety which they themselves are now held to be for their treatment of him. The feelings with which mankind now regards these lamentable transactions, especially the later of the two, render them extremely unjust in their judgment of the unhappy actors. These were, to all appearance, not bad men—not worse than men commonly are, but rather the contrary; men who possessed in a full, or somewhat more than a full measure, the religious, moral, and patriotic feelings of their time and people: the very kind of men who, in all times, our own included, have every chance of passing through life blameless and respected. The high-priest who rent his garments when the words were pronounced, which, according to all the ideas of his country, constituted the blackest guilt, was in all probability quite as sincere in his horror and indignation as the generality of respectable and pious men now are in the religious and moral sentiments they profess; and most of those who now shudder at his conduct, if they had lived in his time, and been born Jews, would have acted precisely as he did. Orthodox Christians who are tempted to think that those who stoned to death the first martyrs must have been worse men than they themselves are, ought to remember that one of those persecutors was Saint Paul. . . .

But, indeed, the dictum that truth always triumphs over persecution is one of those pleasant falsehoods which men repeat after one another till they pass into commonplaces, but which all experience refutes. History teems with instances of truth put down by persecution. If not suppressed forever, it may be thrown back for centuries. To speak only of religious opinions: the Reformation broke out at least twenty times before Luther, and was put down. Arnold of Bresica was put down. Fra Dolcino was put down. Savonarola was put down. The Albigeois were put down. The Vaudois were put down. The Lollards were put down. The Hussites were put down. Even after the era of Luther, wherever persecution was persisted in, it was successful. In Spain, Italy, Flanders, the Austrian empire,

Protestantism was rooted out; and, most likely, would have been so in England, had Queen Mary lived, or Queen Elizabeth died. Persecution has always succeeded, save where the heretics were too strong a party to be effectually persecuted. No reasonable person can doubt that Christianity might have been extirpated in the Roman Empire. It spread, and became predominant, because the persecutions were only occasional, lasting but a short time, and separated by long intervals of almost undisturbed propagandism. It is a piece of idle sentimentality that truth, merely as truth, has any inherent power denied to error of prevailing against the dungeon and the stake. Men are not more zealous for truth than they often are for error, and a sufficient application of legal or even of social penalties will generally succeed in stopping the propagation of either. The real advantage which truth has consists in this, that when an opinion is true, it may be extinguished once, twice, or many times, but in the course of ages there will generally be found persons to rediscover it, until some one of its reappearances falls on a time when from favourable circumstances it escapes persecution until it has made such head as to withstand all subsequent attempt to suppress it.

It will be said, that we do not now put to death the introducers of new opinions: we are not like our fathers who slew the prophets, we even build sepulchers to them. It is true we no longer put heretics to death; and the amount of penal infliction which modern feelings would probably tolerate, even against the most obnoxious opinions, is not sufficient to extirpate them. But let us not flatter ourselves that we are yet free from the strain even of legal persecution. Penalties for opinion, or at least for its expression, still exist by law; and their enforcement is not, even in these times, so unexampled as to make it at all incredible that they may some day be revived in full force. . . .

Let us now pass to the second division of the argument, and dismissing the supposition that any of the received opinions may be false, let us assume them to be true, and examine into the worth of the manner in which they are likely to be held, when their truth is not freely and openly canvassed. However unwillingly a person who has a strong opinion may admit the possibility that his opinion may be false, he ought to be moved by the consideration that, however true it may be, if it is not fully, frequently, and fearlessly discussed, it will be held as a dead dogma, not a living truth.

There is a class of persons (happily not quite so numerous as formerly) who think it enough if a person assents undoubtingly to what they think true, though he has no knowledge whatever of the grounds of the opinion, and could not make a tenable defence of it against the most superficial objections. Such persons, if they can once get their creed taught from authority, naturally think that no good, and some harm, comes of its being allowed to be questioned. Where their influence prevails, they make it nearly impossible for the received opinion to be rejected wisely and considerately, though it may still be rejected rashly and ignorantly; for to shut out discussion entirely is seldom possible, and when it once gets in, beliefs not grounded on conviction are apt to give way before the slightest semblance of an argument. Waiving, however, this possibility—assuming that the true opinion abides in the mind, but abides as a prejudice, a belief independent of, and proof against, argument—this is not the way in which truth ought to be held by a rational being. This is not knowing the truth. Truth, thus held, is but one superstition the more, accidentally clinging to the words which enunciate a truth.

If the intellect and judgment of mankind ought to be cultivated, a thing which Protestants at least do not deny, on what can these faculties be more appropriately exercised by anyone, than on the things which concern him so much that it is considered necessary for him to hold opinions on them? If the cultivation of the understanding consists in one thing more than in another, it is surely in learning the grounds of one's own opinions. Whatever people believe, on subjects on which it is of the first importance to believe rightly, they ought to be able to defend against at least the common objections. But, someone may say, "Let them be *taught* the grounds of their opinions. It does not follow that opinions must be merely parroted because they are never heard controverted. Persons who learn geometry do not simply commit the theorems to memory, but understand and learn likewise the demonstrations; and it would be absurd to say that they remain ignorant of the grounds of geometrical truths, because they never hear anyone deny, and attempt to disprove them." Undoubtedly: and such teaching suffices on a subject like mathematics, where there is nothing at all to be said on the wrong side of the question. The peculiarity of the evidence of mathematical truths is that all the argument is on one side. There are no objections, and no answers to objections. But on every subject on which difference of opinion is possible, the truth depends on a balance to be struck between two sets of conflicting reasons. Even in natural philosophy, there is always some other explanation possible of the same facts; some geocentric theory instead of heliocentric, some phlogiston instead of oxygen; and it has to be shown why that other theory cannot be the true one: and until this is shown, and until we know how it is shown, we do not understand the grounds of our opinion. But when we turn to subjects infinitely more complicated, to morals, religion, politics, social relations, and the business of life, three-fourths of the arguments for every disputed opinion consist in dispelling the appearances which favor some opinion different from it. The greatest orator, save one, of antiquity, has left it on record that he always studied his adversary's case with as great, if not still greater, intensity than even his own. What Cicero practised as the means of forensic success requires to be imitated by all who study any subject in order to arrive at the truth. He who knows only his own side of the case knows little of that. His reasons may be good, and no one may have been able to refute them. But if he is equally unable to refute the reasons on the opposite side; if he does not so much as know what they are, he has no ground for preferring either opinion. The rational position for him would be suspension of judgment, and unless he contents himself with that, he is either led by authority, or adopts, like the generality of the world, the side to which he feels most inclination. Nor is it enough that he should hear the arguments of adversaries from his own teachers, presented as they state them, and accompanied by what they offer as refutations. That is not the way to do justice to the arguments, or bring them into real contact with his own mind. He must be able to hear them from persons who actually believe them; who defend them in earnest, and do their very utmost for them. He must know them in their most plausible and persuasive form; he must feel the whole force of the difficulty which the true view of the subject has to encounter and dispose of; else he will never really possess himself of the portion of truth which meets and removes that difficulty. Ninety-nine in a hundred of what are called educated men are in this condition; even of those who can argue fluently for their opinions. Their conclusion may be true, but it might be false for anything they know: they have never thrown themselves into the mental position of those who think differently from them, and considered what such persons may have to say; and consequently they do not, in any proper sense of the word, know the doctrine which they themselves profess. They do not know those parts of it which explain and justify the remainder; the considerations which show that a fact which seemingly conflicts with another is reconcilable with it, or that, of two apparently strong reasons, one and not the other ought to be preferred. All that part of the truth which turns the scale, and decides the judgment of a completely informed mind, they are strangers to; nor is it ever really known, but to those who have attended equally and impartially to both sides, and endeavoured to see the reasons of both in the strongest light. So essential is this discipline to a real understanding of moral and human subjects, that if opponents of all important truths do not exist, it is indispensable to imagine them, and supply them with the strongest arguments which the most skillful devil's advocate can conjure up. . . .

If, however, the mischievous operation of the absence of free discussion, when the received opinions are true, were confined to leaving men ignorant of the grounds of those opinions, it might be thought that this, if an intellectual, is no moral evil, and does not affect the worth of the opinions, regarded in their influence on the character. The fact, however, is, that not only the grounds of the opinion are forgotten in the absence of discussion, but too often the meaning of the opinion itself. The words which convey it cease to suggest ideas, or suggest only a small portion of those they were originally employed to communicate. Instead of a vivid conception and a living belief, there remain only a few phrases retained by rote; or, if any part, the shell and husk only of the meaning is retained, the finer essence being lost. . . .

To what an extent doctrines intrinsically fitted to make the deepest impression upon the mind may remain in it as dead beliefs, without being ever realised in the imagination, the feelings, or the understanding, is exemplified by the manner in which the majority of believers hold the doctrines of Christianity. By Christianity I here mean what is accounted such by all churches and sects—the maxims and precepts contained in the New Testament. These are considered sacred, and accepted as laws, by all professing Christians. Yet it is scarcely too much to say that not one Christian in a thousand guides or tests his individual conduct by reference to those laws. The standard to which he does refer it, is the custom of his nation, his class, or his religious profession. He has thus, on the one hand, a collection of ethical maxims, which he believes to have been vouchsafed to him by infallible wisdom as rules for his government; and on the other a set of everyday judgments and practices, which go a certain length with some of those maxims, not so great a length with others, stand in direct opposition to some, and are, on the whole, a compromise between the Christian creed and the interests and suggestions of wor[l]dly life. To the first of these standards he gives his homage; to the other his real allegiance. All Christians believe that the blessed are the poor and humble, and those who are ill-used by the world; that it is easier for a camel to pass through the eye of a needle than for a rich man to enter the kingdom of heaven; that they should judge not, lest they be judged; that they should swear not at all; that they should love their neighbour as themselves; that if one take their cloak, they should give him their coat also; that they should take no thought for the morrow; that if they would be perfect they should sell all that they have and give it to the poor. They are not insincere when they say that they believe these things. They do believe them, as people believe what they have always heard lauded and never discussed. But in the sense of that living belief which regulates conduct, they believe these doctrines just up to the point to which it is usual to act upon them. The doctrines in their integrity are serviceable to pelt adversaries with; and it is understood that they are to be put forward (when possible) as the reasons for whatever people do that they think laudable. But anyone who reminded them that the maxims require an infinity of things which they never even think of doing, would gain nothing but to be classed among those very unpopular characters who affect to be better than other people. The doctrines have no hold on ordinary believers—are not a power in their minds. They have an habitual respect for the sound of them, but no feeling which spreads from the words to the things signified, and forces the mind to take *them* in, and make them conform to the formula. Whenever conduct is concerned, they look round for Mr. A and B to direct them how far to go in obeying Christ. . . .

But what! (it may be asked) Is the absence of unanimity an indispensable condition of true knowledge? Is it necessary that some part of mankind should persist in error to enable any to realize the truth? Does a belief cease to be real and vital as soon as it is generally received—and is a proposition never thoroughly understood and felt unless some doubt of it remains? As soon as mankind have unanimously accepted a truth, does the truth perish within them? The highest aim and best result of improved intelligence, it has hitherto been thought, is to unite mankind more and more in the acknowledgment of all important truths; and does the intelligence only last as long as it has not achieved its object? Do the fruits of conquest perish by the very completeness of the victory?

I affirm no such thing. As mankind improve, the number of doctrines which are no longer disputed or doubted will be constantly on the increase: and the well-being of mankind may almost be measured by the number and gravity of the truths which have reached the point of being uncontested. The cessation, on one question after another, of serious controversy, is one of the necessary incidents of the consolidation of opinion; a consolidation as salutary in the case of true opinions, as it is dangerous and noxious when the opinions are erroneous. But though this gradual narrowing of the bounds of diversity of opinion is necessary in both senses of the term, being at once inevitable and indispensable, we are not therefore obliged to conclude that all its consequences must be beneficial. The loss of so important an aid to the intelligent and living apprehension of a truth, as is afforded by the necessity of explaining it to, or defending it against, opponents, though not sufficient to outweigh, is no trifling drawback, from the benefit of its universal recognition. Where this advantage can no longer be had, I confess I should like to see the teachers of mankind endeavoring to provide a substitute for it; some contrivance for making the difficulties of the question as present to the learner's consciousness, as if they were pressed upon him by a dissentient champion, eager for his conversion. . . .

It still remains to speak of one of the principal causes which make diversity of opinion advantageous, and will continue to do so until mankind shall have entered a stage of intellectual advancement which at present seems at an incalculable distance. We have hitherto considered only two possibilities: that the received opinion may be false, and some other opinion, consequently, true; or that, the received opinion being true, a conflict with the opposite error is essential to a clear apprehension and deep feeling of its truth. But there is a commoner case than either of these; when the conflicting doctrines, instead of being one true and the other false, share the truth between them; and the nonconforming opinion is needed to supply the remainder of the truth, of which the received doctrine embodies only a part. Popular opinions, on subjects not palpable to sense, are often true, but seldom or never the whole truth. They are a part of the truth; sometimes a greater, sometimes a smaller part, but exaggerated, distorted, and disjointed from the truths by which they ought to be accompanied and limited. Heretical opinions, on the other hand, are generally some of these suppressed and neglected truths, bursting the bonds which kept them down, and either seeking reconciliation with the truth contained in the common opinion, or fronting it as enemies, and setting themselves up, with similar exclusiveness, as the whole truth. The latter case is hitherto the most frequent, as, in the human mind, one-sidedness has always been the rule, and many-sidedness the exception. Hence, even in revolutions of opinion, one part of the truth usually sets while another rises. Even progress, which ought to superadd, for the most part only substitutes, one partial and incomplete truth for another; improvement consisting chiefly in this, that the new fragment of truth is more wanted, more adapted to the needs of the time, than that which it displaces. Such being the partial character of prevailing opinions, even when resting on a true foundation, every opinion which embodies somewhat of the portion of truth which the common opinion omits, ought to be considered precious, with whatever amount of error and confusion that truth may be blended. No sober judge of human affairs will feel bound to be indignant because those who force on our notice truths which we should otherwise have overlooked, overlook some of those which we see. Rather, he will think that so long as popular truth is one-sided, it is more desirable than otherwise that unpopular truth should have one-sided assertors too; such being usually the most energetic, and the most likely to compel reluctant attention to the fragment of wisdom which they proclaim as if it were the whole. . . .

In politics, again, it is almost a commonplace, that a party of order or stability, and a party of progress or reform, are both necessary elements of a healthy state of political life; until the one or the other shall have so enlarged its mental grasp as to be a party equally of order and of progress, knowing and distinguishing what is fit to be preserved from what ought to be swept away. Each of these modes of thinking derives its utility from the deficiencies of the other; but it is in a great measure the opposition of the other that keeps each within the limits of reason and sanity. Unless opinions favourable to democracy and to aristocracy, to property and to equality, to co-operation and to competition, to luxury and to abstinence, to sociality and individuality, to liberty and discipline, and all the other standing antagonisms of practical life, are expressed with equal freedom, and enforced and defended with equal talent and energy, there is no chance of both elements obtaining their due; one scale is sure to go up, and the other down. Truth, in the great practical concerns of life, is so much a question of the reconciling and combining of opposites, that very few have minds sufficiently capacious and impartial to make the adjustment with an approach to correctness, and it has to be made by the rough process of a struggle between combatants fighting under hostile banners. On any of the great open questions just enumerated, if either of the two opinions has a better claim than the other, not merely to be tolerated, but to be encouraged and countenanced, it is the one which happens at the particular time and place to be in a minority. That is the opinion which, for the time being, represents the neglected interests, the side of human well-being which is in danger of obtaining less than its share. I am aware that there is not, in this country, any intolerance of differences of opinion on most of these topics. They are adduced to show, by admitted and multiplied examples, the universality of the fact that only through diversity of opinion is there, in the existing state of human intellect, a chance of fair play to all sides of the truth. When there are persons to be found who form an exception to the apparent unanimity of the world of any subject, even if the world is in the right, it is always probable that dissentients have something worth hearing to say for themselves, and that truth would lose something by their silence. . . .

I do not pretend that the most unlimited use of the freedom of enunciating all possible opinions would put an end to the evils of religious or philosophical sectarianism. Every truth which men of narrow capacity are in earnest about, is sure to be asserted, inculcated, and in many ways even acted on, as if no other truth existed in the world, or at all events none that could limit or qualify the first. I acknowledge that the tendency of all opinions to become sectarian is not cured by the freest discussion, but is often heightened and exacerbated thereby; the truth which ought to have been, but was not, seen, being rejected all the more violently because proclaimed by persons regarded as opponents. But it is not on the impassioned partisan, it is on the calmer and more disinterested bystander, that this collision of opinions works its salutary effect. Not the violent conflict between parts of the truth, but the quiet suppression of half of it, is the formidable evil; there is always hope when people are forced to listen to both sides; it is when they attend only to one that errors harden into prejudices, and truth itself ceases to have the effect of truth, by being exaggerated into falsehood. And since there are few mental attributes more rare than that judicial faculty which can sit in intelligent judgment between two sides of a question, of which only one is represented by an advocate before it, truth has no chance but in proportion as every side of it, every opinion which embodies any fraction of the truth, not only finds advocates, but is so advocated as to be listened to.

We have now recognised the necessity to the mental well-being of mankind (on which all their other well-being depends) of freedom of opinion, and freedom of the expression of opinion, on four distinct grounds; which we will now briefly recapitulate.

First, if any opinion is compelled to silence, that opinion may, for aught we can certainly know, be true. To deny this is to assume our own infallibility.

Secondly, though the silenced opinion be an error, it may, and very commonly does, contain a portion of truth; and since the general or prevailing opinion on any subject is rarely or never the whole truth, it is only by the collision of adverse opinions that the remainder of the truth has any chance of being supplied.

Thirdly, even if the received opinion be not only true, but the whole truth; unless it is suffered to be, and actually is, vigorously and earnestly contested, it will, by most of those who receive it, be held in the manner of a prejudice, with little comprehension or feeling of its rational grounds. And not only this, but, fourthly, the meaning of the doctrine itself will be in danger of being lost or enfeebled, and deprived of its vital effect on the character and conduct: the dogma becoming a mere formal profession, inefficacious for good, but cumbering the ground, and preventing the growth of any real and heartfelt conviction, from reason or personal experience.

Before quitting the subject of freedom of opinion, it is fit to take some notice of those who say that the free expression of all opinions should be permitted, on condition that the manner be temperate, and do not pass the bounds of fair discussion. Much might be said on the impossibility of fixing where these supposed bounds are to be placed; for if the test be offence to those whose opinions are attacked, I think experience testifies that this offence is given whenever the attack is telling and powerful, and that every opponent who pushes them hard, and whom they find it difficult to answer, appears to them, if he shows any strong feeling on the subject, an intemperate opponent. But this, though an important consideration in a practical point of view, merges in a more fundamental objection. Undoubtedly the manner of asserting an opinion, even though it be a true one, may be very objectionable, and may justly incur severe censure. But the principal offences of the kind are such as it is mostly impossible, unless by accidental self-betrayal, to bring home to conviction. The gravest of them is, to argue sophistically, to suppress facts or arguments, to misstate the elements of the case, or misrepresent the opposite opinion. But all this, even to the most aggravated degree, is so continually done in perfect good faith, by persons who are not considered, and in many other respects may not deserve to be considered, ignorant or incompetent, that it is rarely possible, on adequate grounds, conscientiously to stamp the misrepresentation as morally culpable; and still less could law presume to interfere with this kind of controversial misconduct. With regard to what is commonly meant by intemperate discussion, namely invective, sarcasm, personality, and the like, the denunciation of these weapons would deserve more sympathy if it were ever proposed to interdict them equally to both sides; but it is only desired to restrain the employment of them against the prevailing opinion: against the unprevailing they may not only be used without general disapproval, but will be likely to obtain for him who uses them the praise of honest zeal and righteous indignation. Yet whatever mischief arises from their use is greatest when they are employed against the comparatively defenceless; and whatever unfair advantage can be derived by any opinion from this mode of asserting it, accrues almost exclusively to received opinions. The worst offence of this kind which can be committed by a polemic is to stigmatize those who hold the contrary opinion as bad and immoral men. To calumny of this sort, those who hold any unpopular opinion are peculiarly exposed, because they are in general few and uninfluential, and nobody but themselves feels much interested in seeing justice done them; but this weapon is, from the nature of the case, denied to those who attack a prevailing opinion: they can neither use it with safety to themselves, nor, if they could, would it do anything but recoil on their own cause. In general, opinions contrary to those commonly received can only obtain a hearing by studied moderation of language, and the most cautious avoidance of unnecessary offence, from which they hardly ever deviate even in a slight degree without losing ground: while unmeasured vituperation employed on the side of the prevailing opinion really does deter people from professing contrary opinions, and from listening to those who profess them. For the interest, therefore, of truth and justice, it is far more important to restrain this employment of vituperative language than the other; and, for example, if it were necessary to choose, there would be much more need to discourage offensive attacks on infidelity than on religion. It is, however, obvious that law and authority have no business with restraining either, while opinion ought, in every instance, to determine its verdict by the circumstances of the individual case; condemning everyone, on whichever side of the argument he places himself, in whose mode of advocacy either want of candor, or malignity, bigotry, or intolerance of feeling manifest themselves; but not inferring these vices from the side which a person takes, though it be the contrary side of the question to our own; and giving merited honor to every one, whatever opinion he may hold, who has calmness to see and honesty to state what his opponents and their opinions really are, exaggerating nothing to their discredit, keeping nothing back which tells, or can be supposed to tell, in their favor. This is the real morality of public discussion: and if often violated, I am happy to think that there are many controversialists who to a great extent observe it, and a still greater number who conscientiously strive towards it.

3

The Federalist Papers, nos. 10 and 51 (1787–1788)

The Federalist Papers, *written by Alexander Hamilton, John Jay, and James Madison, were originally published in New York City newspapers during the debate over ratification of the Constitution. Intended as a defense of the document, they have become an authoritative interpretation of it.* Federalist *no. 10 outlines the principles of representation and federalism.* Federalist *no. 51 explains the separation of powers and checks and balances.*

Federalist no. 10

AMONG THE NUMEROUS advantages promised by a well-constructed Union, none deserves to be more accurately developed than its tendency to break and control the violence of faction. The friend of popular governments never finds himself so much alarmed for their character and fate as when he contemplates their propensity to this dangerous vice. He will not fail, therefore, to set a due value on any plan which, without violating the principles to which he is attached, provides a proper cure for it. The instability, injustice, and confusion introduced into the public councils have, in truth, been the mortal disease under which popular governments have everywhere perished, as they continue to be the favorite and fruitful topics from which the adversaries to liberty derive their most specious declamations. The valuable improvements made by the American constitutions on the popular models, both ancient and modern, cannot certainly be too much admired; but it would be an unwarrantable partiality to contend that they have as effectually obviated the danger on this side, as was wished and expected. Complaints are everywhere heard from our most considerate and virtuous citizens, equally the friends of public and private faith and of public and personal liberty, that our governments are too unstable, that the public good is disregarded in the conflicts of rival parties, and that measures are too often decided, not according to the rules of justice and the rights of the minor party, but by the superior force of an interested and overbearing majority. However anxiously we may wish that these complaints had no foundation, the evidence of known facts will not permit us to deny that they are in some degree true. It will be found, indeed, on a candid review of our situation, that some of the distresses under which we labor have been erroneously charged on the operation of our governments; but it will be found, at the same time, that other causes will not alone account for many of our heaviest misfortunes; and, particularly, for that prevailing and increasing distrust of public engagements and alarm for private rights which are echoed from one end of the continent to the other. These must be chiefly, if not wholly, effects of the unsteadiness and injustice with which a factious spirit has tainted our public administration.

By a faction I understand a number of citizens, whether amounting to a majority or minority of the whole, who are united and actuated by some common impulse of passion, or of interest, adverse to the rights of other citizens, or to the permanent and aggregate interests of the community.

There are two methods of curing the mischiefs of faction: the one, by removing its causes; the other, by controlling its effects.

There are again two methods of removing the causes of faction: the one, by destroying the liberty which is essential to its existence; the other, by giving to every citizen the same opinions, the same passions, and the same interests.

It could never be more truly said than of the first remedy that it was worse than the disease. Liberty is to faction what air is to fire, an aliment without which it instantly expires. But it could not be a less folly to abolish liberty, which is essential to political life, because it nourishes faction than it would be to wish the annihilation of air, which is essential to animal life, because it imparts to fire its destructive agency.

The second expedient is as impracticable as the first would be unwise. As long as the reason of man continues fallible, and he is at liberty to exercise it, different opinions will be formed. As long as the connection subsists between his reason and his self-love, his opinions and his passions will have a reciprocal influence on each other; and the former will be objects to which the latter will attach themselves. The diversity in the faculties of men, from which the rights of property originate, is not less an insuperable obstacle to a uniformity of interests. The protection of these faculties is the first object of government. From the protection of different and unequal faculties of acquiring property, the possession of different degrees and kinds of property immediately results; and from the influence of these on the sentiments and views of the respective proprietors ensues a division of the society into different interests and parties.

The latent causes of faction are thus sown in the nature of man; and we see them everywhere brought into different degrees of activity, according to the different circumstances of civil society. A zeal for different opinions concerning religion, concerning government, and many other points, as well of speculation as of practice; an attachment to different leaders ambitiously contending for preeminence and power; or to persons of other descriptions whose fortunes have been interesting to the human passions, have, in turn, divided mankind into parties, inflamed them with mutual animosity, and rendered them much more disposed to vex and oppress each other than to co-operate for their common good. So strong is this propensity of mankind to fall into mutual animosities that where no substantial occasion presents itself the most frivolous and fanciful distinctions have been sufficient to kindle their unfriendly passions and excite their most violent conflicts. But the most common and durable source of factions has been the various and unequal distribution of property. Those who hold and those who are without property have ever formed distinct interests in society. Those who are creditors, and those who are debtors, fall under a like discrimination. A landed interest, a manufacturing interest, a mercantile interest, a moneyed interest, with many lesser interests, grow up of necessity in civilized nations, and divide them into different classes, actuated by different sentiments and views. The regulation of these various and interfering interests forms the principal task of modern legislation and involves the spirit of party and faction in the necessary and ordinary operations of government.

No man is allowed to be a judge in his own cause because his interest would certainly bias his judgment, and, not improbably, corrupt his integrity. With equal, nay with greater reason, a body of men are unfit to be both judges and parties at the same time; yet what are many of the most important acts of legislation but so many judicial determinations, not indeed concerning the rights of single persons, but concerning the rights of large bodies of citizens? And what are the different classes of legislators but advocates and parties to the causes which they determine? Is a law proposed concerning private debts? It is a question to which the creditors are parties on one side and debtors on the other. Justice ought to hold the balance between them. Yet the parties are, and must be, themselves the judges; and the most numerous party, or in other words, the most powerful faction must be expected to prevail. Shall domestic manufacturers be encouraged, and in what degree, by restrictions on foreign manufacturers? are questions which would be differently decided by the landed and the manufacturing classes, and probably by neither with a sole regard to justice and the public good. The apportionment of taxes on the various descriptions of property is an act which seems to require the most exact impartiality; yet there is, perhaps, no legislative act in which greater opportunity and temptation are given to a predominant party to trample on the rules of justice. Every shilling with which they overburden the inferior number is a shilling saved to their own pockets.

It is in vain to say that enlightened statesmen will be able to adjust these clashing interests and render them all subservient to the public good. Enlightened statesmen will not always be at the helm. Nor in many cases, can such an adjustment be made at all without taking into view indirect and remote considerations, which will rarely prevail over the immediate interest which one party may find in disregarding the rights of another or the good of the whole.

The inference to which we are brought is that the *causes* of faction cannot be removed and that relief is only to be sought in the means of controlling its *effects*.

If a faction consists of less than a majority, relief is supplied by the republican principle, which enables the majority to defeat its sinister views by regular vote. It may clog the administration, it may convulse the society; but it will be unable to execute and mask its violence under the forms of the Constitution. When a majority is included in a faction, the form of popular government, on the other hand, enables it to sacrifice to its ruling passion or interest both the public good and the rights of other citizens. To secure the public good and private rights against the danger of such a faction, and at the same time to preserve the spirit and the form of popular government, is then the great object to which alone this form of government can be rescued from the opprobrium under which it has so long labored and be recommended to the esteem and adoption of mankind.

By what means is this object attainable? Evidently by one of two only. Either the existence of the same passion or interest in a majority at the same time must be prevented, or the majority, having such coexistent passion or interest, must be rendered, by their number and local situation, unable to concert and carry into effect schemes of oppression. If the impulse and the opportunity be suffered to coincide, we well know that neither moral nor religious motives can be relied on as an adequate control. They are not found to be such on the injustice and violence of individuals, and lose their efficacy in proportion to the number combined together, that is, as their efficacy becomes needful.

From this view of the subject it may be concluded that a pure democracy, by which I mean a society consisting of a small number of citizens, who assemble and administer the government in person, can admit of no cure for the mischiefs of faction. A common passion or interest will, in almost every case, be felt by a majority of the whole; a communication and concert results from the form of government itself; and there is nothing to check the inducements to sacrifice the weaker party or an obnoxious individual. Hence it is that such democracies have ever been spectacles of turbulence and contention; have ever been found incompatible with personal security or the rights of property; and have in general been as short in their lives as they have been violent in their deaths. Theoretic politicians, who have patronized this species of government, have erroneously supposed that by reducing mankind to a perfect equality in their political rights, they would at the same time be perfectly equalized and assimilated in their possessions, their opinions, and their passions.

A republic, by which I mean a government in which the scheme of representation takes place, opens a different prospect and promises the cure for which we are seeking. Let us examine the points in which it varies from pure democracy, and we shall comprehend both the nature of the cure and the efficacy which it must derive from the Union.

The two great points of difference between a democracy and a republic are: first, the delegation of the government, in the latter, to a small number of citizens elected by the rest; secondly, the greater number of citizens and greater sphere of country over which the latter may be extended.

The effect of the first difference is, on the one hand, to refine and enlarge the public views by passing them through the medium of a chosen body of citizens, whose wisdom may best discern the true interest of their country and whose patriotism and love of justice will be least likely to sacrifice it to temporary or partial considerations. Under such a regulation it may well happen that the public voice, pronounced by the representatives of the people, will be more consonant to the public good than if pronounced by the people themselves, convened for the purpose. On the other hand, the effect may be inverted. Men of factious tempers, of local prejudices, or of sinister designs, may, by intrigue, by corruption, or by other means, first obtain the suffrages, and then betray the interests of the people. The question resulting is, whether small or extensive republics are most favorable to the election of proper guardians of the public weal; and it is clearly decided in favor of the latter by two obvious considerations.

In the first place it is to be remarked that however small the republic may be the representatives must be raised to a certain number in order to guard against the cabals of a few; and that however large it may be they must be limited to a certain number in order to guard against the confusion of a multitude. Hence, the number of representatives in the two cases not being in proportion to that of the constituents, and being proportionally greatest in the small republic, it follows that if the proportion of fit characters be not less in the large than in the small republic, the former will present a greater option, and consequently a greater probability of a fit choice.

In the next place, as each representative will be chosen by a greater number of citizens in the large than in the small republic, it will be more difficult for unworthy candidates to practise with success the vicious arts by which elections are too often carried; and the suffrages of the people being more free, will be more likely to center on men who possess the most attractive merit and the most diffusive and established characters.

It must be confessed that in this, as in most other cases, there is a mean, on both sides of which inconveniences will be found to lie. By enlarging too much the number of electors, you render the representative too little acquainted with all their local circumstances and lesser interests; as by reducing it too much, you render him unduly attached to these and too little fit to comprehend and pursue great and national objects. The federal Constitution forms a happy combination in this respect; the great and aggregate interests being referred to the national, the local and particular to the State legislatures.

The other point of difference is the greater number of citizens and extent of territory which may be brought within the compass of republican than of democratic government; and it is this circumstance principally which renders factious combinations less to be dreaded in the former than in the latter. The smaller the society, the fewer probably will be the distinct parties and interests composing it; the fewer the distinct parties and interests, the more frequently will a majority be found of the same party; and the smaller the number of individuals composing a majority, and the smaller the compass within which they are placed, the more easily will they concert and execute their plans of oppression. Extend the sphere and you take in a greater variety of parties and interests; you make it less probable that a majority of the whole will have a common motive to invade the rights of other citizens; or if such a common motive exists, it will be more difficult for all who feel it to discover their own strength and to act in unison with each other. Besides other impediments, it may be remarked that, where there is a consciousness of unjust or dishonorable purposes, communication is always checked by distrust in proportion to the number whose concurrence is necessary.

Hence, it clearly appears that the same advantage which a republic has over democracy in controlling the effects of faction is enjoyed by a large over a small republic—is enjoyed by the Union over the States composing it. Does this advantage consist in the substitution of representatives whose enlightened views and virtuous sentiments render them superior to local prejudices and to schemes of injustice? It will not be denied that the representation of the Union will be most likely to possess these requisite endowments. Does it consist in the greater security afforded by a greater variety of parties, against the event of any one party being able to outnumber and oppress the rest? In an equal degree does the increased variety of parties comprised within the Union increase this security. Does it, in fine, consist in the greater obstacles opposed to the concert and accomplishment of the secret wishes of an unjust and interested majority? Here again the extent of the Union gives it the most palpable advantage.

The influence of factious leaders may kindle a flame within their particular States but will be unable to spread a general conflagration through the other States. A religious sect may degenerate into a political faction in a part of the Confederacy; but the variety of sects dispersed over the entire face of it must secure the national councils against any danger from that source. A rage for paper money, for an abolition of debts, for an equal division of property, or for any other improper or wicked project, will be less apt to pervade the whole body of the Union than a particular member of it, in the same proportion as such a malady is more likely to taint a particular county or district than an entire State.

In the extent and proper structure of the Union, therefore, we behold a republican remedy for the diseases most incident to republican government. And according to the degree of pleasure and pride we feel in being republicans ought to be our zeal in cherishing the spirit and supporting the character of federalists.

Federalist no. 51

To what expedient, then, shall we finally resort, for maintaining in practice the necessary partition of power among the several departments as laid down in the Constitution? The only answer that can be given is that as all these exterior provisions are found to be inadequate the defect must be supplied, by so contriving the interior structure of the government as that its several constituent parts may, by their mutual relations, be the means of keeping each other in their proper places. Without presuming to undertake a full development of this important idea I will hazard a few general observations which may perhaps place it in a clearer light, and enable us to form a more correct judgment of the principles and structure of the government planned by the convention.

In order to lay a due foundation for that separate and distinct exercise of the different powers of government, which to a certain extent is admitted on all hands to be essential to the preservation of liberty, it is evident that each department should have a will of its own; and consequently should be so constituted that the members of each should have as little agency as possible in the appointment of the members of the others. Were this principle rigorously adhered to, it would require that all the appointments for the supreme executive, legislative, and judiciary magistracies should be drawn from the same fountain of authority, the people, through channels having no communication whatever with one another. Perhaps such a plan of constructing the several departments would be less difficult in practice than it may in contemplation appear. Some difficulties, however, and some additional expense would attend the execution of it. Some deviations, therefore, from the principle must be admitted. In the constitution of the judiciary department in particular, it might be inexpedient to insist rigorously on the principle: first, because peculiar qualifications being essential in the members, the primary consideration ought to be to select that mode of choice which best secures these qualifications: second, because the permanent tenure by which the appointments are held in that department must soon destroy all sense of dependence on the authority conferring them.

It is equally evident that the members of each department should be as little dependent as possible on those of the others for the emoluments annexed to their offices. Were the executive magistrate, or the judges, not independent of the legislature in this particular, their independence in every other would be merely nominal.

But the great security against a gradual concentration of the several powers in the same department consists in giving to those who administer each department the necessary constitutional means and personal motives to resist encroachments of the others. The provision for defense must in this, as in all other cases, be made commensurate to the danger of attack. Ambition must be made to counteract ambition. The interest of the man must be connected with the constitutional rights of the place. It may be a reflection on human nature that such devices should be necessary to control the abuses of government. But what is government itself but the greatest of all reflections on human nature? If men were angels, no government would be necessary. If angels were to govern men, neither external nor internal controls on government would be necessary. In framing a government which is to be administered by men over men, the great difficulty lies in this: you must first enable the government to control the governed; and in the next place oblige it to control itself. A dependence on the people is, no doubt, the primary control on the government; but experience has taught mankind the necessity of auxiliary precautions.

This policy of supplying, by opposite and rival interests, the defect of better motives, might be traced through the whole system of human affairs, private as well as public. We see it particularly displayed in all the subordinate distributions of power, where the constant aim is to divide and arrange the several offices in such a manner as that each may be a check on the other—that the private interest of every individual may be a sentinel over the public rights. These inventions of prudence cannot be less requisite in the distribution of the supreme powers of the State.

But it is not possible to give to each department an equal power of self-defense. In republican government, the legislative authority necessarily predominates. The remedy for this inconveniency is to divide the legislature into different branches; and to render them, by different modes of election and different principles of action, as little connected with each other as the nature of their common functions and their common dependence on the society will admit. It may even be necessary to guard against dangerous encroachments by still further precautions. As the weight of the legislative authority requires that it should be thus divided, the weakness of the executive may require, on the other hand, that it should be fortified. An absolute negative on the legislature appears, at first view, to be the natural defense with which the executive magistrate should be armed. But perhaps it would be neither altogether safe nor alone sufficient. On ordinary occasions it might not be exerted with the requisite firmness and on extraordinary occasions it might be perfidiously abused. May not this defect of an absolute negative be supplied by some qualified connection between this weaker department and the weaker branch of the stronger department, by which the latter may be led to support the constitutional rights of the former, without being too much detached from the rights of its own department?

If the principles on which these observations are founded be just, as I persuade myself they are, and they be applied as a criterion to the several State constitutions, and to the federal Constitution, it will be found that if the latter does not perfectly correspond with them, the former are infinitely less able to bear such a test.

There are, moreover, two considerations particularly applicable to the federal system of America, which place that system in a very interesting point of view.

First. In a single republic, all the power surrendered by the people is submitted to the administration of a single government; and the usurpations are guarded against by a division of the government into distinct and separate departments. In the compound republic of America, the power surrendered by the people is first divided between two distinct governments, and then the portion allotted to each subdivided among distinct and separate departments. Hence a double security arises to the rights of the people. The different governments will control each other, at the same time that each will be controlled by itself.

Second. It is of great importance in a republic not only to guard the society against the oppression of its rulers, but to guard one part of the society against the injustice of the other part. Different interests necessarily exist in different classes of citizens. If a majority be united by a common interest, the rights of the minority will be insecure. There are but two methods of providing against this evil: the one by creating a will in the community independent of the majority— that is, of the society itself; the other, by comprehending in the society so many separate descriptions of citizens as will render an unjust combination of a majority of the whole very improbable, if not impracticable. The first method prevails in all governments possessing an hereditary or self-appointed authority. This, at best, is but a precarious security; because a power independent of the society may as well espouse the unjust views of the major as the rightful interests of the minor party, and may possibly be turned against both parties. The second method will be exemplified in the federal republic of the United States. Whilst all authority in it will be derived from and dependent on the society, the society itself will be broken into so many parts, interests and classes of citizens, that the rights of individuals, or of the minority, will be in little danger from interested combinations of the majority. In a free government the security for civil rights must be the multiplicity of interests, and in the other in the multiplicity of sects. The degree of security in both cases will depend on the number of interests and sects; and this may be presumed to depend on the extent of country and number of people comprehended under the same government. This view of the subject must particularly recommend a proper federal system to all the sincere and considerate friends of republican government, since it shows that in exact proportion as the territory of the Union may be formed into more circumscribed Confederacies, or States, oppressive combinations of a majority will be facilitated; the best security, under the republican forms, for the rights of every class of citizen, will be diminished; and consequently the stability and independence of some member of the government, the only other security, must be proportionally increased. Justice is the end of government. It is the end of civil society. It ever has been and ever will be pursued until it be obtained, or until liberty be lost in the pursuit. In a society under the forms of which the stronger faction can readily unite and oppress the weaker, anarchy may as truly be said to reign as in a state of nature, where the weaker individual is not secured against the violence of the stronger; and as, in the latter state, even the stronger individuals are prompted, by the uncertainty of their condition, to submit to a government which may protect the weak as well as themselves; so, in the former state, will the more powerful factions or parties be gradually induced, by a like motive, to wish for a government which will protect all parties, the weaker as well as the more powerful. It can be little doubted that if the State of Rhode Island was separated from the Confederacy and left to itself, the insecurity of rights under the popular form of government within such narrow limits would be displayed by such reiterated oppressions of factious majorities that some power altogether independent of the people would soon be called for by the voice of the very factions whose misrule had proved the necessity of it. In the extended republic of the United States, and among the great variety of interests, parties, and sects which it embraces, a coalition of a majority of the whole society could seldom take place on any other principles than those of justice and the general good; whilst there being less pretext, also, to provide for the security of the former, by introducing into the government a will not dependent on the latter, or, in other words, a will independent of the society itself. It is no less certain than it is important, notwithstanding the contrary opinions which have been entertained, that the larger the society, provided it lie within a practicable sphere, the more duly capable it will be of self-government. And happily for the *republican cause,* the practicable sphere may be carried to a very great extent by a judicious modification and mixture of the *federal principle.*

4

Thomas Hill Green

"Lecture on Liberal Legislation and Freedom of Contract" (1881)

Thomas Hill Green (1836–1882) was the leader of the British Idealist move-
ment, a school of liberal philosophers committed to radical political reforms,
including education for women. As a student and later teacher at Balliol
College, Oxford, he was inspired by Hegel's and Fichte's ideas of moral com-
munity. His "Lecture on Liberal Legislation and Freedom of Contract" is the
best-known statement of his egalitarian liberalism. Due to his sudden death
from blood poisoning in 1882, many of his important writings were published
posthumously, including Prolegomena to Ethics *and* Lectures on the
Principles of Political Obligation.

WE SHALL PROBABLY all agree that freedom, rightly understood, is the greatest of
blessings; that its attainment is the true end of all our effort as citizens. But when
we thus speak of freedom, we should consider carefully what we mean by it. We
do not mean merely freedom from restraint or compulsion. We do not mean
merely freedom to do as we like irrespectively of what it is that we like. We do
not mean a freedom that can be enjoyed by one man or one set of men at the
cost of a loss of freedom to others. When we speak of freedom as something to
be so highly prized, we mean a positive power or capacity of doing or enjoying
something worth doing or enjoying, and that, too, something that we do or
enjoy in common with others. We mean by it a power which each man exercises
through the help or security given him by his fellow-men, and which he in turn
helps to secure for them. When we measure the progress of a society by its

growth in freedom, we measure it by the increasing development and exercise on the whole of those powers of contributing to social good with which we believe the members of the society to be endowed; in short, by the greater power on the part of the citizens as a body to make the most and best of themselves. Thus, though of course there can be no freedom among men who act not willingly but under compulsion, yet on the other hand the mere removal of compulsion, the mere enabling a man to do as he likes, is in itself no contribution to true freedom. In one sense no man is so well able to do as he likes as the wandering savage. He has no master. There is no one to say him nay. Yet we do not count him really free, because the freedom of savagery is not strength, but weakness. The actual powers of the noblest savage do not admit of comparison with those of the humblest citizen of a law-abiding state. He is not the slave of man, but he is the slave of nature. Of compulsion by natural necessity he has plenty of experience, though of restraint by society none at all. Nor can he deliver himself from that compulsion except by submitting to this restraint. So to submit is the first step in true freedom, because the first step towards the full exercise of the faculties with which man is endowed. But we rightly refuse to recognise the highest development on the part of an exceptional individual or exceptional class, as an advance towards the true freedom of man, if it is founded on a refusal of the same opportunity to other men. The powers of the human mind have probably never attained such force and keenness, the proof of what society can do for the individual has never been so strikingly exhibited, as among the small groups of men who possessed civil privileges in the small republics of antiquity. The whole framework of our political ideas, to say nothing of our philosophy, is derived from them. But in them this extraordinary efflorescence of the privileged class was accompanied by the slavery of the multitude. That slavery was the condition on which it depended, and for that reason it was doomed to decay. There is no clearer ordinance of that supreme reason, often dark to us, which governs the course of man's affairs, than that no body of men should in the long run be able to strengthen itself at the cost of others' weakness. The civilisation and freedom of the ancient world were shortlived because they were partial and exceptional. If the ideal of true freedom is the maximum of power for all members of human society alike to make the best of themselves, we are right in refusing to ascribe the glory of freedom to a state in which the apparent elevation of the few is founded on the degradation of the many, and in ranking modern society, founded as it is on free industry, with all its confusion and ignorant licence and waste of effort, above the most splendid of ancient republics.

If I have given a true account of that freedom which forms the goal of social effort, we shall see that freedom of contract, freedom in all the forms of doing what one will with one's own, is valuable only as a means to an end. That end is what I call freedom in the positive sense: in other words, the liberation of the powers of all men equally for contributions to a common good. No one has a right to do what he will with his own in such a way as to contravene this end. It is only through the guarantee which society gives him that he has property at all, or, strictly speaking, any right to his possessions. This guarantee is founded on a sense of common interest. Every one has an interest in securing to every one else the free use and enjoyment and disposal of his possessions, so long as that freedom on the part of one does not interfere with a like freedom on the part of others, because such freedom contributes to that equal development of the faculties of all which is the highest good for all. This is the true and the only justification of rights of property. Rights of property, however, have been and are claimed which cannot be thus justified. We are all now agreed that men cannot rightly be the property of men. The institution of property being only justifiable as a means to the free exercise of the social capabilities of all, there can be no true right to property of a kind which debars one class of men from such free exercise altogether. We condemn slavery no less when it arises out of a voluntary agreement on the part of the enslaved person. A contract by which any one agreed for a certain consideration to become the slave of another we should reckon a void contract. Here, then, is a limitation upon freedom of contract which we all recognise as rightful. No contract is valid in which human persons, willingly or unwillingly, are dealt with as commodities, because such contracts of necessity defeat the end for which alone society enforces contracts at all.

Are there no other contracts which, less obviously perhaps but really, are open to the same objection? In the first place, let us consider contracts affecting labour. Labour, the economist tells us, is a commodity exchangeable like other commodities. This is in a certain sense true, but it is a commodity which attaches in a peculiar manner to the person of man. Hence restrictions may need to be placed on the sale of this commodity which would be unnecessary in other cases, in order to prevent labour from being sold under conditions which make it impossible for the person selling it ever to become a free contributor to social good in any form. This is most plainly the case when a man bargains to work under conditions fatal to health, *e.g.,* in an unventilated factory. Every injury to the health of the individual is, so far as it goes, a public injury. It is an impediment to the general freedom; so much deduction from our power, as members of society, to make the best of ourselves. Society is, therefore, plainly within its right when it limits freedom of contract for the sale of labour, so far as is done by our laws for the sanitary regulations of factories, workshops, and mines. It is equally within its right in prohibiting the labour of women and young persons beyond certain hours. If they work beyond those hours, the result is demonstrably physical deterioration; which, as demonstrably, carries with it a lowering of the moral forces of society. For the sake of that general freedom of its members to make the best of themselves, which it is the object of civil society to secure, a prohibition should be put by law, which is the deliberate voice of society, on all such contracts of service as in a general way yield such a result. The purchase or hire of unwholesome dwellings is properly forbidden on the same principle. Its application to compulsory education may not be quite so obvious, but it will appear on a little reflection. Without a command of certain elementary arts and knowledge, the individual in modern society is as effectually crippled as by the loss of a limb or a broken constitution. He is not free to develop his faculties. With a view to securing such freedom among its members it is as certainly within the province of the state to prevent children from growing up in that kind of ignorance which practically excludes them from a free career in life, as it is within its province to require the sort of building and drainage necessary for public health.

Our modern legislation then with reference to labour, and education, and health, involving as it does manifold interference with freedom of contract, is justified on the ground that it is the business of the state, not indeed directly to promote moral goodness, for that, from the very nature of moral goodness, it cannot do, but to maintain the conditions without which a free exercise of the human faculties is impossible. It does not indeed follow that it is advisable for the state to do all which it is justified in doing. We are often warned nowadays against the danger of over-legislation: or, as I heard it put in a speech of the present home[i] secretary in days when he was sowing his political wild oats, of 'grandmotherly government.' There may be good ground for the warning, but at any rate we should be quite clear what we mean by it. The outcry against state interference is often raised by men whose real objection is not to state interference but to centralisation, to the constant aggression of the central executive upon local authorities. As I have already pointed out, compulsion at the discretion of some elected municipal board proceeds just as much from the state as does compulsion exercised by a government office in London. No doubt, much needless friction is avoided, much is gained in the way of elasticity and adjustment to circumstances, by the independent local administration of general laws; and most of us would agree that of late there has been a dangerous tendency to override municipal discretion by the hard and fast rules of London 'departments.' But centralisation is one thing: over-legislation, or the improper exercise of the power of the state, quite another. It is one question whether of late the central government has been unduly trenching on local government, and another question whether the law of the state, either as administered by central or by

i [Sir William Vernon-Harcourt.]

provincial authorities, has been unduly interfering with the discretion of individuals. We may object most strongly to advancing centralisation, and yet wish that the law should put rather more than less restraint on those liberties of the individual which are a social nuisance. But there are some political speculators whose objection is not merely to centralisation, but to the extended action of law altogether. They think that the individual ought to be left much more to himself than has of late been the case. Might not our people, they ask, have been trusted to learn in time for themselves to eschew unhealthy dwellings, to refuse dangerous and degrading employment, to get their children the schooling necessary for making their way in the world? Would they not for their own comfort, if not from more chivalrous feeling, keep their wives and daughters from overwork? Or, failing this, ought not women, like men, to learn to protect themselves? Might not all the rules, in short, which legislation of the kind we have been discussing is intended to attain, have been attained without it; not so quickly, perhaps, but without tampering so dangerously with the independence and self-reliance of the people?

Now, we shall probably all agree that a society in which the public health was duly protected, and necessary education duly provided for, by the spontaneous action of individuals, was in a higher condition than one in which the compulsion of law was needed to secure these ends. But we must take men as we find them. Until such a condition of society is reached, it is the business of the state to take the best security it can for the young citizens' growing up in such health and with so much knowledge as is necessary for their real freedom. In so doing it need not at all interfere with the independence and self-reliance of those whom it requires to do what they would otherwise do for themselves. The man who, of his own right feeling, saves his wife from overwork and sends his children to school, suffers no moral degradation from a law which, if he did not do this for himself, would seek to make him do it. Such a man does not feel the law as constraint at all. To him it is simply a powerful friend. It gives him security for that being done efficiently which, with the best wishes, he might have much trouble in getting done efficiently if left to himself. No doubt it relieves him from some of the responsibility which would otherwise fall to him as head of a family, but, if he is what we are supposing him to be, in proportion as he is relieved of responsibilities in one direction he will assume them in another. The security which the state gives him for the safe housing and sufficient schooling of his family will only make him the more careful for their well-being in other respects, which he is left to look after for himself. We need have no fear, then, of such legislation having an ill effect on those who, without the law, would have seen to that being done, though probably less efficiently, which the law requires to be done. But it was not their case that the laws we are considering were especially meant to meet. It was the overworked women, the ill-housed and untaught families, for whose benefit they were intended. And the question is whether without these laws the suffering classes could have been delivered quickly or slowly from the condition they were in. Could the enlightened self-interest or benevolence of individuals, working under a system of unlimited freedom of contract, have ever brought them into a state compatible with the free development of the human faculties? No one considering the facts can have any doubt as to the answer to this question. Left to itself, or to the operation of casual benevolence, a degraded population perpetuates and increases itself. Read any of the authorised accounts, given before royal or parliamentary commissions, of the state of the labourers, especially of the women and children, as they were in our great industries before the law was first brought to bear on them, and before freedom of contract was first interfered with in them. Ask yourself what chance there was of a generation, born and bred under such conditions, ever contracting itself out of them. Given a certain standard of moral and material wellbeing, people may be trusted not to sell their labour, or the labour of their children, on terms which would not allow that standard to be maintained. But with large masses of our population, until the laws we have been considering took effect, there was no such standard. There was nothing on their part, in the way either of self-respect or established demand for comforts, to prevent them from working and living, or from putting their children to work and live, in a way in which no one who is to be a healthy and free citizen can work and live. No doubt there were many high-minded employers who did their best for their workpeople before the days of state-interference, but they could not prevent less scrupulous hirers of labour from hiring it on the cheapest terms. It is true that cheap labour is in the long run dear labour, but it is so only in the long run, and eager traders do not think of the long run. If labour is to be had under conditions incompatible with the health or decent housing or education of the labourer, there will always be plenty of people to buy it under those conditions, careless of the burden in the shape of rates and taxes which they may be laying up for posterity. Either the standard of well-being on the part of the sellers of labour must prevent them from selling their labour under those conditions, or the law must prevent it. With a population such as ours was forty years ago, and still largely is, the law must prevent it and continue the prevention for some generations, before the sellers will be in a state to prevent it for themselves.

As there is practically no danger of a reversal of our factory and school laws, it may seem needless to dwell at such length on their justification. I do so for two reasons; partly to remind the younger generation of citizens of the great blessing which they inherited in those laws, and of the interest which they still have in their completion and extension; but still more in order to obtain some clear principles for our guidance when we approach those difficult questions of the immediate future, the questions of the land law and the liquor law. . . .

. . . There is no right to freedom in the purchase and sale of a particular commodity, if the general result of allowing such freedom is to detract from freedom in the higher sense, from the general power of men to make the best of themselves. Now with anyone who looks calmly at the facts, there can be no doubt that the present habits of drinking in England do lay a heavy burden on the free development of man's powers for social good, a heavier burden probably than arises from all other preventible causes put together. It used to be the fashion to look on drunkenness as a vice which was the concern only of the person who fell into it, so long as it did not lead him to commit an assault on his neighbours. No thoughtful man any longer looks on it in this way. We know that, however decently carried on, the excessive drinking of one man means an injury to others in health, purse, and capability, to which no limits can be placed. Drunkenness in the head of a family means, as a rule, the impoverishment and degradation of all members of the family; and the presence of a drink-shop at the corner of a street means, as a rule, the drunkenness of a certain number of heads of families in that street. Remove the drink-shops, and, as the experience of many happy communities sufficiently shows, you almost, perhaps in time altogether, remove the drunkenness. Here, then, is a wide-spreading social evil, of which society may, if it will, by a restraining law, to a great extent, rid itself, to the infinite enhancement of the positive freedom enjoyed by its members. All that is required for the attainment of so blessed a result is so much effort and self-sacrifice on the part of the majority of citizens as is necessary for the enactment and enforcement of the restraining law. The majority of citizens may still be far from prepared for such an effort. That is a point on which I express no opinion. To attempt a restraining law, in advance of the social sentiment necessary to give real effect to it, is always a mistake. But to argue that an effectual law in restraint of the drink-traffic would be a wrongful interference with individual liberty, is to ignore the essential condition under which alone every particular liberty can rightly be allowed to the individual, the condition, namely, that the allowance of that liberty is not, as a rule, and on the whole, an impediment to social good.

The more reasonable opponents of the restraint for which I plead, would probably argue not so much that it was necessarily wrong in principle, as that it was one of those short cuts to a good end which ultimately defeat their own object. They would take the same line that has been taken by the opponents of state-interference in all its forms. 'Leave the people to themselves,' they would say; 'as their standard of self-respect rises, as they become better housed and better educated, they will gradually shake off the evil habit. The cure so effected may not be so rapid as that brought by a repressive law, but it will be more lasting. Better that it should come more slowly through the spontaneous action of individuals, than more quickly through compulsion.'

But here again we reply that it is dangerous to wait. The slower remedy might be preferable if we were sure that it was a remedy at all, but we have no such assurance. There is strong reason to think the contrary. Every year that the evil is left to itself, it becomes greater. The vested interest in the encouragement of the vice becomes larger, and the persons affected by it more numerous. If any abatement of it has already taken place, we may fairly argue that this is because it has not been altogether left to itself; for the licensing law, as it is, is much more stringent and more stringently administered than it was ten years ago. A drunken population naturally perpetuates and increases itself. Many families, it is true, keep emerging from the conditions which render them specially liable to the evil habit, but on the other hand descent through drunkenness from respectability to squalor is constantly going on. The families of drunkards do not seem to be smaller than those of sober men, though they are shorter-lived; and that the children of a drunkard should escape from drunkenness is what we call almost a miracle. Better education, better housing, more healthy rules of labour, no doubt lessen the temptations to drink for those who have the benefit of these advantages, but meanwhile drunkenness is constantly recruiting the ranks of those who cannot be really educated, who will not be better housed, who make their employments dangerous and unhealthy. An effectual liquor law in short is the necessary complement of our factory acts, our education acts, our public health acts. Without it the full measure of their usefulness will never be attained. They were all opposed in their turn by the same arguments that are now used against a restraint of the facilities for drinking. Sometimes it was the argument that the state had no business to interfere with the liberties of the individual. Sometimes it was the dilatory plea that the better nature of man would in time assert itself, and that meanwhile it would be lowered by compulsion. Happily a sense of the facts and necessities of the case got the better of the delusive cry of liberty. Act after act was passed preventing master and workman, parent and child, house-builder and householder, from doing as they pleased, with the result of a great addition to the real freedom of society. The spirit of self-reliance and independence was not weakened by those acts. Rather it received a new development. The dead weight of ignorance and unhealthy surroundings, with which it would otherwise have had to struggle, being partially removed by law, it was more free to exert itself for higher objects. When we ask for a stringent liquor law, which should even go to the length of allowing the householders of a district to exclude the drink traffic altogether, we are only asking for a continuation of the same work, a continuation necessary to its complete success. It is a poor sophistry to tell us that it is moral cowardice to seek to remove by law a temptation which every one ought to be able to resist for himself. It is not the part of a considerate self-reliance to remain in presence of a temptation merely for the sake of being tempted. When all temptations are removed which law can remove, there will still be room enough, nay, much more room, for the play of our moral energies. The temptation to excessive drinking is one which upon sufficient evidence we hold that the law can at least greatly diminish. If it can, it ought to do so. This then, along with the effectual liberation of the soil, is the next great conquest which our democracy, on behalf of its own true freedom, has to make. The danger of legislation, either in the interests of a privileged class or for the promotion of particular religious opinions, we may fairly assume to be over. The popular jealousy of law, once justifiable enough, is therefore out of date. The citizens of England now make its law. We ask them by law to put a restraint on themselves in the matter of strong drink. We ask them further to limit, or even altogether to give up, the not very precious liberty of buying and selling alcohol, in order that they may become more free to exercise the faculties and improve the talents which God has given them.

Franklin D. Roosevelt

"The Continuing Struggle for Liberalism" (1941)

Franklin Delano Roosevelt (1882–1945) began the first of four terms as president of the United States in 1932. The nation was deep in depression, and Roosevelt responded with a series of reforms to provide relief to the unemployed and rebuild the economy. In this introduction to a collection of his papers and addresses, FDR argues that government should act to protect the economic and political rights of "the average person." Along with his New Deal programs, FDR is known for his efforts to enlarge the Supreme Court, to keep the United States out of World War II, and to plan the United Nations.

Introduction

IT HAS FREQUENTLY been said that eternal vigilance is necessary to preserve our liberties. It is equally true that eternal vigilance is necessary to keep democracies and their governments truly liberal. We in the United States have had first hand experience with that truism since the end of 1933, when, for the first time, the full effects of our program of recovery and reform began to be felt. For, as soon as the clear action of the new administration in 1933 had started the wheels of industry turning, there came the demand from some sources to stop all of the reforms, and to let things begin again to run on as they had during the previous decade.

Source: The Public Papers and Addresses of Franklin D. Roosevelt, With a Special Introduction and Explanatory Notes by President Roosevelt, vol. 38 (New York: The MacMillan Company, 1941), xxi–xxxiii.

Of course, the people of the United States have always understood that the new administration never intended to be a mere rescue party—organized to save the economic system and turn it back to the small, powerful group which had formerly controlled it through their concentrated economic power. The Government in 1933 was determined not only to save the system, but also to remove from it the abuses, evils, and widespread maladjustments which had brought it to the very brink of destruction. The Government was determined that the system, thus preserved and reformed, should no longer be subject to the control of the handful of men and corporations that had dominated it in the false boom days before 1929.

To carry out that determination was to resist, from 1933 down to date, all the efforts of mighty forces—day by day, year by year. These forces had tremendous interests at stake—wealth, privilege, economic power, political power. Although few in number, they had the resources which enabled them to make the most noise, and to become the most vociferous in the press, over the radio, through newspaper and outdoor advertising, by floods of telegrams and letters to the Congress, by employment of professional lobbyists, by all the many means of propaganda and public pressure which have been developed in recent years.

In 1938 the efforts of this minority, consistent in its opposition since 1933, rose to new heights. They had tried stubbornly at the polls in 1936 to stop our program of reform. They had failed. They had tried in 1937 to stop it in the courts, where they had been so successful during 1935 and 1936. Here, too, they had failed. Therefore, through the years of 1937 and 1938, their activities to impede progress and to bring about a repeal or emasculation of the New Deal measures of reform were redoubled.

There were several reasons for this particular burst of effort this year. First, the Supreme Court fight, although it had been finally successful in obtaining its objective, had been defeated in the Congress. The enemies of liberal government tried to hail that loss of a single battle as a defeat of the entire progressive program of the administration. A strong "putsch" was organized to try to make it appear as though the representatives of the people in the Congress had, by failing to pass the Supreme Court bill, repudiated the principles and conduct of the New Deal.

Second, there had come a substantial business recession—commencing in the fall of 1937, and continuing through the first half of 1938. That recession has been discussed at length in various items and notes in these volumes. These same minority groups sought at once to take advantage of it by blaming it exclusively on the attitude and legislation of the Government, claiming that the administration was "strangling business" and "ruining confidence," and preventing "full recovery."

In 1932, the national income had fallen as low as $38,000,000,000 from a high in 1929 of about $80,000,000,000. Since 1932, and for each and every year thereafter, up to and including 1937, the national income had gradually risen until it reached the figure of $68,000,000,000.

This consistent and continuous recovery was stopped short in 1937 by several factors. First, the production and speculative buying of heavy and consumer goods had been increased by industry at such a rapid pace that they had completely outstripped the ability of the people of the country to buy such goods. The same thing happened in 1937 on a small scale, that had happened in 1929 on a prodigious scale, namely, the purchasing power of the consumers of goods had been exceeded too quickly and too greatly by the amount of merchandise manufactured. The result was that large inventories of stocks had accumulated, which could not be sold.

In addition, the prices of merchandise had been forced up by business too drastically during the year 1937, in spite of all the efforts of the Government to discourage such inordinate increases. The mounting prices, in turn, contributed also to the inability to sell the goods manufactured, and helped to create a large excess of goods which could not be sold.

At the same time, with the steady rise of business through 1936 and early 1937, the Government had begun to cut down its own expenditures for relief and work relief. It did so with the reasonable expectation that private industry, with its increased markets and output, would take up some of the slack, and provide some of the employment which had previously been furnished by the Government through public works projects. In this the Government miscalculated.

It soon became obvious that 1937 was too early to begin to cut down drastically on the expenditure of public funds which had been furnishing the necessary purchasing power for those who could not otherwise get it. The Government's expectations that industry would take up the process of giving employment were not fulfilled. Industry failed to supply jobs to replace those which had been lost by curtailment of Federal work relief.

At the same time, it is also undoubtedly true that, in some quarters, labor had gone too far in its demands and in its conduct, especially with respect to sit-down strikes.

The explanation for the recession may, therefore, legitimately be placed at the door of all three—Government, capital, and labor. It should be remembered that at no time did this recession ever reach alarming proportions. There was never any semblance of the panic or stagnation or hopelessness which had developed in 1932. Our Government had been adequately prepared to deal with it—and did deal with it quickly and effectively. However, the recession, such as it was, was seized upon by the opponents of reform and liberal government, as a great talking point from which to urge that, unless the whole business of reform and progress were stopped right away, the industrial system of America would collapse, and the Government itself would become bankrupt.

All of the big guns and resources of pressure politics and modern propaganda were brought into play in late 1937 and 1938, to try to strike down liberalism in the Congress and in the executive branch of the Government.

The policy of the Federal Government, however, continued to follow the only path of true recovery and the only assurance of preservation of our system of private profit and free enterprise—the continuance and strengthening of social reform and progressive legislation.

When I called the Congress into extraordinary session in 1937, I pointed this out; and I announced the determination of the Federal Government to proceed with its program on all fronts with full speed.

Accordingly, I recommended the enactment of new farm legislation. I called for a comprehensive farm program—not only to replace the old measures which had been declared unconstitutional by the Supreme Court, but one which would go forward. I called for legislation for soil conservation and for regulation of crop production so as to furnish an ever-normal granary which would give the farmer a fair share of the national income, and at the same time, would also assure the consumer a steady supply of food and textile fibre at reasonable prices.

I also recommended to this extraordinary session of the Congress the enactment of legislation providing for minimum wages and maximum hours and the abolition of child labor in all interstate occupations. Only in this way could sweatshop conditions be eliminated and workers receive a reasonable purchasing power—to enable them to live with some degree of decency, and to provide a market for the products of the farms and factories of the nation.

And, in order to make government more efficient in planning and in executing its duties and responsibilities, I recommended a comprehensive plan of reorganization of the administrative branch of the Federal Government and a great expansion of the planning functions of government.

These recommendations were renewed by me when the Congress reassembled in regular session in January, 1938. In addition, I made other recommendations showing that the New Deal was determined not to stop in its tracks, but to press forward in its program of progress. I recommended, for example, that new tax legislation was necessary—first, to prevent continued tax evasion by some few individuals and corporations; and, second, to make sure that the principle of ability to pay was not violated by the tax structure.

I also called attention to some of the grave social abuses which had grown up in the use of capital—not all capital, but in a limited portion thereof. In other words, I made it clear that what I was attacking was not business in general or all business practices, but certain clearly wrongful business practices which were ruinous to the rest of the economic system of the country. I pointed out that, in addition to tax avoidance, these practices included: excessive capitalization, continued write-ups of investment values, security manipulations, collusive bidding and price rigging, high-pressure salesmanship which creates cycles of overproduction and recessions in production, the use of patent laws for monopolistic purposes, and unfair competition. I also called attention to the unfortunate practice of industry to move from one locality or region of the country to another—in an effort to find the cheapest possible wage scales, or in order to try to intimidate local and state governments from the passage of progressive legislation for the protection of labor.

Above all, I stressed the grave danger and serious problems which had arisen, and which always arise, out of the growing concentration of economic power, involving, as it did, the control by a relatively few men of other people's money, other people's labor, and other people's lives.

In a special message to the Congress on April 29, 1938, I pointed out that this concentration was seriously impairing the economic effectiveness of private enterprise as a way of providing employment for labor and capital, and as a way of assuring a more equitable distribution of income and earnings among the people of the nation as a whole. To meet this situation I recommended a thorough study of the concentration of economic power in American industry and the effect of that concentration upon the decline of competition. I suggested that this investigation should include an examination of the existing price system and price policies of industry to determine their effect upon the general level of trade, upon employment, upon long term profits and upon consumption. Such a survey, I pointed out, should not be confined to the traditional anti-trust field, but should review critically the social and economic effects of tax, patent and other government policies.

Much of the legislation which I recommended was passed during 1938. For example, a new farm program was adopted; legislation establishing minimum wages and maximum hours and outlawing child labor was finally passed; additional funds were provided for the construction of public works to furnish employment; and a congressional and administrative committee was set up to study the whole subject of monopolies and the concentration of economic power. Administrative reorganization was delayed until 1939.

Many of the great measures debated in 1937 and 1938—farm legislation, reorganization of government, minimum wages and maximum hours, increased public works, monopoly controls, judicial reforms, water power development, low-cost housing—have, by now, become more or less accepted as part of our economic life. It is a little difficult, therefore, to look back even across the short period to 1938 and remember how bitter and how difficult was the struggle—in the Congress and out of the Congress—which was necessary in order to have some of these laws adopted. The opposition to them—chiefly from the same sources which had opposed the whole program of reform since 1933—developed into "blitzkrieg" proportions. Misrepresentation as to motives, and falsehoods as to objectives and results, became common practice, especially in the columns of some of the large newspapers.

In that struggle, a few Democratic members of the House and Senate—who had been elected in 1936 and in earlier years on liberal platforms, and who had pledged themselves to support the great objectives and social measures enunciated in those platforms—had definitely allied themselves with the opponents of the program. I do not mean merely that these members had disagreed with one or two or more items in the program, and had suggested other measures which they thought more likely to obtain the same results. Obviously, no fault could have been found in any respect with legislators who thought that the liberal principles of the Democratic platform of 1936 could be carried out by other measures, and who proposed and fought for such other measures. But that was not what was happening. The blunt fact is that these men were deliberately repudiating the very principles of progress which they had espoused in order to be elected—and which were, in some cases, the only reason that they had been elected.

It became quite obvious that this kind of conduct was not only a renunciation of platform pledges, but was actually endangering the successful accomplishment of the Federal Government's determination to preserve a liberal, progressive administration.

The primary obligation and responsibility for determining the general objectives and direction of any administration naturally lie with the President himself. However, he can do little alone, without the cooperation of the Congress. In this particular instance the vast majority of the Congress were members of my own party. The number of Democrats in the Congress had been increased during each and every Congressional election commencing with 1932. They had each time been elected on a platform which expressly called for the adoption of liberal legislation. But, in spite of this, that type of legislation had begun to be repudiated by several of them; so that if the process were not checked, the whole liberal program might eventually become jeopardized.

I believe it to be my sworn duty, as President, to take all steps necessary to insure the continuance of liberalism in our government. I believe, at the same time, that it is my duty as the head of the Democratic party to see to it that my party remains the truly liberal party in the political life of America.

There had been many periods in American history, unfortunately, when one major political party was no different from the other major party—except only in name. In a system of party government such as ours, however, elections become meaningless when the two major parties have no differences other than their labels. For such elections do not give the people of the United States an opportunity to decide upon the type of government which they prefer for themselves for the next two or the next four years, as the case may be. I do not mean necessarily that expression of choice at the polls should concern itself with details, or with particular methods. But it is essential that the general trend and direction of government should be left to the determination of a majority of the people; and the only way that they can express their will is by voting for the candidates of that party which espouses the particular trend in government which they prefer.

Generally speaking, in a representative form of government there are usually two general schools of political belief—liberal and conservative. The system of party responsibility in America requires that one of its parties be the liberal party and the other be the conservative party. This has been the division by which the major parties in American history have identified themselves whenever crises have developed which required definite choice of direction. In Jefferson's day, in Jackson's day, and in Lincoln's, and Theodore Roosevelt's, and Wilson's day, one group emerged clearly as liberals, opposed to the other—the conservatives.

One great difference which has characterized this division has been that the liberal party—no matter what its particular name was at the time—believed in the wisdom and efficacy of the will of the great majority of the people, as distinguished from the judgment of a small minority of either education or wealth. The liberal group has always believed that control by a few—political control or economic control—if exercised for a long period of time, would be destructive of a sound representative democracy. For this reason, for example, it has always advocated the extension of the right of suffrage to as many people as possible, trusting the combined judgment of all the people in political matters rather than the judgment of a small minority.

The other great difference between the two parties has been this: The liberal party is a party which believes that, as new conditions and problems arise beyond the power of men and women to meet as individuals, it becomes the duty of the Government itself to find new remedies with which to meet them. The liberal party insists that the Government has the definite duty to use all its power and resources to meet new social problems with new social controls—to insure to the average person the right to his own economic and political life, liberty, and the pursuit of happiness. That theory of the role of government was expressed by Abraham Lincoln when he said, "the legitimate object of government is to do for a community of people whatever they need to have done, but cannot do at all, or cannot do so well, for themselves, in their separate and individual capacities."

The conservative party in government honestly and conscientiously believes the contrary. It believes that there is no necessity for the Government to step in, even when new conditions and new problems arise. It believes that, in the long run, individual initiative and private philanthropy can take care of all situations. The test of allegiance to one or the other of these schools of political and economic thought cannot be based on a person's views with respect to one particular measure or policy or even several of them. The test is rather whether a person adheres to the broad general objectives of the particular party as expressed in its fundamental principles.

The clear and undisputed fact is that in these later years, at least since 1932, the Democratic party has been the liberal party, and the Republican party has been the conservative party.

There can, of course, be no quarrel by anybody with anyone who sincerely subscribes either to the principles of liberalism or conservatism. The quarrel in 1938 was with those who said they were liberals, but who, nevertheless, proceeded to stand in the way of all social progress by objecting to any measure to carry out liberal objectives. The usual procedure of this type of liberal is to say that he believes in the objective, but that he does not like the details of the particular method proposed to carry out the objective. He says, *"Yes"*—that he is in favor of the end; *but* he objects to the means—at the same time offering no alternative method, and seldom, if ever, raising a finger of his own to try to obtain the ultimate objective. I have frequently referred to this type of individual as a "yes, but—" fellow.

The true liberal does not claim, of course, that the remedies with which he proposes to attain his objectives are perfect. But he is willing to start with something less than perfect in this imperfect world. The conservative, on the other hand, believes generally that all remedies proposed by the Government itself are usually unnecessary, and that perfection can be obtained more readily and more quickly through private initiative.

It is a comparatively simple thing for a nation to determine, by its votes, whether it chooses the liberal or the conservative form of government. On the other hand, a nation can never intelligently determine its policy, if it has to go through the confusion of voting for candidates who pretend to be one thing but who act the other.

I have always believed, and I have frequently stated, that my own party can succeed at the polls only so long as it continues to be the party of militant liberalism. I do not mean to imply that only enrolled Democrats are liberal voters, or even that all enrolled Democrats are liberal voters. I do not mean to imply, on the other hand, that only enrolled Republicans are conservative voters, or that all enrolled Republicans are conservative voters. There is a vast number of independent voters who are unwilling to become affiliated with either party, but whose social and political outlook is definitely liberal, and whose votes have been cast for liberal candidates. On the other hand, millions of enrolled Republican voters— affiliated under the conservative Republican leadership for one reason or another— have nevertheless consistently voted for the type of government and candidates who appear under the liberal banner.

But, as the head of the Democratic party, I think that it is nothing more nor less than political consistency for the candidates standing for election on the liberal program of my party to act like liberals after the election is over.

It was that belief, and the complete realization of the fact that some Democratic candidates had acted in repudiation of progressive and liberal government, that I took an active part in some of the primary elections of 1938—in an effort to keep liberalism in the foreground in the councils of my own party, as well as in the legislative and executive branches of the Government itself.

My participation in these primary campaigns was slurringly referred to, by those who were opposed to liberalism, as a "purge." The word became a slogan for those who tried to misrepresent my conduct to make it appear to be an effort to defeat certain Senators and Representatives who had voted against one measure or another recommended by me—particularly those who had voted against the Supreme Court bill of 1937. Nothing could be further from the truth. I was not interested in personalities. Nor was I interested in particular measures— because most of the liberal measures I had recommended had already been passed. I was, however, primarily interested in seeing to it that the Democratic party and the Republican party should not be merely Tweedledum and Tweedledee to each other. I was chiefly interested in continuing the Democratic party as the liberal, forward-looking, progressive party in the United States.

The primary campaigns in which I actively spoke, consisted of one congressional campaign in my own home State, one senatorial campaign in my other home State of Georgia, one in Kentucky (where the choice was not between a conservative and a liberal, but between two liberals, one of whom was the experienced Democratic leader of the Senate), and one senatorial campaign in the State of Maryland, where I was accompanied by the chairman of the Democratic National Committee. It must be remembered, also, that in some of these States, and in some other States, a definite misuse was being made of my name by one candidate or the other, falsely claiming that I favored his election. Under such circumstances I exercised my clear right to speak out in the interest of truth.

In these primary campaign speeches, I made it clear that I was not trying to dictate to the people of any State as to how they should vote. What I was trying to do was to impress upon them the necessity of voting for liberal candidates— if they wanted a continuation of the liberal kind of government which they had had since 1933.

Looking back on the domestic issues of 1937 and 1938, there is much satisfaction in realizing that the American people, as a whole, were not taken in by the bitter accusations and dire predictions of those who cried "dictatorship," "imminent bankruptcy," or "strangulation of business." The determination of the people to continue the same liberal program of progressive reform was clearly expressed at the polls in 1938. As was to be expected, after the steady and continued increase in Democratic representation in the Congress in 1932, 1934, and 1936, the Democratic majority fell off somewhat in 1938. But the fact that, after the elections of 1938, there were 69 Democratic Senators and 262 Democratic Representatives, as against 23 Republican Senators and 169 Republican Representatives, shows that the cause of progressive government had found definite approval with the people, and that the people were determined that it be continued.

The political struggle of 1938 had not been in vain. Liberalism in Government was still triumphant.

> Franklin D. Roosevelt
> *White House,*
> *Washington, D. C.,*
> *June 16, 1941.*

6

Milton Friedman

———

Capitalism and Freedom (1962)

Milton Friedman (b. 1912), recipient of a Nobel Prize in economics, is an emeritus professor at the University of Chicago, a Fellow at the Hoover Institute, and the founder of the Chicago School of monetary economics. Described as an economic liberal, he emphasizes the relationship between capitalism and freedom. After Capitalism and Freedom, *his best-known work is* Free to Choose *(1980), written with his wife, Rose Friedman.* Two Lucky People, *their joint memoir, was published in 1998.*

Chapter 1
The Relation between Economic Freedom and Political Freedom

IT IS WIDELY BELIEVED that politics and economics are separate and largely unconnected; that individual freedom is a political problem and material welfare an economic problem; and that any kind of political arrangements can be combined with any kind of economic arrangements. The chief contemporary manifestation of this idea is the advocacy of "democratic socialism" by many who condemn out of hand the restrictions on individual freedom imposed by "totalitarian socialism" in Russia, and who are persuaded that it is possible for a country to adopt the essential features of Russian economic arrangements and yet to ensure individual freedom through political arrangements. The thesis of this chapter is that such a view is a delusion, that there is an intimate connection between economics and politics, that only certain combinations of political and economic arrangements are possible, and that in particular, a society which is socialist cannot also be democratic, in the sense of guaranteeing individual freedom.

Economic arrangements play a dual role in the promotion of a free society. On the one hand, freedom in economic arrangements is itself a component of freedom broadly understood, so economic freedom is an end in itself. In the second place, economic freedom is also an indispensable means toward the achievement of political freedom.

The first of these roles of economic freedom needs special emphasis because intellectuals in particular have a strong bias against regarding this aspect of freedom as important. They tend to express contempt for what they regard as material aspects of life, and to regard their own pursuit of allegedly higher values as on a different plane of significance and as deserving of special attention. For most citizens of the country, however, if not for the intellectual, the direct importance of economic freedom is at least comparable in significance to the indirect importance of economic freedom as a means to political freedom.

The citizen of Great Britain, who after World War II was not permitted to spend his vacation in the United States because of exchange control, was being deprived of an essential freedom no less than the citizen of the United States, who was denied the opportunity to spend his vacation in Russia because of his political views. The one was ostensibly an economic limitation on freedom and the other a political limitation, yet there is no essential difference between the two.

The citizen of the United States who is compelled by law to devote something like 10 percent of his income to the purchase of a particular kind of retirement contract, administered by the government, is being deprived of a corresponding part of his personal freedom. How strongly this deprivation may be felt and its closeness to the deprivation of religious freedom, which all would regard as "civil" or "political" rather than "economic," were dramatized by an episode involving a group of farmers of the Amish sect. On grounds of principle, this group regarded compulsory federal old age programs as an infringement of their personal individual freedom and refused to pay taxes or accept benefits. As a result, some of their livestock were sold by auction in order to satisfy claims for social security levies. True, the number of citizens who regard compulsory old-age insurance as a deprivation of freedom may be few, but the believer in freedom has never counted noses.

A citizen of the United States who under the laws of various states is not free to follow the occupation of his own choosing unless he can get a license for it, is likewise being deprived of an essential part of his freedom. So is the man who would like to exchange some of his goods with, say, a Swiss for a watch but is prevented from doing so by a quota. So also is the Californian who was thrown into jail for selling Alka-Seltzer at a price below that set by the manufacturer under so-called "fair trade" laws. So also is the farmer who cannot grow the amount of wheat he wants. And so on. Clearly, economic freedom, in and of itself, is an extremely important part of total freedom.

Viewed as a means to the end of political freedom, economic arrangements are important because of their effect on the concentration or dispersion of power. The kind of economic organization that provides economic freedom directly, namely, competitive capitalism, also promotes political freedom because it separates economic power from political power and in this way enables the one to offset the other.

Historical evidence speaks with a single voice on the relation between political freedom and a free market. I know of no example in time or place of a society that has been marked by a large measure of political freedom, and that has not also used something comparable to a free market to organize the bulk of economic activity.

Because we live in a largely free society, we tend to forget how limited is the span of time and the part of the globe for which there has ever been anything like political freedom: the typical state of mankind is tyranny, servitude, and misery. The nineteenth century and early twentieth century in the Western world stand out as striking exceptions to the general trend of historical development. Political freedom in this instance clearly came along with the free market and the development of capitalist institutions. So also did political freedom in the golden age of Greece and in the early days of the Roman era.

History suggests only that capitalism is a necessary condition for political freedom. Clearly it is not a sufficient condition. Fascist Italy and Fascist Spain, Germany at various times in the last seventy years, Japan before World Wars I and II, tzarist Russia in the decades before World War I—are all societies that cannot conceivably be described as politically free. Yet, in each, private enterprise was the dominant form of economic organization. It is therefore clearly possible to have economic arrangements that are fundamentally capitalist and political arrangements that are not free.

Even in those societies, the citizenry had a good deal more freedom than citizens of a modern totalitarian state like Russia or Nazi Germany, in which economic totalitarianism is combined with political totalitarianism. Even in Russia under the Tzars, it was possible for some citizens, under some circumstances, to change their jobs without getting permission from political authority because capitalism and the existence of private property provided some check to the centralized power of the state.

The relation between political and economic freedom is complex and by no means unilateral. In the early nineteenth century, [Jeremy] Bentham and the Philosophical Radicals were inclined to regard political freedom as a means to economic freedom. They believed that the masses were being hampered by the restrictions that were being imposed upon them, and that if political reform gave the bulk of the people the vote, they would do what was good for them, which was to vote for laissez faire. In retrospect, one cannot say that they were wrong. There was a large measure of political reform that was accompanied by economic reform in the direction of a great deal of laissez faire. An enormous increase in the well-being of the masses followed this change in economic arrangements.

The triumph of Benthamite liberalism in nineteenth-century England was followed by a reaction toward increasing intervention by government in economic affairs. This tendency to collectivism was greatly accelerated, both in England and elsewhere, by the two World Wars. Welfare rather than freedom became the dominant note in democratic countries. Recognizing the implicit threat to individualism, the intellectual descendants of the Philosophical Radicals—Dicey, Mises, Hayek, and Simons, to mention only a few—feared that a continued movement toward centralized control of economic activity would prove *The Road to Serfdom,* as Hayek entitled his penetrating analysis of the process. Their emphasis was on economic freedom as a means toward political freedom.

Events since the end of World War II display still a different relation between economic and political freedom. Collectivist economic planning has indeed interfered with individual freedom. At least in some countries, however, the result has not been the suppression of freedom, but the reversal of economic policy. England again provides the most striking example. The turning point was perhaps the "control of engagements" order which, despite great misgivings, the Labour party found it necessary to impose in order to carry out its economic policy. Fully enforced and carried through, the law would have involved centralized allocation of individuals to occupations. This conflicted so sharply with personal liberty that it was enforced in a negligible number of cases, and then repealed after the law had been in effect for only a short period. Its repeal ushered in a decided shift in economic policy, marked by reduced reliance on centralized "plans" and "programs," by the dismantling of many controls, and by increased emphasis on the private market. A similar shift in policy occurred in most other democratic countries.

The proximate explanation of these shifts in policy is the limited success of central planning or its outright failure to achieve stated objectives. However, this failure is itself to be attributed, at least in some measure, to the political implications of central planning and to an unwillingness to follow out its logic when doing so requires trampling rough-shod on treasured private rights. It may well be that the shift is only a temporary interruption in the collectivist trend of this century. Even so, it illustrated the close relation between political freedom and economic arrangements.

Historical evidence by itself can never be convincing. Perhaps it was sheer coincidence that the expansion of freedom occurred at the same time as the development of capitalist and market institutions. Why should there be a connection? What are the logical links between economic and political freedom? In discussing these questions we shall consider first the market as a direct component of freedom, and then the indirect relation between market arrangements and political freedom. A by-product will be an outline of the ideal economic arrangements for a free society.

As liberals, we take freedom of the individual, or perhaps the family, as our ultimate goal in judging social arrangements. Freedom as a value in this sense has to do with the interrelations among people; it has no meaning whatsoever to a Robinson Crusoe on an isolated island (without his Man Friday). Robinson Crusoe on his island is subject to "constraint," he has limited "power," and he has only a limited number of alternatives, but there is no problem of freedom in the sense that is relevant to our discussion. Similarly, in a society freedom has nothing to say about what an individual does with his freedom; it is not an all-embracing ethic. Indeed, a major aim of the liberal is to leave the ethical problem for the individual to wrestle with. The "really" important ethical problems are those that face an individual in a free society—what he should do with his freedom. There are thus two sets of values that a liberal will emphasize—the values that are relevant to relations among people, which is the context in which he assigns first priority to freedom; and the values that are relevant to the individual in the exercise of his freedom, which is the realm of individual ethics and philosophy.

The liberal conceives of men as imperfect beings. He regards the problem of social organization to be as much a negative problem of preventing "bad" people from doing harm as of enabling "good" people to do good; and, of course, "bad" and "good" people may be the same people, depending on who is judging them.

The basic problem of social organization is how to co-ordinate the economic activities of large numbers of people. Even in relatively backward societies, extensive division of labor and specialization of function is required to make effective use of available resources. In advanced societies, the scale on which co-ordination is needed, to take full advantage of the opportunities offered by modern science and technology, is enormously greater. Literally millions of people are involved in providing one another with their daily bread, let alone with their yearly automobiles. The challenge to the believer in liberty is to reconcile this widespread interdependence with individual freedom.

Fundamentally, there are only two ways of co-ordinating the economic activities of millions. One is central direction involving the use of coercion—the technique of the army and of the modern totalitarian state. The other is voluntary co-operation of individuals—the technique of the market place.

The possibility of co-ordination through voluntary co-operation rests on the elementary—yet frequently denied—proposition that both parties to an economic transaction benefit from it, provided the transaction is bilaterally voluntary and informed.

Exchange can therefore bring about co-ordination without coercion. A working model of a society organized through voluntary exchange is a free private enterprise exchange economy—what we have been calling competitive capitalism.

In its simplest form, such a society consists of a number of independent households—a collection of Robinson Crusoes, as it were. Each household uses the resources it controls to produce goods and services that it exchanges for goods and services produced by other households, on terms mutually acceptable to the two parties to the bargain. It is thereby enabled to satisfy its wants indirectly by producing goods and services for others, rather than directly by producing goods for its own immediate use. The incentive for adopting this indirect route is, of course, the increased product made possible by division of labor and specialization of function. Since the household always has the alternative of producing directly for itself, it need not enter into any exchange unless it benefits from it. Hence, no exchange will take place unless both parties so benefit from it. Co-operation is thereby achieved without coercion.

Specialization of function and division of labor would not go far if the ultimate productive unit were the household. In a modern society, we have gone much farther. We have introduced enterprises which are intermediaries between individuals in their capacities as suppliers of service and as purchasers of goods. And similarly, specialization of function and division of labor could not go very far if we had to continue to rely on the barter of product for product. In consequence, money has been introduced as a means of facilitating exchange, and of enabling the acts of purchase and of sale to be separated into two parts.

Despite the important role of enterprises and of money in our actual economy, and despite the numerous and complex problems they raise, the central characteristic of the market technique of achieving co-ordination is fully displayed in the simple exchange economy that contains neither enterprises nor money. As in that simple model, so in the complex enterprise and money-exchange economy, co-operation is strictly individual and voluntary *provided:* (a) that enterprises are private, so that the ultimate contracting parties are individuals, and (b) that individuals are effectively free to enter or not to enter into any particular exchange, so that every transaction is strictly voluntary.

It is far easier to state these provisos in general terms than to spell them out in detail, or to specify precisely the institutional arrangements most conducive to their maintenance. Indeed, much of technical economic literature is concerned with precisely these questions. The basic requisite is the maintenance of law and order to prevent physical coercion of one individual by another and to enforce contracts voluntarily entered into, thus giving substance to "private." Aside from this, perhaps the most difficult problems arise from monopoly—which inhibits effective freedom by denying individuals alternatives to the particular exchange—and from "neighborhood effects"—effects on third parties for which it is not feasible to charge or recompense them. These problems will be discussed in more detail in the following chapter.

So long as effective freedom of exchange is maintained, the central feature of the market organization of economic activity is that it prevents one person from interfering with another in respect of most of his activities. The consumer is protected from coercion by the seller because of the presence of other sellers with whom he can deal. The seller is protected from coercion by the consumer because of other consumers to whom he can sell. The employee is protected from coercion by the employer because of other employers for whom he can work, and so on. And the market does this impersonally and without centralized authority.

Indeed, a major source of objection to a free economy is precisely that it does this task so well. It gives people what they want instead of what a particular group thinks they ought to want. Underlying most arguments against the free market is a lack of belief in freedom itself.

The existence of a free market does not of course eliminate the need for government. On the contrary, government is essential both as a forum for determining the "rules of the game" and as an umpire to interpret and enforce the rules decided on. What the market does is to reduce greatly the range of issues that must be decided through political means, and thereby to minimize the extent to which government need participate directly in the game. The characteristic feature of action through political channels is that it tends to require or enforce substantial conformity. The great advantage of the market, on the other hand, is that it permits wide diversity. It is, in political terms, a system of proportional representation. Each man can vote, as it were, for the color of tie he wants and get it; he does not have to see what color the majority wants and then, if he is in the minority, submit.

It is this feature of the market that we refer to when we say that the market provides economic freedom. But this characteristic also has implications that go far beyond the narrowly economic. Political freedom means the absence of coercion of a man by his fellow men. The fundamental threat to freedom is power to coerce, be it in the hands of a monarch, a dictator, an oligarchy, or a momentary majority. The preservation of freedom requires the elimination of such concentration of power to the fullest possible extent and the dispersal and distribution of whatever power cannot be eliminated—a system of checks and balances. By removing the organization of economic activity from the control of political authority, the market eliminates this source of coercive power. It enables economic strength to be a check to political power rather than a reinforcement.

Economic power can be widely dispersed. There is no law of conservation which forces the growth of new centers of economic strength to be at the expense of existing centers. Political power, on the other hand, is more difficult to decentralize. There can be numerous small independent governments. But it is far more difficult to maintain numerous equipotent small centers of political power in a single large government than it is to have numerous centers of economic strength in a single large economy. There can be many millionaires in one large economy. But can there be more than one really outstanding leader, one person on whom the energies and enthusiasms of his countrymen are centered? If the central government gains power, it is likely to be at the expense of local governments. There seems to be something like a fixed total of political power to be distributed. Consequently, if economic power is joined to political power, it can serve as a check and a counter to political power.

The force of this abstract argument can perhaps best be demonstrated by example. Let us consider first, a hypothetical example that may help to bring out the principles involved, and then some actual examples from recent experience that illustrate the way in which the market works to preserve political freedom.

One feature of a free society is surely the freedom of individuals to advocate and propagandize openly for a radical change in the structure of the society—so long as the advocacy is restricted to persuasion and does not include force or other forms of coercion. It is a mark of the political freedom of a capitalist society that men can openly advocate and work for socialism. Equally, political freedom in a socialist society would require that men be free to advocate the introduction of capitalism. How could the freedom to advocate capitalism be preserved and protected in a socialist society?

In order for men to advocate anything, they must in the first place be able to earn a living. This already raises a problem in a socialist society, since all jobs are under the direct control of political authorities. It would take an act of self-denial whose difficulty is underlined by experience in the United States after World War II with the problem of "security" among Federal employees, for a socialist government to permit its employees to advocate policies directly contrary to official doctrine.

But let us suppose this act of self-denial to be achieved. For advocacy of capitalism to mean anything, the proponents must be able to finance their cause—to hold public meetings, publish pamphlets, buy radio time, issue newspapers and magazines, and so on. How could they raise the funds? There might and probably would be men in the socialist society with large incomes, perhaps even large capital sums in the form of government bonds and the like, but these would of necessity be high public officials. It is possible to conceive of a minor socialist

official retaining his job although openly advocating capitalism. It strains cre-
dulity to imagine the socialist top brass financing such "subversive" activities.

The only recourse for funds would be to raise small amounts from a large number of minor officials. But this is no real answer. To tap these sources, many people would already have to be persuaded, and our whole problem is how to initiate
and finance a campaign to do so. Radical movements in capitalist societies
have never been financed this way. They have typically been supported by a few
wealthy individuals who have become persuaded—by a Frederick Vanderbilt
Field, or an Anita McCormick Blaine, or a Corliss Lamont, to mention a few
names recently prominent, or by a Friedrich Engels, to go farther back. This is a
role of inequality of wealth in preserving political freedom that is seldom noted—
the role of the patron.

In a capitalist society, it is only necessary to convince a few wealthy people to
get funds to launch any idea, however strange, and there are many such persons,
many independent foci of support. And, indeed, it is not even necessary to persuade people or financial institutions with available funds of the soundness of
the ideas to be propagated. It is only necessary to persuade them that the propagation can be financially successful; that the newspaper or magazine or book or
other venture will be profitable. The competitive publisher, for example, cannot
afford to publish only writing with which he personally agrees; his touchstone
must be the likelihood that the market will be large enough to yield a satisfactory
return on his investment.

In this way, the market breaks the vicious circle and makes it possible ultimately to finance such ventures by small amounts from many people without
first persuading them. There are no such possibilities in the socialist society;
there is only the all-powerful state.

Let us stretch our imagination and suppose that a socialist government is
aware of this problem and is composed of people anxious to preserve freedom.
Could it provide the funds? Perhaps, but it is difficult to see how. It could establish a bureau for subsidizing subversive propaganda. But how could it choose
whom to support? If it gave to all who asked, it would shortly find itself out of
funds, for socialism cannot repeal the elementary economic law that a sufficiently high price will call forth a large supply. Make the advocacy of radical
causes sufficiently remunerative, and the supply of advocates will be unlimited.

Moreover, freedom to advocate unpopular causes does not require that such
advocacy be without cost. On the contrary, no society could be stable if advocacy
of radical change were costless, much less subsidized. It is entirely appropriate
that men make sacrifices to advocate causes in which they deeply believe. Indeed,
it is important to preserve freedom only for people who are willing to practice
self-denial, for otherwise freedom degenerates into license and irresponsibility.

What is essential is that the cost of advocating unpopular causes be tolerable and not prohibitive.

But we are not yet through. In a free market society, it is enough to have the funds. The suppliers of paper are as willing to sell it to the *Daily Worker* as to the *Wall Street Journal*. In a socialist society, it would not be enough to have the funds. The hypothetical supporter of capitalism would have to persuade a government factory making paper to sell to him, the government printing press to print his pamphlets, a government post office to distribute them among the people, a government agency to rent him a hall in which to talk, and so on.

Perhaps there is some way in which one could overcome these difficulties and preserve freedom in a socialist society. One cannot say it is utterly impossible. What is clear, however, is that there are very real difficulties in establishing institutions that will effectively preserve the possibility of dissent. So far as I know, none of the people who have been in favor of socialism and also in favor of freedom have really faced up to this issue, or made even a respectable start at developing the institutional arrangements that would permit freedom under socialism. By contrast, it is clear how a free market capitalist society fosters freedom.

A striking practical example of these abstract principles is the experience of Winston Churchill. From 1933 to the outbreak of World War II, Churchill was not permitted to talk over the British radio, which was, of course, a government monopoly administered by the British Broadcasting Corporation. Here was a leading citizen of his country, a Member of Parliament, a former cabinet minister, a man who was desperately trying by every device possible to persuade his countrymen to take steps to ward off the menace of Hitler's Germany. He was not permitted to talk over the radio to the British people because the BBC was a government monopoly and his position was too "controversial."

Another striking example, reported in the January 26, 1959, issue of *Time*, has to do with the "Blacklist Fadeout." Says the *Time* story,

> The Oscar-awarding ritual is Hollywood's biggest pitch for dignity, but two years ago dignity suffered. When one Robert Rich was announced as top writer for *The Brave One*, he never stepped forward. Robert Rich was a pseudonym, masking one of about 150 writers . . . blacklisted by the industry since 1947 as suspected Communists or fellow travelers. The case was particularly embarrassing because the Motion Picture Academy had barred any Communist or Fifth Amendment pleader from Oscar competition. Last week both the Communist rule and the mystery of Rich's identity were suddenly rescripted.
>
> Rich turned out to be Dalton (*Johnny Got His Gun*) Trumbo, one of the original "Hollywood Ten" writers who refused to testify at the 1947 hearings on Communism in the movie industry. Said producer Frank King, who had stoutly insisted that Robert Rich was "a young guy in Spain with a beard":

"We have an obligation to our stockholders to buy the best script we can. Trumbo brought us *The Brave One* and we bought it."

In effect it was the formal end of the Hollywood blacklist. For barred writers, the informal end came long ago. At least 15 percent of current Hollywood films are reportedly written by blacklist members. Said Producer King, "There are more ghosts in Hollywood than in Forest Lawn. Every company in town has used the work of blacklisted people. We're just the first to confirm what everybody knows."

One may believe, as I do, that communism would destroy all of our freedoms, one may be opposed to it as firmly and as strongly as possible, and yet, at the same time, also believe that in a free society it is intolerable for a man to be prevented from making voluntary arrangements with others that are mutually attractive because he believes in or is trying to promote communism. His freedom includes his freedom to promote communism. Freedom also, of course, includes the freedom of others not to deal with him under those circumstances. The Hollywood blacklist was an unfree act that destroys freedom because it was a collusive arrangement that used coercive means to prevent voluntary exchanges. It didn't work precisely because the market made it costly for people to preserve the blacklist. The commercial emphasis, the fact that people who are running enterprises have an incentive to make as much money as they can, protected the freedom of the individuals who were blacklisted by providing them with an alternative form of employment, and by giving people an incentive to employ them.

If Hollywood and the movie industry had been government enterprises or if in England it had been a question of employment by the British Broadcasting Corporation it is difficult to believe that the "Hollywood Ten" or their equivalent would have found employment. Equally, it is difficult to believe that under those circumstances, strong proponents of individualism and private enterprise—or indeed strong proponents of any view other than the status quo—would be able to get employment.

Another example of the role of the market in preserving political freedom was revealed in our experience with McCarthyism. Entirely aside from the substantive issues involved, and the merits of the charges made, what protection did individuals, and in particular government employees, have against irresponsible accusations and probings into matters that it went against their conscience to reveal? Their appeal to the Fifth Amendment would have been a hollow mockery without an alternative to government employment.

Their fundamental protection was the existence of a private-market economy in which they could earn a living. Here again, the protection was not absolute. Many potential private employers were, rightly or wrongly, averse to hiring those pilloried. It may well be that there was far less justification for the costs imposed on many of the people involved than for the costs generally imposed on people who advocate unpopular causes. But the important point is that the costs were limited and not prohibitive, as they would have been if government employment had been the only possibility.

It is of interest to note that a disproportionately large fraction of the people involved apparently went into the most competitive sectors of the economy— small business, trade, farming—where the market approaches most closely the ideal free market. No one who buys bread knows whether the wheat from which it is made was grown by a Communist or a Republican, by a constitutionalist or a Fascist, or, for that matter, by a Negro or a white. This illustrates how an impersonal market separates economic activities from political views and protects men from being discriminated against in their economic activities for reasons that are irrelevant to their productivity—whether these reasons are associated with their view or their color.

As this example suggests, the groups in our society that have the most at stake in the preservation and strengthening of competitive capitalism are those minority groups which can most easily become the object of the distrust and enmity of the majority—the Negroes, the Jews, the foreign-born, to mention only the most obvious. Yet, paradoxically enough, the enemies of the free market—the Socialists and Communists—have been recruited in disproportionate measure from these groups. Instead of recognizing that the existence of the market has protected them from the attitudes of their fellow countrymen, they mistakenly attribute the residual discrimination to the market.

Chapter 2
The Role of Government in a Free Society

A common objection to totalitarian societies is that they regard the end as justifying the means. Taken literally, this objection is clearly illogical. If the end does not justify the means, what does? But this easy answer does not dispose of the objection; it simply shows that the objection is not well put. To deny that the end justifies the means is indirectly to assert that the end in question is not the ultimate end, that the ultimate end is itself the use of the proper means. Desirable or not, any end that can be attained only by the use of bad means must give way to the more basic end of the use of acceptable means.

To the liberal, the appropriate means are free discussion and voluntary cooperation, which implies that any form of coercion is inappropriate. The ideal is unanimity among responsible individuals achieved on the basis of free and full discussion. This is another way of expressing the goal of freedom emphasized in the preceding chapter.

From this standpoint, the role of the market, as already noted, is that it permits unanimity without conformity; that it is a system of effectively proportional representation. On the other hand, the characteristic feature of action through explicitly political channels is that it tends to require or to enforce substantial conformity. The typical issue must be decided "yes" or "no"; at most, provision can be made for a fairly limited number of alternatives. Even the use of proportional representation in its explicitly political form does not alter this conclusion. The number of separate groups that can in fact be represented is narrowly limited, enormously so by comparison with the proportional representation of the market. More important, the fact that the final outcome generally must be a law applicable to all groups, rather than separate legislative enactments for each "party" represented, means that proportional representation in its political version, far from permitting unanimity without conformity, tends toward ineffectiveness and fragmentation. It thereby operates to destroy any consensus on which unanimity with conformity can rest.

There are clearly some matters with respect to which effective proportional representation is impossible. I cannot get the amount of national defense I want and you, a different amount. With respect to such indivisible matters we can discuss, and argue, and vote. But having decided, we must conform. It is precisely the existence of such indivisible matters—protection of the individual and the nation from coercion are clearly the most basic—that prevents exclusive reliance on individual action through the market. If we are to use some of our resources for such indivisible items, we must employ political channels to reconcile differences.

The use of political channels, while inevitable, tends to strain the social cohesion essential for a stable society. The strain is least if agreement for joint action need be reached only on a limited range of issues on which people in any event have common views. Every extension of the range of issues for which explicit agreement is sought strains further the delicate threads that hold society together. If it goes so far as to touch an issue on which men feel deeply yet differently, it may well disrupt the society. Fundamental differences in basic values can seldom if ever be resolved at the ballot box; ultimately they can only be decided, though not resolved, by conflict. The religious and civil wars of history are a bloody testament to this judgment.

The widespread use of the market reduces the strain on the social fabric by rendering conformity unnecessary with respect to any activities it encompasses. The wider the range of activities covered by the market, the fewer are the issues on which explicitly political decisions are required and hence on which it is necessary to achieve agreement. In turn, the fewer the issues on which agreement is necessary, the greater is the likelihood of getting agreement while maintaining a free society.

Unanimity is, of course, an ideal. In practice, we can afford neither the time nor the effort that would be required to achieve complete unanimity on every issue. We must perforce accept something less. We are thus led to accept majority rule in one form or another as an expedient. That majority rule is an expedient rather than itself a basic principle is clearly shown by the fact that our willingness to resort to majority rule, and the size of the majority we require, themselves depend on the seriousness of the issue involved. If the matter is of little moment and the minority has no strong feelings about being overruled, a bare plurality will suffice. On the other hand, if the minority feels strongly about the issue involved, even a bare majority will not do. Few of us would be willing to have issues of free speech, for example, decided by a bare majority. Our legal structure is full of such distinctions among kinds of issues that require different kinds of majorities. At the extreme are those issues embodied in the Constitution. These are the principles that are so important that we are willing to make minimal concessions to expediency. Something like essential consensus was achieved initially in accepting them, and we require something like essential consensus for a change in them.

The self-denying ordinance to refrain from majority rule on certain kinds of issues that is embodied in our Constitution and in similar written or unwritten constitutions elsewhere, and the specific provisions in these constitutions or their equivalents prohibiting coercion of individuals, are themselves to be regarded as reached by free discussion and as reflecting essential unanimity about means.

I turn now to consider more specifically, though still in very broad terms, what the areas are that cannot be handled through the market at all, or can be handled only at so great a cost that the use of political channels may be preferable.

Government as Rule-maker and Umpire

It is important to distinguish the day-to-day activities of people from the general customary and legal framework within which these take place. The day-to-day activities are like the actions of the participants in a game when they are playing it; the framework, like the rules of the game they play. And just as a good game requires acceptance by the players both of the rules and of the umpire to interpret and enforce them, so a good society requires that its members agree on the general conditions that will govern relations among them, on some means of arbitrating different interpretations of these conditions, and on some device for enforcing compliance with the generally accepted rules. As in games, so also in society, most of the general conditions are the unintended outcome of custom, accepted unthinkingly. At most, we consider explicitly only minor modifications in them, though the cumulative effect of a series of minor modifications may be a drastic alteration in the character of the game or of the society. In both games and society also, no set of rules can prevail unless most participants most of the time conform to them without external sanctions; unless, that is, there is a broad underlying social consensus. But we cannot rely on custom or on this consensus alone to interpret and to enforce the rules; we need an umpire. These then are the basic roles of government in a free society: to provide a means whereby we can modify the rules, to mediate differences among us on the meaning of the rules, and to enforce compliance with the rules on the part of those few who would otherwise not play the game.

The need for government in these respects arises because absolute freedom is impossible. However attractive anarchy may be as a philosophy, it is not feasible in a world of imperfect men. Men's freedoms can conflict, and when they do, one man's freedom must be limited to preserve another's—as a Supreme Court Justice once put it, "My freedom to move my fist must be limited by the proximity of your chin."

The major problem in deciding the appropriate activities of government is how to resolve such conflicts among the freedoms of different individuals. In some cases, the answer is easy. There is little difficulty in attaining near unanimity to the proposition that one man's freedom to murder his neighbor must be sacrificed to preserve the freedom of the other man to live. In other cases, the answer is difficult. In the economic area, a major problem arises in respect of the conflict between freedom to combine and freedom to compete. What meaning is to be attributed to "free" as modifying "enterprise"? In the United States, "free" has been understood to mean that anyone is free to set up an enterprise, which means that existing enterprises are not free to keep out competitors except by selling a better product at the same price or the same product at a lower price. In the continental tradition, on the other hand, the meaning has generally been that enterprises are free to do what they want, including the fixing of prices, division of markets, and the adoption of other technique to keep out potential competitors. Perhaps the most difficult specific problem in this area arises with respect to combinations among laborers, where the problem of freedom to combine and freedom to compete is particularly acute.

A still more basic economic area in which the answer is both difficult and important is the definition of property rights. The notion of property, as it has developed over centuries and as it is embodied in our legal codes, has become so much a part of us that we tend to take it for granted, and fail to recognize the extent to which just what constitutes property and what rights the ownership of property confers are complex social creations rather than self-evident propositions. Does my having title to land, for example, and my freedom to use my property as I wish, permit me to deny to someone else the right to fly over my land in his airplane? Or does his right to use his airplane take precedence? Or does this depend on how high he flies? Or how much noise he makes? Does voluntary exchange require that he pay me for the privilege of flying over my land? Or that I must pay him to refrain from flying over it? The mere mention of royalties, copyrights, patents; shares of stock in corporations; riparian rights, and the like, may perhaps emphasize the role of generally accepted social rules in the very definition of property. It may suggest also that, in many cases, the existence of a well specified and generally accepted definition of property is far more important than just what the definition is.

Another economic area that raises particularly difficult problems is the monetary system. Government responsibility for the monetary system has long been recognized. It is explicitly provided for in the constitutional provision which gives Congress the power "to coin money, regulate the value thereof, and of foreign coin." There is probably no other area of economic activity with respect to which government action has been so uniformly accepted. This habitual and by now almost unthinking acceptance of governmental responsibility makes thorough understanding of the grounds for such responsibility all the more necessary, since it enhances the danger that the scope of government will spread from activities that are, to those that are not, appropriate in a free society, from providing a monetary framework to determining the allocation of resources among individuals. We shall discuss this problem in detail in chapter 3.

In summary, the organization of economic activity through voluntary exchange presumes that we have provided, through government, for the maintenance of law and order to prevent coercion of one individual by another, the enforcement of contracts voluntarily entered into, the definition of the meaning of property rights, the interpretation and enforcement of such rights, and the provision of a monetary framework.

Action Through Government on Grounds of Technical Monopoly and Neighborhood Effects

The role of government just considered is to do something that the market cannot do for itself, namely, to determine, arbitrate, and enforce the rules of the game. We may also want to do through government some things that might conceivably be done through the market but that technical or similar conditions render it difficult to do in that way. These all reduce to cases in which strictly voluntary exchange is either exceedingly costly or practically impossible. There are two general classes of such cases: monopoly and similar market imperfections, and neighborhood effects. Exchange is truly voluntary only when nearly equivalent alternatives exist. Monopoly implies the absence of alternatives and thereby inhibits effective freedom of exchange. In practice, monopoly frequently, if not generally, arises from government support or from collusive agreements among individuals. With respect to these, the problem is either to avoid governmental fostering of monopoly or to stimulate the effective enforcement of rules such as those embodied in our anti-trust laws. However, monopoly may also arise because it is technically efficient to have a single producer or enterprise. I venture to suggest that such cases are more limited than is supposed but they unquestionably do arise. A simple example is perhaps the provision of telephone services within a community. I shall refer to such cases as "technical" monopoly.

When technical conditions make a monopoly the natural outcome of competitive market forces, there are only three alternatives that seem available: private monopoly, public monopoly, or public regulation. All three are bad so we must choose among evils. Henry Simons, observing public regulation of monopoly in the United States found the results so distasteful that he concluded public monopoly would be a lesser evil. Walter Eucken, a noted German liberal, observing public monopoly in German railroads, found the results so distasteful that he concluded public regulation would be a lesser evil. Having learned from both, I reluctantly concluded that, if tolerable, private monopoly may be the least of the evils.

If society were static so that the conditions which give rise to a technical monopoly were sure to remain, I would have little confidence in this solution. In a rapidly changing society, however, the conditions making for technical monopoly frequently change and I suspect that both public regulation and public monopoly are likely to be less responsive to such changes in conditions, to be less readily capable of elimination, than private monopoly.

Railroads in the United States are an excellent example. A large degree of monopoly in railroads was perhaps inevitable on technical grounds in the nineteenth century. This was the justification for the Interstate Commerce Commission. But conditions have changed. The emergence of road and air transport has reduced the monopoly element in railroads to negligible proportions. Yet we have not eliminated the ICC. On the contrary, the ICC, which started out as an agency to protect the public from exploitation by the railroads, has become an agency to protect railroads from competition by trucks and other means of transport, and more recently even to protect existing truck companies from competition by new entrants. Similarly, in England, when the railroads were nationalized, trucking was at first brought into the state monopoly. If railroads had never been subjected to regulation in the United States, it is nearly certain that by now transportation, including railroads, would be a highly competitive industry with little or no remaining monopoly elements.

The choice between the evils of private monopoly, public monopoly, and public regulation cannot, however, be made once and for all, independently of the factual circumstances. If the technical monopoly is of a service or commodity that is regarded as essential and if its monopoly power is sizable, even the short-run effects of private unregulated monopoly may not be tolerable, and either public regulation or ownership may be a lesser evil.

Technical monopoly may on occasion justify a *de facto* public monopoly. It cannot by itself justify a public monopoly achieved by making it illegal for anyone else to compete. For example, there is no way to justify our present public monopoly of the post office. It may be argued that the carrying of mail is a technical monopoly and that a government monopoly is the least of evils. Along these lines, one could perhaps justify a government post office but not the present law, which makes it illegal for anybody else to carry mail. If the delivery of mail is a technical monopoly, no one will be able to succeed in competition with the government. If it is not, there is no reason why the government should be engaged in it. The only way to find out is to leave other people free to enter.

The historical reason why we have a post office monopoly is because the Pony Express did such a good job of carrying the mail across the continent that, when the government introduced transcontinental service, it couldn't compete effectively and lost money. The result was a law making it illegal for anybody else to carry the mail. That is why the Adams Express Company is an investment trust today instead of an operating company. I conjecture that if entry into the mail-carrying business were open to all, there would be a large number of firms entering it and this archaic industry would become revolutionized in short order.

A second general class of cases in which strictly voluntary exchange is impossible arises when actions of individuals have effects on other individuals for which it is not feasible to charge or recompense them. This is the problem of "neighborhood effects." An obvious example is the pollution of a stream. The man who pollutes a stream is in effect forcing others to exchange good water for bad. These others might be willing to make the exchange at a price. But it is not feasible for them, acting individually, to avoid the exchange or to enforce appropriate compensation.

A less obvious example is the provision of highways. In this case, it is technically possible to identify and hence charge individuals for their use of the roads and so to have private operation. However, for general access roads, involving many points of entry and exit, the costs of collection would be extremely high if a charge were to be made for the specific services received by each individual, because of the necessity of establishing toll booths or the equivalent at all entrances. The gasoline tax is a much cheaper method of charging individuals roughly in proportion to their use of the roads. This method, however, is one in which the particular payment cannot be identified closely with the particular use. Hence, it is hardly feasible to have private enterprise provide the service and collect the charge without establishing extensive private monopoly.

These considerations do not apply to long-distance turnpikes with high density of traffic and limited access. For these, the costs of collection are small and in many cases are now being paid, and there are often numerous alternatives, so that there is no serious monopoly problem. Hence, there is every reason why these should be privately owned and operated. If so owned and operated, the enterprises running the highway should receive the gasoline taxes paid on account of travel on it.

Parks are an interesting example because they illustrate the difference between cases that can and cases that cannot be justified by neighborhood effects, and because almost everyone at first sight regards the conduct of National Parks as obviously a valid function of government. In fact, however, neighborhood effects may justify a city park; they do not justify a national park, like Yellowstone National Park or the Grand Canyon. What is the fundamental difference between the two? For the city park, it is extremely difficult to identify the people who benefit from it and to charge them for the benefits which they receive. If there is a park in the middle of the city, the houses on all sides get the benefit of the open space, and people who walk through it or by it also benefit. To maintain toll collectors at the gates or to impose annual charges per window overlooking the park would be very expensive and difficult. The entrances to a national park like Yellowstone, on the other hand, are few; most of the people who come stay for a considerable period of time and it is perfectly feasible to set up toll gates and collect admission charges. This is indeed now done, though the charges do not cover the whole costs. If the public wants this kind of an activity enough to pay for it, private enterprises will have every incentive to provide such parks. And, of course, there are many private enterprises of this nature now in existence. I cannot myself conjure up any neighborhood effects or important monopoly effects that would justify governmental activity in this area.

Considerations like those I have treated under the heading of neighborhood effects have been used to rationalize almost every conceivable intervention. In many instances, however, this rationalization is special pleading rather than a legitimate application of the concept of neighborhood effects. Neighborhood effects cut both ways. They can be a reason for limiting the activities of government as well as for expanding them. Neighborhood effects impede voluntary exchange because it is difficult to identify the effects on third parties and to measure their magnitude; but this difficulty is present in governmental activity as well. It is hard to know when neighborhood effects are sufficiently large to justify particular costs in overcoming them and even harder to distribute the costs in an appropriate fashion. Consequently, when government engages in activities to overcome neighborhood effects, it will in part introduce an additional set of neighborhood effects by failing to charge or to compensate individuals properly. Whether the original or the new neighborhood effects are the more serious can only be judged by the facts of the individual case, and even then, only very approximately. Furthermore, the use of government to overcome neighborhood effects itself has an extremely important neighborhood effect which is unrelated to the particular occasion for government action. Every act of the government intervention limits the area of individual freedom directly and threatens the preservation of freedom indirectly for reasons elaborated in the first chapter.

Our principles offer no hard and fast line how far it is appropriate to use government to accomplish jointly what it is difficult or impossible for us to accomplish separately through strictly voluntary exchange. In any particular case of proposed intervention, we must make up a balance sheet, listing separately the advantages and disadvantages. Our principles tell us what items to put on the one side and what items on the other and they give us some basis for attaching importance to the different items. In particular, we shall always want to enter on the liability side of any proposed government intervention, its neighborhood effect in threatening freedom, and give this effect considerable weight. Just how much weight to give to it, as to other items, depends upon the circumstances. If, for example, existing government intervention is minor, we shall attach a smaller weight to the negative effects of additional government intervention. This is an important reason why many earlier liberals, like Henry Simons, writing at a time when government was small by today's standards, were willing to have government undertake activities that today's liberals would not accept now that government has become so overgrown.

Action Through Government on Paternalistic Grounds

Freedom is a tenable objective only for responsible individuals. We do not believe in freedom for madmen or children. The necessity of drawing a line between responsible individuals and others is inescapable, yet it means that there is an essential ambiguity in our ultimate objective of freedom. Paternalism is inescapable for those whom we designate as not responsible.

The clearest case, perhaps, is that of madmen. We are willing neither to permit them freedom nor to shoot them. It would be nice if we could rely on voluntary activities of individuals to house and care for the madmen. But I think we cannot rule out the possibility that such charitable activities will be inadequate, if only because of the neighborhood effect involved in the fact that I benefit if another man contributes to the care of the insane. For this reason, we may be willing to arrange for their care through government.

Children offer a more difficult case. The ultimate operative unit in our society is the family, not the individual. Yet the acceptance of the family as the unit rests in considerable part on expediency rather than principle. We believe that parents are generally best able to protect their children and to provide for their development into responsible individuals for whom freedom is appropriate. But we do not believe in the freedom of parents to do what they will with other people. The children are responsible individuals in embryo, and a believer in freedom believes in protecting their ultimate rights.

To put this in a different and what may seem a more callous way, children are at one and the same time consumer goods and potentially responsible members of society. The freedom of individuals to use their economic resources as they want includes the freedom to use them to have children—to buy, as it were, the services of children as a particular form of consumption. But once this choice is exercised, the children have a value in and of themselves and have a freedom of their own that is not simply an extension of the freedom of the parents.

The paternalistic ground for governmental activity is in many ways the most troublesome to a liberal; for it involves the acceptance of a principle—that some shall decide for others—which he finds objectionable in most applications and which he rightly regards as a hallmark of his chief intellectual opponents, the proponents of collectivism in one or another of its guises, whether it be communism, socialism, or a welfare state. Yet there is no use pretending that problems are simpler than in fact they are. There is no avoiding the need for some measure of paternalism. As Dicey wrote in 1914 about an act for the protection of mental defectives, "The Mental Deficiency Act is the first step along a path on which no sane man can decline to enter, but which, if too far pursued, will bring statesmen across difficulties hard to meet without considerable interference with individual liberty." There is no formula that can tell us where to stop. We must rely on our fallible judgment and, having reached a judgment, on our ability to persuade our fellow men that it is a correct judgment, on their ability to persuade us to modify our views. We must put our faith, here as elsewhere, in a consensus reached by imperfect and biased men through free discussion and trial and error.

Conclusion

A government which maintained law and order, defined property rights, served as a means whereby we could modify property rights and other rules of the economic game, adjudicated disputes about the interpretation of the rules, enforced contracts, promoted competition, provided a monetary framework, engaged in activities to counter technical monopolies and to overcome neighborhood effects widely regarded as sufficiently important to justify government intervention, and which supplemented private charity and the private family in protecting the irresponsible, whether madman or child—such a government would have clearly important functions to perform. The consistent liberal is not an anarchist.

Yet it is also true that such a government would have clearly limited functions and would refrain from a host of activities that are now undertaken by federal and state governments in the United States, and their counterparts in other Western countries. Succeeding chapters will deal in some detail with some of these activities, and a few have been discussed above, but it may help to give a sense of proportion about the role that a liberal would assign government simply to list, in closing this chapter, some activities currently undertaken by government in the U.S. that cannot, so far as I can see, validly be justified in terms of the principles outlined above:

1. Parity price support programs for agriculture.
2. Tariffs on imports or restrictions on exports, such as current oil import quotas, sugar quotas, etc.
3. Governmental control of output, such as through the farm program, or through prorationing of oil as is done by the Texas Railroad Commission.
4. Rent control, such as is still practiced in New York, or more general price and wage controls such as were imposed during and just after World War II.
5. Legal minimum wage rates, or legal maximum prices, such as the legal maximum of zero on the rate of interest that can be paid on demand deposits by commercial banks, or the legally fixed maximum rates that can be paid on savings and time deposits.
6. Detailed regulation of industries, such as the regulation of transportation by the Interstate Commerce Commission. This had some justification on technical monopoly grounds when initially introduced for railroads; it has none now for any means of transport. Another example is detailed regulation of banking.
7. A similar example, but one which deserves special mention because of its implicit censorship and violation of free speech, is the control of radio and television by the Federal Communications Commission.
8. Present social security programs, especially the old-age and retirement programs compelling people in effect (a) to spend a specified fraction of their income on the purchase of retirement annuity, (b) to buy the annuity from a publicly operated enterprise.
9. Licensure provisions in various cities and states which restrict particular enterprises or occupations or professions to people who have a license, where the license is more than a receipt for a tax which anyone who wishes to enter the activity may pay.

10. So-called "public-housing" and the host of other subsidy programs directed at fostering residential construction such as FHA and VA guarantee of mortgage, and the like.

11. Conscription to man the military services in peacetime. The appropriate free market arrangement is volunteer military forces; which is to say, hiring men to serve. There is no justification for not paying whatever price is necessary to attract the required number of men. Present arrangements are inequitable and arbitrary, seriously interfere with the freedom of young men to shape their lives, and probably are even more costly than the market alternative. (Universal military training to provide a reserve for war time is a different problem and may be justified on liberal grounds.)

12. National parks, as noted above.

13. The legal prohibition on the carrying of mail for profit.

14. Publicly owned and operated toll roads, as noted above.

This list is far from comprehensive.

7

Isaac Kramnick

"Equal Opportunity and the 'Race of Life'" (1981)

Isaac Kramnick (b. 1938) is Richard J. Schwartz Professor, former chair of the Department of Government, and Vice Provost for Undergraduate Education at Cornell University. He is the author of numerous articles on American and English liberalism. His books include Bolingbroke and His Circle *(1968),* The Rage of Edmund Burke *(1977),* Republicanism and Bourgeois Radicalism *(1990), and* Harold Laski: A Life on the Left *(1993).*

A FAIR RACE was what Lyndon Johnson pleaded for in his 1965 commencement address at Howard University that ushered in the era of affirmative action.

> You do not take a person, who for years has been hobbled by chains and liberate him, bring him up to the starting line of a race and then say "you are free to compete with all the others," and still justly believe that you have been completely fair.

Fifteen years later, *Bakke, Weber,* and the politics of affirmative action have stirred up a great public debate. The reasons are obvious. They raise sensitive questions of public policy and have grave implications for how we deal with one another, blacks and whites, men and women, workers and professionals, young and old. The focus of this debate has justifiably been on the here and now. But the doctrine of equal opportunity has occupied a central place in liberal ideology from the seventeenth century to the present, and the

Source: Isaac Kramnick, "Equal Opportunity and the 'Race of Life'" *Dissent* 28, no. 2 (Spring 1981): 178–187. Reprinted by permission of Isaac Kramnick and *Dissent.* Copyright © 1981 *Dissent.*

metaphor of life as a race was used centuries before Johnson's speech at Howard University.

Bakke, Weber, and the debate over affirmative action touch upon the deepest aspects of bourgeois liberalism. They are concerned with the marketplace, open or closed; with access to jobs and high status; with rewards to merit and talent; with privilege and the state. They involve the realization of self through work. They raise to public awareness the insecurity and anxiety inherent in a market society. As these issues are brought into public dialogue today, centuries-old beliefs lurk between every line of the briefs, learned articles, and position papers.

Central and enduring in liberalism is its unique conception of liberty and equality, rooted principally in attitudes toward work and the marketplace, toward achievement and talent. The revolutionary bourgeois attitude is best expressed in two famous cultural documents. The first is Beaumarchais's *Marriage of Figaro,* written in 1783 just before the French Revolution. The play, of course, was the basis of Mozart's opera. The plot, though complicated, is for our purposes, quite simple. It is built around the conflict between the great aristocrat Count Almaviva and a commoner, the hardworking, industrious barber, Figaro. The count seems almost to have outwitted Figaro in Act 5, which prompts Figaro to his famous denunciation:

> Just because you're a great Lord, you think you're a genius. Nobility, fortune, rank, position—you're so proud of those things. What have you done to deserve so many rewards? You went to the trouble of being born, and no more.

So subversive were these sentiments that the play was banned and only surfaced again in France after the Revolution had dealt even more definitively with the Almavivas.

The second document is from Thomas Mann, part of whose genius consisted in his ability to describe with meticulous accuracy European bourgeois civilization. In the *Buddenbrooks* Mann gives a much more vivid summary of these basic liberal beliefs than did Beaumarchais: his nineteenth-century liberal revolutionary Morten Schwartzkopf is speaking, criticizing a friend who has just spoken well of an aristocratic acquaintance:

> They need only to be born to be the pick of everything, and look down on all the rest of us. While we, however hard we strive, cannot climb to their level. We, the bourgeoisie—the Third Estate as we have been called—we recognize only that nobility which consists of merit; we refuse to admit any longer the rights of the indolent aristocracy, we repudiate the class distinctions of the present day, we desire that all men should be free and equal. . . . So that all men, without distinction, shall be able to strive together and receive their reward according to their merit.

Writing at the turn of the twentieth century when these values would be assaulted on the left and right (as he so beautifully depicted in his *Magic Mountain*),

Mann's sense of liberalism is the same as Beaumarchais's. Basic to both the dreams of Figaro and to Schwartzkopf is a vision of society where the rule or privilege is replaced by equal opportunity and where individuals, now masters of their destiny, are no longer the slaves of history, tradition, or birth.

Figaro's and Schwartzkopf's liberal vision of an ideal society is still with us, especially in America. But it is not some timeless, eternal ideal of humanity found, like so much else of our culture, in the antique world of Greece or Rome or the Judeo-Christian tradition. It emerged at a specific historic moment, for specific reasons, and with specific intellectual justifications. That moment was, of course, the grand transformation wrought in the Europe of the sixteenth, seventeenth, and eighteenth centuries by the rise of Protestantism and capitalism. The traditional hierarchical world was replaced in Western Europe by the modern liberal world as we know it. Central to this transformation were new conceptions of self and work.

Ascription, the assignment to some preordained rank in life, came more and more to be replaced by achievement as the major definer of personal identity. Individuals increasingly came to define themselves as active subjects. They no longer tended to see their place in life as part of some natural, inevitable, and eternal plan. Their own enterprise and ability mattered; they possessed the opportunity (a key word) to determine their place through their own voluntary actions in this life and in this world.

Now, and this is the truly critical step, what one did in this world came soon to be understood primarily as what one did economically, what one did in terms of work. In the world of work one was the author of self. Individuality became an internal subjective quality; work became a concrete test and property a material extension of self. Inherent in this is the birth of the market society, where the allocation and distribution of such valuable things as power, wealth, and fame came to be seen as the result of countless individual decisions, not of some authoritative norms set by custom, God, or ruling class decree. Who has more, who has less, whether some get any, is decided less by a social or moral consensus than by the free action of individual actors seeking their own gain in a context of continuous competition. What one has or gets, and therefore who one is, is no longer the appropriate reward fit to one's prescribed place; it is the product of what one can get and what one does in the competitive market.

The new theory of individuality had profound political implications. To be free, truly self-denying, master of the self, the individual had to eliminate all barriers to that individuality. So war was declared against religious restraint on free thought and against economic restraint on a free market. What I am describing is, of course, the gradual liquidation of the aristocratic world and its replacement by the liberal capitalist order. It is the crusade of Figaro and Schwartzkopf.

In the history of the crusade, we can discern familiar philosophic benchmarks. There is Thomas Hobbes's brilliant model of individualistic society, offered in the 1650s with its vision of human beings as self-moving, self-directing independent machines, constantly competing with one another for power, wealth, and glory. A person's value or worth (a fascinating word if one thinks of it) is determined by the market; people are as the market values them. They are whatever their hard work can get. But competitive individuals, constantly seeking power and wealth, are constantly frightened lest the fruits of their work, their property, be stolen by other competing individuals. Enter then the liberal state with the principal task of protecting the fruits of industry and providing safety and a more commodious living for competitive individuals.

John Locke, in turn, introduces a moral revolution, one absolutely essential for the liberal world of individuality and equal opportunity. The unlimited acquisition of money and wealth, he argues, is neither unjust nor morally wrong. God (a very Protestant God) commanded men to work the earth, and those that were hardworking and industrious had the right to what they worked. While there were limits initially to what one could own in terms of what one could use, and what would not spoil, the invention of money put an end to these restraints. One does not eat money; there are no limits to its use; it never spoils. Since God has given "different degrees of industry" to men, some have more talent, and work harder than others. It is just and ethical, then, for them to have as many possessions as they want (as Locke says, to "heap as much of these durable things as he pleased"). The liberal state, then, as Locke never tires of telling us, is really constructed by property-owning individuals to protect their property.

This, indeed, is the critical point. If individuals are to define their individuality in terms of what they achieve, and if this sense of achievement is seen in terms of work in a market society where God-given talent and industry can have their play, then the barriers to unlimited accumulation have to fall. How else can achievement and sense of self be known if not by economic success?

Adam Smith's great contribution to the liberal theory of equality of opportunity was his conviction that at bottom all men were ambitious. Smith saw in bourgeois man a constant striving. Every individual, Smith wrote, "seeks to better his own condition." This ambition, he wrote in his *Wealth of Nations*, is "a desire which comes with us from the womb and never leaves us till we go into the grave." Smith pulled together the diverse strands of emerging liberal-bourgeois thought and produced the first complete statement of liberal social theory. Life, he wrote, was a "race for wealth and honours and preferments." What a revolution is in this metaphor! Life is no longer a hierarchical ladder or chain of being. It is a race. And this race should be fair; each and every runner in it should have an equal opportunity to win. Each competitor will "run as hard as he can, and strain every move and every muscle, in order to outstrip all his competitors." Interfering with other runners or seizing special advantages is "a violation of fair play." But merit, talent, virtue, and ability are, alas, no sure indicators of success, because government is too involved in the race, according to Smith. By reserving offices, power, and authority for the privileged it tilts the competition in favor of an idle aristocracy devoid of talent and virtue.

Smith has no illusions, however. Even if the unproductive aristocratic social order were eliminated and the race could be run with equal opportunity for all, only some would win. There would remain obvious differences in how each was able to "better his own condition." An unexpected note of pessimism sneaks in with Smith's acknowledgment that the race seldom provides "real satisfaction," and that it is often really "contemptible and trifling." Equally seldom, however, Smith admits, does anyone look at the race in such an "abstract and philosophical light"—and a good thing, too. The race, the competition, the illusion that everyone can win, and the alleged pleasures of victory are all necessary and worthwhile deceptions. "It is this deception which rouses and keeps in continual motion the industry of mankind."

II

Life as a race becomes the central metaphor in liberal ideology. One group of writers and activists, relatively unknown today, popularized the metaphor and its corollary of equal opportunity more than any other and deserves special mention. In England in the last two decades of the eighteenth century, an amazing group of radical Protestant dissenters (non-Anglicans, that is, Baptists, Presbyterians, Independents, Unitarians, and Quakers) articulated the principles of revolutionary bourgeois ideology in a devastating attack on the aristocracy and the aristocratic world view. The group included the Reverend Joseph Priestley, the eminent scientist, the Reverend Richard Price, Tom Paine, Mary Wollstonecraft, William Godwin, James Burgh, Anna Barbauld, and others. They spoke for a dissenter community very much involved in the creation of a new England. Incredible achievers, the Protestant dissenters, while only 7 percent of the population, were found as leaders in every new and successful enterprise that marked the industrial revolution.

The dissenters operated at the margins of English life in the eighteenth century. For most of the century, it was technically illegal, for example, to carry on a Unitarian service. But much more onerous than this were the dreaded Test and Corporation Acts, which required all holders of offices under the British Crown to receive the sacrament according to the rites of the Anglican Church. The Acts also excluded nonsubscribers to the Anglican creed from any office in an incorporated municipality. Exclusion from public jobs meant that legions of these talented dissenters were denied one of the most important rewards of the successful, prestigious positions in the military or civil establishment.

Priestley warned that if preferment would not come to talented dissenters, then as "citizens of the world" they would get up and go to where their virtuous achievements were rewarded. This was shorthand for America and there, indeed, Priestley went, emigrating to Pennsylvania in 1794. The fiery Anna Barbauld, another dissenter, did not leave, however, and in making her case for the repeal of the Test and Corporation Acts in 1790 she addressed the social issue straight on. It was no favor she asked, but "a natural and inalienable right," which she claimed. The issue was "power, place and influence."

> To exclude us from jobs is no more reasonable than to exclude all those above five feet high or those whose birthdays are before the summer solstice. These are arbitrary and whimsical distinctions. . . . We want civil offices. And why should citizens not aspire to civil offices? Why should not the fair field of generous competition be freely opened to every one. . . .

Barbauld articulates the very core of liberal-bourgeois social theory. In the competitive scramble of the marketplace, all citizens are equal in their opportunity to win; no one has built-in advantages of birth or status. Freedom involves unrestrained individual competition and equality, and absence of built-in handicaps. No cooperation, no collective good is sought.

These early bourgeois ideologues were extremely sensitive lest their assault on hierarchy and aristocratic privilege be construed as a mere leveling to an absolute equality of conditions. Nothing could be further from their intentions; bourgeois society, they assumed, would still have inequalities. Thomas Walker, a Manchester cotton manufacturer, dissenting layman and political activist, summed up the essence of this new radical creed in 1794:

> We do not seek an equality of wealth and possessions, but an equality of rights. What we seek is that all may be equally entitled to the protection and benefit of society, may equally have a voice in elections . . . and may have a fair opportunity of exerting to advantage any talents he may possess. The rule is not "let all mankind be perpetually equal." God and nature have forbidden it. But "let all mankind start fair in the race of life." The inequality derived from labour and successful enterprise, the result of superior industry and good fortune, is an inequality essential to the very existence of society.

What distressed Mary Wollstonecraft, particularly, was not only that in this race the winners were always men, but that women did not even bother to run. She lamented their socially conditioned lack of ambition. "Woman," she wrote in her *Vindication,* was just like the useless aristocrat "in her self complete" possessed of "all those frivolous accomplishments." Unlike bourgeois man she lacked any desire to improve herself.

Women were socialized to avoid the race, to avoid the ambitious individual scramble for rewards to talent and merit. Wollstonecraft's message was that women should become more like the assertive men of the middle class. Instead, "women were always on the watch to please." Instead of "laudable ambitions," they were ruled by "romantic wavering feelings." Only education and political rights could fit them for the race.

These eighteenth-century dissenting radicals reveal a crucial contradiction at the heart of liberal social theory. The ideal of equality of opportunity at its origins was both an effort to reduce inequality and to perpetuate it. It was egalitarian at its birth because it lashed out at the exclusiveness of aristocratic privilege, but it sought to replace an aristocratic elite with a new elite, albeit one more broadly based on talent and merit. Equality of opportunity is not really a theory of equality, but of justified and morally acceptable inequality. What can legitimate some having more than others? Only that all have had an equal opportunity to have more. Equality for liberals really means fairness. Let the race be fair, let all have an equal chance to win.

Equality of opportunity presumes a noncooperative vision of society. There is no ideal of community or quest for the common good. Individuals compete on an equal footing and as in any race, some win, others lose. According to the theory, those that win do so because they are more talented and work harder than the losers. Equality of opportunity presumes that people have different abilities and talents. This basic human inequality in talents will, in a free society, legitimize status differentials. The society is free if the race is fair. The race is not fair; there is no equality of opportunity when freedom to realize oneself through success and achievement is impaired, and this occurs whenever ethical, religious, or social limitations are placed on economic activity, whenever governments interfere in the race by favoring some privileged class, whose members could not win on their own. Equality of opportunity, then, is historically the ideal of the revolutionary middle class, perhaps the most powerful weapon in its battle, ultimately successful, to end the rule of aristocratic privilege.

III

In the nineteenth century, two important social groups called upon this doctrine of equal opportunity: women, again, and the working class. John Stuart Mill in his essay *The Subjection of Women* (1869) offers the classic plea that equality of opportunity be extended to women. All the themes discussed here are repeated.

Women are ambitious, he writes; they are not totally socialized to be different from men. The problem is that they are barred from market society. They are not allowed to achieve, to compete freely, to have the status they want. They are treated by the modern liberal as if they were living in the feudal, precapitalist world. They were perceived as creatures of status and told to accept their dependent place. They have no opportunity to be or do anything else, no internal subjective mastery and direction of self. In short, the liberal revolution has passed them by. Mill's essay is one long plea for the extension of liberal emancipation to women. He even invokes Figaro. Men rule like aristocrats, regardless of their merit, simply because they have taken the trouble to be born.

The place of the laboring poor in liberal social theory is ambivalent at best. On the one hand, seventeenth- and eighteenth-century theorists saw the competitive society, the race of life, peopled only by middle-class men. Equal opportunity was their subversive weapon against the world of privilege. Workers, like women, lived outside market society. They were expected to accept their place as dependent subordinates barred from the race. This is clearly how Locke and Smith perceived the working class, and why many writers opposed education for the poor lest they become discontented and seek ambitiously to join or even replace their middle-class betters. One of the serious crimes in the ante-bellum South was teaching a slave to read and write; one of the great themes of feminism from Wollstonecraft to this day is equal access to education.

Alongside a conviction that the laboring poor are excluded from the race, that they are naturally dependent, there is in liberal theory another strain insisting that they be treated as if they were free contracting individuals, equal members of market society. This may take the form of ideological myth, rags to riches, Horatio Alger, and so on, or a more commonplace defense of laissez-faire. Workers are surely free individuals, and if they contract for low or subsistence wages or for long hours, it's their own voluntary act. The state ought not to intervene in their behalf. They are free individuals who can raise themselves by talent and hard work, just as their employers have done.

By the latter part of the nineteenth century, more and more European liberals began to have second thoughts and to call upon the state to protect workers with factory legislation, health and education acts, and so on. This came much later (not, indeed, until deep into this century) in America. A principal theorist of this shift in liberal attitudes was T. H. Green, the Oxford philosopher. What Green did in the 1870s was, in fact, to call upon the doctrine of equal opportunity to assist the working-class cause. Workers, he wrote, were not in fact free to act voluntarily in the market. Poorly paid, uneducated, starving, or sick, they could not make the best of themselves; they could not compete on equal terms. He called upon the state, therefore, to establish the conditions that would enable workers to join the race. This meant public schools, factory laws, prohibition, and public health.

But the continuous liberal commitment to individuality and equal opportunity persists in Green's writings. Once that ideal had involved emancipating the individual from feudal restrictions, opening up the market. Now, in the writings of Green, it involved restricting market freedoms to provide conditions that would allow the proletariat to acquire the skills necessary to compete. The state had to augment workers' power and resources, even at the expense of cherished contractual rights. The aim however, is the same as it was earlier: a fair race. The liberal model endures in T. H. Green. He still assumes that life is a scramble for self-realization through achievement and success, and that this is a moral vision of society and of life.

We can readily recognize T. H. Green's vision as the ideology of the American New Deal in the twentieth century. T. H. Green is, in fact, an intellectual ancestor of all those defenders of state action from the New Deal to the present whom Americans describe in their own peculiar way as liberals! They are committed ultimately to individualism, equal opportunity, and a competitive society.

And here we return to the LBJ commencement speech at Howard University. Racial issues were brought to political saliency in this century by these very same liberal descendants of T. H. Green. Their commitment is to that same liberal vision of the race of life. Positive state action is needed, it is argued, to enable blacks to compete on equal terms—which brings us full-circle back to Lyndon Johnson, *Bakke,* and *Weber.*

IV

One often-noted feature of the contemporary crisis is the pervasive anxiety among whites (and men in general) about the possible loss of status, wealth, and privilege in the wake of an aggressive affirmative action policy. This, too, is nothing new. It has always been a part of the historical legacy of liberal ideology. For all its optimism, assertiveness, and self-confidence, liberalism has another face, a frightened and fearful view of market society and the race of life as fraught with dangers, the most horrible of which, in fact, is the possibility of losing.

A convincing case can be made (as it was twenty years ago by Sheldon Wolin) that liberal social theorists of the seventeenth and eighteenth centuries presumed fear and anxiety to be the basic motive in human nature that first sets men and women running—or, in Smith's words, "rouses and keeps in continual motion the industry of mankind." We are, of course, familiar with the religious interpretation of this linkage from the more recent writings of Max Weber and

R. H. Tawney, but less familiar with the explicit claims of the early liberals them-selves. Locke, for example, held in his *Essay on Human Understanding* that "the chief, if not the only spur to human industry and action is uneasiness." This feel-ing of uneasiness, a desire for "some absent good," drives men to enterprise. But men are ever fearful; once driven to the race they never lose their uneasiness. They are permanently cursed, wrote Locke, with "an itch after honour, power, and riches," which in turn unleashes more "fantastical uneasiness."

Anxiety forever haunts bourgeois man. "Fear and anxiety," Smith wrote, are the "two great tormentors of the human breast." They persist because the race of life has winners and losers and, above all else, bourgeois man fears failure. For [Jeremy] Bentham all life was "a universal scramble" for "money, power and pres-tige," and the "suffering from loss," he wrote, was infinitely greater than "the enjoyment from gain." For Smith the possibility of losing ground was "worse than death."

Runners in the race of life fear losing what they have, or losing simply, be-cause to lose is to become a nonperson. Only success in the marketplace brings the notice and valuation of others. To understand the fear and anxiety of whites and males in the face of affirmative action today one need only reread these early liberal theorists who knew very well what insecurity lurks in the heart of bourgeois man. To be a loser is to be invisible, according to Smith in his *Theory of Moral Sentiment:*

> What are the advantages which we propose by that great purpose of human life which we call bettering our condition? To be observed, to be attended to, to be taken notice of . . . the poor man, on the contrary, is ashamed of his poverty. He feels that it . . . places him out of the sight of mankind. . . . To feel that we are taken no notice of, necessarily damps the most agreeable hope, and disappoints the most ardent desire, of human nature. The poor man goes out and comes in unheeded, and when in the midst of a crowd is in the same obscu-rity as if shut up in his own house. . . . They turn away their eyes from him.

John Adams repeated this judgement on failure 132 years later in his *Discourses on Davila.* The pain of being a loser consisted not so much in being hated as in being invisible. What motivated men to public and economic activity was a pas-sion for distinction, "the desire to be observed, considered, esteemed, praised, beloved and admired by his fellows." Of those who failed in this quest he wrote:

> Mankind takes no notice of him. He rambles and wanders unheeded. In the midst of a crowd, at church, in the market, at a play, at an execution, or coro-nation, he is in such obscurity as he would be in a garret or a cellar. He is not disapproved, censured, or reproached, he is only not seen.

Anxiety over failure in the race of life, over becoming invisible, haunts today's marketplace as it did the world of Smith and Adams. And here is the heart of the matter, the grand historical reversal produced by today's crisis of liberal ideology. What whites and men fear in the loss of wealth and status is what the poor, women, and blacks have experienced throughout liberal hegemony. But the age-old invisibility of these latter groups and the fear of invisibility among today's privileged groups follow alike from the inner logic of liberal ideology, where self-esteem and a sense of personality are inextricably tied to degrees of accumulation and success in the race of life.

V

We can now better appreciate the profound impact of *Bakke, Weber,* and affirmative action on our lives. They are much more than political bombshells. They involve an intellectual crisis that goes to the very heart of liberalism. Two important forms of liberal doctrine are being played off against one another. There is the traditional eighteenth-century middle-class meritocratic ideal, and there is the latter-day liberal vision of intervention in the race of life to aid and perhaps award victory to handicapped competitors. A doctrine originally designed to serve the class interests of the talented "have-nots" against the untalented "haves" now pits the talented "haves" against the allegedly untalented "have-nots." Here is the real source of contemporary tension. In historical terms, the talented class has remained the same. What has happened, however, is that it has changed from a revolutionary class to the status quo defender of a new elite, the meritocracy. Its ideology remains the same: that is why certain social policies of recent years, for instance, headstart programs, were not challenged by the meritocrats. Unlike affirmative action, giving children intensive and special preschooling is quite comparable with simply making the race fair. It doesn't definitely give the victory, that is, jobs or medical degrees, to anyone, especially not to anyone seen as untalented and therefore undeserving.

Each of the issues raised in the current debate speaks to a part of the liberal ideological heritage. Are individuals being treated unfairly in the effort to deal equally with groups? Are fundamental beliefs about individual responsibility for achievement and success being violated? Can groups or individuals ever be in a truly competitive position leading to equal opportunity? Can past privations be countered by eliminating present competitive disadvantages? Are governments once again interfering with the race of life and saying who will win? Is this being done not in terms of talent but to meet political considerations? Is past injustice a more solid moral basis of desert than talent? As we grapple with these issues we must realize how the very language of our dilemmas presumes a framework of beliefs centering on individuality, equality of opportunity, and a market society.

These are values at the very core of liberal society, and since *Bakke, Weber,* and affirmative action involve contradictions and strains within that set of values, the current crisis is bound to be far-reaching and painful.

But we ought also to be clear that certain questions are not confronted by the ideological tradition traced here. What if our talents are in fact ascriptive, given to us by dint not of our worth and intrinsic achievements or merit, but simply, as Figaro and Schwartzkopf noted, by our being born? What if the basic liberal assumptions about the conditioning role of environment, education, and nurturing are wrong? Is it not then possible that the distribution of valuable things to the talented is inherently unjust to those born less privileged?

There are other questions *Bakke* and *Weber* do not confront: Is life truly a race? Is life a marketplace? Is it basic to our humanity to compete with one another? Are winners real people and losers deservedly unnoticed and invisible? Is a race with winners and losers ever fair or moral, no matter how equal the conditions at the starting line? The time has come to go beyond the framework of the current debate and question the very metaphors and assumptions that inform both it and the problems it has created. Difficult as it may be, the time has come to abandon our old and dear friends, Figaro and Schwartzkopf.

What might a new world view look like? It would involve a fundamental abandonment of our sense of life as a competitive race. This means that some appealing suggestions for changing public policy premised on this view would have to be called inadequate. Expanding the number of places in medical schools or the number of medical schools themselves, providing more jobs in the building trades, more jobs for faculty in an expanded system of higher education—all these are no doubt desirable, but in the end they serve merely to enlarge the field of runners. Just as quotas and affirmative action often set blacks to run only with other blacks, whites only with other whites, so a larger pie means simply a larger race. Even more far-reaching alternatives preserve the competitive race. Proposals to broaden the notion of deserving talent and merit beyond successful market skills and to reward the generous, the loving, the kind, the good, the cooperative would again simply provide new races. The same can be said for instituting nonpecuniary rewards for work, effort, and achievement. A society of Stakhanovites is no more congenial, for by definition it assumes the continuation of the race, albeit for lower stakes. Similarly, the lowering of stakes inherent in proposals that would narrow the range of prizes is mere tinkering. It ends the ability of winners to set their own prizes, to be sure, but it keeps the race intact. Like affirmative action itself, all these proposals would promote greater justice and equality. They are but temporary expedients, however, for they assume the context of a competitive race.

One possible way to transcend the world of Figaro and Schwartzkopf is a retreat from meritocracy itself, a tabooed subject for intellectuals whose very place in society may well be owed to that principle. One need not be one of Michael Young's fanciful "prols" to propose a less slavish preoccupation with merit and talent in our society. Imagine the transformation of American life that would come from implementing Robert Wolff's suggestion of two decades ago that students be assigned to universities at random by computers. What would America look like if random chance distributed as many valuable things as test scores did? How essential is the expert medical education sought by [Allan] Bakke to the health needs of inner cities of rural America? What are the trade-offs between pushing the advance of America's highly technological medicine for the few or seeking an improved health system for the many provided by a less than expert corps of lay practitioners emphasizing prevention and lacking the talents of an expertly trained medical elite? Might this calculation not be made in other areas of society as well, with greater justice and equality flowing from less obsession with meritocracy?

Abandoning the worship of talent and merit might also introduce new attitudes to work. Capitalists (and even Marxists) are convinced that individuals find fulfillment primarily through productive work. But why should work alone or even principally define one's sense of self? This is not to advocate an updated Consciousness III, but to offer the heretical suggestion that a sense of identity can come just as meaningfully from play, love, spirituality, place or affiliation, as from work. To transcend Figaro and Schwartzkopf may well require a return to some of what they in fact repudiated. Much of the ambience of affirmative action already points to a renaissance of a world where extrinsic affiliation not individual achievement is critical, where ascriptive identity with a geographic place, a race, a sex, or ethnic group helps define one's sense of self, rather than simply the unique talent or merit of that self. This utopian ideal need not revive the entire world that was lost to liberal hegemony. Nor is romantic nostalgia for the stable, ordered, and noncompetitive Middle Ages what I would offer. It is a moral economy, as E. P. Thompson has called it, which flourished before the advent of the free economy of market society, that I want to revive. Drawn from diverse sources, the moral economy assumes that buying and selling is subordinate to the moral purposes of community and social life. It need not be a completely socialist economy with collectivization of the means of production. A moral and natural economy, according to Aristotle, could well blend private ownership of property with public and common use. "Moral goodness," he wrote, "will ensure that the property of each is made to serve the use of all." Public interests and social needs, not individual free choices in the pursuit of private gain, would be the organizing principle of a moral economic life.

In a moral economy individual freedom in the market is subordinate to the constraints of a moral and social consensus insisting that there are natural levels of profit, of income, and of wealth; that the poor have rights to a decent life; that there are moral limits to accumulation. The sense of self in a moral economy comes not from success or failure in the competitive market but from the identification with and the quest to realize the collective moral purpose to which individual economic activity is ultimately subject. A moral economy in the 1980s requires restricting the freedom of economic actors. Just as affirmative action temporarily introduces moral purpose and public good into the market economy while restricting the play of free choice, so the solution to most of our contemporary ills requires public restraint of market freedom. Only in a moral economy can the inevitable bourgeois linkage of work and success with personal identity be broken. And only then can the preoccupation with equal opportunity be transcended, and affirmative action redefined to encompass real equality.

Since metaphors have hovered closely over these reflections, let me end by offering another. Life should be neither a race nor a chain of being; it should be understood as a kind of play. Races begin and end; they must have winners and losers. One runs not only against the others in adjoining lanes, but against the records and achievements of those running in other races or of all those who have ever run. Play need never end, nor need it have winners and losers. In play fulfillment and joy is a product of the common purpose, the shared experience. A market economy is inevitably a race; a moral economy can be play.

There was a time in the West when play not races preoccupied us. [Johan] Huizinga noted in his *Homo Ludens* that the bourgeois era with its utilitarianism, its efficiency, its preoccupation with serious work, has killed off what he called the "play-factor" in social life and ended the imaginative and fanciful sense of self. Another victim has surely been the moral sense of self. Whatever just and progressive purposes the ideal of equal opportunity has served at various historical moments, it still envisages life as a war of all against all with persons of worth as victor. The first great utopian thinker knew already that such an ideal was morally unsatisfactory. Plato wrote:

> Every man and every woman should live life accordingly, and play the noblest games, and be of another mind from what they are at present. For they deem war a serious thing, though in war there is neither play nor culture worthy the name, which are the things we deem most serious. Hence all must live in peace as well as they possibly can. What, then, is the right way of living? Life must be lived as play, playing certain games, making sacrifices, singing and dancing.

PART TWO

———◆◆———

Conservatism

THE LIBERALS MUST be the conservatives in America today . . . the greatest need is not so much the creation of more liberal institutions as the successful defense of those which already exist."[1] With these words, Samuel Huntington both acknowledges the tensions within contemporary liberalism and responds to them with a more traditional conservatism. At first glance, his conservatism seems to fit popular usage: today's laissez-faire liberals—those who question the welfare state, who would return to a free market—are often labeled "conservative." But this label is misleading. Milton Friedman, for example, argues that such liberals are, in fact, radicals because they demand greater freedom and prosperity, and he would have them recapture the "liberal" label from welfare staters. Yet this group, too, are radicals, though their demands for greater equality and democracy reflect a far different agenda. Indeed, both camps within liberal politics today are radical when compared to traditional conservatism. In other words, the debate between the so-called liberals and conservatives in popular politics actually occurs within liberalism. In contrast, conservatives, such as Huntington, articulate a different ideology, in which freedom and prosperity, equality and democracy, play only minor parts.

Why, then, should both groups of American liberals become conservatives? Or, why is conservatism thriving in America today? To answer these questions, we must examine the peculiar character of conservatism. Huntington discusses three theories of conservative ideology. The first, aristocratic theory, defines it as feudal aristocrats' reaction to the French Revolution. This definition seems too narrow, for nothing limits conservatism to that historical situation. Second, the autonomous theory portrays conservatism as a general system of ideas. This portrayal is too broad: as we see in this section, conservatives attack abstract philosophical principles. Third, conservatism is defined situationally as "that system of ideas employed to justify any established social order, no matter where or when it exists, against any fundamental challenge to its nature or being, no matter from what quarter."[2] This definition finds a middle ground, placing conservatism in historical context yet maintaining its theoretical substance. But what is that substance? And does it constitute an ideology? Huntington says yes. He describes conservatism as a nonideational ideology whose substance is "the articulate, systematic, theoretical resistance to change."[3]

In "On Being Conservative," Michael Oakeshott clarifies this nonideational character of conservatism. He acknowledges the controversy over whether conservatism is an ideology, and he claims that it may well be one. Yet Oakeshott's "theme is not a creed or a doctrine, but a disposition." He discusses three characteristics of the conservative disposition. First, conservatives "delight in what is present rather than what was or what may be." Second, and closely related, conservatives are "cool and critical in respect of change and innovation." Third, conservatives recognize that change is sometimes necessary, but they ask that it occur gradually in order to maintain as much as possible of our previous identity.

This conservative disposition seems to fit Huntington's situational definition. According to Huntington, conservatism has no inherent affiliation with or opposition to any ideational ideology; conservatives can love any "familiar present." In particular, Huntington argues, "No necessary dichotomy exists . . . between conservatism and liberalism."[4] But, even if "no necessary dichotomy" exists, the liberals' progressive spirit does create tensions with a conservative disposition. (It is for this reason that Friedman rejects the conservative label.) Those tensions appear clearly in the selection from Edmund Burke. Huntington notes that Burke defended "Whig institutions in England, democratic institutions in America, autocratic institutions in France, and Hindu institutions in India."[5] But Burke attacked the French Revolution. Conservatives have their doubts about liberal democracy.

Burke has been called the father of conservatism. His *Reflections on the Revolution in France* outlines the fundamental principles of that ideology.[6] First, for conservatives, society is not a mere contract, but a moral order: "It is a partnership in all science; a partnership in all art; a partnership in every virtue, and in all perfection." That partnership exists "between those who are living, those who are dead, and those who are to be born." Second, in keeping with this moral continuum, it is history, not nature, that confers individual rights, which thus constitute an "entailed inheritance." "Prescription," Burke says, "is the most solid of all titles." Third, humanity is largely irrational. Our survival and our success depend on the accumulated wisdom of generations. For this reason, tradition and authority, better yet traditional authorities, should guide politics. Fourth, humanity is also imperfect, marred by original sin. Abstract rights only unleash human passions; instead, individuals require restraint, or an "ordered liberty." Burke puts this well: "Government is a contrivance of human wisdom to provide for human wants. . . . Among these wants is to be reckoned the want, out of civil society, of a sufficient restraint upon their passions." He adds, "Men have no right to what is not reasonable." Fifth, equality (except in an ultimate moral sense) is unreasonable. "In this partnership all men have equal rights, but not to equal things." Equality violates the natural hierarchy of wisdom and virtue. Sixth, politics requires prudence. Society is complex and change has hidden costs. Citizens should moderate their demands; reformers should "conserve and correct." According to Burke, the English and American revolutions, unlike the French, achieved this balance.

Like the conservative disposition, this conservative doctrine creates some tensions with liberalism, which may explain why, until recently, America has not been congenial to conservatism. Still, conservative principles have played a part in our history. Working with the limited history they have, American conservatives have stressed the cautious side of liberalism. During the nation's founding, the Federalists defended liberalism from democracy: conservative caution appeared in Madison's fear of majority tyranny, in Hamilton's call for a strong central government, and especially in John Adams's defense of natural aristocracy. Adams argued that "inequalities are part of the natural history of mankind"; despite their best efforts, the Americans and the French could not make all equally wise, attractive, strong, and/or moral. In fact, "the more you educate . . . the more aristocratic the peoples and the government will be."[7] Adams thus paralleled Burke: "Real merit should govern the world; men ought to be respected only in proportion to their talents, virtues, and services."[8] The political problem, of course, was how to ensure that these natural aristocrats became our public officials. Fisher Ames, writing after the 1800 election of Thomas Jefferson, doubted Americans could solve that problem: "Our materials for a government were all democratic," and "a democracy cannot last." The American Constitution presumes "the supposed existence of sufficient political virtue and the permanency and authority of the public morals," but American institutions do not encourage these sustaining qualities. Ames feared that the revolution would "proceed in exactly the same way, but not with so rapid a pace, as that of France."[9]

For these early American conservatives, democracy posed a threat to liberal institutions. Is this the threat conservatives think liberals face today? Is this why they too should become conservatives? Yes, according to the remaining authors in this section. In "The Neoconservative Persuasion, *What it was, and what it is,*" Irving Kristol outlines "the historical task and political purpose of neoconservatism": "to convert the Republican party, and American conservatism in general, against their respective wills, into a new kind of conservative politics suitable to governing a modern democracy." His *new* conservatism is "distinctly American," the first such variation on conservative themes. Earlier conservatism, including the Old Right and Reagan Republicans, grew from European ideas transplanted to American soil. By comparison, Kristol's neoconservatism is "hopeful, not lugubrious; forward-looking, not nostalgic; and its general tone is cheerful, not grim or dyspeptic." This optimism reflects a compromise or adjustment of conservatism to the twentieth-century realities of economic growth and big government. Even Kristol has moderated his earlier critique of liberals' tendency to "think economically," a tendency he once charged with creating excessive demands on government. What Kristol's New Right still shares with the Old Right is a commitment to traditional moral and religious values; Kristol celebrates the "unexpected alliance" between neoconservatives and "religious traditionalists." He also reaffirms patriotic loyalty as a crucial feature of American politics. The United States, he argues, is "uniquely powerful" and, hence, responsible for international order—a responsibility the second Bush administration has wholeheartedly embraced. Although tensions persist between the social agenda of traditional conservatism and the economic freedoms of classical liberalism, the "war on terror" has, at least temporarily, obscured them for neoconservatives.

Among the traditional values neoconservatives would uphold is the stability of the family, and, especially, women's traditional role within it. According to Phyllis Schlafly, the "positive woman" understands that "men and women are different and that those very differences provide the key to her success as a person and fulfillment as a woman." Women's liberationists, who regard bearing and rearing children as "handicaps," mistakenly try to "neuterize society." Schlafly blames feminists' pursuit of equal rights for the decline of the family, and her arguments strike a powerful chord in many women. Do feminists really respect wives and mothers? Do they propose a unisex society? Is this, Schlafly asks, really liberation? She concludes, "It is no gain for women, for children, for families, or for America to propel us into a unisex society. Our strength is in our diversity, not in our sameness." In the feminism section, we explore other arguments on the ways different identities shape politics and society.

The final selection in this part focuses on another American institution that neoconservatives revere: the university. "The Democratization of the University" is an early essay by Allan Bloom, author of the best-seller, *The Closing of the American Mind*. According to Bloom, universities provide an aristocratic influence in democratic societies: preserving tradition, establishing authority, and teaching morality. Or this is what they should do. When universities adopt the market mentality and participatory politics of the larger society, however, they undermine their ability to perform these functions. Bloom fears the results, for liberal democracy depends on the university to balance equality with excellence and consent with reason. He warns: "If neither reason nor tradition can bring about consensus, then the force of the first man resourceful and committed enough must needs do so."

Common themes emerge in these conservatives' writings: morality, tradition, authority, imperfection, inequality, and above all, prudence. Some Americans have become conservatives, as Huntington counseled, to save liberalism from itself. But their conservatism—as disposition and doctrine—still fits uneasily with some aspects of liberalism, especially in the United States. Are such tensions unavoidable in a situational ideology? Might they suggest that conservatism is really an autonomous ideology? Or is conservatism not an ideology at all? Is it merely a continual process of adjustment to changing political contexts?

NOTES

1. Samuel Huntington, "Conservatism as an Ideology," *American Political Science Review* 51 (June 1957): 452–473.

2. Ibid., 455.

3. Ibid., 461. According to Huntington, conservatism is nonideational because it lacks a substantive ideal. Instead, "the essence of conservatism is the rationalization of existing institutions in terms of history, God, nature, and man" (p. 457).

4. Ibid., 460.

5. Ibid., 463.

6. As Huntington notes, there are many lists with various numbers of conservative principles. This list, adapted from his summary of Burke, captures the essential ideas.

7. John Adams, "On Natural Aristocracy." In *The Portable Conservative Reader,* ed. Russell Kirk (New York: Penguin Books, 1982), 67.

8. Ibid., 69.

9. Fisher Ames, "The Dangers of American Liberty," in ibid., 84–112.

8

Michael Oakeshott

<hr/>

"On Being Conservative" (1962)

Born in Cambridge, England, Michael Oakeshott (1901–1990) was educated and lectured at Cambridge University before accepting a chair at the London School of Economics. Perhaps best known for his moderate conservatism, encapsulated in the phrase "the purpose of government is simply to rule," Oakeshott advocated a "conservative disposition" partly in response to the extremism of fascist and socialist politics in twentieth-century Europe. The essay reprinted here appears in his collection Rationalism in Politics and Other Essays.

1

THE COMMON BELIEF that it is impossible (or, if not impossible, then so unpromising as to be not worth while attempting) to elicit explanatory general principles from what is recognized to be conservative conduct is not one that I share. It may be true that conservative conduct does not readily provoke articulation in the idiom of general ideas, and that consequently there has been a certain reluctance to undertake this kind of elucidation; but it is not to be presumed that conservative conduct is less eligible than any other for this sort of interpretation, for what it is worth. Nevertheless, this is not the enterprise I propose to engage in here. My theme is not a creed or a doctrine, but a disposition. To be conservative is to be disposed to think and behave in certain manners; it is to prefer certain kinds of conduct and certain conditions of human circumstances to others; it is to be

From *Rationalism in Politics and Other Essays* by Michael Oakeshott, pp. 168–196. © 1962 by Michael Oakeshott. Reprinted with permission of Basic Books, a member of Perseus Books, L.L.C., and Liberty Fund, Inc.

disposed to make certain kinds of choices. And my design here is to construe this disposition as it appears in contemporary character, rather than to transpose it into the idiom of general principles.

The general characteristics of this disposition are not difficult to discern, although they have often been mistaken. They centre upon a propensity to use and to enjoy what is available rather than to wish for or to look for something else; to delight in what is present rather than what was or what may be. Reflection may bring to light an appropriate gratefulness for what is available, and consequently the acknowledgement of a gift or an inheritance from the past; but there is no mere idolizing of what is past and gone. What is esteemed is the present; and it is esteemed not on account of its connections with a remote antiquity, nor because it is recognized to be more admirable than any possible alternative, but on account of its familiarity: not, *Verweile doch, du bist so schön,* but *Stay with me because I am attached to you.*

If the present is arid, offering little or nothing to be used or enjoyed, then this inclination will be weak or absent; if the present is remarkably unsettled, it will display itself in a search for a firmer foothold and consequently in a recourse to and an exploration of the past; but it asserts itself characteristically when there is much to be enjoyed, and it will be strongest when this is combined with evident risk of loss. In short, it is a disposition appropriate to a man who is acutely aware of having something to lose which he has learned to care for; a man in some degree rich in opportunities for enjoyment, but not so rich that he can afford to be indifferent to loss. It will appear more naturally in the old than in the young, not because the old are more sensitive to loss but because they are apt to be more fully aware of the resources of their world and therefore less likely to find them inadequate. In some people this disposition is weak merely because they are ignorant of what their world has to offer them: the present appears to them only as a residue of inopportunities.

To be conservative, then, is to prefer the familiar to the unknown, to prefer the tried to the untried, fact to mystery, the actual to the possible, the limited to the unbounded, the near to the distant, the sufficient to the superabundant, the convenient to the perfect, present laughter to utopian bliss. Familiar relationships and loyalties will be preferred to the allure of more profitable attachments; to acquire and to enlarge will be less important than to keep, to cultivate and to enjoy; the grief of loss will be more acute than the excitement of novelty or promise. It is to be equal to one's own fortune, to live at the level of one's own means, to be content with the want of greater perfection which belongs alike to oneself and one's circumstances. With some people this is itself a choice; in others it is a disposition which appears, frequently or less frequently, in their preferences and aversions, and is not itself chosen or specifically cultivated.

Now, all this is represented in a certain attitude towards change and innovation; change denoting alterations we have to suffer and innovation those we design and execute.

Changes are circumstances to which we have to accommodate ourselves, and the disposition to be conservative is both the emblem of our difficulty in doing so and our resort in the attempts we make to do so. Changes are without effect only upon those who notice nothing, who are ignorant of what they possess and apathetic to their circumstances; and they can be welcomed indiscriminately only by those who esteem nothing, whose attachments are fleeting and who are strangers to love and affection. The conservative disposition provokes neither of these conditions: the inclination to enjoy what is present and available is the opposite of ignorance and apathy and it breeds attachment and affection. Consequently, it is averse from change, which appears always, in the first place, as deprivation. A storm which sweeps away a copse and transforms a favourite view, the death of friends, the sleep of friendship, the desuetude of customs of behavior, the retirement of a favourite clown, involuntary exile, reversals of fortune, the loss of abilities enjoyed and their replacement by others—these are changes, none perhaps without its compensations, which the man of conservative temperament unavoidably regrets. But he has difficulty in reconciling himself to them, not because what he has lost in them was intrinsically better than any alternative might have been or was incapable of improvement, nor because what takes its place is inherently incapable of being enjoyed, but because what he has lost was something he actually enjoyed and had learned how to enjoy and what takes its place is something to which he has acquired no attachment. Consequently, he will find small and slow changes more tolerable than large and sudden; and he will value highly every appearance of continuity. Some changes, indeed, will present no difficulty; but, again, this is not because they are manifest improvements but merely because they are easily assimilated: the changes of the seasons are mediated by their recurrence and the growing up of children by its continuousness. And, in general, he will accommodate himself more readily to changes which do not offend expectation than to the destruction of what seems to have no ground of dissolution within itself.

Moreover, to be conservative is not merely to be averse from change (which may be an idiosyncrasy); it is also a manner of accommodating ourselves to changes, an activity imposed upon all men. For, change is a threat to identity, and every change is an emblem of extinction. But a man's identity (or that of a community) is nothing more than an unbroken rehearsal of contingencies, each at the mercy of circumstance and each significant in proportion to its familiarity. It is not a fortress into which we may retire, and the only means we have of defending it (that is, ourselves) against the hostile forces of change is in the open field of our experience; by throwing our weight upon the foot which for the time being is most firmly placed, by cleaving to whatever familiarities are not immediately threatened and thus assimilating what is new without becoming unrecognizable to ourselves. The Masai, when they were moved from their old country to the present Masai reserve in Kenya, took with them the names of their hills and plains and rivers and gave them to the hills and plains and rivers of the new country. And it is by some such subterfuge of conservatism that every man or people compelled to suffer a notable change avoids the shame of extinction.

Changes, then, have to be suffered; and a man of conservative temperament (that is, one strongly disposed to preserve his identity) cannot be indifferent to them. In the main, he judges them by the disturbance they entail and, like everyone else, deploys his resources to meet them. The idea of innovation, on the other hand, is improvement. Nevertheless, a man of this temperament will not himself be an ardent innovator. In the first place, he is not inclined to think that nothing is happening unless great changes are afoot and therefore he is not worried by the absence of innovation: the use and enjoyment of things as they are occupies most of his attention. Further, he is aware that not all innovation is, in fact, improvement; and he will think that to innovate without improving is either designed or inadvertent folly. Moreover, even when an innovation commends itself as a convincing improvement, he will look twice at its claims before accepting them. From his point of view, because every improvement involves change, the disruption entailed has always to be set against the benefit anticipated. But when he has satisfied himself about this, there will be other considerations to be taken into the account. Innovating is always an equivocal enterprise, in which gain and loss (even excluding the loss of familiarity) are so closely interwoven that it is exceedingly difficult to forecast the final up-shot: there is no such thing as an unqualified improvement. For, innovating is an activity which generates not only the "improvement" sought, but a new and complex situation of which this is only one of the components. The total change is always more extensive than the change designed; and the whole of what is entailed can neither be foreseen nor circumscribed. Thus, whenever there is innovation there is the certainty that the change will be greater than was intended, that there will be loss as well as gain and that the loss and the gain will not be equally distributed among the people affected; there is the chance that the benefits derived will be greater than those which were designed; and there is the risk that they will be off-set by change for the worse.

From all this the man of conservative temperament draws some appropriate conclusions. First, innovation entails certain loss and possible gain, therefore, the onus of proof, to show that the proposed change may be expected to be on the whole beneficial, rests with the would-be innovator. Secondly, he believes that the more closely an innovation resembles growth (that is, the more clearly it is intimated in and not merely imposed upon the situation), the less likely it is to result in a preponderance of loss. Thirdly, he thinks that an innovation which is a response to some specific defect, one designed to redress some specific disequilibrium, is more desirable than one which springs from a notion of a generally improved condition of human circumstances, and is far more desirable than one generated by a vision of perfection. Consequently, he prefers small and limited innovations to large and indefinite. Fourthly, he favours a slow rather than a rapid pace, and pauses to observe current consequences and make appropriate adjustments. And lastly, he believes the occasion to be important; and, other things being equal, he considers the most favourable occasion for innovation to be when the projected change is most likely to be limited to what is intended and least likely to be corrupted by undesired and unmanageable consequences.

The disposition to be conservative is, then, warm and positive in respect of enjoyment, and correspondingly cool and critical in respect of change and innovation: these two inclinations support and elucidate one another. The man of conservative temperament believes that a known good is not lightly to be surrendered for an unknown better. He is not in love with what is dangerous and difficult; he is unadventurous; he has no impulse to sail uncharted seas; for him there is no magic in being lost, bewildered or shipwrecked. If he is forced to navigate the unknown, he sees virtue in heaving the lead every inch of the way. What others plausibly identify as timidity, he recognizes in himself as rational prudence; what others interpret as inactivity, he recognizes as a disposition to enjoy rather than to exploit. He is cautious, and he is disposed to indicate his assent or dissent, not in absolute, but in graduated terms. He eyes the situation in terms of its propensity to disrupt the familiarity of the features of his world.

2

It is commonly believed that this conservative disposition is pretty deeply rooted in what is called "human nature." Change is tiring, innovation calls for effort, and human beings (it is said) are more apt to be lazy than energetic. If they have found a not unsatisfactory way of getting along in the world, they are not disposed to go looking for trouble. They are naturally apprehensive of the unknown and prefer safety to danger. They are reluctant innovators, and they accept change not because they like it but (as Rochefoucauld says, they accept death) because it is inescapable. Change generates sadness rather than exhilaration: heaven is the dream of a changeless no less than of a perfect world. Of course, those who read "human nature" in this way agree that this disposition does not stand alone; they merely contend that it is an exceedingly strong, perhaps the strongest, of human propensities. And, so far as it goes, there is something to be said for this belief: human circumstances would certainly be very different from what they are if there were not a large ingredient of conservatism in human preferences. Primitive peoples are said to cling to what is familiar and to be averse from change; ancient myth is full of warnings against innovation; our folklore and proverbial wisdom about the conduct of life abounds in conservative precepts; and how many tears are shed by children in their unwilling accommodation to change. Indeed, wherever a firm identity has been achieved, and wherever identity is felt to be precariously balanced, a conservative disposition is likely to prevail. On the other hand, the disposition of adolescence is often predominantly adventurous and experimental: when we are young, nothing seems more desirable than to take a chance; *pas de risque, pas de plaisir.* And while some peoples, over long stretches of time, appear successfully to have avoided change, the history of others displays periods of intense and intrepid innovation. There is, indeed, not much profit to be had from general speculation about "human nature," which is no steadier than anything else in our acquaintance. What is more to the point is to consider current human nature, to consider ourselves.

With us, I think, the disposition to be conservative is far from being notably strong. Indeed, if he were to judge by our conduct during the last five centuries or so, an unprejudiced stranger might plausibly suppose us to be in love with change, to have an appetite only for innovation and to be either so out of sympathy with ourselves or so careless of our identity as not to be disposed to give it any consideration. In general, the fascination of what is new is felt far more keenly than the comfort of what is familiar. We are disposed to think that nothing important is happening unless great innovations are afoot, and that what is not being improved must be deteriorating. There is a positive prejudice in favour of the yet untried. We readily presume that all change is, somehow, for the better, and we are easily persuaded that all the consequences of our innovating activity are either themselves improvements or at least a reasonable price to pay for getting what we want. While the conservative, if he were forced to gamble, would bet on the field, we are disposed to back our individual fancies with little calculation and no apprehension of loss. We are acquisitive to the point to greed; ready to drop the bone we have for its reflection magnified in the mirror of the future. Nothing is made to outlast probable improvement in a world where everything is undergoing incessant improvement: the expectation of life of everything except human beings themselves continuously declines. Pieties are fleeting, loyalties evanescent and the pace of change warns us against too deep attachments. We are willing to try anything once, regardless of the consequences. One activity vies with another in being "up-to-date": discarded motor-cars and television sets have their counterparts in discarded moral and religious beliefs: the eye is ever on the new model. To see is to imagine what might be in the place of what is; to touch is to transform. Whatever the shape or quality of the world, it is not for long as we want it. And those in the van of movement infect those behind with their energy and enterprise. *Omnes eodem cogemur:* when we are no longer light-footed we find a place for ourselves in the band.[1]

Of course, our character has other ingredients besides this lust for change (we are not devoid of the impulse to cherish and preserve), but there can be little doubt about its pre-eminence. And, in these circumstances, it seems appropriate that a conservative disposition should appear, not as an intelligible (or even plausible) alternative to our mainly "progressive" habit of mind, but either as an unfortunate hindrance to the movement afoot, or as the custodian of the museum in which quaint examples of superseded achievement are preserved for children to gape at, and as the guardian of what from time to time is considered not yet ripe for destruction, which we call (ironically enough) the amenities of life.

Here our account of the disposition to be conservative and its current fortunes might be expected to end, with the man in whom this disposition is strong last seen swimming against the tide, disregarded not because what he has to say is necessarily false but because it has become irrelevant; outmanœuvred, not on account of any intrinsic demerit but merely by the flow of circumstance; a faded, timid, nostalgic character, provoking pity as an outcast and contempt as a reactionary. Nevertheless, I think there is something more to be said. Even in these circumstances, when a conservative disposition in respect of things in general is unmistakably at a discount, there are occasions when this disposition remains not only appropriate, but supremely so; and there are connections in which we are unavoidably disposed in a conservative direction.

In the first place, there is a certain kind of activity (not yet extinct) which can be engaged in only in virtue of a disposition to be conservative, namely, activities where what is sought is present enjoyment and not a profit, a reward, a prize or a result in addition to the experience itself. And when these activities are recognized as the emblems of this disposition, to be conservative is disclosed, not as prejudiced hostility to a "progressive" attitude capable of embracing the whole range of human conduct, but as a disposition exclusively appropriate in a large and significant field of human activity. And the man in whom this disposition is pre-eminent appears as one who prefers to engage in activities where to be conservative is uniquely appropriate, and not as a man inclined to impose his conservatism indiscriminately upon all human activity. In short, if we find ourselves (as most of us do) inclined to reject conservatism as a disposition appropriate in respect of human conduct in general, there still remains a certain kind of human conduct for which this disposition is not merely appropriate but a necessary condition.

There are, of course, numerous human relationships in which a disposition to be conservative, a disposition merely to enjoy what they offer for its own sake, is not particularly appropriate: master and servant, owner and bailiff, buyer and seller, principal and agent. In these, each participant seeks some service or some recompense for a service. A customer who finds a shopkeeper unable to supply his wants either persuades him to enlarge his stock or goes elsewhere; and a shopkeeper unable to meet the desires of a customer tries to impose upon him others which he can satisfy. A principal ill-served by his agent, looks for another. A servant ill-recompensed for his service, asks for a rise; and one dissatisfied with his conditions of work, seeks a change. In short, these are all relationships in which some result is sought; each party is concerned with the ability of the other to provide it. If what is sought is lacking, it is to be expected that the relationship will lapse or be terminated. To be conservative in such relationships, to enjoy what is present and available regardless of its failure to satisfy any want and merely because it has struck our fancy and become familiar, is conduct which discloses a *jusqu'aubuiste* conservatism, an irrational inclination to refuse all relationships which call for the exercise of any other disposition. Though even these relationships seem to lack something appropriate to them when they are confined to a nexus of supply and demand and allow no room for the intrusion of the loyalties and attachments which spring from familiarity.

But there are relationships of another kind in which no result is sought and which are engaged in for their own sake and enjoyed for what they are and not for what they provide. This is so of friendship. Here, attachment springs from an intimation of familiarity and subsists in a mutual sharing of personalities. To go on changing one's butcher until one gets the meat one likes, to go on educating one's agent until he does what is required of him, is conduct not inappropriate to the relationship concerned; but to discard friends because they do not behave as we expected and refuse to be educated to our requirements is the conduct of a man who has altogether mistaken the character of friendship. Friends are not concerned with what might be made of one another, but only with the enjoyment of one another; and the condition of this enjoyment is a ready acceptance of what is and the absence of any desire to change or to improve. A friend is not somebody one trusts to behave in a certain manner, who supplies certain wants, who has certain useful abilities, who possesses certain merely agreeable qualities, or who holds certain acceptable opinions; he is somebody who engages the imagination, who excites contemplation, who provokes interest, sympathy, delight and loyalty simply on account of the relationship entered into. One friend cannot replace another; there is all the difference in the world between the death of a friend and the retirement of one's tailor from business. The relationship of friend to friend is dramatic, not utilitarian; the tie is one of familiarity, not usefulness; the disposition engaged is conservative, not "progressive." And what is true of friendship is not less true of other experiences—of patriotism, for example, and of conversation—each of which demands a conservative disposition as a condition of its enjoyment.

But further, there are activities, not involving human relationships, that may be engaged in, not for a prize, but for the enjoyment they generate, and for which the only appropriate disposition is the disposition to be conservative. Consider fishing. If your project is merely to catch fish it would be foolish to be unduly conservative. You will seek out the best tackle, you will discard practices which prove unsuccessful, you will not be bound by unprofitable attachments to particular localities, pieties will be fleeting, loyalties evanescent; you may even be wise to try anything once in the hope of improvement. But fishing is an activity that may be engaged in, not for the profit of a catch, but for its own sake; and the fisherman may return home in the evening not less content for being empty-handed. Where this is so, the activity has become a ritual and a conservative disposition is appropriate. Why worry about the best gear if you do not care whether or not you make a catch? What matters is the enjoyment of exercising skill (or, perhaps, merely passing, the time),[2] and this is to be had with any tackle, so long as it is familiar and is not grotesquely inappropriate.

All activities, then, where what is sought is enjoyment springing, not from the success of the enterprise but from the familiarity of the engagement, are emblems of the disposition to be conservative. And there are many of them. Fox placed gambling among them when he said that it gave two supreme pleasures, the pleasure of winning and the pleasure of losing. Indeed, I can think of only one activity of this kind which seems to call for a disposition other than conservative: the love of fashion, that is, wanton delight in change for its own sake no matter what it generates.

But, besides the not inconsiderable class of activities which we can engage in only in virtue of a disposition to be conservative, there are occasions in the conduct of other activities when this is the most appropriate disposition; indeed there are few activities which do not, at some point or other, make a call upon it. Whenever stability is more profitable than improvement, whenever certainty is more valuable than speculation, whenever familiarity is more desirable than perfection, whenever agreed error is superior to controversial truth, whenever the disease is more sufferable than the cure, whenever the satisfaction of expectations is more important than the "justice" of the expectations themselves, whenever a rule of some sort is better than the risk of having no rule at all, a disposition to be conservative will be more appropriate than any other; and on any reading of human conduct these cover a not negligible range of circumstances. Those who see the man of conservative disposition (even in what is vulgarly called a "progressive" society) as a lonely swimmer battling against the overwhelming current of circumstance must be thought to have adjusted their binoculars to exclude a large field of human occasion.

In most activities not engaged in for their own sake a distinction appears, a certain level of observation, between the project undertaken and the means employed, between the enterprise and the tools used for its achievement. This is not, of course, an absolute distinction; projects are often provoked and governed by the tools available, and on rarer occasions the tools are designed to fit a particular project. And what on one occasion is a project, on another is a tool. Moreover there is at least one significant exception: the activity of being a poet. It is, however, a relative distinction of some usefulness because it calls our attention to an appropriate difference of attitude towards the two components of the situation.

In general, it may be said that our disposition in respect of tools is appropriately more conservative than our attitude towards projects; or, in other words, tools are less subject to innovation than projects because, except on rare occasions, tools are not designed to fit a particular project and then thrown aside, they are designed to fit a whole class of projects. And this is intelligible because most tools call for skill in use and skill is inseparable from practice and familiarity: a skilled man, whether he is a sailor, a cook or an accountant, is a man familiar with a certain stock of tools. Indeed, a carpenter is usually more skilful in handling his own tools than in handling other examples of the kind of tools commonly used by carpenters; and the solicitor can use his own (annotated) copy of Pollock on *Partnership* or Jarman on *Wills* more readily than any other. Familiarity is the essence of tool using; and in so far as man is a tool using animal he is disposed to be conservative.

Many of the tools in common use have remained unchanged for generations; the design of others has undergone considerable modification; and our stock of tools is always being enlarged by new inventions and improved by new designs. Kitchens, factories, workshops, building sites and offices disclose a characteristic mixture of long-tried and newly invented equipment. But, be that how it may, when business of any kind is afoot, when a particular project has been engaged in—whether it is baking a pie or shoeing a horse, floating a loan or a company, selling fish or insurance to a customer, building a ship or a suit of clothes, sowing wheat or lifting potatoes, laying down port or putting up a barrage—we recognize it to be an occasion when it is particularly appropriate to be conservative about the tools we employ. If it is a large project, we put it in charge of a man who has the requisite knowledge, and we expect him to engage subordinates who know their own business and are skilled in the use of certain stocks of tools.

At some point in this hierarchy of tool-users the suggestion may be made that in order to do this particular job an addition or modification is required in the available stock of tools. Such a suggestion is likely to come from somewhere about the middle of the hierarchy: we do not expect a designer to say "I must go away and do some fundamental research which will take me five years before I can go on with the job" (his bag of tools is a body of knowledge and we expect him to have it handy and to know his way about it); and we do not expect the man at the bottom to have a stock of tools inadequate for the needs of his particular part. But even if such a suggestion is made and is followed up, it will not disrupt the appropriateness of a conservative disposition in respect of the whole stock of tools being used. Indeed, it is clear enough that no job would ever get done, no piece of business could ever be transacted, if, on the occasion, our disposition in respect of our tools were not, generally speaking, conservative. And since doing business of one sort or another occupies most of our time and little can be done without tools of some kind, the disposition to be conservative occupies an unavoidably large place in our character.

The carpenter comes to do a job, perhaps one the exact like of which he has never before tackled; but he comes with his bag of familiar tools and his only chance of doing the job lies in the skill with which he uses what he has at his disposal. When the plumber goes to fetch his tools he would be away even longer than is usually the case if his purpose were to invent new or to improve old ones. Nobody questions the value of money in the market place. No business would ever get done if, before a pound of cheese were weighed or a pint of beer drawn, the relative usefulness of these particular scales of weight and measurement as compared with others were threshed out. The surgeon does not pause in the middle of an operation to redesign his instruments. The MCC does not authorize a new width of bat, a new weight of ball or a new length of wicket in the middle of a Test Match, or even in the middle of a cricket season. When your house is on fire you do not get in touch with a fire-prevention research station to design a new appliance; as Disraeli pointed out, unless you are a lunatic, you send for the parish fire-engine. A musician may improvise music, but he would think himself hardly done-by if, at the same time, he were expected to improvise an instrument. Indeed, when a particularly tricky job is to be done, the workman will often prefer to use a tool that he is thoroughly familiar with rather than another he has in his bag, of new design, but which he has not yet mastered the use of. No doubt there is a time and a place to be radical about such things, for promoting innovation and carrying out improvements in the tools we employ, but these are clearly occasions for the exercise of a conservative disposition.

Now, what is true about tools in general, as distinct from projects, is even more obviously true about a certain kind of tool in common use, namely, general rules of conduct. If the familiarity that springs from relative immunity from change is appropriate to hammers and pincers and to bats and balls, it is supremely appropriate, for example, to an office routine. Routines, no doubt, are susceptible of improvement; but the more familiar they become, the more useful they are. Not to have a conservative disposition in respect of a routine is obvious folly. Of course, exceptional occasions occur which may call for a dispensation; but an inclination to be conservative rather than reformist about a routine is unquestionably appropriate. Consider the conduct of a public meeting, the rules of debate in the House of Commons or the procedure of a court of law. The chief virtue of these arrangements is that they are fixed and familiar; they establish and satisfy certain expectations, they allow to be said in a convenient order whatever is relevant, they prevent extraneous collisions and they conserve human energy. They are typical tools—instruments eligible for use in a variety of different but similar jobs. They are the product of reflection and choice, there is nothing sacrosanct about them, they are susceptible of change and improvement; but if our disposition in respect of them were not, generally speaking, conservative, if we were disposed to argue about them and change them on every occasion, they would rapidly lose their value. And while there may be rare occasions when it is useful to suspend them, it is pre-eminently appropriate that they should not be innovated upon or improved while they are in operation. Or again, consider the rules of a game. These, also, are the product of reflection and choice, and there are occasions when it is appropriate to reconsider them in the light of current experience; but it is inappropriate to have anything but a conservative disposition towards them or to consider putting them all together at one time into the melting-pot; and it is supremely inappropriate to change or improve upon them in the heat and confusion of play. Indeed, the more eager each side is to win, the more valuable is an inflexible set of rules. Players in the course of play may devise new tactics, they may improvise new methods of attack and defence, they may do anything they choose to defeat the expectations of their opponents, except invent new rules. That is an activity to be indulged sparingly and then only in the off-season.

There is much more that might be said about the relevance of the disposition to be conservative and its appropriateness even in a character, such as ours, chiefly disposed in the opposite direction. I have said nothing of morals, nothing of religion; but perhaps I have said enough to show that, even if to be conservative on all occasions and in all connections is so remote from our habit of thought as to be almost unintelligible, there are nevertheless, few of our activities which do not on all occasions call into partnership a disposition to be conservative and on some occasions recognize it as the senior partner; and there are some activities where it is properly master.

3

How, then, are we to construe the disposition to be conservative in respect of politics? And in making this inquiry what I am interested in is not merely the intelligibility of this disposition in any set of circumstances, but its intelligibility in our own contemporary circumstances.

Writers who have considered this question commonly direct our attention to beliefs about the world in general, about human beings in general, about associations in general and even about the universe; and they tell us that a conservative disposition in politics can be correctly construed only when we understand it as a reflection of certain beliefs of these kinds. It is said, for example, that conservatism in politics is the appropriate counterpart of a generally conservative disposition in respect of human conduct: to be reformist in business, in morals or in religion and to be conservative in politics is represented as being inconsistent. It is said that the conservative in politics is so by virtue of holding certain religious beliefs; a belief, for example, in a natural law to be gathered from human experience, and in a providential order reflecting a divine purpose in nature and in human history to which it is the duty of mankind to conform its conduct and departure from which spells injustice and calamity. Further, it is said that a disposition to be conservative in politics reflects what is called an "organic" theory of human society; that it is tied up with a belief in the absolute value of human personality, and with a belief in a primordial propensity of human beings to sin. And the "conservatism" of an Englishman has ever been connected with Royalism and Anglicanism.

Now, setting aside the minor complaints one might be moved to make about this account of the situation, it seems to me to suffer from one large defect. It is true that many of these beliefs have been held by people disposed to be conservative in political activity, and it may be true that these people have also believed their disposition to be in some way confirmed by them, or even to be founded upon them; but, as I understand it, a disposition to be conservative in politics does not entail either that we should hold these beliefs to be true or even that we should suppose them to be true. Indeed, I do not think it is necessarily connected with any particular beliefs about the universe, about the world in general or about human conduct in general. What it is tied to is certain beliefs about the activity of governing and the instruments of government, and it is in terms of beliefs on these topics, and not on others, that it can be made to appear intelligible. And, to state my view briefly before elaborating it, what makes a conservative disposition in politics intelligible is nothing to do with a natural law or a providential order, nothing to do with morals or religion; it is the observation of our current manner of living combined with the belief (which from our point of view need be regarded as no more than an hypothesis) that governing is a specific and limited activity, namely the provision and custody of general rules of conduct, which are understood, not as plans for imposing substantive activities, but as instruments enabling people to pursue the activities of their own choice with the minimum frustration, and therefore something which it is appropriate to be conservative about.

Let us begin at what I believe to be the proper starting-place; not in the empyrean, but with ourselves as we have come to be. I and my neighbours, my associates, my compatriots, my friends, my enemies and those who I am indifferent about, are people engaged in a great variety of activities. We are apt to entertain a multiplicity of opinions on every conceivable subject and are disposed to change these beliefs as we grow tired of them or as they prove unserviceable. Each of us is pursuing a course of his own; and there is no project so unlikely that somebody will not be found to engage in it, no enterprise so foolish that somebody will not undertake it. There are those who spend their lives trying to sell copies of the Anglican Catechism to the Jews. And one half of the world is engaged in trying to make the other half want what it has hitherto never felt the lack of. We are all inclined to be passionate about our own concerns, whether it is making things or selling them, whether it is business or sport, religion or learning, poetry, drink or drugs. Each of us has preferences of his own. For some, the opportunities of making choices (which are numerous) are invitations readily accepted; others welcome them less eagerly or even find them burdensome. Some dream dreams of new and better worlds: others are more inclined to move in familiar paths or even to be idle. Some are apt to deplore the rapidity of change, others delight in it; all recognize it. At times we grow tired and fall asleep: it is a blessed relief to gaze in a shop window and see nothing we want; we are grateful for ugliness merely because it repels attention. But, for the most part, we pursue happiness by seeking the satisfaction of desires which spring from one another inexhaustibly. We enter into relationships of interest and of emotion, of competition, partnership, guardianship, love, friendship, jealousy and hatred, some of which are more durable than others. We make agreements with one another; we have expectations about one another's conduct; we approve, we are indifferent and we disapprove. This multiplicity of activity and variety of opinions is apt to produce collisions: we pursue courses which cut across those of others, and we do not all approve the same sort of conduct. But, in the main, we get along with one another, sometimes by giving way, sometimes by standing fast, sometimes in a compromise. Our conduct consists of activity assimilated to that of others in small, and for the most part unconsidered and unobtrusive, adjustments.

Why all this should be so, does not matter. It is not necessarily so. A different condition of human circumstances can easily be imagined, and we know that elsewhere and at other times activity is, or has been, far less multifarious and changeful and opinion far less diverse and far less likely to provoke collision; but, by and large, we recognize this to be our condition. It is an acquired condition, though nobody designed or specifically chose it in preference to all others. It is the product, not of "human nature" let loose, but of human beings impelled by an acquired love of making choices for themselves. And we know as little and as much about where it is leading us as we know about the fashion in hats in twenty years' time or the design of motor-cars.

Surveying the scene, some people are provoked by the absence of order and coherence which appears to them to be its dominant feature; its wastefulness, its frustration, its dissipation of human energy, its lack not merely of a premeditated destination but even of any discernible direction of movement. It provides an excitement similar to that of a stock-car race; but it has none of the satisfaction of a well-conducted business enterprise. Such people are apt to exaggerate the current disorder; the absence of plan is so conspicuous that the small adjustments, and even the more massive arrangements, which restrain the chaos seem to them nugatory; they have no feeling for the warmth of untidiness but only for its inconvenience. But what is significant is not the limitations of their powers of observation, but the turn of their thoughts. They feel that there ought to be something that ought to be done to convert this so-called chaos into order for this is no way for rational human beings to be spending their lives. Like Apollo when he saw Daphne with her hair hung carelessly about her neck, they sigh and say to themselves: "What if it were properly arranged." Moreover, they tell us that they have seen in a dream the glorious, collisionless manner of living proper to all mankind, and this dream they understand as their warrant for seeking to remove the diversities and occasions of conflict which distinguish our current manner of living. Of course, their dreams are not all exactly alike; but they have this in common: each is a vision of a condition of human circumstances from which the occasion of conflict has been removed, a vision of human activity co-ordinated and set going in a single direction and of every resource being used to the full. And such people appropriately understand the office of government to be the imposition upon its subjects of the condition of human circumstances of their dream. To govern is to turn a private dream into a public and compulsory manner of living. Thus, politics becomes an encounter of dreams and the activity in which government is held to this understanding of its office and provided with the appropriate instruments.

I do not propose to criticize this jump to glory style of politics in which governing is understood as a perpetual take-over bid for the purchase of the resources of human energy in order to concentrate them in a single direction; it is not at all unintelligible, and there is much in our circumstances to provoke it. My purpose is merely to point out that there is another quite different understanding of government, and that it is no less intelligible and in some respects perhaps more appropriate to our circumstances.

The spring of this other disposition in respect of governing and the instruments of government—a conservative disposition—is to be found in the acceptance of the current condition of human circumstances as I have described it: the propensity to make our own choices and to find happiness in doing so, the variety of enterprises each pursued with passion, the diversity of beliefs each held with the conviction of its exclusive truth; the inventiveness, the changefulness and the absence of any large design; the excess, the over-activity and the informal compromise. And the office of government is not to impose other beliefs and activities upon its subjects, not to tutor or to educate them, not to make them better or happier in another way, not to direct them, to galvanize them into action, to lead them or to coordinate their activities so that no occasion of conflict shall occur; the office of government is merely to rule. This is a specific and limited activity, easily corrupted when it is combined with any other, and, in the circumstances, indispensable. The image of the ruler is the umpire whose business is to administer the rules of the game, or the chairman who governs the debate according to known rules but does not himself participate in it.

Now people of this disposition commonly defend their belief that the proper attitude of government towards the current condition of human circumstance is one of acceptance by appealing to certain general ideas. They contend that there is absolute value in the free play of human choice, that private property (the emblem of choice) is a natural right, that it is only in the enjoyment of diversity of opinion and activity that true belief and good conduct can be expected to disclose themselves. But I do not think that this disposition requires these or any similar beliefs in order to make it intelligible. Something much smaller and less pretentious will do: the observation that this condition of human circumstance is, in fact, current, and that we have learned to enjoy it and how to manage it; that we are not children in statu pupillari but adults who do not consider themselves under any obligation to justify their preference for making their own choices; and that it is beyond human experience to suppose that those who rule are endowed with a superior wisdom which discloses them a better range of beliefs and activities and which gives them authority to impose upon their subjects a quite different manner of life. In short, if the man of this disposition is asked: Why ought governments to accept the current diversity of opinion and activity in preference to imposing upon their subjects a dream of their own? it is enough for him to reply: Why not? Their dreams are no different from those of anyone else; and if it is boring to have to listen to dreams of others being recounted, it is insufferable to be forced to re-enact them. We tolerate monomaniacs, it is our habit to do so; but why should we be *ruled* by them? Is it not (the man of conservative disposition asks) an intelligible task for a government to protect its subjects against the nuisance of those who spend their energy and their wealth in the service of some pet indignation, endeavouring to impose it upon everybody, not by suppressing their activities in favour of others of a similar kind, but by setting a limit to the amount of noise anyone may emit?

Nevertheless, if this acceptance is the spring of the conservative's disposition in respect of government, he does not suppose that the office of government is to do nothing. As he understands it, there is work to be done which can be done only in virtue of a genuine acceptance of current beliefs simply because they are current and current activities simply because they are afoot. And, briefly, the office he attributes to government is to resolve some of the collisions which this variety of beliefs and activities generates; to preserve peace, not by placing an interdict upon choice and upon the diversity that springs from the exercise of preference, not by imposing substantive uniformity, but by enforcing general rules of procedure upon all subjects alike.

Government, then, as the conservative in this matter understands it, does not begin with a vision of another, different and better world, but with the observation of the self-government practised even by men of passion in the conduct of their enterprises; it begins in the informal adjustments of interests to one another which are designed to release those who are apt to collide from the mutual frustrations of a collision. Sometimes these adjustments are no more than agreements between two parties to keep out of each other's way; sometimes they are of wider application and more durable character, such as the International Rules for the prevention of collisions at sea. In short, the intimations of government are to be found in ritual, not in religion or philosophy; in the enjoyment of orderly and peaceable behaviour, not in the search for truth or perfection.

But the self-government of men of passionate belief and enterprise is apt to break down when it is most needed. It often suffices to resolve minor collisions of interest, but beyond these it is not to be relied upon. A more precise and a less easily corrupted ritual is required to resolve the massive collisions which our manner of living is apt to generate and to release us from the massive frustrations in which we are apt to become locked. The custodian of this ritual is "the government," and the rules it imposes are "the law." One may imagine a government engaged in the activity of an arbiter in cases of collisions of interest but doing its business without the aid of laws, just as one may imagine a game without rules and an umpire who was appealed to in cases of dispute and who on each occasion merely used his judgement to devise *ad hoc* a way of releasing the disputants from their mutual frustration. But the diseconomy of such an arrangement is so obvious that it could only be expected to occur to those inclined to believe the ruler to be supernaturally inspired and to those disposed to attribute to him a quite different office—that of leader, or tutor, or manager. At all events the disposition to be conservative in respect of government is rooted in the belief that where government rests upon the acceptance of the current activities and beliefs of its subjects, the only appropriate manner of ruling is by making and enforcing rules of conduct. In short, to be conservative about government is a reflection of the conservatism we have recognized to be appropriate in respect of rules of conduct.

To govern, then, as the conservative understands it, is to provide a *vinculum juris* for those manners of conduct which, in the circumstances, are least likely to result in a frustrating collision of interests; to provide redress and means of compensation for those who suffer from others behaving in a contrary manner; sometimes to provide punishment for those who pursue their own interests regardless of the rules; and, of course, to provide a sufficient force to maintain the authority of an arbiter of this kind. Thus, governing is recognized as a specific and limited activity; not the management of an enterprise, but the rule of those engaged in a great diversity of self-chosen enterprises. It is not concerned with concrete persons, but with activities; and with activities only in respect of their propensity to collide with one another. It is not concerned with moral right and wrong, it is not designed to make men good or even better; it is not indispensable on account of "the natural depravity of mankind" but merely because of their current disposition to be extravagant; its business is to keep its subjects at peace with one another in the activities in which they have chosen to seek their happiness. And if there is any general idea entailed in this view, it is, perhaps, that a government which does not sustain the loyalty of its subjects is worthless; and that while one which (in the old puritan phrase) "commands for truth" is incapable of doing so (because some of its subjects will believe its "truth" to be error), one which is indifferent to "truth" and "error" alike, and merely pursues peace, presents no obstacle to the necessary loyalty.

Now, it is intelligible enough that any man who thinks in this manner about government should be averse from innovation: government is providing rules of conduct, and familiarity is a supremely important virtue in a rule. Nevertheless, he has room for other thoughts. The current condition of human circumstances is one in which new activities (often springing from new inventions) are constantly appearing and rapidly extend themselves, and in which beliefs are perpetually being modified or discarded; and for the rules to be inappropriate to the current activities and beliefs is as unprofitable as for them to be unfamiliar. For example, a variety of inventions and considerable changes in the conduct of business, seem now to have made the current law of copyright inadequate. And it may be thought that neither the newspaper nor the motor-car nor the aeroplane have yet received proper recognition in the law of England; they have all created nuisances that call out to be abated. Or again, at the end of the last century our governments engaged in an extensive codification of large parts of our law and in this manner both brought it into closer relationship with current beliefs and manners of activity and insulated it from the small adjustments to circumstances which are characteristic of the operation of our common law. But many of these Statutes are now hopelessly out of date. And there are older Acts of Parliament (such as the Merchant Shipping Act), governing large and important departments of activity, which are even more inappropriate to current circumstances. Innovation, then, is called for if the rules are to remain appropriate to the activities they govern. But, as the conservative understands it, modification of the rules should always reflect, and never impose, a change in the activities and beliefs of those who are subject to them, and should never on any occasion be so great as to destroy the *ensemble*. Consequently, the conservative will have nothing to do with innovations designed to meet merely hypothetical situations; he will prefer to enforce a rule he has got rather than invent a new one; he will think it appropriate to delay a modification of the rules until it is clear that the change of circumstance it is designed to reflect has come to stay for a while; he will be suspicious of proposals for change in excess of what the situation calls for, of rulers who demand extra-ordinary powers in order to make great changes and whose utterances are tied to generalities like "the public good" or "social justice," and of Saviours of Society who buckle on armour and seek dragons to slay; he will think it proper to consider the occasion of the innovation with care; in short, he will be disposed to regard politics as an activity in which a valuable set of tools is renovated from time to time and kept in trim rather than as an opportunity for perpetual re-equipment.

All this may help to make intelligible the disposition to be conservative in respect of government; and the detail might be elaborated to show, for example, how a man of this disposition understands the other great business of a government, the conduct of a foreign policy; to show why he places so high a value upon the complicated set of arrangements we call "the institution of private property"; to show the appropriateness of his rejection of the view that politics is a shadow thrown by economics; to show why he believes that the main (perhaps the only) specifically economic activity appropriate to government is the maintenance of a stable currency. But, on this occasion, I think there is something else to be said.

To some people, "government" appears as a vast reservoir of power which inspires them to dream of what use might be made of it. They have favourite projects, of various dimensions, which they sincerely believe are for the benefit of mankind, and to capture this source of power, if necessary to increase it, and to use it for imposing their favourite projects upon their fellows is what they understand as the adventure of governing men. They are, thus, disposed to recognize government as an instrument of passion; the art of politics is to inflame and direct desire. In short, governing is understood to be just like any other activity—making and selling a brand of soap, exploiting the resources of a locality, or developing a housing estate—only the power here is (for the most part) already mobilized, and the enterprise is remarkable only because it aims at monopoly and because of its promise of success once the source of power has been captured. Of course a private enterprise politician of this sort would get nowhere in these days unless there were people with wants so vague that they can be prompted to ask for what he has to offer, or with wants so servile that they prefer the promise of a provided abundance to the opportunity of choice and activity on their own account. And it is not all as plain sailing as it might appear: often a politician of this sort misjudges the situation; and then, briefly, even in democratic politics, we become aware of what the camel thinks of the camel driver.

Now, the disposition to be conservative in respect of politics reflects a quite different view of the activity of governing. The man of this disposition understands it to be the business of a government not to inflame passion and give it new objects to feed upon, but to inject into the activities of already too passionate men an ingredient of moderation; to restrain, to deflate, to pacify and to reconcile; not to stoke the fires of desire, but to damp them down. And all this, not because passion is vice and moderation virtue, but because moderation is indispensable if passionate men are to escape being locked in an encounter of mutual frustration. A government of this sort does not need to be regarded as the agent of a benign providence, as the custodian of a moral law, or as the emblem of a divine order. What it provides is something that its subjects (if they are such people as we are) can easily recognize to be valuable; indeed, it is something that, to some extent, they do for themselves in the ordinary course of business or pleasure. They scarcely need to be reminded of its indispensability, as Sextus Empiricus tells us the ancient Persians were accustomed periodically to remind themselves by setting aside all laws for five hair-raising days on the death of a king. Generally speaking, they are not averse from paying the modest cost of this service; and they recognize that the appropriate attitude to a government of this sort is loyalty (sometimes a confident loyalty, at others perhaps the heavy-hearted loyalty of Sidney Godolphin), respect and some suspicion, not love or devotion or affection. Thus, governing is understood to be a secondary activity; but it is recognized also to be a specific activity, not easily to be combined with any other, because all other activities (except the mere contemplation of the scene) entail taking sides and the surrender of the indifference appropriate (on this view of things) not only to the judge but also to the legislator, who is understood to occupy a judicial office. The subjects of such a government require that it shall be strong, alert, resolute, economical and neither capricious nor over-active: they have no use for a referee who does not govern the game according to the rules, who takes sides, who plays a game of his own, or who is always blowing his whistle; after all, the game's the thing, and in playing the game we neither need to be, nor at present are disposed to be, conservative.

But there is something more to be observed in this style of governing than merely the restraint imposed by familiar and appropriate rules. Of course, it will not countenance government by suggestion or cajolery or by any other means than by law; an avuncular Home Secretary or a threatening Chancellor of the Exchequer. But the spectacle of its indifference to the beliefs and substantive activities of its subjects may itself be expected to provoke a habit of restraint. Into the heat of our engagements, into the passionate clash of beliefs, into our enthusiasm for saving the souls of our neighbours or of all mankind, a government of this sort injects an ingredient, not of reason (how should we expect that?) but of the irony that is prepared to counteract one vice by another, of the raillery that deflates extravagance without itself pretending to wisdom, of the mockery that disperses tension, of inertia, and of scepticism: indeed, it might be said that we keep a government of this sort to do for us the scepticism we have neither the time nor the inclination to do for ourselves. It is like the cool touch of the mountain that one feels in the plain even on the hottest summer day. Or, to leave metaphor behind, it is like the "governor" which, by controlling the speed at which its parts move, keeps an engine from racketing itself to pieces.

It is not, then, mere stupid prejudice which disposes a conservative to take this view of the activity of governing; nor are any highfalutin metaphysical beliefs necessary to provoke it or make it intelligible. It is connected merely with the observation that where activity is bent upon enterprise the indispensable counterpart is another order of activity, bent upon restraint, which is unavoidably corrupted (indeed, altogether abrogated) when the power assigned to it is used for advancing favourite projects. An "umpire" who at the same time is one of the players is no umpire; "rules" about which we are not disposed to be conservative are not rules but incitements to disorder; the conjunction of dreaming and ruling generates tyranny.

4

Political conservatism is, then, not at all unintelligible in a people disposed to be adventurous and enterprising, a people in love with change and apt to rationalize their affections in terms of "progress."[3] And one does not need to think that the belief in "progress" is the most cruel and unprofitable of all beliefs, arousing cupidity without satisfying it, in order to think it inappropriate for a government to be conspicuously "progressive." Indeed, a disposition to be conservative in respect of government would seem to be pre-eminently appropriate to men who have something to do and something to think about on their own account, who have a skill to practice or an intellectual fortune to make, to people whose passions do not need to be inflamed, whose desires do not need to be provoked and whose dreams of a better world need no prompting. Such people know the value of a rule which imposes orderliness without directing enterprise, a rule which concentrates duty so that room is left for delight. They might even be prepared to suffer a legally established ecclesiastical order; but it would not be because they believed it to represent some unassailable religious truth, but merely because it restrained the indecent competition of sects and (as Hume said) moderated "the plague of a too diligent clergy."

Now, whether or not these beliefs recommend themselves as reasonable and appropriate to our circumstances and to the abilities we are likely to find in those who rule us, they and their like are in my view what make intelligible a conservative disposition in respect of politics. What would be the appropriateness of this disposition in circumstances other than our own, whether to be conservative in respect of government would have the same relevance in the circumstances of an unadventurous, a slothful or a spiritless people, is a question we need not try to answer: we are concerned with ourselves as we are. I myself think that it would occupy an important place in any set of circumstances. But what I hope I have made clear is that it is not at all inconsistent to be conservative in respect of government and radical in respect of almost every other activity. And, in my opinion, there is more to be learnt about this disposition from Montaigne, Pascal, Hobbes and Hume than from Burke or Bentham.

Of the many entailments of this view of things that might be pointed to, I will notice one, namely, that politics is an activity unsuited to the young, not on account of their vices but on account of what I at least consider to be their virtues.

Nobody pretends that it is easy to acquire or to sustain the mood of indifference which this manner of politics calls for. To rein-in one's own beliefs and desires, to acknowledge the current shape of things, to feel the balance of things in one's hand, to tolerate what is abominable, to distinguish between crime and sin, to respect formality even when it appears to be leading to error, these are difficult achievements; and they are achievements not to be looked for in the young.

Everybody's young days are a dream, a delightful insanity, a sweet solipsism. Nothing in them has a fixed shape, nothing a fixed price; everything is a possibility, and we live happily on credit. There are no obligations to be observed; there are no accounts to be kept. Nothing is specified in advance; everything is what can be made of it. The world is a mirror in which we seek the reflection of our own desires. The allure of violent emotions is irresistible. When we are young we are not disposed to make concessions to the world; we never feel the balance of a thing in our hands—unless it be a cricket bat. We are not apt to distinguish between our liking and our esteem; urgency is our criterion of importance; and we do not easily understand that what is humdrum need not be despicable. We are impatient of restraint; and we readily believe, like Shelley, that to have contracted a habit is to have failed. These, in my opinion, are among our virtues when we are young; but how remote they are from the disposition appropriate for participating in the style of government I have been describing. Since life is a dream, we argue (with plausible but erroneous logic) that politics must be an encounter of dreams, in which we hope to impose our own. Some unfortunate people, like Pitt (laughably called "the Younger"), are born old, and are eligible to engage in politics almost in their cradles; others, perhaps more fortunate, belie the saying that one is young only once, they never grow up. But these are exceptions. For most there is what Conrad called the "shadow line" which, when we pass it, discloses a solid world of things, each with its fixed shape, each with its own point of balance, each with its price; a world of fact, not poetic image, in which what we have spent on one thing we cannot spend on another; a world inhabited by others besides ourselves who cannot be reduced to mere reflections of our own emotions. And coming to be at home in this commonplace world qualifies us (as no knowledge of "political science" can ever qualify us), if we are so inclined and have nothing better to think about, to engage in what the man of conservative disposition understands to be political activity.

NOTES

1. "Which of us," asks a contemporary (not without some equivocation), "would not settle, at whatever cost in nervous anxiety, for a febrile and creative rather than a static society?"

2. When Prince Wen Wang was on a tour of inspection in Tsang, he saw an old man fishing. But his fishing was not real fishing, for he did not fish in order to catch fish, but to amuse himself. So Wen Wang wished to employ him in the administration of government, but he feared his own ministers, uncles and brothers might object. On the other hand, if he let the old man go, he could not bear to think of the people being deprived of his influence. *Chuang Tzu.*

3. I have not forgotten to ask myself the question: Why, then, have we so neglected what is appropriate to our circumstances as to make the activist dreamer the stereotype of the modern politician? And I have tried to answer it elsewhere.

9

Edmund Burke

———◦•◦———

Reflections on the Revolution in France (1790)

Edmund Burke was born in Dublin, Ireland, in 1729 and served as a Whig member of Parliament until his death in 1797. In Parliament he worked for the improvement of British colonial relations, especially between England and Ireland. Reflections on the Revolution in France, *his most famous work, greatly influenced British perceptions of and policies toward postrevolutionary France. The British conservatives adopted Burke's philosophy, and today he is rightly called the father of conservatism.*

Dear Sir,

You are pleased to call again, and with some earnestness, for my thoughts on the late proceedings in France. I will not give you reason to imagine, that I think my sentiments of such value as to wish myself to be solicited about them. They are of too little consequence to be very anxiously either communicated or withheld. It was from attention to you, and to you only, that I hesitated at the time, when you first desired to receive them. In the first letter I had the honour to write to you, and which at length I send, I wrote neither for nor from any description of men; nor shall I in this. My errors, if any, are my own. My reputation alone is to answer for them.

You see, Sir, by the long letter I have transmitted to you, that, though I do most heartily wish that France may be animated by a spirit of rational liberty, and that I think you bound, in all honest policy, to provide a permanent body, in which that spirit may reside, and an effectual organ, by which it may act, it is my misfortune to entertain great doubts concerning several material points in your late transactions. . . .

[Liberty and Order]

I flatter myself that I love a manly, moral, regulated liberty as well as any gentleman of that society, be he who he will; and perhaps I have given as good proofs of my attachment to that cause, in the whole course of my public conduct. I think I envy liberty as little as they do, to any other nation. But I cannot stand forward, and give praise or blame to any thing which relates to human actions, and human concerns, on a simple view of the object, as it stands stripped of every relation, in all the nakedness and solitude of metaphysical abstraction. Circumstances (which with some gentlemen pass for nothing) give in reality to every political principle its distinguishing colour, and discriminating effect. The circumstances are what render every civil and political scheme beneficial or noxious to mankind. Abstractedly speaking, government, as well as liberty, is good; yet could I, in common sense, ten years ago, have felicitated France on her enjoyment of a government (for she then had a government) without enquiry what the nature of that government was, or how it was administered? Can I now congratulate the same nation upon its freedom? Is it because liberty in the abstract may be classed amongst the blessings of mankind, that I am seriously to felicitate a madman, who has escaped from the protecting restraint and wholesome darkness of his cell, on his restoration to the enjoyment of light and liberty? Am I to congratulate an highwayman and murderer, who has broke prison, upon the recovery of his natural rights? This would be to act over again the scene of the criminals condemned to the gallies, and their heroic deliverer, the metaphysic Knight of the Sorrowful Countenance.

When I see the spirit of liberty in action, I see a strong principle at work; and this, for a while, is all I can possibly know of it. The wild *gas,* the fixed air is plainly broke loose: but we ought to suspend our judgment until the first effervescence is a little subsided, till the liquor is cleared, and until we see something deeper than the agitation of a troubled and frothy surface. I must be tolerably sure, before I venture publicly to congratulate men upon a blessing, that they have really received one. Flattery corrupts both the receiver and the giver; and adulation is not of more service to the people than to kings. I should therefore suspend my congratulations on the new liberty of France, until I was informed how it had been combined with government; with public force; with the discipline and obedience of armies; with the collection of an effective and well-distributed revenue; with morality and religion; with the solidity of property; with peace and order; with civil and social manners. All these (in their way) are good things too; and, without them, liberty is not a benefit whilst it lasts, and is not likely to continue long. The effect of liberty to individuals is, that they may do what they please: We ought to see what it will please them to do, before we risque congratulations, which may be soon turned into complaints. Prudence would dictate this in the case of separate insulated private men; but liberty, when men act in bodies, is *power*. Considerate people, before they declare themselves, will observe the use which is made of *power;* and particularly of so trying a thing as *new* power in *new* persons, of whose principles, tempers, and dispositions, they have little or no experience, and in situations where those who appear the most stirring in the scene may possibly not be the real movers. . . .

[Continuity and Change]

It is far from impossible to reconcile, if we do not suffer ourselves to be entangled in the mazes of metaphysic sophistry, the use both of a fixed rule and an occasional deviation; the sacredness of an hereditary principle of succession in our government, with a power of change in its application in cases of extreme emergency. Even in that extremity (if we take the measure of our rights by our exercise of them at the Revolution) the change is to be confined to the peccant part only; to the part which produced the necessary deviation; and even then it is to be effected without a decomposition of the whole civil and political mass, for the purpose of originating a new civil order out of the first elements of society.

A state without the means of some change is without the means of its conservation. Without such means it might even risque the loss of that part of the constitution which it wished the most religiously to preserve. The two principles of conservation and correction operated strongly at the two critical periods of the Restoration and Revolution, when England found itself without a king. At both those periods the nation had lost the bond of union in their ancient edifice; they did not however, dissolve the whole fabric. On the contrary, in both cases they regenerated the deficient part of the old constitution through the parts which were not impaired. They kept these old parts exactly as they were, that the part recovered might be suited to them. They acted by the ancient organized states in the shape of their old organization, and not by the organic *moleculae* of a disbanded people. At no time, perhaps, did the sovereign legislature manifest a more tender regard to that fundamental principle of British constitutional policy, than at the time of the Revolution, when it deviated from the direct line of hereditary succession. The crown was carried somewhat out of the line in which it had before moved; but the new line was derived from the same stock. It was still a line of hereditary descent; still an hereditary descent in the same blood, though an hereditary descent qualified with protestantism. When the legislature altered the direction, but kept the principle, they shewed that they held it inviolable. . . .

The speculative line of demarcation, where obedience ought to end, and resistance must begin, is faint, obscure, and not easily definable. It is not a single act, or a single event, which determines it. Governments must be abused and deranged indeed, before it can be thought of; and the prospect of the future must be as bad as the experience of the past. When things are in that lamentable condition, the nature of the disease is to indicate the remedy to those whom nature has qualified to administer in extremities this critical, ambiguous, bitter portion to a distempered state. Times and occasions, and provocations, will teach their own lessons. The wise will determine from the gravity of the case; the irritable from sensibility to oppression; the high-minded from disdain and indignation at abusive power in unworthy hands; the brave and bold from the love of honourable danger in a generous cause: but, with or without right, a revolution will be the very last resource of the thinking and the good. . . .

The very idea of the fabrication of a new government, is enough to fill us with disgust and horror. We wished at the period of the Revolution, and do now wish, to derive all we possess as *an inheritance from our forefathers.* Upon that body and stock of inheritance we have taken care not to inoculate any cyon [scion] alien to the nature of the original plant. All the reformations we have hitherto made, have proceeded upon the principle of reference to antiquity; and I hope, nay I am persuaded, that all those which possibly may be made hereafter, will be carefully formed upon analogical precedent, authority, and example. . . .

Our political system is placed in a just correspondence and symmetry with the order of the world, and with the mode of existence decreed to a permanent body composed of transitory parts; wherein, by the disposition of a stupendous wisdom, moulding together the great mysterious incorporation of the human race, the whole, at one time, is never old, or middle-aged, or young, but in a condition of unchangeable constancy, moves on through the varied tenour of perpetual decay, fall, renovation, and progression. Thus, by preserving the method of nature in the conduct of the state, in what we improve we are never wholly new; in what we retain we are never wholly obsolete. By adhering in this manner and on those principles to our forefathers, we are guided not by the superstition of antiquarians, but by the spirit of philosophic analogy. In this choice of inheritance we have given to our frame of polity the image of a relation in blood; binding up the constitution of our country with our dearest domestic ties; adopting our fundamental laws into the bosom of our family affections; keeping inseparable, and cherishing with the warmth of all their combined and mutually reflected charities, our state, our hearths, our sepulchres, and our altars.

Through the same plan of a conformity to nature in our artificial institutions, and by calling in the aid of her unerring and powerful instincts, to fortify the fallible and feeble contrivances of our reason, we have derived several other, and those no small benefits, from considering our liberties in the light of an inheritance. Always acting as if in the presence of canonized forefathers, the spirit of freedom, leading in itself to misrule and excess, is tempered with an awful gravity. This idea of a liberal descent inspires us with a sense of habitual native dignity, which prevents that upstart insolence almost inevitably adhering to and disgracing those who are the first acquirers of any distinction. By this means our liberty becomes a noble freedom. It carries an imposing and majestic aspect. It has a pedigree and illustrating ancestors. It has its bearings and its ensigns armorial. It has its gallery of portraits; its monumental inscriptions; its records, evidences, and titles. We procure reverence to our civil institutions on the principle upon which nature teaches us to revere individual men; on account of their age; and on account of those from whom they are descended. All your sophisters cannot produce any thing better adapted to preserve a rational and manly freedom than the course that we have pursued, who have chosen our nature rather than our speculations, our breasts rather than our inventions, for the great conservatories and magazines of our rights and privileges.

You might, if you pleased, have profited of our example, and have given to your recovered freedom a correspondent dignity. Your privileges, though discontinued, were not lost to memory. Your constitution, it is true, whilst you were out of possession, suffered waste and dilapidation; but you possessed in some parts the walls, and in all the foundations of a noble and venerable castle. You might have repaired those walls; you might have built on those old foundations. Your constitution was suspended before it was perfected; but you had the elements of a constitution very nearly as good as could be wished. In your old states you possessed that variety of parts corresponding with the various descriptions of which your community was happily composed; you had all that combination, and all that opposition of interests, you had that action and counteraction which, in the natural and in the political world, from the reciprocal struggle of discordant powers, draws out the harmony of the universe. These opposed and conflicting interests, which you considered as so great a blemish in your old and in our present constitution, interpose a salutary check to all precipitate resolutions; they render deliberation a matter not of choice, but of necessity; they make all change a subject of *compromise,* which naturally begets moderation; they produce *temperaments,* preventing the sore evil of harsh, crude, unqualified reformations; and rendering all the headlong exertions of arbitrary power, in the few or in the many, for ever impracticable. Through that diversity of members and interests, general liberty had as many securities as there were separate views in the several orders; whilst by pressing down the whole by the weight of a real monarchy, the separate parts would have been prevented from warping and starting from their allotted places. . . .

[Real Rights]

They have "the rights of men." Against these there can be no prescription; against these no agreement is binding: these admit no temperament, and no compromise: any thing withheld from their full demand is so much of fraud and injustice. Against these their rights of men let no government look for security in the length of its continuance, or in the justice and lenity of its administration. The objections of these speculatists, if its forms do not quadrate with their theories, are as valid against such an old and beneficent government as against the most violent tyranny, or the greenest usurpation. They are always at issue with governments, not on a question of abuse, but a question of competency, and a question of title. I have nothing to say to the clumsy subtilty of their political metaphysics. Let them be their amusement in the schools—"*Illa se jactet in aula—Aeolus, et clauso ventorum carcere regnet.*" But let them not break prison to burst like a *Levanter,* to sweep the earth with their hurricane, and to break up the fountains of the great deep to overwhelm us. . . .

Far am I from denying in theory; full as far is my heart from withholding in practice (if I were of power to give or to withhold) the *real* rights of men. In denying their false claims of right, I do not mean to injure those which are real, and are such as their pretended rights would totally destroy. If civil society be made for the advantage of man, all the advantages for which it is made become his right. It is an institution of beneficence; and law itself is only beneficence acting by a rule. Men have a right to live by that rule; they have a right to justice: as between their fellows, whether their fellows are in politic function or in ordinary occupation. They have a right to the fruits of their industry; and to the means of making their industry fruitful. They have a right to the acquisitions of their parents; to the nourishment and improvement of their offspring; to instruction in life, and to consolation in death. Whatever each man can separately do, without trespassing upon others, he has a right to do for himself; and he has a right to a fair portion of all which society, with all its combinations of skill and force, can do in his favour. In this partnership all men have equal rights; but not to equal things. He that has but five shillings in the partnership, has as good a right to it, as he that has five hundred pounds has to his larger proportion. But he has not a right to an equal dividend in the product of the joint stock; and as to the share of power, authority, and direction which each individual ought to have in the management of the state, that I must deny to be amongst the direct original rights of man in civil society;

for I have in my contemplation the civil social man, and no other. It is a thing to be settled by convention. . . .

If civil society be the offspring of convention, that convention must be its law. That convention must limit and modify all the descriptions of constitution which are formed under it. Every sort of legislative, judicial, or executory power are its creatures. They can have no being in any other state of things; and how can any man claim, under the conventions of civil society, rights which do not so much as suppose its existence? Rights which are absolutely repugnant to it? One of the first motives to civil society, and which becomes one of its fundamental rules, is, *that no man should be judge in his own cause.* By this each person has at once divested himself of the first fundamental right of uncovenanted man, that is, to judge for himself, and to assert his own cause. He abdicates all right to be his own governor. He inclusively, in a great measure, abandons the right of self-defence, the first law of nature. Men cannot enjoy the rights of an uncivil and of a civil state together. That he may obtain justice he gives up his right of determining what it is in points the most essential to him. That he may secure some liberty, he makes a surrender in trust of the whole of it. . . .

Government is not made in virtue of natural rights, which may and do exist in total independence of it; and exist in much greater clearness, and in a much greater degree of abstract perfection: but their abstract perfection is their practical defect. By having a right to every thing they want every thing. Government is a contrivance of human wisdom to provide for human *wants.* Men have a right that these wants should be provided for by this wisdom. Among these wants is to be reckoned the want, out of civil society, of a sufficient restraint upon their passions. Society requires not only that the passions of individuals should be subjected, but that even in the mass and body as well as in the individuals, the inclinations of men should frequently be thwarted, their will controlled, and their passions brought into subjection. This can only be done *by a power out of themselves;* and not, in the exercise of its function, subject to that will and to those passions which it is its office to bridle and subdue. In this sense the restraints on men, as well as their liberties, are to be reckoned among their rights. But as the liberties and the restrictions vary with times and circumstances, and admit of infinite modifications, they cannot be settled upon any abstract rule; and nothing is so foolish as to discuss them upon the principle. . . .

[Prudence]

The science of government being therefore so practical in itself, and intended for such practical purposes, a matter which requires experience, and even more experience than any person can gain in his whole life, however sagacious and observing he may be, it is with infinite caution that any man ought to venture upon pulling down an edifice which has answered in any tolerable degree for ages the common purposes of society, or on building it up again, without having models and patterns of approved utility before his eyes.

These metaphysic rights entering into common life, like rays of light which pierce into a dense medium, are, by the laws of nature, refracted from their straight line. Indeed in the gross and complicated mass of human passions and concerns, the primitive rights of men undergo such a variety of refractions and reflections, that it becomes absurd to talk of them as if they continued in the simplicity of their original direction. The nature of man is intricate; the objects of society are of the greatest possible complexity; and therefore no simple disposition of direction of power can be suitable either to man's nature, or to the quality of his affairs. When I hear the simplicity of contrivance aimed at and boasted of in any new political constitutions, I am at no loss to decide that the artificers are grossly ignorant of their trade, or totally negligent of their duty. . . .

[Tradition]

It is now sixteen or seventeen years since I saw the queen of France, then the dauphiness, at Versailles; and surely never lighted on this orb, which she hardly seemed to touch, a more delightful vision. I saw her just above the horizon, decorating and cheering the elevated sphere she just began to move in,—glittering like the morningstar, full of life, and splendor, and joy. Oh! What a revolution! and what an heart must I have, to contemplate without emotion that elevation and that fall! Little did I dream when she added titles of veneration to those of enthusiastic, distant, respectful love, that she should ever be obliged to carry the sharp antidote against disgrace concealed in that bosom; little did I dream that I should have lived to see such disasters fallen upon her in a nation of gallant men, in a nation of men of honour and of cavaliers. I thought ten thousand swords must have leaped from their scabbards to avenge even a look that threatened her with insult.—But the age of chivalry is gone.—That of sophisters, œconomists, and calculators, has succeeded; and the glory of Europe is extinguished for ever. Never, never more, shall we behold that generous loyalty to rank and sex, that proud submission, that dignified obedience, that subordination of the heart, which kept alive, even in servitude itself, the spirit of an exalted freedom. The unbought grace of life, the cheap defence of nations, the nurse of manly sentiment and heroic enterprize is gone! It is gone, that sensibility of principle, that chastity of honour, which felt a stain like a wound, which inspired courage whilst it mitigated ferocity, which ennobled whatever it touched, and under which vice itself lost half its evil, by losing all its grossness.

This mixed system of opinion and sentiment had its origin in the ancient chivalry; and the principle, though varied in its appearance by the varying state of human affairs, subsisted and influenced through a long succession of generations, even to the time we live in. If it should ever be totally extinguished, the loss I fear will be great. It is this which has given its character to modern Europe. It is this which has distinguished it under all its forms of government, and distinguished it to its advantage, from the states of Asia, and possibly from those states which flourished in the most brilliant periods of the antique world. It was this, which, without confounding ranks, had produced a noble equality, and handed it down through all the gradations of social life. It was this opinion which mitigated kings into companions, and raised private men to be fellows with kings. Without force, or opposition, it subdued the fierceness of pride and power; it obliged sovereigns to submit to the soft collar of social esteem, compelled stern authority to submit to elegance, and gave a domination vanquisher of laws, to be subdued by manners.

But now all is to be changed. All the pleasing illusions, which made power gentle, and obedience liberal, which harmonized the different shades of life, and which, by a bland assimilation, incorporated into politics the sentiments which beautify and soften private society, are to be dissolved by this new conquering empire of light and reason. All the decent drapery of life is to be rudely torn off. All the super-added ideas, furnished from the wardrobe of a moral imagination, which the heart owns, and the understanding ratifies, as necessary to cover the defects of our naked shivering nature, and to raise it to dignity in our own estimation, are to be exploded as a ridiculous, absurd, and antiquated fashion.

On this scheme of things, a king is but a man; a queen is but a woman; a woman is but an animal; and an animal not of the highest order. All homage paid to the sex in general as such, and without distinct views, is to be regarded as romance and folly. Regicide, and parricide, and sacrilege, are but fictions of superstition corrupting jurisprudence by destroying its simplicity. The murder of a king, or a queen, or a bishop, or a father, are only common homicide; and if the people are by any chance, or in any way gainers by it, a sort of homicide much the most pardonable, and into which we ought not to make too severe a scrutiny.

On the scheme of this barbarous philosophy, which is the offspring of cold hearts and muddy understandings, and which is as void of solid wisdom, as it is destitute of all taste and elegance, laws are to be supported only by their own terrors, and by the concern, which each individual may find in them, from his own private speculations, or can spare to them from his own private interests. In the groves of *their* academy, at the end of every vista, you see nothing but the gallows. Nothing is left which engages the affections on the part of the commonwealth. On the principles of this mechanic philosophy, our institutions can never be embodied, if I may use the expression, in persons; so as to create in us love, veneration, admiration, or attachment. But that sort of reason which banishes the affections is incapable of filling their place. These public affections, combined with manners, are required sometimes as supplements, sometimes as correctives, always as aids to law. . . .

Thanks to our sullen resistance to innovation, thanks to the cold sluggishness of our national character, we still bear the stamp of our forefathers. We have not (as I conceive) lost the generosity and dignity of thinking of the fourteenth century; nor as yet have we subtilized ourselves into savages. We are not the converts of Rousseau; we are not the disciples of Voltaire; Helvetius has made no progress amongst us. Atheists are not our preachers; madmen are not our lawgivers. We know that *we* have made no discoveries; and we think that no discoveries are to be made, in morality; nor many in the great principles of government, nor in the ideas of liberty, which were understood long before we were born, altogether as well as they will be after the grave has heaped its mould upon our presumption, and the silent tomb shall have imposed its law on our pert loquacity. . . .

You see, Sir, that in this enlightened age I am bold enough to confess, that we are generally men of untaught feelings; that instead of casting away all our old prejudices, we cherish them to a very considerable degree, and, to take more shame to ourselves, we cherish them because they are prejudices; and the longer they have lasted, and the more generally they have prevailed, the more we cherish them. We are afraid to put men to live and trade each on his own private stock of reason; because we suspect that this stock in each man is small, and that the individuals would do better to avail themselves of the general bank and capital of nations, and of ages. Many of our men of speculation, instead of exploding general prejudices, employ their sagacity to discover the latent wisdom which prevails in them. If they find what they seek, and they seldom fail, they think it more wise to continue the prejudice, with the reason involved, than to cast away the coat of prejudice, and to leave nothing but the naked reason; because prejudice, with its reason, has a motive to give action to that reason, and an affection which will give it permanence. Prejudice is of ready application in the emergency; it previously engages the mind in a steady course of wisdom and virtue, and does not leave the man hesitating in the moment of decision, skeptical, puzzled, and unresolved. Prejudice renders a man's virtue his habit; and not a series of unconnected acts. Through just prejudice, his duty becomes a part of his nature.

But one of the first and most leading principles on which the commonwealth and the laws are consecrated, is lest the temporary possessors and life-renters in it, unmindful of what they have received from their ancestors, or of what is due to their posterity, should act as if they were the entire masters; that they should not think it amongst their rights to cut off the entail, or commit waste on the inheritance, by destroying at their pleasure the whole original fabric of their society; hazarding to leave to those who come after them, a ruin instead of an habitation— and teaching these successors as little to respect their contrivances, as they had themselves respected the institutions of their forefathers. By this unprincipled facility of changing the state as often, and as much, and in as many ways as there are floating fancies or fashions, the whole chain and continuity of the commonwealth would be broken. No one generation could link with the other. Men would become little better than the flies of a summer. . . .

[The Social Contract]

Society is indeed a contract. Subordinate contracts for objects of mere occasional interest may be dissolved at pleasure—but the state ought not to be considered as nothing better than a partnership agreement in a trade of pepper and coffee, calico or tobacco, or some other such low concern, to be taken up for a little temporary interest, and to be dissolved by the fancy of the parties. It is to be looked on with other reverence; because it is not a partnership in things subservient only to the gross animal existence of a temporary and perishable nature. It is a partnership in all science; a partnership in all art; a partnership in every virtue, and in all perfection. As the ends of such a partnership cannot be obtained in many generations, it becomes a partnership not only between those who are living, but between those who are living, those who are dead, and those who are to be born. Each contract of each particular state is but a clause in the great primaeval contract of eternal society, linking the lower with the higher natures, connecting the visible and invisible world, according to a fixed compact sanctioned by the inviolable oath which holds all physical and all moral natures, each in their appointed place. This law is not subject to the will of those, who by an obligation above them, and infinitely superior, are bound to submit their will to that law. The municipal corporations of that universal kingdom are not morally at liberty at their pleasure, and on their speculations of a contingent improvement, wholly to separate and tear asunder the bands of their subordinate community, and to dissolve it into an unsocial, uncivil, unconnected chaos of elementary principles. It is the first and supreme necessity only, a necessity that is not chosen but chooses, a necessity paramount to deliberation, that admits no discussion, and demands no evidence, which alone can justify a resort to anarchy. This necessity is no exception to the rule; because this necessity itself is a part too of that moral and physical disposition of things to which man must be obedient by consent or force; but if that which is only submission to necessity should be made the object of choice, the law is broken, nature is disobeyed, and the rebellious are outlawed, cast forth, and exiled, from this world of reason, and order, and peace, and virtue, and fruitful penitence, into the antagonist world of madness, discord, vice, confusion, and unavailing sorrow. . . .

[Prescription]

With the national assembly of France, possession is nothing; law and usage are nothing. I see the national assembly openly reprobate the doctrine of prescription, which one of the greatest of their own lawyers tells us, with great truth, is a part of the law of nature. He tells us, that the positive ascertainment of its limits, and its security from invasion, were among the causes for which civil society itself has been instituted. If prescription be once shaken, no species of property is secure, when it once becomes an object large enough to tempt the cupidity of indigent power. I see a practice perfectly correspondent to their contempt of this great fundamental part of natural law. I see the confiscators begin with bishops, and chapters, and monasteries; but I do not see them end there. I see the princes of the blood, who, by the oldest usages of that kingdom, held large landed estates (hardly with the compliment of a debate), deprived of their possessions, and in lieu of their stable independent property, reduced to the hope of some precarious, charitable pension, at the pleasure of an assembly, which of course will pay little regard to the rights of pensioners at pleasure, when it despises those of legal proprietors. Flushed with the insolence of their first inglorious victories, and pressed by the distresses caused by their lust of unhallowed lucre, disappointed but not discouraged, they have at length ventured completely to subvert all property of all descriptions throughout the extent of a great kingdom. They have compelled all men, in all transactions of commerce, in the disposal of lands, in civil dealing, and through the whole communion of life, to accept as perfect payment and good and lawful tender, the symbols of their speculations on a projected sale of their plunder. What vestiges of liberty or property have they left? The tenant-right of a cabbage-garden, a year's interest in a hovel, the good-will of an alehouse, or a baker's shop, the very shadow of a constructive property, are more ceremoniously treated in our parliament than with you the oldest and most valuable landed possessions, in the hands of the most respectable personages, or than the whole body of the monied and commercial interest of your country. We entertain an high opinion of the legislative authority; but we have never dreamt that parliaments had any right whatever to violate property, to overrule prescription, or to force a currency of their own fiction in the place of that which is real, and recognized by the law of nations. But you, who began with refusing to submit to the most moderate restraints, have ended by establishing an unheard of despotism. I find the ground upon which your confiscators go is this; that indeed their proceedings could not be supported in a court of justice; but that the rules of prescription cannot bind a legislative assembly. So that this legislative assembly of a free nation sits, not for the security, but for the destruction of property, and not of property only, but of every rule and maxim which can give it stability, and of those instruments which can alone give it circulation.

10

Irving Kristol

"The Neoconservative Persuasion: *What it was, and what it is*" (2003)

Irving Kristol (b. 1920) is a prominent voice in the neoconservative movement in America. Since 1965, he has been the editor, with Nathan Glazer, of The Public Interest. *He is the author of numerous books, among them* Two Cheers for Capitalism *(1978),* Reflections of a Neoconservative *(1983); and* Neoconservatism: The Autobiography of an Idea *(1995). In 2002 Kristol was awarded the Presidential Medal of Freedom by President George W. Bush.*

"[President Bush is] an engaging person, but I think for some reason he's been captured by the neoconservatives around him."
Howard Dean, *U.S. News & World Report,* August 11, 2003

WHAT EXACTLY IS neoconservatism? Journalists, and now even presidential candidates, speak with an enviable confidence on who or what is "neoconservative," and seem to assume the meaning is fully revealed in the name. Those of us who are designated as "neocons" are amused, flattered, or dismissive, depending on the context. It is reasonable to wonder: Is there any "there" there?

Even I, frequently referred to as the "godfather" of all those neocons, have had my moments of wonderment. A few years ago I said (and, alas, wrote) that neoconservatism had had its own distinctive qualities in its early years, but by now had been absorbed into the mainstream of American conservatism. I was wrong, and the reason I was wrong is that, ever since its origin among disillusioned liberal

Source: Irving Kristol, "The Neoconservative Persuasion: *What it was, and what it is,*" *The Weekly Standard* 8, no. 47 (August 2003): 23–25.

intellectuals in the 1970s, what we call neoconservatism has been one of those intellectual undercurrents that surface only intermittently. It is not a "movement," as the conspiratorial critics would have it. Neoconservatism is what the late historian of Jacksonian America, Marvin Meyers, called a "persuasion," one that manifests itself over time, but erratically, and one whose meaning we clearly glimpse only in retrospect.

Viewed in this way, one can say that the historical task and political purpose of neoconservatism would seem to be this: to convert the Republican party, and American conservatism in general, against their respective wills, into a new kind of conservative politics suitable to governing a modern democracy. That this new conservative politics is distinctly American is beyond doubt. There is nothing like neoconservatism in Europe, and most European conservatives are highly skeptical of its legitimacy. The fact that conservatism in the United States is so much healthier than in Europe, so much more politically effective, surely has something to do with the existence of neoconservatism. But Europeans, who think it absurd to look to the United States for lessons in political innovation, resolutely refuse to consider this possibility.

Neoconservatism is the first variant of American conservatism in the past century that is in the "American grain." It is hopeful, not lugubrious; forward-looking, not nostalgic; and its general tone is cheerful, not grim or dyspeptic. Its 20th-century heroes tend to be TR, FDR, and Ronald Reagan. Such Republican and conservative worthies as Calvin Coolidge, Herbert Hoover, Dwight Eisenhower, and Barry Goldwater are politely overlooked. Of course, those worthies are in no way overlooked by a large, probably the largest, segment of the Republican party, with the result that most Republican politicians know nothing and could not care less about neoconservatism. Nevertheless, they cannot be blind to the fact that neoconservative policies, reaching out beyond the traditional political and financial base, have helped make the very idea of political conservatism more acceptable to a majority of American voters. Nor has it passed official notice that it is the neoconservative public policies, not the traditional Republican ones, that result in popular Republican presidencies.

One of these policies, most visible and controversial, is cutting tax rates in order to stimulate steady economic growth. This policy was not invented by neocons, and it was not the particularities of tax cuts that interested them, but rather the steady focus on economic growth. Neocons are familiar with intellectual history and aware that it is only in the last two centuries that democracy has become a respectable option among political thinkers. In earlier times, democracy meant an inherently turbulent political regime, with the "have-nots" and the "haves" engaged in a perpetual and utterly destructive class struggle. It was only the prospect of economic growth in which everyone prospered, if not equally or simultaneously, that gave modern democracies their legitimacy and durability.

The cost of this emphasis on economic growth has been an attitude toward public finance that is far less risk averse than is the case among more traditional conservatives. Neocons would prefer not to have large budget deficits, but it is in the nature of democracy—because it seems to be in the nature of human nature—that political demagogy will frequently result in economic recklessness, so that one sometimes must shoulder budgetary deficits as the cost (temporary, one hopes) of pursuing economic growth. It is a basic assumption of neoconservatism that, as a consequence of the spread of affluence among all classes, a property-owning and taxpaying population will, in time, become less vulnerable to egalitarian illusions and demagogic appeals and more sensible about the fundamentals of economic reckoning.

This leads to the issue of the role of the state. Neocons do not like the concentration of services in the welfare state and are happy to study alternative ways of delivering these services. But they are impatient with the Hayekian notion that we are on "the road to serfdom." Neocons do not feel that kind of alarm or anxiety about the growth of the state in the past century, seeing it as natural, indeed inevitable. Because they tend to be more interested in history than economics or sociology, they know that the 19th-century idea, so neatly propounded by Herbert Spencer in his *The Man Versus the State,* was a historical eccentricity. People have always preferred strong government to weak government, although they certainly have no liking for anything that smacks of overly intrusive government. Neocons feel at home in today's America to a degree that more traditional conservatives do not. Though they find much to be critical about, they tend to seek intellectual guidance in the democratic wisdom of Tocqueville, rather than in the Tory nostalgia of say, Russell Kirk.

But it is only to a degree that neocons are comfortable in modern America. The steady decline in our democratic culture, sinking to new levels of vulgarity, does unite neocons with traditional conservatives—though not with those libertarian conservatives who are conservative in economics but unmindful of the culture. The upshot is a quite unexpected alliance between neocons, who include a fair proportion of secular intellectuals, and religious traditionalists. They are united on issues concerning the quality of education, the relations of church and state, the regulation of pornography, and the like, all of which they regard as proper candidates for the government's attention. And since the Republican party now has a substantial base among the religious, this gives neocons a certain influence and even power. Because religious conservatism is so feeble in Europe, the neoconservative potential there is correspondingly weak.

And then, of course, there is foreign policy, the area of American politics where neoconservatism has recently been the focus of media attention. This is surprising since there is no set of neoconservative beliefs concerning foreign policy, only a set of attitudes derived from historical experience. (The favorite neoconservative text on foreign affairs, thanks to professors Leo Strauss of Chicago and Donald Kagan of Yale, is Thucydides on the Peloponnesian War.) These attitudes can be summarized in the following "theses" (as a Marxist would say): First, patriotism is a natural and healthy sentiment and should be encouraged by both private and public institutions. Precisely because we are a nation of immigrants, this is a powerful American sentiment. Second, world government is a terrible idea since it can lead to world tyranny. International institutions that point to an ultimate world government should be regarded with the deepest suspicion. Third, statesmen should, above all, have the ability to distinguish friends from enemies. This is not as easy as it sounds, as the history of the Cold War revealed. The number of intelligent men who could not count the Soviet Union as an enemy, even though this was its own self-definition, was absolutely astonishing.

Finally, for a great power, the "national interest" is not a geographical term, except for fairly prosaic matters like trade and environmental regulation. A smaller nation might appropriately feel that its national interest begins and ends at its borders, so that its foreign policy is almost always in a defensive mode. A larger nation has more extensive interests. And large nations, whose identity is ideological, like the Soviet Union of yesteryear and the United States of today, inevitably have ideological interests in addition to more material concerns. Barring extraordinary events, the United States will always feel obliged to defend, if possible, a democratic nation under attack from nondemocratic forces, external or internal. That is why it was in our national interest to come to the defense of France and Britain in World War II. That is why we feel it necessary to defend Israel today, when its survival is threatened. No complicated geopolitical calculations of national interest are necessary.

Behind all this is a fact: the incredible military superiority of the United States vis-à-vis the nations of the rest of the world, in any imaginable combination. This superiority was planned by no one, and even today there are many Americans who are in denial. To a large extent, it all happened as a result of our bad luck. During the 50 years after World War II, while Europe was at peace and the Soviet Union largely relied on surrogates to do its fighting, the United States was involved in a whole series of wars: the Korean War, the Vietnam War, the Gulf War, the Kosovo conflict, the Afghan War, and the Iraq War. The result was that our military spending expanded more or less in line with our economic growth, while Europe's democracies cut back their military spending in favor of social welfare programs. The Soviet Union spent profusely but wastefully, so that its military collapsed along with its economy.

Suddenly, after two decades during which "imperial decline" and "imperial overstretch" were the academic and journalistic watchwords, the United States emerged as uniquely powerful. The "magic" of compound interest over half a century had its effect on our military budget, as did the cumulative scientific and technological research of our armed forces. With power come responsibilities, whether sought or not, whether welcome or not. And it is a fact that if you have the kind of power we now have, either you will find opportunities to use it, or the world will discover them for you.

The older, traditional elements in the Republican party have difficulty coming to terms with this new reality in foreign affairs, just as they cannot reconcile economic conservatism with social and cultural conservatism. But by one of those accidents historians ponder, our current president and his administration turn out to be quite at home in this new political environment, although it is clear they did not anticipate this role any more than their party as a whole did. As a result, neoconservatism began enjoying a second life, at a time when its obituaries were still being published.

11

Phyllis Schlafly

The Power of the Positive Woman (1977)

Phyllis Schlafly (b. 1924) is best known for her work as national chair of "Stop ERA." Under her leadership, the Equal Rights Amendment was identified with unisex toilets and women in combat, contributing to its eventual defeat. Schlafly continues to argue that feminism "is no gain for women, for children, for families, or for America." Her latest book on the subject is Feminist Fantasies *(2003), a series of essays on feminism in the media, the military, at work, and at home.* Ladies' Home Journal *recently recognized her as among the 100 most important women of the twentieth century.*

THE FIRST REQUIREMENT for the acquisition of power by the Positive Woman is to understand the differences between men and women. Your outlook on life, your faith, your behavior, your potential for fulfillment, all are determined by the parameters of your original premise. The Positive Woman starts with the assumption that the world is her oyster. She rejoices in the creative capability within her body and the power potential of her mind and spirit. She understands that men and women are different, and that those very differences provide the key to her success as a person and fulfillment as a woman.

The women's liberationist, on the other hand, is imprisoned by her own negative view of herself and of her place in the world around her. This view of women was most succinctly expressed in an advertisement designed by the principal women's liberationist organization, the National Organization for Women

(NOW), and run in many magazines and newspapers and as spot announce-ments on many television stations. The advertisement showed a darling curly-headed girl with the caption: "This healthy, normal baby has a handicap. She was born female."

This is the self-articulated dog-in-the-manger, chip-on-the-shoulder, funda-mental dogma of the women's liberation movement. Someone—it is not clear who, perhaps God, perhaps the "Establishment," perhaps a conspiracy of male chauvinist pigs—dealt women a foul blow by making them female. It becomes necessary, therefore, for women to agitate and demonstrate and hurl demands on society in order to wrest from an oppressive male-dominated social structure the status that has been wrongfully denied to women through the centuries.

By its very nature, therefore, the women's liberation movement precipitates a series of conflict situations—in the legislatures, in the courts, in the schools, in industry—with man targeted as the enemy. Confrontation replaces cooperation as the watchword of all relationships. Women and men become adversaries instead of partners.

The second dogma of the women's liberationists is that, of all the injustices perpetrated upon women through the centuries, the most oppressive is the cruel fact that women have babies and men do not. Within the confines of the women's liberationist ideology, therefore, the abolition of this overriding inequality of women becomes the primary goal. This goal must be achieved at any and all costs—to the woman herself, to the baby, to the family, and to society. Women must be made equal to men in their ability *not* to become pregnant and *not* to be expected to care for babies they may bring into the world.

This is why women's liberationists are compulsively involved in the drive to make abortion and child-care centers for all women, regardless of religion or income, both socially acceptable and government-financed. Former Congress-woman Bella Abzug has defined the goal: "to enforce the constitutional right of females to terminate pregnancies that they do not wish to continue."

If man is targeted as the enemy, and the ultimate goal of women's liberation is independence from men and the avoidance of pregnancy and its conse-quences, then lesbianism is logically the highest form in the ritual of women's liberation. Many, such as Kate Millett, come to this conclusion, although many others do not.

The Positive Woman will never travel that dead-end road. It is self-evident to the Positive Woman that the female body with its baby-producing organs was not designed by a conspiracy of men but by the Divine Architect of the human race. Those who think it is unfair that women have babies, whereas men cannot, will have to take up their complaint with God because no other power is capable of changing that fundamental fact. On some college campuses,

I have been assured that other methods of reproduction will be developed. But most of us must deal with the real world rather than with the imagination of dreamers.

Another feature of the woman's natural role is the obvious fact that women can breast-feed babies and men cannot. This functional role was not imposed by conspiratorial males seeking to burden women with confining chores, but must be recognized as part of the plan of the Divine Architect for the survival of the human race through the centuries and in the countries that know no pasteurization of milk or sterilization of bottles.

The Positive Woman looks upon her femaleness and her fertility as part of her purpose, her potential, and her power. She rejoices that she has a capability for creativity that men can never have.

The third basic dogma of the women's liberation movement is that there is no difference between male and female except the sex organs, and that all those physical, cognitive, and emotional differences you *think* are there, are merely the result of centuries of restraints imposed by a male-dominated society and sex-stereotyped schooling. The role imposed on women is, by definition, inferior, according to the women's liberationists.

The Positive Woman knows that, while there are some physical competitions in which women are better (and can command more money) than men, including those that put a premium on grace and beauty, such as figure skating, the superior physical strength of males over females in competitions of strength, speed, and short-term endurance is beyond rational dispute.

In the Olympic Games, women not only cannot win any medals in competition with men, the gulf between them is so great that they cannot even qualify for the contests with men. No amount of training from infancy can enable women to throw the discus as far as men, or to match men in pushups or in lifting weights. In track and field events, individual male records surpass those of women by 10 to 20 percent.

Female swimmers today are beating Johnny Weissmuller's records, but today's male swimmers are better still. Chris Evert can never win a tennis match against Jimmy Connors. If we removed lady's tees from golf courses, women would be out of the game. Putting women in football or wrestling matches can only be an exercise in laughs.

The Olympic Games, whose rules require strict verification to ascertain that no male enters a female contest and, with his masculine advantage, unfairly captures a woman's medal, formerly insisted on a visual inspection of the contestants' bodies. Science, however, has discovered that men and women are so innately different physically that their maleness/femaleness can be conclusively established by means of a simple skin test of fully clothed persons.

If there is *anyone* who should oppose enforced sex equality, it is the women athletes. Babe Didrickson, who played and defeated some of the great male athletes of her time, is unique in the history of sports.

If sex equality were enforced in professional sports, it would mean that men could enter the women's tournaments and win most of the money. Bobby Riggs has already threatened: "I think that men 55 years and over should be allowed to play women's tournaments—like the Virginia Slims. Everybody ought to know there's no sex after 55 anyway."

The Positive Woman remembers the essential validity of the old prayer: "Lord, give me the strength to change what I can change, the serenity to accept what I cannot change, and the wisdom to discern the difference." The women's liberationists are expending their time and energies erecting a make-believe world in which they hypothesize that *if* schooling were gender-free, and *if* the same money were spent on male and female sports programs, and *if* women were permitted to compete on equal terms, *then* they would prove themselves to be physically equal. Meanwhile, the Positive Woman has put the ineradicable physical differences into her mental computer, programmed her plan of action, and is already on the way to personal achievement.

Thus, while some militant women spend their time demanding more money for professional sports, ice skater Janet Lynn, a truly Positive Woman, quietly signed the most profitable financial contract in the history of women's athletics. It was not the strident demands of the women's liberationists that brought high prizes to women's tennis, but the discovery by sports promoters that beautiful female legs gracefully moving around the court made women's tennis a highly marketable television production to delight male audiences.

Many people thought that the remarkable filly named Ruffian would prove that a female race horse could compete equally with a male. Even with the handicap of extra weights placed on the male horse, the race was a disaster for the female. The gallant Ruffian gave her all in a noble effort to compete, but broke a leg in the race and, despite the immediate attention of top veterinarians, had to be put away.

Despite the claims of the women's liberation movement, there are countless physical differences between men and women. The female body is 50 to 60 percent water, the male 60 to 70 percent water; which explains why males can dilute alcohol better than women and delay its effect. The average woman is about 25 percent fatty tissue, while the male is 15 percent, making women more buoyant in water and able to swim with less effort. Males have a tendency to color blindness. Only 5 percent of persons who get gout are female. Boys are born bigger. Women live longer in most countries of the world, not only in the United States where we have a hard-driving competitive pace. Women excel in manual dexterity, verbal skills, and memory recall.

Arianna Stassinopoulos [Huffington] in her book *The Female Woman* has done a good job of spelling out the many specific physical differences that are so innate and so all-pervasive that

> even if Women's Lib was given a hundred, a thousand, ten thousand years in which to eradicate *all* the differences between the sexes, it would still be an impossible undertaking. . . .
>
> It is inconceivable that millions of years of evolutionary selection during a period of marked sexual division of labor have not left pronounced traces on the innate character of men and women. Aggressiveness, and mechanical and spatial skills, a sense of direction, and physical strength—all masculine characteristics—are the qualities essential for a hunter; even food gatherers need these same qualities for defense and exploration. The prolonged period of dependence of human children, the difficulty of carrying the peculiarly heavy and inert human baby—a much heavier, clumsier burden than the monkey infant and much less able to cling on for safety—meant that women could not both look after their children and be hunters and explorers. Early humans learned to take advantage of this period of dependence to transmit rules, knowledge and skills to their offspring—women needed to develop verbal skills, a talent for personal relationships, and a predilection for nurturing going even beyond the maternal instinct.

Does the physical advantage of men doom women to a life of servility and subservience? The Positive Woman knows that she has a complementary advantage which is at least as great—and, in the hands of a skillful woman, far greater. The Divine Architect who gave men a superior strength to lift weights also gave women a different kind of superior strength.

The women's liberationists and their dupes who try to tell each other that the sexual drive of men and women is really the same, and that it is only societal restraints that inhibit women from an equal desire, an equal enjoyment, and an equal freedom from the consequences, are doomed to frustration forever. It just isn't so, and pretending cannot make it so. The differences are not a woman's weakness but her strength.

Dr. Robert Collins, who has had ten year's experience in listening to and advising young women at a large eastern university, put his finger on the reason why casual "sexual activity" is such a cheat on women:

> A basic flaw in this new morality is the assumption that males and females are the same sexually. The simplicity of the male anatomy and its operation suggest that to a man, sex can be an activity apart from his whole being, a drive related to the organs themselves.
>
> In a woman, the complex internal organization, correlated with her other hormonal systems, indicates her sexuality must involve her total self. On the other hand, the man is orgasm-oriented with a drive that ignores most other aspects

of the relationship. The woman is almost totally different. She is engulfed in romanticism and tries to find and express her total feelings for her partner.

A study at a midwestern school shows that 80 percent of the women who had intercourse hoped to marry their partner. Only 12 percent of the men expected the same.

Women say that soft, warm promises and tender touches are delightful, but that the act itself usually leads to a "Is that all there is to it?" reaction. . . .

[A typical reaction is]: "It sure wasn't worth it. It was no fun at the time. I've been worried ever since. . . ."

The new morality is a fad. It ignores history, it denies the physical and mental composition of human beings, it is intolerant, exploitative, and is oriented toward intercourse, not love.

The new generation can brag all it wants about the new liberation of the new morality, but it is still the woman who is hurt the most. The new morality isn't just a "fad"—it is a cheat and a thief. It robs the woman of her virtue, her youth, her beauty, and her love—for nothing, just nothing. It has produced a generation of young women searching for their identity, bored with sexual freedom, and despondent from the loneliness of living a life without commitment. They have abandoned the old commandments, but they can't find any new rules that work.

The Positive Woman recognizes the fact that, when it comes to sex, women are simply not the equal of men. The sexual drive of men is much stronger than that of women. That is how the human race was designed in order that it might perpetuate itself. The other side of the coin is that it is easier for women to control their sexual appetites. A Positive Woman cannot defeat a man in a wrestling or boxing match, but she can motivate him, inspire him, encourage him, teach him, restrain him, reward him, and have power over him that he can never achieve over her with all his muscle. How or whether a Positive Woman uses her power is determined solely by the way she alone defines her goals and develops her skills.

The differences between men and women are also emotional and psychological. Without woman's innate maternal instinct, the human race would have died out centuries ago. There is nothing so helpless in all earthly life as the newborn infant. It will die within hours if not cared for. Even in the most primitive, uneducated societies, women have always cared for their newborn babies. They didn't need any schooling to teach them how. They didn't need any welfare workers to tell them it is their social obligation. Even in societies to whom such concepts as "ought," "social responsibility," and "compassion for the helpless" were unknown, mothers cared for their new babies.

Why? Because caring for a baby serves the natural maternal need of a woman. Although not nearly so total as the baby's need, the woman's need is nonetheless real.

The overriding psychological need of a woman is to love something alive. A baby fulfills this need in the lives of most women. If a baby is not available to fill that need, women search for a baby-substitute. This is the reason why women have traditionally gone into teaching and nursing careers. They are doing what comes naturally to the female psyche. The schoolchild or the patient of any age provides an outlet for a woman to express her natural maternal need.

This maternal need in women is the reason why mothers whose children have grown up and flown from the nest are sometimes cut loose from their psychological moorings. The maternal need in women can show itself in love for grandchildren, nieces, nephews, or even neighbors' children. The maternal need in some women has even manifested itself in an extraordinary affection lavished on a dog, a cat, or a parakeet.

This is not to say that every woman must have a baby in order to be fulfilled. But it is to say that fulfillment for most women involves expressing their natural maternal urge by loving and caring for someone.

The women's liberation movement complains that traditional stereotyped roles assume that women are "passive" and that men are "aggressive." The anomaly is that a woman's most fundamental emotional need is not passive at all, but active. A woman naturally seeks to love affirmatively and to show that love in an active way by caring for the object of her affections.

The Positive Woman finds somebody on whom she can lavish her maternal love so that it doesn't well up inside her and cause psychological frustrations. Surely no woman is so isolated by geography or insulated by spirit that she cannot find someone worthy of her maternal love. All persons, men and women, gain by sharing something of themselves with their fellow humans, but women profit most of all because it is part of their very nature.

One of the strangest quirks of women's liberationists is their complaint that societal restraints prevent men from crying in public or showing their emotions, but permit women to do so, and that therefore we should "liberate" men to enable them, too, to cry in public. The public display of fear, sorrow, anger, and irritation reveals a lack of self-discipline that should be avoided by the Positive Woman just as much as by the Positive Man. Maternal love, however, is not a weakness but a manifestation of strength and service, and it should be nurtured by the Positive Woman.

Most women's organizations, recognizing the preference of most women to avoid hard-driving competition, handle the matter of succession of officers by the device of a nominating committee. This eliminates the unpleasantness and the tension of a competitive confrontation every year or two. Many women's organizations customarily use a prayer attributed to Mary, Queen of Scots, which is an excellent analysis by a woman of women's faults:

Keep us, O God, from pettiness; let us be large in thought, in word, in deed. Let us be done with fault-finding and leave off self-seeking. . . . Grant that we may realize it is the little things that create differences, that in the big things of life we are at one.

Another silliness of the women's liberationists is their frenetic desire to force all women to accept the title *Ms.* in place of *Miss* or *Mrs.* If Gloria Steinem and Betty Friedan want to call themselves *Ms.* in order to conceal their marital status, their wishes should be respected.

But that doesn't satisfy the women's liberationists. They want all women to be compelled to use *Ms.* whether they like it or not. The women's liberation movement has been waging a persistent campaign to browbeat the media into using *Ms.* as the standard title for all women. The women's liberationists have already succeeded in getting the Department of Health, Education, and Welfare to forbid schools and colleges from identifying women students as *Miss* or *Mrs.*

All polls show that the majority of women do not care to be called *Ms.* A Roper poll indicated that 81 percent of the women questioned said they prefer *Miss* or *Mrs.* Most married women feel they worked hard for the *r* in their names, and they don't care to be gratuitously deprived of it. Most single women don't care to have their name changed to an unfamiliar title that at best conveys overtones of feminist ideology and is polemical in meaning, and at worst connotes misery instead of joy. Thus, Kate Smith, a very Positive Woman, proudly proclaimed on television that she is "Miss Kate Smith, not Ms." Like other Positive Women, she has been succeeding while negative women have been complaining.

Finally, women are different from men in dealing with the fundamentals of life itself. Men are philosophers, women are practical, and 'twas ever thus. Men may philosophize about how life began and where we are heading; women are concerned about feeding the kids today. No woman would ever, as Karl Marx did, spend years reading political philosophy in the British Museum while her child starved to death. Women don't take naturally to a search for the intangible and the abstract. The Positive Woman knows who she is and where she is going, and she will reach her goal because the longest journey starts with a very practical first step.

Amaury de Riencourt, in his book *Sex and Power in History,* shows that a successful society depends on a delicate balancing of different male and female factors, and that the women's liberation movement, which promotes unisexual values and androgyny, contains within it "a social and cultural death wish and the end of the civilization that endorses it."

One of the two scholarly works dealing with woman's role, *Sex and Power in History,* synthesizes research from a variety of disciplines—sociology, biology, history, anthropology, religion, philosophy, and psychology. De Reincourt traces distinguishable types of women in different periods in history, from prehistoric to modern times. The "liberated" Roman matron, who is most similar to the present-day feminist, helped bring about the fall of Rome through her unnatural emulation of masculine qualities, which resulted in large-scale breakdown of the family and ultimately of the empire.

De Riencourt examines the fundamental, inherent differences between men and women. He argues that man is the more aggressive, rational, mentally creative, analytical-minded sex because of his early biological role as hunter and provider. Woman, on the other hand, represents stability, flexibility, reliance on intuition, and harmony with nature, stemming from her procreative function.

Where man is discursive, logical, abstract, or philosophical, woman tends to be emotional, personal, practical, or mystical. Each set of qualities is vital and complements the other. Among the many differences explained in de Riencourt's book are the following:

> Women tend more toward conformity than men—which is why they often excel in such disciplines as spelling and punctuation where there is only one correct answer, determined by social authority. Higher intellectual activities, however, require a mental independence and power of abstraction that they usually lack, not to mention a certain form of aggressive boldness of the imagination which can only exist in a sex that is basically aggressive for biological reasons.

> To sum up: The masculine proclivity in problem solving is analytical and categorical; the feminine, synthetic and contextual. . . . Deep down, man tends to focus on the object, on external results and achievements; woman focuses on subjective motives and feelings. If life can be compared to a play, man focuses on the theme and structure of the play, woman on the innermost feelings displayed by the actors.

De Riencourt provides impressive refutation of two of the basic errors of the women's liberation movement: (1) that there are no emotional or cognitive differences between the sexes, and (2) that women should strive to be like men.

A more colloquial way of expressing the de Riencourt conclusion that men are more analytical and women more personal and practical is in the different answers that one is likely to get to the question, "Where did you get that steak?" A man will reply, "At the corner market," or wherever he bought it. A woman will usually answer, "Why? What's the matter with it?"

An effort to eliminate the differences by social engineering or legislative or constitutional tinkering cannot succeed, which is fortunate, but social relationships and spiritual values can be ruptured in the attempt. Thus the role reversals being forced upon high school students, under which guidance counselors urge reluctant girls to take "shop" and boys to take "home economics," further confuse a generation already unsure about its identity. They are as wrong as efforts to make a left-handed child right-handed.

The Five Principles

When the women's liberationists enter the political arena to promote legislation and litigation in pursuit of their goals, their specific demands are based on five principles.

1. They demand that a "gender-free" rule be applied to every federal and state law, bureaucratic regulation, educational institution, and expenditure of public funds. Based on their dogma that there is no real difference between men and women (except in sex organs), they demand that males and females have identical treatment always. Thus, if fathers are not expected to stay home and care for their infant children, then neither should mothers be expected to do so; and, therefore, it becomes the duty of the government to provide kiddy-care centers to relieve mothers of that unfair and unequal burden.

The women's lib dogma demands that the courts treat sex as a "suspect" classification—just as race is now treated—so that no difference of treatment or separation between the sexes will ever be permitted, no matter how reasonable or how much it is desired by reasonable people.

The nonsense of these militant demands was illustrated by the Department of Health, Education, and Welfare (HEW) ruling in July 1976 that all public school "functions such as father-son or mother-daughter breakfasts" would be prohibited because this "would be subjecting students to separate treatment." It was announced that violations would lead to a cutoff of federal assistance or court action by the Justice Department.

When President Gerald Ford read this in the newspaper, he was described by his press secretary as being "quite irritated" and as saying that he could not believe that this was the intent of Congress in passing a law against sex discrimination in education. He telephoned HEW Secretary David Mathews and told him to suspend the ruling.

The National Organization for Women, however, immediately announced opposition to President Ford's action, claiming that such events (fashion shows, softball games, banquets, and breakfasts) are sex-discriminatory and must be eliminated. It is clear that a prohibition against your right to make any difference or separation between the sexes anytime anywhere is a primary goal of the women's liberation movement.

No sooner had the father-son, mother-daughter flap blown over than HEW embroiled itself in another controversy by a ruling that an after-school choir of

fifth and sixth grade boys violates the HEW regulation that bars single-sex choruses. The choir in Wethersfield, Connecticut, that precipitated the ruling had
been established for boys whose "voices haven't changed yet," and the purpose
was "to get boys interested in singing" at an early age so they would be willing
to join coed choruses later. Nevertheless, HEW found that such a boy's chorus is
by definition sex discriminatory.

The Positive Woman rejects the "gender-free" approach. She knows that there
are many differences between male and female and that we are entitled to have
our laws, regulations, schools, and courts reflect these differences and allow for
reasonable differences in treatment and separations of activities that reasonable
men and women want.

The Positive Woman also rejects the argument that sex discrimination should
be treated the same as race discrimination. There is vastly more difference
between a man and a woman than there is between a black and a white, and it is
nonsense to adopt a legal and bureaucratic attitude that pretends that those differences do not exist. Even the U.S. Supreme Court has, in recent and relevant
cases, upheld "reasonable" sex-based differences of treatment by legislatures and
by the military.

2. The women's lib legislative goals seek an irrational mandate of "equality"
at the expense of justice. The fact is that equality cannot always be equated with
justice, and may sometimes even be highly unjust. If we had absolutely equal
treatment in regard to taxes, then everyone would pay the same income tax, or
perhaps the same rate of income tax, regardless of the size of the income.

If we had absolutely equal treatment in regard to federal spending programs,
we would have to eliminate welfare, low-income housing benefits, food stamps,
government scholarships, and many other programs designed to benefit low-
income citizens. If we had absolutely equal treatment in regard to age, then
seventeen-year-olds, or even ten-year-olds, would be permitted to vote, and we
would have to eliminate Social Security unless all persons received the same benefits that only those over sixty-two receive now.

Our legislatures, our administrative departments, and our courts have always
had and still retain the discretion to make reasonable differences in treatment
based on age, income, or economic situation. The Positive Woman believes that
it makes no sense to deprive us of the ability to make reasonable distinctions
based on sex that reasonable men and women want.

3. The women's liberation movement demands that women be given the benefit of "reverse discrimination." The Positive Woman recognizes that this is mutually exclusive with the principle of equal opportunity for all. Reverse discrimination is based on the theory that "group rights" take precedence over individual
rights, and that "reverse discrimination" (variously called "preferential treatment,"

"remedial action," or "affirmative action") should be imposed in order to compensate some women today for alleged past discriminations against other women. The word "quotas" is usually avoided, but it amounts to the same thing.

The fallacy of reverse discrimination has been aptly exposed by Professor Sidney Hook. No one would argue, he wrote, that because many years ago blacks and women were denied the right to vote, we should now compensate by giving them an extra vote or two, or by barring white men from voting at all.

But that is substantially what the women's liberationists are demanding—and getting by federal court orders—in education, employment, and politics when they ask for "affirmative action" to remedy past discrimination.

The Positive Woman supports equal opportunity for individuals of both sexes, as well as of all faiths and races. She rejects the theories of reverse discrimination and "group rights." It does no good for the woman who may have been discriminated against twenty-five years ago to know that an unqualified woman today receives preferential treatment at the expense of a qualified man. Only the vindictive radical would support such a policy of revenge.

4. The women's liberation movement is based on the unproven theory that uniformity should replace diversity—or, in simpler language, the federalization of all remaining aspects of our life. The militant women demand that *all* educational institutions conform to federally determined rules about sex discrimination.

There is absolutely no evidence that HEW bureaucrats can do a better or fairer job of regulating our schools and colleges than local officials. Nor is there any evidence that individuals, or women, or society as a whole, would be better off under a uniform system enforced by the full power of the federal government than they would be under a free and competitive system, under local control, using diverse methods and regulations. It is hard to see why anyone would want to put more power into the hands of federal bureaucrats who cannot cope with the problems they already have.

The militant women demand the HEW regulations enforce a strict gender-free uniformity on all schools and colleges. Everything from sports to glee clubs must be coed, regardless of local customs or wishes. The militants deplore the differences from state to state in the laws governing marriage and divorce. Yet does anyone think our nation would be improved if we were made subject to a national divorce law devised by HEW?

The Positive Woman rejects the theory that Washington, D.C., is the fountainhead of all wisdom and professional skill. She supports the principle of leaving all possible control and discretion in the hands of local school and college officials and their elected boards.

5. The women's liberation movement pushes its proposals on the premise that everything must be neutral as between morality and immorality, and as between

the institution of the family and alternate lifestyles: for example, that homosexuals and lesbians should have just as much right to teach in the schools and to adopt children as anyone else; and that illegitimate babies and abortions by married or single mothers should be accepted as normal behavior for teachers—and funded by public money.

A good example of the rabid determination of the militant radicals to push every law and regulation to the far-out limit of moral neutrality is the HEW regulation on sex discrimination that implements the Education Amendments of 1972. Although the federal statute simply prohibits sex discrimination, the HEW regulation (1) requires that any medical benefit program administered by a school or college pay for abortions for married and unmarried students, (2) prohibits any school or college from refusing to employ or from firing an unmarried pregnant teacher or a woman who has had, or plans to have, an abortion, and (3) prohibits any school or college from refusing admission to any student who has had, or plans to have, an abortion. Abortion is referred to by the code words "termination of pregnancy."

This HEW regulation is illogical, immoral, and unauthorized by any reasonable reading of the 1972 Education Act. But the HEW regulation became federal law on 18 July 1975, after being signed by the president and accepted by Congress.

The Positive Woman believes that our educational institutions have not only the right, but the obligation, to set minimum standards of moral conduct at the local level. She believes that schools and colleges have no right to use our public money to promote conduct that is offensive to the religious and moral values of parents and taxpayers.

Neuterizing Society

A basic objective and tactic of the women's liberationists is to neuterize all laws, textbooks, and language in newspapers, radio, and television. Their friends in state legislatures are ordering computer printouts of all laws that use such "sexist" words as *man, woman, husband,* and *wife.* They are to be expunged and replaced with neuter equivalents. Some state legislators have acquiesced rather than face charges of "sexism." Others have rejected this effort and labeled it the silliness that it is.

The feminists look upon textbooks as a major weapon in their campaign to eliminate what they call our "sex-stereotyped society" and to restructure it into one that is sex-neutral from cradle to grave. Under liberationist demands, the Macmillan Publishing Company issued a booklet called *Guidelines for Creating Positive Sexual and Racial Images in Educational Materials.* Its purpose is to instruct authors in the use of sex-neutral language, concepts, and illustrations in order to conform to the new Macmillan censorship code. (The McGraw-Hill Book Company has issued a similar pamphlet, *Guidelines for Equal Treatment of the Sexes*.)

Henceforth, you may not say *mankind*, it should be *humanity*. You may not say *brotherhood*, it should be *amity*. *Manpower* must be replaced by *human energy*, *forefathers* should give way to *precursors*. *Chairman* and *salesman* are out; and "in" words are *chairperson* and *salesperson*.

You are forbidden to say "man the sailboat." The acceptable substitute is not given; presumably it is "person the sailboat." You must not say "the conscientious housekeeper dusts *her* furniture at least once a week"; you must say "*the* furniture," because otherwise you would imply that the housekeeper is a woman—and that would be intolerable. You may not say "the cat washed herself"; it must be "the cat washed itself," because it would be sexist to imply that the cat is female.

The section forbidding sexism in textbook illustrations is even more amusing. According to the Macmillan guidelines, males must be shown wearing aprons just as often as females. Father should be pictured doing household chores and nursing a sick child, mother working at her desk while dad clears the dining-room table, little girls reaching toward snakes instead of recoiling from them, boys crying or preening in front of a mirror, and fathers using hair spray.

Women must be shown participating actively "in exciting worthwhile pursuits," which, by apparent definition, do not include being a homemaker. The guidelines warn that books will not be tolerated that indicate that "homemaking is the true vocation for a woman."

The Macmillan guidelines reach the height of absurdity when they deliver a stern rebuke to the history book that refers to Sacajawea as "an amazing Shoshoni Indian woman" because she led the Lewis and Clark expedition through the Rockies "with a young baby strapped to her back." According to the Macmillan guidelines, the use of the word *amazing* is intolerable sexist propaganda that perpetuates "the myth of feminine fragility." It is a pity that our school children can no longer be told that Sacajawea was "amazing" because the historical fact is that her physical accomplishment was unique.

The Macmillan guidelines reserve their most stinging rebuke for the four-letter word *lady*, terming it "distasteful" specifically because it connotes "lady-like" behavior.

The Macmillan guidelines are not only a good source of laughs, but are a healthy exposure to the hypocrisy of the liberals who pilloried the West Virginia parents who tried to censor obnoxious four-letter words from their children's textbooks. It all depends on which four-letter words you want to censor.

Baby-care doctor Benjamin Spock was one of those whom the feminists targeted as obnoxious because of the alleged "sexism" in his bestselling baby books.

His principal offense was that, in advising mothers how to care for their babies, he repeatedly used the pronoun *he* instead of *she*. Obviously, it would be a semantic hurdle of significant magnitude to write a baby book and say "he or she" every time the author refers to the baby. Until women's liberationists became so vocal, normal mothers understood that *he* is used in the generic sense to mean babies of both sexes.

The feminists continued their campaign against Dr. Spock's "sexism" until they finally convinced him that modern liberated society should treat males and females exactly the same. In his latest book he eliminated "sexist" language. The only trouble was, Dr. Spock bought the whole bag of "liberation." He walked out on his faithful wife Jane, to whom he had been married for forty-eight years, and took up with a younger woman. Dr. Spock was truly "liberated" from traditional restraints.

It is no gain for women, for children, for families, or for America to propel us into a unisex society. Our strength is in our diversity, not in our sameness.

12

Allan Bloom

———·◦·———

"The Democratization of the University"
(1969)

*"The Democratization of the University" is an early essay by Allan Bloom
(1930–1992), author of the best-selling* The Closing of the American Mind
*(1987). The themes Bloom introduces here, which he developed further in that
later work—the threats egalitarianism and relativism pose to the liberal university and to a democratic society—are based on his experiences with student
protests in the 1960s at Cornell University. Bloom left Cornell to teach at the
University of Toronto; he later taught on the Committee on Social Thought at
the University of Chicago, where he remained until his death.*

"Do you too believe, as do the many, that certain young men are corrupted
by sophists, and that there are certain sophists who in a private capacity corrupt to an extent worth mentioning? Isn't it rather the very men who say this
who are the biggest sophists, who educate most perfectly and who turn out
young and old, men and women, just the way they want them to be?"

"But when do they do that?" he said.

"When many gathered together sit down in assemblies, courts, theaters,
army camps, or any other common meeting of a multitude, and, with a great
deal of uproar, blame some of the things said or done, and praise others, both
in excess, shouting and clapping; and, besides, the rocks and the very place
surrounding them echo and redouble the uproar of blame and praise. Now
in such circumstances, as the saying goes, what do you suppose is the state of
the young man's heart? Or what kind of private education will hold out for

Reprinted by permission of the Public Affairs Conference Center at Kenyon College.

him and not be swept away by such blame and praise and go, borne by the flood, wherever it tends so that he'll say the same things are noble and base as they do, practice what they practice, and be such as they are?"

"The necessity is great, Socrates," he said.

"And yet," I said, "we still haven't mentioned the greatest necessity."

"What?" he said.

"What these educators and sophists inflict in deed when they fail to persuade in speech. Or don't you know that they punish the man who's not persuaded with dishonor, fines and death? . . . So what other sophist or what sort of private speeches do you suppose will go counter to these and prevail? . . . Even the attempt is a great folly."[1]

THE MODERN UNIVERSITY was that great folly of an attempt to establish a center for reflection and education independent of the regime and the pervasive influence of its principles, free of the overwhelming effect of public opinion in its crude and subtle forms, devoted to the dispassionate quest for the important and comprehensive truths. It was to be an independent island within civil society, the sovereign Republic of Letters. It tried to disprove the Socratic contention that he who shares bed and board with the rulers, be they kings or peoples, would soon have to share their tastes and way of life, and that thus the thinker must separate himself in heart and mind from the currents of party passion in order to liberate himself from prejudice. The modern university has as its premises that free thought can exist in full view of the community unthreatened by the public passions and that it can be of service while preserving its integrity. Academic freedom was to protect scholars from the most obtrusive violations of their independence and was designed to draw them from private isolation into the public institutions; tenure is the most visible expression of that principle in the modern university.

Previously, it had been understood that democracies were in particular need of the enlightening function of the university, both because democracies necessarily have a large proportion of uneducated rulers and because public opinion reigns supreme in them without the counterpoising effect exercised by an aristocratic class which incorporates different principles and to the protection of which dissenters can repair. The presence of the university was the means of combining excellence with egalitarianism, reason with the consent of the governed. But precisely because it is so necessary to democracies, it is particularly threatened in nations where equality takes on the character of a religion and can call forth all the elements of fanaticism. In the first place this is so because democracy's fundamental beliefs are difficult to question; flattery of the regime and of the people at large is hard to avoid. Democratic sycophancy becomes a great temptation; one not resisted without difficulty and risk. And, in the second place, the university is, willy-nilly, in some sense aristocratic in both the conventional and natural senses of the term. It cannot, within broad limits, avoid being somewhat more accessible to the children of men of means than to the children of the poor, and it forms men of different tastes from those of the people at large who are, it is not to be forgotten, the real rulers. And the university is supposed to educate those who are more intelligent and to set up standards for their achievement which cannot be met by most men. This cannot but be irritating to democratic sensibilities.

Now the most obvious, the most comprehensive, the truest explanation of what is going on in our universities today is the triumph of a radical egalitarian view of democracy over the last remnants of the liberal university. This kind of egalitarianism insists that the goal of a democratic society is not equality of opportunity but factual equality; it comes equipped with all the doctrines which are necessary to persuade its adherents that such an equality is possible and that its not being actual is a result of vicious special interests; it will brook no vestige of differentiation in qualities of men. It would more willingly accept a totalitarian regime than a free one in which the advantages of money, position, education, and even talent are unevenly distributed. The liberal university with its concentration on a humane education and high standards had already been almost engulfed by the multiversity which is directed to the service of the community and responsive to the wishes of its constituency.

Now the universities have become the battleground of a struggle between liberal democracy and radical, or, one might say, totalitarian, egalitarianism. Therefore, it is not only the fact that universities are so much in the news that makes them central to any discussion of how democratic America is, it is also because they educate the best of our young, now more than half of them; because what they teach will ultimately determine the thought of the nation; and because the struggle going on in them concerns the interpretation of the meaning of our institutions and their goodness or badness. All this discussion takes place within the context of democracy, for both the defenders and critics of our regime accept the premise that democracy is the one legitimate regime, the only issue being whether the United States is sufficiently or truly a democracy.

The gradual politicization of the university can be seen partially by the extent of the concern expressed about it in society at large. Political men are constantly talking about universities and what they should or should not do. The universities have lost their neutrality as well as control of their destinies. Previously matters of curricula and student conduct were thought to be properly matters of internal university policy. Now the sense of the university's mission has been lost, and at the same time, what has been going on within it has succeeded in frightening and arousing the political community. The former secretary of Health, Education and Welfare, Robert Finch, has even gone so far as to make an attack

on the tenure system, the vital heart of academic freedom. Following professorial and student radicals, he accurately assessed the fact that it is the faculties
which are most likely to be recalcitrant in an attempt to make the universities
responsive to immediate concerns and that tenure protects them. He characterized faculties in much the same way as Marxists do the bourgeoisie in a capitalist system. They are, according to him, a privileged class protecting special and
private interests. He sees no principle embodied in their unusual status; the issues
are so clear, as he sees them, that only private vice could be the source of their
unwillingness to change with the times. We are overburdened by the pontifica-
tions of journalists as well as politicians, and professors, administrators, and students look to the newspapers and television for publicity and support. All of this
indicates the extent to which universities have become a part of the system of
public opinion.

But these are only symptoms. One must look within the universities themselves to see the full magnitude of what has happened. The primary fact is the
advent of student power, which, if it means anything, means an extreme democratization of the university. It is a democratization in several senses: it extends the
range of power to everyone present (things have gone so far that maintenance
personnel are to sit in some university legislative bodies); even the usually accepted
notions of age and stake in the community as standards for participation are considered discriminatory; and, most important of all, the special claim of competence is ignored or rejected. Professors, as well as students, frequently deny that
their learning gives them title to govern the university or to determine what is
important for it to represent. Everyone is listening to young people these days,
and they are talking.

The most stunning example of this about which I know is what happened at
Cornell. When black students carrying guns and thousands of white students
supporting them insisted that the faculty abandon the university's judicial system, the minimal condition of civil community within the university, and backed
up that insistence with threats, the faculty capitulated. Most of the faculty members who voted for capitulation argued that this was the will of the community,
what the students wanted. They had talked to many students, and the students
strongly desired that the faculty reverse itself. These professors could satisfy their
consciences by turning to public opinion. So democratic had they become that
they accepted a mob gathered in an atmosphere of violence as a true public. So
weak were their convictions about what a university is that they could find legitimacy only in public approval by their student constituency; their scholarly competence provided no source for independent judgment. Their souls had become
democratic and egalitarian to a degree far greater than that demanded by the
principles of the regime; the regime requires that every citizen abide by the duly

expressed will of the majority, not that the mind of man be determined by the taste of the community at large. In this instance there was a realization of Socrates' comic comparison of a democracy to the solemn deliberations of a group of children who are empowered to choose between the dietary prescriptions of a doctor and those of a pastry chef. Here, though, the doctors accepted the legitimacy of the tribunal.

In order to see the full dimensions of the situation and to recognize that the only real element in the changes occurring and the reforms demanded is radical egalitarianism, one must listen carefully to what is said. The key word is *relevance*. The whole of education must be guided by the standard of relevance. Now, of course, no curriculum was ever intended to be irrelevant; and even if scholars have lost the habit of justifying the importance of their disciplines, there is imbedded in each a serious argument for its study. Relevance is obviously a relative term, implying a standard by which relevant and irrelevant things are judged. Classical liberal education set as its standard the formation of a man possessing intellectual and moral virtue; relevant studies were those that tended to the perfection of the natural faculties, independent of the particular demands of time or place.

This is not the criterion of relevance referred to by today's students. Those students who are doing most of the talking and popularizing the notion of a relevance—that is, the leftist students—mean that education must be directed to the problems of war, poverty, and particularly, racism as they now present themselves, in other words, to the problems of contemporary democratic society. They not only argue that these are the fundamental issues to which the universities should address themselves, they also insist that certain kinds of solutions are self-evident. When they talk about justice they do not regard knowledge of justice as a problem; it is almost inconceivable to them that there can be a theoretical questioning of the principle of equality, let alone a practical doubt about it. The universities, as they are seen by these students, are meant to preach certain principles and to study their implementation. The movement is anti-intellectual and has the character of a democratic crusade. The theoretical man who stands outside of the movement, who urges that the university's primary function is the pursuit of clarity about such questions, is easily accused of complacency. Such idle lack of commitment can only be tolerated when we have brought peace, prosperity, and equality to the earth. Not even the richest country ever known can afford to devote any of its resources to the useless cultivation of the mind.

The relevant curriculum is to be promoted, watched over, and used by students. Student participation is the catchword in all talk of university reform. The goals to be achieved by student participation are never explicitly defined. It is enough to refer to the democratic view: everyone has the right to a vote. Faculties and administrations everywhere are bustling to "restructure" the universities with a view to greater student participation in everything; it has become an end in itself. To point out that students do not participate in disciplinary procedures, choice of faculty, establishment of curricula, and so forth is sufficient to demonstrate that decisions are illegitimate. There is almost no concern to show that such participation improves the quality of those decisions or contributes in any way to serious educational goals or even that it satisfies the students' wishes, let alone their real needs. I would venture to suggest that none of the moves toward student participation made in the last four or five years has done anything but generate new demands on their part and cause a deterioration of academic standards, an increase of demagogic teaching, and a loss of the sense of a university's purpose. There is a craze for change, but educators have no vision of the purposes of this change; they have nothing to offer but change itself. The direction is given to the drift by the prevailing winds of democratic extremism. Whether an educational institution can be treated as a political community or whether democracy needs any restraints seems never to be a question.

This is a democratic age and democracy is the special place of the young. According to Plato's analysis, the young in their turn exacerbate the weaknesses of democracy and impel it toward anarchy and ultimately tyranny. He describes our situation before the fact:

> As the teacher in such a situation is frightened of the pupils and fawns on them, so the students make light of their teachers, as well as their attendants. And, generally, the young copy their elders and compete with them in speeches and deeds while the old come down to the level of the young, imitating the young, they are overflowing with facility and charm, and that's so that they won't seem to be unpleasant or despotic.[2]

The young are powerful in democracies for many reasons. Estates are not easily transferable within them, so the authority of fathers is diminished. The hierarchies from which the young are excluded and which characterize other regimes are absent in a democracy. The older people lose their special privileges; and, in the atmosphere of liberty, the bodily pleasures, of which the young are more capable, are emancipated and have a higher status. Equality renders most claims to rule over the young illegitimate: age, wisdom, wealth, moral virtue, good family, are all banished, leaving only number, or consent, and force; and it is more difficult to exclude the young from ruling on the basis of these titles. All of this gives ground for believing that when the young become more demanding and the old more compliant, a new stage of democracy has been reached. The young are taking full advantage of their condition, making use of both their special claims to rule, consent and violence, however contradictory the two may appear to be.

In our democracy there is a further reason, of which Plato did not speak, for the dominance of the young. The radical political movements attempt to establish new kinds of societies, to find solutions to what older wisdom said was insoluble, to overcome necessity and master chance or, as Machiavelli put it, fortune.

> I judge that it is better to be impetuous than circumspect, because fortune is a woman; to keep her down it is necessary to beat her and thrash her. One sees that she lets herself be conquered by the impetuous rather than by those who proceed coldly. And, of course, as a woman she is always a friend to the young, because they are less circumspect, more brutal, and command her with greater audacity.[3]

Those who wish to ride the wave of the future know that the young are most skilled at it and do deference to them as such. Only those who have some conviction of the rightness of their principles can stand against the sea of change, and as we shall see, this conviction is what seems no longer to be generally possessed.

The democratic ruling body constituted by the students establishes, as do all ruling bodies, policies which further its interests. The substantive reforms, as I have said, have no basis other than that they conduce to the equality of all. Open admissions is the new cry. All citizens must go to college; everyone must be allowed into the halls of learning. And this means, in effect, that everyone must graduate from college, for it will soon be found that it is impossible to fail great masses of students in the age of student power. It immediately follows that standards must be lowered or, rather, utterly abandoned, no matter under what shining banner this change is presented. One of the first points of attack is grading; grades are said to degrade, to make students "grinds" rather than independently thoughtful, to make students part of the system, to encourage bad motivations for study. Although these allegations are not without merit, the real reason for the criticism is that grades make distinctions and indicate that some are better, at least as students, than others. Similarly, required courses and traditional majors begin to be abandoned. It would be hard to argue that these courses and programs of study were very well conceived, but they represented the tattered remnants of some thought about the natural articulation of the kinds of knowledge and what a man must know in order to be called minimally educated. A vacuum called freedom takes their place.

Each student is to be permitted to construct his own curriculum and discover his special genius or realize his unique self. The university can no longer provide guidance as to what is important and set standards based on a view of human perfection. It is blithely assumed that the student is capable of doing so for himself and that he has no need of sublimating discipline. In technical studies, of course, fixed courses of study will remain, because, for example, professors of engineering know what they must teach and what a student must know. But the best students in the better universities are no longer interested in a technical education; they are strongly inclined to what are very loosely called the humanities and the social sciences, and here the universities have abandoned their pedagogic function. It is a perfect solution for educators: in the hallowed name of freedom they are relieved of the responsibility of elaborating a curriculum. The true result of all of this is that the most vulgar and philistine things which proliferate in society at large will dominate the university, for the university cannot, as it should, counterpoise them. If the university does not provide alternatives to the prevalent, where else could the student find them?

One thing is certain: the serious study of classic literature will be sacrificed to the reforming spirit. It does not seem relevant to our students, and it is not to be expected that it would. The importance of classic literature, particularly the philosophic literature, could be recognized by young people only after long and exacting discipline. This is particularly true in America where nothing in the students' past or the world outside the university attests to the significance, or even the existence, of these rare and fine things. It was because the university insisted on them that they were preserved and that a university education could be understood to be a transforming experience rather than an exercise in self-expression or "doing one's own thing," no matter what it may happen to be.

The fate of classical languages is the model for what is happening in general. They are less and less studied, for they require an effort which seems pedantic and constraining, and they do not simply relate to the students' untutored, unguided experience. In the absence of knowledge of the languages, there can be no serious study of the texts written in them. In our current atmosphere everything has its place, and no one need feel uncomfortable or left out. At the end, whole new kinds of ephemeral study programs emerge, brought into being by the most popular issues of the day or the inclinations of groups of students.

Finally, the criticism is turned on the professors who not only are the protectors of the old ways but also are charged with being negligent of their students. The professors are understood to be primarily teachers who have lost their taste for teaching. The notion that a professor in a university is, in the first place, a scholar and that this must take most of his time is gradually becoming unintelligible. It used to be considered something of a vice for a man to be too much of a teacher because that would lead him into the temptation of adapting his thought to the demands of the market. He should not have to attract students but should provide a model for them of integrity and independence, of a higher motivation, whether they like it or not. The opportunity to be with a learned man should be considered a privilege and not a right, a privilege reserved for the competent and respectful. This was believed to be for the good not only of science but also of the student. But now it is everywhere deemed appropriate that the professor should teach more, be in closer contact with students, and accept their judgments as to his competence. It is not to be denied that a professor sometimes learns from students, that many professors are bad teachers and also bad scholars, and that often criticism can help him to right his ways in both respects. But to assert that students, as a matter of principle, have a right to judge the value of a professor or what he teaches is to convert the university into a market in which the sellers must please the buyers and the standard of value is determined by demand.

It was precisely to provide a shelter from the suffrages of the economic system and the popular will they represent that universities were founded. Now that the student right to judge has become dogma, the universities have become democracies in which the students are the constituencies to which the professors are responsible; the professors no longer look upward toward the gods but downward toward the people, or rather, *vox populi* has become *vox dei*. A whole new race of charlatans or pastry chefs has come into being who act as the tribunes of the people. One can expect a wholesale departure from the universities of professors of manly independence.

Thus we have gone very far down the road toward equality. It is somehow now held morally reprehensible to believe that equality is limited by natural differences in men's gifts and that a reasonable understanding of democracy is as a regime which allows men to develop those gifts without conventional or arbitrary hindrances. It is now doctrine that all men are factually equal, and if they do not meet high standards it is due to deprivation or the falseness of the standards. In the theory and practice of our universities we have come to that stage of democratic sentiment at which Tocqueville warned that men prefer equality to freedom, where they are willing to overturn the institutions and laws necessary to freedom in order to gain the sense of equality, where they level rather than raise, indifferent to the deprivations they impose on the superior and on the community at large.

I

What, then, is the future of liberal education in the face of these powerful tides? By *liberal* education I mean education for freedom, particularly the freedom of the mind, which consists primarily in the awareness of the most important human alternatives. Such an education is largely dedicated to the study of the deepest thinkers of the past, because their works constitute the body of learning which we must preserve in order to remain civilized and because anything new that is serious must be based on, and take account of, them. Without such a study a man's mind is almost necessarily a prisoner of the horizon of his particular time and place, and in a democracy that means of the most fundamental premises or prejudices of public opinion. This study has long had only frail support in the United States, and it is what is most threatened at this moment. It is the sole reason for the being of the university as anything more than an advanced high school for the training and detention of the young.

Addressing myself to this question four years ago, I wrote an article for this series assessing the condition of universities with respect to liberal education.[4] At that time the picture was bleak, but there was some basis for hope that in the interstices of the universities with all their bigness this small vital center might be maintained, not because it had any place guaranteed in the principle of the university but simply out of habit supported by the great wealth and diversity of the American university. That hope has all but disappeared. I saw then that the multiversity had no principle of organization, that it was directed to public usefulness rather than knowledge for its own sake, that the university had lost any sense of the unity of knowledge. It had become a place for specialists without any view of, or longing for, wholeness. The students were beginning to be aroused, and their stirrings seemed to express that longing for wholeness which was absent in the rest of the university. However, they too shared the belief of the specialists that the end of the university is public service, practice not theory. And the intensity of their demands, in sharp contrast to the easygoing, live-and-let-live disposition of the specialists, could easily result in a deterioration of the university's intellectual atmosphere. The liberal arts were likely to be crushed between the aimless diversity of the specialists and the spirit of political reform of the students.

I also saw that administrators were likely to become accomplices of the students for they have almost no education other than that in efficiency; without a clear view of the goals of a university they would, I knew, give in to the greatest pressures. But I based what hopes I had on my belief that the undergraduates did have a *feeling* of what was lacking in the specialist's education; and that their concern for living their lives well might be a wedge for the development of some liberal curricula which would respond to that concern and help to restore some limited sense of the unity of education in a rational and scholarly way. What I did not foresee was, on the one hand, the speed of the collapse of the administrators, and, on the other, the lack of conviction of the professors about the importance of what they were doing. The pieties of the professors about academic freedom and civility have turned out to be largely empty. They are ready to transform the university totally in terms of the untutored wishes of the students. The professors have proved to be so accommodating because they lack clarity, or because they too wish to share the students' idealism, or because they make the interested calculation that their specialties will be spared.

As for the students, I saw in them a potentiality for good or evil. They were freer in some senses than their parents. Necessities of life were better provided to them, and they lived in a world in which most principles of morals, religion, and politics were without great persuasiveness or binding force. This gave them the equipment for a reconsideration of such questions without external constraint. But they were lacking in rootedness, and their almost total lack of education in the tradition gave them no experience of greatness in thought or deed; no books meant much to them. There was that longing for wholeness, partly genuine, partly spurious (in order to have the exhilaration of the sense of depth). Properly controlled and guided, I believed, this longing could be the motor which would drive them to the effort requisite to learn.

But somewhere along the line this dangerous mixture has begun to fall out of balance; perhaps it is, and was always, inevitable, for there is not enough intellectual and moral substance available to discipline their aimless freedom. It was only a small minority of well-endowed students who could have been touched and finally trained, but they required protection and, at the least, an atmosphere of calm in which there is some respect for liberal studies. I suppose that this minority still remains, but all the honors go to a loud group of protestors furnished with easy and appealing ideologies as a substitute for thought; they either attract the really able students, because they appear to represent the only thing that has real force, or they reduce them to a confused silence. At first they seemed to be questing for guidance and leadership of a sort to respond to their sentiments. But, of course, they are easily dupes of movements, political and intellectual, which play to their tastes and are largely sham.

How can they judge, having neither experience nor knowledge? Every year their souls are thinner from want of spiritual nourishment; their openness becomes emptiness, the soil within incapable of sustaining any deep-rooted plant. They test the possible authorities to which they turn and find that none has the power to inspire them or resist them. The adult world makes itself contemptible, seeming to represent nothing itself, and, in what can only appear to the young to be cowardly flattery, praises the idealism and morality of those who have never had the chance to practice either. The great change comes when students no longer quest but teach, confident that they know the answers and are sufficient unto themselves. One of the ugliest spectacles is that of a young person who has no awe, who is shameless, who does not sense his imperfection, for it is the charm of youth to be potentiality striving to perfect itself, to be an essential incompleteness which may one day be truly complete. Adults are almost always imperfect; a youth is surely imperfect, but he at least offers the hope of development. But self-contempt is the basis of self-improvement, and this generation has nothing left in god or man against which to measure itself. Plato's description of the democratic man now seems most appropriate:

> . . . he doesn't admit it . . . if someone says that there are some pleasures belonging to fine and good desires and some belonging to bad desires. . . . He shakes his head at all this and says that all are alike and must be honored on an equal basis. . . . He lives along day by day, gratifying the desire that occurs to him, at one time drinking and listening to the flute, at another downing water and reducing; now practicing gymnastics, and again idling and neglecting everything; and sometimes spending his time as though he were occupied with philosophy. Often he engages in politics and jumping up, says and does whatever chances to come to him. . . .[5]

To Plato's account must be added a somewhat more sinister element: a rage at the emptiness of this life, and a desire to commit oneself to acts of revolutionary violence. Nonviolence has more or less silently been dropped from the creed of the New Left. College now means to more and more students a place where the young educate the nation and practice self-expression. It should not be surprising that the aristocratic aspiration which democracy frustrates should find its outlet on the radical left. Under the banner of equality these privileged students can lead and, with impunity, express their contempt for the people.

The universities were a fertile field for this development. A survey of the so-called liberal arts segments of the universities reveals that they are unarticulated heaps of departments, each teaching specialized disciplines which have presuppositions that are hardly discussed and are frequently incompatible with those of other disciplines. These disciplines have aggregated to the university at various times over the last one thousand years. There is little coherence to them nor does a view of life and the world evidently emerge from any separately or all together. The most important question has been forgotten, and even the means for a rational discussion of the unity of the university or the unity of life seem to have been lost. We seem to have to make do with tradition or whatever the winds of the day bring along. The state of academic philosophy, which should be the unifying discipline, indicates the severity of the problem. Today it is largely dominated by linguistic analysis which is merely a method for studying discourse rather than itself a source of discourse; it is a universal rule book for playing the game, but it does not tell us what the game is or play it itself. The natural sciences are a world unto themselves, dealing with what are presumably important problems, but they are unable to do anything about conveying their meaning within the total picture. The humanities have also become specialties, and it is rare to find a convincing explanation of their importance; the literatures studied are very rarely understood to be of vital significance for life today, and certainly they are undermined by the notion that science is the domain of reason and cannot understand the world of poetry. And the social sciences are slavishly imitating the natural sciences and are further hampered by their own principle, the fact-value distinction, from speaking about the moral and political good, which is what agitates the students.

Thus when students ask about the good life and the nature of our world, they are met by a deafening silence, for there are no men in the university whose competence enables them to respond to such questions. Many professors are answering the students but not on the basis of their competence; they are biologists or psychologists, or whatever else, speaking about what they have never studied, never adequately reflected on, and what is in no way connected with the things they can claim to know. The questions and pressures of students during these past six years have created a stir among academic men, but it has not caused them to undertake a serious reconsideration of the state of our learning or to look toward a philosophic and scholarly treatment of the issues raised. That just seems impossible; the whole is approached by way of feeling, by identification with popular movements, by "commitment" or "concern." The professors do not try to educate these longings; they try to share them without transforming them. What some social scientists proudly name "postbehavioralism" consists in nothing more than an attempt to keep the "value" hungry wolves from the door.

The university has proved itself incapable of teaching students about the good life because that is not a subject that any part of our universities even knows how to discuss; it belongs to no department nor any group of them added together. The education of our professors has been a specialized, technical one, with more or less old-style humanities mixed in but not really taken seriously or penetrating the special discipline. We have hardly a reminiscence of what was once the central business of universities. During and just after World War II, America was the beneficiary of many generally and humanely educated European scholars. Whatever the difficulties of the teachings many brought with them, these men had roots deep in the best thinkers and had the habit of justifying what they taught by them. One might have thought that the example of their learning and persons would fundamentally affect our universities. But the enormous expansion of higher education and the growth of the multiversity simply drowned their influence. Now, even in the unlikely event that it were to be thought that the philosophic, unifying, synoptic education needed to be reestablished, we would not be in a position to do so, for we no longer have the teachers who sufficiently know or care for the great tradition or are capable of working through the prejudices which seem to have rendered it meaningless and irrelevant.

Until the students became vocal, the university was characterized by easygoing indifference to larger purposes; each discipline followed its own internal development and the administration held the whole together. In the new era, scientists and humanists have come out to meet the students, praise them, agree to reorder "the priorities" and announce that the real purposes of the universities are those proposed by the political movements of the left. Thus a direction and purpose is again given to the university, and a community is established around this purpose. The only problem is whether that purpose is in any way consistent with the premises of science and scholarship.

Some professors become disturbed when they recognize that they must change their teaching in order to fit the movement and that the integrity of their discipline is threatened, that the passionate desires of the indignant are not consonant with the results of dispassionate rational inquiry. But such worried professors are more than counterbalanced by those professors who, excited by their new roles and liberated from what they now recognize to be the fragmented character of their existence, are willing to make their disciplines "relevant." The strength of this group is reinforced by the more or less active support of another group of professors, composed most particularly of natural scientists, who see no threat of a new Lysenkoism in their disciplines and who therefore are of the opinion they can have their cake and eat it. The fact that the interests of the professors can differ so much indicates how little of a real *intellectual* community there was and hence how partial the lives of the professors had become. In these circumstances, the university was an easy conquest for the first movement which exposed its lack of purpose or conviction and which proposed to restore the wholeness of life, the absence of which was even beginning to trouble the complacent professors. This movement usurped the position in the university which by right belonged to liberal education and in the process abolished the throne—occupied by weak and illegitimate pretenders—of the only legitimate ruler, philosophy.

II

Although the universities have had little to offer in the way of reflection or leadership in recent years, there are those who have jumped into the void created by the absence of philosophy and spoken to the general issues. There is not much thought reflected in what they say but there is the decay of a certain kind of thought here and its language is the only language which appeals to students. Although there have been few political movements which make such modest demands on the minds of their adherents or which have been so profoundly anti-intellectual, this one too is, of course, founded on a comprehensive view of things and is guided by that view. That view was not a product of the founders of the movement, and, because its followers are so unselfconscious, they are unaware of its sources and its implications. They are prisoners of certain European, particularly German, teachings which migrated to the United States and have been so successfully assimilated that they now seem native and part of common sense. We have adopted the language and the consequences of these teachings from the European professors who helped to bring them but have absorbed almost none of the learning which should accompany them. At all events, when thought out, these teachings lead to views and ways of life which are antithetical to this regime, and their dominance would surely undermine it. The German thought reflected in the current language of politics is the thought which is at the roots of both communism and fascism. Although the present political movements are democratic in that they propose to speak for all men, and they are egalitarian, they are based on a critique of liberal democracy and a hostility to it. The egalitarian movement has gathered into its bosom the teachings of men who were, to say the least, not friends of democracy and has used them to the furtherance of equality. The only sacrifice is free society as we know it. Prudent observers who know something of modern philosophy were not surprised to find that kind of irrationalism which is open to violence, tyranny, and racism emerging in the New Left. This was a necessity of its principles, as I shall try to show.

In the events that have occurred within the universities these past few years, the most sobering fact which has emerged is that neither in the things that are taught in them nor in the actions or reactions of those who are supposed to be responsible for their preservation is there much evidence of a conviction of the truth of the principles on which liberal democracy and the liberal university are founded. When such conviction is lacking, institutions and laws have lost their vitality and maintain themselves only by inertia; their replacement by new modes and orders is only a matter of time. This is not to suggest that by preaching the principles one can give them life; it is only meant as an observation. Somehow our principles are no longer persuasive. Our condition is beautifully characterized by a passage in Dostoyevsky's *Possessed:*

> Do you know that we are tremendously powerful already? Our party does not consist only of those who commit murder and arson, fire off pistols in the traditional way, or bite colonels. . . . Listen. I've reckoned them all up: a teacher who laughs with children at their God and at their cradle is on our side. The lawyer who defends an educated murderer because he is more cultured than his victims and could not help murdering them to get money is one of us. The schoolboys who murder a peasant for the sake of sensation are ours. The juries who acquit every criminal are ours. The prosecutor who trembles at a trial for fear he should not seem advanced enough is ours, ours. Among officials and literary men we have lots, lots, and they don't know it themselves. . . . Do you know how many we shall catch by little, ready-made ideas? When I left Russia, Littre's dictum that crime is insanity was all the rage; I came back and find that crime is no longer insanity, but simply common sense, almost a duty; anyway, a gallant protest.

That is a nihilist speaking, looking at the dissolution of the horizon within which his people had lived. The similarity of this situation to our own is no accident. The speaker is not referring essentially to the decay of the Czarist regime but of Western justice and morality and that is what we are experiencing in all liberal society today. Dostoyevsky was one of a small group of clairvoyant men in the last half of the nineteenth century who saw that somehow the old world was sick and dying, not meaning by the "old world" states or regimes, but the Biblical and classical morality which stood behind and made possible all states and regimes as we have known them or can imagine them. Nihilism was a response to the incipient death of all that had gone before, an expression of the meaninglessness of life without a compelling horizon of values, an attempt to destroy the lifeless body which remained after the vital center had died, and, perhaps, a hope of a new world, the outlines of which we cannot yet perceive but to which we must be dedicated for the sake of life. Civil societies are constituted by what they respect, by what men bow their heads before in reverence. When they no longer have anything before which they can bow, their world is near its end, and all the suppressed and lawless monsters within man reemerge. One might suggest that our New Left is a strange mixture of nihilism with respect to past and present and a naive faith in a future of democratic progress.

To put this more compellingly for Americans, the old liberalism is no longer of real concern to today's students. By the old liberalism I mean either the thought of the founding fathers who believed in the natural rights of man, established by reason and applicable to all men, and who constructed a nation dedicated to life, liberty, and the pursuit of happiness, or that of men like John Stuart Mill who believed in the open society dedicated to free speech and the self-determined private life. To the extent that Locke, the Declaration of Independence, *The Federalist,* or Mill are taught in the universities, they are historical matter and hardly anyone supposes that they can be believed or taken as guides for our lives. Without entering into the merits of that older liberal thought, it somehow no longer satisfies the soul for this generation of mankind and seems to be taking its place alongside the teachings which legitimized monarchy and aristocracy in the graveyard of history. Adults still refer to its principles, but when protests against war, poverty, or racism contradict them, those protests carry the day. It is not believed that liberal society insures substantive justice. And anyone whose "life style" is hostile to that of liberal society is considered justified or even heroic in "opting out" of it. What appeals to students now is the language of Marxism and existentialism; it seems to them to describe their situation.

It is a most striking fact that since Mill there has not been a single really influential book supporting liberal democratic society, and Mill cannot be compared in power or depth to men like Marx or Nietzsche, who were his critics. Liberal democracy has come to seem to be negative; it wishes to provide the conditions for freedom or the good life, but it does not give prescriptions for the use of freedom or define the good life. Its neutrality permits the dominance of any one of very many possible ways of life, some of them unattractive. Marx could plausibly assert that it was merely the condition for the existence of bourgeois capitalism, and that freedom meant primarily freedom to be a worker or an owner in this kind of system. And Nietzsche argued that liberal democracy was the home of "the last man," a being without heart or conviction, a shriveled manikin dedicated only to preservation and comfort. All of this criticism has become commonplace in the unremitting attack on white, complacent, middle-class America; it was vulgarized in America by men like [Erich] Fromm and [Herbert] Marcuse. The models for admiration are no longer statesmen but bohemians or revolutionaries.

But in the improbable wedding of Marx and Nietzsche which has recently been arranged, it is clear that Nietzsche is the dominant partner in spite of his rightist inclinations. Marx's egalitarianism, concentration on the poor, hatred of imperialism, and so forth, have been maintained, and leftists would still like to style themselves Marxists. But they no longer read the serious Marx; *Capital* seems both boring and irrelevant; the only Marx which is attractive is found in the early, so-called humanistic, writings, the study of which is of very recent origin. And the attack on reason, the use of terms like self, authenticity, and commitment, which are on everybody's lips, show plainly enough to what extent the Marxist teaching has been adulterated by a newer and more compelling kind of thought and a different understanding of the goals of politics. The New Left is not the Old Left, but is rather a result of the assimilation of the thought of Nietzsche and [Martin] Heidegger to that of the Old Left. However this may be, the prevalent discussion in the highest seats of learning is, to a greater or lesser degree, in the terms of postliberal thought, and this means that soon everyone will think in this way.

But it would perhaps be best to see the changes in our thought by looking to the recent history of the social sciences in America. The social sciences are the disciplines in which one would most expect the political and moral life of man to be discussed and are the sources of our understanding of them. For more than thirty years the social sciences have been dominated by the fact-value distinction. This distinction was made by German sociologists in the 1890s and most influentially propounded by Max Weber. It was imported to this country by sociologists and political scientists in the 1920s. This distinction was based on the assertion that no judgments of good and bad, no moral distinctions, could be grounded on reason, that they were subjective acts of the mind, preferences. The goals by which we guide our lives constitute a horizon by which we orient ourselves, but that horizon is an act of human creativity, not one of reason; no horizon can claim to be authoritative or demonstrable. Weber was persuaded of the truth of this analysis and attempted to salvage some possibility for the existence of science, of the reasonable quest for objective truth. Science was to be the noble endeavor of overcoming one's own values in the name of truth. The consequences of all this for our lives are, as Weber knew, quite far-reaching. Little attention was, however, given by American social scientists to assessing the effect of the distinction or, for that matter, to proving its validity. They accepted it and devoted themselves to the elaboration of an objective social science based on it; they were enchanted by the vision of a value-free social science which would be comparable to the natural sciences.

Although the science itself has not been very impressive, the success of the viewpoint has been breathtaking. Today even school children use the word *value* where another generation would have spoken of good and evil. The new social science had the effect of banishing good and bad, the discussion of the ends, from the domain of the sciences or reason. That was no longer a scholarly theme. The social scientists still had to live as men as well as scholars; but they were almost to a man liberal democrats; they accepted that as their value. And, unlike Weber, they used the fact-value distinction as a means of sparing themselves the necessity of being concerned about the status of their value. This was just fine until that value was challenged. It had lost its dignity; liberal democracy was just one value among many, and it had eroded from long neglect.

When the students wanted to implement certain policies and found apathy and indifference among adults, they, and their professorial camp followers, launched an attack on value-free social science, insisting that the social sciences should be primarily concerned with values. They accused the social scientists of being easygoing accomplices of the established order. The social scientists were indeed supporters of this order and were also unable to give an account of their reasons for being so. They simply believed that no sane man would question the superiority of liberal democracy to all available alternatives. Indeed, the fact-value distinction had become the last intellectual bastion of liberal democracy: in the absence of any demonstrable superiority of one value over another, that regime which tolerated all values might be understood to be preferable to one which did not. Moreover, since values are equal, they seem to be democratic. Every man has a right to his own values; no one need feel inferior. But the social scientists were utterly unprepared to resist a large group who insisted that its values had to be accepted no matter what others wanted. After all, why not?

It is to be noted that the students, as was to be expected, themselves adopted the fact-value distinction. They made no attempt to return to Marx, who thought that the true goals of human life could be determined by reason. They merely looked at the fact-value distinction and recognized that there was no intrinsic reason why we should concentrate on facts; that choice in itself is a value judgment. Science seems to have demonstrated that the most important thing—the right way of life is the most important thing—is not amenable to scientific, that is rational, treatment. This means men must abandon reason and turn to the establishment of values. This is precisely the analysis made by the profoundest European thinkers in the last century who took the value question seriously. The positing of values is, in this perspective, the most important human activity, and all the specialized activities are guided by the values posited. Thus the social scientists, men so dedicated to reason, were astonished to see their students, even their own children, denying reason, turning to Eastern religions, addicted to drugs, toying with violence, becoming a new breed or species unintelligible to rationalists. But in a sense they were going to the end of roads which their teachers and parents had opened but had themselves not traveled. Phenomena such as the use of drugs cannot be understood on mere sociological and psychological grounds. They are the consequences of the problems in our thought. If reason is superficial, then the irrational must be cultivated for the enrichment of life.

Much of what we recognize to be the most advanced contemporary opinion follows as a consequence from the fact-value distinction. Man is the value-producing being; that is the great discovery implicit in the distinction. If it is values which guide reason, then one must look beneath rational consciousness, the *ego,* to an unconscious, an *id,* a self, in order to find out what man is and discover a source for a meaningful life. This self cannot be understood by reason; it must be creative and hence beyond prediction; it must be listened to as an oracle. One cannot know what it will produce or whether what it produces is good or bad. It is the absolute beginning. With this we see the origin of our concentration on the self and its fulfillment. It is the modern substitute for the soul, which is a rationally ordered structure and is dependent on and subordinate to the order of the *cosmos.* The self has no order and it is dependent on nothing; it makes a *cosmos* out of the chaos that is really outside by imposing an order of values upon it.

In most discussion today one finds little elaboration of what the self is; rather the self is defined by what it is opposed to. The great illness of modern man, according to our critics, is alienation or other-directedness. This means to live according to other people's values, whether they are expressed in laws, schools, work, or whatever. A man who lives in that way is divorced from his self and is hollow. Education must not impose values on the student but let his own values develop and grow. In the absence of any objective standard for judging a man's words or deeds, the only test can be whether they are his own or another's whether he is a true self or alienated, inner-directed or other-directed, authentic or hypocritical. Authentic is really the word, the replacement for good. Many different ways of life can be authentic; the standard is only in the honesty or sincerity of the expression of that way of life. No matter how criminal or foul you may be, you are cleansed if you are sincere about it; hypocritical obedience to law is the human crime; Jean Gênet is superior by far to the bourgeois father and citizen.

How can one then be sure that one is sincere, that one's values are authentic? Such assurance cannot be achieved by comparison of one man's values with those of another. The only proof is in the intensity of one's *commitment,* in the ultimate case by being willing to die for one's value, in the assertion of one's value against the chaotic outside, bravely facing all risks. It is the strong-willed versus the weak-willed instead of the good versus the bad. We praise men now, not for the rightness of their cause, but because they care; the primary thing is not truth but concern. This, of course, puts a premium on fanaticism, not to speak of fakery.

At all events, man as the value-needing and value-producing animal leads directly to the view that the good society is one which allows selves to commit themselves to authentic values and to grow in terms of them. This is exactly the prescription of the New Left. It is, of course, in the absence of elaboration, empty. One has no idea what such a society would be like; it is utterly unprogrammatic. But it is just such a vision which allows for the most complete rejection and destruction of the present regime and the greatest self-indulgence without guilt; and to be committed to this vision gratifies moralistic vanity at the same time. It is the best of many possible worlds.

Nietzsche, who was the first to present a profound teaching of the self, understood it to be an aristocratic teaching, for true selves are rare. The kind of man who can create a horizon for a whole people and make his values theirs and thus ennoble their lives is extremely rare. This is a natural distinction among men, and democratic society, according to him, effaces this distinction. But, as is easy to see, this teaching, or a corruption of it, easily becomes grist for the mill for radical egalitarianism. Objective standards encourage distinctions of rank among men; each self is a standard unto itself, and there is no rational basis for comparison of one self with another. The self justifies the most extreme freedom, for there is nothing in nature to which the self is subservient; the self is the creator, the Biblical God possessed uniquely by everyone.

In politics, teachings tend to be transformed by what is most powerful in the regime and in turn transform the regime in the direction of its most dangerous tendencies. The corruption of a teaching which was intended to be noble is peculiarly revolting. Not content with understanding democratic citizens as self-regarding but decent men who try to live by laws they themselves set down for the good of the community, we have had to make them into gods to whom nothing can be compared. Every man must be understood to be creative, no matter how much the standards of art and taste have to be debauched in order to do so. Political restraint and moderation must give way to ugly fanaticism in order to give everyone the chance to be committed. The grossest indecencies are permitted in the name of sincerity. And the wisdom of the ages must be forgotten in order to avoid alienating a growing self.

All of this tends to intensify the conformism—the increasingly monolithic quality of life—which it is supposed to overcome; for in the absence of real goals to strive for, men are most likely to fall back into their animal sameness, into the common instincts in the satisfaction of which all men are alike. Real diversity is never the result of the concentration on diversity. And at the same time as we are likely to produce greater conformity, we do not stop to consider whether the *laissez aller* we encourage is consonant with civility or political justice. No one asks whether we have any right to be so hopeful that every healthy self will posit nice civil values for itself which are consonant with everyone else's self-realization. Is there any built-in assurance that the unrestrained growth of each individual will not encroach on the vital space of other individuals? Yet this is all that seems to be talked about; the situation is parallel to that in which Rousseau's rhetoric of compassion was used by every dry, self-serving French bureaucrat in the nineteenth century. One thing at least is certain: in all of this there is no concern for justifying or preserving those restraints which have been necessary to the life of every community ever known to man. If neither reason nor tradition can bring about consensus, then the force of the first man resourceful and committed enough must needs do so.

It cannot be doubted that the status of values is a most perplexed and difficult question. Great men have contributed to the present view of things. They must be studied carefully, and the alternatives to them must be equally considered. Reason can only be abandoned reasonably; without this serious examination the modern view becomes empty and dangerous nonsense. It is precisely in this context that the value of liberal democracy becomes manifest; it is the only regime which permits and encourages such a quest. It should be the university's vocation to carry out this quest. In order for it to restore itself today, its faculties would have to make common cause in defense of free inquiry and at the same time protect and encourage those students who wish to learn. It is highly questionable whether it would any longer be capable of such an effort, for it lacks the awareness, the desire, and the personnel. Instead radical egalitarianism is a dogma within it. Given the increasing and menacing pressures for conformity growing up within the university, it seems reasonable to ask whether it will not be necessary for thinking men to return to the isolation of private life in order to be able to think freely. This is not a happy thought for our universities. However, there is also a larger question: is liberal democracy conceivable in the absence of the liberal university?

The liberal university appears to be both the highest expression of liberal democracy and a condition of its perpetuation.

Appendix

These reflections were set to paper in 1969. The following academic year, 1969–70, only hastened the progress of the disease I have described, culminating in faculties and presidents of major universities, under extreme pressure from students and in their desire to recapture their students' respect, taking political stands on current issues. It was accepted that the business of the university can be interrupted in the name of political activism and that students who abandon their studies to participate will suffer no consequences, that they will receive credit equally with those who do the work of students.

At the moment there appears to be a calm on our campuses, and it may very well endure for a time. But one should not be misled as to the meaning of that calm. The principle of student power has been largely victorious; the students are now at something of a loss as to what to do with that victory. Nothing has been done to reestablish respect for the proper purposes of the university or the rules requisite to the fulfillment of those purposes. The relative quiet results also in part from outside pressure. Hostility to universities has expressed itself in many ways but in particular of the tightening of the purse strings. The highly favorable disposition of the general public toward universities, which was an essential element in the possibility of their success, has been undermined. The public has apparently finally been persuaded of the view of our universities so loudly propounded by students and professors and has come to wonder why it should support such institutions. Economic motivations do indeed seem to have some effect on this generation of idealists.

NOTES

1. Plato, *Republic,* VI 492 a–e.
2. Ibid., VIII 563 a–b.
3. Machiavelli, *The Prince,* chap. 25.
4. Allan Bloom, "The Crisis of Liberal Education," in *Higher Education and Modern Democracy,* ed. Robert A. Goldwin (Chicago: Rand McNally, 1967).
5. Plato, *Republic,* VIII 561 c–d.

PART THREE

Socialism

KARL MARX WAS not the first, though he is the most famous, socialist.[1] Socialist themes are as old as Plato's *Republic* (the ideal city requires communal property, including women and children) and Christ's Sermon on the Mount (the poor in spirit are blessed; the reign of God is theirs). Marx discusses his more immediate predecessors in part 3 of *The Communist Manifesto*. Most important among them are the utopian socialists Charles Fourier (1772–1837), Robert Owen (1771–1858), and Claude-Henri Saint Simon (1760–1825). Like Marx, Saint Simon portrayed history as a conflict between productive and unproductive classes. Owen was an industrialist who founded New Lanark, a model factory based on the principle that better working conditions improve productivity. But it was Charles Fourier, included here, who had the greatest influence upon Marx.

According to Fourier, philosophers typically treat human passions as problems, but this is true, he argues, only in badly organized societies. Fourier claims that God created the passions and that He rules by attraction. If society organizes itself by harnessing the energy of "passionate attraction," then it will be harmonious. Fourier's schemes for promoting a harmonious society, however, are often bizarre. His utopian vision incorporates "little hordes" of children, whose love of dirt naturally suits them to collect the garbage—and so "filth . . . become[s] their path to glory." Fourier also proposes a court of love ruled by the "butterfly principle," where more mature individuals are encouraged to "flit" from one sexual encounter to another. What Marx found most useful in this fantastic social program was the idea that work, if properly organized, is desirable. What he missed was Fourier's sensuous side—nothing in Marx's writings even approaches the sexual troubadours![2]

Although Marx learned from the utopian socialists, he also criticized them for neglecting the laws of economics and the necessity for political action. Their naiveté, he feared, would undermine the class struggle.[3] That "the history of all hitherto existing society is the history of class struggle" is the central thesis of Marx and Engels's *Communist Manifesto*.[4] To understand it, an introduction to their theory of history is necessary.

According to Marx, humans are producers. But they do not produce merely to meet physical needs. "Rather it [production] is a definite form of activity . . . , a definite form of expressing their life, a definite mode of life on their part."[5] Human productive powers expand historically: as one need is satisfied, another is generated, and then a way of satisfying it. "Their history is . . . the history of the evolving productive forces . . . and is, therefore, the history of the development of the forces of the individuals themselves."[6] Marx and Engels argue that the productive forces are crucial for understanding a society, for they shape its division of labor, class relations, state institutions, and basic values. When productive forces outgrow class relations, social revolution occurs.

Classes are defined by relations of ownership (and with it control) of the productive forces. Marx distinguishes between classes in themselves and classes for themselves: the first is an objective class, defined by shared economic circumstances; the second adds subjective components, consciousness of class interests and collective activity to promote them.[7] The problem for socialist revolutionaries is moving from the first to the second. The *Manifesto* is, in part, an explanation of the development of class consciousness in capitalist society.

The classes in capitalist society are the bourgeoisie (owners of productive forces and buyers of labor power) and the proletariat (sellers of labor power who do not own productive forces). In a sense, both are revolutionary. The bourgeoisie revolutionizes production—centralizing, expanding, internationalizing, and mechanizing it—and, in the process, it makes work less attractive, less lucrative, and less accessible for the proletariat. This class conflict manifests itself in periodic crises of overproduction and underconsumption, as the bourgeoisie produces vast quantities of goods and impoverishes potential consumers. As Marx puts it, the bourgeoisie both "forges the weapons which bring death to itself" and "calls into existence the men who are to wield those weapons." It not only makes work intolerable, but also organizes the proletariat economically and politically, inadvertently preparing it for revolution.

What does that revolution entail? Marx and Engels say only what communism abolishes: the division of labor, private property, nation-states, classes, families, truths. What replaces them remains unclear. Marx and Engels cannot say more because their ideas are also shaped by the productive forces: "They merely express . . . actual relations springing from an existing class struggle, from a historical movement going on under our very eyes." To say more would be utopian.

The *Manifesto* emphasizes the inevitability of socialist revolution. The next two selections in this part explain its desirability. "Estranged Labor" is from Marx's early, unpublished *Economic and Philosophical Manuscripts*. Most simply, estrangement, or alienation, refers to a loss of meaning in life. Marx discusses four aspects of such alienation. First, workers are alienated from their products, which they produce for the bourgeoisie. Second, they are alienated from their productive activity, which is forced labor. Third, workers' alienation from their species-being manifests itself in attitudes toward nature (as an object to be manipulated and possessed) and society (as a mere means to self-preservation). Fourth, workers experience alienation from their fellow men, with whom they interact through competitive exchanges. According to Marx, alienation pervades capitalist societies and is a necessary result of their mode of production.

Alienation is only one of the problems of capitalism. Another, exploitation, is equally important. Whereas alienation involves a loss of meaning, exploitation involves being used by others.[8] Marx's labor theory of value, outlined in "Value, Price, and Profit," explains the nature of capitalist exploitation. He begins by arguing that profit comes from production, not exchange: some (capitalists) profit from others' (proletarians') labor. Is this fair? Yes and no. Capitalists pay workers the full exchange value of their labor power. But labor power is a peculiar commodity in that it creates more value than it has. The surplus value it creates is the capitalists' profit. Not surprisingly, capitalists try to increase this surplus value, gaining absolute surplus value by lengthening the working day and relative surplus value by improving productivity. These strategies, both of which disadvantage the laborer, create the conditions for revolution—the crises of overproduction and underconsumption—described in the *Manifesto*. The labor theory of value also shows why liberation requires revolution: a higher wage and a shorter day are only better conditions for a "slave."

Yet the inevitable revolution has not occurred. Why? Twentieth-century socialists differ in their responses to this question. Lenin responds to it by developing the theory of the party vanguard and the proletarian dictatorship. Whereas Marx theorized that capitalist production created the essential preconditions—economic crisis and class consciousness—for socialist revolution, Lenin argues that left to its own devices, the proletariat is capable of developing only trade union consciousness, the desire for "bread and butter" reforms. Therefore, the communist party, a small, secret cadre of professional revolutionaries who see the future direction of history, must bring revolutionary consciousness to the proletariat from without. These professional revolutionaries must lead the proletariat in insurrection, even seizing power in their name. In *State and Revolution*, Lenin explains how the party transforms the proletariat along with the bourgeoisie during a transitional dictatorship. As Lenin puts it, "We want the socialist revolution with human nature as it is now, with human nature that cannot do without subordination, control and managers."

By emphasizing the party and its rule, Lenin modifies Marx's connection between socialist revolution and capitalist development. For Lenin, political changes can lead to economic changes. He even considers the possibility that socialists could "skip" the capitalist stage. Does Lenin provide an appropriate adaptation of socialism to changing circumstances, a reinterpretation that sustains the fundamental features of Marx's theory? Lenin does offer an explanation for why European revolutions failed, and he also makes socialist revolution applicable to conditions in less developed countries. In *Imperialism, the Highest Stage of Capitalism,* Lenin argues that late or monopoly capitalism involves continuing struggles among imperialist powers over the "division and redivision of the world." The superprofits colonial powers receive allow the imperialist bourgeoisie to buy off a part of their national proletariat, while promises of investment give them control over politico-economic elites in colonized nations. However, these imperialist strategies are temporary, for the imperialist powers are simultaneously creating the conditions for worldwide socialist revolution—that is, an international proletariat and a global production system. Controversy persists over how significant the differences are between Marx and Lenin: does Lenin adapt or reject Marx's theory of revolution?

Whereas Lenin brings socialist revolution to the Third World, Eduard Bernstein revises it for a new Europe. As the theorist of the German SPD, the largest democratic socialist party in nineteenth-century Europe, Bernstein agreed with Lenin that European workers lacked revolutionary consciousness. However, his analysis of the problem and his solution to it differ from Lenin's. According to Bernstein, capitalism has not created the economic preconditions for socialist revolution and can no longer be expected to do so. As he succinctly puts it: "Peasants do not sink; middle class does not disappear; crises do not grow ever larger; misery and serfdom do not increase. There is increase in insecurity, dependence, social distance, social character of production, functional superfluity of property owners."[9] Bernstein concludes that a new Marxist theory is required, and in *Evolutionary Socialism,* he presents that theory. He argues that current economic and political factors—trade unions and socialist parties and voters—will eventually lead to socialism. Gradual change is not only possible but also preferable to revolution: "A greater surety of lasting success lies in a steady advance than in a revolutionary cataclysm."[10] In contrast to Lenin, and perhaps also to Marx, Bernstein argues that socialists should accept workers as they are. This means listening to their desires, even for "bread and butter" reforms, and working to fulfill them. But what if workers never want socialism? If, as in England, they are content with a welfare state? Or if, as in Germany, they choose fascism? This is the continuing dilemma faced by democratic socialists.

The final selection in this part, "The Port Huron Statement at 40," discusses this dilemma in the context of American politics. Marx and Engels were fascinated by the United States, where "classes . . . have not yet become fixed but, in continual flux, perpetually change and interchange their elements."[11] But they saw social mobility, along with southern slavery, as obstacles to socialism. "Labor," Marx said, "cannot emancipate itself in the white skin when in the black it is branded."[12] After the Civil War, Marx expected a "serious workers' party" to emerge in the United States,[13] but this was not to be. Like conservatism, socialism remained marginal for most of American political history.[14] However, foreign affairs (Vietnam, the Cold War, nuclear weapons) and domestic issues (racism and poverty), helped to create a "new" left on college campuses in the 1960s. Forty years later, Tom Hayden and Dick Flacks look back on their manifesto, "The Port Huron Statement," which presents the vision of Students for a Democratic Society (SDS), a loosely organized group of student activists, many of them leaders in student government and writers for student newspapers. Equally critical of Soviet Marxism and welfare liberalism, their manifesto envisions a populist, pragmatic, participatory democracy of ordinary citizens and calls for "new modes of organization (decentralization, consensus methods of decision-making, leadership rotation and avoidance of hierarchy)" that are anarchist in style and spirit. What began as a call for student participation on campus was ultimately destined to become a demand for a more democratic society.[15]

However, the New Left fulfilled only part of its agenda in the sixties. Looking forward at the turn of the twenty-first century, Hayden and Flacks ask whether "participatory democracy" may have renewed relevance in American politics today. The war on terrorism and the war in Iraq, they argue, parallel the Cold War and the Vietnam War; like those earlier conflicts, our current crises inspire calls for citizens of conscience to protest, to demand that their political leaders seek "peace with justice." Again, the question arises: What does socialism mean today? In our postcommunist world, is it possible to imagine new and democratic socialist alternatives, or has socialism been reduced to a utopian dream?

NOTES

1. I am indebted to Isaac Kramnick for this insight.

2. Feminists have criticized Marx (see Heidi Hartmann in part six of this book) for overemphasizing material production and ignoring sexual reproduction.

3. Again, Fourier is instructive. He reportedly advertised for wealthy patrons to "fund a phalanstery" (cooperative community). They were to contribute over lunch at a Paris cafe. He waited; none came.

4. Marx and Engels wrote the *Manifesto* for the Communist League on the eve of the 1848 revolutions, which explains its polemical tone and its sense of urgency. Although the failure of those revolutions forced them to revise their claims, they continued to see the *Manifesto* as the best single statement of their views.

5. Karl Marx and Friedrich Engels, *The German Ideology*, tr. C. J. Arthur (London: Lawrence and Wishart, 1970), 42.

6. Ibid., 87.

7. For this distinction, see Karl Marx, *The Eighteenth Brumaire of Louis Bonaparte*, in *The Portable Karl Marx*, ed. Eugene Kamenka (New York: Viking Penguin, 1983), 312.

8. Exploitation and alienation may be related as cause and effect (though workers may be exploited without experiencing alienation, e.g., if they lack class consciousness).

9. Quoted in Peter Gay, *The Dilemma of Democratic Socialism* (New York: Collier, 1962), 250.

10. Eduard Bernstein, *Evolutionary Socialism* (1961; 7th printing, New York: Schocken, 1975), xxviii.

11. Marx, *Eighteenth Brumaire*, 297.

12. Karl Marx, "The American Question in England," *New York Daily Tribune*, September 18, 1861, reprinted in *The American Journalism of Marx and Engels, a Selection from the New York Daily Tribune*, ed. Henry M. Christman (New York: New American Library, 1966), 211–222.

13. Karl Marx, "Preface to the Russian edition of the Communist Manifesto," in Kamenka, *Portable Karl Marx*, 556.

14. In addition to social mobility and lingering racism, many other explanations have been offered for the marginality of American socialism. Among them are our history of agrarian radicalism, the safety valve provided by the frontier, and the presence of numerous immigrants. The classic on this topic is Werner Sombart, *Why Is There No Socialism in the United States?* ed. C. T. Husbands (White Plains, N.Y.: International Arts and Sciences Press, 1976).

15. See James Miller, *"Democracy Is In the Streets": From Port Huron to the Siege of Chicago* (Cambridge, Mass.: Harvard University Press, 1994); Sohnya Sayres et al., eds., *The 60s Without Apology* (Minneapolis: University of Minnesota Press, 1984); and Christopher Lasch, *The Agony of the American Left* (New York: Knopf, 1969).

13

Charles Fourier

"Utopian Socialism" (*ca.* 1808–1851)

Charles Fourier, a utopian socialist, lived in Paris from 1772 until 1837. Following the French Revolution, during which he was imprisoned and nearly executed, he began to work for a new social order. His ideal system of social organization was the phalanstery, a group of 1,700 to 1,800 people whose different psychological traits would be complementary and would produce happiness. The following selections come from an anthology of translations of his major works: Théorie des Quatre Mouvements et des Destinées Générales *(1808)*, Le Nouveau Monde Industriel et Sociétare *(1829), and* Le Nouveau Monde Amoureux *(1851).*

Commerce, Industry, and Work in Civilization

True Freedom and Work

AFTER HEALTH AND wealth nothing is more precious than freedom. But there are two sorts of freedom: physical freedom and social freedom. The second variety is not the one that the sophists wish to procure for us.

The sophists are used to considering nature in a simplistic manner, and they have allowed their mania for simplification to confuse the debate about freedom. They have not been able to distinguish between the simple, compound and bi-compound varieties of freedom. For more than a thousand years they neglected

Source: The Utopian Vision of Charles Fourier. Copyright © 1971 by Jonathan Beecher and Richard Bienvenu. Reprinted by permission of Beacon Press, Boston.

the first of the freedoms, material or bodily freedom. It was the Christian religion which finally intervened powerfully to emancipate the slaves. But before Christianity the philanthropists of antiquity were used to turning human beings into beasts of burden and to obliging slaves to kill each other in mass combats for the amusement of the virtuous citizens of Rome. When the Romans did not wish to see twenty thousand slaves slaughtered en masse, they had two hundred massacred one by one in gladiatorial combats. These performances repeated with more civic pomp by the virtuous republicans of Sparta. To reduce their slave population the Spartans would gather two thousand of their most faithful slaves, crown them with flowers, parade them around the city, and then slaughter them. The Spartans dispatched their most faithful slaves in this way because they did not want to see them die of slow torture in the galleys. Such were, for a thousand years, the noble ideas of Philosophy about physical freedom. Every good republican applauded these massacres; and if Christianity had not intervened, things might still be at the same point.

If someone had consulted the oracles of wisdom, the Platos and the Aristotles about the emancipation of the slaves, they would have replied with the fine word "impossibility" which France has inherited. The enlightened Aristotle was so sure that slaves were beasts of burden, creatures outside the human race, that he laid down the principle that "there is no virtue proper to a slave." He wished to reduce them to the status of brute beasts, devoid of the rational faculty and of virtue itself. . . .

Under the last Caesars the philosophers saw the granting of bodily freedom, which they had so long regarded as impossible, was in fact quite feasible. They should then have recognized the error of their science with its assumptions about impossibility and its conviction that "nature is limited to known means." But they learned nothing from this lesson, and their secret indifference with regard to freedom is proven by the fact that they made no effort to analyze and spread word of the means by which emancipation had been brought about.

The ideas that people now have about emancipation are superficial and highly impractical. Thus in recent times the attempt to grant bodily freedom to the Negroes was a failure. It was in 1789 that Philosophy undertook the task. Instead of seeking appropriate methods and adopting a policy of judicious philanthropy, Philosophy relied solely on the spirit of partisan politics. It succeeded only in turning Santo Domingo into a bloody battle-ground under the banal pretext of liberty.[1]

Philosophy thus stands convicted of complete incompetence in matters related to bodily or physical freedom and the process of emancipation, whether sudden or gradual. . . . Has Philosophy shown any more skill in the matter of social freedom? This question prompts us to distinguish three kinds of freedom. . . .

1. *Simple or Physical Freedom* without social freedom. This is the condition of a poor man who has a very small fixed income, only enough to provide the barest necessities, a military ration. He enjoys an *active physical* freedom because he is not forced to work like the laborer who has no independent income. Yet his passions are completely unsatisfied. Phebon is quite free to go to the opera. But it costs a crown to get in and Phebon has only enough money to feed himself poorly and to dress himself shabbily. He is free to aspire to the rank of Deputy, but this requires a far greater income than he has. He may take pride in the fine title of Free Man, but his social freedom is a sham. The doors of the inn and the opera are closed to him, and he has no place among the electorate.[2] He is only a passive member of society. His passions cannot express themselves in an active way, and his opinions are held in contempt.

Such a man is, nonetheless, considerably more free than the laborer who is obliged to work lest he die of starvation and who has just one day a week of *active* physical freedom—Sunday. For the other six days of the week the laborer is in a state of passive physical freedom. He has consented to the form of slavery represented by the workshop. But compared to the idleness and well-being which he enjoys on Sunday, this indirect form of slavery is not any less physically constraining than real slavery.

A distinction can also be made between active and passive social freedom. For the time being let us simply point out that the two classes of men just cited do not enjoy social freedom. They only possess simple or physical freedom: it is active for the man with a small fixed income and passive for the laborer. But the laborer is himself much better off than the slave who is denied physical freedom in both its active and its passive forms.

2. *Divergent Compound Freedom.* This includes *active physical* freedom and *active social freedom,* and it permits the complete satisfaction of the passions. Such is the condition of the savages, for they enjoy both these freedoms. A savage deliberates on questions of peace and war just like a cabinet member in civilization. He enjoys, insofar as it is possible in his horde, the complete satisfaction of his soul's passions. Above all, he enjoys freedom from worry, a good almost unknown to civilized men. It is true that he must hunt and fish for his subsistence, but this work is attractive to him and no threat to his active physical freedom. Work which is pleasing is not a form of servitude. While the savage would feel enslaved behind a plow, his hunting is an amusement just as selling is the merchant's amusement. Do you think that a merchant has experienced physical discomfort when he spends his morning setting out a hundred bolts of cloth, lying to his clients and selling many pairs of breeches? The fatigue he may feel is a pleasure,

for his work is attractive and he possesses physical freedom. This is proved by the fact that our merchant who is quite content today will be glum and surly tomorrow if the customers don't come and he is unable to lie and to sell.

We have seen that the freedom of the savage is a compound freedom because it is both physically and socially active. But these two *activities* are *divergent* from man's destiny which is attractive labor. If the savage is to enjoy *active, convergent* freedom, he must be offered attractive *productive* work which is carried out in passionate series. Then he will advance to the third type of freedom.

3. *Convergent Compound or Bi-compound Freedom.* This consists of two independent elements, *active physical* freedom and *active social* freedom in alliance with *attractive productive work.* It presupposes unified adherence, the individual consent of every worker—man, woman and child—and their impassioned collaboration in the performance of work and in the maintenance of the established order. This third sort of liberty is the destiny of man. (*Œuvres Complètes,* 3:152–156. Hereafter cited as *OC.*)

Work and Compulsion

Freedom from worry is a form of happiness experienced by the animals. But it is also a human right, although it can only be enjoyed in civilization by the very rich. Far from being careless of the morrow, nine-tenths of civilized men are worried about the present day because they are obliged to devote themselves to loathsome work that is forced upon them. And so on Sunday they go to cafes and places of amusement to enjoy a few moments of the sort of carefreeness that is vainly sought by so many rich men who are themselves pursued by anxiety. *"Post equitem sedet atra cura."*[3]

Quibblers will say that freedom from worry is a state of mind and not a right. But it becomes a right insofar as it is proscribed in the state of civilization where any sign of carelessness is held in dishonor and resolutely condemned. Let the father of a poor family try to devote himself to his own pleasures without worrying about his workshop and without saving up money for taxes, rent and future needs. Then public opinion through its criticism and the tax collector through his agents will let him know that he does not have the right to be carefree, to enjoy life like the savages and animals. They will tell him that he must master his carefree inclinations. Civilized education, moreover, intervenes systematically to fight against our desire to be carefree, a desire that will be unfettered in Harmony.

As for the Savage, it is obvious that he enjoys his carefree life and does not want to concern himself with the future. Otherwise he would worry that his children and his horde might suffer from hunger. He would then accept the agricultural implements and farming equipment that civilized governments try to offer him. But he doesn't want to give up any of his seven rights. In this he is correct because if he gave up his right to freedom from worry he would lose all his other rights one after the other. Doubtless he does this without calculating, but nature has done his thinking for him. Attraction leads him along the right path. . . .

The only plausible objection that can be raised against the happiness of the Savages is that women do not share it. Although women constitute one-half of the human race, their condition among the Savages is quite servile and very unfortunate. . . .

I have already established that the savage is more advanced than we are in his enjoyment of freedom because he has achieved *compound divergent* freedom. That is, savage males enjoy the seven natural rights. They are thus quite superior to us because we deprive the vast majority of either sex of the advantage. . . .

To indemnify a civilized man for the loss of his seven rights our publicists fob him off with a few promises and tall stories. They offer him the dignity of possessing the fine title of a free man and the happiness of living under the Charter of 1815. These silly promises don't even deserve to be called illusions. They are incapable of satisfying a wage earner who wants above all to eat to fill, to live happily and free from worry, to hunt, fish, intrigue and steal like the Savage. . . .

When it deprives man of his seven natural rights, Civilization never gives him agreed-upon equivalents. Take an unfortunate worker who has neither work nor bread and is pursued by creditors and tax collector. Ask him if he would not prefer to enjoy the rights of hunting and fishing and to have trees and flocks like the Savage? He will not fail to prefer the life of the Savage. What is he given as an equivalent? The happiness of living under the Charter. But an indigent man cannot satisfy himself by reading the Charter instead of eating dinner. To offer him that sort of compensation is to insult his poverty. He would consider himself happy if he could enjoy the seven natural rights and freedom as does the Savage. But he will not find these in the civilized order. (*OC*, 3:167–170)

The exercise of the industrial faculty which is a delight for the free animals— the beavers, bees, wasps and ants—is a torment for man, who escapes it as soon as he acquires his freedom. Civilized man aspires only to inertia, and the supreme curse which the savage shouts at his enemy is this: "May you be reduced to plowing a field!"

Since we are evidently destined by God for agricultural and manufacturing labor, how has it happened that we have thus far received from him neither a social code regulating our industrial relations nor a natural enticement to work? Why is work, which is said to be our destiny, only a torment for civilized and barbarian wage earners and slaves, who are in constant rebellion against the obligation to work and who would quit working altogether if they were no longer constrained by the fear of punishment?

Work is nonetheless a delight for many creatures such as the beavers, bees, wasps, and ants, who are perfectly free to lapse into a state of inertia. God has provided them with a social mechanism which attracts them to work and makes it a source of happiness for them. Why should he have failed to grant us a benefit which he bestows upon the animals? There is a huge difference between their work and ours! The Russians and the Algerians work out of fear of the whip or the cudgel; the English and the French work from fear of the hunger which besets their poor households. The liberty of the Greeks and Romans is much vaunted, but they had slaves who worked out of fear of being executed just like the Negroes in our colonies today. Such is the happiness of man in the absence of the *attractive industrial code;* such is the result of human laws and of the philosophical constitutions: they make humanity envy the lot of the industrious animals, for whom Attraction turns wearisome tasks into sources of pleasure.

Our happiness would be great indeed if God had treated us like these animals, if he endowed us with *passionate attraction* for the work which we are destined to perform! Our life would be but a succession of delights, and these delights would be a source of great wealth to us. In the absence of the system of attractive labor, however, we are no more than a society of slave-laborers in which a few people manage to avoid the necessity of working and form coalitions in order to remain in a state of idleness. These people are hated by the masses who share their desire to free themselves from work. This is the source of revolutionary ferment. Agitators promise to make the people happy, rich and idle; but once they have gained power, they oppress the multitude and reduce it to a more complete state of servitude in order to consolidate their own position as idlers or as managers of those who work. The latter are no different from the idlers.

In this miserable condition we are reduced to envying the lot of the animals and insects, and bemoaning a providence which appears to have regarded these creatures with a solicitude which it has not had for us. For, if one is to believe the philosophical prejudices, God has not prepared a social code for us, nor a sure industrial mechanism, nor industrial attraction to make our work enjoyable, nor even the guarantee of the work we need for our subsistence. . . .

Our philosophers would be vain in claiming that their vague wisdom and their oppressive laws could ever provide us with an attractive *industrial code.* They are vain in promising in their innumerable constitutions to make life enchanting for our wage-earners. All their theories only serve to make work more loathsome and to add to the horror of the seven limbic calamities. (*OC,* 3:249–251)

The Worker's Misfortunes

The common people have not even reached the level of simple pleasure on the scale of happiness. They do not have enough for subsistence or to satisfy their sense of taste. This is the most imperious of all the senses and its satisfaction is the *sine qua non* of happiness. Rather, the common people are overwhelmed by a host of privations which transform their lives into a permanent hell. These privations constitute all of the degrees of unhappiness: simple, compound, super-compound, bi-compound, and quintessentially subversive or omni-compound, unhappiness.

As many as sixteen causes of despair can be enumerated. They assail the common people of civilization in varying degrees at every moment according to the following scheme.

Misfortunes of Working People

PRESSING EVIL

1. The burden of taxes: pursuits of fiscal agents who come to extract the few pennies that a man has painfully amassed to support his unfortunate family.
2. The necessity of endangering his health in excessive and unhealthy work in order to provide for his own subsistence and that of his children.

DIRECT EVIL

3. Repercussion of poverty, shared suffering, or the faculty of feeling the misfortunes of his family whose privations add to his own pain.
4. New misfortunes that redouble his suffering just when he thinks he has endured the worst that fate had in store for him.
5. Unjust stigma of shame: the opprobrium and defamation which plague the poor man because of his destitution and expose him to a disdain which merely increases with his penury.

INDIRECT EVIL

6. The sight of fortune's favorites to whom chance, intrigue or crime brings affluence. This can only increase the despair of the honest worker who is led by his own probity deeper and deeper into the abyss of indigence.
7. Relative regression caused by the progress of luxury which increases the sufferings of the multitude in the same proportion that it creates new means of pleasure for the rich. Deprived of life's necessities, the civilized worker is tormented by a display of increased affluence which the savage does not see.
8. Frustration in seeking legal redress through lawsuits and other claims. He lacks the money and the credit to pay lawyers' fees.

ACCESSORY EVIL

9. Social snare, or the constant danger of being cheated by his fellow citizens, of meeting nothing but a swarm of cheats or disguised enemies in the social world.

10. Poverty anticipated in the present, or the fear of unemployment, which never troubles the savages and the animals.

11. Scientific mockery, or the illusory help of literary charlatans who, while promising the people that they will soften their misfortunes, overwhelm them with new calamities.

12. The trap of morality, or the persecution he attracts when he practices virtue, because virtue shames perverse rivals, excites them to calumny which is always well-received in civilization.

PIVOTS

Y. Loathing for work, and deprivation of the prerogatives enjoyed by animals such as beavers, bees, etc., who are attracted to work and find their happiness in that work which is the civilized man's torture.

YY. Betrayal of nature, or the martyrdom of attraction. The goad of numerous desires which the civilized man cannot satisfy and which lead him to ruin; whereas nature endows animals with only those passions which are suited to guide them and which they have the right to satisfy.

TRANSITIONS

KK. Wearisome reflections on the past, the memory of numerous miseries already endured and yet to be feared.

K. Suffering anticipated in the future, or the awareness that in his old age, in the distant future, he will meet with increased misfortunes and be unable to escape them.

Such is the lot of the common people whom the sophists describe as making great strides toward perfectibility. In fact their condition is worse than that of the wild animals. The lion, for example, is well clothed, well armed, and takes its subsistence where it finds it; it is a hundred times more fortunate than the common people of civilization who are dragged off to the gallows if they ask for any one of their natural rights or for the primordial social right to a *minimum* of subsistence.

Is someone going to object that the common people are so brutish that they are incapable of feeling the enormity of their misfortunes? In that case just what is the significance of the pretension of our sages to spread enlightenment, to give us delicate senses and to refine our minds' perceptions of sensations? Here one might be inclined to praise the obscurantists who want to brutalize the common people. Since all of civilization turns in a vicious circle, the obscurantists may well be right in more than one case. (*OC*, 4:191–193)

Attractive Work

Loathsome Work: God's Curse

"We must love work," say our sages. Well! How can we? What is lovable about work in civilization? For nine-tenths of all men work procures nothing but profitless boredom. Rich men, consequently, find work loathsome and do only the easiest and most lucrative kinds of work such as managing companies. How can you make a poor man love work when you are not even able to make work agreeable for the rich? This would require elegant workshops, division of tasks and courteous, loyal, and polished fellow-workers. All of these conditions are impractical in civilization. They can exist only when work is organized in passionate series.

In addition to all the obvious drawbacks of civilized work such as the filthiness of certain workshops, the coarseness of the peasants, theft, complications, isolation, boredom, the risk of loss, etc., there is a still greater drawback. That is the necessity of watching over all phases of a particular kind of work and often of performing all of them oneself. A certain rich man, for example, would very much like to grow flowers and fruits. But he hasn't the courage to order seeds and plants because he is afraid of being cheated by the merchants. (He most certainly will be cheated.) He is discouraged at the prospect that a negligent son or son-in-law may allow his plantings to perish after him. He is surrounded by maladroit, careless, thieving, and hateful workers; by mocking and ignorant neighbors who ridicule his work; by children who come and spitefully lay waste to his flower beds; and by women who devastate his gardens even more stupidly. For women know nothing about flowers and think that they are doing the flower-grower a great honor by cutting and chopping up his flower beds, when they are not able to recognize the different species nor praise the grower intelligently. How can we make work agreeable for the poor man when all kinds of obstacles conspire to disgust even the rich? (*OC*, 4:520–521)

Work, say the Scriptures, is a punishment for man: Adam and his children were condemned to earn their bread by the sweat of their brows. Before the infliction of this punishment, man's primeval happiness consisted in having nothing to do, as in the case now for our populace on Sunday. It is thus well recognized, even by religion, that civilized work is a state of unhappiness for man. Religion admits that man is closer to nature when he indulges in enchanting illusion rather than when he listens to philosophy's promises about the charms of life in a thatched hut. Yet when Scripture told us the truth concerning the unhappiness attached to work today, it did not say that this punishment would not end one day, nor did it claim that man would never be able to return to the happy state he first enjoyed. (*OC*, 4:554–555)

Drudgery: Work Devoid of Attraction

Drudge duty (40th series) includes all jobs which are isolated and devoid of attraction. These include coach driving, mail delivery, sentry duty at the watchtower, the operation of the telegraph, the guarding of the colors, the playing of the carillon, the night watch at the porter's lodge both at the Phalanstery itself and at the stables, the night patrol, the fire-watch, the tending of the beacon light, etc., etc.

The series of Drudges will receive a substantial dividend in addition to the exemption fees paid by the rich who will be able, as they are today, to purchase exemptions from guard duty. These fees will be allocated to the series as a whole and not to individuals, since individual service for wages would be dishonorable in association.

The Drudges will also be encouraged by various favors such as the right to eat at the second class tables. (Most of them would otherwise eat with the third class.) Our intention is to make the day on which they perform their chores—which recurs about once every two weeks—a day of gaiety for them.

These precautions will seem quite superfluous to the civilized, all of whom are accustomed to regarding oppression as moral wisdom. They tend to forget that every page of this book is concerned with the creation of industrial attraction, the harmonious distribution of wealth, and the fusion of the three classes. It is very important, therefore, to avoid degrading any job or displeasing any class. It is necessary to possess reliable methods capable of infusing repugnant and disdained work with gaiety. (See the section on the Little Hordes.)[4] (*OC*, 6:136–137)

The Little Hordes and Disgusting Work

We shall now see that morality has failed to understand the principles governing education and that, according to its habit, it has classed as vices all of the impulses which nature would employ to create virtues.

Conflict between the instincts and the sexes yields prodigious results in work and virtue. To create such conflict we will divide children between the ages of four and fifteen and a half (the four tribes of Cherubs, Seraphs, Pupils and Students) into two instinctual corps. These are:

The Little Hordes, who perform tasks which are repugnant either to the senses or to self-esteem.

The Little Bands, who are responsible for the maintenance of collective luxury.[5]

These two contrasting corporations will usefully employ the instincts that morality vainly seeks to suppress in both sexes: the taste that little boys have for filth, and the love that little girls have for finery. By setting these two tastes off against each other, societary education will lead both sexes to the same goal by different paths. It will lead the Little Hordes to the beautiful by way of the good, and the Little Bands to the good by way of the beautiful.

This method gives children a freedom of choice which they do not enjoy in a society such as ours, which forces them to accept a single system of morals. The societary state will permit them to choose between two contrasting paths which favor opposite penchants: the penchants for finery and filth.

Two-thirds of all boys have a penchant for filth. They love to wallow in the mire and play with dirty things. They are unruly, peevish, scurrilous and over-bearing, and they will brave any storm or peril simply for the pleasure of wreak-ing havoc. These children will enroll in the Little Hordes whose task is to per-form, dauntlessly and as a point of honor, all those loathsome tasks that ordinary workers would find debasing. This corporation is a kind of half-savage legion whose wild ways contrast with the refined courtesy of Harmony. But this con-trast is one of style and not of sentiment; for the Little Hordes are the most ardently patriotic of corporations.

The other third of little boys have a taste for good manners and tranquil occu-pations. They will enroll in the Little Bands. By contrast, a third of all girls have boyish inclinations and love to horn in on boys' games. They are called tomboys. Such girls will join the Little Hordes. Thus the Little Hordes will include ⅔ boys and ⅓ girls, and the Little Bands will include ⅔ girls and ⅓ boys. Each of these two corps will be subdivided into three sections which must be given names. The Little Hordes will adopt vulgar sobriquets, while the Little Bands will assume romantic names. This will emphasize the contrast between these two groups which are both vital to the working of industrial attraction.

Let us first analyze the duties and civic virtues of the Little Hordes. . . . The Little Hordes have the rank of *God's Militia* in the service of industrial unity. By virtue of this title, they should be the first to enter the breach whenever unity is threatened. To maintain unity the Little Hordes will be asked to perform a num-ber of tasks which are so disgusting that it would otherwise be necessary to call upon the services of wage-laborers. In performing these tasks they will be divided into three corps: the first is assigned to foul functions such as sewer-cleaning, tending the dung heap, working in the slaughter-houses, etc.; the sec-ond is assigned to dangerous functions such as the hunting of reptiles or to jobs requiring dexterity; the third will participate in both these kinds of work. The older members of the Little Hordes will ride on their own dwarf horses.

One of the tasks assigned to the Little Hordes will be the maintenance of roads. They will make it a point of pride to keep the roads of Harmony lined with shrubs and flowers and in more splendid condition than the lanes of our country estates. If a highway is damaged in any way, the alarm will be given at once. The Little Hordes will immediately make temporary repairs and raise a warning flag to make sure that no passer-by might have grounds for accusing the community of having a bad Horde. The same reproach would be made if anyone found a dangerous reptile or a caterpillar's nest or heard the croaking of toads near a highway. The presence of such unclean objects would make people scornful of a Phalanx, and the value of its shares would fall.

Although the Little Hordes perform the most difficult tasks in the Phalanx—tasks which are totally lacking in *direct* attraction—they receive the least retribution. They would accept nothing at all if that were permitted in association. The fact that they receive the smallest share, however, does not prevent any of the members of the Little Hordes from receiving large shares for work performed in other groups and series. But as members of the unitary and philanthropic brotherhood of the Little Hordes, their work is inspired by devotion to the community and not by the hope of remuneration. . . .

Since the Little Hordes are the seedbed of all the civic virtues, they should serve society through the practice of the Christian virtue of *self-abnegation* and the philosophical virtue of *contempt for wealth*. They should exemplify and practice all the virtues that civilization dreams of but only counterfeits. As the guardians of social honor, they should crush evil in all its guises. While ridding the countryside of poisonous reptiles, they will purge society of a poison worse than the viper's, the poison of greed. . . . And in performing their foul tasks, they will eradicate the feelings of pride which make men disdain the laborious class and which tend to promote the spirit of caste, to impair social friendship, and to prevent the fusion of classes. . . .

It might seem that to make children so prodigiously virtuous it would be necessary to resort to supernatural means, as do our monastic orders when they accustom the neophyte to self-abnegation through austere novitiates. We will follow an entirely different course; nothing but the enticement of pleasure will be used with the Little Hordes.

Let us analyze the sources of their virtues. They are four in number, and all of them are condemned by morality. They are the penchant for dirt, and the feelings of pride, impudence and insubordination. It is by abandoning themselves to these so-called vices that the Little Hordes will become virtuous. As we consider this paradox, let us recall that the theory of attraction must restrict itself to utilizing the passions as God made them, without modifying them in any way. In support of this principle I have shown that there are a number of infantile attractions which we are wrong to regard as harmful. *Curiosity* and *flightiness,* for instance, are designed to attract the child to a host of Seristeries where he will discover his industrial vocations. The penchant for *running around with older, tougher children* is also useful; for the example of such children will teach the infant to be enthusiastic about his work in Harmony. *Disobedience toward the father and the teacher* is likewise a perfectly natural impulse. For these are not the persons who should educate the child; his education will be provided by cabalistic rivalries in work groups. Thus all youthful impulses are good in infancy and also in later childhood, provided that they are exercised in passionate series.

The Little Hordes will not be inspired to perform disgusting work from the very outset: they must be gradually introduced to it. First their pride must be aroused by giving them a sense of their own preeminence. All authorities, even monarchs, owe the first salute to the Little Hordes. With their dwarf horses the Little Hordes comprise the globe's foremost regiments of cavalry; no industrial army[6] may begin a campaign without them. They also have the prerogative of initiating all work done in the name of unity. They report to the army on the day set for the beginning of the project. After the engineers have laid out the work, the Little Hordes parade across the battlefield, and in their first charge they are cheered on by the whole army. They spend several days with the army and distinguish themselves in a number of tasks.

During religious ceremonies the Little Hordes are seated in the sanctuary, and on all other festive occasions they are given the place of honor. The purpose of all these distinctions is to utilize their penchant for foul tasks. They must be impassioned for such tasks by the trappings of glory, which cost nothing. Filth must become their path to glory, and it is for this reason that we encourage their pride, impudence and insubordination.

The Little Hordes have their own slang or cabalistic language, as well as their own miniature artillery. They also have their Druids and Druidesses, who are acolytes chosen from those elderly persons who have retained their taste for foul tasks. This service brings the elderly numerous advantages.

The method to follow with the Little Hordes is to utilize their enthusiasm for filth, but not to *use it up* by fatiguing them. In order to avoid exhausting their enthusiasm, they must be made to work gaily, honorifically, and in short sessions. If, for example, there is a particularly filthy job to be done, the Hordes from four or five neighboring Phalanxes are assembled. They arrive to take part in the *delite* or matinal meal which is served at four forty-five. Then after the religious hymn at five and the parade of out-going work groups, the charge of the Little Hordes is sounded in an uproar of bells, chimes, drums and trumpets, a howling of dogs and a bellowing of bulls. Then the Hordes, led by their Khans and Druids, rush forward with a great shout, passing before the priests who sprinkle them with holy water. They run off frenetically to their work, which they perform piously as an act of charity toward the Phalanx, a gesture of devotion to God and to unity.

The job done, they proceed to wash and dress. Then, dispersing into the gardens and workshops until eight, they return triumphantly to breakfast. There each Horde receives a crown of oak leaves which is attached to its banner. After breakfast, they remount their horses and return to their respective Phalanxes.

The Little Hordes should be associated with the priesthood as members of a religious brotherhood. When performing their work they should wear a religious symbol, such as a cross or other emblem, on their clothing. Among their work stimulants we must not forget the religious spirit, which is a very powerful means of inspiring education in children.

After the Little Hordes have developed an enthusiasm for collective work at difficult tasks, it will be easy to accustom them to unattractive day-to-day jobs in the apartments, slaughterhouses, kitchens, stables and laundries. They will always be up at three in the morning, taking the initiative at work on the Phalanx as they do in the industrial army.

The Little Hordes have supreme jurisdiction over the animal kingdom. They watch over the slaughterhouses to prevent unnecessary suffering and to insure every animal the most gentle death. Anyone who mistreats a quadruped, bird, fish or insect by abusing it in any way or by making it suffer at the slaughterhouse will have to answer to the Divan of the Little Hordes. Whatever his age, he will be brought before a tribunal of children because his reason is inferior even to that of children. Since animals are productive only when they are well treated, it is a rule in Harmony that a man who mistreats them is himself more of an animal than the defenseless beasts he persecutes. . . .

I have now said enough to make it clear that this corps of children, who indulge all the inclinations that morality forbids, is a device which will realize all the virtuous fancies with which the moralists feed their imaginations:

1. *Sweet Fraternity.* If a particular task is disdained because it is filthy, the men who perform it will become a class of pariahs, degraded beings with whom the rich will not wish to associate. In Harmony all of the tasks which might lead to such bad consequences are performed by the Little Hordes. The Little Hordes ennoble loathsome work and thereby promote unity and social harmony, the fusion of the rich, middle and poor classes.

2. *Contempt for Wealth.* The Little Hordes do not disdain wealth as such, but rather its egotistical use. They will sacrifice a portion of their own wealth to increase that of the whole Phalanx and to maintain the true source of wealth: industrial attraction. When all three classes—rich, middle and poor—become subject to industrial attraction, they will work together affectionately on all sorts of tasks, even including the dirty work which is reserved for children. For children of rich parents will be as eager as those of the poor to join the ranks of the Little Hordes. It is personality that determines which corporation a child will choose. . . .

If our moralists had studied human nature, they would have recognized that most male children like filth and they would have sought to employ this inclination usefully. This is what the societary order does; it makes use of the taste for filth to form a corporation of industrial Deciuses. It encourages the dirty inclinations which are repressed with heavy-handed whippings by a tender morality that makes no effort to utilize the passions as God gave them to us. (*OC*, 6:206–214)

Work, Love, and the Industrial Armies

Love, which is a source of disorder, idleness and expense in civilization, will become a source of profit and industrial miracles in the combined order. I am going to demonstrate this through a discussion of one of the most difficult administrative problems of civilization: the recruitment of armies. In the combined order this task will be accomplished by means of amorous strategy.

In each Phalanx there are two major series devoted to love, the *half-type* and the *whole type*. The latter is divided into nine groups beginning with the Vestalate which I shall now discuss.[7]

In each Phalanx the virginal members of the choir of Striplings[8] elect a quadrille of Vestals consisting of two parading couples and two meritorious couples. The former are chosen for their beauty and the latter for their accomplishments in the sciences and the arts or for their dedication to work.

The Vestals hold the rank of Magnates. When the poorest girl is elected a Vestal, she travels in a carriage which is studded with jewels and drawn by six white horses. . . . This youthful elite has the privilege of voyaging with the industrial armies. It is during their magnificent campaigns that the Vestals have their first love affairs.

Every day after their work is done the industrial armies hold magnificent festivities. These festivities are all the more splendid in that they bring together young people who have been chosen for their great beauty and talent. They also offer an excellent occasion for displays of courtliness. For each of the Vestals has numerous suitors and he or she must choose between them during the course of the campaign. Those who wish to form bonds with a single love join the ranks of the Damsels who are constant lovers representing the second of the nine amorous types. Others who have penchants for inconstancy take their places in the seven remaining categories. The principal result of these diversions is that immense industrial armies are formed without any constraint. The only ruse employed is that of showing off and honoring those virgins whom the philosophers would like to keep hidden and surrounded by chaperons and prejudices.

Scenes and Episodes from the New Amorous World

A Session of the Court of Love

The band of adventurers moves forward through a cloud of perfume and a rain of flowers. The choral groups and musicians of the Phalanx welcome them with hymns of joy. As soon as the visitors have reached the colonnades of the Phalanstery, bowls of flaming punch are brought in and a hundred different nectars spurt from the opened fountains. All the knights and ladies are wearing their most seductive clothing. Two hundred priests and priestesses, who are dressed no less elegantly, greet their guests and perform the introductions. After refreshments have been served, the whole group mounts to the throne room where the pontiff Isis is seated. The welcoming ceremonies are concluded there and, after washing, all the visitors proceed to the confessional.

The high priests begin to examine the adventurers and to read their written declarations. A few adventurers, who have been examined at their last stop, give the priests the commentaries written by their previous confessors. Everyone hands over a written summary of his or her most recent confession together with whatever observations may have been added by the consistory of the last Phalanx visited.

While the visitors are eating a light snack, the work of analyzing and classifying their confessions goes on in the consistory. A list of five or six sympathetic relationships is drawn up for each knight and lady on the basis of the examinations conducted by the young priests and priestesses who wish to become sympathetic with the adventurers. Before the snack is over the fairies and genies have completed their task of match-making. Their recommendations are delivered to the office of the High Matron along with a summary of each confession. Sympathetic matching takes everything into account, and the final choices made are those which seem most likely to complement previous encounters either through contrast or identity.

I am only speaking here about young adventurers. The amorous affairs of the older adventurers are handled by the fakirs who use other methods. . . .

The first moments of the visit are taken up by ceremonial activities which should always include an informal meal. This meal will give everyone a chance to satisfy his curiosity, to move about from one person to another and to form some general impression of the visitors. Of course they too need to see how the land lies. People should get a brief look at one another before amorous affairs get underway. This interlude also allows time for the theoretical determination of sympathies; it enables everyone to have his own list of partners in time for the opening of the court of love. It should be added that up until the opening of the court of love the Vestals and the children are free to mingle with the visitors and to satisfy their curiosity about them. This is a most important precaution since the children might otherwise wish to enter the court of love, which they are not allowed to do. Thus the session does not begin until they have seen all they want of the visitors and are quite ready for bed. Only then do the adventurers go to the office of the High Matron to get back their papers and to look at the portraits of their designated sympathetic partners.

When the preludes are over the adventurers and their hosts gather in the salon. A salvo is fired to announce the opening of the session. On one side of the salon stands the whole band of adventurers. On the other side the priesthood is gathered along with other people who have been designated as sympathetic partners or who have come to take part in the amorous activities. The priests are placed opposite the adventuresses and the priestesses opposite the adventurers.

When the Head Fairy waves her wand a semi-bacchanalia gets underway. The members of both groups rush into each other's arms, and in the ensuing scramble caresses are liberally given and received. Everyone strokes and investigates whatever comes to hand and surrenders himself or herself to the unfettered impulses of simple nature. Each participant flits from one person to another, bestowing kisses everywhere with as much eagerness as rapidity. Everyone also makes a special point of encountering those individuals who caught his or her eye earlier. This brief bacchanalia allows people to verify the physical attributes of those to whom they are attracted, and it can lay the ground work for the establishment of sympathetic relationships between people who are more inclined to physical than spiritual pleasure.

It would be wrong, however, to suppose that this first confused skirmish exercises a decisive influence on the match-making that is to follow. Indeed, it would be bad form for anyone to make a binding commitment at the outset before formally encountering his designated sympathetic partners. People who have gotten together in the scramble will be able to renew their acquaintance later, and they will only love each other all the more if it turns out that their calculated sympathies, of which they are as yet unaware, are consistent with the preferences revealed in the bacchanalia.

Some of our civilized materialists might wish to conclude their investigations at this point. They would claim that this opening skirmish is all they need to make their choice. It will, in fact, be enough for monogynies dominated by the passion of touch; and they will not be prevented from forming sensual relationships with like-minded partners encountered during the bacchanalia. But such relationships, which are no more than simple amorous ties, deriving from purely physical affinities, will satisfy no more than a twentieth of the lovers in Harmony. . . . For the goal of Harmony is to establish compound amorous relationships based on both physical and spiritual affinities. Thus while the opening sensual skirmish is indispensable, it is only a prelude. It is the first phase in a process which moves, according to the law of progression, from the simple to the compound. Since nature's first thrust is always towards the physical, it would be contrary to the natural order of things to begin by occupying lovers with transcendent and spiritual illusions. The natural impulse should first be reinforced by a little opening bacchanalia, and then the sentiments should be brought into play with the help of the fairies. When sentimental inclinations are linked to the physical ties already established, pleasure will be compounded.

Let us return to our narrative. The opening caresses and exploratory activities should last no more than a few minutes, barely a quarter of an hour. To break up the skirmish, use should be made of a divisive agent. Since everything is done by attraction in Harmony, mixed or homosexual attractions should be employed. Groups of Sapphists and Spartites[9] should therefore be thrown into the fray to attack people of their own kind. Such people are easy to recognize in Harmony since everyone wears plumes or epaulettes designating his passions. These two new groups will create a general distraction and disunite a number of couples. At that point the senior confessors will have no difficulty in calling a halt to the skirmish, and everyone will proceed to the reconnoitering-room.

The reconnoitering-room contains two tiered and elevated stands. These stands face each other in such a way that anyone on one stand can get a good look at everyone on the other. All of the adventurers are placed on one side and all the sympathetic candidates on the other.

The actual matching is done by the matrons each of whom takes charge of five or six lovers. . . . The matrons point out the various partners who have been designated for each individual. The individual has been given a list with precise information concerning the spiritual affinities and temporary inclinations of each of his potential partners. He is also able to determine their physical attraction since they are right before his eyes and since he has perhaps already gotten acquainted with them during the introductory bacchanalia. . . .

When the inspection is over, everyone proceeds to the festival hall where the encounter takes place. The encounter is supervised by the fairies and genies whose tasks are much more delicate than those of the matrons. First of all there will be certain problems to resolve. A number of people may desire the same lover. A given priest may be desired by ten adventuresses and a given priestess by ten adventurers. Such conflicting claims would be very troublesome in civilized gatherings. . . . But anyone who has been in love several times knows that people often develop passionate spiritual sympathies for individuals who did not seem at all attractive to them at first. The whole point of the operations of the court of love is to determine these spiritual sympathies at the very outset in order to minimize competition for the most physically attractive individuals. Such competition leaves some people with throngs of admirers and leaves a great many other people in a state of abandonment.

In Harmony sheer physical attractiveness will not have the colossal influence that it has in civilization where everyone is transfixed by the sight of a beautiful woman. Of course the Harmonians will not fail to appreciate physical beauty; in fact their judgement will be considerably more discerning than ours. But when it comes to the selection of sympathetic partners their choices will not be determined by physical charm. For their desire for sensual gratification will be satisfied in several different ways.

First of all the adventurers will never fail to ask for an exhibition of simple nature, a session in which the amorous notabilities of the area, and of their own band, show off their most remarkable attributes. A woman who has only a beautiful bosom exhibits only the bosom and leaves the rest of her body covered. Another who has only an attractive waist bares it and leaves the rest covered. Another who wishes to exhibit everything she has appears completely naked. Men do the same. No one can say after this session that he has been denied a chance to admire all the physical attractions of the region.

In addition to this exhibition of simple nature, the visitors will be able to organize orgies to be held the following day. At these orgies, which will be appropriately harmonized, everyone will have ample opportunity to derive satisfaction from the beauties displayed at the exhibition.[10]

The physical needs of the adventurers are satisfied in this way at every Phalanx they visit. Given the human need for variety and contrast, the most pressing desire of the adventurers when they arrive at a new Phalanx will therefore be for spiritual sympathy rather than for mere physical gratification.

It should also be pointed out that if, at the end of a visit, an adventuress takes a fancy to a handsome priest with whom she has not made love, it will be possible for her to obtain satisfaction during the farewell session. Such gestures of traditional courtesy should not be refused to any member of a departing band.

As a result of these measures, no one will suffer from a lack of physical gratification. Thus the important problems to be dealt with at the court of love will concern the establishment of spiritual sympathies. . . . The encounters which take place in the festival hall will be run in an alternating pattern. First of all the adventurers and adventuresses will be taken by their fairies to meet the priests and priestesses whom they have chosen as their most desirable sympathetic partners. Then the priests and priestesses will go to meet the adventurers whom they have selected. No final decisions will be made until everyone has had a chance to converse with all his or her candidates. Everyone must have a chance to present himself to those he desires and to inspect the information recorded on their escutcheons concerning their personalities, their habits, current caprices, most recent passions, and their need of alternating and contrasting pleasures.

Little by little, as alliances are established, the group will grow smaller. The first and most rapid matchings will be dictated by romantic inspiration or by pure sensuality. But these sudden alliances may well be compound sympathies since everyone has already had the opportunity to study his list and to scrutinize his potential partners. . . . All those who are definitively matched up withdraw in order to permit the others to proceed with their encounters. Although it may be necessary for repeated enquiries to be made, this should be done without undue haste. Some alliances take a long time to form: preliminary discussions may go awry and a couple may only come to terms in the ballroom or even at supper. Such delays are commonplace among the more refined individuals.

Those who are the last to make up their minds do not run the risk of being left out or badly matched, for the fakirs may always intervene to satisfy them. But in general the tardy couples. . . . get along particularly well because they have spent a long time flirting with each other. Moreover, if the sympathies which bind the tardy couples are somewhat lacking in intensity, their pleasures are always compound and never simple.

In all of these encounters great care is taken to avoid wounding anyone's pride. This is the particular responsibility of the fairies. Even when they are serving as protectors to just two individuals, they can make sure that no one's feelings are hurt. For if after a conversation one person wishes to refuse his or her suitor, the reason for the refusal is told only to the fairy who explains things to the rejected suitor with the utmost delicacy. The fairies abandon their proteges only when they are no longer needed, when two potential partners have established a sufficiently intimate relationship to reach an agreement of their own accord.

I have only described a single phase in the workings of the court of love. But it is already clear that in just two or three hours' time it can cement a host of happy alliances or compound sympathetic relationships of a sort that it takes months to establish in civilization. For it takes an extremely long time to understand the character of any civilized individual, and especially of a civilized woman.

The sympathetic intrigue which take place on the morning after the arrival of a group of visitors will be even more lively than those of the night before. For affairs which miscarried or failed to ripen will be renewed, and there will also be cases of infidelity to lend a touch of variety. The sympathetic relationships which endure will be particularly noteworthy in view of the fact that there will be many temptations to overcome. During a visit of three days almost all the adventurers and adventuresses will waver in their sympathies, finally returning to partners whom they barely got to know in the opening session. All this of course is quite independent of their participation in the orgies, the exposition of simple nature, the bacchanalias, etc. These material distractions are interludes in which both partners in a sympathetic relationship generally participate by mutual consent. They are moments of respite which do not destroy a relationship and which are not even considered to be acts of infidelity when they have been mutually agreed upon. Momentary respites of this sort are widely practiced in Harmony not only by sympathetic partners but also by the most faithful lovers. For on special occasions such as the visit of a band of adventurers. . . . there are so many temptations that even the most faithful are likely to succumb. In order to avoid losing the privileges of fidelity they agree to break off their relationship for a stipulated period in accordance with the provision of the code of love. . . .

It is evident that the task of arranging sympathetic relationships cannot be assumed by young people. . . . Decisions must be made which can only be entrusted to elderly and experienced individuals. Without their cooperation a band of visitors would be reduced to forming brutish relationships like the dirty and dangerous orgies of civilization in which partners are chosen uniquely on the basis of simple love and physical attraction. . . .

Let us consider the benefits that the elderly will derive from their services as amorous intermediaries. The task will not be at all wearisome for them. A skilled and knowledgeable pontiff will take pride in his or her abilities as a match-maker. . . . It will also be common for a traveler to become passionately attached to his confessors. For apart from the fact that many individuals have an innate penchant for elderly people when they are agreeable, there will also be times when this penchant will be aroused by the methodical progression of sympathies. A skillful confessoress will manage to discern this need in the soul of her client and she will even try to call it forth. No one will be taken by surprise in such cases since, according to the custom of the court of love, the confessoress herself will be wearing medals or epaulettes indicating her own spiritual situation, her character, and her most recent impressions. Whenever the need for a sympathetic union between persons of divergent ages arises, it will be very much to the advantage of the confessors and confessoresses.

They say that no one does anything for nothing in this world; and if it is right for the elderly to assist the young in amorous affairs, it is just as right for them to be repaid for their services. . . . I cannot repeat too often, however, that customs so alien to ours cannot be established during the first years of Harmony. It will first be necessary to purge the globe of syphilis and other skin diseases. Until this is accomplished, Harmony will be more circumspect about love than civilization now is. (*OC*, 7:209–220)

NOTES

1. Fourier refers to the decade of fighting which followed the Negro rebellion led by Toussaint L'Ouverture in Haiti during the French Revolution.

2. According to the French electoral laws which prevailed in 1822, when this text was published, the right to vote was contingent upon the payment of at least 300 francs a year in direct taxes. To run for elective office a man had to pay at least 1,000 francs in taxes. In all of France only 110,000 "electors" and 16,000 eligible office holders met these qualifications.

3. "Black care rides behind the horseman." Horace, *Odes* bk. III, i. 40.

4. Elsewhere (*OC,* 4:37) Fourier notes that drudge duty "will be assigned to a few individuals whose temperaments are appropriate to such tasks, which they will transform into games."

5. The Little Bands, most of whom were girls, were to provide material adornment and moral uplift in Harmony. Although their contribution was less essential than that of the Little Hordes, it should not be neglected. The following account of their functions is drawn from *OC,* 6:214–216:

> The Little Bands are the guardians of *social charm.* Their job is less spectacular than that of the Little Hordes, who are entrusted with the defense of *social harmony.* However, great importance is attached to finery and to collective luxury in the societary system, and the Little Bands make a valuable contribution in this domain. Their main function is the *physical and spiritual* adornment of the whole community. . . .

> Completely different in style from the Little Hordes, they are devotees of Attic restraint and purity. They are very polite; it is the girls rather than the boys who set the tone among them. . . . Only a third of the members of the Little Bands are boys, and they are the studious ones, the precocious scholars like Pascal, as well as those effeminate young lads who show early tendencies to indolence.

> Less active than the Little Hordes, the Little Bands are slower to rise and they do not get to the workshops until four o'clock in the morning. They wouldn't be needed earlier since they have little to do with the care of the larger animals. But they are devoted to those species which are difficult to raise and tame, such as passenger pigeons and other birds, beavers and zebras.

> The Little Bands have jurisdiction over the vegetable kingdom. Anyone who breaks a tree-branch, picks a forbidden flower or an unripe fruit, or accidentally steps on a plant is brought before the Senate of the Little Bands. This Senate renders judgment by virtue of a special penal code similar to the code of animal care which is enforced by the Divan of the Little Hordes.

> Entrusted with the spiritual and physical adornment of the community, the Little Bands perform academic functions similar to those of the French Academy. They censor bad language and faulty pronunciation. . . . The Senate of the Little Bands even has the right to censor literary works produced by adults. It draws up a list of the mistakes in grammar and pronunciation made by every member of the community and forwards the list to the guilty parties, advising them not to repeat the same mistakes. . . .

Just as the Little Hordes have their Druids and Druidesses, the Little Bands have their own adult associates, who are known as Corybants. They also have their own allies among the groups of voyagers who travel about Harmony. Whereas the Little Hordes are allied to the big hordes of Adventurers and Adventuresses who belong to the industrial armies, the Little Bands are affiliated with the big bands of Knights and Ladies Errant who are dedicated to the fine arts.

6. On the industrial armies see below. . . .

7. On the Vestals see below. . . .

8. Young men and women between the ages of 15½ and 20.

9. Female and male homosexuals.

10. Elsewhere in *Le Nouveau monde amoureux* (*OC*, 7:329–332) Fourier discusses a variation on these proceedings: a type of "museum orgy" offering no more than visual gratification and designed to encourage the development of the aesthetic faculties of the Harmonians. His discussion concludes: "In civilization such meetings would be no more than bawdy gatherings because artistic taste and knowledge are not widespread. Our generation lacks the means to ennoble the amorous orgy, and especially the museum orgy. We are even more lacking in the general goodwill which will prevail among the Harmonians. Thus it is not surprising that the expression 'amorous orgy' evokes ideas of secret debauchery" (*OC*, 7:331).

14

Karl Marx

"Estranged Labor"[1] (1844)

Karl Marx (1818–1883) is widely regarded as the foremost socialist thinker. Although born and educated in Germany, Marx spent most of his life in political exile, first in France and later in England. His writings combine philosophy and politics, demonstrating the commitment he stated in his famous phrase: "The philosophers have only interpreted the world, in various ways; the point, however, is to change it." In this first selection from The Economic and Philosophical Manuscripts of 1844, *Marx outlines his theory of alienation (or estrangement), which explains the loss of meaning workers experience due to the dehumanizing conditions of capitalist production. Marx also offers an alternative vision of human fulfillment that is influenced by his early studies with Hegel and by the utopian socialists, including Fourier.*

WE HAVE PROCEEDED from the premises of political economy. We have accepted its language and its laws. We presupposed private property, the separation of labor, capital and land, and of wages, profit of capital and rent of land—likewise division of labor, competition, the concept of exchange-value, etc. On the basis of political economy itself, in its own words, we have shown that the worker sinks to the level of a commodity and becomes indeed the most wretched of commodities; that the wretchedness of the worker is in inverse proportion to the power and magnitude of his production; that the necessary result of competition

Source: Karl Marx. "Estranged Labor" in *Economic and Philosophical Manuscripts.* Ed. Dirk Stuik. Trans. Martin Milligan (Moscow: Progress Publishers, 1959), 106–119. Reprinted with the permission of International Publishers Co.

is the accumulation of capital in a few hands, and thus the restoration of monopoly in a more terrible form; and that finally the distinction between capitalist and land rentier, like that between the tiller of the soil and the factory worker, disappears and that the whole of society must fall apart into the two classes—the property *owners* and the propertyless *workers*.

Political economy starts with the fact of private property, but it does not explain it to us. It expresses in general, abstract formulas the *material* process through which private property actually passes, and these formulas it then takes for *laws*. It does not *comprehend* these laws, i.e., it does not demonstrate how they arise from the very nature of private property. Political economy does not disclose the source of the division between labor and capital, and between capital and land. When, for example, it defines the relationship of wages to profit, it takes the interest of the capitalists to be the ultimate cause, i.e., it takes for granted what it is supposed to explain. Similarly, competition comes in everywhere. It is explained from external circumstances. As to how far these external and apparently accidental circumstances are but the expression of a necessary course of development, political economy teaches us nothing. We have seen how exchange itself appears to it as an accidental fact. The only wheels which political economy sets in motion are *greed* and the war *amongst the greedy—competition*.

Precisely because political economy does not grasp the way the movement is connected, it was possible to oppose, for instance, the doctrine of competition to the doctrine of monopoly, the doctrine of the freedom of the crafts to the doctrine of the guild, the doctrine of the division of landed property to the doctrine of the big estate—for competition, freedom of the crafts and the division of landed property were explained and comprehended only as accidental, premeditated and violent consequences of monopoly, of the guild system, and of feudal property, not as their necessary, inevitable and natural consequences.

Now, therefore, we have to grasp the essential connection between private property, greed, and the separation of labor, capital and landed property; between exchange and competition, value and the devaluation of men, monopoly and competition, etc.—the connection between this whole estrangement and the *money* system.

Do not let us go back to a fictitious primordial condition as the political economist does, when he tries to explain. Such a primordial condition explains nothing; it merely pushes the question away into a gray nebulous distance. It assumes in the form of a fact, of an event, what the economist is supposed to deduce—namely, the necessary relationship between two things—between, for example, division of labor and exchange. Theology in the same way explains the origin of evil by the fall of man; that is, it assumes as a fact, in historical form, what has to be explained.

We proceed from an economic fact *of the present.*

The worker becomes all the poorer the more wealth he produces, the more his production increases in power and size. The worker becomes an ever cheaper commodity the more commodities he creates. With the *increasing value* of the world of things proceeds in direct proportion the *devaluation* of the world of men. Labor produces not only commodities: it produces itself and the worker as a *commodity*—and this in the same general proportion in which it produces commodities.

This fact expresses merely that the object which labor produces—labor's product—confronts it as *something alien, as a power independent* of the producer. The product of labor is labor which has been embodied in an object, which has become material: it is the *objectification*[2] of labor. Labor's realization is its objectification. In the sphere of political economy this realization of labor appears as *loss of realization*[3] for the workers; objectification as *loss of the object* and *bondage to it;* appropriation as *estrangement, as alienation.*[4]

So much does labor's realization appear as loss of realization that the worker loses realization to the point of starving to death. So much does objectification appear as loss of the object that the worker is robbed of the objects most necessary not only for his life but for his work. Indeed, labor itself becomes an object which he can obtain only with the greatest effort and with the most irregular interruptions. So much does the appropriation of the object appear as estrangement that the more objects the worker produces the less he can possess and the more he falls under the sway of his product, capital.

All these consequences result from the fact that the worker is related to the *product of his labor* as to an *alien* object. For on this premise it is clear that the more the worker spends himself, the more powerful becomes the alien world of objects which he creates over and against himself, the poorer he himself— his inner world—becomes, the less belongs to him as his own. It is the same in religion. The more man puts into God, the less he retains in himself. The worker puts his life into the object; but now his life no longer belongs to him but to the object. Hence, the greater this activity, the greater is the worker's lack of objects. Whatever the product of his labor is, he is not. Therefore the greater this product, the less is he himself. The *alienation* of the worker in his product means not only that his labor becomes an object, an *external* existence, but that it exists *outside him,* independently, as something alien to him, and that it becomes a power on its own confronting him. It means that the life which he has conferred on the object confronts him as something hostile and alien.

Let us now look more closely at the *objectification,* at the production of the worker; and in it at the *estrangement,* the *loss* of the object, of his product.

The worker can create nothing without *nature*, without the *sensuous external world*.[5] It is the material on which his labor is realized, in which it is active, from which and by means of which it produces.

But just as nature provides labor with the *means of life* in the sense that labor cannot *live* without objects on which to operate, on the other hand, it also provides the *means of life* in the more restricted sense, i.e., the means for the physical subsistence of the *worker* himself.

Thus the more the worker by his labor *appropriates* the external world, hence sensuous nature, the more he deprives himself of *means of life* in a double manner: first, in that the sensuous external world more and more ceases to be an object belonging to his labor—to be his labor's *means of life;* and secondly, in that it more and more ceases to be *means of life* in the immediate sense, means for the physical subsistence of the worker.

In both respects, therefore, the worker becomes a slave of his object, first, in that he receives an *object of labor,* i.e., in that he receives *work;* and secondly, in that he receives *means of subsistence*. Therefore, it enables him to exist, first, as a *worker;* and, second, as a *physical subject*. The height of this bondage is that it is only as a worker that he continues to maintain himself as a *physical subject,* and that it is only as a physical subject that he is a *worker.*

(The laws of political economy express the estrangement of the worker in his object thus: the more the worker produces, the less he has to consume; the more values he creates, the more valueless, the more unworthy he becomes; the better formed his product, the more deformed becomes the worker; the more civilized his object, the more barbarous becomes the worker; the more powerful labor becomes, the more powerless becomes the worker; the more ingenious labor becomes, the less ingenious becomes the worker and the more he becomes nature's bondsman.)

Political economy conceals the estrangement inherent in the nature of labor by not considering the direct relationship between the worker (labor) *and production*. It is true that labor produces for the rich wonderful things—but for the worker it produces privation. It produces palaces—but for the worker, hovels. It produces beauty but for the worker, deformity. It replaces labor by machines, but it throws a section of the workers back to a barbarous type of labor, and it turns the other workers into machines. It produces intelligence—but for the worker stupidity, cretinism.

The direct relationship of labor to its products is the relationship of the worker to the objects of his production. The relationship of the man of means to the objects of production and to production itself is only a *consequence* of this first relationship— and confirms it. We shall consider this other aspect later.

When we ask, then, what is the essential relationship of labor we are asking about the relationship of the *worker* to production.

Till now we have been considering the estrangement, the alienation of the worker only in one of its aspects, i.e., the worker's *relationship to the products of his labor*. But the estrangement is manifested not only in the result but in the *act of production*, within the *producing activity*, itself. How could the worker come to face the product of his activity as a stranger, were it not that in the very act of production he was estranging himself from himself? The product is after all but the summary of the activity, of production. If then the product of labor is alienation, production itself must be active alienation, the alienation of activity, the activity of alienation. In the estrangement of the object of labor is merely summarized the estrangement, the alienation, in the activity of labor itself.

What, then, constitutes the alienation of labor?

First, the fact that labor is *external* to the worker, i.e., it does not belong to his essential being; that in his work, therefore, he does not affirm himself but denies himself, does not feel content but unhappy, does not develop freely his physical and mental energy but mortifies his body and ruins his mind. The worker therefore only feels himself outside his work, and in his work feels outside himself. He is at home when he is not working, and when he is working he is not at home. His labor is therefore not voluntary, but coerced; it is *forced labor*. It is therefore not the satisfaction of a need; it is merely a *means* to satisfy needs external to it. Its alien character emerges clearly in the fact that as soon as no physical or other compulsion exists, labor is shunned like the plague. External labor, labor in which man alienates himself, is a labor of self-sacrifice, of mortification. Lastly, the external character of labor for the worker appears in the fact that it is not his own, but someone else's, that it does not belong to him, that in it he belongs, not to himself, but to another. Just as in religion the spontaneous activity of the human imagination, of the human brain and the human heart, operates independently of the individual—that is, operates on him as an alien, divine or diabolical activity—so is the worker's activity not his spontaneous activity. It belongs to another; it is the loss of his self.

As a result, therefore, man (the worker) only feels himself freely active in his animal functions—eating, drinking, procreating, or at most in his dwelling and in dressing-up, etc.; and in his human functions he no longer feels himself to be anything but an animal. What is animal becomes human and what is human becomes animal.

Certainly eating, drinking, procreating, etc., are also genuinely human functions. But abstractly taken, separated from the sphere of all other human activity and turned into sole and ultimate ends, they are animal functions.

We have considered the act of estranging practical human activity, labor, in two of its aspects.

1. The relation of the worker to the *product of labor* as an alien object exercising power over him. This relation is at the same time the relation to the

sensuous external world, to the objects of nature, as an alien world inimically opposed to him.

2. The relation of labor to the *act of production* within the *labor* process. This relation is the relation of the worker to his own activity as an alien activity not belonging to him; it is activity as suffering, strength as weakness, begetting as emasculating, the worker's *own* physical and mental energy, his personal life indeed, what is life but activity?—as an activity which is turned against him, independent of him and not belonging to him. Here we have *self-estrangement,* as previously we had the estrangement of the *thing.*

We have still a third aspect of *estranged labor* to deduce from the two already considered.

Man is a species being,[6] not only because in practice and in theory he adopts the species as his object (his own as well as those of other things), but—and this is only another way of expressing it—also because he treats himself as the actual, living species; because he treats himself as a *universal* and therefore a free being.

The life of the species, both in man and in animals, consists physically in the fact that man (like the animal) lives on inorganic nature; and the more universal man is compared with an animal, the more universal is the sphere of inorganic nature on which he lives. Just as plants, animals, stones, air, light, etc., constitute theoretically a part of human consciousness, partly as objects of natural science, partly as objects of art—his spiritual inorganic nature, spiritual nourishment which he must first prepare to make palatable and digestible—so also in the realm of practice they constitute a part of human life and human activity. Physically man lives only on these products of nature, whether they appear in the form of food, heating, clothes, a dwelling, etc. The universality of man appears in practice precisely in the universality which makes all nature his *inorganic body*—both inasmuch as nature is (1) his direct means of life, and (2) the material, the object, and the instrument of his life activity. Nature is man's *inorganic body*—nature, that is, in so far as it is not itself the human body. Man *lives* on nature—means that nature is his *body,* with which he must remain in continuous interchange if he is not to die. That man's physical and spiritual life is linked to nature means simply that nature is linked to itself, for man is a part of nature.

In estranging from man (1) nature, and (2) himself, his own active functions, his life activity, estranged labor estranges the *species* from man. It changes for him the *life of the species* into a means of individual life. First it estranges the life of the species and individual life, and secondly it makes individual life in its abstract form the purpose of the life of the life of the species, likewise in its abstract and estranged form.

Indeed, labor, *life-activity, productive life,* itself, appears in the first place merely as a *means* of satisfying a need—the need to maintain physical existence. Yet the productive life is the species. It is life-engendering life. The whole character of a species—its species character—is contained in the character of its life activity; and free, conscious activity is man's species character. Life itself appears only as a *means to life*.

The animal is immediately one with its life activity. It does not distinguish itself from it. It is *its life activity*. Man makes his life activity itself the object of his will and of his consciousness. He has conscious life activity. It is not a determination with which he directly merges. Conscious life activity distinguishes man immediately from animal life activity. It is just because of this that he is a species being. Or rather, it is only because he is a species being that he is a conscious being, i.e., that his own life is an object for him. Only because of that is his activity free activity. Estranged labor reverses this relationship, so that it is just because man is a conscious being that he makes his life activity, his *essential* being, a mere means to his *existence*.

In creating a *world of objects*[7] by his practical activity, in *his work upon* inorganic nature, man proves himself a conscious species being, i.e., as a being that treats the species as its own essential being, or that treats itself as a species being. Admittedly animals also produce. They build themselves nests, dwellings, like the bees, beavers, ants, etc. But an animal only produces what it immediately needs for itself or its young. It produces one-sidedly, whilst man produces universally. It produces only under the dominion of immediate physical need, whilst man produces even when he is free from physical need and only truly produces in freedom therefore. An animal produces only itself, whilst man reproduces the whole of nature. An animal's product belongs immediately to its physical body, whilst man freely confronts his product. An animal forms things in accordance with the standard and the need of the species to which it belongs, whilst man knows how to produce in accordance with the standard of every species, and knows how to apply everywhere the inherent standard to the object. Man therefore also forms things in accordance with the laws of beauty.

It is just in his work upon the objective world, therefore, that man first really proves himself to be a *species being*. This production is his active species life. Through and because of this production, nature appears as *his* work and his reality. The object of labor is, therefore, the *objectification of man's species life*: for he duplicates himself not only, as in consciousness, intellectually, but also actively, in reality, and therefore he contemplates himself in a world that he has created. In tearing away from man the object of his production, therefore, estranged labor tears from him his *species life*, his real objectivity as a member of the species and transforms his advantage over animals into the disadvantage that his inorganic body, nature, is taken away from him.

Similarly, in degrading spontaneous, free, activity, to a means, estranged labor makes man's species life a means to his physical existence.

The consciousness which man has of his species is thus transformed by estrangement in such a way that species life becomes for him a means.

Estranged labor turns thus:

3. *Man's species being,* both nature and his spiritual species property, into a being *alien* to him, into a *means* to his *individual existence.* It estranges from man his own body, as well as external nature and his spiritual essence, his *human* being.

4. An immediate consequence of the fact that man is estranged from the product of his labor, from his life activity, from his species being is the *estrangement of man* from *man.* When man confronts himself, he confronts the *other* man. What applies to a man's relation to his work, to the product of his labor and to himself, also holds of a man's relation to the other man, and to the other man's labor and object of labor.

In fact, the proposition that man's species nature is estranged from him means that one man is estranged from the other, as each of them is from man's essential nature.

The estrangement of man, and in fact every relationship in which man stands to himself, is first realized and expressed in the relationship in which a man stands to other men.

Hence within the relationship of estranged labor each man views the other in accordance with the standard and the relationship in which he finds himself as a worker.

We took our departure from a fact of political economy—the estrangement of the worker and his production. We have formulated this fact in conceptual terms as *estranged, alienated* labor. We have analyzed this concept—hence analyzing merely a fact of political economy.

Let us now see, further, how the concept of estranged, alienated labor must express and present itself in real life.

If the product of labor is alien to me, if it confronts me as an alien power, to whom, then, does it belong?

If my own activity does not belong to me, if it is an alien, a coerced activity, to whom, then, does it belong?

To a being *other* than myself.

Who is this being?

The *gods?* To be sure, in the earliest times the principal production (for example, the building of temples, etc., in Egypt, India and Mexico) appears to be in the service of the gods, and the product belongs to the gods. However, the gods on their own were never the lords of labor. No more was *nature.* And what a contradiction it would be if, the more man subjugated nature by his labor and the more the miracles of the gods were rendered superfluous by the miracles of industry, the more man were to renounce the joy of production and the enjoyment of the product in favor of these powers.

The *alien* being, to whom labor and the product of labor belongs, in whose service labor is done and for whose benefit the product of labor is provided, can only be *man* himself.

If the product of labor does not belong to the worker, if it confronts him as an alien power, then this can only be because it belongs to some *other man than the worker*. If the worker's activity is a torment to him, to another it must be *delight* and his life's joy. Not the gods, not nature, but only man himself can be this alien power over man.

We must bear in mind the previous proposition that man's relation to himself only becomes for him *objective* and *actual*[8] through his relation to the other man. Thus, if the product of his labor, *objectified*, is for him an *alien*, hostile, powerful object independent of him, then his position towards it is such that someone else is master of this object, someone who is alien, hostile, powerful, and independent of him. If his own activity is to him related as an unfree activity, then he is related to it as an activity performed in the service, under the dominion, the coercion, and the yoke of another man.

Every self-estrangement of man, from himself and from nature, appears in the relation in which he places himself and nature to men other than and differentiated from himself. For this reason religious self-estrangement necessarily appears in the relationship of the layman to the priest, or again to a mediator, etc., since we are here dealing with the intellectual world. In the real practical world self-estrangement can only become manifest through the real practical relationship to other men. The medium through which estrangement takes place is itself *practical*. Thus through estranged labor man not only creates his relationship to the object and to the act of production as to men that are alien and hostile to him; he also creates the relationship in which other men stand to his production and to his product, and the relationship in which he stands to these other men. Just as he creates his own production as the loss of his reality, as his punishment; his own product as a loss, as a product not belonging to him; so he creates the domination of the person who does not produce over production and over the product. Just as he estranges his own activity from himself, so he confers to the stranger an activity which is not his own.

We have until now only considered this relationship from the standpoint of the worker and later we shall be considering it also from the standpoint of the non-worker.

Through *estranged, alienated labor*, then, the worker produces the relationship to this labor of a man alien to labor and standing outside it. The relationship of the worker to labor created the relation to it of the capitalist (or whatever one chooses to call the master of labor). *Private property* is thus the product, the result, the necessary consequence, of *alienated labor*, of the external relation of the worker to nature and to himself.

Private property thus results by analysis from the concept of *alienated labor*, i.e., of *alienated man*, of estranged labor, of estranged life, of *estranged* man.

True, it is as a result of the *movement of private property* that we have obtained the concept of *alienated labor (of alienated life)* from political economy. But on analysis of this concept it becomes clear that though private property appears to be the source, the cause of alienated labor, it is rather its consequence, just as the gods are *originally* not the cause but the effect of man's intellectual confusion. Later this relationship becomes reciprocal.

Only at the last culmination of the development of private property does this, its secret, appear again, namely, that on the one hand it is the *product* of alienated labor, and that on the other it is the *means* by which labor alienates itself, the *realization of this alienation.*

This exposition immediately sheds light on various hitherto unsolved conflicts.

1. Political economy starts from labor as the real soul of production; yet to labor it gives nothing, and to private property everything. Confronting this contradiction, [Pierre-Joseph] Proudhon has decided in favor of labor against private property. We understand, however, that this apparent contradiction is the contradiction of *estranged labor* with itself, and that political economy has merely formulated the laws of estranged labor.

We also understand, therefore, that *wages* and *private property* are identical: since the product, as the object of labor pays for labor itself, therefore the wage is but a necessary consequence of labor's estrangement. After all, in the wage of labor, labor does not appear as an end in itself but as the servant of the wage. We shall develop this point later, and meanwhile will only derive some conclusions.[9]

An enforced increase of wages (disregarding all other difficulties, including the fact that it would only be by force, too, that higher wages, being an anomaly, could be maintained) would therefore be nothing but *better payment for the slave*, and would not win either for the worker or for labor their human status and dignity.

Indeed, even the *equality of wages* demanded by Proudhon only transforms the relationship of the present-day worker to his labor into the relationship of all men to labor. Society is then conceived as an abstract capitalist.

Wages are a direct consequence of estranged labor, and estranged labor is the direct cause of private property. The downfall of the one must involve the downfall of the other.

2. From the relationship of estranged labor to private property it follows further that the emancipation of society from private property, etc., from servitude,

is expressed in the *political* form of the *emancipation of the workers;* not that *their* emancipation alone is at stake, but because the emancipation of the workers contains universal human emancipation—and it contains this, because the whole of human servitude is involved in the relation of the worker to production, and every relation of servitude is but a modification and consequence of this relation.

Just as we have derived the concept of *private property* from the concept of *estranged, alienated labor* by *analysis,* so we can develop every *category* of political economy with the help of these two factors; and we shall find again in each category, e.g., trade, competition, capital, money, only a *definite* and *developed expression* of these first elements.

Before considering this aspect, however, let us try to solve two problems.

1. To define the general *nature of private property,* as it has arisen as a result of estranged labor, in its relation to truly *human* and *social property.*

2. We have accepted the *estrangement of labor,* its *alienation,* as a fact, and we have analyzed this fact. How, we now ask, does *man* come to *alienate,* to estrange, *his labor?* How is this estrangement rooted in the nature of human development? We have already gone a long way to the solution of this problem by *transforming* the question of the *origin of private property* into the question of the relation of *alienated labor* to the course of humanity's development. For when one speaks of *private property,* one thinks of dealing with something external to man. When one speaks of labor, one is directly dealing with man himself. This new formulation of the question already contains its solution.

As to (1): The general nature of private property and its relation to truly human property.

Alienated labor has resolved itself for us into two elements which mutually condition one another, or which are but different expressions of one and the same relationship. *Appropriation* appears as *estrangement,* as *alienation;* and *alienation* appears as *appropriation, estrangement* as true introduction into society.[10]

We have considered the one side—*alienated* labor in relation to the *worker* himself, i.e., the *relation of alienated labor to itself.* The *property relation of the non-worker to the worker and to labor* we have found as the product, the necessary outcome of this relationship. *Private property,* as the material, summary expression of alienated labor, embraces both relations—the *relation of the worker to work and to the product of his labor and to the non-worker,* and the relation of the *non-worker to the worker and to the product of his labor.*

Having seen that in relation to the worker who *appropriates* nature by means of his labor, this appropriation appears as estrangement, his own spontaneous activity as activity for another and as activity of another, vitality as a sacrifice of life, production of the object as loss of the object to an alien power, to an *alien* person—we shall now consider the relation to the worker, to labor and its object of this person who is *alien* to labor and the worker.

First it has to be noted that everything which appears in the worker as an *activity of alienation, of estrangement*, appears in the non-worker as a *state of alienation, of estrangement.*

Secondly, that the worker's *real, practical attitude* in production and to the product (as a state of mind) appears in the non-worker confronting him as a *theoretical* attitude.

Thirdly, the non-worker does everything against the worker which the worker does against himself; but he does not do against himself what he does against the worker.

Let us look more closely at these three relations.

[*At this point the first manuscript breaks off unfinished.*]

NOTES

1. Estranged Labor—*Die Entfremdete Arbeit.*
2. Objectification, *Vergegenständlichung:* the process of becoming an object.
3. Loss of realization, *Entwirklichung.* A better translation might be "devaluation." Marx, in true Hegel fashion, opposes *Verwirklichung*, here translated as *realization*, to *Entwirklichung*, the taking away of reality. Here *realization* is meant as accomplishment, performance, making something real. Marx states that the accomplishment of labor turns into its opposite.
4. Alienation, *Entäusserung.*
5. Sensuous, *sinnlich:* what can be observed by means of the senses.
6. Species being, *Gattungswesen*, a term used by Feuerbach, who takes as the *Gattung* mankind as a whole, hence the human species.

Species nature (just like species being), *Gattungswesen:* man's essential nature, *menschliches Wesen.*

The following passages from Feuerbach's *Essence of Christianity* may help readers to understand the ideological background to this part of Marx's thought, and incidentally, to see how Marx accepted but infused with new content concepts made current by Feuerbach as well as by Hegel and the political economists:

"What is this essential difference between man and the brute? . . . Consciousness—but consciousness in the strict sense; for the consciousness implied in the feeling of self as an individual, in discrimination by the senses, in the perception and even judgment of outward things according to definite sensible signs, cannot be denied to the brutes. Consciousness in the strictest sense is present only in a being to whom his species, his essential nature, is an object of thought. The brute is indeed conscious of himself as an individual—and he has accordingly the feeling of self as the common center of successive sensations—but not as a species. . . . In practical life we have to do with individuals; in science, with species. . . . But only a being to whom his own species, his own nature, is an object of thought, can make the essential nature of other things or beings an object of thought. . . . The brute has only a simple, man a twofold life; in the brute, the inner life is one with the outer. Man has both an inner and an outer life.

The inner life of man is the life which has relation to his species—to his general, as distinguished from his individual nature. . . . The brute can exercise no function which has relation to its species without another individual external to itself; but man can perform the functions of thought and speech, which strictly imply such a relation, apart from another individual. . . . Man is in fact at once I and Thou; he can put himself in the place of another, for this reason, that to him his species, his essential nature, and not merely his individuality, is an object of thought. . . . An object to which a subject essentially, necessarily relates, is nothing else than this subject's own, but objective nature. . . ."

The relation of the sun to the earth is, therefore, at the same time a relation of the earth to itself, or to its own nature, for the measure of the size and of the intensity of light which the sun possesses as the object of the earth, is the measure of the distance, which determines the peculiar nature of the earth. . . . In the object which he contemplates, therefore, man becomes acquainted with himself. . . . The power of the object over him is therefore the power of his own nature." (*The Essence of Christianity*, by Ludwig Feuerbach, translated from the second German edition by Marian Evans, London, 1854, pp. 1–5.)

7. Marx's term *gegenständlich* can be translated by "objective," but what is meant is an adjective belonging to *Gegenstand*, object. We believe that *gegenständliche Welt* may be rendered best by "world of objects."

8. *Gegenständlich, wirklich*, in Marx, see previous note. Just as *gegenständlich* belongs to *Gegenstand*, so does *wirklich* belong to *Wirken*, to work. A better translation might be: "man's relation to himself only becomes for him a relation of objects and of work."

9. This obscure sentence becomes somewhat more intelligible, if we remember that in Hegelian terminology "identity" often stands for "unity." There is, Marx seems to say, a unity of opposites between wages and private property, since wages result in private property, and private property is the result of the wage system. Labor, in this process, plays only a mediating role: wages and property are the real poles.

10. Marx calls estrangement *die wahre Einbürgerung*. This means "truly becoming a part of society." The sentence seems to mean that alienation is the key to society.

15

Karl Marx and Friedrich Engels

The Communist Manifesto (1848)

Marx and Engels wrote The Communist Manifesto *for the Communist League, an association of radical workers, on the eve of the revolutions of 1848. Although the failure of those revolutions forced them to rethink some of its claims, Marx and Engels continued to regard the* Manifesto *as the best single statement of their theory of history as class struggle. Here they portray the victory of socialism as the inevitable outcome of the self-destructive tendencies of capitalist economies, especially the increasing exploitation of the working class.*

A SPECTRE IS haunting Europe—the spectre of Communism. All the Powers of old Europe have entered into a holy alliance to exorcize this spectre: Pope and Czar, Metternich and Guizot, French Radicals and German policy spies.

Where is the party in opposition that has not been decried as Communistic by its opponents in power? Where the Opposition that has not hurled back the branding reproach of Communism, against the more advanced opposition parties as well as against its reactionary adversaries?

Two things result from this fact:

I. Communism is already acknowledged by all European Powers to be itself a Power.

II. It is high time that Communists should openly, in the face of the whole world, publish their views, their aims, their tendencies, and meet this nursery tale of the Spectre of Communism with a Manifesto of the party itself.

To this end, Communists of various nationalities have assembled in London, and sketched the following Manifesto, to be published in the English, French, German, Italian, Flemish and Danish languages.

Bourgeois and Proletarians[i]

The history of all hitherto existing society[ii] is the history of class struggles.

Freeman and slave, patrician and plebeian, lord and serf, guild-master and journeyman, in a word, oppressor and oppressed, stood in constant opposition to one another, carried on an uninterrupted, now hidden, now open fight, a fight that each time ended, either in a revolutionary reconstitution of society at large, or in the common ruin of the contending classes.

In the earlier epochs of history, we find almost everywhere a complicated arrangement of society into various orders, a manifold gradation of social rank. In ancient Rome we have patricians, knights, plebeians, slaves; in the Middle Ages, feudal lords, vassals, guild-masters, journeymen, apprentices, serfs; in almost all of these classes, again, subordinate gradations.

The modern bourgeois society that has sprouted from the ruins of feudal society has not done away with class antagonisms. It has but established new classes, new conditions of oppression, new forms of struggle in place of the old ones.

Our epoch, the epoch of the bourgeoisie, possesses, however, this distinctive feature: it has simplified the class antagonisms. Society as a whole is more and more splitting up into two great hostile camps, into two great classes directly facing each other: Bourgeoisie and Proletariat.

From the serfs of the Middle Ages sprang the chartered burghers of the earliest towns. From these burgesses the first elements of the bourgeoisie were developed.

The discovery of America, the rounding of the Cape, opened up fresh ground for the rising bourgeoisie. The East-Indian and Chinese markets, the colonization of America, trade with the colonies, the increase in the means of exchange and in commodities generally, gave to commerce, to navigation, to industry, an

---

i By bourgeoisie is meant the class of modern Capitalists, owners of the means of social production and employers of wage labor. By proletariat, the class of modern wage-laborers who, having no means of production of their own, are reduced to selling their labor power in order to live. [Note by Engels to the English edition of 1888.]

ii That is, all *written* history. In 1847, the pre-history of society, the social organization existing previous to recorded history, was all but unknown. Since then, Haxthausen discovered common ownership of land in Russia, Maurer proved it to be the social foundation from which all Teutonic races started in history, and by and by village communities were found to be, or to have been the primitive form of society everywhere from India to Ireland. The inner organization of this primitive Communistic society was laid bare, in its typical form, by Morgan's crowning discovery of the true nature of the *gens* and its relation to the tribe. With the dissolution of these primeval communities society begins to be differentiated into separate and finally antagonistic classes. I have attempted to retrace this process of dissolution in: *Der Ursprung der Familie, des Privateigenthums und des Staats (The Origin of the Family, Private Property and the State)*, 2d edition, Stuttgart 1886. [Note by Engels to the English edition of 1888.]

impulse never before known, and thereby, to the revolutionary element in the tottering feudal society, a rapid development.

The feudal system of industry, under which industrial production was monopolized by closed guilds, now no longer sufficed for the growing wants of the new markets. The manufacturing system took its place. The guild-masters were pushed on one side by the manufacturing middle class; division of labour between the different corporate guilds vanished in the face of division of labour in each single workshop.

Meantime the markets kept ever growing, the demand ever rising. Even manufacture no longer sufficed. Thereupon, steam and machinery revolutionized industrial production. The place of manufacture was taken by the giant, Modern Industry, the place of the industrial middle class, by industrial millionaires, the leaders of whole industrial armies, the modern bourgeois.

Modern industry has established the world market, for which the discovery of America paved the way. This market has given an immense development to commerce, to navigation, to communication by land. This development has, in its turn, reacted on the extension of industry; and in proportion as industry, commerce, navigation, railways extended, in the same proportion the bourgeoisie developed, increased its capital, and pushed into the background every class handed down from the Middle Ages.

We see, therefore, how the modern bourgeoisie is itself the product of a long course of development, of a series of revolutions in the modes of production and of exchange.

Each step in the development of the bourgeoisie was accompanied by a corresponding political advance of that class. An oppressed class under the sway of the feudal nobility, an armed and self-governing association in the medieval commune; here independent urban republic (as in Italy and Germany), there taxable "third estate" of the monarchy (as in France), afterwards, in the period of manufacture proper, serving either the semi-feudal or the absolute monarchy as a counterpoise against the nobility, and, in fact, corner-stone of the great monarchies in general, the bourgeoisie has at last, since the establishment of Modern Industry and of the world market, conquered for itself, in the modern representative State, exclusive political sway. The executive of the modern State is but a committee for managing the common affairs of the whole bourgeoisie.

The bourgeoisie, historically, has played a most revolutionary part.

The bourgeoisie, wherever it has got the upper hand, has put an end to all feudal, patriarchal, idyllic relations. It has pitilessly torn asunder the motley feudal ties that bound man to his "natural superiors," and has left remaining no other nexus between man and man than naked self-interest, than callous "cash payment." It has drowned the most heavenly ecstasies of religious fervour, of chivalrous enthusiasm, of philistine sentimentalism, in the icy water of egotistical calculation. It has resolved personal worth into exchange value, and in place of the numberless indefeasible chartered freedoms, has set up that single, unconscionable freedom—Free Trade. In one word, for exploitation, veiled by religious and political illusions, it has substituted naked, shameless, direct, brutal exploitation.

The bourgeoisie has stripped of its halo every occupation hitherto honoured and looked up to with reverent awe. It has converted the physician, the lawyer, the priest, the poet, the man of science, into paid wage-labourers.

The bourgeoisie has torn away from the family its sentimental veil, and has reduced the family relation to a mere money relation.

The bourgeoisie has disclosed how it came to pass that the brutal display of vigour in the Middle Ages, which Reactionists so much admire, found its fitting complement in the most slothful indolence. It has been the first to show what man's activity can bring about. It has accomplished wonders far surpassing Egyptian pyramids, Roman aqueducts, and Gothic cathedrals; it has conducted expeditions that put in the shade all former Exoduses of nations and crusades.

The bourgeoisie cannot exist without constantly revolutionizing the instruments of production, and thereby the relations of production, and with them the whole relations of society. Conservation of the old modes of production in unaltered form, was, on the contrary, the first condition of existence for all earlier industrial classes. Constant revolutionizing of production, uninterrupted disturbance of all social conditions, everlasting uncertainty and agitation distinguish the bourgeois epoch from all earlier ones. All fixed, fast-frozen relations, with their train of ancient and venerable prejudices and opinions are swept away, all new-formed ones become antiquated before they can ossify. All that is solid melts into air, all that is holy is profaned, and man is at last compelled to face with sober senses, his real conditions of life, and his relations with his kind.

The need of a constantly expanding market of its products chases the bourgeoisie over the whole surface of the globe. It must nestle everywhere, settle everywhere, establish connexions everywhere.

The bourgeoisie has through its exploitation of the world market given a cosmopolitan character to production and consumption in every country. To the great chagrin of Reactionists, it has drawn from under the feet of industry the national ground on which it stood. All old-established national industries have been destroyed or are daily being destroyed. They are dislodged by new industries, whose introduction becomes a life and death question for all civilized nations, by industries that no longer work up indigenous raw material, but raw material drawn from the remotest zones; industries whose products are consumed, not only at home, but in every quarter of the globe. In place of the old wants, satisfied by the productions of the country, we find new wants, requiring for their satisfaction the products of distant lands and climes. In place of the old local and national seclusion and self-sufficiency, we have intercourse in every direction, universal interdependence of nations. And as in material, so also in intellectual production. The intellectual creations of individual nations become property. National one-sidedness and narrow-mindedness become more and more impossible, and from the numerous national and local literatures, there arises a world literature.

The bourgeoisie, by the rapid improvement of all instruments of production, by the immensely facilitated means of communication, draws all, even the most barbarian, nations into civilization. The cheap prices of its commodities are the heavy artillery with which it batters down all Chinese walls, with which it forces the barbarians' intensely obstinate hatred of foreigners to capitulate. It compels all nations, on pain of extinction, to adopt the bourgeois mode of production; it compels them to introduce what it calls civilization into their midst, i.e., to become bourgeois themselves. In one word, it creates a world after its own image.

The bourgeoisie has subjected the country to the rule of the towns. It has created enormous cities, has greatly increased the urban population as compared with the rural, and has thus rescued a considerable part of the population from the idiocy of rural life. Just as it has made the country dependent on the towns, so it has made barbarian and semi-barbarian countries dependent on the civilized ones, nations of peasants on nations of bourgeois, the East on the West.

The bourgeoisie keeps more and more doing away with the scattered state of the population, of the means of production, and of property. It has agglomerated population, centralized means of production, and has concentrated property in a few hands. The necessary consequence of this was political centralization. Independent, or but loosely connected, provinces with separate interests, laws, governments and systems of taxation, became lumped together into one nation, with one government, one code of laws, one national class-interest, one frontier and one customs-tariff.

The bourgeoisie, during its rule of scarce one hundred years, has created more massive and more colossal productive forces than have all preceding generations together. Subjection of Nature's forces to man, machinery, application of chemistry to industry and agriculture, steam-navigation, railways, electric telegraphs, clearing of whole continents for cultivation, canalization of rivers, whole populations conjured out of the ground—what earlier century had even a presentiment that such productive forces slumbered in the lap of social labour?

We see then: the means of production and of exchange, on whose foundation the bourgeoisie built itself up, were generated in feudal society. At a certain stage in the development of these means of production and of exchange, the conditions under which feudal society produced and exchanged, the feudal organization of agriculture and manufacturing industry, in one word, the feudal relations of property became no longer compatible with the already developed productive forces; they became so many fetters. They had to be burst asunder; they were burst asunder.

Into their place stepped free competition, accompanied by a social and political constitution adapted to it, and by the economical and political sway of the bourgeois class.

A similar movement is going on before our own eyes. Modern bourgeois society with its relations of production, of exchange and of property, a society that has conjured up such gigantic means of production and of exchange, is like the sorcerer, who is no longer able to control the powers of the nether world whom he has called up by his spells. For many a decade past the history of industry and commerce is but the history of the revolt of modern productive forces against modern conditions of production, against the property relations that are the conditions for the existence of the bourgeoisie and of its rule. It is enough to mention the commercial crises that by their periodical return put on its trial, each time more threateningly, the existence of the entire bourgeois society. In these crises a great part not only of the existing products, but also of the previously created productive forces, are periodically destroyed. In these crises there breaks out an epidemic that, in all earlier epochs, would have seemed an absurdity— the epidemic of overproduction. Society suddenly finds itself put back into a state of momentary barbarism; it appears as if a famine, a universal war of devastation had cut off the supply of every means of subsistence; industry and commerce seem to be destroyed; and why? Because there is too much civilization, too much means of subsistence, too much industry, too much commerce. The productive forces at the disposal of society no longer tend to further the development of the conditions of bourgeois property; on the contrary, they have become too powerful for these conditions, by which they are fettered, and so soon as they overcome these fetters, they bring disorder into the whole of bourgeois society, endanger the existence of bourgeois property. The conditions of bourgeois society are too narrow to comprise the wealth created by them. And how does the bourgeoisie get over these crises? On the one hand by enforced destruction of a mass of productive forces; on the other, by the conquest of new markets, and by the more thorough exploitation of the old ones. That is to say, by paving the way for more extensive and more destructive crises, and by diminishing the means whereby crises are prevented.

The weapons with which the bourgeoisie felled feudalism to the ground are now turned against the bourgeoisie itself.

But not only has the bourgeoisie forged the weapons that bring death to itself; it has also called into existence the men who are to wield those weapons—the modern working class—the proletarians.

In proportion as the bourgeoisie, i.e., capital, is developed, in the same proportion is the proletariat, the modern working class, developed—a class of labourers, who live only so long as they find work, and who find work only so long as their labour increases capital. These labourers, who must sell themselves piecemeal, are a commodity, like every other article of commerce, and are consequently exposed to all the vicissitudes of competition, to all the fluctuations of the market.

Owing to the extensive use of machinery and to division of labour, the work of the proletarians has lost all individual character, and, consequently, all charm for the workman. He becomes an appendage of the machine, and it is only the most simple, most monotonous, and most easily acquired knack, that is required of him. Hence, the cost of production of a workman is restricted, almost entirely, to the means of subsistence that he requires for his maintenance, and for the propagation of his race. But the price of a commodity, and therefore also of labour, is equal to its cost of production. In proportion, therefore, as the repulsiveness of the work increases, the wage decreases. Nay more, in proportion as the use of machinery and division of labour increases, in the same proportion the burden of toil also increases, whether by prolongation of the working hours, by increase of the work exacted in a given time or by increased speed of the machinery, etc.

Modern industry has converted the little workshop of the patriarchal master into the great factory of the industrial capitalist. Masses of labourers, crowded into the factory, are organized like soldiers. As privates of the industrial army they are placed under the command of a perfect hierarchy of officers and sergeants. Not only are they slaves of the bourgeois class, and of the bourgeois State; they are daily and hourly enslaved by the machine, by the overlooker, and, above all, by the individual bourgeois manufacturer himself. The more openly this despotism proclaims gain to be its end aim, the more petty, the more hateful and the more embittering it is.

The less the skill and exertion of strength implied in manual labour, in other words, the more modern industry becomes developed, the more is the labour of men superseded by that of women. Differences of age and sex have no longer any distinctive social validity for the working class. All are instruments of labour, more or less expensive to use, according to their age and sex.

No sooner is the exploitation of the labourer by the manufacturer, so far, at an end, that he receives his wages in cash, than he is set upon by the other portions of the bourgeoisie, the landlord, the shopkeeper, the pawnbroker, etc.

The lower strata of the middle class—the small trades people, shopkeepers, and retired tradesmen generally, the handicraftsmen and peasants—all these sink gradually into the proletariat, partly because their diminutive capital does not suffice for the scale on which Modern Industry is carried on, and is swamped in the competition with the large capitalists, partly because their specialized skill is rendered worthless by new methods of production. Thus the proletariat is recruited from all classes of the population.

The proletariat goes through various stages of development. With its birth begins its struggle with the bourgeoisie. At first the contest is carried on by individual labourers, then by the work-people of a factory, then by the operatives of one trade, in one locality, against the individual bourgeois who directly exploits them. They direct their attacks not against the bourgeois conditions of production, but against the instruments of production themselves; they destroy imported wares that compete with their labour, they smash to pieces machinery, they set factories ablaze, they seek to restore by force the vanished status of the workman of the Middle Ages.

At this stage the labourers still form an incoherent mass scattered over the whole country, and broken up by their mutual competition. If anywhere they unite to form more compact bodies, this is not yet the consequence of their own active union, but of the union of the bourgeoisie, which class, in order to attain its own political ends, is compelled to set the whole proletariat in motion, and is moreover yet, for a time, able to do so. At this stage, therefore, the proletarians do not fight their enemies, but the enemies of their enemies, the remnants of absolute monarchy, the landowners, the non-industrial bourgeois, the petty bourgeoisie. Thus the whole historical movement is concentrated in the hands of the bourgeoisie; every victory so obtained is a victory for the bourgeoisie.

But with the development of industry the proletariat not only increases in number; it becomes concentrated in greater masses, its strength grows, and it feels that strength more. The various interests and conditions of life within the ranks of the proletariat are more and more equalized, in proportion as machinery obliterates all distinctions of labour, and nearly everywhere reduces wages to the same low level. The growing competition among the bourgeois, and the resulting commercial crises, make the wages of the workers ever more fluctuating. The unceasing improvement of machinery, ever more rapidly developing, makes their livelihood more and more precarious; the collision between individual workmen and individual bourgeois take more the character of collision between two classes. Thereupon the workers begin to form combinations (Trades Unions) against the bourgeois; they club together in order to keep up the rate of wages; they found permanent associations in order to make provision beforehand for these occasional revolts. Here and there the contest breaks out into riots.

Now and then the workers are victorious, but only for a time. The real fruit of their battles lies, not in the immediate result, but in the ever-expanding union of the workers. This union is helped on by the improved means of communication that are created by modern industry and that place the workers of different localities in contact with one another. It was just this contact that was needed to centralize the numerous local struggles, all of the same character, into one national struggle between classes. But every class struggle is a political struggle. And that union, to attain which the burghers of the Middle Ages, with their miserable highways, required centuries, the modern proletarians, thanks to railways, achieve in a few years.

This organization of the proletarians into a class, and consequently into a political party, is continually being upset again by the competition between the workers themselves. But it ever rises up again, stronger, firmer, mightier. It compels legislative recognition of particular interests of the workers, by taking advantage of the divisions among the bourgeoisie itself. Thus the Ten Hours bill in England was carried.

Altogether collisions between the classes of the old society further, in many ways, the course of development of the proletariat. The bourgeoisie finds itself involved in a constant battle. At first with the aristocracy; later on, with those portions of the bourgeoisie itself, whose interests have become antagonistic to the progress of industry; at all times, with the bourgeoisie of foreign countries. In all these battles it sees itself compelled to appeal to the proletariat, to ask for its help, and thus, to drag it into the political arena. The bourgeoisie itself, therefore, supplies the proletariat with its own elements of political and general education, in other words, it furnishes the proletariat with weapons for fighting the bourgeoisie.

Further, as we have already seen, entire sections of the ruling classes are, by the advance of industry, precipitated into the proletariat, or are at least threatened in their conditions of existence. These also supply the proletariat with fresh elements of enlightenment and progress.

Finally, in times when the class struggle nears the decisive hour, the process of dissolution going on within the ruling class, in fact within the whole range of old society, assumes such a violent, glaring character, that a small section of the ruling class cuts itself adrift, and joins the revolutionary class, the class that holds the future in its hands. Just as, therefore, at an earlier period, a section of the nobility went over to the bourgeoisie, so now a portion of the bourgeoisie goes over to the proletariat, and in particular, a portion of the bourgeois ideologists, who have raised themselves to the level of comprehending theoretically the historical movement as a whole.

Of all the classes that stand face to face with the bourgeoisie today, the proletariat alone is a really revolutionary class. The other classes decay and finally disappear in the face of modern industry; the proletariat is its special and essential product.

The lower middle class, the small manufacturer, the shopkeeper, the artisan, the peasant, all these fight against the bourgeoisie, to save from extinction their existence as fractions of the middle class. They are therefore not revolutionary, but conservative. Nay more, they are reactionary, for they try to roll back the wheel of history. If by chance they are revolutionary, they are so only in view of their impending transfer into the proletariat, they thus defend not their present, but their future interests, they desert their own standpoint to place themselves at that of the proletariat.

The "dangerous class," the social scum, that passively rotting mass thrown off by the lowest layers of old society, may, here and there, be swept into the movement by a proletarian revolution; its conditions of life, however, prepare it far more for the part of a bribed tool of reactionary intrigue.

In the conditions of the proletariat, those of old society at large are already virtually swamped. The proletarian is without property; his relation to his wife and children has no longer anything in common with the bourgeois family relations; modern industrial labour, modern subjection to capital, the same in England as in France, in America as in Germany, has stripped him of every trace of national character. Law, morality, religion, are to him so many bourgeois prejudices, behind which lurk in ambush just as many bourgeois interests.

All the preceding classes that got the upper hand sought to fortify their already acquired status by subjecting society at large to their conditions of appropriation. The proletarians cannot become masters of the productive forces of society, except by abolishing their own previous mode of appropriation, and thereby also every other previous mode of appropriation. They have nothing of their own to secure and to fortify; their mission is to destroy all previous securities for, and insurances of, individual property.

All previous historical movements were movements of minorities, or in the interest of minorities. The proletarian movement is the self-conscious, independent movement of the immense majority, in the interest of the immense majority. The proletariat, the lowest stratum of our present society, cannot stir, cannot raise itself up, without the whole superincumbent strata of official society being sprung into the air.

Though not in substance, yet in form, the struggle of the proletariat with the bourgeoisie is at first a national struggle. The proletariat of each country must, of course, first of all settle matters with its own bourgeoisie.

In depicting the most general phases of the development of the proletariat, we traced the more or less veiled civil war, raging within existing society, up to the point where that war breaks out into open revolution, and where the violent overthrow of the bourgeoisie lays the foundation for the sway of the proletariat.

Hitherto, every form of society has been based, as we have already seen, on the antagonism of oppressing and oppressed classes. But in order to oppress a class, certain conditions must be assured to it under which it can, at least, continue its slavish existence. The serf, in the period of serfdom, raised himself to membership in the commune, just as the petty bourgeois, under the yoke of feudal absolutism, managed to develop into a bourgeois. The modern labourer, on the contrary, instead of rising with the progress of industry, sinks deeper and deeper below the conditions of existence of his own class. He becomes a pauper, and pauperism develops more rapidly than population and wealth. And here it becomes evident, that the bourgeoisie is unfit any longer to be the ruling class in society, and to impose its condition of existence upon society as an overriding law. It is unfit to rule because it is incompetent to assure an existence to its slave within his slavery, because it cannot help letting him sink into such a state, that it has to feed him, instead of being fed by him. Society can no longer live under this bourgeoisie, in other words, its existence is no longer compatible with society.

The essential condition for the existence, and for the sway of the bourgeois class, is the formation and augmentation of capital; the condition for capital is wage labour. Wage labour rests exclusively on competition between the labourers. The advance of industry, whose involuntary promoter is the bourgeoisie, replaces the isolation of the labourers, due to competition, by their revolutionary combination, due to association. The development of Modern Industry, therefore, cuts from under its feet the very foundation on which the bourgeoisie produces and appropriates products. What the bourgeoisie, therefore, produces, above all, is its own grave-diggers. Its fall and the victory of the proletariat are equally inevitable.

2. Proletarians and Communists

In what relation do the Communists stand to the proletarians as a whole?

The Communists do not form a separate party opposed to other working-class parties.

They have no interests separate and apart from those of the proletariat as a whole.

They do not set up any sectarian principles of their own, by which to shape and mould the proletarian movement.

The Communists are distinguished from the other working-class parties by this only:

1. In the national struggles of the proletarians of the different countries, they point out and bring to the front the common interests of the entire proletariat, independently of all nationality.

2. In the various stages of development which the struggle of the working class against the bourgeoisie has to pass through, they always and everywhere represent the interests of the movement as a whole.

The Communists, therefore, are on the one hand, practically, the most advanced and resolute section of the working-class parties of every country, that section which pushes forward all others; on the other hand, theoretically, they have over the great mass of the proletariat the advantage of clearly understanding the line of march, the conditions, and the ultimate general results of the proletarian movement.

The immediate aim of the Communists is the same as that of all the other proletarian parties: formation of the proletariat into a class, overthrow of the bourgeois supremacy, conquest of political power by the proletariat.

The theoretical conclusions of the Communists are in no way based on ideas or principles that have been invented, or discovered, by this or that would-be universal reformer.

They merely express, in general terms, actual relations springing from an existing class struggle, from a historical movement going on under our very eyes. The abolition of existing property relations is not at all a distinctive feature of Communism.

All property relations in the past have continually been subject to historical change consequent upon the change in historical conditions.

The French Revolution, for example, abolished feudal property in favour of bourgeois property.

The distinguishing feature of Communism is not the abolition of property generally, but the abolition of bourgeois property. But modern bourgeois private property is the final and most complete expression of the system of producing and appropriating products, that is based on class antagonisms, on the exploitation of the many by the few.

In this sense, the theory of the Communists may be summed up in the single sentence: Abolition of private property.

We Communists have been reproached with the desire of abolishing the right of personally acquiring property as the fruit of a man's own labour, which property is alleged to be the ground work of all personal freedom, activity and independence.

Hard-won, self-acquired, self-earned property! Do you mean the property of the petty artisan and of the small peasant, a form of property that preceded the bourgeois form? There is no need to abolish that; the development of industry has to a great extent already destroyed it, and is still destroying it daily.

Or do you mean modern bourgeois private property?

But does wage labour create any property for the labourer? Not a bit. It creates capital, i.e., that kind of property which exploits wage labour, and which cannot increase except upon condition of begetting a new supply of wage labour for fresh exploitation. Property, in its present form, is based on the antagonism of capital and wage labour. Let us examine both sides of this antagonism.

To be a capitalist is to have not only a purely personal but a social *status* in production. Capital is a collective product, and only by the united action of many members, nay, in the last resort, only by the united action of all members of society, can it be set in motion.

Capital is, therefore, not a personal, it is a social power.

When, therefore, capital is converted into common property, into the property of all members of society, personal property is not thereby transformed into social property. It is only the social character of the property that is changed. It loses its class character.

Let us now take wage labour.

The average price of wage labour is the minimum wage, i.e., that quantum of the means of subsistence which is absolutely requisite to keep the labourer in bare existence as a labourer. What, therefore, the wage-labourer appropriates by means of his labour, merely suffices to prolong and reproduce a bare existence. We by no means intend to abolish this personal appropriation of the products of labour, an appropriation that is made for the maintenance and reproduction of human life, and that leaves no surplus wherewith to command the labour of others. All that we want to do away with is the miserable character of this appropriation, under which the labourer lives merely to increase capital, and is allowed to live only in so far as the interest of the ruling class requires it.

In bourgeois society, living labour is but a means to increase accumulated labour. In Communist society, accumulated labour is but a means to widen, to enrich, to promote the existence of the labourer.

In bourgeois society, therefore, the past dominates the present; in Communist society, the present dominates the past. In bourgeois society capital is independent and has individuality, while the living person is dependent and has no individuality.

And the abolition of this state of things is called by the bourgeois, abolition of individuality and freedom! And rightly so. The abolition of bourgeois individuality, bourgeois independence, and bourgeois freedom is undoubtedly aimed at.

By freedom is meant, under the present bourgeois conditions of production, free trade, free selling and buying.

But if selling and buying disappears, free selling and buying disappears also. This talk about free selling and buying, and all the other "brave words" of our bourgeoisie about freedom in general, have a meaning, if any, only in contrast with restricted selling and buying, with the fettered traders of the Middle Ages, but have no meaning when opposed to the Communistic abolition of buying and selling, of the bourgeois conditions of production, and of the bourgeoisie itself.

You are horrified at our intending to do away with private property. But in your existing society, private property is already done away with for nine-tenths of the population; its existence for the few is solely due to its non-existence in the hands of those nine-tenths. You reproach us, therefore, with intending to do away with a form of property the necessary condition for whose existence is the non-existence of any property for the immense majority of society.

In one word, you reproach us with intending to do away with your property. Precisely so; that is just what we intend.

From the moment when labour can no longer be converted into capital, money, or rent, into a social power capable of being monopolized, i.e., from the moment when individual property can no longer be transformed into bourgeois property, into capital, from that moment, you say, individuality vanishes.

You must, therefore, confess that by "individual" you mean no other person than the bourgeois, than the middle-class owner of property. This person must, indeed, be swept out of the way, and made impossible.

Communism deprives no man of the power to appropriate the products of society; all that it does is to deprive him of the power to subjugate the labour of others by means of such appropriation.

It has been objected that upon the abolition of private property all work will cease, and universal laziness will overtake us.

According to this, bourgeois society ought long ago to have gone to the dogs through sheer idleness; for those of its members who work, acquire nothing, and those who acquire anything, do not work. The whole of this objection is but another expression of the tautology: that there can no longer be any wage labour when there is no longer any capital.

All objections urged against the Communistic mode of producing and appropriating material products, have, in the same way, been urged against the Communistic modes of producing and appropriating intellectual products. Just as, to the bourgeois, the disappearance of class property is the disappearance of production itself, so the disappearance of class culture is to him identical with the disappearance of all culture.

That culture, the loss of which he laments, is, for the enormous majority, a mere training to act as a machine.

But don't wrangle with us so long as you apply, to our intended abolition of bourgeois property, the standard of your bourgeois notions of freedom, culture, law, etc. Your very ideas are but the outgrowth of the conditions of your bourgeois production and bourgeois property, just as your jurisprudence is but the will of your class made into a law for all, a will, whose essential character and direction are determined by the economical conditions of existence of your class.

The selfish misconception that induces you to transform into eternal laws of nature and of reason, the social forms springing from your present mode of production and form of property—historical relations that rise and disappear in the progress of production—this misconception you share with every ruling class that has preceded you. What you see clearly in the case of ancient property, what you admit in the case of feudal property, you are of course forbidden to admit in the case of your own bourgeois form of property.

Abolition of the family! Even the most radical flare up at this infamous proposal of the Communists.

On what foundation is the present family, the bourgeois family, based? On capital, on private gain. In its completely developed form this family exists only among the bourgeoisie. But this state of things finds its complement in the practical absence of the family among the proletarians, and in public prostitution.

The bourgeois family will vanish as a matter of course when its complement vanishes, and both will vanish with the vanishing of capital.

Do you charge us with wanting to stop the exploitation of children by their parents? To this crime we plead guilty.

But, you will say, we destroy the most hallowed of relations, when we replace home education by social.

And your education! Is not that also social, and determined by the social conditions under which you educate, by the intervention, direct or indirect, of society, by means of schools, etc.? The Communists have not invented the intervention of society in education; they do but seek to alter the character of that intervention, and to rescue education from the influence of the ruling class.

The bourgeois clap-trap about the family and education, about the hallowed co-relation of parent and child, becomes all the more disgusting, the more, by the action of Modern Industry, all family ties among the proletarians are torn asunder, and their children transformed into simple articles of commerce and instruments of labour.

But you Communists would introduce community of women, screams the whole bourgeoisie in chorus.

The bourgeois sees in his wife a mere instrument of production. He hears that the instruments of production are to be exploited in common, and, naturally, can come to no other conclusion than that the lot of being common to all will likewise fall to the women.

He has not even a suspicion that the real point aimed at is to do away with the status of women as mere instruments of production.

For the rest, nothing is more ridiculous than the virtuous indignation of our bourgeois at the community of women which, they pretend, is to be openly and officially established by the Communists. The Communists have no need to introduce community of women; it has existed almost from time immemorial.

Our bourgeois, not content with having the wives and daughters of their proletarians at their disposal, not to speak of common prostitutes, take the greatest pleasure in seducing each other's wives.

Bourgeois marriage is in reality a system of wives in common and thus, at the most, what the Communists might possibly be reproached with, is that they desire to introduce, in substitution for a hypocritically concealed, an openly legalized community of women. For the rest, it is self-evident that the abolition of the present system of production must bring with it the abolition of the community of women springing from that system, i.e., of prostitution both public and private.

The Communists are further reproached with desiring to abolish countries and nationality.

The working men have no country. We cannot take from them what they have not got. Since the proletariat must first of all acquire political supremacy, must rise to be the leading class of the nation, must constitute itself *the* nation, it is, so far, itself national, though not in the bourgeois sense of the word.

National differences and antagonism between peoples are daily more and more vanishing, owing to the development of the bourgeoisie, to freedom of commerce, to the world market, to uniformity in the mode of production and in the conditions of life corresponding thereto.

The supremacy of the proletariat will cause them to vanish still faster. United action, of the leading civilized countries at least, is one of the first conditions for the emancipation of the proletariat.

In proportion as the exploitation of one individual by another is put an end to, the exploitation of one nation by another will also be put an end to. In proportion as the antagonism between classes within the nation vanishes, the hostility of one nation to another will come to an end.

The charges against Communism made from a religious, a philosophical, and, generally, from an ideological standpoint, are not deserving of serious examination.

Does it require deep intuition to comprehend that man's ideas, views and conceptions, in one word, man's consciousness, changes with every change in the conditions of his material existence, in his social relations and in his social life?

What else does the history of ideas prove, than that intellectual production changes in character in proportion as material production is changed? The ruling ideas of each age have ever been the ideas of its ruling class.

When people speak of ideas that revolutionize society, they do but express the fact, that within the old society, the elements of a new one have been created, and that the dissolution of the old ideas keeps even pace with the dissolution of the old conditions of existence.

When the ancient world was in its last throes, the ancient religions were overcome by Christianity. When Christian ideas succumbed in the eighteenth century to rationalist ideas, feudal society fought its death battle with the then revolutionary bourgeoisie. The ideas of religious liberty and freedom of conscience, merely gave expression to the sway of free competition within the domain of knowledge.

"Undoubtedly," it will be said, "religious, moral, philosophical and juridical ideas have been modified in the course of historical development. But religion, morality, philosophy, political science, and law, constantly survived this change.

"There are, besides, eternal truths, such as Freedom, Justice, etc., that are common to all states of society. But Communism abolishes eternal truths, it abolishes all religion, and all morality, instead of constituting them on a new basis; it therefore acts in contradiction to all past historical experience."

What does this accusation reduce itself to? The history of all past society has consisted in the development of class antagonisms, antagonisms that assumed different forms at different epochs.

But whatever form they may have taken, one fact is common to all past ages, viz., the exploitation of one part of society by the other. No wonder, then, that the social consciousness of past ages, despite all the multiplicity and variety it displays, moves within certain common forms, or general ideas, which cannot completely vanish except with the total disappearance of class antagonisms.

The Communist revolution is the most radical rupture with traditional property relations; no wonder that its development involves the most radical rupture with traditional ideas.

But let us have done with the bourgeois objections to Communism.

We have seen above, that the first step in the revolution by the working class, is to raise the proletariat to the position of ruling class, to win the battle of democracy.

The proletariat will use its political supremacy to wrest, by degrees, all capital from the bourgeoisie, to centralize all instruments of production in the hands of the State, i.e., of the proletariat organized as the ruling class; and to increase the total of productive forces as rapidly as possible.

Of course, in the beginning, this cannot be effected except by means of despotic inroads on the rights of property, and on the conditions of bourgeois production; by means of measures, therefore, which appear economically insufficient and untenable, but which, in the course of the movement, outstrip themselves, necessitate further inroads upon the old social order, and are unavoidable as a means of entirely revolutionizing the mode of production.

The measures will of course be different in different countries.

Nevertheless, in the most advanced countries, the following will be pretty generally applicable:

1. Abolition of property in land and application of all rents of land to public purposes.

2. A heavy progressive or graduated income tax.

3. Abolition of all right of inheritance.

4. Confiscation of the property of all emigrants and rebels.

5. Centralization of credit in the hands of the State, by means of a national bank with State capital and an exclusive monopoly.

6. Centralization of the means of communication and transport in the hands of the State.

7. Extension of factories and instruments of production owned by the State; the bringing into cultivation of wastelands, and the improvement of the soil generally in accordance with a common plan.

8. Equal liability of all to labour. Establishment of industrial armies, especially for agriculture.

9. Combination of agriculture with manufacturing industries; gradual abolition of the distinction between town and country, by a more equable distribution of the population over the country.

10. Free education for all children in public schools. Abolition of children's factory labour in its present form. Combination of education with industrial production, etc., etc.

When, in the course of development, class distinctions have disappeared, and all production has been concentrated in the whole nation, the public power will lose its political character. Political power, properly so called, is merely the organized power of one class for oppressing another. If the proletariat during its contest with the bourgeoisie is compelled, by the force of circumstances, to organize itself as a class, if, by means of a revolution, it makes itself the ruling class, and, as such, sweeps away by force the old conditions of production, then it will, along with these conditions, have swept away the conditions for the existence of class antagonisms and of classes generally, and will thereby have abolished its own supremacy as a class.

In place of the old bourgeois society, with its classes and class antagonisms, we shall have an association, in which the free development of each is the condition for the free development of all.

3. Socialist and Communist Literature

I. Reactionary Socialism

a. Feudal Socialism.—Owing to their historical position, it became the vocation of the aristocracies of France and England to write pamphlets against modern bourgeois society. In the French revolution of July 1830, and in the English reform agitation, these aristocracies again succumbed to the hateful upstart.

Thenceforth, a serious political contest was altogether out of question. A literary battle alone remained possible. But even in the domain of literature the old cries of the restoration period had become impossible.

In order to arouse sympathy, the aristocracy were obliged to lose sight, apparently, of their own interests, and to formulate their indictment against the bourgeoisie in the interest of the exploited working class alone. Thus the aristocracy took their revenge by singing lampoons on their new master, and whispering in his ears sinister prophecies of coming catastrophe.

In this way arose feudal Socialism: half lamentation, half lampoon; half echo of the past, half menace of the future; at times, by its bitter, witty and incisive criticism, striking the bourgeoisie to the very heart's core; but always ludicrous in its effect, through total incapacity to comprehend the march of modern history.

The aristocracy, in order to rally the people to them, waved the proletarian alms-bag in front for a banner. But the people, so often as it joined them, saw on their hindquarters the old feudal coats of arms, and deserted with loud and irreverent laughter.

One section of the French Legitimist and 'Young England' exhibited this spectacle.

In pointing out that their mode of exploitation was different to that of the bourgeoisie, the feudalists forget that they exploited under circumstances and conditions that were quite different, and that are now antiquated. In showing that, under their rule, the modern proletariat never existed, they forget that the modern bourgeoisie is the necessary offspring of their own form of society.

For the rest, so little do they conceal the reactionary character of their criticism that their chief accusation against the bourgeoisie amounts to this, that under the bourgeois *regime* a class is being developed, which is destined to cut up root and branch the old order of society.

What they upbraid the bourgeoisie with is not so much that it creates a proletariat, as that it creates a *revolutionary* proletariat.

In political practice, therefore, they join in all coercive measures against the working class; and in ordinary life, despite their high-falutin phrases, they stoop to pick up the golden apples dropped from the tree of industry, and to barter truth, love, and honour for traffic in wool, beetroot-sugar, and potato spirits.

As the parson has ever gone hand in hand with the landlord, so has Clerical Socialism with Feudal Socialism.

Nothing is easier than to give Christian asceticism a Socialist tinge. Has not Christianity declaimed against private property, against marriage, against the State? Has it not preached in the place of these, charity and poverty, celibacy and mortification of the flesh, monastic life and Mother Church? Christian Socialism is but the holy water with which the priest consecrates the heart-burnings of the aristocrat.

b. Petty-Bourgeois Socialism.—The feudal aristocracy was not the only class that was ruined by the bourgeoisie, not the only class whose conditions of existence pined and perished in the atmosphere of modern bourgeois society. The medieval burgesses and the small peasant proprietors were the precursors of the modern bourgeoisie. In those countries which are but little developed, industrially and commercially, these two classes still vegetate side by side with the rising bourgeoisie.

In countries where modern civilization has become fully developed, a new class of petty bourgeois has been formed, fluctuating between proletariat and bourgeoisie and ever renewing itself as a supplementary part of bourgeois society. The individual members of this class, however, are being constantly hurled down into the proletariat by the action of competition, and, as modern industry develops, they even see the moment approaching when they will completely disappear as an independent section of modern society, to be replaced, in manufacture, agriculture and commerce, by overlookers, bailiffs and shopmen.

In countries like France, where the peasants constitute far more than half of the population, it was natural that writers who sided with the proletariat against the bourgeoisie, should use, in their criticism of the bourgeois *regime,* the standard of the peasant and petty bourgeois, and from the standpoint of these intermediate classes should take up the cudgels for the working class. Thus arose petty-bourgeois Socialism. [Jean Charles] Sismondi was the head of this school, not only in France but also in England.

This school of Socialism dissected with great acuteness the contradictions in the conditions of modern production. It laid bare the hypocritical apologies of economists. It proved, incontrovertibly, the disastrous effects of machinery and division of labour; the concentration of capital and land in a few hands; over-production and crises; it pointed out the inevitable ruin of the petty bourgeois and peasant, the misery of the proletariat, the anarchy in production, the crying inequalities in the distribution of wealth, the industrial war of extermination between nations, the dissolution of old moral bonds, of the old family relations, of the old nationalities.

In its positive aims, however, this form of Socialism aspires either to restoring the old means of production and of exchange, and with them the old property relations, and the old society, or to cramping the modern means of production and of exchange, within the framework of the old property relations that have been, and were bound to be, exploded by those means. In either case, it is both reactionary and Utopian.

Its last words are: corporate guilds for manufacture; patriarchal relations in agriculture.

Ultimately, when stubborn historical facts had dispersed all intoxicating effects of self-deception, this form of Socialism ended in a miserable fit of the blues.

c. German, or "True," Socialism.—The Socialist and Communist literature of France, a literature that originated under the pressure of a bourgeoisie in power, and that was the expression of the struggle against this power, was introduced into Germany at a time when the bourgeoisie, in that country, had just begun its contest with feudal absolutism.

German philosophers, would-be philosophers, and *beaux esprits,* eagerly seized on this literature, only forgetting, that when these writings immigrated from France into Germany, French social conditions had not immigrated along with them. In contact with German social conditions, this French literature lost all its immediate practical significance, and assumed a purely literary aspect. Thus, to the German philosophers of the Eighteenth Century, the demands of the first French Revolution were nothing more than the demands of "Practical Reason" in general, and the utterance of the will of the revolutionary French bourgeoisie signified in their eyes the laws of pure Will, of Will as it was bound to be, of true human Will generally.

The work of the German *literati* consisted solely in bringing the new French ideas into harmony with their ancient philosophical conscience, or rather, in annexing the French ideas without deserting their own philosophic point of view.

This annexation took place in the same way in which a foreign language is appropriated, namely, by translation.

It is well known how the monks wrote silly lives of Catholic Saints *over* the manuscripts on which the classical works of ancient heathendom had been written. The German *literati* reversed this process with the profane French literature. They wrote their philosophical nonsense beneath the French original. For instance, beneath the French criticism of the economic functions of money, they wrote "Alienation of Humanity," and beneath the French criticism of the bourgeois State they wrote, "Dethronement of the Category of the General," and so forth.

The introduction of these philosophical phrases at the back of the French historical criticisms they dubbed "Philosophy of Action," "The Socialism," "German Science of Socialism," "Philosophical Foundation of Socialism," and so on.

The French Socialist and Communist literature was thus completely emasculated. And, since it ceased in the hands of the German to express the struggle of one class with the other, he felt conscious of having overcome "French

one-sidedness" and of representing, not true requirements, but the requirements of Truth; not the interests of the proletariat, but the interests of Human
Nature, of Man in general, who belongs to no class, has no reality, who exists
only in the misty realm of philosophical fantasy.

This German Socialism, which took its schoolboy task so seriously and
solemnly, and extolled its poor stock-in-trade in such mountebank fashion,
meanwhile gradually lost its pedantic innocence.

The fight of the German, and, especially of the Prussian bourgeoisie, against
feudal aristocracy and absolute monarchy, in other words, the liberal movement,
became more earnest.

By this, the long wished-for opportunity was offered to "True" Socialism of
confronting the political movement with the Socialist demands, of hurling the traditional anathemas against liberalism, against representative government, against
bourgeois competition, bourgeois freedom of the press, bourgeois legislation,
bourgeois liberty and equality, and of preaching to the masses that they had
nothing to gain, and everything to lose, by this bourgeois movement. German
Socialism forgot, in the nick of time, that the French criticism, whose silly echo
it was, presupposed the existence of modern bourgeois society, with its corresponding economic conditions of existence, and the political constitution
adapted thereto, the very things whose attainment was the object of the pending
struggle in Germany.

To the absolute governments, with their following of parsons, professors,
country squires and officials, it served as a welcome scarecrow against the threatening bourgeoisie.

It was a sweet finish after the bitter pills of floggings and bullets with which
these same governments, just at that time, dosed the German working-class
risings.

While this "True" Socialism thus served the governments as a weapon for
fighting the German bourgeoisie, it, at the same time, directly represented a
reactionary interest, the interest of the German Philistines. In Germany the
petty-bourgeois class, a relic of the sixteenth century, and since then constantly
cropping up again under various forms, is the real social basis of the existing state
of things.

To preserve this class is to preserve the existing state of things in Germany.
The industrial and political supremacy of the bourgeoisie threatens it with certain destruction; on the one hand, from the concentration of capital; on the
other, from the rise of a revolutionary proletariat. "True" Socialism appeared to
kill these two birds with one stone. It spread like an epidemic.

The robe of speculative cobwebs, embroidered with flowers of rhetoric,
steeped in the dew of sickly sentiment, this transcendental robe in which the

German Socialists wrapped their sorry "eternal truths," all skin and bone, served to wonderfully increase the sale of their goods amongst such a public.

And on its part, German Socialism recognized, more and more, its own calling as the bombastic representative of the petty-bourgeois Philistine.

It proclaimed the German nation to be the model nation, and the German petty Philistine to be the typical man. To every villainous meanness of this model man it gave a hidden, higher, Socialistic interpretation, the exact contrary of its real character. It went to the extreme length of directly opposing the "brutally destructive" tendency of Communism, and of proclaiming its supreme and impartial contempt of all class struggles. With very few exceptions, all the so-called Socialist and Communist publications that now (1847) circulate in Germany belong to the domain of this foul and enervating literature.

II. Conservative, or Bourgeois, Socialism

A part of the bourgeoisie is desirous of redressing social grievances, in order to secure the continued existence of bourgeois society.

To this section belong economists, philanthropists, humanitarians, improvers of the condition of the working class, organizers of charity, members of societies for the prevention of cruelty to animals, temperance fanatics, hole-and-corner reformers of every imaginable kind. This form of Socialism has, moreover, been worked out into complete systems.

We may cite Proudhon's *Philosophie de la Misère* as an example of this form.

The Socialistic bourgeois want all the advantages of modern social conditions without the struggles and dangers necessarily resulting therefrom. They desire the existing state of society minus its revolutionary and disintegrating elements. They wish for a bourgeoisie without a proletariat. The bourgeoisie naturally conceives the world in which it is supreme to be the best; and bourgeois Socialism develops this comfortable conception into various more or less complete systems. In requiring the proletariat to carry out such a system, and thereby to march straightway into the social New Jerusalem, it but requires in reality, that the proletariat should remain within the bounds of existing society, but should cast away all its hateful ideas concerning the bourgeoisie.

A second and more practical, but less systematic, form of this Socialism sought to depreciate every revolutionary movement in the eyes of the working class, by showing that no mere political reform, but only a change in the material conditions of existence, in economical relations, could be of any advantage to them. By changes in the material conditions of existence, this form of Socialism, however, by no means understands abolition of the bourgeois relations of production, an abolition that can be effected only by a revolution, but administrative reforms, based on the continued existence of these relations; reforms, therefore, that in no respect affect the relations between capital and labour, but, at the best, lessen the cost, and simplify the administrative work, of bourgeois government.

Bourgeois Socialism attains adequate expression, when, and only when, it becomes a mere figure of speech.

Free trade: for the benefit of the working class. Protective duties: for the benefit of the working class. Prison Reform: for the benefit of the working class. This is the last word and the only seriously meant word of bourgeois Socialism.

It is summed up in the phrase: the bourgeois is a bourgeois—for the benefit of the working class.

III. Critical-Utopian Socalism and Communism

We do not here refer to that literature which, in every great modern revolution, has always given voice to the demands of the proletariat, such as the writings of [François-Noël] Babeuf and others.

The first direct attempts of the proletariat to attain its own ends, made in times of universal excitement, when feudal society was being overthrown, these attempts necessarily failed, owing to the then undeveloped state of the proletariat, as well as to the absence of the economic conditions for its emancipation, conditions that had yet to be produced, and could be produced by the impending bourgeois epoch alone. The revolutionary literature that accompanied these first movements of the proletariat had necessarily a reactionary character. It inculcated universal asceticism and social levelling in its crudest form.

The Socialist and Communist systems properly so called, those of Saint-Simon, Fourier, Owen and others, spring into existence in the early undeveloped period, described above, of the struggle between proletariat and bourgeoisie (see Section I, Bourgeois and Proletarians).

The founders of these systems see, indeed, the class antagonisms, as well as the action of the decomposing elements in the prevailing form of society. But the proletariat, as yet in its infancy, offers to them the spectacle of a class without any historical initiative or any independent political movement.

Since the development of class antagonism keeps even pace with the development of industry, the economic situation, as they find it, does not as yet offer to them the material conditions for the emancipation of the proletariat. They therefore search after a new social science, after new social laws, that are to create these conditions.

Historical action is to yield to their personal inventive action, historically created conditions of emancipation to fantastic ones, and the gradual, spontaneous class organization of the proletariat to an organization of society specially contrived by these inventors. Future history resolves itself, in their eyes, into the propaganda and the practical carrying out of their social plans.

In the formation of their plans they are conscious of caring chiefly for the interests of the working class, as being the most suffering class. Only from the point of view of being the most suffering class does the proletariat exist for them.

The undeveloped state of the class struggle, as well as their own surroundings, causes Socialists of this kind to consider themselves far superior to all class antagonisms. They want to improve the condition of every member of society, even that of the most favoured. Hence, they habitually appeal to society at large, without distinction of class; nay, by preference, to the ruling class. For how can people, when once they understand their system, fail to see in it the best possible plan of the best possible state of society?

Hence, they reject all political, and especially all revolutionary, action; they wish to attain their ends by peaceful means, and endeavour, by small experiments, necessarily doomed to failure, and by the force of example, to pave the way for the new social Gospel.

Such fantastic pictures of future society, painted at a time when the proletariat is still in a very undeveloped state and has but a fantastic conception of its own position correspond with the first instinctive yearnings of that class for a general reconstruction of society.

But these Socialist and Communist publications contain also a critical element. They attack every principle of existing society. Hence they are full of the most valuable materials for the enlightenment of the working class. The practical measures proposed in them—such as the abolition of the distinction between town and country, of the family, of the carrying on of industries for the account of private individuals, and of the wage system, the proclamation of social harmony, the conversion of the functions of the State into a mere superintendence of production, all these proposals point solely to the disappearance of class antagonisms which were, at that time, only just cropping up, and which, in these publications, are recognized in their earliest indistinct and undefined forms only. These proposals, therefore, are of a purely Utopian character.

The significance of Critical-Utopian Socialism and Communism bears an inverse relation to historical development. In proportion as the modern class struggle develops and takes definite shape, this fantastic standing apart from the contest, these fantastic attacks on it, lose all practical value and all theoretical justification. Therefore, although the originators of these systems were, in many respects, revolutionary, their disciples have, in every case, formed mere reactionary sects. They hold fast by the original views of their masters, in opposition to the progressive historical development of the proletariat. They, therefore, endeavour, and that consistently, to deaden the class struggle and to reconcile the class antagonisms. They still dream of experimental realization of their social Utopias, of founding isolated 'phalanstères,' of establishing 'Home Colonies,' of setting up a 'Little Icaria'—duodecimo editions of the New Jerusalem—and to realize all these castles in the air, they are compelled to appeal to the feelings and purses of the bourgeois. By degrees they sink into the category of the reactionary conservative Socialists depicted above, differing from these only by more systematic pedantry, and by their fanatical and superstitious belief in the miraculous effects of their social science.

They, therefore, violently oppose all political action on the part of the working class; such action, according to them, can only result from blind unbelief in the new Gospel.

The Owenites in England, and the Fourierists in France, respectively oppose the Chartists and the *Réformistes*.

4. Position of the Communists in Relation to the Various Existing Opposition Parties

Section 2 has made clear the relations of the Communists to the existing working-class parties, such as the Chartists in England and the Agrarian Reformers in America.

The Communists fight for the attainment of the immediate aims, for the enforcement of the momentary interests of the working class; but in the movement of the present, they also represent and take care of the future of that movement. In France the Communists ally themselves with the Social-Democrats, against the conservative and radical bourgeoisie, reserving, however, the right to take up a critical position in regard to phrases and illusions traditionally handed down from the great Revolution.

In Switzerland they support the Radicals, without losing sight of the fact that this party consists of antagonistic elements, partly of Democratic Socialists, in the French sense, partly of radical bourgeois.

In Poland they support the party that insists on an agrarian revolution as the prime condition for national emancipation, that party which fomented the insurrection of Cracow in 1846.

In Germany they fight with the bourgeoisie whenever it acts in a revolutionary way, against the absolute monarchy, the feudal squirearchy, and the petty bourgeoisie.

But they never cease, for a single instant, to instil into the working class the clearest possible recognition of the hostile antagonism between bourgeoisie and proletariat, in order that the German workers may straightway use, as so many weapons against the bourgeoisie, the social and political conditions that the bourgeoisie must necessarily introduce along with its supremacy, and in order that, after the fall of the reactionary classes in Germany, the fight against the bourgeoisie itself may immediately begin.

The Communists turn their attention chiefly to Germany, because that country is on the eve of a bourgeois revolution that is bound to be carried out under more advanced conditions of European civilization, and with a much more developed proletariat, than that of England was in the seventeenth, and of France in the eighteenth century, and because the bourgeois revolution in Germany will be but the prelude to an immediately following proletarian revolution.

In short, the Communists everywhere support every revolutionary movement against the existing social and political order of things.

In all these movements they bring to the front, as the leading question in each, the property question, no matter what its degree of development at the time.

Finally, they labour everywhere for the union and agreement of the democratic parties of all countries.

The Communists disdain to conceal their views and aims. They openly declare that their ends can be attained only by the forcible overthrow of all existing social conditions. Let the ruling classes tremble at a Communistic revolution. The proletarians have nothing to lose but their chains. They have a world to win.

WORKING MEN OF ALL COUNTRIES, UNITE!

16

Karl Marx

"Value, Price, and Profit" (1865)

Marx's most important work was his three-volume Das Kapital, *an analysis of the "internal laws of motion" of capitalist societies. While writing* Capital, *Marx also lectured on his economic theory to British trade unionists fighting for better working conditions. In this lecture, "Value, Price, and Profit," he provides a popular summary of the labor theory of value—his explanation for how capitalist profits originate from the exploitation of labor. Some scholars contrast this "scientific" analysis of capitalism with Marx's earlier "humanistic" critique of alienation; others maintain that Marx's vision of human fulfillment continues to inform his later works.*

VI.
Value and Labour

CITIZENS, I HAVE now arrived at a point where I must enter upon the real development of the question. I cannot promise to do this in a very satisfactory way, because to do so I should be obliged to go over the whole field of political economy. I can, as the French would say, but *effleurer la question,* touch upon the main points.

The first question we have to put is: what is the *value* of a commodity? How is it determined?

At first sight it would seem that the value of a commodity is a thing quite *relative,* and not to be settled without considering one commodity in its relations to all other commodities. In fact, in speaking of the value, the value in exchange of

Source: Eleanor Marx Aveling, ed. *Value, Price, and Profit* (New York: International Publishers Co., 1935).

a commodity, we mean the proportional quantities in which it exchanges with all other commodities. But then arises the question: How are the proportions in which commodities exchange with each other regulated?

We know from experience that these proportions vary infinitely. Taking one single commodity, wheat, for instance, we shall find that a quarter of wheat exchanges in almost countless variations of proportion with different commodities. Yet, *its value remaining always the same,* whether expressed in silk, gold, or any other commodity, it must be something distinct from, and independent of, these *different rates of exchange* with different articles. It must be possible to express, in a very different form, these various equations with various commodities.

Besides, if I say a quarter of wheat exchanges with iron in a certain proportion, or the value of a quarter of wheat is expressed in a certain amount of iron, I say that the value of wheat and its equivalent in iron are equal *to some third thing,* which is neither wheat nor iron, because I suppose them to express the same magnitude in two different shapes. Either of them, the wheat or the iron, must, therefore, independently of the other, be reducible to this third thing which is their common measure.

To elucidate this point I shall recur to a very simple geometrical illustration. In comparing the areas of triangles of all possible forms and magnitudes, or comparing triangles with rectangles, or any other rectilinear figure, how do we proceed? We reduce the area of any triangle whatever to an expression quite different from its visible form. Having found from the nature of the triangle that its area is equal to half the product of its base by its height, we can then compare the different values of all sorts of triangles, and of all rectilinear figures whatever, because all of them may be resolved into a certain number of triangles.

The same mode of procedure must obtain with the values of commodities. We must be able to reduce all of them to an expression common to all, and distinguishing them only by the proportions in which they contain that same and identical measure.

As the *exchangeable values* of commodities are only *social functions* of those things, and have nothing at all to do with the *natural* qualities, we must first ask: What is the common *social substance* of all commodities? It is *labour.* To produce a commodity a certain amount of labour must be bestowed upon it, or worked up in it. And I say not only *labour,* but *social labour.* A man who produces an article for his own immediate use, to consume it himself, creates a *product,* but not a *commodity.* As a self-sustaining producer he has nothing to do with society. But to produce a *commodity,* a man must not only produce an article satisfying some *social* want, but his labour itself must form part and parcel of the total sum of labour expended by society. It must be subordinate to the *division of labour within society.* It is nothing without the other division of labour, and on its part is required to *integrate* them.

If we consider *commodities as values,* we consider them exclusively under the single aspect of *realised, fixed,* or, if you like, *crystallised social labour.* In this respect they can *differ* only by representing greater or smaller quantities of labour, as, for example, a greater amount of labour may be worked up in a silken handkerchief than in a brick. But how does one measure *quantities of labour?* By the *time the labour lasts,* in measuring the labour by the hour, the day, etc. Of course, to apply this measure, all sorts of labour are reduced to average or simple labour as their unit.

We arrive, therefore, at this conclusion. A commodity has a *value,* because it is a *crystallisation of social labour.* The *greatness* of its value, or its *relative* value, depends upon the greater or less amount of that social substance contained in it; that is to say, on the relative mass of labour necessary for its production. The *relative values of commodities* are, therefore, determined by the *respective quantities or amounts of labour, worked up, realised, fixed in them.* The *correlative* quantities of commodities which can be produced in the *same time of labour are equal.* Or the value of one commodity is to the value of another commodity as the quantity of labour fixed in the one is to the quantity of labour fixed in the other.

I suspect that many of you will ask: Does then, indeed, there exist such a vast, or any difference whatever, between determining of values of commodities by *wages,* and determining them by the *relative quantities of labour* necessary for their production? You must, however, be aware that the *reward* for labour, and *quantity* of labour, are quite disparate things. Suppose, for example, *equal quantities of labour* to be fixed in one quarter of wheat and one ounce of gold. I resort to the example because it was used by Benjamin Franklin in his first essay published in 1721 and entitled: *A Modest Enquiry into the Nature and Necessity of a Paper Currency,* where he, one of the first, hit upon the true nature of value. Well. We suppose, then, that one quarter of wheat and one ounce of gold are *equal values or equivalents,* because they are *crystallisations of equal amounts of average labour,* of so many days' or so many weeks' labour respectively fixed in them. In thus determining the relative values of gold and corn, do we refer in any way whatever to the *wages* of the agricultural labourer and the miner? Not a bit. We leave it quite *indeterminate how* their day's or weeks' labour was paid, or even whether wages labour was employed at all. If it was, wages may have been very unequal. The labourer whose labour is realised in the quarter of wheat may receive two bushels only, and the labourer employed in mining may receive one-half of the ounce of gold. Or, supposing their wages to be equal, they may deviate in all possible proportions from the values of the commodities produced by them. They may amount to one-half, one-third, one-fourth, one-fifth, or any other proportional part of the one-quarter of corn or the one ounce of gold. Their *wages* can, of course, not *exceed,* not be more than the values of the commodities they produced, but they can be *less* in every possible degree. Their *wages* will be *limited* by the *values* of the products, but the *values of their products* will not be limited by the wages. And above all, the values, the relative values of corn and gold, for example, will have been settled without any regard whatever to the value of the labour employed, that is to say, to *wages.* To determine the values of commodities by the *relative quantities of labour fixed in them,* is, therefore, a thing quite different from the tautological method of determining the values of commodities by the value of labour, or by wages. This point, however, will be further elucidated in the progress of our inquiry.

In calculating the exchangeable value of a commodity we must add to the quantity of labour *last* employed the quantity of labour *previously* worked up in the raw material of the commodity, and the labour bestowed on the implements, tools, machinery, and buildings, with which such labour is assisted. For example, the value of a certain amount of cotton yarn is the crystallisation of the quantity of labour added to the cotton during the spinning process, the quantity of labour previously realised in the cotton itself, the quantity of labour realised in the coal, oil, and other auxiliary matter used, the quantity of labour fixed in the steam-engine, the spindles, the factory building, and so forth. Instruments of production properly so-called, such as tools, machinery, buildings, serve again and again for a longer or shorter period during repeated processes of production. If they were used up at once, like the raw material, their whole value would at once be transferred to the commodities they assist in producing. But as a spindle, for example, is but gradually used up, an average calculation is made, based upon the average time it lasts, and its average waste or wear and tear during a certain period, say a day. In this way we calculate how much of the value of the spindle is transferred to the yarn daily spun, and how much, therefore, of the total amount of labour realised in a pound of yarn, for example, is due to the quantity of labour previously realised in the spindle. For our present purpose it is not necessary to dwell any longer upon this point.

It might seem that if the value of a commodity is determined by the *quantity of labour bestowed upon its production,* the lazier a man, or the clumsier a man, the more valuable his commodity, because the greater the time of labour required for finishing the commodity. This, however, would be a sad mistake. You will recollect that I used the word *"social* labour," and many points are involved in this qualification of "social." In saying that the value of a commodity is determined by the *quantity of labour* worked up or crystallised in it, we mean the *quantity of labour necessary* for its production in a given state of society, under certain social average conditions of production, with a given social average intensity, and average skill of the labour employed. When, in England, the power-loom came to compete with the hand-loom, only one-half the former time of labour was wanted to convert a given amount of yarn into a yard of cotton or cloth. The poor hand-loom weaver now worked seventeen and eighteen hours daily, instead of the nine or ten hours he had worked before. Still the product of twenty hours of his labour represented now only ten social hours of labour, or ten hours of labour socially necessary for the conversion of a certain amount of yarn into textile stuffs. His product of twenty hours had, therefore, no more value than his former product of ten hours.

If then the quantity of socially necessary labour realised in commodities regulates their exchangeable values, every increase in the quantity of labour wanted for the production of a commodity must augment its value, as every diminution must lower it.

If the respective quantities of labour necessary for the production of the respective commodities remained constant, their relative values also would be constant. But such is not the case. The quantity of labour necessary for the production of a commodity changes continuously with the changes in the productive powers of the labour employed. The greater the productive powers of labour, the more produce is finished in a given time of labour; and the smaller the productive powers of labour, the less produce is finished in the same time. If, for example, in the progress of population it should become necessary to cultivate less fertile soils, the same amount of produce would be only attainable by a greater amount of labour spent, and the value of agricultural produce would consequently rise. On the other hand, if with the modern means of production, a single spinner converts into yarn, during one working day, many thousand times the amount of cotton which he could have spun during the same time with the spinning wheel, it is evident that every single pound of cotton will absorb many thousand times less of spinning labour than it did before, and, consequently, the value added by spinning to every single pound of cotton will be a thousand times less than before. The value of yarn will sink accordingly.

Apart from the different natural energies and acquired working abilities of different peoples, the productive powers of labour must principally depend:

Firstly. Upon the *natural* conditions of labour, such as fertility of soil, mines, and so forth.

Secondly. Upon the progressive improvement of the *social powers of labour,* such as are derived from production on a grand scale, concentration of capital and combination of labour, subdivision of labour, machinery, improved methods, appliance of chemical and other natural agencies, shortening of time and space by means of communication and transport, and every other contrivance by which science presses natural agencies into the service of labour, and by which the social or co-operative character of labour is developed. The greater the productive powers of labour, the less labour is bestowed upon a given amount of produce; hence the smaller the value of this produce. The smaller the productive powers of labour, the more labour is bestowed upon the same amount of produce; hence the greater its value. As a general law we may, therefore, set it down that:

The values of commodities are directly as the times of labour employed in their production, and are inversely as the productive powers of the labour employed.

Having till now only spoken of *value*, I shall add a few words about *price*, which is a peculiar form assumed by value.

Price, taken by itself, is nothing but the *monetary expression of value*. The values of all commodities of this country, for example, are expressed in gold prices, while on the Continent they are mainly expressed in silver prices. The value of gold or silver, like that of all other commodities, is regulated by the quantity of labour necessary for getting them. You exchange a certain amount of your national products, in which a certain amount of your national labour is crystallised, for the produce of the gold and silver producing countries, in which a certain quantity of *their* labour is crystallised. It is in this way, in fact by barter, that you learn to express in gold and silver the values of all commodities, that is the respective quantities of labour bestowed upon them. Looking somewhat closer into *the monetary expression of value*, or, what comes to the same, the *conversion of value into price*, you will find that it is a process by which you give to the *values* of all commodities an *independent* and *homogeneous form*, or by which you express them as quantities of *equal* social labour. So far as it is but the monetary expression of value, price has been called *natural price* by Adam Smith, *prix nécessaire* by the French physiocrats.

What then is the relation between *value* and *market prices*, or between *natural prices* and *market prices?* You all know that the *market price* is the *same* for all commodities of the same kind, however the conditions of production may differ for the individual producers. The market price expresses only the *average amount of social labour* necessary, under the average conditions of production, to supply the market with a certain mass of a certain article. It is calculated upon the whole lot of a commodity of a certain description.

So far the *market price* of a commodity coincides with its *value*. On the other hand, the oscillations of market prices, rising now over, sinking now under the value or natural price, depend upon the fluctuations of supply and demand. The deviations of market prices from values are continual, but as Adam Smith says: "The natural price is the central price to which the prices of commodities are continually gravitating. Different accidents may sometimes keep them suspended a good deal above it, and sometimes force them down even somewhat below it.

But whatever may be the obstacles which hinder them from settling in this center of repose and continuance, they are constantly tending towards it."

I cannot now sift this matter. It suffices to say that *if* supply and demand equilibrate each other, the market prices of commodities will correspond with their natural prices, that is to say with their values, as determined by the respective quantities of labour required for their production. But supply and demand *must* constantly tend to equilibrate each other, although they do so only by compensating one fluctuation by another, a rise by a fall, and *vice versa*. If instead of considering only the daily fluctuations you analyse the movement of market price for longer periods, as Mr. [Thomas] Tooke, for example, has done in his *History of Prices*, you will find that the fluctuations of market prices, their deviations from values, their ups and downs, paralyse and compensate each other; so that apart from the effect of monopolies and some other modifications I must now pass by, all descriptions of commodities are, on the average, sold at their respective *values* or natural prices. The average periods during which the fluctuations of market prices compensate each other are different for different kinds of commodities, because with one kind it is easier to adapt supply to demand than with the other.

If then, speaking broadly, and embracing somewhat longer periods, all descriptions of commodities sell at their respective values, it is nonsense to suppose that profit, not in individual cases, but that the constant and usual profits of different trades spring from surcharging the prices of commodities or selling them at a price over and above their *value*. The absurdity of this notion becomes evident if it is generalized. What a man would constantly win as a seller he would as constantly lose as a purchaser. It would not do to say that there are men who are buyers without being sellers, or consumers without being producers. What these people pay to the producers, they must first get from them for nothing. If a man first takes your money and afterwards returns that money in buying your commodities, you will never enrich yourselves by selling your commodities too dear to that same man. This sort of transaction might diminish a loss, but would never help in realising a profit.

To explain, therefore, the *general nature of profits*, you must start from the theorem that, on an average, commodities are *sold at their real values*, and that *profits are derived from selling them at their values*, that is, in proportion to the quantity of labour realised in them. If you cannot explain profit upon this supposition, you cannot explain it at all. This seems paradox and contrary to everyday observation. It is also paradox that the earth moves round the sun, and that water consists of two highly inflammable gases. Scientific truth is always paradox, if judged by everyday experience, which catches only the delusive appearance of things.

VII.
Labouring Power[i]

Having now, as far as it could be done in such a cursory manner, analysed the nature of *Value,* of the *Value of any commodity whatever,* we must turn our attention to the specific *Value of Labour.* And here, again, I must startle you by a seeming paradox. All of you feel sure that what they daily sell is their Labour; that, therefore, Labour has a Price, and that, the price of a commodity being only the monetary expression of its value, there must certainly exist such a thing as the *Value of Labour.* However, there exists no such thing as the *Value of Labour* in the common acceptance of the word. We have seen that the amount of necessary labour crystallised in a commodity constitutes its value. Now, applying this notion of value, how could we define, say, the value of a ten hours' working day? How much labour is contained in that day? Ten hours' labour. To say that the value of a ten hours' working day is equal to ten hours labour, or the quantity of labour contained in it, would be a tautological and, moreover, a nonsensical expression. Of course, having once found out the true but hidden sense of the expression *"Value of Labour,"* we shall be able to interpret this irrational, and seemingly impossible application of value, in the same way that, having once made sure of the real movement of the celestial bodies, we shall be able to explain their apparent or merely phenomenal movements.

What the working man sells is not directly his *Labour,* but his *Labouring Power,* the temporary disposal of which he makes over to the capitalist. This is so much the case that I do not know whether by the English laws, but certainly by some Continental laws, the *maximum time* is fixed for which a man is allowed to sell his labouring power. If allowed to do so for any indefinite period whatever, slavery would be immediately restored. Such a sale, if it comprised his lifetime, for example, would make him at once the lifelong slave of his employer.

One of the oldest economists and most original philosophers of England—Thomas Hobbes—has already, in his *Leviathan,* instinctively hit upon this point overlooked by all his successors. He says: *"The value or worth of a man is,* as in all other things, his *price:* that is so much as would be given for the *Use of his Power."*

Proceeding from this basis, we shall be able to determine the *Value of Labour* as that of all other commodities.

But before doing so, we might ask, how does this strange phenomenon arise, that we find on the market a set of buyers, possessed of land, machinery, raw material, and the means of life, all of them, save land in its crude state, the *products of labour,* and on the other hand, a set of sellers who have nothing to sell

---

i "Labour Power" in the English translation of *Capital.*

except their labouring power, their working arms and brains? That the one set buys continually in order to make a profit and enrich themselves, while the other set continually sells in order to earn their livelihood? The inquiry into this question would be an inquiry into what the economists call *"Previous, or Original Accumulation,"* but which ought to be called *Original Expropriation.* We should find that this so-called *Original Accumulation* means nothing but a series of historical processes, resulting in a *Decomposition of the Original Union* existing between the Labouring Man and his Means of Labour. Such an inquiry, however, lies beyond the pale of my present subject. The *Separation* between the Man of Labour and the Means of Labour once established, such a state of things will maintain itself and reproduce itself upon a constantly increasing scale, until a new and fundamental revolution in the mode of production should again overturn it, and restore the original union in a new historical form.

What, then, is the *Value of Labouring Power?*

Like that of every other commodity, its value is determined by the quantity of labour necessary to produce it. The labouring power of a man exists only in his living individuality. A certain mass of necessaries must be consumed by a man to grow up and maintain his life. But the man, like the machine, will wear out, and must be replaced by another man. Beside the mass of necessaries required for *his own* maintenance, he wants another amount of necessaries to bring up a certain quota of children that are to replace him on the labour market and to perpetuate the race of labourers. Moreover, to develop his labouring power, and acquire a given skill, another amount of values must be spent. For our purpose it suffices to consider only average labour, the costs of whose education and development are vanishing magnitudes. Still I must seize upon this occasion to state that, as the costs of producing labouring powers of different quality do differ, so must differ the values of the labouring powers employed in different trades. The cry for an *equality of wages* rests, therefore, upon a mistake, is an inane wish never to be fulfilled. It is an offspring of that false and superficial radicalism that accepts premises and tries to evade conclusions. Upon the basis of the wages system the value of labouring power is settled like that of every other commodity; and as different kinds of labouring power have different values, or require different quantities of labour for their production, they *must* fetch different prices in the labour market. To clamour for *equal or even equitable retribution* on the basis of the wages system is the same as to clamour for *freedom* on the basis of the slavery system. What you think just or equitable is out of the question. The question is: What is necessary and unavoidable with a given system of production?

After what has been said, the *value of labouring power* is determined by the *value of the necessaries* required to produce, develop, maintain, and perpetuate the labouring power.

VIII.
Production of Surplus Value

Now suppose that the average amount of the daily necessaries of a labouring man require *six hours of average labour* for their production. Suppose, moreover, six hours of average labour to be also realised in a quantity of gold equal to 3s. [shillings]. Then 3s. would be the *Price*, or the monetary expression of the *Daily Value* of that man's *Labouring Power*. If he worked daily six hours he would daily produce a value sufficient to buy the average amount of his daily necessaries, or to maintain himself as a labouring man.

But our man is a wages labourer. He must, therefore, sell his labouring power to a capitalist. If he sells it at 3s. daily, or 18s. weekly, he sells it at its value. Suppose him to be a spinner. If he works six hours daily he will add to the cotton a value of 3s. daily. This value, daily added by him, would be an exact equivalent for the wages, or the price of his labouring power, received daily. But in that case no *surplus value* or *surplus produce* whatever would go to the capitalist. Here, then, we come to the rub.

In buying the labouring power of the workman, and paying its value, the capitalist, like every other purchaser, has acquired the right to consume or use the commodity bought. You consume or use the labouring power of a man by making him work, as you consume or use a machine by making it run. By paying the daily or weekly value of the labouring power of the workman, the capitalist has, therefore, acquired the right to use or make that labouring power work during the *whole day or week*. The working day or the working week has, of course, certain limits, but those we shall afterwards look more closely at.

For the present I want to turn your attention to one decisive point.

The *value* of the labouring power is determined by the quantity of labour necessary to maintain or reproduce it, but the *use* of that labouring power is only limited by the active energies and physical strength of the labourer. The daily or weekly *value* of the labouring power is quite distinct from the daily or weekly exercise of that power, the same as the food a horse wants and the time it can carry the horseman are quite distinct. The quantity of labour by which the *value* of the workman's labouring power is limited forms by no means a limit to the quantity of labour which his labouring power is apt to perform. Take the example of our spinner. We have seen that, to daily reproduce his labouring power, he must daily reproduce a value of 3s., which he will do by working six hours daily. But this does not disable him from working ten or twelve or more hours a day. But by paying the daily or weekly *value* of the spinner's labouring power the capitalist has acquired the right of using that labouring power during *the whole day or week*. He will, therefore, make him work daily, say, *twelve* hours. *Over and above* the six hours required to replace his wages, or the value of his labouring power, he will, therefore, have to work *six other hours,* which I shall call hours of *surplus labour,* which surplus labour will realise itself in a *surplus value* and *a surplus produce.* If our spinner, for example, by his daily labour of six hours, added 3s. value to the cotton, a value forming an exact equivalent to his wages, he will, in twelve hours, add 6s. worth to the cotton, and produce *a proportional surplus of yarn.* As he has sold his labouring power to the capitalist, the whole value or produce created by him belongs to the capitalist, the owner *pro tem.* of his labouring power. By advancing 3s., the capitalist will, therefore, realise a value of 6s., because, advancing a value in which six hours of labour are crystallised, he will receive in return a value in which twelve hours of labour are crystallised. By repeating this same process daily, the capitalist will daily advance 3s. and daily pocket 6s., one half of which will go to pay wages anew, and the other half of which will form the *surplus value,* for which the capitalist pays no equivalent. It is this *sort of exchange between capital and labour* upon which capitalistic production, or the wages system, is founded, and which must constantly result in reproducing the working man as a working man, and the capitalist as a capitalist.

The rate of surplus value, all other circumstance remaining the same, will depend on the proportion between that part of the working day necessary to reproduce the value of the labouring power and the *surplus time or surplus labour* performed for the capitalist. It will, therefore, depend on the *ratio in which the working day is prolonged over and above that extent,* by working which the working man would only reproduce the value of his labouring power, or replace his wages.

IX.
Value of Labour

We must now return to the expression, *"Value, or Price of Labour."*

We have seen that, in fact, it is only the value of the labouring power, measured by the values of commodities necessary for its maintenance. But since the workman receives his wages *after* his labour is performed, and knows, moreover, that what he actually gives to the capitalist is his labour, the value or price of his labouring power necessarily appears to him as the *price or value of his labour itself.* If the price of his labouring power is 3s., in which six hours of labour are realised, and if he works twelve hours, he necessarily considers these 3s. as the value or price of twelve hours of labour, although these twelve hours of labour realise themselves in a value of 6s. A double consequence flows from this.

Firstly. *The value or price of the labouring power* takes the semblance of the *price or value of labour itself,* although, strictly speaking, value and price of labour are senseless terms.

Secondly. Although one part only of the workman's daily labour is *paid,* while the other part is *unpaid,* and while that unpaid or surplus labour constitutes exactly the fund out of which *surplus value* or *profit* is formed, it seems as if the aggregate labour was paid labour.

This false appearance distinguishes *wages labour* from other *historical* forms of labour. On the basis of the wages system even the *unpaid* labour seems to be *paid* labour. With the *slave,* on the contrary, even that part of his labour which is paid appears to be unpaid. Of course, in order to work the slave must live, and one part of his working day goes to replace the value of his own maintenance. But since no bargain is struck between him and his master, and no acts of selling and buying are going on between the two parties, all his labour seems to be given away for nothing.

Take, on the other hand, the peasant serf, such as he, I might say, until yesterday existed in the whole east of Europe. This peasant worked, for example, three days for himself on his own field or the field allotted to him, and the three subsequent days he performed compulsory and gratuitous labour on the estate of his lord. Here, then, the paid and unpaid parts of labour were visibly separated, separated in time and space; and our Liberal overflowed with moral indignation at the preposterous notion of making a man work for nothing.

In point of fact, however, whether a man works three days of the week for himself on his own field and three days for nothing on the estate of his lord, or whether he works in the factory or the workshop six hours daily for himself and six for his employer, comes to the same, although in the latter case the paid and unpaid portions of labour are inseparably mixed up with each other, and the nature of the whole transaction is completely masked by the *intervention of a contract* and the *pay* received at the end of the week. The gratuitous labour appears to be voluntarily given in the one instance, and to be compulsory in the other. That makes all the difference.

In using the expression *"value of labour,"* I shall only use it as a popular slang term for *"value of labouring power."*

X.
Profit Is Made by Selling a Commodity at Its Value

Suppose an average hour of labour to be realised in a value equal to sixpence, or twelve average hours of labour to be realised in 6s. Suppose, further, the value of labour to be 3s. or the produce of six hours' labour. If, then, in the raw material, machinery, and so forth, used in a commodity, twenty-four average hours of labour were realised, its value would amount to 12s. If, moreover, the workman employed by the capitalist added twelve hours of labour to those means of production, these twelve hours would be realised in an additional value of 6s. The *total value of the product* would, therefore, amount to thirty-six hours of realised labour, and be equal to 18s. But as the value of labour, or the wages paid to the workman, would be 3s. only, no equivalent would have been paid by the capitalist for the six hours of surplus labour worked by the workman, and realised in the value of the commodity. By selling this commodity at its value for 18s., the capitalist would, therefore, realise a value of 3s., for which he had paid no equivalent. These 3s. would constitute the surplus value or profit pocketed by him. The capitalist would consequently realise the profit of 3s., not by selling his commodity at a price *over and above* its value, but by selling it *at its real value.*

The value of a commodity is determined by the *total quantity of labour* contained in it. But part of that quantity of labour is realised in a value, for which an equivalent has been paid in the form of wages; part of it is realised in a value for which *no* equivalent has been paid. Part of the labour contained in the commodity is *paid* labour; part is *unpaid* labour. By selling, therefore, the commodity *at its value,* that is, as the crystallisation of the *total quantity of labour* bestowed upon it, the capitalist must necessarily sell it at a profit. He sells not only what has cost him an equivalent, but he sells also what has cost him nothing, although it has cost the labour of his workman. The cost of the commodity to the capitalist and its real cost are different things. I repeat, therefore, that normal and average profits are made by selling commodities not *above,* but *at their real values.*

XI.
The Different Parts into Which Surplus Value Is Decomposed

The *surplus value,* or that part of the total value of the commodity in which the *surplus labour* or *unpaid labour* of the working man is realised, I call *Profit.* The whole of that profit is not pocketed by the employing capitalist. The monopoly of land enables the landlord to take one part of that *surplus value,* under the name of *rent,* whether the land is used for agriculture or buildings or railways, or for any other productive purpose. On the other hand, the very fact that the possession of the *means of labour* enables the employing capitalist to produce a *surplus value,* or, what comes to the same, to *appropriate to himself a certain amount of unpaid labour,* enables the owner of the means of labour, which he lends wholly or partly to the employing capitalist—enables, in one word, the *money-lending capitalist* to claim for himself under the name of *interest* another part of that surplus value, so that there remains to the employing capitalist *as such* only what is called *industrial* or *commercial profit*.

By what laws this division of the total amount of surplus value amongst the three categories of people is regulated is a question quite foreign to our subject. This much, however, results from what has been stated.

Rent, Interest, and Industrial Profits are only *different names for different parts* of the *surplus value* of the commodity, or the *unpaid labour realised in it,* and they are *equally derived from this source, and from this source alone.* They are not derived from *land* as such nor from *capital* as such, but land and capital enable their owners to get their respective shares out of the surplus value extracted by the employing capitalist from the labourer. For the labourer himself it is a matter of subordinate importance whether that surplus value, the result of his surplus labour, or unpaid labour, is altogether pocketed by the employing capitalist or whether the latter is obliged to pay portions of it, under the names of rent and interest, away to third parties. Suppose the employing capitalist to use only his own capital and to be his own landlord, then the whole surplus value would go into his pocket.

It is the employing capitalist who immediately extracts from the labourer this surplus value, whatever part of it he may ultimately be able to keep for himself. Upon this relation, therefore, between the employing capitalist and the wages labourer the whole wages system and the whole present system of production hinge. Some of the citizens who took part in our debate were, therefore, wrong in trying to mince matters, and to treat this fundamental relation between the employing capitalist and the working man as a secondary question, although they were right in stating that, under given circumstances, a rise of prices might affect in very unequal degrees the employing capitalist, the landlord, the moneyed capitalist, and, if you please, the taxgatherer.

Another consequence follows from what has been stated.

That part of the value of the commodity which represents only the value of the raw materials, the machinery, in one word, the value of the means of production used up, forms *no revenue* at all, but replaces *only capital*. But, apart from this, it is false that the other part of the value of the commodity *which forms revenue,* or may be spent in the form of wages, profits, rent, interest, is *constituted* by the value of wages, the value of rent, the value of profit, and so forth. We shall, in the first instance, discard wages, and only treat industrial profits, interest, and rent. We have just seen that the *surplus value* contained in the commodity, or that part of its value in which *unpaid labour* is realised, resolves itself into different fractions, bearing three different names. But it would be quite the reverse of the truth to say that its value is *composed* of, or *formed* by, the *addition* of the *independent values of these three constituents.*

If one hour of labour realises itself in a value of sixpence, if the working day of the labourer comprises twelve hours, if half of this time is unpaid labour, that surplus labour will add to the commodity a *surplus value* of 3s., that is of value for which no equivalent has been paid. This surplus value of 3s. constitutes the *whole fund* which the employing capitalist may divide, in whatever proportions, with the landlord and the money-lender. The value of these 3s. constitutes the limit of the value they have to divide amongst them. But it is not the employing capitalist who adds to the value of the commodity an arbitrary value for his profit, to which another value is added for the landlord, and so forth, so that the addition of these arbitrarily fixed values would constitute the total value. You see, therefore, the fallacy of the popular notion, which confounds the *decomposition* of a *given value* into three parts, with the *formation* of that value by the addition of three *independent* values, thus converting the aggregate value, from which rent, profit, and interest are derived, into an arbitrary magnitude.

If the total profit realised by a capitalist be equal to 100, we call this sum, considered as absolute magnitude, the *amount of profit*. But if we calculate the ratio which those 100 bear to the capital advanced, we call this relative magnitude, the *rate of profit*. It is evident that this rate of profit may be expressed in a double way.

Suppose 100 to be the capital *advanced in wages*. If the surplus value created is also 100—and this would show us that half the working day of the labourer consists of *unpaid* labour—and if we measured this profit by the value of the capital advanced in wages, we should say that the *rate of profit* amounted to 100 percent, because the value advanced would be 100 and the value realised would be 200.

If, on the other hand, we should not only consider the *capital advanced in wages,* but the *total capital* advanced, say, for example, 500, of which 400 represented the value of raw materials, machinery, and so forth, we should say that the *rate of profit* amounted only to 20 percent, because the profit of 100 would be but the fifth part of the *total* capital advanced.

The first mode of expressing the rate of profit is the only one which shows you the real ratio between paid and unpaid labour, the real degree of the *exploitation* (you must allow me this French word) *of labour.* The other mode of expression is that in common use, and is, indeed, appropriate for certain purposes. At all events, it is very useful for concealing the degree in which the capitalist extracts gratuitous labour from the workman.

In the remarks I have still to make I shall use the word *profit* for the whole amount of the surplus value extracted by the capitalist without any regard to the division of that surplus value between different parties, and in using the words *Rate of Profit,* I shall always measure profits by the value of the capital advanced in wages.

XII.
General Relation of Profits, Wages and Prices

Deduct from the value of a commodity the value replacing the value of the raw materials, and other means of production used upon it, that is to say, deduct the value representing the *past* labour contained in it, and the remainder of its value will resolve into the quantity of labour added by the working man *last* employed. If that working man works twelve hours daily, if twelve hours of average labour crystallise themselves in an amount of gold equal to 6s., this additional value of 6s. is the *only* value his labour will have created. This given value, determined by the time of his labour, is the only fund from which both he and the capitalist have to draw their respective shares or dividends, the only value to be divided into wages and profits. It is evident that this value itself will not be altered by the variable proportions in which it may be divided amongst the two parties. There will also be nothing changed if in the place of one working man you put the whole working population, twelve million working days, for example, instead of one.

Since the capitalist and workman have only to divide this limited value, that is, the value measured by the total labour of the working man, the more the one gets the less will the other get, and *vice versa*. Whenever a quantity is given, one part of it will increase inversely as the other decreases. If the wages change, profits will change in an opposite direction. If wages fall, profits will rise, and if wages rise, profits will fall. If the working man, on our former supposition gets 3s., equal to one-half of the value he has created, or if his whole working day consists half of paid, half of unpaid labour, the *rate of profit* will be 100 percent because the capitalist would also get 3s. If the working man receives only 2s. or works only one-third of the whole day for himself, the capitalist will get 4s., and the rate of profit will be 200 percent. If the working man receives 4s., the capitalist will only receive 2s., and the rate of profit would sink to 50 percent, but all these variations will not affect the value of the commodity. A general rise of wages would, therefore, result in a fall of the general rate of profit, but not affect values. But although the values of commodities, which must ultimately regulate their market prices, are exclusively determined by the total quantities of labour fixed in them, and not by the division of that quantity in to paid and unpaid labour, it by no means follows that the values of the single commodities, or lots of commodities, produced during twelve hours, for example, will remain constant. The *number* or mass of commodities produced in a given time of labour, or by a given quantity of labour, depends upon the *productive power* of the labour employed, and not upon its *extent* or length. With one degree of the productive power of spinning labour, for example, a working day of twelve hours may produce twelve pounds of yarn, with a lesser degree of productive power only two pounds. If then twelve hours' average labour were realised in the value of 6s. in the one case, the twelve pounds of yarn would cost 6s., in the other case the two pounds of yarn would also cost 6s. One pound of yarn would, therefore, cost sixpence in the one case, and 3s. in the other. This difference of price would result from the difference in the productive powers of labour employed. One hour of labour would be realised in one pound of yarn with the greater productive power, while with the smaller productive power, six hours of labour would be realised in one pound of yarn. The price of a pound of yarn would, in the one instance, be only sixpence, although wages were relatively high and the rate of profit low; it would be 3s. in the other instance, although wages were low and the rate of profit high. This would be so because the price of the pound of yarn is regulated by the *total amount of labour worked up in it,* and not by the *proportional division of that total amount into paid and unpaid labour.* The fact I have before mentioned that high-priced labour may produce cheap, and low-priced labour may produce dear commodities, loses, therefore, its paradoxical appearance. It is only the expression of the general law that the value of a commodity is regulated by the quantity of labour worked up in it, but that quantity of labour worked up in it depends altogether upon the productive powers of the labour employed, and will, therefore, vary with every variation in the productivity of labour.

17

V. I. Lenin

State and Revolution (1917)

Vladimir Ilyich Ulyanov (1870–1924)—or Lenin, as he is better known—adapted Marxism to conditions in Russia by arguing that socialist revolution could succeed without an industrialized economy or a proletarian majority. He proposed that a small, secret party of professional revolutionaries seize power in the name of the proletariat and then use the state to modernize society. In the following selection from State and Revolution, *which he wrote when he returned from Europe to Russia to lead the Bolshevik Revolution, Lenin explains how he plans to continue the revolution and consolidate its gains. Unlike Marx, he provides a detailed description of the transition from bourgeois democracy to proletarian dictatorship to higher communism.*

A MOST DETAILED elucidation of this question is given by Marx in his *Critique of the Gotha Programme* (letter to [Wilhelm] Bracke, 15 May 1875, printed only in 1891 in the *Neue Zeit,* IX-1, and in a special Russian edition).[1] The polemical part of this remarkable work, consisting of a criticism of Lassalleanism, has, so to speak, overshadowed its positive part, namely, the analysis of the connection between the development of Communism and the withering away of the state.

1. Formulation of the Question by Marx

From a superficial comparison of the letter of Marx to Bracke (15 May 1875) with Engels's letter to [August] Bebel (28 March 1875), analysed above, it might appear

Source: Vladimir Lenin, *State and Revolution* (New York: International Publishers Co., 1932), 5–25, 99–122. Reprinted with the permission of International Publishers Co.

that Marx was much more "pro-state" than Engels, and that the difference of opinion between the two writers on the question of the state is very considerable.

Engels suggests to Bebel that all the chatter about the state should be thrown overboard; that the word "state" should be eliminated from the programme and replaced by "community"; Engels even declares that the Commune was really no longer a state in the proper sense of the word. And Marx even speaks of the "future state in Communist society," i.e., he is apparently recognising the necessity of a state even under Communism.

But such a view would be fundamentally incorrect. A closer examination shows that Marx's and Engels's views on the state and its withering away were completely identical, and that Marx's expression quoted above refers merely to this withering away of the state.

It is clear that there can be no question of defining the exact moment of the *future* withering away—the more so as it must obviously be a rather lengthy process. The apparent difference between Marx and Engels is due to the different subjects they dealt with, the different aims they were pursuing. Engels set out to show to Bebel, in plain, bold and broad outline, all the absurdity of the current superstitions concerning the state, shared to no small degree by [Ferdinand] Lassalle himself. Marx, on the other hand, only touches upon *this* question in passing, being interested mainly in another subject—the *evolution* of Communist society.

The whole theory of Marx is an application of the theory of evolution—in its most consistent, complete, well considered and fruitful form—to modern capitalism. It was natural for Marx to raise the question of applying this theory both to the *coming* collapse of capitalism and to the *future* evolution of *future* Communism.

On the basis of what *data* can the future evolution of future Communism be considered?

On the basis of the fact that *it has its origin* in capitalism, that it develops historically from capitalism, that it is the result of the action of a social force to which capitalism *has given birth*. There is no shadow of an attempt on Marx's part to conjure up a Utopia, to make idle guesses about that which cannot be known. Marx treats the question of Communism in the same way as a naturalist would treat the question of the evolution of, say, a new biological species, if he knew that such and such was its origin, and such and such the direction in which it changed.

Marx, first of all, brushes aside the confusion the Gotha Programme brings into the question of the interrelation between state and society.

> "Contemporary society" is the capitalist society—he writes—which exists in all civilised countries, more or less free of medieval admixture, more or less modified by each country's particular historical development, more or less

developed. In contrast with this, the "contemporary state" varies with every state boundary. It is different in the Prusso-German Empire from what it is in Switzerland, and different in England from what it is in the United States. The "contemporary state" is therefore a fiction.

Nevertheless, in spite of the motley variety of their forms, the different states of the various civilised counties all have this in common: they are all based on modern bourgeois society, only a little more or less capitalistically developed. Consequently, they also have certain essential characteristics in common. In this sense, it is possible to speak of the "contemporary state" in contrast to the future, when its present root, bourgeois society, will have perished.

Then the question arises: what transformation will the state undergo in a Communist society? In other words, what social functions analogous to the present functions of the state will then still survive? This question can only be answered scientifically, and however many thousand times the word people is combined with the word state, we get not a flea-jump closer to the problem. . . .[2]

Having thus ridiculed all talk about a "people's state," Marx formulates the question and warns us, as it were, that to arrive at a scientific answer one must rely only on firmly established scientific data.

The first fact that has been established with complete exactness by the whole theory of evolution, by science as a whole—a fact which the Utopians forgot, and which is forgotten by the present-day opportunists who are afraid of the Socialist revolution—is that, historically, there must undoubtedly be a special stage or epoch of *transition* from capitalism to Communism.

2. Transition from Capitalism to Communism

Between capitalist and Communist society—Marx continues—lies the period of the revolutionary transformation of the former into the latter. To this also corresponds a political transition period, in which the state can be no other than *the revolutionary dictatorship of the proletariat.*[3]

This conclusion Marx bases on an analysis of the role played by the proletariat in modern capitalist society, on the data concerning the evolution of this society, and on the irreconcilability of the opposing interests of the proletariat and the bourgeoisie.

Earlier the question was put thus: to attain its emancipation, the proletariat must overthrow the bourgeoisie, conquer political power and establish its own revolutionary dictatorship.

Now the question is put somewhat differently: the transition from capitalist society, developing towards Communism, towards a Communist society, is impossible without a "political transition period," and the state in this period can only be the revolutionary dictatorship of the proletariat.

What, then, is the relation of this dictatorship to democracy?

We have seen that the *Communist Manifesto* simply places side by side the two ideas: the "transformation of the proletariat into the ruling class," and the "establishment of democracy." On the basis of all that has been said above, one can define more exactly how democracy changes in the transition from capitalism to Communism.

In capitalist society, under the conditions most favourable to its development, we have more or less complete democracy in the democratic republic. But this democracy is always bound by the narrow framework of capitalist exploitation, and consequently always remains, in reality, a democracy for the minority, only for the possessing classes, only for the rich. Freedom in capitalist society always remains just about the same as it was in the ancient Greek republics: freedom for the slave-owners. The modern wage-slaves, owing to the conditions of capitalist exploitation, are so much crushed by want and poverty that "democracy is nothing to them," "politics is nothing to them"; that, in the ordinary peaceful course of events, the majority of the population is debarred from participating in social and political life.

The correctness of this statement is perhaps most clearly proved by Germany, just because in this state constitutional legality lasted and remained stable for a remarkably long time—for nearly half a century (1871–1914)—and because Social-Democracy in Germany during that time was able to achieve far more than in other countries in "utilising legality," and was able to organise into a political party a larger proportion of the working class than anywhere else in the world.

What, then, is this largest proportion of politically conscious and active wage-slaves that has so far been observed in capitalist society? One million members of the Social-Democratic Party—out of fifteen million wage-workers! Three million organised in trade unions—out of fifteen million!

Democracy for an insignificant minority, democracy for the rich—that is the democracy of capitalist society. If we look more closely into the mechanism of capitalist democracy, everywhere, both in the "petty"—so-called petty—details of the suffrage (residential qualification, exclusion of women, etc.), and in the technique of the representative institutions, in the actual obstacles to the right of assembly (public buildings are not for "beggars"!), in the purely capitalist organisation of the daily press, etc., etc.—on all sides we see restriction after restriction upon democracy. These restrictions, exceptions, exclusions, obstacles for the poor, seem slight, especially in the eyes of one who has himself never known want and has never been in close contact with the oppressed classes in their mass life (and nine-tenths, if not ninety-nine hundredths, of the bourgeois publicists and politicians are of this class), but in their sum total these restrictions exclude and squeeze out the poor from politics and from an active share in democracy.

Marx splendidly grasped this *essence* of capitalist democracy, when, in analysing the experience of the Commune, he said that the oppressed were allowed, once every few years, to decide which particular representatives of the oppressing class should be in parliament to represent and repress them!

But from this capitalist democracy—inevitably narrow, subtly rejecting the poor, and therefore hypocritical and false to the core—progress does not march onward, simply, smoothly and directly, to "greater and greater democracy," as the liberal professors and petty-bourgeois opportunists would have us believe.

No, progress marches onward, i.e., towards Communism, through the dictatorship of the proletariat; it cannot do otherwise, for there is no one else and no other way to *break the resistance* of the capitalist exploiters.

But the dictatorship of the proletariat—i.e., the organisation of the vanguard of the oppressed as the ruling class for the purpose of crushing the oppressors— cannot produce merely an expansion of democracy. *Together* with an immense expansion of democracy which *for the first time* becomes democracy for the poor, democracy for the people, and not democracy for the rich folk, the dictatorship of the proletariat produces a series of restrictions of liberty in the case of the oppressors, the exploiters, the capitalists. We must crush them in order to free humanity from wage-slavery; their resistance must be broken by force; it is clear that where there is suppression there is also violence, there is no liberty, no democracy.

Engels expressed this splendidly in his letter to Bebel when he said, as the reader will remember, that "as long as the proletariat still *needs* the state, it needs it not in the interests of freedom, but for the purpose of crushing its antagonists; and as soon as it becomes possible to speak of freedom, then the state, as such, ceases to exist."

Democracy for the vast majority of the people, and suppression by force, i.e., exclusion from democracy, of the exploiters and oppressors of the people— this is the modification of democracy during the *transition* from capitalism to Communism.

Only in Communist society, when the resistance of the capitalists has been completely broken, when the capitalists have disappeared, when there are no classes (i.e., there is no difference between the members of society in their relation to the social means of production), *only then* "the state ceases to exist," and *"it becomes possible to speak of freedom."* Only then a really full democracy, a democracy without any exceptions, will be possible and will be realised. And only then will democracy itself begin to *wither away* due to the simple fact that, freed from capitalist slavery, from the untold horrors, savagery, absurdities and infamies of capitalist exploitation, people will gradually *become accustomed* to the observance of the elementary rules of social life that have been known for centuries and repeated for thousands of years in all school books; they will become accustomed to observing them without force, without compulsion, without subordination, without the *special apparatus* for compulsion which is called the state.

The expression "the state *withers away,*" is very well chosen, for it indicates both the gradual and the elemental nature of the process. Only habit can, and undoubtedly will, have such an effect; for we see around us millions of times how readily people get accustomed to observe the necessary rules of life in common, if there is no exploitation, if there is nothing that causes indignation, that calls forth protest and revolt and has to be *suppressed.*

Thus, in capitalist society, we have a democracy that is curtailed, poor, false; a democracy only for the rich, for the minority. The dictatorship of the proletariat, the period of transition to Communism, will, for the first time, produce democracy for the people, for the majority, side by side with the necessary suppression of the minority—the exploiters. Communism alone is capable of giving a really complete democracy, and the more complete it is the more quickly will it become unnecessary and wither away of itself.

In other words: under capitalism we have a state in the proper sense of the word, that is, special machinery for the suppression of one class by another, and of the majority by the minority at that. Naturally, for the successful discharge of such a task as the systematic suppression by the exploiting minority of the exploited majority, the greatest ferocity and savagery of suppression are required, seas of blood are required, through which mankind is marching in slavery, serfdom, and wage-labour.

Again, during the *transition* from capitalism to Communism, suppression is *still* necessary; but it is the suppression of the minority of exploiters by the majority of exploited. A special apparatus, special machinery for suppression, the "state," is *still* necessary, but this is now a transitional state, no longer a state in the usual sense, for the suppression of the minority of exploiters, by the majority of the wage slaves of *yesterday,* is a matter comparatively so easy, simple and natural that it will cost far less bloodshed than the suppression of the risings of slaves, serfs or wage labourers, and will cost mankind far less. This is compatible with the diffusion of democracy among such an overwhelming majority of the population, that the need for *special machinery* of suppression will begin to disappear. The exploiters are, naturally, unable to suppress the people without a most complex machinery for performing this task; but *the people* can suppress the exploiters even with very simple "machinery," almost without any "machinery," without any special apparatus, by the simple *organisation of the armed masses* (such as the Soviets of Workers' and Soldiers' Deputies, we may remark, anticipating a little).

Finally, only Communism renders the state absolutely unnecessary, for there is *no one* to be suppressed—"no one" in the sense of a *class*, in the sense of a systematic struggle with a definite section of the population. We are not Utopians, and we do not in the least deny the possibility and inevitability of excesses on the part of *individual persons*, nor the need to suppress *such* excesses. But, in the first place, no special machinery, no special apparatus of repression is needed for this; this will be done by the armed people itself, as simply and as readily as any crowd of civilised people, even in modern society, parts a pair of combatants or does not allow a woman to be outraged. And, secondly, we know that the fundamental social cause of excesses which consist in violating the rules of social life is the exploitation of the masses, their want and their poverty. With the removal of this chief cause, excesses will inevitably begin to *"wither away."* We do not know how quickly and in what succession, but we know that they will wither away. With their withering away, the state will also *wither away.*

Without going into Utopias, Marx defined more fully what can *now* be defined regarding this future, namely, the difference between the lower and the higher phases (degrees, stages) of Communist society.

3. First Phase of Communist Society

In the *Critique of the Gotha Programme,* Marx goes into some detail to disprove the Lassallean idea of the workers' receiving under Socialism the "undiminished" or the "full product of their labour." Marx shows that out of the whole of the social labour of society, it is necessary to deduct a reserve fund, a fund for the expansion of production, for the replacement of worn-out machinery, and so on; then, also, out of the means of consumption must be deducted a fund for the expenses of management, for schools, hospitals, homes for the aged, and so on.

Instead of the hazy, obscure, general phrase of Lassalle's—"the full product of his labour for the worker"—Marx gives a sober estimate of exactly how a Socialist society will have to manage its affairs. Marx undertakes a *concrete* analysis of the condition of life of a society in which there is no capitalism, and says:

> What we are dealing with here [analysing the programme of the party] is not a Communist society which has *developed* on its own foundations, but, on the contrary, one which is just *emerging* from capitalist society, and which therefore in all respects—economic, moral and intellectual—still bears the birthmarks of the old society from whose womb it sprung.[4]

And it is this Communist society—a society which has just come into the world out of the womb of capitalism, and which, in all respects, bears the stamp of the old society—that Marx terms the "first," or lower, phase of Communist society.

The means of production are no longer the private property of individuals. The means of production belong to the whole of society. Every member of society, performing a certain part of socially necessary work, receives a certificate from society to the effect that he has done such and such a quantity of work. According to this certificate, he receives from the public warehouses, where articles of consumption are stored, a corresponding quantity of products. Deducting that proportion of labour which goes to the public fund, every worker, therefore, receives from society as much as he has given it.

"Equality" seems to reign supreme.

But when Lassalle, having in view such a social order (generally called Socialism, but termed by Marx the first phase of Communism), speaks of this as "just distribution," and says that this is "the equal right of each to an equal product of labour," Lassalle is mistaken, and Marx exposes his error.

"Equal right," says Marx, we indeed have here; but it is *still* a "bourgeois right," which, like every right, *presupposes inequality.* Every right is an application of the *same* measure to *different* people who, in fact, are not the same and are not equal to one another; this is why "equal right" is really a violation of equality, and an injustice. In effect, every man having done as much social labour as every other, receives an equal share of the social products (with the above-mentioned deductions).

But different people are not alike: one is strong, another is weak; one is married, the other is not; one has more children, another has less, and so on.

> . . . With equal labour—Marx concludes—and therefore an equal share in the social consumption fund, one man in fact receives more than the other, one is richer than the other, and so forth. In order to avoid all these defects, rights, instead of being equal, must be unequal.[5]

The first phase of Communism, therefore, still cannot produce justice and equality; differences, and unjust differences, in wealth will still exist, but the *exploitation* of man by man will have become impossible, because it will be impossible to seize as private property the *means of production,* the factories, machines, lands, and so on. In tearing down Lassalle's petty-bourgeois, confused phrase about "equality" and "justice" *in general,* Marx shows the *course of development* of Communist society, which is forced at first to destroy *only* the "injustice" that consists in the means of production having been seized by private individuals, and which *is not capable* of destroying at once the further injustice consisting in the distribution of the articles of consumption "according to work performed" (and not according to need).

The vulgar economists, including the bourgeois professors and also "our" Tugan-Baranovsky, constantly reproach the Socialists with forgetting the inequality of people and with "dreaming" of destroying this inequality. Such a reproach, as we see, only proves the extreme ignorance of the gentlemen pro-pounding bourgeois ideology.

Marx not only takes into account with the greatest accuracy the inevitable inequality of men; he also takes into account the fact that the mere conver-sion of the means of production into the common property of the whole of society ("Socialism" in the generally accepted sense of the word) *does not remove* the defects of distribution and the inequality of "bourgeois right" which *continue to rule* as long as the products are divided "according to work performed."

> But these defects—Marx continues—are unavoidable in the first phase of Communist society, when, after long travail, it first emerges from capitalist society. Justice can never rise superior to the economic conditions of society and the cultural development conditioned by them.[6]

And so, in the first phase of Communist society (generally called Socialism) "bourgeois right" is *not* abolished in its entirety, but only in part, only in propor-tion to the economic transformation so far attained, i.e., only in respect of the means of production. "Bourgeois right" recognises them as the private property of separate individuals. Socialism converts them into common property. *To that extent,* and to that extent alone, does "bourgeois right" disappear.

However, it continues to exist as far as its other part is concerned; it remains in the capacity of regulator (determining factor) distributing the products and allotting labour among the members of society. "He who does not work, shall not eat"—this Socialist principle is *already* realised; "for an equal quantity of labour, an equal quantity of products"—this Socialist principle is also *already* realised. However, this is not yet Communism, and this does not abolish "bourgeois right," which gives to unequal individuals, in return for an unequal (in reality unequal) amount of work, an equal quantity of products.

This is a "defect," says Marx, but it is unavoidable during the first phase of Communism; for, if we are not to fall into Utopianism, we cannot imagine that, having overthrown capitalism, people will at once learn to work for society *with-out any standards of right;* indeed, the abolition of capitalism *does not immediately lay* the economic foundations for *such* a change.

And there is no other standard yet than that of "bourgeois right." To this extent, therefore, a form of state is still necessary, which, while maintaining pub-lic ownership of the means of production, would preserve the equality of labour and equality in the distribution of products.

The state is withering away in so far as there are no longer any capitalists, any classes, and, consequently, no *class* can be suppressed.

But the state has not yet altogether withered away, since there still remains the protection of "bourgeois right" which sanctifies actual inequality. For the complete extinction of the state, complete Communism is necessary.

4. Higher Phase of Communist Society

Marx continues:

> In a higher phase of Communist society, when the enslaving subordination of individuals in the division of labour has disappeared, and with it also the antagonism between mental and physical labour; when labour has become not only a means of living, but itself the first necessity of life; when, along with the allround development of individuals, the productive forces too have grown, and all the springs of social wealth are flowing more freely—it is only at that stage that it will be possible to pass completely beyond the narrow horizon of bourgeois rights, and for society to inscribe on its banners: from each according to his ability; to each according to his needs![7]

Only now can we appreciate the full correctness of Engels's remarks in which he mercilessly ridiculed all the absurdity of combining the words "freedom" and "state." While the state exists there is no freedom. When there is freedom, there will be no state.

The economic basis for the complete withering away of the state is that high stage of development of Communism when the antagonism between mental and physical labour disappears, that is to say, when one of the principal sources of modern *social* inequality disappears—a source, moreover, which it is impossible to remove immediately by the mere conversion of the means of production into public property, by the mere expropriation of the capitalists.

This expropriation will make a gigantic development of the productive forces *possible*. And seeing how incredibly, even now, capitalism *retards* this development, how much progress could be made even on the basis of modern technique at the level it has reached, we have a right to say, with the fullest confidence, that the expropriation of the capitalists will inevitably result in a gigantic development of the productive forces of human society. But how rapidly this development will go forward, how soon it will reach the point of breaking away from the division of labour, of removing the antagonism between mental and physical labour, of transforming work into the "first necessity of life"—this we do not and *cannot* know.

Consequently, we have a right to speak solely of the inevitable withering away of the state, emphasising the protracted nature of this process and its dependence upon the rapidity of development of the *higher phase* of Communism; leaving quite open the question of lengths of time, or the concrete forms of withering away, since material for the solution of such questions is *not available*.

The state will be able to wither away completely when society has realised the rule: "From each according to his ability; to each according to his needs," i.e., when people have become accustomed to observe the fundamental rules of social life, and their labour is so productive, that they voluntarily work *according to their ability*. "The narrow horizon of bourgeois rights," which compels one to calculate, with the hard-heartedness of a Shylock, whether he has not worked half an hour more than another, whether he is not getting less pay than another—this narrow horizon will then be left behind. There will then be no need for any exact calculation by society of the quantity of products to be distributed to each of its members; each will take freely "according to his needs."

From the bourgeois point of view, it is easy to declare such a social order "a pure Utopia," and to sneer at the Socialists for promising each the right to receive from society, without any control of the labour of the individual citizen, any quantity of truffles, automobiles, pianos, etc. Even now, most bourgeois "savants" deliver themselves of such sneers, thereby displaying at once their ignorance and their self-seeking defence of capitalism.

Ignorance—for it has never entered the head of any Socialist to "promise" that the highest phase of Communism will arrive; while the great Socialists, in *foreseeing* its arrival, presupposed both a productivity of labour unlike the present and a person not like the present man in the street, capable of spoiling, without reflection, like the seminary students in Pomyalovsky's book,[8] the stores of social wealth, and of demanding the impossible.

Until the "higher" phase of Communism arrives, the Socialists demand the *strictest* control, *by society and by the state,* of the quantity of labour and the quantity of consumption; only this control must *start* with the expropriation of the capitalists, with the control of the workers over the capitalists, and must be carried out, not by a state of bureaucrats, but by a state of *armed workers.*

Self-seeking defence of capitalism by the bourgeois ideologists (and their hangers-on like Tsereteli, Chernov and Co.) consists in that they *substitute* disputes and discussions about the distant future for the essential imperative questions of present-day policy: the expropriation of the capitalists, the conversion of *all* citizens into workers and employees of *one* huge "syndicate"—the whole state—and the complete subordination of the whole of the work of this syndicate to the really democratic state of the *Soviets of Workers' and Soldiers' Deputies.*

In reality, when a learned professor, and following him some philistine, and following the latter Messrs. Tsereteli and Chernov, talk of the unreasonable Utopias, of the demagogic promises of the Bolsheviks, of the impossibility of "introducing" Socialism, it is the higher stage or phase of Communism which they have in mind, and which no one has ever promised, or even thought of "introducing," for the reason that, generally speaking, it cannot be "introduced."

And here we come to that question of the scientific difference between Socialism and Communism, upon which Engels touched in his above-quoted discussion on the incorrectness of the name "Social-Democrat." The political difference between the first, or lower, and the higher phase of Communism will in
time, no doubt, be tremendous; but it would be ridiculous to emphasise it now,
under capitalism, and only, perhaps, some isolated Anarchist could invest it with
primary importance (if there are still some people among the Anarchists who
have learned nothing from the Plekhanov-like conversion of the Kropotkins, the
Graveses, the Cornelissens, and other "leading lights" of Anarchism to social-
chauvinism or Anarcho-*Jusquaubout*-ism,[9] as Ge, one of the few Anarchists still
preserving honour and conscience, has expressed it).

But the scientific difference between Socialism and Communism is clear.
What is generally called Socialism was termed by Marx the "first" or lower phase
of Communist society. In so far as the means of production become *public* property, the word "Communism" is also applicable here, providing we do not forget
that it is *not* full Communism. The great significance of Marx's elucidations consists in this: that here, too, he consistently applies materialist dialectics, the doctrine of evolution, looking upon Communism as something which evolves *out* of
capitalism. Instead of artificial, "elaborate," scholastic definitions and profitless
disquisitions on the meaning of words (what Socialism is, what Communism is),
Marx gives an analysis of what may be called stages in the economic ripeness of
Communism.

In its first phase or first stage Communism *cannot* as yet be economically ripe
and entirely free of all tradition and of all taint of capitalism. Hence the interesting phenomenon of Communism retaining, in its first phase, "the narrow
horizon of bourgeois rights." Bourgeois rights, with respect to distribution of
articles of *consumption,* inevitably presupposes, of course, the existence of the
bourgeois state, for rights are nothing without an apparatus capable of *enforcing*
the observance of the rights.

Consequently, for a certain time not only bourgeois rights, but even the bourgeois state remains under Communism, without the bourgeoisie!

This may look like a paradox, or simply a dialectical puzzle for which Marxism
is often blamed by people who would not make the least effort to study its
extraordinarily profound content.

But, as a matter of fact, the old surviving in the new confronts us in life at
every step, in nature as well as in society. Marx did not smuggle a scrap of "bourgeois" rights into Communism of his own accord; he indicated what is economically and politically inevitable in a society issuing *from the womb* of capitalism.

Democracy is of great importance for the working class in its struggle for freedom against the capitalists. But democracy is by no means a limit one may not

overstep; it is only one of the stages in the course of development from feudalism to capitalism, and from capitalism to Communism.

Democracy means equality. The great significance of the struggle of the proletariat for equality, and the significance of equality as a slogan, are apparent, if we correctly interpret it as meaning the abolition of *classes*. But democracy means only *formal* equality. Immediately after the attainment of equality for all members of society *in respect of* the ownership of the means of production, that is, of equality of labour and equality of wages, there will inevitably arise before humanity the question of going further from formal equality to real equality, i.e., to realising the rule, "From each according to his ability; to each according to his needs." By what stages, by means of what practical measures humanity will proceed to this higher aim—this we do not and cannot know. But it is important to realise how infinitely mendacious is the usual bourgeois presentation of Socialism as something lifeless, petrified, fixed once for all, whereas in reality, it is *only* with Socialism that there will commence a rapid, genuine, real mass advance, in which first the *majority* and then the whole of the population will take part—an advance in all domains of social and individual life.

Democracy is a form of the state—one of its varieties. Consequently, like every state, it consists in organised, systematic application of force against human beings. This on the one hand. On the other hand, however, it signifies the formal recognition of the equality of all citizens, the equal right of all to determine the structure and administration of the state. This, in turn, is connected with the fact that, at a certain stage in the development of democracy, it first rallies the proletariat as a revolutionary class against capitalism, and gives it an opportunity to crush, to smash to bits, to wipe off the face of the earth the bourgeois state machinery—even its republican variety: the standing army, the police, and bureaucracy; then it substitutes for all this a *more* democratic, but still a state machinery in the shape of armed masses of workers, which becomes transformed into universal participation of the people in the militia.

Here "quantity turns into quality": *such* a degree of democracy is bound up with the abandonment of the framework of bourgeois society, and the beginning of its Socialist reconstruction. If *every one* really takes part in the administration of the state, capitalism cannot retain its hold. In its turn, capitalism, as it develops, itself creates *prerequisites* for "every one" *to be able* really to take part in the administration of the state. Among such prerequisites are: universal literacy, already realised in most of the advanced capitalist countries, then the "training and disciplining" of millions of workers by the huge, complex, and socialised apparatus of the post-office, the railways, the big factories, large-scale commerce, banking, etc., etc.

With such *economic* prerequisites it is perfectly possible, immediately, within twenty-four hours after the overthrow of the capitalists and bureaucrats, to replace them, in the control of production and distribution, in the business of *control* of labour and products, by the armed workers, by the whole people in arms. (The question of control and accounting must not be confused with the question of the scientifically educated staff of engineers, agronomists and so on. These gentlemen work today, obeying the capitalists; they will work even better tomorrow, obeying the armed workers.)

Accounting and control—these are the *chief* things necessary for the organising and correct functioning of the *first phase* of Communist society. *All* citizens are here transformed into hired employees of the state, which is made up of the armed workers. *All* citizens become employees and workers of *one* national state "syndicate." All that is required is that they should work equally, should regularly do their share of work, and should receive equal pay. The accounting and control necessary for this have been *simplified* by capitalism to the utmost, till they have become the extraordinarily simple operations of watching, recording and issuing receipts, within the reach of anybody who can read and write and knows the first rules of arithmetic.[10]

When the *majority* of the people begin everywhere to keep such accounts and maintain such control over the capitalists (now converted into employees) and over the intellectual gentry, who still retain capitalist habits, this control will really become universal, general, national; and there will be no way of getting away from it, there will be "nowhere to go."

The whole of society will have become one office and one factory, with equal work and equal pay.

But this "factory" discipline, which the proletariat will extend to the whole of society after the defeat of the capitalists and the overthrow of the exploiters, is by no means our ideal, or our final aim. It is but a *foothold* necessary for the radical cleansing of society of all the hideousness and foulness of capitalist exploitation, *in order to advance further.*

From the moment when all members of society, or even only the overwhelming majority, have learned how to govern the state *themselves,* have taken this business into their own hands, have "established" control over the insignificant minority of capitalists, over the gentry with capitalist leanings, and the workers thoroughly demoralised by capitalism—from this moment the need for any government begins to disappear. The more complete the democracy, the nearer the moment when it begins to be unnecessary. The more democratic the "state" consisting of armed workers, which is "no longer a state in the proper sense of the word," the more rapidly does *every* state begin to wither away.

For when *all* have learned to manage, and independently are actually managing by themselves social production, keeping accounts, controlling the idlers, the gentlefolk, the swindlers and similar "guardians of capitalist traditions," then the escape from this national accounting and control will inevitably become so increasingly difficult, such a rare exception, and will probably be accompanied by such swift and severe punishment (for the armed workers are men of practical life, not sentimental intellectuals, and they will scarcely allow any one to trifle with them), that very soon the *necessity* of observing the simple, fundamental rules of every-day social life in common will have become a *habit*.

The door will then be wide open for the transition from the first phase of Communist society to its higher phase, and along with it to the complete withering away of the state.

NOTES

1. English translation in *Critique of the Social-Democratic Programmes.*—Ed.

2. Ibid.—Ed.

3. Ibid.—Ed.

4. Ibid.—Ed.

5. Ibid.—Ed.

6. Ibid.—Ed.

7. Ibid.—Ed.

8. Pomyalovsky's *Seminary Sketches* depicted a group of student ruffians who engaged in destroying things for the pleasure it gave them.—Ed.

9. *Jusquaubout*—combination of French words meaning "until the end." Thus, Anarcho-*Jusquaubout*-ism—Anarcho-until-the-End-ism.—Ed.

10. When most of the functions of the state are reduced to this accounting and control by the workers themselves, then it ceases to be a "political state," and the "public functions will lose their political character and be transformed into simple administrative functions" (cf. Chap. IV, 2 on Engels's polemic against the Anarchists).

18

V. I. Lenin

―――

Imperialism, The Highest Stage
of Capitalism: A Popular Outline (1917)

Lenin began writing Imperialism, the Highest Stage of Capitalism: A
Popular Outline *during World War I, though he waited until 1917 to publish it. Among his most famous writings, it presents the first theory of international relations from a Marxist perspective. Lenin traces the causes of the
war to the imperialist tendencies of capitalist nations, and he argues that
their colonial policies will eventually prompt socialist revolutions in less
developed countries.*

Chapter X
The Place of Imperialism in History

WE HAVE SEEN that the economic quintessence of imperialism is monopoly capitalism. This very fact determines its place in history, for monopoly that grew up
on the basis of free competition, and precisely out of free competition, is the
transition from the capitalist system to a higher social-economic order. We must
take special note of the four principal forms of monopoly, or the four principal
manifestations of monopoly capitalism, which are characteristic of the epoch
under review.

Firstly, monopoly arose out of the concentration of production at a very
advanced stage of development. This refers to the monopolist capitalist combines,

From *Imperialism, The Highest Stage of Capitalism: A Popular Outline* (New York: International Publishers
Co., 1989), 123–128. Reprinted with the permission of International Publishers Co.

cartels, syndicates and trusts. We have seen the important part that these play in modern economic life. At the beginning of the twentieth century, monopolies acquired complete supremacy in the advanced countries. And although the first steps towards the formation of the cartels were first taken by countries enjoying the protection of high tariffs (Germany, America), Great Britain, with her system of free trade, was not far behind in revealing the same basic phenomenon, namely, the birth of monopoly out of the concentration of production.

Secondly, monopolies have accelerated the capture of the most important sources of raw materials, especially for the coal and iron industries, which are the basic and most highly cartelised industries in capitalist society. The monopoly of the most important sources of raw materials has enormously increased the power of big capital, and has sharpened the antagonism between cartelised and non-cartelised industry.

Thirdly, monopoly has sprung from the banks. The banks have developed from modest intermediary enterprises into the monopolists of finance capital. Some three or five of the biggest banks in each of the foremost capitalist countries have achieved the "personal union" of industrial and bank capital, and have concentrated in their hands the disposal of thousands upon thousands of millions which form the greater part of the capital and income of entire countries. A financial oligarchy, which throws a close net of relations of dependence over all the economic and political institutions of contemporary bourgeois society without exception—such is the most striking manifestation of this monopoly.

Fourthly, monopoly has grown out of colonial policy. To the numerous "old" motives of colonial policy, finance capital has added the struggle for the sources of raw materials, for the export of capital, for "spheres of influence," *i.e.,* for spheres for profitable deals, concessions, monopolist profits and so on; in fine, for economic territory in general. When the colonies of the European powers in Africa, for instance, comprised only one-tenth of that territory (as was the case in 1876), colonial policy was able to develop by methods other than those of monopoly—by the "free grabbing" of territories, so to speak. But when nine-tenths of Africa had been seized (approximately by 1900), when the whole world had been divided up, there was inevitably ushered in a period of colonial monopoly and, consequently, a period of particularly intense struggle for the division and the redivision of the world.

The extent to which monopolist capital has intensified all the contradictions of capitalism is generally known. It is sufficient to mention the high cost of living and the oppression of the cartels. This intensification of contradictions constitutes the most powerful driving force of the transitional period of history, which began from the time of the definite victory of world finance capital.

Monopolies, oligarchy, the striving for domination instead of the striving for liberty, the exploitation of an increasing number of small or weak nations by an extremely small group of the richest or most powerful nations—all these have given birth to those distinctive characteristics of imperialism which compel us to define it as parasitic or decaying capitalism. More and more prominently there emerges, as one of the tendencies of imperialism, the creation of the "bondholding" (rentier) state, the usurer state, in which the bourgeoisie lives on the proceeds of capital exports and by "clipping coupons." It would be a mistake to believe that this tendency to decay precludes the possibility of the rapid growth of capitalism. It does not. In the epoch of imperialism, certain branches of industry, certain strata of the bourgeoisie and certain countries betray, to a more or less degree, one or other of these tendencies. On the whole, capitalism is growing far more rapidly than before. But this growth is not only becoming more and more uneven in general; its unevenness also manifests itself, in particular, in the decay of the countries which are richest in capital (such as England).

In regard to the rapidity of Germany's economic development, Riesser, the author of the book on the big German banks, states:

> "The progress of the preceding period (1848–70), which had not been exactly slow, stood in about the same ratio to the rapidity with which the whole of Germany's national economy, and with it German banking, progressed during this period (1870–1905) as the mail coach of the Holy Roman Empire of the German nation stood to the speed of the present-day automobile . . . which in whizzing past, it must be said, often endangers not only innocent pedestrians in its path, but also the occupants of the car."[1]

In its turn, this finance capital which has grown so rapidly is not unwilling (precisely because it has grown so quickly) to pass on to a more "tranquil" possession of colonies which have to be seized—and not only by peaceful methods—from richer nations. In the United States, economic development in the last decades has been even more rapid than in Germany, and *for this very reason* the parasitic character of modern American capitalism has stood out with particular prominence. On the other hand, a comparison of, say, the republican American bourgeoisie with the monarchist Japanese or German bourgeoisie shows that the most pronounced political distinctions diminish to an extreme degree in the epoch of imperialism—not because they are unimportant in general, but because in all these cases we are discussing a bourgeoisie which has definite features of parasitism.

The receipt of high monopoly profits by the capitalists in one of the numerous branches of industry, in one of numerous countries, etc., makes it economically possible for them to corrupt certain sections of the working class, and for a time a fairly considerable minority, and win them to the side of the bourgeoisie of a given industry or nation against all the others. The intensification of antagonisms between imperialist nations for the division of the world increases this striving. And so there is created that bond between imperialism and opportunism, which revealed itself first and most clearly in England, owing to the fact that certain features of imperialist development were observable there much earlier than in other countries.

Some writers, L. Martov, for example, try to evade the fact that there is a connection between imperialism and opportunism in the labour movement—which is particularly striking at the present time—by resorting to "official optimistic" arguments (*à la* Kautsky and Huysmans) like the following: the cause of the opponents of capitalism would be hopeless if it were precisely progressive capitalism that led to the increase of opportunism, or, if it were precisely the best paid workers who were inclined towards opportunism, etc. We must have no illusion regarding "optimism" of this kind. It is optimism in regard to opportunism; it is optimism which serves to conceal opportunism. As a matter of fact the extraordinary rapidity and the particularly revolting character of the development of opportunism is by no means a guarantee that its victory will be durable: the rapid growth of a malignant abscess on a healthy body only causes it to burst more quickly and thus to relieve the body of it. The most dangerous people of all in this respect are those who do not wish to understand that the fight against imperialism is a sham and humbug unless it is inseparably bound up with the fight against opportunism.

From all that has been said in this book on the economic nature of imperialism, it follows that we must define it as capitalism in transition, or, more precisely, as moribund capitalism. It is very instructive in this respect to note that the bourgeois economists, in describing modern capitalism, frequently employ terms like "interlocking," "absence of isolation," etc.; "in conformity with their functions and course of development," banks are "not purely private business enterprises; they are more and more outgrowing the sphere of purely private business regulation." And this very Riesser, who uttered the words just quoted, declares with all seriousness that the "prophecy" of the Marxists concerning "socialisation" has "not come true"!

What then does this word "interlocking" express? It merely expresses the most striking feature of the process going on before our eyes. It shows that the observer counts the separate trees, but cannot see the wood. It slavishly copies the superficial, the fortuitous, the chaotic. It reveals the observer as one who is overwhelmed by the mass of raw material and is utterly incapable of appreciating its meaning and importance. Ownership of shares and relations between owners of private property "interlock in a haphazard way." But the underlying factor of this interlocking, its very base, is the changing social relations of production. When a big enterprise assumes gigantic proportions, and, on the basis of exact computation of mass data, organises according to plan the supply of primary raw materials to the extent of two-thirds, or three-fourths of all that is necessary for tens of millions of people; when the raw materials are transported to the most suitable place of production, sometimes hundreds or thousands of miles away, in a systematic and organised manner; when a single centre directs all the successive stages of work right up to the manufacture of numerous varieties of finished articles; when these products are distributed according to a single plan among tens and hundreds of millions of consumers (as in the case of the distribution of oil in America and Germany by the American "oil trust")—then it becomes evident that we have socialisation of production, and not mere "interlocking"; that private economic relations and private property relations constitute a shell which is no longer suitable for its contents, a shell which must inevitably begin to decay if its destruction be delayed by artificial means; a shell which may continue in a state of decay for a fairly long period (particularly if the cure of the opportunist abscess is protracted), but which will inevitably be removed.

The enthusiastic admirer of German imperialism, Schulze-Gaevernitz, exclaims:

> "Once the supreme management of the German banks has been entrusted to the hands of a dozen persons, their activity is even today more significant for the public good than that of the majority of the Ministers of State." (The "interlocking" of bankers, ministers, magnates of industry and rentiers is here conveniently forgotten.) . . . "If we conceive of the tendencies of development which we have noted as realised to the utmost: the money capital of the nation united in the banks; the banks themselves combined into cartels; the investment capital of the nation cast in the shape of securities, then the brilliant forecast of Saint-Simon will be fulfilled: 'The present anarchy of production caused by the fact that economic relations are developing without uniform regulation must make way for organisation in production. Production will no longer be shaped by isolated manufacturers, independent of each other and ignorant of man's economic needs, but by a social institution. A central body of management, being able to survey the large fields of social economy from a more elevated point of view, will regulate it for the benefit of the whole of society, will be able to put the means of production into suitable hands, and above all will take care that there be constant harmony between production and consumption. Institutions already exist which have assumed as part of their task a certain organisation of economic labour: the banks.' The fulfillment of the forecasts of Saint-Simon still lies in the future, but we are on the way to its fulfillment—Marxism, different from what Marx imagined, but different only in form."[2]

A crushing "refutation" of Marx, indeed! It is a retreat from Marx's precise, scientific analysis to Saint-Simon's guesswork, the guesswork of a genius, but guesswork all the same.

January–July, 1916.

NOTES

1. Riesser, *op. cit.*, third ed., p. 354.—*Ed.*
2. Schulze-Gaevernitz, in *Grundriss der Socialökonomik*, pp. 145–46.

19

Eduard Bernstein

Evolutionary Socialism (1899)

In 1906 Lenin said of his What Is to Be Done?: *"The Economists have gone to one extreme. To straighten matters out somebody had to pull in the opposite direction—that is what I have done." The democratic socialist Eduard Bernstein (1850–1932) was among the economists to whom Lenin referred. Bernstein's life spanned the rise and fall of German social democracy, from defeat in the 1848 revolution to dominance in the Reichstag to co-optation in the Weimar Republic.* Evolutionary Socialism, *his statement of social democratic principles, adapts Marxism to a new Europe in which the proletariat has greater economic prosperity and increased political power.*

Chapter 2
The Economic Development of Modern Society

d. The Crises and Possibilities of Adjustment in Modern Economy

THE CONTRADICTIONS INHERENT in the movement of capitalist society impress themselves upon the practical bourgeoisie most strikingly in the changes of the periodic cycle through which modern industry runs, and whose crowning point is the universal crisis.

—Marx, Preface to the second edition of Capital.

. . . The time that has elapsed since this was written has left the question unanswered. Signs of an economic world-wide crash of unheard-of violence have not

Source: Eduard Bernstein, *Evolutionary Socialism* (New York: Schocken Books, 1972), 18–27, 73–94, 135–165.

314

been established, nor can one describe the improvement of trade in the intervals between the crises as particularly short-lived. Much more does a third question arise which after all is partly contained already in the second—namely: (1) whether the enormous extension of the world market, in conjunction with the extraordinary shortening of time necessary for the transmission of news and for the transport trade, has so increased the possibilities of adjustment of disturbances; and (2) whether the enormously increased wealth of the European states, in conjunction with the elasticity of the modern credit system and the rise of industrial Kartels, has so limited the reacting force of local or individual disturbances that, at least for some time, general commercial crises similar to the earlier ones are to be regarded as improbable.

This question, raised by me in an essay on the "Socialist Theory of a Catastrophic Development of Society," has experienced all kinds of opposition.[1] Among others it has caused Rosa Luxemburg to lecture me in a series of articles published in the *Leipzig Volkszeitung* of September, 1898, on the nature of credit and the possibilities of capitalism in regard to adaptation. As these articles, which have also passed into other socialist papers, are true examples of false dialectics, but handled at the same time with great skill, it appears to me to be opportune to examine them here.

Rosa Luxemburg maintains that the credit system, far from working against crises, is the means of pushing them to an extremity. It first made possible the unmeasured extension of capitalistic production, the acceleration of the exchange of goods and of the cyclic course of the process of production, and in this way it is the means of bringing into active conflict as often as possible the differences between production and consumption. It puts into the hand of the capitalist the disposal of the capital of others, and with it the means of foolhardy speculation, and if depression sets in it intensifies the crisis. Its function is to banish the residue of stability from all capitalist conditions, to make all capitalist forces in the highest degree elastic, relative, and sensitive.

Now all that is not exactly new to anyone who knows a little of the literature of socialism in general and of Marxist socialism in particular. The only question is whether it rightly represents the real facts of the case to-day, or whether the picture has not another side. According to the laws of dialectic evolution to which Rosa Luxemburg so much likes to give play, it ought certainly to be the case; but even without falling back upon these, one should realise that a thing like credit, capable of so many forms, must under different conditions work in different ways. Marx treats credit by no means from the point of view that it is only a destructive agent in the capitalist system. He assigns to it, amongst other things,[2] the function of "creating the form of transition to a new modus of production," and with regard to it he expressly brings into prominence "the double-sided characteristics of the credit system." Frau Luxemburg knows the passage referred to very well; she even reprints the sentence from it where Marx speaks of the mixed character, "half swindler, half prophet," of the chief promulgators of credit (John Law, Isaac Pereire, etc.). But she refers exclusively to the destructive side of the credit system, and mentions not a word of its capacity for establishing and creating, which Marx expressly includes. Why this amputation, why this noteworthy silence with respect to the "double-sided characteristics"? The brilliant dialectical fireworks by means of which the power of the credit system is represented as a means of adaptation in the light of a "one-day fly," end in smoke and mist as soon as one looks more closely at this other side which Frau Luxemburg passes by so shyly.

That the credit system makes speculation easier is an experience centuries old; and very old, too, is the experience that speculation does not stop production when industrial circumstances are far enough developed to suit it. Meanwhile, speculation is conditioned by the relation of the knowable to the unknown circumstances. The more the latter predominate the more will speculation flourish; the more it is restrained by the former, the more the ground is cut from under its feet. Therefore the maddest outbursts of commercial speculation come to pass at the dawn of the capitalistic era, and speculation celebrates its wildest orgies usually in the countries where the capitalistic development is youngest. In the domain of industry speculation flourished most luxuriantly in new branches of production. The older a branch of production is under modern forms—with the exception of the manufacture of mere articles of fashion—the more does the speculative momentum cease to play a decisive part in it. The conditions and movements of the market are then more exactly foreseen and are taken into consideration with greater certainty.

Nevertheless, this certainty is only relative, because competition and technical development exclude an absolute control of the market. Over-production is to a certain extent unavoidable. But over-production in single industries does not mean general crises. If it leads to such a one, either the industries concerned must be of such importance as consumers of the manufactures of other industries, as that their stagnation also stops these industries, or indeed they must take from them, through the medium of the money market—that is, through the paralysis of general credit—the means of carrying on production. But it is evident that there is always a lessening probability of this latter result. The richer a country is, the more developed its credit organisation—which is not to be confused with a more widely spread habit to produce with a borrowed capital. For here the possibilities of adjustment multiply in an increasing measure. In some passage, which I cannot find at the moment, Marx said once—and the correctness of the sentence can be proved by the most abundant evidence—that the contractions in the centre of the money market are much more quickly over-come than in the different points of the circumference. But the change of the means of communication brought about in the meantime has more than neu-tralized the consequences of great distances in this respect.[3]

If the crises of the money market are not quite banished from the world yet, as far as concerns us here, the tightenings of that market by vast commercial undertakings controlled with difficulty are very much reduced.

The relations of financial crises to trade and business crises are not yet so fully explained that one can say with any certainty when both happen together that it was the trade crisis—*i.e.,* over-production—which directly caused the money cri-sis. In most cases it was quite clear that it was not actual over-production, but over-speculation, which paralysed the money market, and by this depressed the whole business. That is proved from the isolated facts which Marx mentions in the third volume of *Capital,* taken from the official inquiries into the crises of 1847 and 1857, as well as from the facts which Professor Herkner adduces on these and other crises in his sketch of the history of trade crises in his *Hand-wörterbuch der Staatswissenschaften.* Frau Luxemburg deduces on the basis of the facts adduced by Herkner that the crises hitherto have not at all been the right crises, but that they were only infantile illnesses of the capitalistic economy, the accompanying phenomena not of narrowing but of widening the domain of the capitalistic economy—that we "have not yet entered upon that phase of perfect capitalistic maturity which is presumed in the Marxist scheme of the periodicity of crises." According to her, we find ourselves "in a phase where crises no longer accompany the rise of capital nor yet its decline." This time will only come when the world market is fully developed and can be enlarged by no sudden extensions. Then the struggle between the productive powers and the limits of exchange will become continually sharper and more stormy.

To that one must observe that the formula of the crises in and for Marx was no picture of the future, but a picture of the present day which it was expected would recur in the future in always sharper forms and in greater acuteness. As soon as Frau Luxemburg denies to it the significance which Marx imputed to it for the whole epoch lying behind us, and sets it up as a deduction which did not yet correspond with reality, but was only a logical forecast based on the existence of certain elements in an embryonic state, she immediately questions the whole Marxist prediction of the coming social evolution, so far as this is based on the theory of crises. For if this was not based on experience at the time when it was set up, and has not become manifest in the interval between then and now, in what more distant future can one place its formula as coming true? Its relegation to the time when the world market has been fully developed is a flight into the next world.

No one knows when the world market will be fully developed. Frau Luxemburg is not ignorant of the fact that there is an intensive as well as an extensive broadening of the world market, and that the former is to-day of much greater importance than the latter.

In the trade statistics of the great industrial countries exports play by far the greatest part in regard to the countries longest occupied. England exports to the whole of Australia (all the Australian colonies, New Zealand, etc.) values less in amount than to a single country, France; to the whole of British North America (Canada, British Columbia, etc.) not so much as to Russia only; to both colonial territories together, which are indeed of a respectable age, not so much as to Germany. Its trade with all its colonies, including the whole of the immense Indian Empire, is not a third of its trade with the rest of the world; and as regards the colonial acquisitions of the last twenty years, the exports thither have been ridiculously small. The extensive widenings of the world market are accomplished much too slowly to allow sufficient outlet for the actual increase of production, if the countries already drawn into it did not offer it an increasing market. A limit to this increasing and intensive amplifying of the world market, along with the extension of its area, cannot be set up *a priori*. If the universal crisis is the inherent law of capitalistic production, it must prove its reality now or in the near future. Otherwise the proof of its inevitableness hovers in the air of abstract speculation.

We have seen that the credit system to-day undergoes less, not more, contractions, leading to the general paralysis of production, and so far, therefore, takes a minor place as a factor in forming crises. But so far as it is a means of a hot-house forcing of over-production, the associations of manufacturers met this inflation of production in separate countries, and even internationally here and there, ever more frequently, by trying to regulate production as a Kartel, a syndicate, or a trust. Without embarking in prophecies as to its final power of life and work, I have recognised its capacity to influence the relation of productive activity to the condition of the market so far as to diminish the danger of crises. Frau Luxemburg refutes this also.

First she denies that the association of manufacturers can be general. She says the final aim and effect of such associations are, by excluding competition within a branch, to increase their share of the total amount of profit gained in the market of commodities. But, she adds, one branch of industry could only attain this at the cost of another, and the organisation could not possibly, therefore, be general. "Extended into all branches of production it would itself put an end to its effect."

This proof does not differ by a hair's-breadth from the proof, long ago abandoned, of the uselessness of trades unions. Its support is even immeasurably more fragile than the wages fund theory of blessed memory. It is the presumption unproven, unprovable, or, rather, proved to be false, that in the commodity market only a fixed amount of profit is to be divided. It presumes, amongst other things, a fixing of prices independently of the movements in the cost of production. But even given a fixed price, and, moreover, a fixed technological basis of production, the amount of profit in a branch of industry can be raised without thereby lessening the profits of another—namely, by the lessening of unproductive expenses, the ceasing of cutting competition, better organisation of production, and the like. That the association of manufacturers is an effective means towards this is self-evident. The problem of the division of profits is the last obstacle of all which stands in the way of a general union of associations of employers.

It stands somewhat better with the last objection of Frau Luxemburg. According to it, the Kartels are unsuitable for preventing the anarchy of production because the Kartels of manufacturers as a rule obtain their higher profit rate on the home market, because they use the portion of capital that cannot be applied to this for manufacturing products for foreign countries at a much less profit rate. The consequence is, increased anarchy on the world market—the opposite to the object aimed at.

"As a rule" this manœuvre can only be upheld where a protective duty affords the Kartel protection, so as to make it impossible for the foreign country to repay it in like coin. Meanwhile we are concerned here neither with denying the harmful effects of the present simple and high protectionist system, nor with an apology for the syndicates of manufacturers. It has not occurred to me to maintain that Kartels, etc., are the last world of economic development, and are suited to remove for ever the contradictions of modern industrial life. I am, on the contrary, convinced that where in modern industrial countries Kartels and trusts are supported and strengthened by protective duties, they must, in fact, become factors of the crises in the industry concerned—also, if not at first, in any case finally, for the "protected" land itself. The question only arises how long the people concerned will be content with this arrangement. Protective tariffs are in themselves no product of economy, but an encroachment on economy by the political power seeking to secure economic results. It is otherwise with the industrial Kartel. It has—although favoured by protective tariffs—grown out of the economic soil, and is a national means of adapting production to the movements of the market. That it is, or can be, at the same time the means of monopolist exploitation is another matter. But it is just as much beside the question that in the former capacity it means an increase of all earlier remedial measures for overproduction. With much less risk than the individual undertaking, it can, in times of a glut on the market, temporarily limit production. Better than this, it is also in a position to meet foreign cutting competition abroad [*sic*]. To deny this is to deny the superiority of organisation over anarchic competition. But we do so, if we deny on principle that Kartels can work as a modifying influence on the nature and frequency of crises. How *far* they can do so is for the present a matter for conjecture, for we have not sufficient experience to allow of a conclusive judgment in this respect. But still fewer conclusive facts can be given under these circumstances for anticipating future general crises as they hovered before Marx and Engels, repetitions on a larger scale of the crises of 1825, 1836, 1847, 1857, 1873. The mere fact that whilst for a long time socialists generally believed in an increasing contraction of the industrial cycle as the natural consequence of the increasing concentration of capital—a development in the form of a spiral— Friedrich Engels in 1894 found himself driven to question whether a new enlarging of the cycle was not in front of us, and thus to suggest the exact contrary of the former assumption, and he warned us against the abstract deduction that these crises must repeat themselves in the old form.[4]

The history of individual industries shows that their crises by no means always coincide with the so-called general crises. Marx, as we have seen, believed he could establish on the need of an accelerated renewal of fixed capital (implements of production, etc.) a material foundation for periodic crises,[5] and it is undoubtedly true that an important reason for crises is to be found here. But it is not accurate, or not more accurate, that these periods of renewal coincide as to time in the various industries. And therewith a further factor of the great general crisis is done away with.

There remains then only so much, that the capacity for production in modern society is much greater than the actual demand for products determined by the buying capacity; that millions live insufficiently housed, insufficiently clad, and insufficiently nourished, in spite of abundant means at hand for sufficient housing, nourishment, and clothing; that out of this incongruity, over-production appears again and again in different branches of production, so that either actually certain articles are produced in greater amounts than can be used—for example, more yarn than the present weaving mills can work—or that certain articles are produced not indeed in a greater quantity than can be used, but in greater quantity than can be bought; that in consequence of this, great irregularity occurs in the employment of the workers, which makes their situation extremely insecure, weighs them down in unworthy dependence, brings forth over-work here and want of work there; and that of the means employed to-day to counteract the most visible part of this evil, the Kartels represent monopolist unions—on the one side against the workers, and on the other against the great public—which have a tendency to carry on warfare over the heads of these and at their cost with the same kind of monopolist unions in other industries or other lands, or, by international or interindustrial agreements, arbitrarily to adapt production and prices to their need of profit. The capitalistic means of defence against crises virtually bear within themselves the possibilities of a new and more hopeless serfdom for the working classes, as well as of privileges of production which revive in acute form the old guild privileges. It appears to me to be much more important at present, from the standpoint of the workers, to keep before our eyes the possibilities of Kartels and trusts than to prophesy their "impotence." It is for the working class a subordinate question whether these combinations will be able, in the course of time, to attain their first-mentioned object—the warding off of crises. But it becomes a question full of importance as soon as expectations of any kind as regards the movement for the emancipation of the working classes are made dependent upon the question of the general crisis. For then the belief that Kartels are of no effect against crises may be the cause of very disastrous neglect.

The short sketch which we gave in the introduction to this chapter of the Marx-Engels explanations of economic crises will suffice, in conjunction with the corresponding facts adduced, to show that the problem of crises cannot be solved by a few well-preserved catch-words. We can only investigate what elements of modern economy work in favour of crises and what work against them. It is impossible to pre-judge *a priori* the ultimate relation of these forces to one another, or their development. Unless unforeseen external events bring about a general crisis—and as we have said, that can happen any day—there is no urgent reason for concluding that such a crisis will come to pass for purely economic reasons. Local and partial depressions are unavoidable; general stagnation is not unavoidable with the present organisation and extension of the world market, and particularly with the great extension of the production of articles of food. The latter phenomenon is of peculiar importance for our problem. Perhaps nothing has contributed so much to the mitigation of commercial crises or to the stopping of their increase as the fall of rent and of the price of food.[6]

Chapter 3
The Tasks and Possibilities of Social Democracy

c. Democracy and Socialism

On February 24th, 1848, broke the first dawn of a new period of history. Who speaks of universal suffrage utters a cry of reconciliation.

—Lassalle, *Workers' Programme*

. . . The trade unions are the democratic element in industry. Their tendency is to destroy the absolutism of capital, and to procure for the worker a direct influence in the management of an industry. It is only natural that great differences of opinion should exist on the degree of influence to be desired. To a certain mode of thought it may appear a breach of principle to claim less for the union than an unconditional right of decision in the trade. The knowledge that such a right under present circumstances is just as Utopian as it would be contrary to the nature of a socialist community, has led others to deny trade unions any lasting part in economic life, and to recognise them only temporarily as the lesser of various unavoidable evils. There are socialists in whose eyes the union is only an object lesson to prove the uselessness of any other than political revolutionary action. As a matter of fact, the union to-day—and in the near future—has very important social tasks to fulfil for the trades, which, however, do not demand, nor are even consistent with, its omnipotence in any way.

The merit of having first grasped the fact that trade unions are indispensable organs of the democracy, and not only passing coalitions, belongs to a group of English writers. This is not wonderful if one considers that trade unions attained importance in England earlier than anywhere else, and that England in the last third of the nineteenth century passed through a change from an oligarchic to an almost democratic state of government. The latest and most thorough work on this subject, the book on the theory and the practice of the British Trade Unions, by Sydney and Beatrice Webb, has been rightly described by the authors as a treatment of *Industrial Democracy*. Before them the late Thorold Rogers, in his lectures on the *Economic Interpretation of History* (which, in the passing, has little in common with the materialist conception of history, but only touches it in single points), called the trade union, Labour Partnership—which comes to the same thing in principle, but at the same time points out the limits to which the function of a trade union can extend in a democracy, and beyond which it has no place in a democratic community. Independently of whether the state, the community, or capitalists are employers, the trade union as an organisation of all persons occupied in certain trades can only further simultaneously the interests of its members and the general good as long as it is content to remain a partner. Beyond that it would run into danger of degenerating into a close corporation with all the worst qualities of a monopoly. It is the same as with the co-operative society. The trade union, as mistress of a whole branch of production, the ideal of various older socialists, would really be only a monopolist productive association, and as soon as it relied on its monopoly or worked upon it, it would be antagonistic to socialism and democracy, let its inner constitution be what it may. Why it is contrary to socialism needs no further explanation. Associations against the community are as little socialism as is the oligarchic government of the state. But why should such a trade union not be in keeping with the principle of a democracy?

This question necessitates another. What is the principle of democracy?

The answer to this appears very simple. At first one would think it settled by the definition "government by the people." But even a little consideration tells us that by that only quite a superficial, purely formal definition is given, whilst nearly all who use the word democracy to-day understand by it more than a mere form of government. We shall come much nearer to the definition if we express ourselves negatively, and define democracy as an absence of class government, as the indication of a social condition where a political privilege belongs to no one class as opposed to the whole community. By that the explanation is already given as to why a monopolist corporation is in principle anti-democratic. This negative definition has, besides, the advantage that it gives less room than the phrase "government by the people" to the idea of the oppression of the individual by the majority which is absolutely repugnant to the modern mind. To-day we find the oppression of the minority by the majority "undemocratic," although it was originally held to be quite consistent with government by the people.[7] The idea of democracy includes, in the conception of the present day, a notion of justice—an equality of rights for all members of the community, and in that principle the rule of the majority, to which in every concrete case the rule of the people extends, finds its limits. The more it is adopted and governs the general consciousness, the more will democracy be equal in meaning to the highest possible degree of freedom for all.

Democracy is in principle the suppression of class government, though it is not yet the actual suppression of classes. They speak of the conservative character of the democracy, and to a certain degree rightly. Absolutism, or semi-absolutism, deceives its supporters as well as its opponents as to the extent of their power. Therefore in countries where it obtains, or where its traditions still exist, we have flitting plans, exaggerated language, zigzag politics, fear of revolution, hope in oppression. In a democracy the parties, and the classes standing behind them, soon learn to know the limits of their power, and to undertake each time only as much as they can reasonably hope to carry through under the existing circumstances. Even if they make their demands rather higher than they seriously mean in order to give way in the unavoidable compromise—and democracy is the high school of compromise—they must still be moderate. The right to vote in a democracy makes its members virtually partners in the community, and this virtual partnership must in the end lead to real partnership. With a working class undeveloped in numbers and culture the general right to vote may long appear as the right to choose "the butcher"; with the growing number and knowledge of the workers it is changed, however, into the implement by which to transform the representatives of the people from masters into real servants of the people.

Universal suffrage in Germany could serve Bismarck temporarily as a tool, but finally it compelled Bismarck to serve it as a tool. It could be of use for a time to the squires of the East Elbe district, but it has long been the terror of these same squires. In 1878 it could bring Bismarck into a position to forge the weapon of socialistic law, but through it this weapon became blunt and broken, until by the help of it Bismarck was thoroughly beaten. Had Bismarck in 1878, with his then majority, created a politically exceptional law, instead of a police one, a law which would have placed the worker outside the franchise, he would for a time have hit social democracy more sharply than with the former. It is true, he would then have hit other people also. Universal franchise is, from two sides, the alternative to a violent revolution. But universal suffrage is only a part of democracy, although a part which in time must draw the other parts after it as the magnet attracts to itself the scattered portions of iron. It certainly proceeds more slowly than many would wish, but in spite of that it is at work. And social democracy can not further this work better than by taking its stand unreservedly on the theory of democracy—on the ground of universal suffrage with all the consequences resulting therefrom to its tactics.

In practice—that is, in its actions—it has in Germany always done so. But in their explanations its literary advocates have often acted otherwise, and still often do so to-day. Phrases which were composed in a time when the political privilege of property ruled all over Europe, and which under these circumstances were explanatory, and to a certain degree also justified, but which to-day are only a dead weight, are treated with such reverence as though the progress of the movement depended on them and not on the understanding of what can be done, and what should be done. Is there any sense, for example, in maintaining the phrase of the "dictatorship of the proletariat" at a time when in all possible places representatives of social democracy have placed themselves practically in the arena of Parliamentary work, have declared for the proportional representation of the people, and for direct legislation—all of which is inconsistent with a dictatorship.

The phrase is to-day so antiquated that it is only to be reconciled with reality by stripping the word dictatorship of its actual meaning and attaching to it some kind of weakened interpretation. The whole practical activity of social democracy is directed towards creating circumstances and conditions which shall render possible and secure a transition (free from convulsive outbursts) of the modern social order into a higher one. From the consciousness of being the pioneers of a higher civilisation, its adherents are ever creating fresh inspiration and zeal. In this rests also, finally, the moral justification of the socialist expropriation towards which they aspire. But the "dictatorship of the classes" belongs to a lower civilisation, and apart from the question of the expediency and practicability of the thing, it is only to be looked upon as a reversion, as political atavism.

If the thought is aroused that the transition from a capitalist to a socialist society must necessarily be accomplished by means of the development of forms of an age which did not know at all, or only in quite an imperfect form, the present method of the initiating and carrying of laws, and which was without the organs fit for the purpose, reaction will set in.

I say expressly transition from a capitalist to a socialist society, and not from a "civic society," as is so frequently the expression used to-day. This application of the word "civic" is also much more an atavism, or in any case an ambiguous way of speaking, which must be considered an inconvenience in the phraseology of German social democracy, and which forms an excellent bridge for mistakes with friend and foe. The fault lies partly in the German language, which has no special word for the idea of the citizen with equal civic rights separate from the idea of privileged citizens.

What is the struggle against, or the abolition of, a civic society? What does it mean specially in Germany, in whose greatest and leading state, Prussia, we are still constantly concerned with first getting rid of a great part of feudalism which stands in the path of civic development? No man thinks of destroying civic society as a civilised ordered system of society. On the contrary, social democracy does not wish to break up this society and make all its members proletarians together; it labours rather incessantly at raising the worker from the social position of a proletarian to that of a citizen, and thus to make citizenship universal. It does not want to set up a proletarian society instead of a civic society, but a socialist order of society instead of a capitalist one. It would be well if one, instead of availing himself of the former ambiguous expression, kept to the latter quite clear declaration. Then one would be quite free of a good portion of other contradictions which opponents, not quite without reason, assert do exist between the phraseology and the practice of social democracy. A few socialist newspapers find a pleasure to-day in forced anti-civic language, which at the most would be in place if we lived in a sectarian fashion as anchorites, but which is absurd in an age which declares it to be no offence to the socialist sentiment to order one's private life throughout in a "bourgeois fashion."[8]

Finally, it is to be recommended that some moderation should be kept in the declaration of war against "liberalism." It is true that the great liberal movement of modern times arose for the advantage of the capitalist bourgeoisie first of all, and the parties which assumed the names of liberals were, or became in due course, simple guardians of capitalism. Naturally, only opposition can reign between these parties and social democracy. But with respect to liberalism as a great historical movement, socialism is its legitimate heir, not only in chronological sequence, but also in its spiritual qualities, as is shown moreover in every question of principle in which social democracy has had to take up an attitude.

Wherever an economic advance of the socialist programme had to be carried out in a manner, or under circumstances, that appeared seriously to imperil the development of freedom, social democracy has never shunned taking up a position against it. The security of civil freedom has always seemed to it to stand higher than the fulfillment of some economic progress.

The aim of all socialist measures, even of those which appear outwardly as coercive measures, is the development and the securing of a free personality. Their more exact examination always shows that the coercion included will raise the sum total of liberty in society, and will give more freedom over a more extended area than it takes away. The legal day of a maximum number of hours' work, for example, is actually a fixing of a minimum of freedom, a prohibition to sell freedom longer than for a certain number of hours daily, and, in principle, therefore, stands on the same ground as the prohibition agreed to by all liberals against selling oneself into personal slavery. It is thus no accident that the first country where a maximum hours' day was carried out was Switzerland, the most democratically progressive country in Europe, and democracy is only the political form of liberalism. Being in its origin a counter-movement to the oppression of nations under institutions imposed from without or having a justification only in tradition, liberalism first sought its realisation as the principle of the sovereignty of the age and of the people, both of which principles formed the everlasting discussion of the philosophers of the rights of the state in the seventeenth and eighteenth centuries, until Rousseau set them up in his *Contrat Social* as the fundamental conditions of the legitimacy of every constitution, and the French Revolution proclaimed them—in the Democratic Constitution of 1793 permeated with Rousseau's spirit—as inalienable rights of men.[9]

The Constitution of 1793 was the logical expression of the liberal ideas of the epoch, and a cursory glance over its contents shows how little it was, or is, an obstacle to socialism. Babeuf, and the believers in absolute equality, saw in it an excellent starting point for the realisation of their communistic strivings, and accordingly wrote "The Restoration of the Constitution of 1793" at the head of their demands.

There is actually no really liberal thought which does not also belong to the elements of the ideas of socialism. Even the principle of economic personal responsibility which belongs apparently so entirely to the Manchester School cannot, in my judgment, be denied in theory by socialism nor be made inoperative under any conceivable circumstances. Without responsibility there is no freedom; we may think as we like theoretically about man's freedom of action, we must practically start from it as the foundation of the moral law, for only under this condition is social morality possible. And similarly, in our states which reckon with millions, a healthy social life is, in the age of traffic, impossible if the economic personal responsibility of all those capable of work is not assumed. The recognition of individual responsibility is the return of the individual to society for services rendered or offered him by society. . . .

Socialism will create no new bondage of any kind whatever. The individual is to be free, not in the metaphysical sense, as the anarchists dreamed—*i.e.*, free from all duties towards the community—but free from every economic compulsion in his action and choice of a calling. Such freedom is only possible for all by means of organisation. In this sense one might call socialism "organising liberalism," for when one examines more closely the organisations that socialism wants and how it wants them, he will find that what distinguishes them above all from the feudalistic organisations, outwardly like them, is just their liberalism, their democratic constitution, their accessibility. Therefore the trade union, striving after an arrangement similar to a guild, is in the eyes of the socialist, the product of self-defence against the tendency of capitalism to overstock the labour market; but, at the same, just on account of its tendency towards a guild, and to the degree in which that obtains, is it an unsocialistic corporate body.

The work here indicated is no very simple problem; it rather conceals within itself a whole series of dangers. Political equality alone has never hitherto sufficed to secure the healthy development of communities whose centre of gravity was in the giant towns. It is, as France and the United States show, no unfailing remedy against the rank growth of all kinds of social parasitism and corruption. If solidity did not reach so far down in the constitution of the French nation, and if the country were not so well favoured geographically, France would have long since been ruined by the land plague of the official class which has gained a footing there. In any case this plague forms one of the causes why, in spite of the great keenness of the French mind, the industrial development of France remains more backward than that of the neighbouring countries. If democracy is not to excel centralised absolutism in the breeding of bureaucracies, it must be built up on an elaborately organised self-government with a corresponding economic, personal responsibility of all the units of administration as well as of the adult citizens of the state. Nothing is more injurious to its healthy development than enforced uniformity and a too abundant amount of protectionism or subventionism.

To create the organisations described—or, so far as they are already begun, to develop them further—is the indispensable preliminary to what we call socialism of production. Without them the so-called social appropriation of the means of production would only result presumably in reckless devastation of productive forces, insane experimentalising and aimless violence, and the political sovereignty of the working class would, in fact, only be carried out in the form of a dictatorial, revolutionary, central power, supported by the terrorist dictatorship of revolutionary clubs. . . .

There is not the least doubt (and it has since then been proved many times practically) that the general development of modern society is along the line of a constant increase of the duties of municipalities and the extension of municipal freedom, that the municipality will be an ever more important lever of social emancipation. It appears to me doubtful if it was necessary for the first work of democracy to be such a dissolution of the modern state system and complete transformation of its organisation as Marx and Proudhon pictured (the formation of the national assembly out of delegates from provincial or district assemblies, which in their turn were composed of delegates from municipalities) so that the form the national assemblies had hitherto taken had to be abolished. Evolution has given life to too many institutions and bodies corporate, whose sphere has outgrown the control of municipalities and even of provinces and districts for it to be able to do without the control of the central governments unless or before their organisation is transformed. The absolute sovereignty of the municipality, etc., is besides no ideal for me. The parish or commune is a component part of the nation, and hence has duties towards it and rights in it. We can as little grant the district, for example, an unconditional and exclusive right to soil as we can to the individual. Valuable royalties, rights of forest and river, etc., belong, in the last instance, not to the parishes or the districts, which indeed only are their usufructuaries, but to the nation. Hence an assembly in which the national, and not the provincial or local, interest stands in the forefront or is the first duty of the representatives, appears to be indispensable, especially in an epoch of transition. But beside it, those other assemblies and representative bodies will attain an ever greater importance, so that Revolution or not, the functions of the central assemblies become constantly narrowed, and therewith the danger of these assemblies or authorities to the democracy is also narrowed. It is already very little in advanced countries to-day.

But we are less concerned here with a criticism of separate items in the quoted programme than with bringing into prominence the energy with which it emphasises autonomy as the preliminary condition of social emancipation, and with showing how the democratic organisation from the bottom upwards is depicted as the way to the realisation of socialism, and how the antagonists Proudhon and Marx meet again in—liberalism.

The future itself will reveal how far the municipalities and other self-governing bodies will discharge their duties under a complete democracy, and how far they will make use of these duties. But so much is clear: the more suddenly they come in possession of their freedom, the more experiments they will make in number and in violence and therefore be liable to greater mistakes, and the more experience the working class democracy has had in the school of self-government, the more cautiously and practically will it proceed.

Simple as democracy appears to be at the first glance, its problems in such a complicated society as ours are in no way easy to solve. Read only in the volumes of *Industrial Democracy* by Mr. and Mrs. Webb how many experiments the English trade unions had to make and are still making in order to find out the most serviceable forms of government and administration, and of what importance this question of constitution is to trade unions. The English trade unions have been able to develop in this respect for over seventy years in perfect freedom. They began with the most elementary form of self-government and have been forced to convince themselves that this form is only suited to the most elementary organisms, for quite small, local unions. As they grew they gradually learned to renounce as injurious to their successful development certain cherished ideas of doctrinaire democracy (the imperative mandate, the unpaid official, the powerless central representation), and to form instead of it a democracy capable of governing with representative assemblies, paid officials, and central government with full powers. This section of the history of the development of "trade union democracy" is extremely instructive. If all that concerns trade unions does not quite fit the units of national administration, yet much of it does. The chapter referred to in *Industrial Democracy* belongs to the theory of democratic government. In the history of the development of trade unions is shown how the executive central management—their state government—can arise simply from division of labour which becomes necessary through the extension in area of the society and through the number of its members. It is possible that with the socialist development of society this centralisation may also later on become superfluous. But for the present it cannot be dispensed with in democracy. As was demonstrated at the end of the first division of this chapter it is an impossibility for the municipalities of great towns or industrial centres to take over under their own management all local productive and commercial undertakings. It is also, on practical grounds, improbable—not to mention grounds of equity which are against it—that they should "expropriate" those undertakings each and all offhand in revolutionary upheaval. But even if they did (whereby in the majority of cases would only empty husks come into their hands) they would be obliged to lease the mass of the businesses to associations, whether individual or trade union, for associated management.[10]

In every one of these cases, as also in the municipal and national undertakings, certain interests of the different trades would have to be protected, and so there would always remain a need for active supervision on the part of trade unions. In the transition period particularly, the multiplicity of organs will be of great value.

Meantime we are not yet so far on, and it is not my intention to unfold pictures of the future. I am not concerned with what will happen in the more distant future, but with what can and ought to happen in the present, for the present and the nearest future. And so the conclusion of this exposition is the very banal statement that the conquest of the democracy, the formation of political and social organs of the democracy, is the indispensable preliminary condition to the realisation of socialism.

Feudalism, with its unbending organisations and corporations, had to be destroyed nearly everywhere by violence. The liberal organisations of modern society are distinguished from those exactly because they are flexible, and capable of change and development. They do not need to be destroyed, but only to be further developed. For that we need organisation and energetic action, but not necessarily a revolutionary dictatorship. "As the object of the class war is especially to destroy distinctions of class," wrote some time since (October, 1897) a social democratic Swiss organ, the *Vorwärts* of Basle, "a period must logically be agreed upon in which the realisation of this object, of this ideal, must be begun. This beginning, these periods following on one another, are already founded in our democratic development; they come to our help, to serve gradually as a substitute for the class war, to absorb it into themselves by the building up of the social democracy." "The bourgeoisie, of whatever shade of opinion it may be," declared lately the Spanish socialist, Pablo Iglesias, "must be convinced of this, that we do not wish to take possession of the Government by the same means that were once employed, by violence and bloodshed, but by lawful means which are suited to civilisation" (*Vorwärts*, October 16, 1898). From a similar point of view the *Labour Leader*, the leading organ of the English Independent Labour Party, agreed unreservedly with the remarks of Vollmar on the Paris Commune. But no one will accuse this paper of timidity in fighting capitalism and the capitalist parties. And another organ of the English socialist working class democracy, the *Clarion*, accompanied an extract from my article on the theory of catastrophic evolution with the following commentary:

"The formation of a true democracy—I am quite convinced that that is the most pressing and most important duty which lies before us. This is the lesson which the socialist campaign of the last ten years has taught us. That is the doctrine which emerges out of all my knowledge and experiences of politics. We must build up a nation of democrats before socialism is possible."

NOTES

1. The essay criticised the opinion laid down in a resolution of the International Socialist Congress of 1896 that we were on the eve of a great catastrophic crisis that would produce a

total revolution of social conditions. The said resolution ran thus: "The economic and industrial development is going on with such rapidity that a crisis may occur within a comparatively short time. The Congress, therefore, impresses upon the proletariat of all countries the imperative necessity of learning, as class-conscious citizens, how to administer the business of their respective countries for the common good." I gladly recognised the usefulness of the final recommendation, but I boldly disputed the truth of the premise. This occasioned some violent attacks, to which I replied in the letter reprinted in the preface of this book.

2. Vol. 3, i, p. 429.

3. Engels calculates that America and India have been brought nearer to the industrial countries of Europe, by means of the Suez Canal, steamer transport, etc., by 70 to 90 per cent, and adds "that owing to this the two great incubators of crises from 1825 to 1857 lost a great part of their destructive power" (*Capital*, vol. 3, Part 1, p. 45). On p. 395, of the same volume, Engels maintains that certain speculative businesses formed on risky schemes of credit, which Marx pictures as factors of crises in the money market, have been brought to an end through the oceanic cable. The correcting parenthesis of Engels on p. 56 of the second part of vol. 3 is also worthy of notice for its criticism of the development of the credit system.

4. We are, of course, only speaking here of the purely economic foundation of crises. Crises as results of political events (wars and serious threatenings of war) or of very widespread failures of crops—local failures no longer exercise any effect in this respect—are of course always possible.

5. The use of the word "material" in the passage mentioned (vol. 2, p. 164) is not without interest in judging how Marx understood this word. According to the present usual definition of the word the explanation of crises from under-consumption would be quite as materialistic as founding it on changes in the process of production, or in implements.

6. *Note to the English edition.*—This was written in the winter of 1898–1899 before the South African War had produced new conditions on the money market and a great increase in armaments. In spite of these facts the crisis that broke out in 1901 was of shorter life than a good many of the earlier crises, and was followed by a longer period of prosperity.

7. The consistent advocates of Blanquism also always conceived of democracy as at first an oppressive force. Thus Hippolyte Castille publishes a preliminary introduction to his *History of the Second Republic* which culminates in a veritable glorification of the Reign of Terror. "The most perfect community," he says, "would be where tyranny was an affair of the whole community. That proves fundamentally that the most perfect society would be one where there is least freedom in the satanic (*i.e.*, individualistic) meaning of this word. . . . What is called political freedom is only a beautiful name to adorn the justifiable tyranny of the many. Political freedom is only the sacrifice of the freedom of a number of individuals to the despotic God of human societies, to social reason, to the social contract." "From this epoch (the time from October, 1793, to April, 1794, when Girondists, Hebertists, Dantonists, were beheaded one after the other) dates in truth the re-incarnation of the principle of authority, of this eternal defensive warfare of human societies. Freed from the moderates and the ultras, secured against every conflict of authority, the committee of public safety acquires the form of government necessitated by the given circumstances, the necessary force and unity to maintain its position and to protect France from a threatening anarchy. . . . No, it is not the government that killed the first French Republic, but the Parliamentarians, the traitors of Thermidor. The anarchist and liberal republicans whose swarming hordes covered France,

continue in vain the old calumny. Robespierre remains a remarkable man, not on account of his talents and virtues, which are here incidental, but on account of his genius for authority, on account of his strong political instinct."

This worship of Robespierre was not to outlast the second Empire. To the younger generation of the Blanquist socialist revolutionaries who stepped on the stage in the middle of the 'sixties and who were above all anti-clerical, Robespierre was too philistine on account of his Deism. They swore by Hebert and Anacharsis Cloots. But for the rest they reasoned like Castille—*i.e.,* they carried out to extremes, like him, the just idea of the subordination of individual interests to the general interests of the community.

8. In this point Lassalle was much more logical than we are to-day, granted that it was one-sidedness to derive the ideal of the bourgeois simply from political privilege instead of at least from his economic position of power also. But for the rest he was sufficient realist to blunt beforehand the point of the above contradiction when he declared in the *Workers' Programme:* "In the German language the word 'bourgeoisie' had to be translated by 'Bürgerthum' (citizendom). But it has not this meaning with me. We are all citizens ('Bürger')—the workman, the poor citizen, the rich citizen, and so forth. In the course of history the word 'bourgeoisie' has rather acquired a meaning by which to denote a well defined, political line of thought" (*Collected Works,* 2, p. 27). What Lassalle further says there of the distorted logic of Sansculottism is especially to be recommended to writers in the *belles lettres* style who study the middle class "naturalistically" in the *café* and then judge the whole class according to their dried fruits, as the philistine thinks he sees the type of the modern workman in his fellow tippler. I feel no hesitation in declaring that I consider the middle class—not excepting the German—in their bulk to be still fairly healthy, not only economically, but also morally.

9. Sovereignty "rests with the people. It is indivisible, imprescriptible, inalienable" (Article 25). "A people has at any time the right to revise, reform and alter its constitution. No generation can bind the next to its laws" (Article 28).

10. This would certainly bring about complicated problems. Think of the many joint undertakings of modern times which employ members of all possible trades.

20

Tom Hayden and Dick Flacks

"The Port Huron Statement at 40" (2002)

"The Port Huron Statement" was adopted by the Students for a Democratic Society (SDS) at their convention in Port Huron, Michigan, June 11–15, 1962. It is widely regarded as "one of the best pronouncements of New Left democratic theorizing." The primary author of the original draft was Tom Hayden, a leader of the sixties' student movement, who has since been elected to the California Assembly (in 1982) and to the California Senate (in 1992). In the following article, Hayden and Dick Flacks, a close associate, reconsider the statement and its legacy. A short excerpt from the original statement follows their analysis.

IN THE MOVIE *The Big Lebowski*, the aging, stoned hippie played by Jeff Bridges announces that he helped write the Port Huron Statement. We don't remember the "dude" being there, but it's gratifying that the founding manifesto of Students for a Democratic Society still lives in the nostalgia and imagination of so many.

A glance at the web will show tens of thousands of references to "participatory democracy," the central focus of that document, which still appears as a live alternative to the top-down construction of most institutions. Participatory democracy has surfaced in the campaigns of the global justice movement, in utopian visions of telecommunications, in struggles around workplace and neighborhood empowerment, in Paulo Freire's "pedagogy of the oppressed," in grassroots environmental crusades and antipoverty programs, in political plat-

Source: Tom Hayden and Dick Flacks, "The Port Huron Statement at 40," reprinted from the August 5, 2002 issue of *The Nation*. Portions of each week's *Nation* can be accessed at www.thenation.com.

forms from Green parties to the Zapatistas, in participatory management theory, in liberation theology's emphasis on base communities of the poor and even in the current efforts of most Catholics to carve out a participatory role for laity in their church. The Port Huron Statement appears in numerous textbooks and has been the subject of thousands of student papers. This continued interest is the more impressive, since the statement was never marketed or even reissued as a book. It was produced only as a mimeographed pamphlet in 20,000 copies, which sold for 35 cents. We were jaundiced toward the very notion of public relations.

Recent celebrants of the Port Huron Statement include authors Gary Wills and E. J. Dionne, who see in its pages a bright promise of rational reform that was later lost, when they say SDS became too radical. At the other end of the political spectrum, Robert Bork says the "authentic spirit of Sixties radicalism issued" from Port Huron in "a document of ominous mood and aspiration" because it embodied a millennial vision of human possibility. The former radical David Horowitz reads the statement as encoding a "self-conscious effort to rescue the Communist project from its Soviet fate." At different moments, both Democrats and Republicans (under Richard Nixon) have invoked the rhetoric of participatory democracy in campaigns. This perplexing spectrum of reaction reflects, we believe, the statement's attempt at a new departure from the conventional dogmas of left and liberal thought.

Did we succeed, and if so, how? This year's occasion of the Port Huron Statement's fortieth anniversary provides a chance to ask whether its importance today is primarily symbolic and nostalgic, or whether, as we believe, the core of the statement is still relevant for all those trying to create a world where each person has a voice in the decisions affecting his or her life. It remains, as we described it then, "a living document open to change with our times and experiences."

The original idea, conceived at a winter meeting in Ann Arbor in 1961, was modest: to produce an organizing tool for the movement we were trying to spread through SDS. Then the statement became more audacious. The roughly sixty young people who finalized the statement during a week at a United Auto Workers retreat in Port Huron, Michigan, experienced what one could only call an inspirational moment. As the words flowed night and day, we felt we were giving voice to a new generation of rebels.

The two of us had arrived in Port Huron from different paths that symbolized the cultural fusion that happened at the beginning of the 1960s. Tom was a Midwestern populist by nature, rebelling apolitically against the boring hypocrisy of suburban life—until the Southern black student sit-in movement showed him that a committed life was possible. Tom was drawn to the mystique of citizen action and away from left ideologies based on systems far different from America, with its vast middle-class status system. Many others of Port Huron were mainstream student leaders inspired by the civil rights movement, the South African antiapartheid movement and even the youthful ideals of John Kennedy's New Frontier. Dick, on the other hand, was a New York "red diaper baby" whose parents had been fired as schoolteachers during the McCarthy period. Disillusioned by both Stalinism and the conformity of cold war America, he and his wife, Mickey, questioned whether an effective left could be built at all from its quarrelsome subculture of factions. The fusion of these paths yielded a vision informed by a democratic American radicalism going back to Tom Paine, one that attempted to transcend the stale dogmas of the dying left as well as the liberal celebration of the New Frontier as Camelot.

In its beginning, SDS was the student wing of one of those historic factions, the New York–based League for Industrial Democracy (LID), whose definition of anti-Communism was so far-reaching that it prohibited working with anyone who sympathized with Castro's Cuban Revolution or blamed both superpowers for the nuclear arms race instead of the Soviets alone. Soon the LID would endorse the war in Vietnam. In those days, *The Nation* itself was beyond the pale of legitimacy, as was our journalistic hero, I. F. Stone. While the draft Port Huron Statement included a strong denunciation of the Soviet Union, it wasn't enough for LID leaders like Michael Harrington. They wanted absolute clarity, for example, that the United States was blameless for the nuclear arms race. They were offended at our suggestion that the labor movement was losing its vitality. In truth, they seemed threatened by the independence of the new wave of student activism, which they believed should be a kind of youth division of the older non-Communist left, an overreaction that Harrington later regretted. Starting in Port Huron, such frictions continued to wound the New Left through the 1960s, until SDS itself succumbed and splintered under the weight of the very factionalism Port Huron sought to transcend.

Like today, 1962 was a time when many students were waking up, but the vast majority were smothered in apathy. We couldn't resist racism and war, we realized, without first piercing this freezing indifference bred by affluence, conformity and the legacy of McCarthyism. The independent sociologist C. Wright Mills had written a compelling essay titled "Out of Apathy," which helped us understand that apathy was engineered by elites that benefited from our silent condition. Psychologically, it was also a defense mechanism against deeper feelings of helplessness. "Students don't even give a damn about the apathy," the statement dryly observed. Therefore, to "break out of apathy" became the first task in building a movement to challenge what Mills called a "mass society" of drifting individuals without access to power or information. The vast majority of students internalized the message of their elders that they were too young, too inexperienced, too unqualified to make a difference. Most students could not vote, and the universities acted as our substitute parents under the doctrine of *in loco parentis.* Nor was there much record of student activism in American history to bolster us. In the class discourse of the traditional left, students amounted to nothing. But now the black student revolt in the South was setting an example of a different way to see ourselves in history. On some campuses, professors and students were questioning the cold war arms race. There were stirrings on the fringe, too, where students were listening to Bob Dylan and rock and roll. SDS represented the first defections from the mainstream. The student government leaders and campus newspaper editors who came to Port Huron asserted the notion of student "rights" for the first time. It was natural to call on others, as the opening lines of the statement did: "We are people of this generation, bred in at least modest comfort, housed now in universities, looking uncomfortably at the world we inherit. . ." It was a timid trumpet, not yet a call to the barricades, but the tone touched its audience as true, not rhetorical. The need to declare ourselves, to find our voice, came from the powerlessness of everywhere being treated as "kids."

It was no wonder, then, that the statement was inspired by participatory democracy. Participation is what we were denied, and what we hungered for. Without it, there was no dignity. Parents and professors lectured us, administrators ordered us, draft boards conscripted us, the whole system channeled us, all to please authority and take place in line. Now it was our turn. What became a worldwide youth revolt began, it should be remembered, in the multiple failures of the elders.

The denial of dignity and the vote among blacks was a window into powerlessness in many forms. Young male students could be drafted to kill, but not to vote for peace candidates. A majority of Americans were denied any participation in decisions that were being made every day in their workplaces. Women were second class in every sphere of life. We agreed on a core principle: We demanded the right to vote as a first step toward a right to a voice and vote in all decisions that affected our lives.

At the time, as disfranchised students, embracing such an expansive idea required a wrenching re-examination of common assumptions. What, for example, was the view of human nature that underlay our assertion that all people had basic rights to participation, or that democracy was the system best suited to respecting human dignity? All-night discussions ensued, often concluding at daybreak. On the one hand, there were followers of the theologian Reinhold Niebuhr, influenced by the atrocities of the Holocaust and Stalinism, who had asserted that "the children of darkness," the political realists, were in their generation wiser than "the foolish children of light," the pacifists and idealists. On the other side were the Enlightenment humanists who believed in infinite perfectibility through education and nonviolence as adopted by Gandhi and Martin Luther King Jr. The dominant view was that we were children of light. We chose utopia and rejected cynicism. The statement ended on an apocalyptic note: "If we appear to seek the unattainable, as it has been said, then let it be known that we do so to avoid the unimaginable." But, reflecting our mostly mainstream backgrounds, we also wanted to be relevant, effective. Agreement was reached when Mary Varela, a Catholic Worker activist, inspired by Pope John XXIII, suggested that we follow the doctrine that humans have "unfulfilled" rather than "unlimited" capacities for good, and are "infinitely precious" rather than "infinitely perfectible." The theological amendment drew no objections and was incorporated without citation.

Participatory democracy sought to expand the sphere of public decisions from the mere election of representatives to the deeper role of "bringing people out of isolation and into community" in decentralized forms of decision-making. The same democratic humanism was applied to the economy in calls for "incentives worthier than money," and for work to be "self-directed, not manipulated." The statement was not an endorsement of the liberal welfare state or the managerial democracy of the New Frontier, but a call for a thorough, bottom-up reclaiming of the public sector for public, rather than military, purposes. Only then might corporations be made "publicly responsible." In today's terms, we were trying to transform the mass society into a civic society, spark a social awareness in the vast world of private lives and voluntary associations that most people inhabited far from the centers of power.

The phrase "participatory democracy" derived from the influence of Arnold Kaufman, a professor of philosophy at the University of Michigan who had taught Tom and other early SDSers, and who attended the convention as a speaker. Kaufman used the term to signify that democracy, as defined in conventional liberal discourse, was far too limited when reduced to electoral choice and concepts like the free marketplace of ideas. Kaufman's case for participatory democracy flowed directly from John Dewey's writings in the 1920s and '30s. Alongside his mainstream popularity, Dewey was very much a man of the left. One of his longstanding organizational involvements, interestingly, was active membership in SDS's parent organization, LID, which he joined soon after its founding before serving as president and honorary president in the 1940s. Dewey was not at all satisfied with the state of left politics in his time; for most of his life he searched for a "new left" himself, an alternative to the ideology and practice of the established socialist organizations of his day. What motivated that search was a deep sense that a radical political and cultural force was needed if democracy in its fullest sense was to be made possible.

Dewey's definition of democracy was explicitly participatory: "All those who are affected by social institutions must have a share in producing and managing them," he declared, adding that "a democracy is more than a form of government; it is primarily a mode of associated living, of conjoint community experience." He argued that such participation is necessary both for the general welfare and for the fullest development of individuals, and that such a principle should be applied not only in the political sphere as we understand it but in the spheres of family and childraising, in school, in business and in religion.

A more immediate intellectual influence on the framers at Port Huron was C. Wright Mills, who died that year of heart failure. Mills was a follower of Dewey, who shared the same desire to establish a real American left. From Texas, a descendant of Irish immigrants, he too was a native populist. Intellectually, he combated the dogmas of Marxism, for example, the idea that the vast American society was controlled by a narrow economic ruling class. At the same time, he rejected the pluralist argument that America was a balanced society of interest groups. Instead he painstakingly constructed the notion of a fluid but uncoordinated power elite that presided over a mass society of apathetic individuals. Mills was a democratic populist whose vision also encouraged "plain Marxism," in which he sought to revive the humanistic values of the early Marx that preceded dialectical materialism. In his "Letter to the New Left" Mills passionately urged young intellectuals to see themselves as revolutionary and not to become either compromised celebrants of the status quo or blind followers of leftist orthodoxy. It is interesting, in light of later attacks on the Port Huron Statement as a mask for Marxism, that Dewey and Mills were its primary influences. Port Huron marked a milestone in the search for genuine American radicalism based on many traditions, but most of all an egalitarian, almost anarchistic belief in democracy. It also anticipated a post-Communist left, if not the decline of the Soviet Union. Quoting Henry David Thoreau, movement activists said: Vote not with a strip of paper alone, but with your whole life. Or as the novelist Ignazio Silone wrote in *Bread and Wine*, the Italian peasants showed their organizers a new way to live.

The statement also contained a strategic vision of energizing a new insurgency to shift priorities from cold war militarism to the quality of life at home, spearheaded by the civil rights revolution, the revival of peace sentiment, a labor movement committed to organizing and a new consciousness among students and intellectuals in the universities. Michael Harrington's *The Other America*, recovering attention to the invisible poor, was a bestseller then being read by President Kennedy. Serious advocacy of planned economic conversion from military to civilian production was gaining ground. The President would soon question the cold war itself. For the first time since the 1930s, the possibility of bringing domestic priorities front and center was at hand. Politically, it meant realigning the Democratic Party toward its historic liberalism by splitting off the segregationist Dixiecrat South. Accordingly, the statement called for demonstrations at "every Congressional or convention seating of Dixiecrats," anticipating the challenge made in 1964 by the inclusive Mississippi Freedom Democratic Party. Following the example of SNCC, hundreds of early SDSers established community organizing projects in Northern ghettos in 1964, fully expecting to galvanize social reform—even a gradual revolution—on the home front.

But we could not imagine that Vietnam was just around the corner. The Port Huron Statement made just a passing reference condemning aid to the South Vietnamese dictatorship. Unexpectedly, the American commitment deepened in the year following Port Huron. When the moment of choice arrived in 1964–65, the Democratic administration sent 150,000 troops to Vietnam, guaranteeing that the commitment to ending poverty and racism would ebb. The visionary promise of Port Huron died on a battlefield that triggered a radical polarization instead of reform at home. Our difference with Wills and Dionne is that they blame the New Left for becoming too destructive and extreme in the later 1960s, while we would locate the responsibility for things falling apart on our leaders' choice to create a slaughterhouse in Southeast Asia.

Perhaps the most important legacy of the Port Huron Statement is the fact that it introduced the concept of participatory democracy to popular discourse and practice. It made sense of the fact that ordinary people were making history, and not waiting for parties or traditional organizations. The notion was used to define modes of organization (decentralization, consensus methods of decision-making, leadership rotation and avoidance of hierarchy) that would lead to social transformation, not simply concessions from existing institutions. It proved to be a contagious idea, spreading from its academic origins to the very process of movement decision-making, to the subsequent call for women's liberation. These participatory practices, which had their roots in the town hall, Quaker meetings, anarchist collectives and even sensitivity training, are carried on today in grassroots movements such as the one against corporate globalization. The strength of organizations like the early SDS or SNCC, or today's Seattle-style direct-action networks, or ACT UP, is catalytic, not bureaucratic. They empower the passion of spontaneous, communal revolt, continue a few years, succeed in achieving reforms and yet have difficulty in becoming institutionalized. But while hierarchical mass organizations boast more staying power, they have trouble attracting the personal creativity or the energy of ordinary people taking back power over their lives. Participatory democracy offers a lens for looking at all hierarchies critically and not taking them as inevitable. Perhaps the two strands—the grassroots radical democratic thrust and the need for an organization with a program—can never be fused, but neither can one live without the other.

The Port Huron Statement claimed to be articulating an "Agenda for a Generation." Some of that agenda has been fulfilled: The cold war is no more, voting rights for blacks and youth have been won, and much has changed for the better in the content of university curriculums. Yet our dreams have hardly been realized. The Port Huron Statement was composed in the heady interlude of inspiration between the apathetic 1950s and the 1960s' sudden traumas of political assassinations and body counts. Forty years later, we may stand at a similar crossroads. The war on terrorism has revived the cold war framework. An escalating national security state attempts to rivet our attention and invest our resources on fighting an elusive, undefined enemy for years to come, at the inevitable price of our civil liberties and continued neglect of social justice. To challenge the framework of the war on terrorism, to demand a search for real peace with justice, is as difficult today as challenging the cold war was at Port Huron. Yet there is a new movement astir in the world, against the inherent violence of globalization, corporate rule and fundamentalism, that reminds us strongly of the early 1960s. Is history repeating? If so, "participatory democracy" and the priorities of Port Huron continue to offer clues to building a committed movement toward a society responsive to the needs of the vast majority. Many of those who came to Port Huron have been on that quest ever since.

"The Port Huron Statement" (1962)

Introduction: Agenda for a Generation

We are people of this generation, bred in at least modest comfort, housed now in universities, looking uncomfortably to the world we inherit.

When we were kids the United States was the wealthiest and strongest country in the world; the only one with the atom bomb, the least scarred by modern war, and initiator of the United Nations that we thought would distribute Western influence throughout the world. Freedom and equality for each individual, government of, by, and for the people—these American values we found good, principles by which we could live as men. Many of us began maturing in complacency.

As we grew, however, our comfort was penetrated by events too troubling to dismiss. First, the permeating and victimizing fact of human degradation, symbolized by the Southern struggle against racial bigotry, compelled most of us from silence to activism. Second, the enclosing fact of the Cold War, symbolized by the presence of the Bomb, brought awareness that we ourselves, and our friends, and millions of abstract "others" we knew more directly because of our common peril, might die at any time. We might deliberately ignore, or avoid, or fail to feel all other human problems, but not these two, for these were too immediate and crushing in their impact, too challenging in the demand that we as individuals take the responsibility for encounter and resolution.

While these and other problems either directly oppressed us or rankled our consciences and became our own subjective concerns, we began to see complicated and disturbing paradoxes in our surrounding America. The declaration "all men are created equal" rang hollow before the facts of Negro life in the South and the big cities of the North. The proclaimed peaceful intentions of the United States contradicted its economic and military investments in the Cold War status quo.

We witnessed, and continue to witness, other paradoxes. With nuclear energy whole cities can easily be powered, yet the dominant nation-states seem more likely to unleash destruction greater than that incurred in all wars of human history. Although our own technology is destroying old and creating new forms of social organization, men still tolerate meaningless work and idleness. While two-thirds of mankind suffers undernourishment, our own upper classes revel amidst superfluous abundance. Although world population is expected to double in forty years, the nations still tolerate anarchy as a major principle of international conduct and uncontrolled exploitation governs the sapping of the earth's physical resources. Although mankind desperately needs revolutionary leadership, America rests in national stalemate, its goals ambiguous and tradition-bound instead of informed and clear, its democratic system apathetic and manipulated rather than "of, by, and for the people."

Not only did tarnish appear on our image of American virtue, not only did disillusion occur when the hypocrisy of American ideals was discovered, but we began to sense that what we had originally seen as the American Golden Age was actually the decline of an era. The worldwide outbreak of revolution against colonialism and imperialism, the entrenchment of totalitarian states, the menace of war, overpopulation, international disorder, supertechnology—these trends were testing the tenacity of our own commitment to democracy and freedom and our abilities to visualize their application to a world in upheaval.

Our work is guided by the sense that we may be the last generation in the experiment with living. But we are a minority—the vast majority of our people regard the temporary equilibriums of our society and world as eternally functional parts. In this is perhaps the outstanding paradox: we ourselves are imbued with urgency, yet the message of our society is that there is no viable alternative to the present. Beneath the reassuring tones of the politicians, beneath the common opinion that America will "muddle through," beneath the stagnation of those who have closed their minds to the future, is the pervading feeling that there simply are no alternatives, that our times have witnessed the exhaustion not only of Utopias, but of any new departures as well. Feeling the press of complexity upon the emptiness of life, people are fearful of the thought that at any moment things might be thrust out of control. They fear change itself, since change might smash whatever invisible framework seems to hold back chaos for them now. For most Americans, all crusades are suspect, threatening. The fact that each individual sees apathy in his fellows perpetuates the common reluctance to organize for change. The dominant institutions are complex enough to blunt the minds of their potential critics, and entrenched enough to swiftly dissipate or entirely repel the energies of protest and reform, thus limiting human expectancies. Then, too, we are a materially improved society, and by our own improvements we seem to have weakened the case for further change.

Some would have us believe that Americans feel contentment amidst prosperity—but might it not better be called a glaze above deeply felt anxieties about their role in the new world? And if these anxieties produce a developed indifference to human affairs, do they not as well produce a yearning to believe there *is* an alternative to the present, that something *can* be done to change circumstances in the school, the workplaces, the bureaucracies, the government? It is to this latter yearning, at once the spark and engine of change, that we direct our present appeal. The search for truly democratic alternatives to the present, and a commitment to social experimentation with them, is a worthy and fulfilling human enterprise, one which moves us and, we hope, others today. On such a basis do we offer this document of our convictions and analysis: as an effort in understanding and changing the conditions of humanity in the late twentieth century, an effort rooted in the ancient, still unfulfilled conception of man attaining determining influence over his circumstances of life.

Values

Making values explicit—an initial task in establishing alternatives—is an activity that has been devalued and corrupted. The conventional moral terms of the age, the politician moralities—"free world," "people's democracies"—reflect realities poorly, if at all, and seem to function more as ruling myths than as descriptive principles. But neither has our experience in the universities brought us moral enlightenment. Our professors and administrators sacrifice controversy to public relations; their curriculums change more slowly than the living events of the world; their skills and silence are purchased by investors in the arms race; passion is called unscholastic. The questions we might want raised—what is really important? can we live in a different and better way? if we wanted to change society, how would we do it?—are not thought to be questions of a "fruitful, empirical nature," and thus are brushed aside.

Unlike youth in other countries, we are used to moral leadership being exercised and moral dimensions being clarified by our elders. But today, for us, not even the liberal and socialist preachments of the past seem adequate to the forms of the present. Consider the old slogans: Capitalism Cannot Reform Itself, United Front Against Fascism, General Strike, All Out on May Day. Or, more recently, No Cooperation with Commies and Fellow Travellers, Ideologies Are Exhausted, Bipartisanship, No Utopias. These are incomplete, and there are few new prophets. It has been said that our liberal and socialist predecessors were plagued by vision without program, while our own generation is plagued by program without vision. All around us there is astute grasp of method, technique—the committee, the ad hoc group, the lobbyist, the hard and soft sell, the make, the projected image—but, if pressed critically, such expertise is incompetent to explain its implicit ideals. It is highly fashionable to identify oneself by old categories, or by naming a respected political figure, or by explaining "how we would vote" on various issues.

Theoretic chaos has replaced the idealistic thinking of old—and, unable to reconstitute theoretic order, men have condemned idealism itself. Doubt has replaced hopefulness—and men act out a defeatism that is labelled realistic. The decline of utopia and hope is in fact one of the defining features of social life today. The reasons are various: the dreams of the older left were perverted by Stalinism and never re-created; the congressional stalemate makes men narrow their view of the possible; the specialization of human activity leaves little room for sweeping thought; the horrors of the twentieth century, symbolized in the gas ovens and concentration camps and atom bombs, have blasted hopefulness. To be idealistic is to be considered apocalyptic, deluded. To have no serious aspirations, on the contrary, is to be "tough-minded."

In suggesting social goals and values, therefore, we are aware of entering a sphere of some disrepute. Perhaps matured by the past, we have no sure formulas, no closed theories—but that does not mean values are beyond discussion and tentative determination. A first task of any social movement is to convince people that the search for orienting theories and the creation of human values is complex but worthwhile. We are aware that to avoid platitudes we must analyze the concrete conditions of social order. But to direct such an analysis we must use the guideposts of basic principles. Our own social values involve conceptions of human beings, human relationships, and social systems.

We regard *men* as infinitely precious and possessed of unfulfilled capacities for reason, freedom, and love. In affirming these principles we are aware of countering perhaps the dominant conceptions of man in the twentieth century: that he is a thing to be manipulated, and that he is inherently incapable of directing his own affairs. We oppose the depersonalization that reduces human beings to the status of things—if anything, the brutalities of the twentieth century teach that means and ends are intimately related, that vague appeals to "posterity" cannot justify the mutilations of the present. We oppose, too, the doctrine of human incompetence because it rests essentially on the modern fact that men have been "competently" manipulated into incompetence—we see little reason why men cannot meet with increasing skill the complexities and responsibilities of their situation, if society is organized not for minority, but for majority, participation in decision-making.

Men have unrealized potential for self-cultivation, self-direction, self-understanding, and creativity. It is this potential that we regard as crucial and to which we appeal, not to the human potentiality for violence, unreason, and sub-mission to authority. The goal of man and society should be human indepen-dence: a concern not with the image of popularity but with finding a meaning in life that is personally authentic; a quality of mind not compulsively driven by a sense of powerlessness, nor one which unthinkingly adopts status values, nor one which represses all threats to its habits, but one which has full, spontaneous access to present and past experiences, one which easily unites the fragmented parts of personal history, one which openly faces problems which are troubling and unresolved; one with an intuitive awareness of possibilities, an active sense of curiosity, an ability and willingness to learn.

This kind of independence does not mean egotistic individualism—the object is not to have one's way so much as it is to have a way that is one's own. Nor do we deify man—we merely have faith in his potential.

Human relationships should involve fraternity and honesty. Human interde-pendence is contemporary fact; human brotherhood must be willed, however, as a condition of future survival and as the most appropriate form of social rela-tions. Personal links between man and man are needed, especially to go beyond the partial and fragmentary bonds of function that bind men only as worker to worker, employer to employee, teacher to student, American to Russian.

Loneliness, estrangement, isolation describe the vast distance between man and man today. These dominant tendencies cannot be overcome by better per-sonnel management, nor by improved gadgets, but only when a love of man overcomes the idolatrous worship of things by man. As the individualism we affirm is not egoism, the selflessness we affirm is not self-elimination. On the contrary, we believe in generosity of a kind that imprints one's unique individual qualities in the relation to other men, and to all human activity. Further, to dis-like isolation is not to favor the abolition of privacy; the latter differs from isola-tion in that it occurs or is abolished according to individual will.

We would replace power rooted in possession, privilege, or circumstance by power and uniqueness rooted in love, reflectiveness, reason, and creativity. As a *social system* we seek the establishment of a democracy of individual participa-tion, governed by two central aims: that the individual share in those social decisions determining the quality and direction of his life; that society be organized to encourage independence in men and provide the media for their common participation.

In a participatory democracy, the political life would be based in several root principles:

> that decision-making of basic social consequence be carried on by public groupings;
>
> that politics be seen positively, as the art of collectively creating an acceptable pattern of social relations;
>
> that politics has the function of bringing people out of isolation and into community, thus being a necessary, though not sufficient, means of finding meaning in personal life;
>
> that the political order should serve to clarify problems in a way instrumental to their solution; it should provide outlets for the expression of personal grievance and aspiration; opposing views should be organized so as to illuminate choices and facilitate the attainment of goals; channels should be commonly available to relate men to knowledge and to power so that private problems—from bad recreation facilities to personal alienation—are formulated as general issues.

The economic sphere would have as its basis the principles:

> that work should involve incentives worthier than money or survival. It should be educative, not stultifying; creative, not mechanical; self-directed, not manipulated, encouraging independence, a respect for others, a sense of dignity, and a willingness to accept social responsibility, since it is this experience that has crucial influence on habits, perceptions, and individual ethics;
>
> that the economic experience is so personally decisive that the individual must share in its full determination;
>
> that the economy itself is of such social importance that its major resources and means of production should be open to democratic participation and subject to democratic social regulation.

Like the political and economic ones, major social institutions—cultural, educational, rehabilitative, and others—should be generally organized with the well-being and dignity of man as the essential measure of success.

In social change or interchange, we find violence to be abhorrent because it requires generally the transformation of the target, be it a human being or a community of people, into a depersonalized object of hate. It is imperative that the means of violence be abolished and the institutions—local, national, international—that encourage non-violence as a condition of conflict be developed.

These are our central values, in skeletal form. It remains vital to understand their denial or attainment in the context of the modern world.

PART FOUR

Anarchism

EMMA GOLDMAN introduces her essay, "Anarchism: What It Really Stands For," with the words of John Henry Mackay: "I am an Anarchist! Wherefore I will / Not rule, and also ruled I will not be!" Most simply, *anarchism* means "without government." Its popular meaning—chaos or disorder—has been inferred from that. But anarchists resist the association of government with order, freedom with chaos. Instead, they maintain that anarchism involves a natural, not an artificial, order; it is the order of "organized, living society." Goldman's complete definition of anarchism reads: "The philosophy of a new social order based on liberty unrestricted by man-made law; the theory that all forms of government rest on violence, and are therefore wrong and harmful, as well as unnecessary." Anarchists destroy all forms of government in order to create a new social order.

In her essay, Goldman attacks four standard defenses of government. First, she questions claims that the state rests upon natural law. Nature works freely and spontaneously; for example, human needs for food, sex, light, air, and exercise are natural laws. By requiring coercion to maintain themselves, however, states reveal their opposition to nature. Second, Goldman argues that states do not manage to maintain order, their supposed purpose. She writes, "Order derived through submission and maintained by terror is not much of a safe guaranty; yet that is the only 'order' that governments have ever maintained." Third, she asserts that the state not only fails to prevent crime but also creates criminals by misdirecting human energies. The state itself is the greatest criminal: it breaks written and natural laws, stealing through taxes and killing with wars. Fourth, Goldman suggests that states neither increase productivity nor promote prosperity; instead, they protect the property of the nonproductive, who make labor unbearable for others. To arguments that human nature nonetheless requires states, Goldman responds: "Poor human nature, what horrible crimes have been committed in thy name! Every fool . . . presumes to speak authoritatively of human nature. . . . Yet, how can any one speak of it today, with every soul in a prison, with every heart fettered, wounded, and maimed?" In short, humanity has yet to see what it is capable of without government.

Nevertheless, Goldman's essay leaves the constructive side of anarchism vague, only remarking that "it is the philosophy of the sovereignty of the individual. It is the theory of social harmony." These two themes of her positive vision are not easily combined, however. Since anarchists usually emphasize one or the other, their proposals can be divided into two categories: individualist anarchism and socialist anarchism.[1]

In his defense of limited government, Milton Friedman said, "The consistent liberal is not an anarchist." Yet individualist anarchists claim to be just that— consistent liberals who see even limited government as a violation of individual freedom. As Max Stirner puts it, "There is no freedom but that which the individual conquers for himself. Freedom given or conceded [by the state] is not freedom but 'stolen goods.' "[2] That liberal government is also popular government does not help. Votes only mask power; liberal democracy is constitutional tyranny. In addition to freedom, individualist anarchists stress responsibility. According to William Godwin, "A virtuous disposition is principally generated by the uncontrolled exercise of private judgment and the rigid conformity of every man to the dictates of his conscience."[3]

In Henry David Thoreau's "Essay on Civil Disobedience," this combination of freedom and responsibility emerges clearly. Thoreau begins with a seemingly liberal argument: that government is best which governs least. But he quickly adds that no government would be better still. Government saps human vitality; individuals serve it as machines, not men. It also undermines integrity: in innumerable acts of daily life, individuals sanction state policies with which they might on reflection disagree. Thoreau asks us to consult our consciences and not to "lend [ourselves] to the wrong which [we] condemn." He maintains, "The only obligation which I have a right to assume is to do at any time what I think right." This means that the majority cannot bind me: "Any man more right than his neighbors constitutes a majority of one."

What kind of society results when individuals act from principle? Individualist anarchists generally say little about this; like Goldman, they are clearer about what they attack than about what they defend. It is socialist anarchists who outline a new social order. Like individualist anarchists, they claim to be consistent— in this case, consistent socialists. Each of the two socialist anarchists included in this part, Petyr Kropotkin and Mikhail Bakunin, provides a more complete picture of his vision of an ideal society.

In *Mutual Aid,* Kropotkin, a Russian aristocrat who wrote in the late nineteenth and early twentieth centuries, responds to charges that anarchists overestimate human nature—specifically, our capacity to cooperate. Unlike Darwin, Kropotkin finds that mutual aid better guarantees species survival than does mutual struggle. He does not romanticize humanity, however, for he asserts that it is an instinct of human solidarity, not love or even sympathy, that prompts mutual aid: "It is the conscience—be it only at the stage of an instinct—of human solidarity. It is the unconscious recognition of the force that is borrowed by each man from the practice of mutual aid; of the close dependency of every one's happiness upon the happiness of all." Historically, the state has superseded mutual aid institutions, thus absorbing our social functions, undermining social responsibility, and fostering "the development of an unbridled, narrow-minded individualism." According to Kropotkin, "The result is, that the theory which maintains that men can, and must, seek their own happiness in a disregard of other people's wants is now triumphant all round—in law, in science, in religion." Still, some mutual aid survives: "In our mutual relations every one of us has his moments of revolt against the fashionable individualist creed of the day."

Although Kropotkin's concept of mutual aid is fundamental for social anarchists, Mikhail Bakunin is better known. This is largely because of his conflict with Karl Marx, which destroyed the First International.[4] That conflict was, in part, personal: despite the fact that Bakunin claimed to be Marx's disciple, Marx called him "an ass" and his work "an assembled rubbish mishmash." Their more important doctrinal differences center on the relationship between economics and politics. For Marx, politics is ultimately determined by economics; this economic determinism diminishes the importance and the dangers of political power. Hence, Marx advises the revolutionary proletariat to seize the state and remains confident that the state will eventually wither away. Bakunin disagrees. He warns that all men—even "sincere socialist revolutionaries"—possess a natural instinct for power. "A government that does not abuse its power," he says, "is, like squaring the circle, an unattainable ideal because it runs counter to human nature.... Take the most radical revolutionist and place him upon the all-Russian throne or give him dictatorial power ... and within a year he will have become worse than the Emperor himself."[5] Struggle against the state is, then, as important as struggle against capital: "In order to humanize society as a whole, it is necessary ruthlessly to destroy all the causes and all the economic, political, and social conditions which produce within individuals a tradition of evil."[6]

Bakunin's and Marx's revolutionary strategies differ accordingly. Bakunin argues that economic and political revolution must occur simultaneously. Otherwise, the revolution will stop halfway, and the transitional proletarian dictatorship will become a permanent proletarian state. Bakunin asks: "What does it mean for the proletariat to be organized as the ruling class? Can it really be that the entire proletariat will stand at the head of the new socialist administration?"[7] He answers: "It will be the reign of the scientific mind, the most aristocratic, despotic, arrogant, and contemptuous of all regimes. There will be a new class, a new hierarchy of real and bogus learning. . . . Let the masses Beware."[8] Revolutions, this suggests, must occur spontaneously, arising "from the very depths of the soul of the people." They come like "thiefs in the night," prompted by the "force of events." The people need to be educated and organized, but not by a party vanguard. Bakunin's revolutionary leaders are "midwives" to the masses' "self-liberation." They direct, not by "ostensible power," but by "a dictatorship without insignia, title, or official rights, all the more powerful because it will have none of the marks of power."[9]

Throughout their debate, Marx and Bakunin had different concerns. Marx feared proletarian disorganization and capitalist opposition; he believed that revolutions are authoritarian and must remain so, at least temporarily, to consolidate their power. In a short piece, "On Authority," Engels scoffs at the anarchists: "Have these gentlemen ever seen a revolution? A revolution is the most authoritarian thing there is . . . and if the victorious party does not want to have fought in vain, it must maintain this rule by means of . . . terror."[10] In contrast, Bakunin feared corruption of revolutionaries and continuation of state power. History suggests that Bakunin was right. The antistatist Marx inspired a massive state; his means betrayed his ends. Was Marx also right, that nonauthoritarian revolution is a utopian dream? (To answer this question you might want to explore anarchist social movements.[11])

Whatever one concludes, it is important to remember that anarchism survives. Today, individualist strains appear among libertarians or anarcho-capitalists who would create free markets by eliminating states. According to Murray Rothbard, "The state provides a legal, orderly, systematic channel for the predation of private property."[12] Private corporations could assume public services such as police, roads, and schools, and better protect private property. Since national security problems would decrease—it is states that make wars—even armies could be privately funded. This libertarian agenda is far more radical than the demands of classical liberals, such as Milton Friedman, for decreased government regulation of economic activities. For Friedman and other liberals, the state remains necessary to perform crucial, though limited, functions. Socialist anarchism also persists, most prominently, among anarcho-feminists and environmental activists. Monique Wittig's "One Is Not Born a Woman" discusses how anarchism intersects radical and postmodern feminism, while the debate between Murray Bookchin and Dave Foreman represents anarchist philosophy on environmental issues. (Since these selections are included later, I do not discuss their ideas here.)

Although their political tactics vary, anarchists agree on the dangers of the state, the importance of individual responsibility, and the possibility of social harmony. While other ideologies debate the nature of government, anarchists ask the fundamental question: Is government necessary at all?

NOTES

1. Daniel Guerin suggests this categorization in *Anarchism: From Theory to Practice* (New York: Monthly Review Press, 1970), pt. 1.

2. Quoted in ibid., 28.

3. William Godwin, "The Rights of Man and the Principles of Society," in *The Anarchists*, ed. Irving L. Horowitz (New York: Dell, 1964), 118.

4. The First International, or International Workingmen's Association, was organized by Marx and Engels in 1864 to unite trade unions across nations. For a discussion of Marx's and Bakunin's differences, see Alvin Gouldner, "Marx's Last Battle: Bakunin and the First International," *Theory and Society* 11 (1982): 853–884. Also see Paul Thomas, *Karl Marx and the Anarchists* (London: Routledge and Kegan Paul, 1980).

5. Mikhail Bakunin, "The Social and Economic Bases of Anarchism," in Horowitz, *Anarchists*, 128.

6. G. P. Maximoff, *The Political Philosophy of Bakunin: Scientific Anarchism* (Glencoe, Ill.: Free Press, 1953), 369.

7. "After the Revolution: Marx Debates Bakunin," quoted in Alvin W. Gouldner, "Bakunin and the First International," *Theory and Society* 11 (1982): 865.

8. Ibid., 866.

9. Quoted in Guerin, *Anarchism*, 33–34.

10. Friedrich Engels, "Versus the Anarchists" in *The Marx-Engels Reader*, ed. Robert C. Tucker (New York: Norton, 1978), 733.

11. For a discussion of anarchism in the Russian Revolution, the Italian Factory Councils, and the Spanish Civil War, see Guerin, *Anarchism*, pt. 3. Specifically on the Spanish Civil War, see George Orwell, *Homage to Catalonia* (New York: Harcourt, Brace, 1952); and Franz Borkenau, *The Spanish Cockpit* (Ann Arbor: University of Michigan Press, 1963).

12. Murray Newton Rothbard, *For a New Liberty: The Libertarian Manifesto* (New York: Collier Books, 1978), 46.

21

Emma Goldman

———•◦•———

"Anarchism: What It Really Stands For" (1910)

Emma Goldman (1869–1940) was born in Russia and emigrated to New York in 1885. There she began her lifelong association with anarchist politics. Often imprisoned for her protest activities, she was deported to Russia in 1919. Like many anarchists, she was disillusioned with the Bolshevik revolution, and in 1921 she fled Soviet Russia and then lived in Canada until her death. Goldman is also known for her feminist writings, published in The Traffic in Women and Other Essays on Feminism.

Anarchy

Ever reviled, accursed, ne'er understood,
　　Thou art the grisly terror of our age.
"Wreck of all order," cry the multitude,
　　"Art thou, and war and murder's endless rage."
O, let them cry. To them that ne'er have striven
　　The truth that lies behind a word to find,
To them the word's right meaning was not given.
　　They shall continue blind among the blind.
But thou, O word, so clear, so strong, so pure,
　　Thou sayest all which I for goal have taken.
I give thee to the future! Thine secure
　　When each at least unto himself shall waken.
Comes it in sunshine? In the tempest's thrill?
　　I cannot tell—but it the earth shall see!
I am an Anarchist! Wherefore I will
　　Not rule, and also ruled I will not be!

—John Henry Mackay

The history of human growth and development is at the same time the history of the terrible struggle of every new idea heralding the approach of a brighter dawn. In its tenacious hold on tradition, the Old has never hesitated to make use of the foulest and cruelest means to stay the advent of the New, in whatever form or period the latter may have asserted itself. Nor need we retrace our steps into the distant past to realize the enormity of opposition, difficulties, and hardships placed in the path of every progressive idea. The rack, the thumbscrew, and the knout are still with us; so are the convict's garb and the social wrath, all conspiring against the spirit that is serenely marching on.

Anarchism could not hope to escape the fate of all other ideas of innovation. Indeed, as the most revolutionary and uncompromising innovator, Anarchism must needs meet with the combined ignorance and venom of the world it aims to reconstruct.

To deal even remotely with all that is being said and done against Anarchism would necessitate the writing of a whole volume. I shall therefore meet only two of the principal objections. In so doing, I shall attempt to elucidate what Anarchism really stands for.

The strange phenomenon of the opposition to Anarchism is that it brings to light the relation between so-called intelligence and ignorance. And yet this is not so very strange when we consider the relativity of all things. The ignorant mass has in its favor that it makes no pretense of knowledge or tolerance. Acting, as it always does, by mere impulse, its reasons are like those of a child. "Why?" "Because." Yet the opposition of the uneducated to Anarchism deserves the same consideration as that of the intelligent man.

What, then, are the objections? First, Anarchism is impractical, though a beautiful ideal. Second, anarchism stands for violence and destruction, hence it must be repudiated as vile and dangerous. Both the intelligent man and the ignorant mass judge not from a thorough knowledge of the subject, but either from hearsay or false interpretation.

A practical scheme, says Oscar Wilde, is either one already in existence or a scheme that could be carried out under the existing conditions; but it is exactly the existing conditions that one objects to, and any scheme that could accept these conditions is wrong and foolish. The true criterion of the practical, therefore, is not whether the latter can keep intact the wrong or foolish; rather is it whether the scheme has vitality enough to leave the stagnant waters of the old, and build, as well as sustain, new life. In the light of this conception, Anarchism is indeed practical. More than any other idea, it is helping to do away with the wrong and foolish; more than any other idea, it is building and sustaining new life.

The emotions of the ignorant man are continuously kept at a pitch by the most blood-curdling stories about Anarchism. Not a thing too outrageous to be employed against this philosophy and its exponents. Therefore Anarchism represents to the unthinking what the proverbial bad man does to the child—a black monster bent on swallowing everything; in short, destruction and violence.

Destruction and violence! How is the ordinary man to know that the most violent element in society is ignorance; that its power of destruction is the very thing Anarchism is combating? Nor is he aware that Anarchism, whose roots, as it were, are part of nature's forces, destroys, not healthful tissue, but parasitic growths that feed on the life's essence of society. It is merely clearing the soil from weeds and sagebrush, that it may eventually bear healthy fruit.

Someone has said that it requires less mental effort to condemn than to think. The widespread mental indolence, so prevalent in society, proves this to be only too true. Rather than to go to the bottom of any given idea, to examine into its origin and meaning, most people will either condemn it altogether, or rely on some superficial or prejudicial definition of non-essentials.

Anarchism urges man to think, to investigate, to analyze every proposition; but that the brain capacity of the average reader be not taxed too much, I also shall begin with a definition, and then elaborate on the latter.

> ANARCHISM: The philosophy of a new social order based on liberty unrestricted by man-made law; the theory that all forms of government rest on violence, and are therefore wrong and harmful, as well as unnecessary.

The new social order rests, of course, on the materialistic basis of life; but while all Anarchists agree that the main evil today is an economic one, they maintain that the solution of that evil can be brought about only through the consideration of *every phase* of life—individual, as well as the collective; the internal, as well as the external phases.

A thorough perusal of the history of human development will disclose two elements in bitter conflict with each other; elements that are only now beginning to be understood, not as foreign to each other, but as closely related and truly harmonious, if only placed in proper environment: the individual and social instincts. The individual and society have waged a relentless and bloody battle for ages, each striving for supremacy, because each was blind to the value and importance of the other. The individual and social instincts—the one a most potent factor for individual endeavor, for growth, aspiration, self-realization; the other an equally potent factor for mutual helpfulness and social well-being.

The explanation of the storm raging within the individual, and between him and his surroundings, is not far to seek. The primitive man, unable to understand his being, much less the unity of all life, felt himself absolutely dependent on blind, hidden forces ever ready to mock and taunt him. Out of that attitude grew the religious concepts of man as a mere speck of dust dependent on superior powers on high, who can only be appeased by complete surrender. All the early sagas rest on that idea, which continues to be the *Leitmotiv* of the biblical tales dealing with the relation of man to God, to the State, to society. Again and again the same motif, *man is nothing, the powers are everything.* Thus Jehovah would only endure man on condition of complete surrender. Man can have all the glories of the earth, but he must not become conscious of himself. The State, society, and moral laws all sing the same refrain: Man can have all the glories of the earth, but he must not become conscious of himself.

Anarchism is the only philosophy which brings to man the consciousness of himself; which maintains that God, the State, and society are non-existent, that their promises are null and void, since they can be fulfilled only through man's subordination. Anarchism is therefore the teacher of the unity of life; not merely in nature, but in man. There is no conflict between the individual and the social instincts, any more than there is between the heart and the lungs: the one the receptacle of a precious life essence, the other the repository of the element that keeps the essence pure and strong. The individual is the heart of society, conserving the essence of social life; society is the lungs which are distributing the element to keep the life essence—that is, the individual—pure and strong.

"The one thing of value in the world," says Emerson, "is the active soul; this every man contains within him. The soul active sees absolute truth and utters truth and creates." In other words, the individual instinct is the thing of value in the world. It is the true soul that sees and creates the truth alive, out of which is to come a still greater truth, the re-born social soul.

Anarchism is the great liberator of man from the phantoms that have held him captive; it is the arbiter and pacifier of the two forces for individual and social harmony. To accomplish that unity, Anarchism has declared war on the pernicious influences which have so far prevented the harmonious blending of individual and social instincts, the individual and society.

Religion, the dominion of the human mind; Property, the dominion of human needs; and Government, the dominion of human conduct, represent the stronghold of man's enslavement and all the horrors it entails. Religion! How it dominates man's mind, how it humiliates and degrades his soul. God is everything, man is nothing, says religion. But out of that nothing God has created a kingdom so despotic, so tyrannical, so cruel, so terribly exacting that naught but gloom and tears and blood have ruled the world since gods began. Anarchism rouses man to rebellion against this black monster. Break your mental fetters, says Anarchism to man, for not until you think and judge for yourself will you get rid of the dominion of darkness, the greatest obstacle to all progress.

Property, the dominion of man's needs, the denial of the right to satisfy his needs. Time was when property claimed a divine right, when it came to man with the same refrain, even as religion, "Sacrifice! Abnegate! Submit!" The spirit of Anarchism has lifted man from his prostrate position. He now stands erect, with his face toward the light. He has learned to see the insatiable, devouring, devastating nature of property, and he is preparing to strike the monster dead.

"Property is robbery," said the great French Anarchist Proudhon. Yes, but without risk and danger to the robber. Monopolizing the accumulated efforts of man, property has robbed him of his birthright, and has turned him loose a pauper and an outcast. Property has not even the time-worn excuse that man does not create enough to satisfy all needs. The ABC student of economics knows that the productivity of labor within the last few decades far exceeds normal demand. But what are normal demands to an abnormal institution? The only demand that property recognizes is its own gluttonous appetite for greater wealth, because wealth means power; the power to subdue, to crush, to exploit, the power to enslave, to outrage, to degrade. America is particularly boastful of her great power, her enormous national wealth. Poor America, of what avail is all her wealth, if the individuals comprising the nation are wretchedly poor? If they live in squalor, in filth, in crime, with hope and joy gone, a homeless, soilless army of human prey.

It is generally conceded that unless the returns of any business venture exceed the cost, bankruptcy is inevitable. But those engaged in the business of producing wealth have not yet learned even this simple lesson. Every year the cost of production in human life is growing larger (50,000 killed, 100,000 wounded in America last year); the returns to the masses, who help to create wealth, are ever getting smaller. Yet America continues to be blind to the inevitable bankruptcy of our business of production. Nor is this the only crime of the latter. Still more fatal is the crime of turning the producer into a mere particle of a machine, with less will and decision than his master of steel and iron. Man is being robbed not merely of the products of his labor, but of the power of free initiative, of originality, and the interest in, or desire for, the things he is making.

Real wealth consists in things of utility and beauty, in things that help to create strong, beautiful bodies and surroundings inspiring to live in. But if man is doomed to wind cotton around a spool, or dig coal, or build roads for thirty years of his life, there can be no talk of wealth. What he gives to the world is only gray and hideous things, reflecting a dull and hideous existence—too weak to live, too cowardly to die. Strange to say, there are people who extol this deadening method of centralized production as the proudest achievement of our age. They fail utterly to realize that if we are to continue in machine subserviency, our slavery is more complete than was our bondage to the King. They do not want to know that centralization is not only the deathknell of liberty, but also of health and beauty, of art and science, all these being impossible in a clocklike, mechanical atmosphere.

Anarchism cannot but repudiate such a method of production: its goal is the freest possible expression of all the latent powers of the individual. Oscar Wilde defines a perfect personality as "one who develops under perfect conditions, who is not wounded, maimed, or in danger." A perfect personality, then, is only possible in a state of society where man is free to choose the mode of work, the conditions of work, and the freedom to work. One to whom the making of a table, the building of a house, or the tilling of the soil, is what the painting is to the artist and the discovery to the scientist—the result of inspiration, of intense longing, and deep interest in work as a creative force. That being the ideal of Anarchism, its economic arrangements must consist of voluntary productive and distributive associations, gradually developing into free communism, as the best means of producing with the least waste of human energy. Anarchism, however, also recognizes the right of the individual, or numbers of individuals, to arrange at all times for other forms of work, in harmony with their tastes and desires.

Such free display of human energy being possible only under complete individual and social freedom, Anarchism directs its forces against the third and greatest foe of all social equality; namely, the State, organized authority, or statutory law—the dominion of human conduct.

Just as religion has fettered the human mind, and as property, or the monopoly of things, has subdued and stifled man's needs, so has the State enslaved his spirit, dictating every phase of conduct. "All government in essence," says Emerson, "is tyranny." It matters not whether it is government by divine right or majority rule. In every instance its aim is the absolute subordination of the individual.

Referring to the American government, the greatest American Anarchist, David Thoreau, said: "Government, what is it but a tradition, though a recent one, endeavoring to transmit itself unimpaired to posterity, but each instance losing its integrity; it has not the vitality and force of a single living man. Law never made man a whit more just; and by means of their respect for it, even the well disposed are daily made agents of injustice."

Indeed, the keynote of government is injustice. With the arrogance and self-sufficiency of the King who could do no wrong, governments ordain, judge, condemn, and punish the most insignificant offenses, while maintaining themselves by the greatest of all offenses, the annihilation of individual liberty. Thus Ouida is right when she maintains that "the State only aims at instilling those qualities in its public by which its demands are obeyed, and its exchequer is filled. Its highest attainment is the reduction of mankind to clockwork. In its atmosphere all those finer and more delicate liberties, which require treatment and spacious expansion, inevitably dry up and perish. The State requires a taxpaying machine in which there is no hitch, an exchequer in which there is never a deficit, and a public, monotonous, obedient, colorless, spiritless, moving humbly like a flock of sheep along a straight high road between two walls."

Yet even a flock of sheep would resist the chicanery of the State, if it were not for the corruptive, tyrannical, and oppressive methods it employs to serve its purposes. Therefore Bakunin repudiates the State as synonymous with the surrender of the liberty of the individual or small minorities—the destruction of social relationship, the curtailment, or complete denial even, of life itself, for its own aggrandizement. The State is the altar of political freedom and, like the religious altar, it is maintained for the purpose of human sacrifice.

In fact, there is hardly a modern thinker who does not agree that government, organized authority, or the State, is necessary *only* to maintain or protect property and monopoly. It has proven efficient in that function only.

Even George Bernard Shaw, who hopes for the miraculous from the State under Fabianism, nevertheless admits that "it is at present a huge machine for robbing and slave-driving of the poor by brute force." This being the case, it is hard to see why the clever prefacer wishes to uphold the State after poverty shall have ceased to exist.

Unfortunately there are still a number of people who continue in the fatal belief that government rests on natural laws, that it maintains social order and harmony, that it diminishes crime, and that it prevents the lazy man from fleecing his fellows. I shall therefore examine these contentions.

A natural law is that factor in man which asserts itself freely and spontaneously without any external force, in harmony with the requirements of nature. For instance, the demand for nutrition, for sex gratification, for light, air, and exercise, is a natural law. But its expression needs not the machinery of government, needs not the club, the gun, the handcuff, or the prison. To obey such laws, if we may call it obedience, requires only spontaneity and free opportunity. That governments do not maintain themselves through such harmonious factors is proven by the terrible array of violence, force, and coercion all governments use in order to live. Thus Blackstone is right when he says, "Human laws are invalid, because they are contrary to the laws of nature."

Unless it be the order of Warsaw after the slaughter of thousands of people, it is difficult to ascribe to governments any capacity for order or social harmony. Order derived through submission and maintained by terror is not much of a safe guaranty; yet that is the only "order" that governments have ever maintained. True social harmony grows naturally out of solidarity of interests. In a society where those who always work never have anything, while those who never work enjoy everything, solidarity of interests is non-existent; hence social harmony is but a myth. The only way organized authority meets this grave situation is by extending still greater privileges to those who have already monopolized the earth, and by still further enslaving the disinherited masses. Thus the entire arsenal of government—laws, police, soldiers, the courts, legislature, prisons—is strenuously engaged in "harmonizing" the most antagonistic elements in society.

The most absurd apology for authority and law is that they serve to diminish crime. Aside from the fact that the State is itself the greatest criminal, breaking every written and natural law, stealing in the form of taxes, killing in the form of war and capital punishment, it has come to an absolute standstill in coping with crime. It has failed utterly to destroy or even minimize the horrible scourge of its own creation.

Crime is naught but misdirected energy. So long as every institution of today, economic, political, social, and moral, conspires to misdirect human energy into wrong channels; so long as most people are out of place doing the things they hate to do, living a life they loathe to live, crime will be inevitable, and all the laws on the statutes can only increase, but never do away with, crime. What does society, as it exists today, know of the process of despair, the poverty, the horrors, the fearful struggle the human soul must pass on its way to crime and degradation. Who that knows this terrible process can fail to see the truth in these words of Peter Kropotkin:

> Those who will hold the balance between the benefits thus attributed to law and punishment and the degrading effect of the latter on humanity; those who will estimate the torrent of depravity poured abroad in human society by the informer, favored by the Judge even, and paid for in clinking cash by governments, under the pretext of aiding to unmask crime; those who will go within prison walls and there see what human beings become when deprived of liberty, when subjected to the care of brutal keepers, to coarse, cruel words, to a thousand stinging, piercing humiliations, will agree with us that the entire apparatus of prison and punishment is an abomination which ought to be brought to an end.

The deterrent influence of law on the lazy man is too absurd to merit consideration. If society were only relieved of the waste and expense of keeping a lazy class, and the equally great expense of the paraphernalia of protection this lazy class requires, the social tables would contain an abundance for all, including even the occasional lazy individual. Besides, it is well to consider that laziness results either from special privileges, or physical and mental abnormalities. Our present insane system of production fosters both, and the most astounding phenomenon is that people should want to work at all now. Anarchism aims to strip labor of its deadening, dulling aspect, of its gloom and compulsion. It aims to make work an instrument of joy, of strength, of color, of real harmony, so that the poorest sort of a man should find in work both recreation and hope.

To achieve such an arrangement of life, government, with its unjust, arbitrary, repressive measures, must be done away with. At best it has but imposed one single mode of life upon all, without regard to individual and social variations and needs. In destroying government and statutory laws, Anarchism proposes to rescue the self-respect and independence of the individual from all restraint and invasion by authority. Only in freedom can man grow to his full stature. Only in freedom will he learn to think and move, and give the very best in him. Only in freedom will he realize the true force of the social bonds which knit men together, and which are the true foundation of a normal social life.

But what about human nature? Can it be changed? And if not, will it endure under Anarchism?

Poor human nature, what horrible crimes have been committed in thy name! Every fool, from king to policeman, from the flatheaded parson to the visionless dabbler in science, presumes to speak authoritatively of human nature. The greater the mental charlatan, the more definite his insistence on the wickedness and weaknesses of human nature. Yet, how can any one speak of it today, with every soul in a prison, with every heart fettered, wounded, and maimed?

John Burroughs has stated that experimental study of animals in captivity is absolutely useless. Their character, their habits, their appetites undergo a complete transformation when torn from their soil in field and forest. With human nature caged in a narrow space, whipped daily into submission, how can we speak of its potentialities?

Freedom, expansion, opportunity, and, above all, peace and repose, alone can teach us the real dominant factors of human nature and all its wonderful possibilities.

Anarchism, then, really stands for the liberation of the human mind from the dominion of religion; the liberation of the human body from the dominion of property; liberation from the shackles and restraint of government. Anarchism stands for a social order based on the free grouping of individuals for the purpose of producing real social wealth; an order that will guarantee to every human being free access to the earth and full enjoyment of the necessities of life, according to individual desires, tastes, and inclinations.

This is not a wild fancy or an aberration of the mind. It is the conclusion arrived at by hosts of intellectual men and women the world over; a conclusion resulting from the close and studious observation of the tendencies of modern society: individual liberty and economic equality, the twin forces for the birth of what is fine and true in man.

As to methods. Anarchism is not, as some may suppose, a theory of the future to be realized through divine inspiration. It is a living force in the affairs of our life, constantly creating new conditions. The methods of Anarchism therefore do not comprise an iron-clad program to be carried out under all circumstances. Methods must grow out of the economic needs of each place and clime, and of the intellectual and temperamental requirements of the individual. The serene, calm character of a Tolstoy will wish different methods for social reconstruction than the intense, overflowing personality of a Michael Bakunin or a Peter Kropotkin. Equally so it must be apparent that the economic and political needs of Russia will dictate more drastic measures than would England or America. Anarchism does not stand for military drill and uniformity; it does, however, stand for the spirit of revolt, in whatever form, against everything that hinders human growth. All Anarchists agree in that, as they also agree in their opposition to the political machinery as a means of bringing about the great social change.

"All voting," says Thoreau, "is a sort of gaming, like checkers, or backgammon, a playing with right and wrong; its obligation never exceeds that of expediency. Even voting for the right thing is doing nothing for it. A wise man will not leave the right to the mercy of chance, nor wish it to prevail through the power of the majority." A close examination of the machinery of politics and its achievements will bear out the logic of Thoreau.

What does the history of parliamentarism show? Nothing but failure and defeat, not even a single reform to ameliorate the economic and social stress of the people. Laws have been passed and enactments made for the improvement and protection of labor. Thus it was proven only last year that Illinois, with the most rigid laws for mine protection, had the greatest mine disasters. In States where child labor laws prevail, child exploitation is at its highest, and though with us the workers enjoy full political opportunities, capitalism has reached the most brazen zenith.

Even were the workers able to have their own representatives, for which our good Socialist politicians are clamoring, what chances are there for their honesty and good faith? One has but to bear in mind the process of politics to realize that its path of good intentions is full of pitfalls: wirepulling, intriguing, flattering, lying, cheating; in fact, chicanery of every description, whereby the political aspirant can achieve success. Added to that is a complete demoralization of character and conviction, until nothing is left that would make one hope for anything from such a human derelict. Time and time again the people were foolish enough to trust, believe, and support with their last farthing aspiring politicians, only to find themselves betrayed and cheated.

It may be claimed that men of integrity would not become corrupt in the political grinding mill. Perhaps not; but such men would be absolutely helpless to exert the slightest influence in behalf of labor, as indeed has been shown in numerous instances. The State is the economic master of its servants. Good men, if such there be, would either remain true to their political faith and lose their economic support, or they would cling to their economic master and be utterly unable to do the slightest good. The political arena leaves one no alternative, one must either be a dunce or a rogue.

The political superstition is still holding sway over the hearts and minds of the masses, but the true lovers of liberty will have no more to do with it. Instead, they believe with [Max] Stirner that man has as much liberty as he is willing to take. Anarchism therefore stands for direct action, the open defiance of, and resistance to, all laws and restrictions, economic, social, and moral. But defiance and resistance are illegal. Therein lies the salvation of man. Everything illegal necessitates integrity, self-reliance, and courage. In short, it calls for free, independent spirits, for "men who are men, and who have a bone in their backs which you cannot pass your hand through."

Universal suffrage itself owes its existence to direct action. If not for the spirit of rebellion, of the defiance on the part of the American revolutionary fathers, their posterity would still wear the King's coat. If not for the direct action of a John Brown and his comrades, America would still trade in the flesh of the black man. True, the trade in white flesh is still going on; but that, too, will have to be abolished by direct action. Trade-unionism, the economic arena of the modern gladiator, owes its existence to direct action. It is but recently that law and government have attempted to crush the trade-union movement, and condemned the exponents of man's right to organize to prison as conspirators. Had they sought to assert their cause through begging, pleading, and compromise, trade-unionism would today be a negligible quantity. In France, in Spain, in Italy, in Russia, nay even in England (witness the growing rebellion of English labor unions), direct, revolutionary, economic action has become so strong a force in the battle for industrial liberty as to make the world realize the tremendous importance of labor's power. The General Strike, the supreme expression of the economic consciousness of the workers, was ridiculed in America but a short time ago. Today every great strike, in order to win, must realize the importance of the solidaric general protest.

Direct action, having proven effective along economic lines, is equally potent in the environment of the individual. There a hundred forces encroach upon his being, and only persistent resistance to them will finally set him free. Direct action against the authority in the shop, direct action against the invasive, meddlesome authority of our moral code, is the logical, consistent method of Anarchism.

Will it not lead to a revolution? Indeed, it will. No real social change has ever come about without a revolution. People are either not familiar with their history, or they have not yet learned that revolution is but thought carried into action.

Anarchism, the great leaven of thought, is today permeating every phase of human endeavor. Science, art, literature, the drama, the effort of economic betterment, in fact every individual and social opposition to the existing disorder of things, is illumined by the spiritual light of Anarchism. It is the philosophy of the sovereignty of the individual. It is the theory of social harmony. It is the great, surging, living truth that is reconstructing the world, and that will usher in the Dawn.

22

Henry David Thoreau

"Essay on Civil Disobedience" (1846)

Henry David Thoreau (1817–1862) is best known for his account of his tranquil experiences at Walden Pond, outside Boston. But in 1846 he was arrested for failing to pay his taxes. That prompted him to write the "Essay on Civil Disobedience," which justifies disobeying the laws of a government whose policies one cannot support. Thoreau's concern was the Mexican-American War, but his essay continues to inspire protests on issues ranging from civil rights to nuclear energy.

I heartily accept the motto, "That government is best which governs least"; and I should like to see it acted up to more rapidly and systematically. Carried out, it finally amounts to this, which also I believe—"That government is best which governs not at all"; and when men are prepared for it, that will be the kind of government which they will have. Government is at best but an expedient; but most governments are usually, and all governments are sometimes, inexpedient. The objections which have been brought against a standing army, and they are many and weighty, and deserve to prevail, may also at last be brought against a standing government. The standing army is only an arm of the standing government. The government itself, which is only the mode which the people have chosen to execute their will, is equally liable to be abused and perverted before the people can act through it. Witness the present Mexican war, the work of comparatively a few individuals using the standing government as their tool; for, in the outset, the people would not have consented to this measure.

This American government—what is it but a tradition, though a recent one, endeavoring to transmit itself unimpaired to posterity, but each instant losing some of its integrity? It has not the vitality and force of a single living man; for a single man can bend it to his will. It is a sort of wooden gun to the people themselves. But it is not the less necessary for this; for the people must have some complicated machinery or other, and hear its din, to satisfy that idea of government which they have. Governments show thus how successfully men can be imposed on, even impose on themselves, for their own advantage. It is excellent, we must all allow. Yet this government never of itself furthered any enterprise, but by the alacrity with which it got out of its way. *It* does not keep the country free. *It* does not settle the West. *It* does not educate. The character inherent in the American people has done all that has been accomplished; and it would have done somewhat more, if the government had not sometimes got in its way. For government is an expedient by which men would fain succeed in letting one another alone; and, as has been said, when it is most expedient, the governed are most let alone by it. Trade and commerce, if they were not made of India-rubber, would never manage to bounce over the obstacles which legislators are continually putting in their way; and, if one were to judge these men wholly by the effects of their actions and not partly by their intentions, they would deserve to be classed and punished with those mischievous persons who put obstructions on the railroads.

But, to speak practically and as a citizen, unlike those who call themselves no-government men, I ask for, not at once no government, but *at once* a better government. Let every man make known what kind of government would command his respect, and that will be one step toward obtaining it.

After all, the practical reason why, when the power is once in the hands of the people, a majority are permitted, and for a long period continue, to rule is not because they are most likely to be in the right, nor because this seems fairest to the minority, but because they are physically the strongest. But a government in which the majority rule in all cases cannot be based on justice, even as far as men understand it. Can there not be a government in which majorities do not virtually decide right and wrong, but conscience?—in which majorities decide only those questions to which the rule of expediency is applicable? Must the citizen ever for a moment, or in the least degree, resign his conscience to the legislator? Why has every man a conscience, then? I think that we should be men first, and subjects afterward. It is not desirable to cultivate a respect for the law, so much as for the right. The only obligation which I have a right to assume is to do at any time what I think right. It is truly enough said, that a corporation has no conscience; but a corporation of conscientious men is a corporation *with* a conscience. Law never made men a whit more just; and, by means of their respect for it, even the well-disposed are daily made the agents of injustice. A common and natural result of an undue respect for law is, that you may see a file of soldiers, colonel, captain, corporal, privates, powder-monkeys, and all, marching in admirable order over hill and dale to the wars, against their wills, ay, against their common sense and consciences, which makes it very steep marching indeed, and produces a palpitation of the heart. They have no doubt that it is a damnable business in which they are concerned; they are all peaceably inclined. Now, what are they? Men at all? or small movable forts and magazines, at the service of some unscrupulous man in power? Visit the Navy-Yard, and behold a marine, such a man as an American government can make, or such as it can make a man with its black arts—a mere shadow and reminiscence of humanity, a man laid out alive and standing, and already, as one may say, buried under arms with funeral accompaniments, though it may be—

> "Not a drum was heard, not a funeral note,
> As his cor[p]se to the rampart we hurried;
> Not a soldier discharged his farewell shot
> O'er the grave where our hero we buried."

The mass of men serve the state thus, not as men mainly, but as machines, with their bodies. They are the standing army, and the militia, jailers, constables, posse comitatus, etc. In most cases there is no free exercise whatever of the judgment or of the moral sense; but they put themselves on a level with wood and earth and stones; and wooden men can perhaps be manufactured that will serve the purpose as well. Such command no more respect than men of straw or a lump of dirt. They have the same sort of worth only as horses and dogs. Yet such as these even are commonly esteemed good citizens. Others—as most legislators, politicians, lawyers, ministers, and office-holders—serve the state chiefly with their heads; and, as they rarely make any moral distinctions, they are as likely to serve the Devil, without *intending* it, as God. A very few, as heroes, patriots, martyrs, reformers in the sense, and *men,* serve the state with their consciences also, and so necessarily resist it for the most part; and they are commonly treated as enemies by it. A wise man will only be useful as a man, and will not submit to be "clay," and "stop a hole to keep the wind away," but leave that office to his dust at least:

> "I am too high-born to be propertied,
> To be a secondary at control,
> Or useful serving-man and instrument
> To any sovereign state throughout the world."

He who gives himself entirely to his fellowmen appears to them useless and selfish; but he who gives himself partially to them is pronounced a benefactor and philanthropist.

How does it become a man to behave toward this American government today? I answer, that he cannot without disgrace be associated with it. I cannot for an instant recognize that political organization as *my* government which is the *slave's* government also.

All men recognize the right of revolution; that is, the right to refuse allegiance to, and to resist, the government, when its tyranny or its inefficiency are great and unendurable. But almost all say that such is not the case now. But such was the case, they think, in the Revolution of '75. If one were to tell me that this was a bad government because it taxed certain foreign commodities brought to its ports, it is most probable that I should not make an ado about it, for I can do without them. All machines have their friction; and possibly this does enough good to counterbalance the evil. At any rate, it is a great evil to make a stir about it. But when the friction comes to have its machine, and oppression and robbery are organized, I say, let us not have such a machine any longer. In other words, when a sixth of the population of a nation which has undertaken to be the refuge of liberty are slaves, and a whole country is unjustly overrun and conquered by a foreign army, and subjected to military law, I think that it is not too soon for honest men to rebel and revolutionize. What makes this duty the more urgent is the fact that the country so overrun is not our own, but ours is the invading army.

[William] Paley, a common authority with many on moral questions, in his chapter on the "Duty of Submission to Civil Government," resolves all civil obligation into expediency; and he proceeds to say, "that so long as the interest of the whole society requires it, that is, so long as the established government cannot be resisted or changed without public inconveniency, it is the will of God that the established government be obeyed, and no longer. . . . This principle being admitted, the justice of every particular case of resistance is reduced to a computation of the quantity of the danger and grievance on the one side, and of the probability and expense of redressing it on the other." Of this, he says, every man shall judge for himself. But Paley appears never to have contemplated those cases to which the rule of expediency does not apply, in which a people, as well as an individual, must do justice, cost what it may. If I have unjustly wrested a plank from a drowning man, I must restore it to him though I drown myself. This, according to Paley, would be inconvenient. But he that would save his life, in such a case, shall lose it. This people must cease to hold slaves, and to make war on Mexico, though it cost them their existence as a people.

In their practice, nations agree with Paley; but does any one think that Massachusetts does exactly what is right at the present crisis?

> "A drab of state, a cloth-o'-silver slut,
> To have her train borne up, and her soul
> trail in the dirt."

Practically speaking, the opponents to a reform in Massachusetts are not a hundred thousand politicians at the South, but a hundred thousand merchants and farmers here, who are more interested in commerce and agriculture than they are in humanity, and are not prepared to do justice to the slave and to Mexico, *cost what it may.* I quarrel not with far-off foes, but with those who, near at home, cooperate with, and do the bidding of, those far away, and without whom the latter would be harmless. We are accustomed to say, that the mass of men are unprepared; but improvement is slow, because the few are not materially wiser or better than the many. It is not so important that many should be as good as you, as that there be some absolute goodness somewhere; for that will leaven the whole lump. There are thousands who are *in opinion* opposed to slavery and to the war, who yet in effect do nothing to put an end to them; who, esteeming themselves children of Washington and Franklin, sit down with their hands in their pockets, and say that they know not what to do, and do nothing; who even postpone the question of freedom to the question of free trade, and quietly read the prices-current along with the latest advices from Mexico, after dinner, and, it may be, fall asleep over them both. What is the price-current of an honest man and patriot today? They hesitate, and they regret, and sometimes they petition; but they do nothing in earnest and with effect. They will wait, well disposed, for others to remedy the evil, that they may no longer have it to regret. At most, they give only a cheap vote, and a feeble countenance and Godspeed, to the right, as it goes by them. There are nine hundred and ninety-nine patrons of virtue to one virtuous man. But it is easier to deal with the real possessor of a thing than with the temporary guardian of it.

All voting is a sort of gaming, like checkers or backgammon, with a slight moral tinge to it, a playing with right and wrong, with moral questions; and betting naturally accompanies it. The character of the voters is not staked. I cast my vote, perchance, as I think right; but I am not vitally concerned that that right should prevail. I am willing to leave it to the majority. Its obligation, therefore, never exceeds that of expediency. Even voting *for the right* is *doing* nothing for it. It is only expressing to men feebly your desire that it should prevail. A wise man will not leave the right to the mercy of chance, nor wish it to prevail through the power of the majority. There is but little virtue in the action of masses of men. When the majority shall at length vote for the abolition of slavery, it will be because they are indifferent to slavery, or because there is but little slavery left to be abolished by their vote. *They* will then be the only slaves. Only *his* vote can hasten the abolition of slavery who asserts his own freedom by his vote.

I hear of a convention to be held at Baltimore, or elsewhere, for the selection of a candidate for the Presidency, made up chiefly of editors, and men who are politicians by profession; but I think, what is it to any independent, intelligent, and respectable man what decision they may come to? Shall we not have the advantage of his wisdom and honesty, nevertheless? Can we not count upon some independent votes? Are there not many individuals in the country who do not attend conventions? But no: I find that the respectable man, so called, has immediately drifted from his position, and despairs of his country, when his country has more reason to despair of him. He forthwith adopts one of the candidates thus selected as the only *available* one, thus proving that he is himself *available* for any purposes of the demagogue. His vote is of no more worth than that of any unprincipled foreigner or hireling native, who may have been bought. O for a man who is a *man,* and, as my neighbor says, has a bone in his back which you cannot pass your hand through! Our statistics are at fault: the population has been returned too large. How many *men* are there to a square thousand miles in this country? Hardly one. Does not America offer any inducement for men to settle here? The American has dwindled into an Odd Fellow—one who may be known by the development of his organ of gregariousness, and a manifest lack of intellect and cheerful self-reliance; whose first and chief concern, on coming into the world, is to see that the almshouses are in good repair; and, before yet he has lawfully donned the virile garb, to collect a fund for the support of the widows and orphans that may be; who, in short, ventures to live only by the aid of the Mutual Insurance company, which has promised to bury him decently.

It is not a man's duty, as a matter of course, to devote himself to the eradication of any, even the most enormous wrong; he may still properly have other concerns to engage him; but it is his duty, at least, to wash his hands of it, and, if he gives it no thought longer, not to give it practically his support. If I devote myself to other pursuits and contemplations, I must first see, at least, that I do not pursue them sitting upon another man's shoulders. I must get off him first, that he may pursue his contemplations too. See what gross inconsistency is tolerated. I have heard some of my townsmen say, "I should like to have them order me out to help put down an insurrection of the slaves, or to march to Mexico; see if I would go"; and yet these very men have each, directly by their allegiance, and so indirectly, at least, by their money, furnished a substitute. The soldier is applauded who refuses to serve in an unjust war by those who do not refuse to sustain the unjust government which makes the war; is applauded by those whose own act and authority he disregards and sets at naught; as if the state were penitent to that degree that it hired one to scourge it while it sinned, but not to that degree that it left off sinning for a moment. Thus, under the name of Order and Civil Government, we all are made at last to pay homage to and support our own meanness. After the first blush of sin comes its indifference; and from immoral it becomes, as it were, *un*moral, and not quite unnecessary to that life which we have made.

The broadest and most prevalent error requires the most disinterested virtue to sustain it. The slight reproach to which the virtue of patriotism is commonly liable, the noble are most likely to incur. Those who, while they disapprove of the character and measures of a government, yield to it their allegiance and support are undoubtedly its most conscientious supporters, and so frequently the most serious obstacles to reform. Some are petitioning the state to dissolve the Union, to disregard the requisitions of the President. Why do they not dissolve it themselves—the union between themselves and the state—and refuse to pay their quota into its treasury? Do not they stand in the same relation to the state that the state does to the Union? And have not the same reasons prevented the state from resisting the Union which have prevented them from resisting the state?

How can a man be satisfied to entertain an opinion merely, and enjoy *it*? Is there any enjoyment in it, if his opinion is that he is aggrieved? If you are cheated out of a single dollar by your neighbor, you do not rest satisfied with knowing that you are cheated, or with saying that you are cheated, or even with petitioning him to pay you your due; but you take effectual steps at once to obtain the full amount, and see that you are never cheated again. Action from principle, the perception and the performance of right, changes things and relations; it is essentially revolutionary, and does not consist wholly with anything which was. It not only divides states and churches, it divides families; ay, it divides the *individual,* separating the diabolical in him from the divine.

Unjust laws exist: shall we be content to obey them, or shall we endeavor to amend them, and obey them until we have succeeded, or shall we transgress them at once? Men generally, under such a government as this, think that they ought to wait until they have persuaded the majority to alter them. They think that, if they should resist, the remedy would be worse than the evil. But it is the fault of the government itself that the remedy is worse than the evil. *It* makes it worse. Why is it not more apt to anticipate and provide for reform? Why does it not cherish its wise minority? Why does it cry and resist before it is hurt? Why does it not encourage its citizens to be on the alert to point out its faults, and do better than it would have them? Why does it always crucify Christ, and excommunicate Copernicus and Luther, and pronounce Washington and Franklin rebels?

One would think, that a deliberate and practical denial of its authority was the only offense never contemplated by government; else, why has it not assigned its definite, its suitable and proportionate penalty? If a man who has no property refuses but once to earn nine shillings for the state, he is put in prison for a period unlimited by any law that I know, and determined only by the discretion of those who placed him there; but if he should steal ninety times nine shillings from the state, he is soon permitted to go at large again.

If the injustice is part of the necessary friction of the machine of government, let it go, let it go: perchance it will wear smooth—certainly the machine will wear out. If the injustice has a spring, or a pulley, or a rope, or a crank, exclusively for itself, then perhaps you may consider whether the remedy will not be worse than the evil; but if it is of such a nature that it requires you to be the agent of injustice to another, then, I say, break the law. Let your life be a counter friction to stop the machine. What I have to do is to see, at any rate, that I do not lend myself to the wrong which I condemn.

As for adopting the ways which the state has provided for remedying the evil, I know not of such ways. They take too much time, and a man's life will be gone. I have other affairs to attend to. I came into this world, not chiefly to make this a good place to live in, but to live in it, be it good or bad. A man has not everything to do, but something; and because he cannot do *everything*, it is not necessary that he should do *something* wrong. It is not my business to be petitioning the Governor or the Legislature any more than it is theirs to petition me; and if they should not hear my petition, what should I do then? But in this case the state has provided no way: its very constitution is the evil. This may seem to be harsh and stubborn and unconciliatory; but it is to treat with the utmost kindness and consideration the only spirit that can appreciate or deserves it. So is all change for the better, like birth and death, which convulse the body.

I do not hesitate to say, that those who call themselves Abolitionists should at once effectually withdraw their support, both in person and property, from the government of Massachusetts, and not wait till they constitute a majority of one, before they suffer the right to prevail through them. I think that it is enough if they have God on their side, without waiting for that other one. Moreover, any man more right than his neighbors constitutes a majority of one already.

23

Petyr Kropotkin

Mutual Aid (1902)

Petyr Kropotkin (1842–1921) was the son of a prince, an aide to Tsar Alexander II, an officer in the Russian army, and a prominent scientist. In the 1870s he became an anarchist and began to organize Russian workers. Imprisoned for his activities, he escaped and fled to western Europe, where he remained until the revolution when, shortly before his death, he returned to Russia. In Mutual Aid, Kropotkin's best-known book, he argues that cooperation is the chief factor in the evolution of species.

Introduction

TWO ASPECTS OF animal life impressed me most during the journeys which I made in my youth in Eastern Siberia and Northern Manchuria. One of them was the extreme severity of the struggle for existence which most species of animals have to carry on against an inclement Nature; the enormous destruction of life which periodically results from natural agencies; and the consequent paucity of life over the vast territory which fell under my observation. And the other was, that even in those few spots where animal life teemed in abundance, I failed to find—although I was eagerly looking for it—that bitter struggle for the means of existence, *among animals belonging to the same species,* which was considered by most Darwinists (though not always by Darwin himself) as the dominant characteristic of struggle for life, and the main factor of evolution.

The terrible snow-storms which sweep over the northern portion of Eurasia in the later part of the winter, and the glazed frost that often follows them; the frosts and the snow-storms which return every year in the second half of May, when the trees are already in full blossom and insect life swarms everywhere; the early frosts and, occasionally, the heavy snowfalls in July and August, which suddenly destroy myriads of insects, as well as the second broods of the birds in the prairies; the torrential rains, due to the monsoons, which fall in more temperate regions in August and September—resulting in inundations on a scale which is only known in America and in Eastern Asia, and swamping, on the plateaus, areas as wide as European States; and finally, the heavy snowfalls, early in October, which eventually render a territory as large as France and Germany, absolutely impracticable for ruminants, and destroy them by the thousand—these were the conditions under which I saw animal life struggling in Northern Asia. They made me realize at an early date the overwhelming importance in Nature of what Darwin described as "the natural checks to over-multiplication," in comparison to the struggle between individuals of the same species for the means of subsistence, which may go on here and there, to some limited extent, but never attains the importance of the former. Paucity of life, under-population—not over-population—being the distinctive feature of that immense part of the globe which we name Northern Asia, I conceived since then serious doubts—which subsequent study has only confirmed—as to the reality of that fearful competition for food and life within each species, which was an article of faith with most Darwinists, and, consequently, as to the dominant part which this sort of competition was supposed to play in the evolution of new species.

On the other hand, wherever I saw animal life in abundance, as, for instance, on the lakes where scores of species and millions of individuals came together to rear their progeny; in the colonies of rodents; in the migrations of birds which took place at that time on a truly American scale along the Usuri; and especially in a migration of fallow-deer which I witnessed on the Amur, and during which scores of thousands of these intelligent animals came together from an immense territory, flying before the coming deep snow, in order to cross the Amur where it is narrowest—in all these scenes of animal life which passed before my eyes, I saw Mutual Aid and Mutual Support carried on to an extent which made me suspect in it a feature of the greatest importance for the maintenance of life, the preservation of each species, and its further evolution.

And finally, I saw among the semi-wild cattle and horses in Transbaikalia, among the wild ruminants everywhere, the squirrels, and so on, that when animals have to struggle against scarcity of food, in consequence of one of the above-mentioned causes, the whole of that portion of the species which is affected by the calamity, comes out of the ordeal so much impoverished in vigour and health, that *no progressive evolution of the species can be based upon such periods of keen competition*.

Consequently, when my attention was drawn, later on, to the relations between Darwinism and Sociology, I could agree with none of the works and pamphlets that had been written upon this important subject. They all endeavoured to prove that Man, owing to his higher intelligence and knowledge, *may* mitigate the harshness of the struggle for life between men; but they all recognized at the same time that the struggle for the means of existence, of every animal against all its congeners, and of every man against all other men, was "a law of Nature." This view, however, I could not accept, because I was persuaded that to admit a pitiless inner war for life within each species, and to see in that war a condition of progress, was to admit something which not only had not yet been proved, but also lacked confirmation from direct observation. . . .

It may be objected to this book that both animals and men are represented in it under too favourable an aspect; that their sociable qualities are insisted upon, while their anti-social and self-asserting instincts are hardly touched upon. This was, however, unavoidable. We have heard so much lately of the "harsh, pitiless struggle for life," which was said to be carried on by every animal against all other animals, every "savage" against all other "savages," and every civilized man against all his co-citizens—and these assertions have so much become an article of faith—that it was necessary, first of all, to oppose to them a wide series of facts showing animal and human life under a quite different aspect. It was necessary to indicate the overwhelming importance which sociable habits play in Nature and in the progressive evolution of both the animal species and human beings: to prove that they secure to animals a better protection from their enemies, very often facilities for getting food (winter provisions, migrations, etc.), longevity, and therefore a greater facility for the development of intellectual faculties; and that they have given to men, in addition to the same advantages, the possibility of working out those institutions which have enabled mankind to survive in its hard struggle against Nature, and to progress, notwithstanding all the vicissitudes of its history. It is a book on the law of Mutual Aid, viewed at as one of the chief factors of evolution—not on *all* factors of evolution and their respective values; and this first book had to be written, before the latter could become possible.

I should certainly be the last to underrate the part which the self-assertion of the individual has played in the evolution of mankind. However, this subject requires, I believe, a much deeper treatment than the one it has hitherto received. In the history of mankind, individual self-assertion has often been, and continually is, something quite different from, and far larger and deeper than, the petty, unintelligent narrowmindedness, which, with a large class of writers, goes for "individualism" and "self-assertion." Nor have history-making individuals been limited to those whom historians have represented as heroes. My intention, consequently, is, if circumstances permit it, to discuss separately the part taken by the self-assertion of the individual in the progressive evolution of mankind. I can only make in this place the following general remark: When the Mutual Aid institutions—the tribe, the village community, the guilds, the mediaeval city—began, in the course of history, to lose their primitive character, to be invaded by parasitic growths, and thus to become hindrances to progress, the revolt of individuals against these institutions took always two different aspects. Part of those who rose up strove to purify the old institutions, or to work out a higher form of commonwealth, based upon the same Mutual Aid principles; they tried, for instance, to introduce the principle of "compensation," instead of the *lex talionis,* and later on, the pardon of offenses, or a still higher ideal of equality before the human conscience, *in lieu* of "compensation," according to class-value. But at the very same time, another portion of the same individual rebels endeavoured to break down the protective institutions of mutual support, with no other intention but to increase their own wealth and their own powers. In this three-cornered contest, between the two classes of revolted individuals and the supporters of what existed, lies the real tragedy of history. But to delineate that contest, and honestly to study the part played in the evolution of mankind by each one of these three forces, would require at least as many years as it took me to write this book. . . .

Chapter 7
Mutual Aid amongst Ourselves

Popular revolts at the beginning of the State-period. Mutual Aid institutions of the present time. The village community: its struggles for resisting its abolition by the State. Habits derived from the village-community life, retained in our modern villages. Switzerland, France, Germany, Russia.

The mutual-aid tendency in man has so remote an origin, and is so deeply interwoven with all the past evolution of the human race, that it has been maintained by mankind up to the present time, notwithstanding all vicissitudes of history. It was chiefly evolved during periods of peace and prosperity; but when even the greatest calamities befell men—when whole countries were laid waste by wars, and whole populations were decimated by misery, or groaned under the yoke of tyranny—the same tendency continued to live in the villages and among the poorer classes in the towns; it still kept them together, and in the long run it reacted even upon those ruling, fighting, and devastating minorities which dismissed it as sentimental nonsense. And whenever mankind had to work out a new social organization, adapted to a new phase of development, its constructive genius always drew the elements and the inspiration for the new departure from that same ever-living tendency. New economical and social institutions, in so far as they were a creation of the masses, new ethical systems, and new religions, all have originated from the same source, and the ethical progress of our race, viewed in its broad lines, appears as a gradual extension of the mutual-aid principles from the tribe to always larger and larger agglomerations, so as to finally embrace one day the whole of mankind, without respect to its divers creeds, languages, and races.

After having passed through the savage tribe, and next through the village community, the Europeans came to work out in mediaeval times a new form of organization, which had the advantage of allowing great latitude for individual initiative, while it largely responded at the same time to man's need of mutual support. A federation of village communities, covered by a network of guilds and fraternities, was called into existence in the mediaeval cities. The immense results achieved under this new form of union—in well-being for all, in industries, art, science, and commerce—were discussed at some length in two preceding chapters, and an attempt was also made to show why, towards the end of the fifteenth century, the mediaeval republics—surrounded by domains of hostile feudal lords, unable to free the peasants from servitude, and gradually corrupted by ideas of Roman Caesarism—were doomed to become a prey to the growing military States.

However, before submitting for three centuries to come, to the all-absorbing authority of the State, the masses of the people made a formidable attempt at reconstructing society on the old basis of mutual aid and support. It is well known by this time that the great movement of the reform was not a mere revolt against the abuses of the Catholic Church. It had its constructive ideal as well, and that ideal was life in free, brotherly communities. Those of the early writings and sermons of the period which found most response with the masses were imbued with ideas of the economical and social brotherhood of mankind. The "Twelve Articles" and similar professions of faith, which were circulated among the German and Swiss peasants and artisans, maintained not only every one's right to interpret the Bible according to his own understanding, but also included the demand of communal lands being restored to the village communities and feudal servitudes being abolished, and they always alluded to the "true" faith—a faith of brotherhood. At the same time scores of thousands of men and women joined the communist fraternities of Moravia, giving them all their fortune and living in numerous and prosperous settlements constructed upon the principles of communism.[1] Only wholesale massacres by the thousand could put a stop to this widely spread popular movement, and it was by the sword, the fire, and the rack that the young States secured their first and decisive victory over the masses of the people.[2]

For the next three centuries the States, both on the Continent and in these islands, systematically weeded out all institutions in which the mutual-aid tendency had formerly found its expression. The village communities were bereft of their folkmotes, their courts and independent administration; their lands were confiscated. The guilds were spoiliated of their possessions and liberties, and placed under the control, the fancy, and the bribery of the State's official. The cities were divested of their sovereignty, and the very springs of their inner life—the folkmote, the elected justices and administration, the sovereign parish and the sovereign guild—were annihilated; the State's functionary took possession of every link of what formerly was an organic whole. Under that fatal policy and the wars it engendered, whole regions, once populous and wealthy, were laid bare; rich cities became insignificant boroughs; the very roads which connected them with other cities became impracticable. Industry, art, and knowledge fell into decay. Political education, science, and law were rendered subservient to the idea of State centralization. It was taught in the Universities and from the pulpit that the institutions in which men formerly used to embody their needs of mutual support could not be tolerated in a properly organized State; that the State alone could represent the bonds of union between its subjects; that federalism and "particularism" were the enemies of progress, and the State was the only proper initiator of further development. By the end of the last century the kings on the Continent, the Parliament in these isles, and the revolutionary Convention in France, although they were at war with each other, agreed in asserting that no separate unions between citizens must exist within the State; that hard labour and death were the only suitable punishments to workers who dared to enter into "coalitions." "No state within the State!" The State alone, and the State's Church, must take care of matters of general interest, while the subjects must represent loose aggregations of individuals, connected by no particular bonds, bound to appeal to the Government each time that they feel a common need. Up to the middle of this century this was the theory and practice in Europe. Even commercial and industrial societies were looked at with suspicion. As to the workers, their unions were treated as unlawful almost within our own lifetime in this country and within the last twenty years on the Continent. The whole system of our State education was such that up to the present time, even in this country, a notable portion of society would treat as a revolutionary measure the concession of such rights as every one, freeman or serf, exercised five hundred years ago in the village folkmote, the guild, the parish, and the city.

The absorption of all social functions by the State necessarily favoured the development of an unbridled, narrow-minded individualism. In proportion as the obligations towards the State grew in numbers the citizens were evidently relieved from their obligations towards each other. In the guild—and in mediaeval times every man belonged to some guild or fraternity—two "brothers" were bound to watch in turns a brother who had fallen ill; it would be sufficient now to give one's neighbour the address of the next paupers' hospital. In barbarian society, to assist at a fight between two men, arisen from a quarrel, and not to prevent it from taking a fatal issue, meant to be oneself treated as a murderer; but under the theory of the all-protecting State the bystander need not intrude: it is the policeman's business to interfere, or not. And while in a savage land, among the Hottentots, it would be scandalous to eat without having loudly called out thrice whether there is not somebody wanting to share the food, all that a respectable citizen has to do now is to pay the poor tax and to let the starving starve. The result is, that the theory which maintains that men can, and must, seek their own happiness in a disregard of other people's wants is now triumphant all round—in law, in science, in religion. It is the religion of the day, and to doubt of its efficacy is to be a dangerous Utopian. Science loudly proclaims that the struggle of each against all is the leading principle of nature, and of human societies as well. To that struggle Biology ascribes the progressive evolution of the animal world. History takes the same line of argument; and political economists, in their naïve ignorance, trace all progress of modern industry and machinery to the "wonderful" effects of the same principle. The very religion of the pulpit is a religion of individualism, slightly mitigated by more or less charitable relations to one's neighbours, chiefly on Sundays. "Practical" men and theorists, men of science and religious preachers, lawyers and politicians, all agree upon one thing—that individualism may be more or less softened in its harshest effects by charity, but that it is the only secure basis for the maintenance of society and its ulterior progress.

It seems, therefore, hopeless to look for mutual-aid institutions and practices in modern society. What could remain of them? And yet, as soon as we try to ascertain how the millions of human beings live, and begin to study their everyday relations, we are struck with the immense part which the mutual-aid and mutual-support principles play even now-a-days in human life. Although the destruction of mutual-aid institutions has been going on in practice and theory, for full three or four hundred years, hundreds of millions of men continue to live under such institutions; they piously maintain them and endeavour to reconstitute them where they have ceased to exist. In our mutual relations every one of us has his moments of revolt against the fashionable individualistic creed of the day, and actions in which men are guided by their mutual-aid inclinations constitute so great a part of our daily intercourse that if a stop to such actions could be put all further ethical progress would be stopped at once. Human society itself could not be maintained for even so much as the lifetime of one single generation. These facts, mostly neglected by sociologists and yet of the first importance for the life and further elevation of mankind, we are now going to analyze, beginning with the standing institutions of mutual support, and passing next to those acts of mutual aid which have their origin in personal or social sympathies. . . .

Conclusion

If we take now the teachings which can be borrowed from the analysis of modern society, in connection with the body of evidence relative to the importance of mutual aid in the evolution of the animal world and of mankind, we may sum up our inquiry as follows.

In the animal world we have seen that the vast majority of species live in societies, and that they find in association the best arms for the struggle for life: understood, of course, in its wide Darwinian sense—not as a struggle for the sheer means of existence, but as a struggle against all natural conditions unfavourable to the species. The animal species, in which individual struggle has been reduced to its narrowest limits, and the practice of mutual aid has attained the greatest development, are invariably the most numerous, the most prosperous, and the most open to further progress. The mutual protection which is obtained in this case, the possibility of attaining old age and of accumulating experience, the higher intellectual development, and the further growth of sociable habits, secure the maintenance of the species, its extension, and its further progressive evolution. The unsociable species, on the contrary, are doomed to decay.

Going next over to man, we found him living in clans and tribes at the very dawn of the stone age; we saw a wide series of social institutions developed already in the lower savage stage, in the clan and the tribe; and we found that the earliest tribal customs and habits gave to mankind the embryo of all the institutions which made later on the leading aspects of further progress. Out of the savage tribe grew up the barbarian village community; and a new, still wider, circle of social customs, habits, and institutions, numbers of which are still alive among ourselves, was developed under the principles of common possession of a given territory and common defence of it, under the jurisdiction of the village folkmote, and in the federation of villages belonging, or supposed to belong, to one stem. And when new requirements induced men to make a new start, they made it in the city, which represented a double network of territorial units (village communities), connected with guilds—these latter arising out of the common prosecution of a given art or craft, or for mutual support and defence.

And finally, in the last two chapters facts were produced to show that although the growth of the State on the pattern of Imperial Rome had put a violent end to all mediaeval institutions for mutual support, this new aspect of civilization could not last. The State, based upon loose aggregations of individuals and undertaking to be their only bond of union, did not answer its purpose. The mutual-aid tendency finally broke down its iron rules; it reappeared and reasserted itself in an infinity of associations which now tend to embrace all aspects of life and to take possession of all that is required by man for life and for reproducing the waste occasioned by life.

It will probably be remarked that mutual aid, even though it may represent one of the factors of evolution, covers nevertheless one aspect only of human relations; that by the side of this current, powerful though it may be, there is, and always has been, the other current—the self-assertion of the individual, not only in its efforts to attain personal or caste superiority, economical, political, and spiritual, but also in its much more important although less evident function of breaking through the bonds, always prone to become crystallized, which the tribe, the village community, the city, and the State impose upon the individual. In other words, there is the self-assertion of the individual taken as progressive element.

It is evident that no review of evolution can be complete, unless these two dominant currents are analyzed. However, the self-assertion of the individual or of groups of individuals, their struggles for superiority, and the conflicts which resulted therefrom, have already been analyzed, described, and glorified from time immemorial. In fact, up to the present time, this current alone has received attention from the epical poet, the annalist, the historian, and the sociologist. History, such as it has hitherto been written, is almost entirely a description of the ways and means by which theocracy, military power, autocracy, and, later on, the richer classes' rule have been promoted, established, and maintained. The struggles between these forces make, in fact, the substance of history. We may thus take the knowledge of the individual factor in human history as granted—even though there is full room for a new study of the subject on the lines just alluded to; while, on the other side, the mutual-aid factor has been hitherto totally lost sight of; it was simply denied, or even scoffed at, by the writers of the present and past generation. It was therefore necessary to show, first of all, the immense part which this factor plays in the evolution of both the animal world and human societies. Only after this has been fully recognized will it be possible to proceed to a comparison between the two factors.

To make even a rough estimate of their relative importance by any method more or less statistical, is evidently impossible. One single war—we all know—may be productive of more evil, immediate and subsequent, than hundreds of years of the unchecked action of the mutual-aid principle may be productive of good. But when we see that in the animal world, progressive development and mutual aid go hand in hand, while the inner struggle within the species is concomitant with retrogressive development; when we notice that with man, even success in struggle and war is proportionate to the development of mutual aid in each of the two conflicting nations, cities, parties, or tribes, and that in the process of evolution war itself (so far as it can go this way) has been made subservient to the ends of progress in mutual aid within the nation, the city or the clan—we already obtain a perception of the dominating influence of the mutual-aid factor as an element of progress. But we see also that the practice of mutual aid and its successive developments have created the very conditions of society life in which man was enabled to develop his arts, knowledge, and intelligence; and that the periods when institutions based on the mutual-aid tendency took their greatest development were also the periods of the greatest progress in arts, industry, and science. In fact, the study of the inner life of the mediaeval city and of the ancient Greek cities reveals the fact that the combination of mutual aid, as it was practised within the guild and the Greek clan, with a large initiative which was left to the individual and the group by means of the federative principle, gave to mankind the two greatest periods of its history—the ancient Greek city and the mediaeval city periods; while the ruin of the above institutions during the State periods of history, which followed, corresponded in both cases to a rapid decay.

As to the sudden industrial progress which has been achieved during our own century, and which is usually ascribed to the triumph of individualism and competition, it certainly has a much deeper origin than that. Once the great discoveries of the fifteenth century were made, especially that of the pressure of the atmosphere, supported by a series of advances in natural philosophy—and they were made under the mediaeval city organization—once these discoveries were made, the invention of the steam-motor, and all the revolution which the conquest of a new power implied, had necessarily to follow. If the mediaeval cities had lived to bring their discoveries to that point, the ethical consequences of the revolution effected by steam might have been different; but the same revolution in technics and science would have inevitably taken place. It remains, indeed, an open question whether the general decay of industries which followed the ruin of the free cities, and was especially noticeable in the first part of the eighteenth century, did not considerably retard the appearance of the steam-engine as well as the consequent revolution in arts. When we consider the astounding rapidity of industrial progress from the twelfth to the fifteenth centuries—in weaving, working of metals, architecture and navigation, and ponder over the scientific discoveries which that industrial progress led to at the end of the fifteenth century—we must ask ourselves whether mankind was not delayed in its taking full advantage of these conquests when a general depression of arts and industries took place in Europe after the decay of mediaeval civilization. Surely it was not the disappearance of the artist-artisan, nor the ruin of large cities and the extinction of intercourse between them, which could favour the industrial revolution; and we know indeed that James Watt spent twenty or more years of his life in order to render his invention serviceable, because he could not find in the last century what he would have readily found in mediaeval Florence of Brügge, that is, the artisans capable of realizing his devices in metal, and of giving them the artistic finish and precision which the steam-engine requires.

To attribute, therefore, the industrial progress of our century to the war of each against all which it has proclaimed, is to reason like the man who, knowing not the causes of rain, attributes it to the victim he has immolated before his clay idol. For industrial progress, as for each other conquest over nature, mutual aid and close intercourse certainly are, as they have been, much more advantageous than mutual struggle.

However, it is especially in the domain of ethics that the dominating importance of the mutual-aid principle appears in full. That mutual aid is the real foundation of our ethical conceptions seems evident enough. But whatever the opinions as to the first origin of the mutual-aid feeling or instinct may be—whether a biological or a supernatural cause is ascribed to it—we must trace its existence as far back as to the lowest stages of the animal world; and from these stages we can follow its uninterrupted evolution, in opposition to a number of contrary agencies, through all degrees of human development, up to the present times. Even the new religions which were born from time to time—always at epochs when the mutual-aid principle was falling into decay in the theocracies and despotic States of the East, or at the decline of the Roman Empire—even the new religions have only reaffirmed that same principle. They found their first supporters among the humble, in the lowest, down-trodden layers of society, where the mutual-aid principle is the necessary foundation of every-day life; and the new forms of union which were introduced in the earliest Buddhist and Christian communities, in the Moravian brotherhoods and so on, took the character of a return to the best aspects of mutual aid in early tribal life.

Each time, however, that an attempt to return to this old principle was made, its fundamental idea itself was widened. From the clan it was extended to the stem, to the federation of stems, to the nation, and finally—in ideal, at least—to the whole of mankind. It was also refined at the same time. In primitive Buddhism, in primitive Christianity, in the writings of some of the Mussulman teachers, in the early movements of the Reform, and especially in the ethical and philosophical movements of the last century and of our own times, the total abandonment of the idea of revenge, or of "due reward"—of good for good and evil for evil—is affirmed more and more vigorously. The higher conception of "no revenge for wrongs," and of freely giving more than one expects to receive from his neighbours, is proclaimed as being the real principle of morality—a principle superior to mere equivalence, equity, or justice, and more conductive to happiness. And man is appealed to be guided in his acts, not merely by love, which is always personal, or at the best tribal, but by the perception of his oneness with each human being. In the practice of mutual aid, which we can retrace to the earliest beginnings of evolution, we thus find the positive and undoubted origin of our ethical conceptions; and we can affirm that in the ethical progress of man, mutual support—not mutual struggle—has had the leading part. In its wide extension, even at the present time, we also see the best guarantee of a still loftier evolution of our race.

NOTES

1. A bulky literature, dealing with this formerly much neglected subject, is now growing in Germany. Keller's works, *Ein Apostel der Wiedertaüfer* and *Geschichte der Wiedertaüfer*, Cornelius's *Geschichte des münsterischen Aufruhrs*, and Jannsen's *Geschichte des deutschen Volkes* may be named as the leading sources. The first attempt at familiarizing English readers with the results of the wide researches made in German in this direction has been made in an excellent little work by Richard Heath—"Anabaptism from Its Rise at Zwickau to Its Fall at Munster, 1521–1236," London, 1895 (*Baptist Manuals*, vol. 1.)—where the leading features of the movement are well indicated, and full bibligraphical information is given. Also K. Kautsky's *Communism in Central Europe in the Time of the Reformation*, London, 1897.

2. Few of our contemporaries realize both the extent of this movement and the means by which it was suppressed. But those who wrote immediately after the great peasant war estimated at from 100,000 to 150,000 men the number of peasants slaughtered after their defeat in Germany. See Zimmermann's *Allgemeine Geschichte des grossen Baurenkrieges*. For the measures taken to suppress the movement in the Netherlands see Richard Heath's "Anabaptism."

24

Mikhail Bakunin

———◆◆———

"Scientific Anarchism" (*ca.* 1869–1873)

Mikhail Bakunin (1814–1876) is best known for his conflict with Karl Marx, which ended in the disintegration of the First International Workingmen's Association. That conflict was personal and political: beneath their genuine dislike, which resulted in petty accusations—as when Marx claimed that Bakunin had embezzled a 300-ruble advance for a Russian translation of Capital*—were serious doctrinal differences. Bakunin supported peasant revolution and stressed the dangers of proletarian dictatorship. His major works include* Marxism, Freedom, and the State *(1870–1872),* God and the State *(1871), and* Statism and Anarchy *(1873).*

Ethics: Truly Human or Anarchist Morality

The Instinct for Individual Self-Preservation and for Preservation of Species. The elements of what we call morality are already found in the animal world. In all the animal species, with no exception, but with a great difference in development, we find two opposed instincts: the instinct for preservation of the individual and the instinct for preservation of the species; or, speaking in human terms, *the egoistic and the social instincts.* From the point of view of science, as well as from the point of view of Nature itself, those two instincts are equally natural and hence equally legitimate, and, what is even more important, they are equally necessary in the natural economy of beings. The individual instinct is in itself the basic condition for the preservation of the species, for if the individuals did not defend themselves with all their power against all the privations and against all the external pressures constantly menacing their existence, the species itself, which only lives in and through the individuals, would not be able to maintain its existence. But if those two drives are to be judged only from the absolute point of view of the exclusive interest of the species, one may say that social instinct is good, and individual instinct, inasmuch as it is opposed to it, is bad.

The Unbalanced Development of Those Instincts in the Animal World and Among Higher Insects. With the ants and bees it is virtue that predominates, for in both of them social instinct appears to over-ride individual instinct. It is altogether different among wild beasts, and in general one may say that in the animal world egoism is the predominant instinct. Here the instinct of the species, on the contrary, awakens only during short intervals and lasts only so long as it is necessary for the procreation and education of the family.

Egoism and Sociability Are Paramount in Man. It is altogether different with man. It seems, and this has provided one of the pillars of his great superiority over other animal species, that both these opposed instincts—egoism and sociability—are much more powerful and much less distinct from each other in man than among all the other animals. He is more ferocious in his egoism than the wildest beasts and at the same time he is more sociable than ants and bees.

Humanity Is Present Even in the Lowest Character. All human morality, every collective and individual morality, rests basically upon *human respect.* What do we mean by human respect? It is recognition of humanity, of human right and of human dignity in every man of whatever race, color, and degree of intellectual and even moral development he may be. But if a man is stupid, wicked, contemptible, can I respect him? If that were the case, no doubt I would find it impossible to respect his villainy, his stupidity, and brutality; they would make me feel disgusted and indignant; and if necessary I would take most energetic measures against them, not even stopping at killing such a man if no other means were left to defend my life against him, my rights, or whatever I respect or is dear to me. But in the midst of the most energetic and fierce—and if necessary even mortal—struggle against him, I would have to respect his human nature.

Regeneration of Character Possible with Change of Social Conditions. Only at the price of showing such respect can I retain my own human dignity. But if he himself does not recognize this dignity in others, can we recognize the same in himself? If he is a kind of ferocious animal, or even worse, as it sometimes happens would it not be to indulge in fictions if we acknowledged human nature in him? Not at all! For whatever depths his intellectual and moral degradation may reach at any particular moment, unless he is congenitally insane or an idiot—in which case he should be treated not as a criminal but as a sick person—and if he is in full possession of the sense and intelligence allotted to him by Nature, then his human character, amid the most monstrous deviations, still exists in him, in a very real manner, *as a possibility, always present with him so long as he lives, that somehow he may become aware of his humanity if only a radical change is effected in the social conditions which made him what he is.*

Social Environment the Determining Factor. Take the most intelligent ape possessing the finest character, put it under the best, most humane conditions—and you will never succeed in making a man out of it. Take the most hardened criminal or a man of the poorest mind, and, provided neither one of them suffers from some organic *lesion* which may bring about either idiocy or incurable madness of the other—you will soon come to recognize that if one has become a criminal and the other has not yet developed to the conscious awareness of his humanity and human duties, *the fault lies not with them nor with their nature, but with the social environment in which they were born and have been developing. . . .*

Socialism Is Based on Determinism. Socialism, being founded upon positive science, absolutely rejects the doctrine of *"free will."* It recognizes that whatever is called human vice and virtue is absolutely the product of the combined action of Nature and society. Nature, through its ethnographical, physiological, and pathological action, creates faculties and dispositions which are called natural, and the organization of society develops them, or on the other hand halts or falsifies their development. All individuals, with no exception, are at every moment of their lives what Nature and society have made them.

Improvement of Man's Morality Is Conditioned by Moralization of Social Environment. Hence it clearly follows that to make men moral it is necessary to make their social environment moral. And that can be done in only one way: by assuring the triumph of justice, that is, the complete liberty of everyone in the most perfect equality for all. Inequality of conditions and rights, and the resulting lack of liberty for all, is the great collective iniquity begetting all individual iniquities. Suppress this source of iniquities and all the rest will vanish along with it.

A Moral Environment Will Be Created by Revolution. In view of the lack of enthusiasm shown by men of privilege for moral improvement—or what is the same thing, for equalizing their rights with others—we fear that the triumph of justice can be effected only through a social revolution.

Three things are necessary for men to become moral, that is, complete men in the full meaning of the word: birth under hygienic conditions; a rational and integral education accompanied by an upbringing based upon respect for work, reason, equality, and liberty; and a social environment wherein the human individual, enjoying full liberty, will be equal, in fact and by right, to all others.

Does such an environment exist? It does not. It follows then that it has to be created. . . .

Freedom Is Not the Negation of Solidarity. Social solidarity is the first human law; freedom is the second law. Both laws interpenetrate each other and, being inseparable, constitute the essence of humanity. Thus freedom is not the negation of solidarity; on the contrary, it represents the development and, so to speak, the humanizing of it.

Thus respect for the freedom of someone else constitutes the highest duty of men. The only virtue is to love this freedom and serve it. This is the basis of all morality, and there is no other basis.

Since freedom is the result and the clearest expression of solidarity, that is, of mutuality of interests, it can be realized only under conditions of equality. Political equality can be based only upon economic and social equality. And justice is precisely the realization of freedom through such equality. . . .

Society and the Individual

Society Is the Basis of Human Existence. Society, preceding in time any development of humanity, and fully partaking of the almighty power of natural laws, actions, and manifestations, constitutes the very essence of human existence. Man is born into society, just as an ant is born into an ant-hill or a bee into its hive; man is born into society from the very moment that he becomes a human being, that is, a being possessing to a greater or lesser extent the power of speech and thought. Man does not choose society; on the contrary, he is the product of the latter, and he is just as inevitably subjected to natural laws governing his necessary development as to all other natural laws which he must obey. Society antedates and at the same time survives every human individual, being in this respect like Nature itself; it is eternal like Nature, or rather, having been born upon this earth, it will last as long as our earth itself.

Revolt Against Society Is Inconceivable. A radical revolt by man against society would therefore be just as impossible as a revolt against Nature, human society being nothing else but the last great manifestation or creation of Nature upon this earth. And an individual who would want to rebel against society, that is, against Nature in general and his own nature in particular, would place himself beyond the pale of real existence, would plunge into nothingness, into an absolute void, into lifeless abstraction, into God. It follows that it is just as impossible to ask whether society is good or evil as it is to ask whether Nature—the universal, material, real, absolute, sole, and supreme being—is good or evil. It is much more than that: it is an immense, overwhelming fact, a positive and primitive fact, having existence prior to all consciousness, to all ideas, to all intellectual and moral discernment. It is the very basis, it is the world in which inevitably, and at a much later stage, there begins to develop what we call good and evil.

There Is No Humanity Outside of Society. During a very long period, lasting thousands of years, our species roamed the earth in isolated herds. That was before, together with the first emergence of speech and the first gleam of thought, there awakened within the social and animal environment of one of those human herds, the first self-conscious or free individuality. Apart from society, man would never cease to be a speechless and an unreasoning animal, a thousand times poorer and more dependent upon external Nature than most of the quadrupeds, above which he now towers so proudly.

Even the most wretched individual of our present society could not exist and develop without the cumulative social efforts of countless generations. Thus the individual, his freedom and reason, are the products of society, and not *vice versa:* society is not the product of individuals comprising it; and the higher, the more fully the individual is developed, the greater his freedom—and the more he is the product of society, the more does he receive from society and the greater his debt to it. . . .

Property Could Arise Only in the State

The doctrinaire philosophers, as well as the jurists and economists, always assume that property came into existence before the rise of the State, whereas it is clear that the juridical idea of property, as well as family law, could arise historically only in the State, the first inevitable act of which was the establishment of this law and of property.

Property is a god. This god already has its theology (which is called State politics and juridical right) and also its morality, the most adequate expression of which is summed up in the phrase: "This man is worth so much."

The Theology and Metaphysics of Property. The property god also has its metaphysics. It is the science of the bourgeois economists. Like any metaphysics it is a sort of twilight, a compromise between truth and falsehood, with the latter benefiting by it. It seeks to give falsehood the appearance of truth and leads truth to falsehood. Political economy seeks to sanctify property through labor and to represent it as the realization, the fruit, of labor. If it succeeds in doing this, it will save property and the bourgeois world. For labor is sacred, and whatever is based upon labor, is good, just, moral, human, legitimate. One's faith, however, must be of the sturdy kind to enable him to swallow this doctrine, for we see the vast majority of workers deprived of all property; and what is more, we have the avowed statements of the economists and their own scientific proofs to the effect that under the present economic organization, which they defend so passionately, the masses *will never come to own property;* that, consequently, their labor does not emancipate and ennoble them, for, all their labor notwithstanding, they are condemned to remain eternally without property—that is, outside of morality and humanity.

Only Non-Productive Labor Yields Property. On the other hand, we see that the richest property owners, and consequently the most worthy, humane, moral, and respectable citizens, are precisely those who work the least or who do not work at all. To that the answer is made that nowadays it is impossible to remain rich—to preserve, and even less so, to increase one's wealth—without working. Well, let us then agree upon the proper use of the term *work:* there is work and work. There is productive labor and there is the labor of exploitation.

The first is the labor of the proletariat; the second that of property owners. He who turns to good account lands cultivated by someone else, simply exploits someone else's labor. And he who increases the value of his capital, whether in industry or in commerce, exploits the labor of others. The banks which grow rich as a result of thousands of credit transactions, the Stock Exchange speculators, the shareholders who get large dividends without raising a finger; Napoleon III, who became so rich that he was able to raise to wealth all his protégés; King William I, who, proud of his victories, is preparing to levy billions upon poor unfortunate France, and who already has become rich and is enriching his soldiers with this plunder—all those people are workers, but what kind of workers! Highway robbers! Thieves and plain ordinary robbers are "workers" to a much greater extent, for in order to get rich in their own way they have to "work" with their own hands.

It is evident to anyone who is not blind about this matter that productive work creates wealth and yields the producers only misery, and that it is only non-productive, exploiting labor that yields property. But since property is morality, it follows that *morality, as the bourgeois understands it, consists in exploiting someone else's labor.*

Criticism of Marxism

... *The Fallacious Premise of the Doctrinaire Revolutionists.* Idealists of all sorts, metaphysicians, positivists, those who uphold the priority of science over life, the doctrinaire revolutionists—all of them champion, with equal zeal although differing in their argumentation, the idea of the State and State power, seeing in them, quite logically from their point of view, the only salvation of society. *Quite logically,* I say, having taken as their basis the tenet—a fallacious tenet in our opinion—that thought is prior to life, and abstract theory is prior to social practice, and that therefore sociological science must become the starting point for social upheavals and social reconstruction—they necessarily arrived at the conclusion that since thought, theory, and science are, for the present at least, the property of only a very few people, those few should direct social life, and not only foment and stimulate but rule all movements of the people; and that on the morrow of the Revolution the new social organization should be set up not by the free integration of workers' associations, villages, communes, and regions from below upward, conforming to the needs and instincts of the people, but solely by the dictatorial power of this learned minority, allegedly expressing the general will of the people.

The Common Ground of the Theory of Revolutionary Dictatorship and the Theory of the State. It is upon this fiction of people's representation and upon the actual fact of the masses of people being ruled by a small handful of privileged individuals elected, or for that matter not even elected, by throngs herded together on election day and ever ignorant of why and whom they elect; it is upon this fictitious and abstract expression of the fancied general will and thought of the people, of which the living and real people have not the slightest conception— that the theory of the State and that of revolutionary dictatorship are based in equal measure.

Between revolutionary dictatorship and the State principle the difference is only in the external situation. In substance both are one and the same: the ruling of the majority by the minority in the name of the alleged stupidity of the first and the alleged superior intelligence of the second. Therefore both are equally reactionary, both having as their result the invariable consolidation of the political and economic privileges of the ruling minority and the political and economic enslavement of the masses of people.

Doctrinaire Socialists Are the Friends of the State. Now it is clear why the doctrinaire Socialists who have for their aim the overthrow of the existing authorities and regimes in order to build upon the ruins of the latter a dictatorship of their own, never were and never will be enemies of the State, but on the contrary that they were and ever will be its zealous champions. They are enemies of the powers-that-be only because they cannot take their places. They are enemies of the existing political institutions because such institutions preclude the possibility of carrying out their own dictatorship, but they are at the same time the most ardent friends of State power, without which the Revolution, by freeing the toiling masses, would deprive this would-be revolutionary minority of all hope of putting the people into a new harness and heap upon them the blessings of their governmental measures. . . .

Socialism via Peaceful Reform. How is the proletariat to capture the State? There are but two means available for that purpose: a political revolution or a lawful agitation on behalf of a peaceful reform. [Ferdinand] Lassalle chose the second course.

In this sense, and for that purpose, he formed a political party of German workers possessing considerable strength, having organized it along hierarchical lines and submitted it to rigorous discipline and to a sort of personal dictatorship; in other words, he did what M. Marx had tried to do to the International during the last three years. Marx's attempt proved to be a failure, while Lassalle was wholly successful. As his direct aim Lassalle set himself the task of impelling a popular movement and agitation for the winning of universal suffrage, for the right of the people to elect State representatives and authorities.

Having won this right, the people would send their own representatives to the Parliament, which in turn, by various decrees and enactments, would transform the given State into a People's State (*Volks-Staat*). And the first task of this People's State would be to open unlimited credit to the producers' and consumers' associations, which only then will be able to combat bourgeois capital, finally succeeding in conquering and assimilating it. When this process of absorption has been completed, then the period of the radical change of society will dawn upon mankind.

The Fiction of the People's State. Such is the program of Lassalle, such is the program of the Social-Democratic Party. Properly speaking, it belongs not to Lassalle but to Marx, who fully expressed it in the well-known *Manifesto of the Communist Party* published by Marx and Engels in 1848. This program is likewise alluded to in the first *Manifesto of the International Association* written by Marx in 1864, in the words: "The first duty of the working class should be to conquer for itself political power," or as the *Manifesto of the Communist Party* says in that respect: "The first step in the revolution by the working class, is to raise the proletariat to the position of a ruling class. . . . The proletariat will centralize the instruments of production in the hands of the State, that is, the proletariat raised to the position of a ruling class."

We already have expressed our abhorrence for the theories of Lassalle and Marx, theories which counseled the workers—if not as their ultimate ideal, at least as their next chief aim—*to form a People's State,* which, according to their interpretation, will only be "the proletariat raised to the position of a ruling class."

. . . But the State connotes domination, and domination connotes exploitation, which proves that the term *the People's State (Volks-Staat),* which unfortunately still remains the watchword of the German Social-Democratic Party, is a ridiculous contradiction, a fiction, a falsehood—doubtless an unconscious falsehood—and for the proletariat a very dangerous pitfall. The State, however popular it be made in form, will always be an institution of domination and exploitation, and it will therefore ever remain a permanent source of slavery and misery. Consequently there is no other means of emancipating the people economically and politically, of providing them with well-being and freedom, but to abolish the State, all States, and once and for all do away with that which until now has been called *politics*.

The Implication of the Dictatorship of the Proletariat. One may ask then: if the proletariat is to be the ruling class, over whom will it rule? The answer is that there will remain another proletariat which will be subjected to this new domination, this new State. It may be, for example, the peasant "rabble," which, as we know, does not stand in great favor with the Marxists, and who, finding themselves on a lower level of culture, probably will be ruled by the city and factory proletariat; or considered from the national point of view, the Slavs, for instance, will assume, for precisely the same reason, the same position of slavish subjection to the victorious German proletariat which the latter now holds with respect to its own bourgeoisie.

If there is a State, there must necessarily be domination, and therefore slavery; a State without slavery, overt or concealed, is unthinkable—and that is why we are enemies of the State.

What does it mean: "the proletariat raised into a ruling class?" Will the proletariat as a whole be at the head of the government? There are about forty million Germans. Will all the forty million be members of the government? The whole people will govern and there will be no one to be governed. It means that there will be no government, no State, but if there is a State in existence there will be people who are governed, and there will be slaves.

This dilemma is solved very simply in the Marxist theory. By a people's government they mean the governing of people by means of a small number of representatives elected by the people. Universal suffrage—the right of the whole people to elect its so-called representatives and rulers of the State—this is the last word of the Marxists as well as of the democratic school. And this is a falsehood behind which lurks the despotism of a governing minority, a falsehood which is all the more dangerous in that it appears as the ostensible expression of a people's will.

Thus, from whatever angle we approach the problem, we arrive at the same sorry result: the rule of great masses of people by a small privileged minority. But, the Marxists say, this minority will consist of workers. Yes, indeed, of *exworkers*, who, once they become rulers or representatives of the people, cease to be workers and begin to look down upon the toiling people. From that time on they represent not the people but themselves and their own claims to govern the people. Those who doubt this know precious little about human nature.

Dictatorship Cannot Beget Freedom. But these elected representatives will be convinced Socialists, and learned Socialists at that. The words "learned Socialist" and "scientific Socialism" which are met with constantly in the works and speeches of the Lassalleans and Marxists, prove only that this would-be people's State will be nothing else but despotic rule over the toiling masses by a new, numerically small aristocracy of genuine or sham scientists. The people lack learning and so they will be freed from the cares of government, will be wholly regimented into one common herd of governed people. Emancipation indeed!

The Marxists are aware of this contradiction, and, realizing that government by scientists (the most distressing, offensive, and despicable type of government in the world) will be, notwithstanding its democratic form, a veritable dictatorship—console themselves with the thought that this dictatorship will be only temporary and of brief duration. They say that the only care and aim of this government will be to educate and uplift the people—economically and politically—to such an extent that no government will be necessary, and that the State, having lost its political character, that is, its character of rule and domination, will turn all by itself into an altogether free organization of economic interest and communes.

Here we have an obvious contradiction. If their State is going to be a genuine people's State, why should it then dissolve itself—and if its rule is necessary for the real emancipation of the people, how dare they call it a people's State? Our polemic had the effect of making them realize that freedom or Anarchism, that is, the free organization of workers from below upward, is the ultimate aim of social development, and that every State, their own people's State included, is a yoke, which means that it begets despotism on one hand and slavery on the other.

They say that this State yoke—the dictatorship—is a necessary transitional means in order to attain the emancipation of the people: Anarchism or freedom is the goal, the State or dictatorship is the means. Thus to free the working masses, it is first necessary to enslave them.

That is as far as our polemic went. They maintain that only a dictatorship—their dictatorship, of course—can create the will of the people, while our answer to this is: No dictatorship can have any other aim but that of self-perpetuation, and it can beget only slavery in the people tolerating it: freedom can be created only by freedom, that is, by a universal rebellion on the part of the people and free organization of the toiling masses from the bottom up.

Powerfully Centralized State the Goal of the Marxists. While the political and social theory of the anti-State Socialists or Anarchists leads them steadily toward a full break with all governments, and with all varieties of bourgeois policy, leaving no other way out but a social revolution, the opposite theory of the State Communists and scientific authority also inevitably draws and enmeshes its partisans, under the pretext of political tactics, into ceaseless compromises with governments and political parties; that is, it pushes them toward downright reaction.

The basic point of Lassalle's politico-social program and the Communist theory of Marx is *the (imaginary) emancipation of the proletariat by means of the State*. But for that it is necessary that the State consent to take upon itself the task of emancipating the proletariat from the yoke of bourgeois capital. How can the State be imbued with such a will? There are only two means whereby that can be done.

The proletariat ought to wage a revolution in order to capture the State—a rather heroic undertaking. And in our opinion, once the proletariat captures the State, it should immediately proceed with its destruction as the everlasting prison for the toiling masses. Yet according to the theory of M. Marx, the people not only should not destroy the State but should strengthen and reinforce it, and transfer it in this form into the hands of its benefactors, guardians, and teachers, the chiefs of the Communist Party—in a word, to M. Marx and his friends, who will begin to emancipate it in their own fashion.

They will concentrate all the powers of government in strong hands, because the very fact that the people are ignorant necessitates strong, solicitous care by the government. They will create a single State bank, concentrating in its hands all the commercial, industrial, agricultural, and even scientific production; and they will divide the mass of people into two armies—industrial and agricultural armies under the direct command of the State engineers who will constitute the new privileged scientific-political class.

One can see then what a shining goal the German Communist school has set up before the people.

Social-Democratic Program Examined

. . . *Political and Social Revolution Must Go Together.* We should ruthlessly eliminate the politics of bourgeois democrats or bourgeois Socialists who, in declaring that "political liberty is the *preliminary* condition of economic emancipation," understand by those words only the following: "Political reforms, or a political revolution, must precede economic reforms or an economic revolution; therefore the workers must ally themselves with the more or less radical bourgeois in order to carry out a political revolution together with the bourgeoisie, and then wage an economic revolution against the latter."

We loudly protest against this baneful theory, which can end only with the workers being used once more as an instrument against themselves and being turned over again to bourgeois exploitation.

To win political freedom first can signify no other thing but to win this freedom only, leaving for the first days at least economic and social relations in the same old state—that is, leaving the proprietors and capitalists with their insolent wealth, and the workers with their poverty.

But, it is argued, this freedom, once won, shall serve the workers later as an instrument with which to win *equality* or *economic justice.*

Freedom is indeed a magnificent and powerful instrument. The question, however, is whether workers really can make use of it, whether it will actually be in their possession, or whether, as has been the case until now, their *political liberty* will prove to be only a deceitful appearance, a mere fiction.

Stateless Socialism: Anarchism

. . . *Organization of Productive Forces in Place of Political Power.* It is necessary to abolish completely, both in principle and in fact, all that which is called political power; for, so long as political power exists, there will be ruler and ruled, masters and slaves, exploiters and exploited. Once abolished, political power should be replaced by an organization of productive forces and economic service.

Notwithstanding the enormous development of modern states—a development which in its ultimate phase is quite logically reducing the State to an absurdity—it is becoming evident that the days of the State and the State principle are numbered. Already we can see approaching the full emancipation of the toiling masses and their free social organization, free from governmental intervention, formed by economic associations of the people and brushing aside all the old State frontiers and national distinctions, and having as its basis only productive labor, humanized labor, having one common interest in spite of its diversity.

The Ideal of the People. This ideal of course appears to the people as signifying first of all the end of want, the end of poverty, and the full satisfaction of all material needs by means of collective labor, equal and obligatory for all, and then, as the end of domination and the free organization of the people's lives in accordance with their needs—not from the top down, as we have it in the State, but from the bottom up, an organization formed by the people themselves, apart from all governments and parliaments, a free union of associations of agricultural and factory workers, of communes, regions, and nations, and finally, in the more remote future, the universal human brotherhood, triumphing above the ruins of all States.

The Program of a Free Society. Outside of the Mazzinian system, which is the system of the republic in the form of a State, there is no other system but that of the republic as a commune, the republic as a federation, a Socialist and a genuine people's republic—the system of Anarchism. It is the politics of the Social Revolution, which aims at the abolition of the State, and the economic, altogether free organization of the people, an organization from below upward, by means of a federation.

. . . There will be no possibility of the existence of a political government, for this government will be transformed into a simple administration of common affairs.

Our program can be summed up in a few words:

Peace, emancipation, and the happiness of the oppressed.

War upon all oppressors and all despoilers.

Full restitution to workers: all the capital, the factories, and all the instruments of work and raw materials to go to the associations, and the land to those who cultivate it with their own hands.

Liberty, justice, and fraternity in regard to all human beings born upon the earth. Equality for all.

To all, with no distinction whatever, all the means of development, education, and upbringing, and the equal possibility of living while working.

Organizing of a society by means of a free federation from below upward, of workers' associations, industrial as well as agricultural, scientific as well as literary associations—first into a commune, then a federation of communes into regions, of regions into nations, and of nations into an international fraternal association.

Correct Tactics During a Revolution. In a social revolution, which in everything is diametrically opposed to a political revolution, the actions of individuals hardly count at all, whereas the spontaneous action of the masses is everything. All that individuals can do is to clarify, propagate, and work out ideas corresponding to the popular instinct, and, what is more, to contribute their incessant efforts to revolutionary organization of the natural power of the masses—but nothing else beyond that; the rest can and should be done by the people themselves. Any other method would lead to political dictatorship, to the reemergence of the State, of privileges, of inequalities, of all the oppressions of the State—that is, it would lead in a roundabout but logical way toward re-establishment of political, social, and economic slavery of the masses of people.

Varlin and all his friends, like all sincere Socialists, and in general like all workers born and brought up among the people, shared to a high degree this perfectly legitimate bias against the initiative coming from isolated individuals, against the domination exercised by superior individuals, and being above all consistent, they extended the same prejudice and distrust to their own persons. . . .

Freedom Must Go Hand-in-Hand with Equality. I am a convinced partisan of *economic and social equality*, for I know that outside of this equality, freedom, justice, human dignity, morality, and the well-being of individuals as well as the prosperity of nations are all nothing but so many falsehoods. But being at the same time a partisan of freedom—the first condition of humanity—I believe that equality should be established in the world by a spontaneous organization of labor and collective property, by the free organization of producers' associations into communes, and the free federation of communes—but nowise by means of the supreme and tutelary action of the State.

The Difference Between Authoritarian and Libertarian Revolutionists. It is this point which mainly divides the Socialists or revolutionary collectivists from the authoritarian Communists, the partisans of the absolute initiative of the State. The goal of both is the same: both parties want the creation of a new social order based exclusively upon collective labor, under economic conditions that are equal for all—that is, under conditions of collective ownership of the tools of production.

Only the Communists imagine that they can attain [this goal] through development and organization of the political power of the working classes, and chiefly of the city proletariat, aided by bourgeois radicalism—whereas the revolutionary Socialists, the enemies of all ambiguous alliances, believe, on the contrary, that this common goal can be attained not through the political but through the social (and therefore anti-political) organization and power of the working masses of the cities and villages, including all those who, though belonging by birth to the higher classes, have broken with their past of their own free will, and have openly joined the proletariat and accepted its program.

The Methods of the Communists and the Anarchists. Hence the two different methods. The Communists believe that it is necessary to organize the forces of the workers in order to take possession of the political might of the State. The revolutionary Socialists organize with the view of destroying, or if you prefer a more refined expression, of liquidating the State. The Communists are the partisans of the principle and practice of authority, while revolutionary Socialists place their faith only in freedom. Both are equally the partisans of science, which is to destroy superstition and take the place of faith; but the first want to impose science upon the people, while the revolutionary collectivists try to diffuse science and knowledge among the people, so that the various groups of human society, when convinced by propaganda, may organize and spontaneously combine into federations, in accordance with their natural tendencies and their real interests, but never according to a plan traced in advance and *imposed upon the ignorant masses* by a few "superior" minds.

Revolutionary Socialists believe that there is much more of practical reason and intelligence in the instinctive aspirations and real needs of the masses of people than in the profound minds of all these learned doctors and self-appointed tutors of humanity, who, having before them the sorry example of so many abortive attempts to make humanity happy, still intend to keep on working in the same direction. But revolutionary Socialists believe, on the contrary, that humanity has permitted itself to be ruled for a long time, much too long, and that the source of its misfortune lies not in this nor in any other form of government but in the principle and the very existence of the government, whatever its nature may be.

It is this difference of opinion, which already has become historic, that now exists between the scientific Communism, developed by the German school and partly accepted by American and English Socialists, and Proudhonism, extensively developed and pushed to its ultimate conclusions, and by now accepted by the proletariat of the Latin countries. Revolutionary Socialism has made its first brilliant and practical appearance in the Paris Commune.

PART FIVE

Fascism

FASCISM ONCE APPEARED to be an isolated development, limited to Germany and Italy, and to a lesser extent, France and Spain in the interwar years. Specific historical factors, among them the Versailles Treaty, economic instability, authoritarian psychology, and charismatic leadership, arguably contributed to those fascist outbreaks. However, a growing number of scholars draw parallels with the rise of right-wing extremism in post-Soviet Europe and the United States today, as globalization poses renewed challenges to the economic security and cultural identity of Western nation-states. Other features of contemporary fascist movements reflect this new global reality: they include reliance on apocalyptic or millennial images of a "global race war"; international alliances between neo-Nazi, white-supremacist, and Christian Identity organizations; sophisticated use of mass communications, including Internet sites and "hate-core" music; and recruitment efforts focused on "vulnerable" populations, such as women and teenagers.[1]

Although these features distinguish neofascism from earlier forms, they also suggest that fascist ideology retains broad appeal. Writing in 1978, David Calleo argued that fascism was not a "German problem," but a human one. He feared then for America's future: "For it is not to Germany that we would go today to find the most egregious examples of ambitions outrunning resources, nor, it might be argued, is it the Germans whose arrogant failure to adjust to a new world strains the international system beyond endurance."[2] Other scholars expressed similar fears. Kenneth Dolbeare wrote that "seasoned observers from across the American political spectrum have warned of the [neofascist] dangers we face from our current political incapacity."[3] Bertram Gross predicted America's future as "friendly fascism," that is, social management by a benevolent bureaucracy.[4]

Nicholas Fraser recently questioned such "alarmists," but also noted that fascists need not "come to power" to achieve "pervasive influence." An interview with Jean-Marie Le Pen, leader of France's ultra-right-wing *Front National* and a presidential candidate in 2002, helped Fraser to understand that influence:

> I didn't understand modern politics, he [Le Pen] told me, gesturing furiously. He meant that he and his ideas had more influence than any number of third-rate so-called democratic hacks whom the rules of the electoral game permitted to say they were in power. I should be looking not at the surfaces, but instead at deep loyalties. And I should examine hatred as if it were a religious movement or a real set of beliefs. Only then would I become capable of acknowledging the real challenge to democracy in Europe.[5]

And, we might add, America.

What, then, is the appeal of fascist ideology? To answer this question, we must examine its essential ideas, one of which is nationalism. As we see later, nationalism can take many forms, ranging from liberal nationalism to the hyper- or ultra-nationalism of fascist ideology. Mussolini clearly articulates fascists' relationship to nationalism: the people crave unity, and the nation—as a living organism whose vitality is embodied in a strong leader—fulfills that need. He writes: "Never before have the peoples thirsted for authority, direction, order, as they do now. If each age has its doctrine, then innumerable symptoms indicate that the doctrine of our age is the Fascist." Mussolini argues that fascism provides an alternative to liberalism and socialism, which are divisive, obsolete, and prosaic ideologies, sharing what he disparages as the "theory of economic man." According to Mussolini, "the economic man does not exist. Man is integral, he is political, he is economic, he is religious, he is saint, he is warrior." The nation and its leader must express all of these aspects of human identity. This theme of "economic" versus "integral" man informs fascist positions on politics and economics.

Fascists argue that the economics of liberalism and socialism undermines the authority of the state. The liberal democratic state is subordinate to individual rights, especially property rights, which it exists to protect, and these individual freedoms potentially threaten national community. Socialists treat states as superstructures, instruments of the ruling class, and they promise that even the proletarian dictatorship will eventually wither away, leaving only freely organized producers. In contrast, the state is the eternal "keystone" of fascist doctrine. Fascists glorify, even spiritualize, the state: it is man's "conscience," his "living, ethical will." Mussolini says, "Thus understood, fascism is totalitarian, and the Fascist State—a synthesis and a unit inclusive of all values—interprets, develops, and potentiates the whole life of a people." As this suggests, fascism "accepts the individual only in so far as his interests coincide with those of the state." Fascists also maintain that the "rights of the state" express "the real essence of the individual." If man is integral, individuals will find meaning through the state, especially through the sacrifices they make for it. Fascists offer a vision of positive liberty (freedom for) which supersedes classical liberals' negative liberty (freedom from). As Mussolini puts it, "Fascism stands for liberty, and for the only liberty worth having, the liberty of the State and of the individual within the State."

Fascists are not only anti-individualistic, but also antimajoritarian. Majority rule divides states, reducing them to the mere sum of individual interests. Hitler speaks contemptuously of representative government—note his description of Parliament, of delegates who are absent, asleep, or engaged in endless, meaningless debates. Representatives, he says, are like "butterflies," for whom each election brings on another metamorphosis: they emerge from their cocoons, pander to their constituents, regain office, then betray their promises and deny responsibility for their actions. According to Hitler, great men cannot win popular elections because the people cannot recognize them. Indeed, he claims that "the revulsion of the masses for every outstanding genius is positively instinctive. Sooner will a camel pass through a needle's eye than a great man be 'discovered' by an election." Yet only great men can embody the collective will. They rule not because of whom they represent, but because of who they are: "The Führer is no 'representative' of a particular group whose wishes he must carry out. . . . He is rather the bearer of the collective will of the people. In his will the will of the people is realized. He transforms the mere feelings of the people into a conscious will."[6] The Führer also takes responsibility for his actions, answering "with his fortune and his life for his choice."

This glorification of the state too easily leads to imperialist politics, for a personified state—a "living, ethical will"—must either grow or die. Mussolini puts it well: "Fascism sees in the imperialistic spirit—i.e., in the tendency of nations to expand—a manifestation of their vitality. In the opposite tendency, which would limit their interests to the home country, it sees a symptom of decadence. Peoples who rise or re-arise are imperialistic; renunciation is characteristic of dying peoples." He insists, however, that this imperialism is not only territorial but also spiritual.

Fascists' attack on "economic man" also involves a critique of capitalist and socialist economics: both the capitalists' free market and the socialists' class war undermine national prosperity. Hitler explains: "Just as surely as a worker sins against the spirit of a real national community when, without regard for the common welfare and the survival of a national economy, he uses his power to raise extortionate demands, an employer breaks this community to the same extent when he conducts his business in an inhuman, exploiting way, misuses the national labor force and makes millions out of its sweat." He concludes that workers and employers should moderate their demands. The "class compromise" he proposes is called corporatism.

Corporatism involves state supervision of production and distribution through functional economic groups. Philippe Schmitter provides the classic definition: "A system of interest and/or attitude representation, a particular model or ideal-typical institutional arrangement for linking the associationally organized interests of civil society with the decisional structures of the state."[7] Schmitter distinguishes corporatism from pluralism: pluralist interest groups are spontaneous, competitive, voluntary, and independent; corporatist ones are functional, cooperative, compulsory, and state-sanctioned. However, he also admits that this distinction is sometimes difficult to draw. Although hardly parallel to Nazi superagencies, many advanced industrialized democracies today have industrial policies and/or planned economies. These also require integrating government, business, and labor. Is this neoliberalism really fascism, albeit a "friendly" variety? Schmitter avoids this conclusion by distinguishing between societal (bottom-up) corporatism and state (top-down) corporatism. Others have argued that these economic arrangements differ only in degree and not in kind, making a continuum more appropriate than a dichotomy.[8] This suggests that the origins of economic arrangements matter less than their outcomes—that state and societal versions of corporatism could converge. If so, fears of a fascist America when government intervenes to manage economic growth may be justified. According to Dolbeare, "an American brand of neofascism" may begin "with the corporatism currently proposed in the neoliberal industrial policy solutions."[9]

So far, I have neglected the most notorious aspect of German fascism: anti-Semitism. In fact, I do not regard anti-Semitism as essential to fascism, though some functional equivalent for it is required. In order to understand this point, it is necessary to delve briefly into the intellectual origins of fascism.[10] Those origins are vast, including the Comte de Gobineau's phrenology, G. W. F. Hegel's *Staatsraison*, Richard Wagner's Bayreuth, and H. S. Chamberlain's Teutonic history, to mention only a few of its sources. However, another influence is most relevant here: the philosophy of Friedrich Nietzsche. Interpreters often try to draw a direct historical connection between Nietzsche and Nazism. Yet this is difficult, because Nietzsche's politics were not overtly Nazi, as he clearly condemned both nationalism and anti-Semitism. A more satisfactory interpretation is that Nietzsche diagnosed a crisis in Western values and then proposed a cure that, tragically, intensified it. Nietzsche speaks of man's need for horizons, for a boundary between what is known and unknown, especially regarding moral values: "This is a universal law: a living thing can only be healthy, strong, and productive within a certain horizon."[11] For Nietzsche, science has demystified the modern world, destroying successive horizons. "God," Nietzsche tells us, "is dead." Yet men continue to crave some higher meaning, some moral purpose, in life. Echoes of conservatism appear here, but for Nietzsche there is no going back to religious or other traditions. His *Übermensch,* an extraordinary individual, will consciously create the new horizons that modern men require.

Hitler and Mussolini are such self-proclaimed creators. Hitler describes propaganda as an "art" that "lies in understanding the emotional ideas of the great masses and finding, through a psychologically correct form, the way to the attention and thence to the heart of the broad masses." To unite the masses, leaders must give them a "scapegoat," a "common enemy" who is morally and/or spiritually depraved. Hitler's history of the struggle between a culture-bearing Aryan and a culture-destroying Jewish race serves this purpose. Mussolini adds the obvious: such myths need not be true. "We have created our myth. The myth is a faith, it is a passion. It is not necessary that it be a reality. It is reality by the fact that it is a goal, a hope, a faith."[12]

Neofascists in more recent years have created new horizons by substituting other functional equivalents for anti-Semitism or combining it with them. Their new "enemies of the people" are drawn from contemporary European and American political contexts. Members of the following groups have been targeted or "scapegoated": "antiracist activists, members of progressive groups, homosexuals, Asians and Asian Americans, Chicanos and Chicanas, Latinos and Latinas, Pakistanis, Indians, doctors and nurses in abortion clinics that serve Aryan women, federal government employees, politicians, lawyers and police officers, and members and clergy of non-Christian religions."[13] More general threats are attributed to terrorists, fundamentalists, and immigrants, who may play the role formerly occupied by Communists. In American politics, racism also persists and has motivated white supremacists from the Ku Klux Klan to align with neo-Nazi groups. Some combination of national identity and national security—even national supremacy—fuels their politics based on hatred of those stigmatized as "Other." Indeed, this extensive list of enemies suggests that when citizens crave meaning and expect to find it in their leaders, democracies may become vulnerable to fascism.

Contemporary right-wing extremist movements exploit that vulnerability. In a recent study, Kathleen Blee discusses four distinct, though connected, racist organizations that operate globally today: (1) the Ku Klux Klan, which is increasingly complex, including a militant branch affiliated with the neo-Nazis and white-power Skinheads, and more domesticated leaders engaged in right-wing electoral politics; (2) the Christian Identity movement, a quasi-religious network of "churches" that regard white Anglo-Saxons as God's "chosen people" and trace the Jews and nonwhite races to Satan's "seed"; (3) the neo-Nazis, a small number of whom retain ties to national socialism while the majority practice cultural separatism and white supremacist racial politics; and (4) the racist Skinheads, youth gangs that are organized around a white-power music culture and are often implicated in murders and other violent crimes.[14]

Blee finds that women are increasingly active in the radical right, despite its outspoken misogyny. Like earlier fascist movements, these groups regard women as "breeders" in the race war and exert strict control over their sexuality. Although some women members may truly believe in racial superiority, many are simply seeking racial safety. In her earlier history of Klanswomen, Blee found that "the main-stay of the 1920s Klan was not the pathological individual," but that, instead, the Klan spoke to "the pervasive strands of racism and unacknowledged privilege that exist among dominant groups in the United States today."[15] Many Klanswomen were good mothers, good neighbors, and good citizens who possessed a "facile ability to fold bitter racial and religious bigotry into progressive politics."[16]

The final two selections in this part illustrate the complex relationships between right-wing extremist groups and the ordinary racism that pervades American society. *The Turner Diaries,* by William Pierce, founder of the Alliance, a neo-Nazi organization, tells the fictitious story of a white revolution against the U.S. government. Written from the perspective of Earl Turner, a "rank and file member of the Organization" who gives his life in a suicide bombing raid on the Pentagon, Pierce's book was "the blueprint" for the 1995 bombing of a federal building in Oklahoma City. It is also well-known to European neofascists: according to Nick Lowles, a writer for *Searchlight,* a British antifascist magazine, "Because of his books, Pierce is undoubtedly the most well-known [American] right-wing figure in Europe. . . . Rightly or wrongly, people here see him as a man who get[s] things done."[17] *The Turner Diaries'* "Epilog," included here, offers Pierce's Leninist model for a global fascist uprising organized by active revolutionary cells in North America, Europe, China, and Russia.

Although the racial violence described and advocated in *The Turner Diaries* remains extreme, Bob Moser's "Age of Rage, Young Extremists Find New Targets—and New Recruits" discusses the increase in hate and hate crimes post–9/11, especially among more affluent white teenagers. Explanations for this phenomenon vary, ranging from increased access to Internet hate sites, "hate-core" music, and neo-Nazi "youth action corps" to more general anger and confusion prompted by a loss of (white) identity in an increasingly complex, global world. Whatever the ultimate explanation, Moser concludes that racial extremists offer "easy answers" that can appeal to the latent racism of white American youth today.

Will fascist movements succeed in their efforts to undermine liberal democracy in the United States and Europe? How deeply rooted are liberal democratic traditions there? How strong are the psyches of contemporary democratic citizens? Milton Mayer's *They Thought They Were Free* is among the most disturbing studies of German fascism. Visiting a German village in the 1940s to learn what fascism meant to its inhabitants, Mayer listened to the villagers describe how good life had been under the Nazis. The villagers had belonged to the party or, at least, to the nation; they had had summer camps and job security. None "knew" Nazism as evil, and none had opposed it. Mayer concludes, "What we call freedom is not, even if they had all the freedom we have, an adequate substitute, in my friends' view, for all that they had and have lost." The danger is that "men who did not know that they were slaves do not know that they have been freed."[18]

NOTES

1. Kathleen M. Blee, *Inside Organized Racism: Women in the Hate Movement* (Berkeley: University of California Press, 2002), 189–191.

2. David Calleo, *The German Problem Reconsidered: Germany and the World Order, 1870 to the Present* (Cambridge and New York: Cambridge University Press, 1978), 209.

3. Kenneth Dolbeare, *Democracy at Risk: The Politics of Economic Renewal* (Chatham, N.J.: Chatham House, 1984), 55.

4. Bertram Myron Gross, *Friendly Fascism: The New Face of Power in America* (New York: M. Evans, 1980).

5. Nicholas Fraser, *The Voice of Modern Hatred: Tracing the Rise of Neo-Fascism in Europe* (Woodstock & New York: Overlook Press, 2000), 23.

6. Ernest Hubber, a Nazi philosopher, as quoted by Leon P. Baradat in *Political Ideologies: Their Origins and Impact,* 5th ed. (Englewood Cliffs, N.J.: Prentice Hall, 1994), 251.

7. Philippe C. Schmitter, "Still the Century of Corporatism," *Review of Politics* 36 (January 1974): 86.

8. Michael Ranis, "On the Centralization of Interest Group Systems: Corporatist Theory in the Western Democratic Context," unpublished manuscript, 1984.

9. Kenneth M. Dolbeare and Linda J. Medcalf, *Neopolitics: American Political Ideas in the 1980s* (New York: Random House, 1985), 121.

10. For a brief discussion, see F. L. Carsten, *The Rise of Fascism* (Berkeley: University of California Press, 1967), chap. 1, "Nationalism and Anti-Semitism before 1914."

11. Friedrich Nietzsche, *The Use and Abuse of History,* trans. Adrian Collins (New York: Bobbs-Merrill, 1957), 7.

12. Mussolini, quoted in Baradat, *Political Ideologies,* 240.

13. Blee, *Inside Organized Racism,* 189–190.

14. Ibid., 7.

15. Kathleen M. Blee, *Women of the Klan: Racism and Gender in the 1920s* (Berkeley: University of California Press, 1991), 7.

16. Ibid., 6.

17. "The Alliance and its Allies: William Pierce builds bridges at home, abroad," at www.splcenter.org/intel/intelreport/article.jsp?aid+358 (accessed October 23, 2004).

18. Milton Mayer, *They Thought They Were Free: The Germans, 1933–45* (Chicago: University of Chicago Press, 1955), 62.

25

Benito Mussolini

Fascism: Doctrine and Institutions (1932)

Benito Mussolini (1883–1945) led the Fascist movement to power in Italy, naming himself head of state in 1925, ending parliamentary government, and outlawing opposing political parties. In 1940 he joined the Axis powers in declaring war on the Allies, but his poor leadership during the war led the Fascist Grand Council to dismiss, arrest, and imprison him in 1943. He was later rescued by the Germans, only to be recaptured and executed by the Italians after the defeat of Germany. Although many of his works were ghost-written, he authored such slogans as "Feel don't think"; "Believe, obey, fight"; and "Fascism is Mussolinism; Mussolini is always right."

Fundamental Ideas

LIKE ALL SOUND political conceptions, Fascism is action and it is thought; action in which doctrine is immanent, and doctrine arising from a given system of historical forces in which it is inserted, and working on them from within (1). It has therefore a form correlated to contingencies of time and space; but it has also an ideal content which makes it an expression of truth in the higher region of the history of thought (2). There is no way of exercising a spiritual influence in the world as a human will dominating the will of others, unless one has a conception both of the transient and the specific reality on which that action is to be exercised, and of the permanent and universal reality in which the transient dwells and has its being. To know men one must know man; and to know man one must be acquainted with reality and its laws. There can be no conception of the State which is not fundamentally a conception of life: philosophy or intuition, system of ideas evolving within the framework of logic or concentrated in a vision or a faith, but always, at least potentially, an organic conception of the world.

Thus many of the practical expressions of Fascism—such as party organisation, system of education, discipline—can only be understood when considered in relation to its general attitude toward life. A spiritual attitude (3). Fascism sees in the world not only those superficial, material aspects in which man appears as an individual, standing by himself, self-centered, subject to natural law which instinctively urges him toward a life of selfish momentary pleasure; it sees not only the individual but the nation and the country; individuals and generations bound together by a moral law, with common traditions and a mission which suppressing the instinct for life closed in a brief circle of pleasure, builds up a higher life, founded on duty, a life free from the limitations of time and space, in which the individual, by self-sacrifice, the renunciation of self-interest, by death itself, can achieve that purely spiritual existence in which his value as a man consists.

The conception is therefore a spiritual one, arising from the general reaction of the century against the fla[c]cid materialistic positivism of the nineteenth century. Anti-positivistic but positive; neither sceptical nor agnostic; neither pessimistic nor supinely optimistic as are, generally speaking, the doctrines (all negative) which place the centre of life outside man; whereas, by the exercise of his free will, man can and must create his own world.

Fascism wants man to be active and to engage in action with all his energies; it wants him to be manfully aware of the difficulties besetting him and ready to face them. It conceives of life as a struggle in which it behooves a man to win for himself a really worthy place, first of all by fitting himself (physically, morally, intellectually) to become the implement required for winning it. As for the individual, so for the nation, and so for mankind (4). Hence the high value of culture in all its forms (artistic, religious, scientific) (5), and the outstanding importance of education. Hence also the essential value of work, by which man subjugates nature and creates the human world (economic, political, ethical, intellectual).

This positive conception of life is obviously an ethical one. It invests the whole field of reality as well as the human activities which master it. No action is exempt from moral judgement; no activity can be despoiled of the value which a moral purpose confers on all things. Therefore life, as conceived of by the Fascist, is serious, austere, religious; all its manifestations are poised in a world sustained by moral forces and subject to spiritual responsibilities. The Fascist disdains an "easy" life (6).

The Fascist conception of life is a religious one (7), in which man is viewed in his immanent relation to a higher law, endowed with an objective will transcending the individual and raising him to conscious membership of a spiritual society. Those who perceive nothing beyond opportunistic considerations in the religious policy of the Fascist regime fail to realize that Fascism is not only a system of government but also and above all a system of thought.

In the Fascist conception of history, man is man only by virtue of the spiritual process to which he contributes as a member of the family, the social group, the nation, and in function of history to which all nations bring their contribution. Hence the great value of tradition in records, in language, in customs, in the rules of social life (8). Outside history man is a nonentity. Fascism is therefore opposed to all individualistic abstractions based on eighteenth century materialism; and it is opposed to all Jacobinistic utopias and innovations. It does not believe in the possibility of "happiness" on earth as conceived by the economistic literature of the eighteenth century, and it therefore rejects the teleological notion that at some future time the human family will secure a final settlement of all its difficulties. This notion runs counter to experience which teaches that life is in continual flux and in process of evolution. In politics Fascism aims at realism; in practice it desires to deal only with those problems which are the spontaneous product of historic conditions and which find or suggest their own solutions (9). Only by entering in to the process of reality and taking possession of the forces at work within it, can man act on man and on nature (10).

Anti-individualistic, the Fascist conception of life stresses the importance of the State and accepts the individual only in so far as his interests coincide with those of the State, which stands for the conscience and the universal will of man as a historic entity (11). It is opposed to classical liberalism which arose as a reaction to absolutism and exhausted its historical function when the State became the expression of the conscience and will of the people. Liberalism denied the State in the name of the individual; Fascism reasserts the rights of the State as expressing the real essence of the individual (12). And if liberty is to be the attribute of living men and not of abstract dummies invented by individualistic liberalism, then Fascism stands for liberty, and for the only liberty worth having, the liberty of the State and of the individual within the State (13). The Fascist conception of the State is all-embracing; outside of it no human or spiritual values can exist, much less have value. Thus understood, Fascism is totalitarian, and the Fascist State—a synthesis and a unit inclusive of all values—interprets, develops, and potentiates the whole life of a people (14).

No individuals or groups (political parties, cultural associations, economic unions, social classes) outside the State (15). Fascism is therefore opposed to Socialism to which unity within the State (which amalgamates classes into a single economic and ethical reality) is unknown, and which sees in history nothing but the class struggle. Fascism is likewise opposed to trade-unionism as a class weapon. But when brought within the orbit of the State, Fascism recognises the real needs which gave rise to socialism and trade-unionism, giving them due weight in the guild or corporative system in which divergent interests are coordinated and harmonised in the unity of the State (16).

Grouped according to their several interests, individuals form classes; they form trade-unions when organised according to their several economic activities; but first and foremost they form the State, which is no mere matter of numbers, the sum of the individuals forming the majority. Fascism is therefore opposed to that form of democracy which equates a nation to the majority, lowering it to the level of the largest number (17); but it is the purest form of democracy if the nation be considered—as it should be—from the point of view of quality rather than quantity, as an idea, the mightiest because the most ethical, the most coherent, the truest, expressing itself in a people as the conscience and will of the few, if not, indeed, of one, and ending to express itself in the conscience and the will of the mass, of the whole group ethnically moulded by natural and historical conditions into a nation, advancing, as one conscience and one will, along the self-same line of development and spiritual formation (18). Not a race, nor a geographically defined region, but a people, historically perpetuating itself; a multitude unified by an idea and imbued with the will to live, the will to power, self-consciousness, personality (19).

In so far as it is embodied in a State, this higher personality becomes a nation. It is not the nation which generates the State; that is an antiquated naturalistic concept which afforded a basis for nineteenth-century publicity in favor of national governments. Rather is it the State which creates the nation, conferring volition and therefore real life on a people made aware of their moral unity.

The right to national independence does not arise from any merely literary and idealistic form of self-consciousness; still less from a more or less passive and unconscious *de facto* situation, but from an active, self-conscious, political will expressing itself in action and ready to prove its rights. It arises, in short, from the existence, at least *in fieri*, of a State. Indeed, it is the State which, as the expression of a universal ethical will, creates the right to national independence (20).

A nation, as expressed in the State, is a living, ethical entity only in so far as it is progressive. Inactivity is death. Therefore the State is not only Authority which governs and confers legal form and spiritual value on individual wills, but it is also Power which makes its will felt and respected beyond its own frontiers, thus affording practical proof of the universal character of the decisions necessary to ensure its development. This implies organisation and expansion, potential if not actual. Thus the State equates itself to the will of man, whose development cannot be checked by obstacles and which, by achieving self-expression, demonstrates its own infinity (21).

The Fascist State, as a higher and more powerful expression of personality, is a force, but a spiritual one. It sums up all the manifestations of the moral and intellectual life of man. Its functions cannot therefore be limited to those of enforcing order and keeping the peace, as the liberal doctrine had it. It is no mere mechanical device for defining the sphere within which the individual may duly exercise his supposed rights. The Fascist State is an inwardly accepted standard and rule of conduct, a discipline of the whole person; it permeates the will no less than the intellect. It stands for a principle which becomes the central motive of man as a member of civilised society, sinking deep down into his personality; it dwells in the heart of the man of action and of the thinker, of the artist and of the man of science: soul of the soul (22).

Fascism, in short, is not only a law-giver and a founder of institutions, but an educator and a promoter of spiritual life. It aims at refashioning not only the forms of life but their content—man, his character, and his faith. To achieve this purpose it enforces discipline and uses authority, entering into the soul and ruling with undisputed sway. Therefore it has chosen as its emblem the Lictor's rods, the symbol of unity, strength, and justice.

Political and Social Doctrine

. . . The Fascist negation of socialism, democracy, liberalism, should not, however, be interpreted as implying a desire to drive the world backwards to positions occupied prior to 1789, a year commonly referred to as that which opened the demo-liberal century. History does not travel backwards. The Fascist doctrine has not taken [Joseph] De Maistre as its prophet. Monarchical absolutism is of the past, and so is ecclesiolatry. Dead and done for are feudal privileges and the division of society into closed, uncommunicating castes. Neither has the Fascist conception of authority anything in common with that of a police-ridden State.

A party governing a nation "totalitarianly" is a new departure in history. There are no points of reference nor of comparison. From beneath the ruins of liberal, socialist, and democratic doctrines, Fascism extracts those elements which are still vital. It preserves what may be described as "the acquired facts" of history; it rejects all else. That is to say, it rejects the idea of a doctrine suited to all times and to all people. Granted that the nineteenth century was the century of socialism, liberalism, democracy, this does not mean that the twentieth century must also be the century of socialism, liberalism, democracy. Political doctrines pass; nations remain. We are free to believe that this is the century of authority, a century tending to the "right," a Fascist century. If the nineteenth century was the century of the individual (liberalism implies individualism), we are free to believe that this is the "collective" century, and therefore the century of the State. It is quite logical for a new doctrine to make use of the still vital elements of other doctrines. No doctrine was ever born quite new and bright and unheard of. No doctrine can boast absolute originality. It is always connected, if only historically, with those which preceded it and those which will follow it. Thus the scientific socialism of Marx links up to the utopian socialism of the Fouriers, the Owens, the Saint-Simons; thus the liberalism of the nineteenth century traces its origin back to the illuministic movement of the eighteenth, and the doctrines of democracy to those of the Encyclopaedists. All doctrines aim at directing the activities of men towards a given objective; but these activities in their turn react on the doctrine, modifying and adjusting it to new needs, or outstripping it. A doctrine must therefore be a vital act and not a verbal display. Hence the pragmatic strain in Fascism, its will to power, its will to live, its attitude toward violence, and its value.

The key-stone of the Fascist doctrine is its conception of the State, of its essence, its functions, and its aims. For Fascism the State is absolute, individuals and groups relative. Individuals and groups are admissible in so far as they come within the State. Instead of directing the game and guiding the material and moral progress of the community, the liberal State restricts its activities to recording results. The Fascist State is wide awake and has a will of its own. For this reason it can be described as "ethical." At the first quinquennial assembly of the regime, in 1929, I said:

> The Fascist State is not a night-watchman, solicitous only of the personal safety of the citizens; nor is it organised exclusively for the purpose of guaranteeing a certain degree of material prosperity and relatively peaceful conditions of life, a board of directors would do as much. Neither is it exclusively political, divorced from practical realities and holding itself aloof from the multifarious activities of the citizens and the nation. The State, as conceived and realised by Fascism, is a spiritual and ethical entity for securing the political, juridical, and economic organisation of the nation, an organisation which in its origin and growth is a manifestation of the spirit. The State guarantees the internal and external safety of the country, but it also safeguards and transmits the spirit of the people, elaborated down the ages in its language, its customs, its faith. The State is not only the present, it is also the past and above all the future. Transcending the individual's brief spell of life, the State stands for the immanent conscience of the nation. The forms in which it finds expression change, but the need for it remains. The State educates the citizens to civism, makes them aware of their mission, urges them to unity; its justice harmonises their divergent interests; it transmits to future generations the conquests of the mind in the fields of science, art, law, human solidarity; it leads men up from primitive tribal life to that highest manifestation of human power, imperial rule. The State hands down to future generations the memory of those who laid down their lives to ensure its safety or to obey its laws; it sets up as examples and records for future ages the names of the captains

who enlarged its territory and of the men of genius who have made it famous. Whenever respect for the State declines and the disintegrating and centrifugal tendencies of individuals and groups prevail, nations are headed for decay.

Since 1929 economic and political development have everywhere emphasised these truths. The importance of the State is rapidly growing. The so-called crisis can only be settled by State action and within the orbit of the State. Where are the shades of the Jules Simons who, in the early days of liberalism, proclaimed that the "State should endeavor to render itself useless and prepare to hand in its resignation"? Or of the MacCullochs who in the second half of last century urged that the State should desist from governing too much? And what of the English Bentham who considered that all industry asked of government was to be left alone, and of the German Humbolt who expressed the opinion that the best government was a "lazy" one? What would they say now to the unceasing, inevitable, and urgently requested interventions of government in business? It is true that the second generation of economists was less uncompromising in this respect than the first, and that even Adam Smith left the door ajar—however cautiously—for government intervention in business.

If liberalism spells individualism, Fascism spells government. The Fascist State is, however, a unique and original creation. It is not reactionary but revolutionary, for it anticipates the solution of certain universal problems which have been raised elsewhere, in the political field by the splitting-up of parties, the usurpation of power by parliaments, the irresponsibility of assemblies; in the economic field by the increasingly numerous and important functions discharged by trade-unions and trade associations with their disputes and ententes, affecting both capital and labor; in the ethical field by the need felt for order, discipline, obedience to the moral dictates of patriotism.

Fascism desires the State to be strong and organic, based on broad foundations of popular support. The Fascist State lays claim to rule in the economic field no less than in others; it makes its action felt throughout the length and breadth of the country by means of its corporative, social, and educational institutions, and all the political, economic, and spiritual forces of the nation, organised in their respective associations, circulate within the State.

A State based on millions of individuals who recognise its authority, feel its action, and are ready to serve its ends is not the tyrannical state of a mediaeval lordling. It has nothing in common with the despotic States existing prior to or subsequent to 1789. Far from crushing the individual, the Fascist State multiplies his energies, just as in a regiment a soldier is not diminished but multiplied by the number of his fellow soldiers.

The Fascist State organises the nation, but it leaves the individual adequate elbow room. It has curtailed useless or harmful liberties while preserving those which are essential. In such matters the individual cannot be the judge, but the State only.

The Fascist State is not indifferent to religious phenomena in general nor does it maintain an attitude of indifference to Roman Catholicism, the special, positive religion of Italians. The State has not got a theology but it has a moral code. The Fascist State sees in religion one of the deepest of spiritual manifestations and for this reason it not only respects religion but defends and protects it. The Fascist State does not attempt, as did Robespierre at the height of the revolutionary delirium of the convention, to set up a "god" of its own; nor does it vainly seek, as does Bolschevism, to efface God from the soul of man. Fascism respects the God of ascetics, saints, and heroes, and it also respects God as conceived by the ingenuous and primitive heart of the people, the God to whom their prayers are raised.

The Fascist State expresses the will to exercise power and to command. Here the Roman tradition is embodied in a conception of strength. Imperial power, as understood by the Fascist doctrine, is not only territorial, or military, or commercial; it is also spiritual and ethical. An imperial nation, that is to say a nation which directly or indirectly is a leader of others, can exist without the need of conquering a single square mile of territory. Fascism sees in the imperialistic spirit—i.e., in the tendency of nations to expand—a manifestation of their vitality. In the opposite tendency, which would limit their interests to the home country, it sees a symptom of decadence. Peoples who rise or rearise are imperialistic; renunciation is characteristic of dying peoples. The Fascist doctrine is that best suited to the tendencies and feelings of a people which, like the Italian, after lying fallow during centuries of foreign servitude, is now reasserting itself in the world.

But imperialism implies discipline, the coordination of efforts, a deep sense of duty and a spirit of self-sacrifice. This explains many aspects of the practical activity of the regime, and the direction taken by many of the forces of the State, as also the severity which has to be exercised towards those who would oppose this spontaneous and inevitable movement of twentieth-century Italy by agitating outgrown ideologies of the nineteenth century, ideologies rejected wherever great experiments in political and social transformations are being dared.

Never before have the peoples thirsted for authority, direction, order, as they do now. If each age has its doctrine, then innumerable symptoms indicate that the doctrine of our age is the Fascist. That it is vital is shown by the fact that it has aroused a faith; that this faith has conquered souls is shown by the fact that Fascism can point to its fallen heroes and its martyrs.

Fascism has now acquired throughout the world that universality which belongs to all doctrines which by achieving self-expression represent a moment in the history of human thought.

The Corporations

The statement I submitted yesterday evening defined the guild as we intend and wish to create it, and it also defined its objectives. The corporation, it says, is formed to expand the wealth, the political power, and the well-being of the Italian people. These three objectives are conditional each on the other.

Political strength creates wealth, and wealth in its turn invigorates political action.

I should like to call your attention to the objective stated: the well-being of the Italian people. It is essential that these institutions we have set up should at a given moment be felt and perceived by the masses themselves as instruments through which those masses improve their standard of life.

At a given moment the worker, the tiller of the soil, must be able to say to himself and to his family: if I am really better off to-day, it is due to the institutions which the Fascist Revolution has created.

In all national societies there is an inevitable residuum of poverty. A certain number of people live on the margin of society; special institutions deal with them. Vice versa, that which distresses our spirit is the poverty of strong, capable men, feverishly and vainly seeking work.

We wish that the Italian workers, who interest us as Italians, as workers, and as Fascists, should feel that we are setting up institutions not only to give expression to our doctrinal views but that we are setting up institutions which at a given moment are to yield positive results; concrete, practical, and tangible.

I will not dwell on the conciliatory functions which the corporations can exercise and I see no drawback to the practice of conciliation.

Whenever the Government has to take measures of some importance it already consults the parties concerned. If to-morrow this consultation on certain specified matters becomes obligatory I see no harm in it, for everything that brings the citizen into closer contact with the State, everything that makes the citizen part of the machinery of the State, is advantageous to the social and national aims of Fascism.

A Step Forward on the Path of the Revolution

We have rejected the theory of the economic man, the liberal theory, and we have risen in indignation every time we have heard labor spoken of as a commodity.

The economic man does not exist. Man is integral, he is political, he is economic, he is religious, he is saint, he is warrior.

To-day we are taking a further step forward on the path of the revolution. . . .

In conclusion, let us ask ourselves: can the guild system be applied to other countries? We should ask this question because it is being asked in all other countries; everywhere the matter is being studied and efforts are being made to understand. There is no doubt that in view of the general crisis of capitalism the guild solution will force itself to the front everywhere, but if the guild system is to be carried out fully, completely, integrally, revolutionarily, three conditions are required:

A single party, so that economic discipline may be accompanied by political discipline and so that rising above contrasting interests all may be bound together by a common faith.

Nor is this enough. After the single party there must be the totalitarian State, that is to say the State which absorbs all the energies, all the interests, all the hopes of a people in order to transform and potentiate them.

And this is not yet enough. The third and last and most important condition is to live a period of high ideal tension.

That is why, step by step, we shall strengthen and consolidate all our achievements, why we shall translate into action our whole doctrine. Who can deny that our Fascist period is a period of high ideal tension? No one can deny it. This is the time in which arms have been crowned with victory; institutions renewed; the land redeemed; new cities founded.

26

Adolf Hitler

<hr>

Mein Kampf (1925)

*The son of a minor customs official, Adolf Hitler (1889–1945) rose to become
the leader of the Third Reich. Early sales of his magnum opus,* Mein Kampf,
*were small, but by the late 1920s the book had become a best seller. The suc-
cess of Hitler and his party, the National Socialists (NSDAP, or Nazis), was
closely linked to the Great Depression. As Germany's economy collapsed,
Hitler offered explanations for its problems and solutions to them. Ironically,
one of his solutions, imperialism, led to his demise. He died in 1945 in a
Berlin bunker encircled by Allied troops.*

[Representative Government]

AT THE HEAD of those institutions which could most clearly have revealed the erosion of the Austrian monarchy, even to a shopkeeper not otherwise gifted with
sharp eyes, was one which ought to have had the greatest strength—parliament,
or, as it was called in Austria, the Reichsrat.

Obviously the example of this body had been taken from England, the land of
classical "democracy." From there the whole blissful institution was taken and
transferred as unchanged as possible to Vienna.

The English two-chamber system was solemnly resurrected in the *Abgeordneten-
haus* and the *Herrenhaus.* Except that the "houses" themselves were somewhat
different. When Barry raised his parliament buildings from the waters of the

Thames, he thrust into the history of the British Empire and from it took the decorations for the twelve hundred niches, consoles, and pillars of his magnificent edifice. Thus, in their sculpture and painting, the House of Lords and the House of Commons became the nation's Hall of Fame.

This was where the first difficulty came in for Vienna. For when Hansen, the Danish builder, had completed the last pinnacle on the marble building of the new parliament, there was nothing he could use as decoration except borrowings from antiquity. Roman and Greek statesmen and philosophers now embellish this opera house of Western democracy, and in symbolic irony the *quadrigae* fly from one another in all four directions above the two houses, in this way giving the best external expression of the activities that went on inside the building.

The "nationalities" had vetoed the glorification of Austrian history in this work as an insult and provocation, just as in the Reich itself it was only beneath the thunder of World War battles that they dared to dedicate Wallot's Reichstag Building to the German people by an inscription.

When, not yet twenty years old, I set foot for the first time in the magnificent building on the Franzensring to attend a session of the House of Deputies as a spectator and listener, I was seized with the most conflicting sentiments.

I had always hated parliament, but not as an institution in itself. On the contrary, as a freedom-loving man I could not even conceive of any other possibility of government, for the idea of any sort of dictatorship would, in view of my attitude toward the House of Habsburg, have seemed to me a crime against freedom and all reason.

What contributed no little to this was that as a young man, in consequence of my extensive newspaper reading, I had, without myself realizing it, been inoculated with a certain admiration for the British Parliament, of which I was not easily able to rid myself. The dignity with which the Lower House there fulfilled its tasks (as was so touchingly described in our press) impressed me immensely. Could a people have any more exalted form of self-government?

But for this very reason I was an enemy of the Austrian parliament. I considered its whole mode of conduct unworthy of the great example. To this the following was now added:

The fate of the Germans in the Austrian state was dependent on their position in the Reichsrat. Up to the introduction of universal and secret suffrage, the Germans had had a majority, though an insignificant one, in parliament. Even this condition was precarious, for the Social Democrats, with their unreliable attitude in national questions, always turned against German interests in critical matters affecting the Germans—in order not to alienate the members of the various foreign nationalities. Even in those days the Social Democracy could not be regarded as a German party. And with the introduction of universal suffrage the

German superiority ceased even in a purely numerical sense. There was no longer any obstacle in the path of the further de-Germanization of the state.

For this reason my instinct of national self-preservation caused me even in those days to have little love for a representative body in which the Germans were always misrepresented rather than represented. Yet these were deficiencies which, like so many others, were attributable, not to the thing in itself, but to the Austrian state. I still believed that if a German majority were restored in the representative bodies, there would no longer be any reason for a principled opposition to them, that is, as long as the old state continued to exist at all.

These were my inner sentiments when for the first time I set foot in these halls as hallowed as they were disputed. For me, to be sure, they were hallowed only by the lofty beauty of the magnificent building. A Hellenic miracle on German soil!

How soon was I to grow indignant when I saw the lamentable comedy that unfolded beneath my eyes!

Present were a few hundred of these popular representatives who had to take a position on a question of most vital economic importance.

The very first day was enough to stimulate me to thought for weeks on end.

The intellectual content of what these men said was on a really depressing level, in so far as you could understand their babbling at all; for several of the gentlemen did not speak German, but their native Slavic languages or rather dialects. I now had occasion to hear with my own ears what previously I had known only from reading the newspapers. A wild gesticulating mass screaming all at once in every different key, presided over by a good-natured old uncle who was striving in the sweat of his brow to revive the dignity of the House by violently ringing his bell and alternating gentle reproofs with grave admonitions.

I couldn't help laughing.

A few weeks later I was in the House again. The picture was changed beyond recognition. The hall was absolutely empty. Down below everybody was asleep. A few deputies were in their places, yawning at one another; one was "speaking." A vice-president of the House was present, looking into the hall with obvious boredom.

The first misgivings arose in me. From now on, whenever time offered me the slightest opportunity, I went back and, with silence and attention, viewed whatever picture presented itself, listened to the speeches in so far as they were intelligible, studied the more or less intelligent faces of the elect of the peoples of this woe-begone state—and little by little formed my own ideas.

A year of this tranquil observation sufficed totally to change or eliminate my former view of the nature of this institution. My innermost position was no longer against the misshapen form which this idea assumed in Austria; no, by now I could no longer accept the parliament as such. Up till then I had seen the misfortune of the Austrian parliament in the absence of a German majority; now I saw that its ruination lay in the whole nature and essence of the institution as such.

A whole series of questions rose up in me.

I began to make myself familiar with the democratic principle of majority rule as the foundation of this whole institution, but devoted no less attention to the intellectual and moral values of these gentlemen, supposedly the elect of the nations, who were expected to serve this purpose.

Thus I came to know the institution and its representatives at once.

In the course of a few years, my knowledge and insight shaped a plastic model of that most dignified phenomenon of modern times: the parliamentarian. He began to impress himself upon me in a form which has never since been subjected to any essential change.

Here again the visual instruction of practical reality had prevented me from being stifled by a theory which at first sight seemed seductive to so many, but which none the less must be counted among the symptoms of human degeneration.

The Western democracy of today is the forerunner of Marxism which without it would not be thinkable. It provides this world plague with the culture in which its germs can spread. In its most extreme form, parliamentarianism created a "monstrosity of excrement and fire,"[1] in which, however, sad to say, the "fire" seems to me at the moment to be burned out.

I must be more than thankful to Fate for laying this question before me while I was in Vienna, for I fear that in Germany at that time I would have found the answer too easily. For if I had first encountered this absurd institution known as "parliament" in Berlin, I might have fallen into the opposite fallacy, and not without seemingly good cause have sided with those who saw the salvation of the people and the Reich exclusively in furthering the power of the imperial idea, and who nevertheless were alien and blind at once to the times and the people involved.

In Austria this was impossible.

Here it was not so easy to go from one mistake to the other. If parliament was worthless, the Habsburgs were even more worthless—in no event, less so. To reject "parliamentarianism" was not enough, for the question still remained open: what then? The rejection and abolition of the Reichsrat would have left the House of Habsburg the sole governing force, a thought which, especially for me, was utterly intolerable.

The difficulty of this special case led me to a more thorough contemplation of the problem as such than would otherwise have been likely at such tender years.

What gave me most food for thought was the obvious absence of any responsibility in a single person.

The parliament arrives at some decision whose consequences may be ever so ruinous—nobody bears any responsibility for this, no one can be taken to account. For can it be called an acceptance of responsibility if, after an unparalleled catastrophe, the guilty government resigns? Or if the coalition changes, or even if parliament is itself dissolved?

Can a fluctuating majority of people ever be made responsible in any case?

Isn't the very idea of responsibility bound up with the individual?

But can an individual directing a government be made practically responsible for actions whose preparation and execution must be set exclusively to the account of the will and inclination of a multitude of men?

Or will not the task of a leading statesman be seen, not in the birth of a creative idea or plan as such, but rather in the art of making the brilliance of his projects intelligible to a herd of sheep and blockheads, and subsequently begging for their kind approval?

Is it the criterion of the statesman that he should possess the art of persuasion in as high degree as that of political intelligence in formulating great policies or decisions? Is the incapacity of a leader shown by the fact that he does not succeed in winning for a certain idea the majority of a mob thrown together by more or less savory accidents?

Indeed, has this mob ever understood an idea before success proclaimed its greatness?

Isn't every deed of genius in this world a visible protest of genius against the inertia of the mass?

And what should the statesman do, who does not succeed in gaining the favor of this mob for his plans by flattery?

Should he buy it?

Or, in view of the stupidity of his fellow citizens, should he renounce the execution of the tasks which he has recognized to be vital necessities? Should he resign or should he remain at his post?

In such a case, doesn't a man of true character find himself in a hopeless conflict between knowledge and decency, or rather honest conviction?

Where is the dividing line between his duty toward the general public and his duty toward his personal honor?

Mustn't every true leader refuse to be thus degraded to the level of a political gangster?

And, conversely, mustn't every gangster feel that he is cut out for politics, since it is never he, but some intangible mob, which has to bear the ultimate responsibility?

Mustn't our principle of parliamentary majorities lead to the demolition of any idea of leadership?

Does anyone believe that the progress of this world springs from the mind of majorities and not from the brains of individuals?

Or does anyone expect that the future will be able to dispense with this premise of human culture?

Does it not, on the contrary, today seem more indispensable than ever?

By rejecting the authority of the individual and replacing it by the numbers of some momentary mob, the parliamentary principle of majority rule sins against the basic aristocratic principle of Nature, though it must be said that this view is not necessarily embodied in the present-day decadence of our upper ten thousand.

The devastation caused by this institution of modern parliamentary rule is hard for the reader of Jewish newspapers to imagine, unless he has learned to think and examine independently. It is, first and foremost, the cause of the incredible inundation of all political life with the most inferior, and I mean the most inferior, characters of our time. Just as the true leader will withdraw from all political activity which does not consist primarily in creative achievement and work, but in bargaining and haggling for the favor of the majority, in the same measure this activity will suit the small mind and consequently attract it.

The more dwarfish one of these present-day leather-merchants is in spirit and ability, the more clearly his own insight makes him aware of the lamentable figure he actually cuts—that much more will he sing the praises of a system which does not demand of him the power and genius of a giant, but is satisfied with the craftiness of a village mayor, preferring in fact this kind of wisdom to that of a Pericles. And this kind doesn't have to torment himself with responsibility for his actions. He is entirely removed from such worry, for he well knows that, regardless what the result of his "statesmanlike" bungling may be, his end has long been written in the stars: one day he will have to cede his place to another equally great mind, for it is one of the characteristics of this decadent system that the number of great statesmen increases in proportion as the stature of the individual decreases. With increasing dependence on parliamentary majorities it will inevitably continue to shrink, since on the one hand great minds will refuse to be the stooges of idiotic incompetents and big-mouths, and on the other, conversely, the representatives of the majority, hence of stupidity, hate nothing more passionately than a superior mind.

For such an assembly of wise men of Gotham, it is always a consolation to know that they are headed by a leader whose intelligence is at the level of those present: this will give each one the pleasure of shining from time to time—and, above all, if Tom can be master, what is to prevent Dick and Harry from having their turn too?

This invention of democracy is most intimately related to a quality which in recent times has grown to be a real disgrace, to wit, the cowardice of a great part of our so-called "leadership." What luck to be able to hide behind the skirts of a so-called majority in all decisions of any real importance!

Take a look at one of these political bandits. How anxiously he begs the approval of the majority for every measure, to assure himself of the necessary accomplices, so he can unload the responsibility at any time. And this is one of the main reasons why this type of political activity is always repulsive and hateful to any man who is decent at heart and hence courageous, while it attracts all low characters—and anyone who is unwilling to take personal responsibility for his acts, but seeks a shield, is a cowardly scoundrel. When the leaders of a nation consist of such vile creatures, the results will soon be deplorable. Such a nation will be unable to muster the courage for any determined act; it will prefer to accept any dishonor, even the most shameful, rather than rise to a decision; for there is no one who is prepared of his own accord to pledge his person and his head for the execution of a dauntless resolve.

For there is one thing which we must never forget: in this, too, the majority can never replace the man. It is not only a representative of stupidity, but of cowardice as well. And no more than a hundred empty heads make one wise man will an heroic decision arise from a hundred cowards.

The less the responsibility of the individual leader, the more numerous will be those who, despite their most insignificant stature, feel called upon to put their immortal forces in the service of the nation. Indeed, they will be unable to await their turn; they stand in a long line, and with pain and regret count the number of those waiting ahead of them, calculating almost the precise hour at which, in all probability, their turn will come. Consequently, they long for any change in the office hovering before their eyes, and are thankful for any scandal which thins out the ranks ahead of them. And if some man is unwilling to move from the post he holds, this in their eyes is practically a breach of a holy pact of solidarity. They grow vindictive, and they do not rest until the impudent fellow is at last overthrown, thus turning his warm place back to the public. And, rest assured, he won't recover the position so easily. For as soon as one of these creatures is forced to give up a position, he will try at once to wedge his way into the "waiting-line" unless the hue and cry raised by the others prevents him.

The consequence of all this is a terrifying turn-over in the most important offices and positions of such a state, a result which is always harmful, but sometimes positively catastrophic. For it is not only the simpleton and incompetent who will fall victim to this custom, but to an even greater extent the real leader, if Fate somehow manages to put one in this place. As soon as this fact has been recognized, a solid front will form against him, especially if such a mind has not arisen from their own ranks, but none the less dares to enter into this exalted society. For on principle these gentry like to be among themselves and they hate as a common enemy any brain which stands even slightly above the zeros. And in this respect their instinct is as much sharper as it is deficient in everything else.

The result will be a steadily expanding intellectual impoverishment of the leading circles. The result for the nation and the state, everyone can judge for himself, excepting in so far as he himself is one of these kind of "leaders."

Old Austria possessed the parliamentary regime in its purest form.

To be sure, the prime ministers were always appointed by the Emperor and King, but this very appointment was nothing but the execution of the parliamentary will. The haggling and bargaining for the individual portfolios represented Western democracy of the first water. And the results corresponded to the principles applied. Particularly the change of individual personalities occurred in shorter and shorter terms, ultimately becoming a veritable chase. In the same measure, the stature of the "statesmen" steadily diminished until finally no one remained but that type of parliamentary gangster whose statesmanship could only be measured and recognized by their ability in pasting together the coalitions of the moment; in other words, concluding those pettiest of political bargains which alone demonstrate the fitness of these representatives of the people for practical work.

Thus the Viennese school transmitted the best impressions in this field.

But what attracted me no less was to compare the ability and knowledge of these representatives of the people and the tasks which awaited them. In this case, whether I liked it or not, I was impelled to examine more closely the intellectual horizon of these elect of the nations themselves, and in so doing, I could not avoid giving the necessary attention to the processes which lead to the discovery of these ornaments of our public life.

The way in which the real ability of these gentlemen was applied and placed in the service of the fatherland—in other words the technical process of their activity—was also worthy of thorough study and investigation.

The more determined I was to penetrate these inner conditions, to study the personalities and material foundations with dauntless and penetrating objectivity, the more deplorable became my total picture of parliamentary life. Indeed, this is an advisable procedure in dealing with an institution which, in the person of its representatives, feels obliged to bring up "objectivity" in every second sentence as the only proper basis for every investigation and opinion. Investigate these gentlemen themselves and the laws of their sordid existence, and you will be amazed at the result.

There is no principle which, objectively considered, is as false as that of parliamentarianism.

Here we may totally disregard the manner in which our fine representatives of the people are chosen, how they arrive at their office and their new dignity. That only the tiniest fraction of them rise in fulfillment of a general desire, let alone a need, will at once be apparent to anyone who realizes that the political understanding of the broad masses is far from being highly enough developed to arrive at definite general political views of their own accord and seek out the suitable personalities.

The thing we designate by the word "public opinion" rests only in the smallest part on experience or knowledge which the individual has acquired by himself, but rather on an idea which is inspired by so-called "enlightenment," often of a highly persistent and obtrusive type.

Just as a man's denominational orientation is the result of upbringing and only the religious need as such slumbers in his soul, the political opinion of the masses represents nothing but the final result of an incredibly tenacious and thorough manipulation of their mind and soul.

By far the greatest share in their political "education," which in this case is most aptly designated by the word "propaganda," falls to the account of the press. It is foremost in performing this "work of enlightenment" and thus represents a sort of school for grown-ups. This instruction, however, is not in the hands of the state, but in the claws of forces which are in part very inferior. In Vienna as a very young man I had the best opportunity to become acquainted with the owners and spiritual manufacturers of this machine for educating the masses. At first I could not help but be amazed at how short a time it took this great evil power within the state to create a certain opinion even where it meant totally falsifying profound desires and views which surely existed among the public. In a few days a ridiculous episode had become a significant state action, while, conversely, at the same time, vital problems fell a prey to public oblivion, or rather were simply filched from the memory and consciousness of the masses.

Thus, in the course of a few weeks it was possible to conjure up names out of the void, to associate them with incredible hopes on the part of the broad public, even to give them a popularity which the really great man often does not obtain his whole life long; names which a month before no one had even seen or heard of, while at the same time old and proved figures of political or other public life, though in the best of health, simply died as far as their fellow men were concerned, or were heaped with such vile insults that their names soon threatened to become the symbol of some definite act of infamy or villainy. We must study this vile Jewish technique of emptying garbage pails full of the vilest slanders and defamations from hundreds and hundreds of sources at once, suddenly and as if by magic, on the clean garments of honorable men, if we are fully to appreciate the entire menace represented by these scoundrels of the press.

There is absolutely nothing one of these spiritual robber-barons will not do to achieve his savory aims.

He will poke into the most secret family affairs and not rest until his truffle-searching instinct digs up some miserable incident which is calculated to finish off the unfortunate victim. But if, after the most careful sniffing, absolutely nothing is found, either in the man's public or private life, one of these scoundrels simply seizes on slander, in the firm conviction that despite a thousand refutations something always sticks and, moreover, through the immediate and hundred-fold repetition of his defamations by all his accomplices, any resistance on the part of the victim is in most cases utterly impossible; and it must be borne in mind that this rabble never acts out of motives which might seem credible or even understandable to the rest of humanity. God forbid! While one of these scum is attacking his beloved fellow men in the most contemptible fashion, the octopus covers himself with a veritable cloud of respectability and unctuous phrases, prates about "journalistic duty" and such-like lies, and even goes so far as to shoot off his mouth at committee meetings and congresses—that is, occasions where these pests are present in large numbers—about a very special variety of "honor," to wit, the journalistic variety, which the assembled rabble gravely and mutually confirm.

These scum manufacture more than three-quarters of the so-called "public opinion," from whose foam the parliamentarian Aphrodite arises. To give an accurate description of this process and depict it in all its falsehood and improbability, one would have to write volumes. But even if we disregard all this and examine only the given product along with its activity, this seems to me enough to make the objective lunacy of this institution dawn on even the naïvest mind.

This human error, as senseless as it is dangerous, will most readily be understood as soon as we compare democratic parliamentarianism with a truly Germanic democracy.

The distinguishing feature of the former is that a body of, let us say five hundred men, or in recent times even women, is chosen and entrusted with making the ultimate decision in any and all matters. And so for practical purposes they alone are the government; for even if they do choose a cabinet which undertakes the external direction of the affairs of state, this is a mere sham. In reality this so-called government cannot take a step without first obtaining the approval of the general assembly. Consequently, it cannot be made responsible for anything, since the ultimate decision never lies with it, but with the majority of parliament. In every case it does nothing but carry out the momentary will of the majority. Its political ability can only be judged according to the skill with which it understands how either to adapt itself to the will of the majority or to pull the majority over to its side. Thereby it sinks from the heights of real government to the level of a beggar confronting the momentary majority. Indeed, its most urgent task becomes nothing more than either to secure the favor of the existing majority, as the need arises, or to form a majority with more friendly inclinations. If this succeeds, it may "govern" a little while longer; if it doesn't succeed, it can resign. The soundness of its purposes as such is beside the point.

For practical purposes, this excludes all responsibility.

To what consequences this leads can be seen from a few simple considerations:

The internal composition of the five hundred chosen representatives of the people, with regard to profession or even individual abilities, gives a picture as incoherent as it is usually deplorable. For no one can believe that these men elected by the nation are elect of spirit or even of intelligence! It is to be hoped that no one will suppose that the ballots of an electorate which is anything else than brilliant will give rise to statesmen by the hundreds. Altogether we cannot be too sharp in condemning the absurd notion that geniuses can be born from general elections. In the first place, a nation only produces a real statesman once in a blue moon and not a hundred or more at once; and in the second place, the revulsion of the masses for every outstanding genius is positively instinctive. Sooner will a camel pass through a needle's eye than a great man be "discovered" by an election.

In world history the man who really rises above the norm of the broad average usually announces himself personally.

As it is, however, five hundred men, whose stature is to say the least modest, vote on the most important affairs of the nation, appoint governments which in every single case and in every special question have to get the approval of the exalted assembly, so that policy is really made by five hundred.

And that is just what it usually looks like.

But even leaving the genius of these representatives of the people aside, bear in mind how varied are the problems awaiting attention, in what widely removed fields solutions and decisions must be made, and you will realize how inadequate a governing institution must be which transfers the ultimate right of decision to a mass assembly of people, only a tiny fraction of which possess knowledge and experience of the matter to be treated. The most important economic measures are thus submitted to a forum, only a tenth of whose members have any economic education to show. This is nothing more nor less than placing the ultimate decision in a matter in the hands of men totally lacking in every prerequisite for the task.

The same is true of every other question. The decision is always made by a majority of ignoramuses and incompetents, since the composition of this institution remains unchanged while the problems under treatment extend to nearly every province of public life and would thereby presuppose a constant turn-over in the deputies who are to judge and decide on them, since it is impossible to let the same persons decide matters of transportation as, let us say, a question of high foreign policy. Otherwise these men would all have to be universal geniuses such as we actually seldom encounter once in centuries. Unfortunately we are here confronted, for the most part, not with "thinkers," but with dilettantes as limited as they are conceited and inflated, intellectual *demi-monde* of the worst sort. And this is the source of the often incomprehensible frivolity with which these gentry speak and decide on things which would require careful meditation even in the greatest minds. Measures of the gravest significance for the future of a whole state, yes, of a nation, are passed as though a game of *Schafkopf* or *Tarock*,[2] which would certainly be better suited to their abilities, lay on the table before them and not the fate of a race.

Yet it would surely be unjust to believe that all of the deputies in such a parliament were personally endowed with so little sense of responsibility.

No, by no means.

But by forcing the individual to take a position on such questions completely ill-suited to him, this system gradually ruins his character. No one will summon up the courage to declare: "Gentlemen, I believe we understand nothing about this matter. I personally certainly do not." (Besides, this would change matters little, for surely this kind of honesty would remain totally unappreciated, and what is more, our friends would scarcely allow one honorable jackass to spoil their whole game.) Anyone with a knowledge of people will realize that in such an illustrious company no one is eager to be the stupidest, and in certain circles honesty is almost synonymous with stupidity.

Thus, even the representative who at first was honest is thrown into this track of general falsehood and deceit. The very conviction that the non-participation of an individual in the business would in itself change nothing kills every honorable impulse which may rise up in this or that deputy. And finally, moreover, he may tell himself that he personally is far from being the worst among the others,[3] and that the sole effect of his collaboration is perhaps to prevent worse things from happening.

It will be objected, to be sure, that though the individual deputy possesses no special understanding in this or that matter, his position has been discussed by the fraction which directs the policy of the gentleman in question, and that the fraction has its special committees which are more than adequately enlightened by experts anyway.

At first glance this seems to be true. But then the question arises: Why are five hundred chosen when only a few possess the necessary wisdom to take a position in the most important matters?

And this is the worm in the apple!

It is not the aim of our present-day parliamentarianism to constitute an assembly of wise men, but rather to compose a band of mentally dependent nonentities who are the more easily led in certain directions, the greater is the personal limitation of the individual. That is the only way of carrying on party politics in the malodorous present-day sense. And only in this way is it possible for the real wirepuller to remain carefully in the background and never personally be called to responsibility. For then every decision, regardless how harmful to the nation, will not be set to the account of a scoundrel visible to all, but will be unloaded on the shoulders of a whole fraction.

And thereby every practical responsibility vanishes. For responsibility can lie only in the obligation of an individual and not in a parliamentary bull session.

Such an institution can only please the biggest liars and sneaks of the sort that shun the light of day, because it is inevitably hateful to an honorable, straightforward man who welcomes personal responsibility.

And that is why this type of democracy has become the instrument of that race which in its inner goals must shun the light of day, now and in all ages of the future. Only the Jew can praise an institution which is as dirty and false as he himself.

Juxtaposed to this is the truly Germanic democracy characterized by the free election of a leader and his obligation fully to assume all responsibility for his actions and omissions. In it there is no majority vote on individual questions, but only the decision of an individual who must answer with his fortune and his life for his choice.

If it be objected that under such conditions scarcely anyone would be prepared to dedicate his person to so risky a task, there is but one possible answer:

Thank the Lord, Germanic democracy means just this: that any old climber or moral slacker cannot rise by devious paths to govern his national comrades,[4] but that, by the very greatness of the responsibility to be assumed, incompetents and weaklings are frightened off.

But if, nevertheless, one of these scoundrels should attempt to sneak in, we can find him more easily, and mercilessly challenge him: Out, cowardly scoundrel! Remove your foot, you are besmirching the steps; the front steps of the Pantheon of history are not for sneak-thieves, but for heroes!

[The State]

With the victorious march of German technology and industry, the rising successes of German commerce, the realization was increasingly lost that all this was only possible on the basis of a strong state. On the contrary, many circles went so far as to put forward the conviction that the state owed its very existence to these phenomena, that the state itself primarily represented an economic institution, that it could be governed according to economic requirements, and that its very existence depended on economics, a state of affairs which was regarded and glorified as by far the healthiest and most natural.

But the state has nothing at all to do with any definite economic conception or development.

It is not a collection of economic contracting parties in a definite delimited living space for the fulfillment of economic tasks, but the organization of a community of physically and psychologically similar living beings for the better facilitation of the maintenance of their species and the achievement of the aim which has been allotted to this species by Providence. This and nothing else is the aim and meaning of a state. Economics is only one of the many instruments required for the achievement of this aim. It is never the cause or the aim of a state unless this state is based on a false, because unnatural, foundation to begin with. Only in this way can it be explained that the state as such does not necessarily presuppose territorial limitation. This will be necessary only among the peoples who want to secure the maintenance of their national comrades by their own resources; in other words, are prepared to fight the struggle for existence by their own labor. Peoples who can sneak their way into the rest of mankind like drones, to make other men work for them under all sorts of pretexts, can form states even without any definitely delimited living space of their own. This applies first and foremost to a people under whose parasitism the whole of honest humanity is suffering, today more than ever: the Jews.

The Jewish state was never spatially limited in itself, but universally unlimited as to space, though restricted in the sense of embracing but one race. Consequently, this people has always formed a state within states. It is one of the most ingenious tricks that was ever devised, to make this state sail under the flag of "religion," thus assuring it of the tolerance which the Aryan is always ready to accord a religious creed. For actually the Mosaic religion is nothing other than a doctrine for the preservation of the Jewish race. It therefore embraces almost all sociological, political, and economic fields of knowledge which can have any bearing on this function.

The urge to preserve the species is the first cause for the formation of human communities; thus the state is a national organism and not an economic organization. A difference which is just as large as it is incomprehensible, particularly to our so-called "statesmen" of today. That is why they think they can build up the state through economics while in reality it results and always will result solely from the action of those qualities which lie in line with the will to preserve the species and race. And these are always heroic virtues and never the egoism of shopkeepers, since the preservation of the existence of a species presupposes a spirit of sacrifice in the individual. The sense of the poet's words, "If you will not stake your life, you will win no life," is that the sacrifice of personal existence is necessary to secure the preservation of the species. Thus, the most sensible prerequisite for the formation and preservation of a state is the presence of a certain feeling of cohesion based on similarity of nature and species, and a willingness to stake everything on it with all possible means, something which in peoples with soil of their own will create heroic virtues, but in parasites will create lying hypocrisy and malignant cruelty, or else these qualities must already be present as the necessary and demonstrable basis for their existence as a state so different in form. The formation of a state, originally at least, will occur through the exercise of these qualities, and in the subsequent struggle for self-preservation those nations will be defeated—this is, will fall a prey to subjugation and thus sooner or later die out—which in the mutual struggle possess the smallest share of heroic virtues, or are not equal to the lies and trickery of the hostile parasite. But in this case, too, this must almost always be attributed less to a lack of astuteness than to a lack of determination and courage, which only tries to conceal itself beneath a cloak of humane convictions.

How little the state-forming and state-preserving qualities are connected with economics is most clearly shown by the fact that the inner strength of a state only in the rarest cases coincides with so-called economic prosperity, but that the latter, in innumerable cases, seems to indicate the state's approaching decline. If the formation of human societies were primarily attributable to economic forces or even impulses, the highest economic development would have to mean the greatest strength of the state and not the opposite.

Belief in the state-forming and state-preserving power of economics seems especially incomprehensible when it obtains in a country which in all things clearly and penetratingly shows the historic reverse. Prussia, in particular, demonstrates with marvelous sharpness that not material qualities but ideal virtues alone make possible the formation of a state. Only under their protection can economic life flourish, until with the collapse of the pure state-forming faculties the economy collapses too; a process which we can observe in so terrible and tragic a form right now. The material interests of man can always thrive best as long as they remain in the shadow of heroic virtues; but as soon as they attempt to enter the primary sphere of existence, they destroy the basis for their own existence.

Always when in Germany there was an upsurge of political power, the economic conditions began to improve; but always when economics became the sole content of our people's life, stifling the ideal virtues, the state collapsed and in a short time drew economic life along with it.

If, however, we consider the question, what, in reality, are the state-forming or even state-preserving forces, we can sum them up under one single head: the ability and will of the individual to sacrifice himself for the totality. That these virtues have nothing at all to do with economics can be seen from the simple realization that man never sacrifices himself for the latter, or, in other words: a man does not die for business, but only for ideals. Nothing proved the English-man's superior psychological knowledge of the popular soul better than the motivation which he gave to his struggle. While we fought for bread, England fought for "freedom"; and not even for her own, no, for that of the small nations. In our country we laughed at this effrontery, or were enraged at it, and thus only demonstrated how empty-headed and stupid the so-called statesmen of Germany had become even before the War. We no longer had the slightest idea concerning the essence of the force which can lead men to their death of their own free will and decision.

In 1914, as long as the German people thought they were fighting for ideals, they stood firm; but as soon as they were told to fight for their daily bread, they preferred to give up the game.

And our brilliant "statesmen" were astonished at this change in attitude. It never became clear to them that from the moment when a man begins to fight for an economic interest, he avoids death as much as possible, since death would forever deprive him of his reward for fighting. Anxiety for the rescue of her own child makes a heroine of even the feeblest mother, and only the struggle for the preservation of the species and the hearth, or the state that protects it, has at all times driven men against the spears of their enemies.

The following theorem may be established as an eternally valid truth:

Never yet has a state been founded by peaceful economic means, but always and exclusively by the instincts of preservation of the species regardless whether these are found in the province of heroic virtue or of cunning craftiness; the one results in Aryan states based on work and culture, the other in Jewish colonies of parasites. As soon as economics as such begins to choke out these instincts in a people or in a state, it becomes the seductive cause of subjugation and oppression.

The belief of pre-war days that the world could be peacefully opened up to, let alone conquered for, the German people by a commercial and colonial policy was a classic sign of the loss of real state-forming and state-preserving virtues and of all the insight, will power, and active determination which follow from them; the penalty for this, inevitable as the law of nature, was the World War with its consequences.

For those who do not look more deeply into the matter, this attitude of the German nation—for it was really as good as general—could only represent an insoluble riddle: for was not Germany above all other countries a marvelous example of an empire which had risen from foundations of pure political power? Prussia, the germ-cell of the Empire, came into being through resplendent heroism and not through financial operations or commercial deals, and the Reich itself in turn was only the glorious reward of aggressive political leadership and the death-defying courage of its soldiers. How could this very German people have succumbed to such a sickening of its political instinct? For here we face, not an isolated phenomenon, but forces of decay which in truly terrifying number soon began to flare up like will-o'-the-wisps, brushing up and down the body politic, or eating like poisonous abscesses into the nation, now here and now there. It seemed as though a continuous stream of poison was being driven into the outermost blood-vessels of this once heroic body by a mysterious power, and was inducing progressively greater paralysis of sound reason and the simple instinct of self-preservation.

As innumerable times I passed in review all these questions, arising through my position on the German alliance policy and the economic policy of the Reich in the years 1912 to 1914—the only remaining solution to the riddle became to an ever-increasing degree that power which, from an entirely different viewpoint, I had come to know earlier in Vienna: the Marxist doctrine and philosophy, and their organizational results.

For the second time I dug into this doctrine of destruction—this time no longer led by the impressions and effects of my daily associations, but directed by the observation of general processes of political life. I again immersed myself in the theoretical literature of this new world, attempting to achieve clarity concerning its possible effects, and then compared it with the actual phenomena and events it brings about in political, cultural, and economic life.

Now for the first time I turned my attention to the attempts to master this world plague.

I studied Bismarck's Socialist legislation[5] in its intention, struggle, and success. Gradually I obtained a positively granite foundation for my own conviction, so that since that time I have never been forced to undertake a shift in my own inner view on this question. Likewise the relation of Marxism to the Jews was submitted to further thorough examination.

Though previously in Vienna, Germany above all had seemed to me an unshakable colossus, now anxious misgivings sometimes entered my mind. In silent solitude and in the small circles of my acquaintance, I was filled with wrath at German foreign policy and likewise with what seemed to me the incredibly frivolous way in which the most important problem then existing for Germany, Marxism, was treated. It was really beyond me how people could rush so blindly into a danger whose effects, pursuant to the Marxists' own intention, were bound some day to be monstrous. Even then, among my acquaintance, just as today on a large scale, I warned against the phrase with which all wretched cowards comfort themselves: "Nothing can happen to us!" This pestilential attitude had once been the downfall of a gigantic empire. Could anyone believe that Germany alone was not subject to exactly the same laws as all other human organisms?

In the years 1913 and 1914, I, for the first time in various circles which today in part faithfully support the National Socialist movement, expressed the conviction that the question of the future of the German nation was the question of destroying Marxism.

In the catastrophic German alliance policy I saw only one of the consequences called forth by the disruptive work of this doctrine; for the terrible part of it was that this poison almost invisibly destroyed all the foundations of a healthy conception of economy and state, and that often those affected by it did not themselves realize to what an extent their activities and desires emanated from this philosophy which they otherwise sharply rejected.

The internal decline of the German nation had long since begun, yet, as so often in life, people had not achieved clarity concerning the force that was destroying their existence. Sometimes they tinkered around with the disease, but confused the forms of the phenomenon with the virus that had caused it. Since they did not know or want to know the cause, the struggle against Marxism was no better than bungling quackery.

[The Spiritualization of Violence]

For me, as for every German, there now began the greatest and most unforgettable time of my earthly existence. Compared to the events of this gigantic struggle, everything past receded to shallow nothingness. Precisely in these days, with the tenth anniversary of the mighty event approaching, I think back with proud sadness on those first weeks of our people's heroic struggle, in which Fate graciously allowed me to take part.

As though it were yesterday, image after image passes before my eyes. I see myself donning the uniform in the circle of my dear comrades, turning out for the first time, drilling, etc., until the day came for us to march off.

A single worry tormented me at that time, me, as so many others: would we not reach the front too late? Time and time again this alone banished all my calm. Thus, in every cause for rejoicing at a new, heroic victory, a slight drop of bitterness was hidden, for every new victory seemed to increase the danger of our coming too late.

At last the day came when we left Munich to begin the fulfillment of our duty. For the first time I saw the Rhine as we rode westward along its quiet waters to defend it, the German stream of streams, from the greed of the old enemy. When through the tender veil of the early morning mist the Niederwald Monument gleamed down upon us in the gentle first rays of the sun, the *old Watch on the Rhine* roared out of the endless transport train into the morning sky, and I felt as though my heart would burst.

And then came a damp, cold night in Flanders, through which we marched in silence, and when the day began to emerge from the mists, suddenly an iron greeting came whizzing at us over our heads, and with a sharp report sent the little pellets flying between our ranks, ripping up the wet ground; but even before the little cloud had passed, from two hundred throats the first hurrah rose to meet the first messenger of death. Then a crackling and a roaring, a singing and a howling began, and with feverish eyes each one of us was drawn forward, faster and faster, until suddenly past turnip fields and hedges the fight began, the fight of man against man. And from the distance the strains of a song reached our ears, coming closer and closer, leaping from company to company, and just as Death plunged a busy hand into our ranks, the song reached us too and we passed it along: *"Deutschland, Deutschland über Alles, Über Alles in der Welt!"*

Four days later we came back. Even our step had changed. Seventeen-year-old boys now looked like men.

The volunteers of the List Regiment may not have learned to fight properly, but they knew how to die like old soldiers.

This was the beginning.

Thus it went on year after year; but the romance of battle had been replaced by horror. The enthusiasm gradually cooled and the exuberant joy was stifled by mortal fear. The time came when every man had to struggle between the instinct of self-preservation and the admonitions of duty. I, too, was not spared by this struggle. Always when Death was on the hunt, a vague something tried to revolt, strove to represent itself to the weak body as reason, yet it was only cowardice, which in such disguises tried to ensnare the individual. A grave tugging and warning set in, and often it was only the last remnant of conscience which decided the issue. Yet the more this voice admonished one to caution, the louder and more insistent its lures, the sharper resistance grew until at last, after a long inner struggle, consciousness of duty emerged victorious. By the winter of 1915–16, this struggle had for me been decided. At last my will was undisputed master. If in the first days I went over the top with rejoicing and laughter, I was I now calm and determined. And this was enduring. Now Fate could bring on the ultimate tests without my nerves shattering or my reason failing.

The young volunteer had become an old soldier.

And this transformation had occurred in the whole army. It had issued old and hard from the eternal battles, and as for those who could not stand up under the storm—well, they were broken.

Now was the time to judge this army. Now, after two or three years, during which it was hurled from one battle into another, forever fighting against superiority in numbers and weapons, suffering hunger and bearing privations, now was the time to test the quality of this unique army.

Thousands of years may pass, but never will it be possible to speak of heroism without mentioning the German army and the World War. Then from the veil of the past the iron front of the gray steel helmet will emerge, unwavering and unflinching, an immortal monument. As long as there are Germans alive, they will remember that these men were sons of their nation. . . .

The application of force alone, without the impetus of a basic spiritual idea as a starting point, can never lead to the destruction of an idea and its dissemination, except in the form of a complete extermination of even the very last exponent of the idea and the destruction of the last tradition. This, however, usually means the disappearance of such a state from the sphere of political importance, often for an indefinite time and sometimes forever; for experience shows that such a blood sacrifice strikes the best part of the people, since every persecution which occurs without a spiritual basis seems morally unjustified and whips up precisely the more valuable parts of a people in protest, which results in an adoption of the spiritual content of the unjustly persecuted movement. In many this occurs simply through a feeling of opposition against the attempt to bludgeon down an idea by brute force.

As a result, the number of inward supporters grows in proportion as the persecution increases. Consequently, the complete annihilation of the new doctrine can be carried out only through a process of extermination so great and constantly increasing that in the end all the truly valuable blood is drawn out of the people or state in question. The consequence is that, though so-called "inner" purge can now take place, it will only be at the cost of total impotence. Such a method will always prove vain in advance if the doctrine to be combated has overstepped a certain small circle.

Consequently, here, too, as in all growth, the first period of childhood is most readily susceptible to the possibility of extermination, while with the mounting years the power of resistance increases and only with the weakness of approaching old age cedes again to new youth, though in another form and for different reasons.

Indeed, nearly all attempts to exterminate a doctrine and its organizational expression, by force without spiritual foundation, are doomed to failure, and not seldom end with the exact opposite of the desired result for the following reason:

The very first requirement for a mode of struggle with the weapons of naked force is and remains persistence. In other words: only the continuous and steady application of the methods for repressing a doctrine, etc., makes it possible for a plan to succeed. But as soon as force wavers and alternates with forbearance, not only will the doctrine to be repressed recover again and again, but it will also be in a position to draw new benefit from every persecution, since, after such a wave of pressure has ebbed away, indignation over the suffering induced leads new supporters to the old doctrine, while the old ones will cling to it with greater defiance and deeper hatred than before, and even schismatic heretics, once the danger has subsided, will attempt to return to their old viewpoint. Only in the steady and constant application of force lies the very first prerequisite for success. This persistence, however, can always and only arise from a definite spiritual conviction. Any violence which does not spring from a firm, spiritual base, will be wavering and uncertain. It lacks the stability which can only rest in a fanatical outlook. It emanates from the momentary energy and brutal determination of an individual, and is therefore subject to the change of personalities and to their nature and strength.

[The Use of Propaganda]

There seems to have been no clarity on the very first question: Is propaganda a means or an end?

It is a means and must therefore be judged with regard to its end. It must consequently take a form calculated to support the aim which it serves. It is also obvious that its aim can vary in importance from the standpoint of general need, and that the inner value of the propaganda will vary accordingly. The aim for which we were fighting the War was the loftiest, the most overpowering, that man can conceive: it was the freedom and independence of our nation, the security of our future food supply, and—our national honor; a thing which, despite all contrary opinions prevailing today, nevertheless exists, or rather should exist, since peoples without honor have sooner or later lost their freedom and independence, which in turn is only the result of a higher justice, since generations of rabble without honor deserve no freedom. Any man who wants to be a cowardly slave can have no honor, or honor itself would soon fall into general contempt.

The German nation was engaged in a struggle for a human existence, and the purpose of war propaganda should have been to support this struggle; its aim to help bring about victory.

When the nations on this planet fight for existence—when the question of destiny, "to be or not to be," cries out for a solution—then all considerations of humanitarianism or aesthetics crumble into nothingness; for all these concepts do not float about in the ether, they arise from man's imagination and are bound up with man. When he departs from this world, these concepts are again dissolved into nothingness, for Nature does not know them. And even among mankind, they belong only to a few nations or rather races, and this in proportion as they emanate from the feeling of the nation or race in question. Humanitarianism and aesthetics would vanish even from a world inhabited by man if this world were to lose the races that have created and upheld these concepts.

But all such concepts become secondary when a nation is fighting for its existence; in fact, they become totally irrelevant to the forms of the struggle as soon as a situation arises where they might paralyze a struggling nation's power of self-preservation. And that has always been their only visible result.

As for humanitarianism, Moltke[6] said years ago that in war it lies in the brevity of the operation, and that means that the most aggressive fighting technique is the most humane.

But when people try to approach these questions with drivel about aesthetics, etc., really only one answer is possible: where the destiny and existence of a people are at stake, all obligation toward beauty ceases. The most unbeautiful thing there can be in human life is and remains the yoke of slavery. Or do these Schwabing[7] decadents view the present lot of the German people as "aesthetic"? Certainly we don't have to discuss these matters with the Jews, the most modern inventors of this cultural perfume. Their whole existence is an embodied protest against the aesthetics of the Lord's image.

And since these criteria of humanitarianism and beauty must be eliminated from the struggle, they are also inapplicable to propaganda.

Propaganda in the War was a means to an end, and the end was the struggle for the existence of the German people; consequently, propaganda could only be considered in accordance with the principles that were valid for this struggle. In this case the most cruel weapons were humane if they brought about a quicker victory; and only those methods were beautiful which helped the nation to safeguard the dignity of its freedom.

This was the only possible attitude toward war propaganda in a life-and-death struggle like ours.

If the so-called responsible authorities had been clear on this point, they would never have fallen into such uncertainty over the form and application of this weapon: for even propaganda is no more than a weapon, though a frightful one in the hand of an expert.

The second really decisive question was this: To whom should propaganda be addressed? To the scientifically trained intelligentsia or to the less educated masses?

It must be addressed always and exclusively to the masses.

What the intelligentsia—or those who today unfortunately often go by that name—what they need is not propaganda but scientific instruction. The content of propaganda is not science any more than the object represented in a poster is art. The art of the poster lies in the designer's ability to attract the attention of the crowd by form and color. A poster advertising an art exhibit must direct the attention of the public to the art being exhibited; the better it succeeds in this, the greater is the art of the poster itself. The poster should give the masses an idea of the significance of the exhibition, it should not be a substitute for the art on display. Anyone who wants to concern himself with the art itself must do more than study the poster; and it will not be enough for him just to saunter through the exhibition. We may expect him to examine and immerse himself in the individual works, and thus little by little form a fair opinion.

A similar situation prevails with what we today call propaganda.

The function of propaganda does not lie in the scientific training of the individual, but in calling the masses' attention to certain facts, processes, necessities, etc., whose significance is thus for the first time placed within their field of vision.

The whole art consists in doing this so skillfully that everyone will be convinced that the fact is real, the process necessary, the necessity correct, etc. But since propaganda is not and cannot be the necessity in itself, since its function, like the poster, consists in attracting the attention of the crowd, and not in educating those who are already educated or who are striving after education and knowledge, its effect for the most part must be aimed at the emotions and only to a very limited degree at the so-called intellect.

All propaganda must be popular and its intellectual level must be adjusted to the most limited intelligence among those it is addressed to. Consequently, the greater the mass it is intended to reach, the lower its purely intellectual level will have to be. But if, as in propaganda for sticking out a war, the aim is to influence a whole people, we must avoid excessive intellectual demands on our public, and too much caution cannot be exerted in this direction.

The more modest its intellectual ballast, the more exclusively it takes into consideration the emotions of the masses, the more effective it will be. And this is the best proof of the soundness or unsoundness of a propaganda campaign, and not success in pleasing a few scholars or young aesthetes.

The art of propaganda lies in understanding the emotional ideas of the great masses and finding, through a psychologically correct form, the way to the attention and thence to the heart of the broad masses. The fact that our bright boys do not understand this merely shows how mentally lazy and conceited they are.

Once we understand how necessary it is for propaganda to be adjusted to the broad mass, the following rule results:

It is a mistake to make propaganda many-sided, like scientific instruction, for instance.

The receptivity of the great masses is very limited, their intelligence is small, but their power of forgetting is enormous. In consequence of these facts, all effective propaganda must be limited to a very few points and must harp on these in slogans until the last member of the public understands what you want him to understand by your slogan. As soon as you sacrifice this slogan and try to be many-sided, the effect will piddle away, for the crowd can neither digest nor retain the material offered. In this way the result is weakened and in the end entirely cancelled out.

Thus we see that propaganda must follow a simple line and correspondingly the basic tactics must be psychologically sound.

[The Purification of Culture]

A further example of the half-heartedness and weakness of the leaders of pre-War Germany in meeting the most important vital questions of the nation is the following: running parallel to the political, ethical, and moral contamination of the people, there had been for many years a no less terrible poisoning of the health of the national body. Especially in the big cities, syphilis was beginning to spread more and more, while tuberculosis steadily reaped its harvest of death throughout nearly the whole country.

Though in both cases the consequences were terrible for the nation, the authorities could not summon up the energy to take decisive measures.

Particularly with regard to syphilis, the attitude of the leadership of the nation and the state can only be designated as total capitulation. To fight it seriously, they would have had to take somewhat broader measures than was actually the case. The invention of a remedy of questionable character and its commercial exploitation can no longer help much against this plague. Here again it was only the fight against causes that mattered and not the elimination of the symptoms. The cause lies, primarily, in our prostitution of love. Even if its result were not this frightful plague, it would nevertheless be profoundly injurious to man, since the moral devastations which accompany this degeneracy suffice to destroy a people slowly but surely. This Jewification of our spiritual life and mammonization of our mating instinct will sooner or later destroy our entire offspring, for the powerful children of a natural emotion will be replaced by the miserable creatures of financial expediency which is becoming more and more the basis and sole prerequisite of our marriages. Love finds its outlet elsewhere.

Here, too, of course, Nature can be scorned for a certain time, but her vengeance will not fail to appear, only it takes a time to manifest itself, or rather: it is often recognized too late by man.

But the devastating consequences of a lasting disregard of the natural requirements for marriage can be seen in our nobility. Here we have before us the results of procreation based partly on purely social compulsion and partly on financial grounds. The one leads to a general weakening, the other to a poisoning of the blood, since every department store Jewess is considered fit to augment the off-spring of His Highness—and, indeed, the offspring look it. In both cases complete degeneration is the consequence.

Today our bourgeoisie strive to go the same road, and they will end up at the same goal.

Hastily and indifferently, people tried to pass by the unpleasant truths, as though by such an attitude events could be undone. No, the fact that our big city population is growing more and more prostituted in its love life cannot just be denied out of existence; it simply is so. The most visible results of this mass con-tamination can, on the one hand, be found in the insane asylums, and on the other, unfortunately, in our—children. They in particular are the sad product of the irresistibly spreading contamination of our sexual life; the vices of the parents are revealed in the sicknesses of the children. . . .

How truly wretched was the attitude of pre-War Germany on this one very question! What was done to check the contamination of our youth in the big cities? What was done to attack the infection and mammonization of our love life? What was done to combat the resulting syphilization of our people?

This can be answered most easily by stating what should have been done. . . .

The very first prerequisite needed for attacking such a difficult stretch of the human road is for the leadership to succeed in representing to the masses of the people the partial goal which now has to be achieved, or rather conquered, as the one which is solely and alone worthy of attention, on whose conquest everything depends. The great mass of the people cannot see the whole road ahead of them without growing weary and despairing of the task. A certain number of them will keep the goal in mind, but will only be able to see the road in small, partial stretches, like the wanderer, who likewise knows and recognizes the end of his journey, but is better able to conquer the endless highway if he divides it into sections and boldly attacks each one as though it represented the desired goal itself. Only in this way does he advance without losing heart.

Thus, by the use of all propagandist means, the question of combating syphilis should have been made to appear as *the* task of the nation. Not just *one more* task. To this end, its injurious effects should have been thoroughly ham-mered into people as the most terrible misfortune, and this by the use of all avail-able means, until the entire nation arrived at the conviction that everything—future or ruin—depended upon the solution of this question.

Only after such a preparation, if necessary over a period of years, will the atten-tion, and consequently the determination, of the entire nation be aroused to such an extent that we can take exceedingly hard measures exacting the greatest sacrifices without running the risk of not being understood or of suddenly being left in the lurch by the will of the masses.

For, seriously to attack this plague, tremendous sacrifices and equally great labors are necessary.

The fight against syphilis demands a fight against prostitution, against prejudices, old habits, against previous conceptions, general views among them not least the false prudery of certain circles.

The first prerequisite for even the moral right to combat these things is the facilitation of earlier marriage for the coming generation. In late marriage alone lies the compulsion to retain an institution which, twist and turn as you like, is and remains a disgrace to humanity, an institution which is damned ill-suited to a being who with his usual modesty likes to regard himself as the "image" of God.

Prostitution is a disgrace to humanity, but it cannot be eliminated by moral lectures, pious intentions, etc.; its limitation and final abolition presuppose the elimination of innumerable preconditions. The first is and remains the creation of an opportunity for early marriage as compatible with human nature—particularly for the man, as the woman in any case is only the passive part.

How lost, how incomprehensible a part of humanity has become today can be seen from the fact that mothers in so-called "good" society can not seldom be heard to say that they are glad to have found their child a husband who has sown his wild oats, etc. Since there is hardly any lack of these, but rather the contrary, the poor girl will be happy to find one of these worn-out Siegfrieds,[8] and the children will be the visible result of this "sensible" marriage. If we bear in mind that, aside from this, propagation as such is limited as much as possible, so that Nature is prevented from making any choice, since naturally every creature, regardless how miserable, must be preserved, the only question that remains is why such an institution exists at all any more and what purpose it is supposed to serve? Isn't it exactly the same as prostitution itself? Hasn't duty toward posterity passed completely out of the picture? Or do people fail to realize what a curse on the part of their children and children's children they are heaping on themselves by such criminal frivolity in observing the ultimate natural law as well as our ultimate natural obligation?[9]

Thus, the civilized peoples degenerate and gradually perish.

And marriage cannot be an end in itself, but must serve the one higher goal, the increase and preservation of the species and the race. This alone is its meaning and its task. . . .

In the second place, education and training must eradicate a number of evils about which today no one bothers at all. Above all, in our present education a balance must be created between mental instruction and physical training. The institution that is called a *Gymnasium* today is a mockery of the Greek model. In our educational system it has been utterly forgotten that in the long run a healthy mind can dwell only in a healthy body. Especially if we bear in mind the mass of the people, aside from a few exceptions, this statement becomes absolutely valid. . . .

The excessive emphasis on purely intellectual instruction and the neglect of physical training also encourage the emergence of sexual ideas at a much too early age. The youth who achieves the hardness of iron by sports and gymnastics succumbs to the need of sexual satisfaction less than the stay-at-home fed exclusively on intellectual fare. And a sensible system of education must bear this in mind. It must, moreover, not fail to consider that the healthy young man will expect different things from the woman than a prematurely corrupted weakling.

Thus, the whole system of education must be so organized as to use the boy's free time for the useful training of his body. He has no right to hang about in idleness during these years, to make the streets and movie-houses unsafe; after his day's work he should steel and harden his young body, so that later life will not find him too soft. To begin this and also carry it out, to direct and guide it, is the task of education, and not just the pumping of so-called wisdom. We must also do away with the conception that the treatment of the body is the affair of every individual. There is no freedom to sin at the cost of posterity and hence of the race.

Parallel to the training of the body, a struggle against the poisoning of the soul must begin. Our whole public life today is like a hothouse for sexual ideas and stimulations. Just look at the bill of fare served up in our movies, vaudeville and theaters, and you will hardly be able to deny that this is not the right kind of food, particularly for the youth. In shop windows and billboards the vilest means are used to attract the attention of the crowd. Anyone who has not lost the ability to think himself into their soul must realize that this must cause great damage in the youth. This sensual, sultry atmosphere leads to ideas and stimulations at a time when the boy should have no understanding of such things. The result of this kind of education can be studied in present-day youth, and it is not exactly gratifying. They mature too early and consequently grow old before their time. Sometimes the public learns of court proceedings which permit shattering insights into the emotional life of our fourteen- and fifteen-year-olds. Who will be surprised that even in these age-groups syphilis begins to seek its victims? And is it not deplorable to see a good number of these physically weak, spiritually corrupted young men obtaining their introduction to marriage through big-city whores?

No, anyone who wants to attack prostitution must first of all help to eliminate its spiritual basis. He must clear away the filth of the moral plague of big-city "civilization" and he must do this ruthlessly and without wavering in the face of all the shouting and screaming that will naturally be let loose. If we do not lift the youth out of the morass of their present-day environment, they will drown in it. Anyone who refuses to see these things supports them, and thereby makes himself an accomplice in the slow prostitution of our future which, whether we like it or not, lies in the coming generation. This cleansing of our culture must be extended to nearly all fields. Theater, art, literature, cinema, press, posters, and window displays must be cleansed of all manifestations of our rotting world and placed in the service of a moral, political, and cultural idea. Public life must be freed from the stifling perfume of our modern eroticism, just as it must be freed from all unmanly, prudish hypocrisy. In all these things the goal and the road must be determined by concern for the preservation of the health of our people in body and soul. The right of personal freedom recedes before the duty to preserve the race.

Only after these measures are carried out can the medical struggle against the plague itself be carried through with any prospect of success. But here, too, there must be no half-measures; the gravest and most ruthless decisions will have to be made. It is a half-measure to let incurably sick people steadily contaminate the remaining healthy ones. This is in keeping with the humanitarianism which, to avoid hurting one individual, lets a hundred others perish. The demand that defective people be prevented from propagating equally defective offspring is a demand of the clearest reason and if systematically executed represents the most humane act of mankind. It will spare millions of unfortunates undeserved sufferings, and consequently will lead to a rising improvement of health as a whole. The determination to proceed in this direction will oppose a dam to the further spread of venereal diseases. For, if necessary, the incurably sick will be pitilessly segregated—a barbaric measure for the unfortunate who is struck by it, but a blessing for his fellow men and posterity. The passing pain of a century can and will redeem millenniums from sufferings.

The struggle against syphilis and the prostitution which prepares the way for it is one of the most gigantic tasks of humanity, gigantic because we are facing, not the solution of a single question, but the elimination of a large number of evils which bring about this plague as a resultant manifestation. For in this case the sickening of the body is only the consequence of a sickening of the moral, social, and racial instincts.

[Nation and Race]

There are some truths which are so obvious that for this very reason they are not seen or at least not recognized by ordinary people. They sometimes pass by such truisms as though blind and are most astonished when someone suddenly discovers what everyone really ought to know. Columbus's eggs lie around by the hundreds of thousands, but Columbuses are met with less frequently.

Thus men without exception wander about in the garden of Nature; they imagine that they know practically everything and yet with few exceptions pass blindly by one of the most patent principles of Nature's rule: the inner segregation of the species of all living beings on this earth.

Even the most superficial observation shows that Nature's restricted form of propagation and increase is an almost rigid basic law of all the innumerable forms of expression of her vital urge. Every animal mates only with a member of the same species. The titmouse seeks the titmouse, the finch the finch, the stork the stork, the field mouse the field mouse, the dormouse the dormouse, the wolf the she-wolf, etc.

Only unusual circumstances can change this, primarily the compulsion of captivity or any other cause that makes it impossible to mate within the same species. But then Nature begins to resist this with all possible means, and her most visible protest consists either in refusing further capacity for propagation to bastards or in limiting the fertility of later offspring; in most cases, however, she takes away the power of resistance to disease or hostile attacks.

This is only too natural.

Any crossing of two beings not at exactly the same level produces a medium between the level of the two parents. This means: the offspring will probably stand higher than the racially lower parent, but not as high as the higher one. Consequently, it will later succumb in the struggle against the higher level. Such mating is contrary to the will of Nature for a higher breeding of all life. The precondition for this does not lie in associating superior and inferior, but in the total victory of the former. The stronger must dominate and not blend with the weaker, thus sacrificing his own greatness. Only the born weakling can view this as cruel, but he after all is only a weak and limited man; for if this law did not prevail, any conceivable higher development of organic living beings would be unthinkable.

The consequence of this racial purity,[10] universally valid in Nature, is not only the sharp outward delimitation of the various races, but their uniform character in themselves. The fox is always a fox, the goose a goose, the tiger a tiger, etc., and the difference can lie at most in the varying measure of force, strength, intelligence, dexterity, endurance, etc., of the individual specimens. But you will never find a fox who in his inner attitude might, for example, show humanitarian tendencies toward geese, as similarly there is no cat with a friendly inclination toward mice.

Therefore, here, too, the struggle among themselves arises less from inner aversion than from hunger and love. In both cases, Nature looks on calmly, with satisfaction, in fact. In the struggle for daily bread all those who are weak and sickly or less determined succumb, while the struggle of the males for the female grants the right or opportunity to propagate only to the healthiest. And struggle is always a means for improving a species' health and power of resistance and, therefore, a cause of its higher development.

If the process were different, all further and higher development would cease and the opposite would occur. For, since the inferior always predominates numerically over the best, if both had the same possibility of preserving life and propagating, the inferior would multiply so much more rapidly that in the end the best would inevitably be driven into the background, unless a correction of this state of affairs were undertaken. Nature does just this by subjecting the weaker part to such severe living conditions that by them alone the number is limited, and by not permitting the remainder to increase promiscuously, but making a new and ruthless choice according to strength and health.

No more than Nature desires the mating of weaker with stronger individuals, even less does she desire the blending of a higher with a lower race, since, if she did, her whole work of higher breeding, over perhaps hundreds of thousands of years, might be ruined with one blow.

Historical experience offers countless proofs of this. It shows with terrifying clarity that in every mingling of Aryan blood with that of lower peoples the result was the end of the cultured people. North America, whose population consists in by far the largest part of Germanic elements who mixed but little with the lower colored peoples, shows a different humanity and culture from Central and South America, where the predominantly Latin immigrants often mixed with the aborigines on a large scale. By this one example, we can clearly and distinctly recognize the effect of racial mixture. The Germanic inhabitant of the American continent, who has remained racially pure and unmixed, rose to be master of the continent; he will remain the master as long as he does not fall a victim to defilement of the blood.

The result of all racial crossing is therefore in brief always the following:

a. Lowering of the level of the higher race;

b. Physical and intellectual regression and hence the beginning of a slowly but surely progressing sickness.

To bring about such a development is, then, nothing else but to sin against the will of the eternal creator.

And as a sin this act is rewarded.

When man attempts to rebel against the iron logic of Nature, he comes into struggle with the principles to which he himself owes his existence as a man. And this attack[11] must lead to his own doom. . . .

Everything we admire on this earth today—science and art, technology and inventions—is only the creative product of a few peoples and originally perhaps of *one* race. On them depends the existence of this whole culture. If they perish, the beauty of this earth will sink into the grave with them.

However much the soil, for example, can influence men, the result of the influence will always be different depending on the races in question. The low fertility of a living space may spur the one race to the highest achievements; in others it will only be the cause of bitterest poverty and final undernourishment with all its consequences. The inner nature of peoples is always determining for the manner in which outward influences will be effective. What leads the one to starvation trains the other to hard work.

All great cultures of the past perished only because the originally creative race died out from blood poisoning.

The ultimate cause of such a decline was their forgetting that all culture depends on men and not conversely; hence that to preserve a certain culture the man who creates it must be preserved. This preservation is bound up with the rigid law of necessity and the right to victory of the best and stronger in this world.[12]

Those who want to live, let them fight, and those who do not want to fight in this world of eternal struggle do not deserve to live.

Even if this were hard—that is how it is! Assuredly, however, by far the harder fate is that which strikes the man who thinks he can overcome Nature, but in the last analysis only mocks her. Distress, misfortune, and diseases are her answer.

The man who misjudges and disregards the racial laws actually forfeits the happiness that seems destined to be his. He thwarts the triumphal march of the best race and hence also the precondition for all human progress, and remains, in consequence, burdened with all the sensibility of man, in the animal realm of helpless misery.[13]

[Corporatism]

This self-sacrificing will to give one's personal labor and if necessary one's own life for others is most strongly developed in the Aryan. The Aryan is not greatest in his mental qualities as such, but in the extent of his willingness to put all his abilities in the service of the community. In him the instinct of self-preservation has reached the noblest form, since he willingly subordinates his own ego to the life of the community and, if the hour demands, even sacrifices it.

Not in his intellectual gifts lies the source of the Aryan's capacity for creating and building culture. If he had just this alone, he could only act destructively, in no case could he organize; for the innermost essence of all organization requires that the individual renounce putting forward his personal opinion and interests and sacrifice both in favor of a larger group. Only by way of this general community does he again recover his share. Now, for example, he no longer works directly for himself, but with his activity articulates himself with the community, not only for his own advantage, but for the advantage of all. The most wonderful elucidation of this attitude is provided by his word "work," by which he does not mean an activity for maintaining life in itself, but exclusively a creative effort that does not conflict with the interests of the community. Otherwise he designates human activity, in so far as it serves the instinct of self-preservation without consideration for his fellow men, as theft, usury, robbery, burglary, etc.

This state of mind, which subordinates the interests of the ego to the conservation of the community, is really the first premise for every truly human culture. From it alone can arise all the great works of mankind, which bring the founder little reward, but the richest blessings to posterity. Yes, from it alone can we understand how so many are able to bear up faithfully under a scanty life which imposes on them nothing but poverty and frugality, but gives the community the foundations of its existence. Every worker, every peasant, every inventor, official, etc., who works without ever being able to achieve any happiness or prosperity for himself, is a representative of this lofty idea, even if the deeper meaning of his activity remains hidden in him.

What applies to work as the foundation of human sustenance and all human progress is true to an even greater degree for the defense of man and his culture. In giving one's own life for the existence of the community lies the crown of all sense of sacrifice. It is this alone that prevents what human hands have built from being overthrown by human hands or destroyed by Nature.

Our own German language possesses a word which magnificently designates this kind of activity: *Pflichterfüllung* (fulfillment of duty); it means not to be self-sufficient but to serve the community.

The basic attitude from which such activity arises, we call—to distinguish it from egoism and selfishness—idealism. By this we understand only the individual's capacity to make sacrifices for the community, for his fellow men. . . .

Organizing the broad masses of our people which are today in the international camp into a national people's community does not mean renouncing the defense of justified class interests. Divergent class and professional interests are not synonymous with class cleavage, but are natural consequences of our economic life. Professional grouping is in no way opposed to a true national community, for the latter consists in the unity of a nation in all those questions which affect this nation as such.

The integration of an occupational group which has become a class with the national community, or merely with the state, is not accomplished by the lowering of higher classes but by uplifting the lower classes. This process in turn can never be upheld by the higher class, but only by the lower class fighting for its equal rights. The present-day bourgeoisie was not organized into the state by measures of the nobility, but by its own energy under its own leadership.

The German worker will not be raised to the framework of the German national community via feeble scenes of fraternization, but by a conscious raising of his social and cultural situation until the most serious differences may be viewed as bridged. A movement which sets this development as its goal will have to take its supporters primarily from this camp.[14] It may fall back on the intelligentsia only in so far as the latter has completely understood the goal to be achieved. This process of transformation and equalization will not be completed in ten or twenty years; experience shows that it comprises many generations.

The severest obstacle to the present-day worker's approach to the national community lies not in the defense of his class interests, but in his international leadership and attitude which are hostile to the people and the fatherland. The same unions with a fanatical national leadership in political and national matters would make millions of workers into the most valuable members of their nation regardless of the various struggles that took place over purely economic matters.

A movement which wants honestly to give the German worker back to his people and tear him away from the international delusion must sharply attack a conception dominant above all in employer circles, which under national community understands the unresisting economic surrender of the employee to the employer and which chooses to regard any attempt at safeguarding even justified interests regarding the employee's economic existence as an attack on the national community. Such an assertion is not only untrue, but a conscious lie, because the national community imposes its obligations not only on one side but also on the other.

Just as surely as a worker sins against the spirit of a real national community when, without regard for the common welfare and the survival of a national economy, he uses his power to raise extortionate demands, an employer breaks this community to the same extent when he conducts his business in an inhuman, exploiting way, misuses the national labor force and makes millions out of its sweat. He then has no right to designate himself as national, no right to speak of a national community; no, he is a selfish scoundrel who induces social unrest and provides future conflicts which whatever happens must end in harming the nation.

Thus, the reservoir from which the young movement must gather its supporters will primarily be the masses of our workers. Its work will be to tear these away from the international delusion, to free them from their social distress, to raise them out of their cultural misery and lead them to the national community as a valuable, united factor, national in feeling and desire.

If, in the circles of the national intelligentsia, there are found men with the warmest hearts for their people and its future, imbued with the deepest knowledge of the importance of this struggle for the soul of these masses, they will be highly welcome in the ranks of this movement, as a valuable spiritual backbone. But winning over the bourgeois voting cattle can never be the aim of this movement.

If it were, it would burden itself with a dead weight which by its whole nature would paralyze our power to recruit from the broad masses. For regardless of the theoretical beauty of the idea of leading together the broadest masses from below and from above within the framework of the movement, there is the opposing fact that by psychological propagandizing of bourgeois masses in general meetings, it may be possible to create moods and even to spread insight, but not to do away with qualities of character or, better expressed, vices, whose development and origin embrace centuries.

NOTES

1. *"Spottgeburt aus Dreck und Feuer."* Should be *"von Dreck und Feuer."* Goethe's *Faust,* Part 1, 5356: Faust to Mephistopheles.

2. *Schaff[s]kopf* is a four-handed card game widely played in Germany. *Tarock* [is a] three-handed card game of Italian origin (*tarocco*), popular in Austria and southern Germany.

3. *"der Schlechteste unter den Anderen."*

4. *"Volksgenosse."* Brockhaus defines: In contrast to the concept of citizen which is based on the idea of legal equality in the state, the designation [is] for all members of the same national community (*Volksgemeinschaft*), especially those who form a working association in the service of the nation as a whole. As used by the National Socialists, it might be translated as "racial comrades." I have chosen the more neutral term "national comrades" because the National Socialists did not coin the term and it occurs frequently in the speeches of parliamentarians who were not even noted for their anti-Semitism.

5. Bismarck's Anti-Socialist Law, put through the Reichstag on 18 October 1878, prohibited meetings, collections of funds, and publications of Social Democrats, Socialists, and Communists; it remained in force until 1890 when the new Emperor, William II, opposed it. Despite the law, Socialist deputies in the Reichstag retained their parliamentary immunity.

6. General Helmuth von Moltke (1800–91) became chief of the Prussian General Staff in 1859. He modernized the Prussian army and was the founder of the German General Staff.

7. Schwabing: the bohemian quarter of Munich, located near the university.

8. The German here has an untranslatable and rather elaborate pun. To sow wild oats is *"sich die Homer abstossen,"* to butt off one's horns. The word I have rendered as "worn-out" is *enthornt*, literally de-horned. Siegfried did not have horns; the reference is to the horny skin which made him invulnerable.

9. *". . . in der Wahrung des letzten Naturrechtes, aber auch der letzten Naturverpflichtung?"*

10. Second edition inserts "urge toward" before "racial purity."

11. Second edition: "so his action against Nature" instead of "this attack."

12. Second edition omits: "in this world."

13. *"und verbleibt in der Folge dann, belastet mit der Empfindlichkeit des Menschen, im Bereich des hilflosen Jammers der Tiere."* Second edition has: *"Er begibt sich in der Folge, belastet mit der Empfindlichkeit des Menschen, ins Bereich des hilflosen Tieres."* This would read: "In consequence, burdened with all the sensibility of man, he moves into the realm of the helpless beast."

14. Changed in second edition to "the workers' camp."

27

Andrew Macdonald

———◦◦◦———

The Turner Diaries (1978)

William Pierce (1933–2002), alias Andrew Macdonald, was the leader of the National Alliance, a neo-Nazi organization, based in West Virginia, that promotes racist and anti-Semitic propaganda. Pierce, who had a Ph.D. in physics and once taught at the University of Oregon, also founded the "Cosmotheists," a Christian Identity group whose believers regard whites as God's "chosen people" and Jews and blacks as "mud people," descended from Satan. His extremist fantasy, The Turner Diaries, *inspired both Timothy McVeigh, the Oklahoma City bomber, and "The Order," a neo-Nazi terrorist group, to commit violent crimes on behalf of the Aryan revolution.*

Foreword

THERE EXISTS SUCH an extensive body of literature on the Great Revolution, including the memoirs of virtually every one of its leading figures who survived into the New Era, that yet another book dealing with the events and circumstances of that time of cataclysmic upheaval and rebirth may seem superfluous. *The Turner Diaries,* however, provides an insight into the background of the Great Revolution which is uniquely valuable for two reasons:

1) It is a fairly detailed and continuous record of a portion of the struggle during the years immediately before the culmination of the Revolution, written as it happened, on a day-to-day basis. Thus, it is free of the distortion which often

Source: Andrew Macdonald, *The Turner Diaries,* 2nd ed. (Washington, D.C.: The National Alliance, 1980).

afflicts hindsight. Although the diaries of other participants in that mighty conflict are extant, none which has yet been published provides as complete and detailed a record.

2) It is written from the viewpoint of a rank-and-file member of the Organization, and, although it consequently suffers from myopia occasionally, it is a totally frank document. Unlike the accounts recorded by some of the leaders of the Revolution, its author did not have one eye on his place in history as he wrote. As we read the pages which follow, we get a better understanding than from any other source, probably, of the true thoughts and feelings of the men and women whose struggle and sacrifice saved our race in its time of greatest peril and brought about the New Era.

Earl Turner, who wrote these diaries, was born in 43 BNE in Los Angeles, which was the name of a vast metropolitan area on the west coast of the North American continent in the Old Era, encompassing the present communities of Eckartsville and Wesselton as well as a great deal of the surrounding countryside. He grew up in the Los Angeles area and was trained as an electrical engineer.

After his education he settled near the city of Washington, which was then the capital of the United States. He was employed there by an electronics research firm.

He first became active in the Organization in 12 BNE. When this record begins, in 8 BNE (1991 according to the old chronology), Turner was 35 years old and had no mate.

These diaries span barely two years in Earl Turner's life, yet they give us an intimate acquaintance with one of those whose name is inscribed in the Record of Martyrs. For that reason alone his words should have a special significance for all of us, who in our school days were given the task of memorizing the names of all the Martyrs in that sacred Record handed down to us by our ancestors.

Turner's diaries consist, in their manuscript form, of five large, cloth-bound ledgers, completely filled, and a few pages at the beginning of a sixth. There are many loose inserts and notes between the ledger pages, apparently written by Turner on those days when he was away from his base and later interpolated into his permanent record.

The ledgers were discovered last year along with a wealth of other historically important material by the same team from the Historical Institute, led by Professor Charles Anderson, which earlier uncovered the Eastern Command Center of the Revolution in its excavations near the Washington ruins. It is fitting that they now be made available to the general public during this, the 100th anniversary year of the Great Revolution.

New Baltimore   *A.M.*
April 100

I

September 16, 1991. Today it finally began! After all these years of talking—and nothing but talking—we have finally taken our first action. We are at war with the System, and it is no longer a war of words.

I cannot sleep, so I will try writing down some of the thoughts which are flying through my head.

It is not safe to talk here. The walls are quite thin, and the neighbors might wonder at a late-night conference. Besides, George and Katherine are already asleep. Only Henry and I are still awake, and he's just staring at the ceiling.

I am really uptight. I am so jittery I can barely sit still. And I'm exhausted. I've been up since 5:30 this morning, when George phoned to warn that the arrests had begun, and it's after midnight now. I've been keyed up and on the move all day.

But at the same time I'm exhilarated. We have finally acted! How long we will be able to continue defying the System, no one knows. Maybe it will all end tomorrow, but we must not think about that. Now that we have begun, we must continue with the plan we have been developing so carefully ever since the Gun Raids two years ago.

What a blow *that* was to us! And how it shamed us! All that brave talk by patriots, "The government will never take *my* guns away," and then nothing but meek submission when it happened.

On the other hand, maybe we should be heartened by the fact that there were still so many of us who had guns then, nearly 18 months after the Cohen Act had outlawed all private ownership of firearms in the United States. It was only because so many of us defied the law and hid our weapons instead of turning them in that the government wasn't able to act more harshly against us after the Gun Raids.

I'll never forget that terrible day: November 9, 1989. They knocked on my door at five in the morning. I was completely unsuspecting as I got up to see who it was.

I opened the door, and four Negroes came pushing into the apartment before I could stop them. One was carrying a baseball bat, and two had long kitchen knives thrust into their belts. The one with the bat shoved me back into a corner and stood guard over me with his bat raised in a threatening position while the other three began ransacking my apartment.

My first thought was that they were robbers. Robberies of this sort had become all too common since the Cohen Act, with groups of Blacks forcing their way into White homes to rob and rape, knowing that even if their victims had guns they probably would not dare use them.

Then the one who was guarding me flashed some kind of card and informed me that he and his accomplices were "special deputies" for the Northern Virginia Human Relations Council. They were searching for firearms, he said.

I couldn't believe it. It just couldn't be happening. Then I saw that they were wearing strips of green cloth tied around their left arms. As they dumped the contents of drawers on the floor and pulled luggage from the closet, they were ignoring things that robbers wouldn't have passed up: my brand-new electric razor, a valuable gold pocket watch, a milk bottle full of dimes. They *were* looking for firearms!

Right after the Cohen Act was passed, all of us in the Organization had cached our guns and ammunition where they weren't likely to be found. Those in my unit had carefully greased our weapons, sealed them in an oil drum, and spent all of one tedious weekend burying the drum in an eight-foot-deep pit 200 miles away in the woods of western Pennsylvania.

But I had kept one gun out of the cache. I had hidden my .357 magnum revolver and 50 rounds of ammunition inside the door frame between the kitchen and the living room. By pulling out two loosened nails and removing one board from the door frame I could get to my revolver in about two minutes flat if I ever needed it. I had timed myself.

But a police search would never uncover it. And these inexperienced Blacks couldn't find it in a million years.

After the three who were conducting the search had looked in all the obvious places, they began slitting open my mattress and the sofa cushions. I protested vigorously at this and briefly considered trying to put up a fight.

About that time there was a commotion out in the hallway. Another group of searchers had found a rifle hidden under a bed in the apartment of the young couple down the hall. They had both been handcuffed and were being forcibly escorted toward the stairs. Both were clad only in their underwear, and the young woman was complaining loudly about the fact that her baby was being left alone in the apartment.

Another man walked into my apartment. He was a Caucasian, though with an unusually dark complexion. He also wore a green armband, and he carried an attache case and a clipboard.

The Blacks greeted him deferentially and reported the negative result of their search: "No guns here, Mr. Tepper."

Tepper ran his finger down the list of names and apartment numbers on his clipboard until he came to mine. He frowned. "This is a bad one," he said. "He has a racist record. Been cited by the Council twice. And he owned eight firearms which were never turned in."

Tepper opened his attache case and took out a small, black object about the size of a pack of cigarettes which was attached by a long cord to an electronic instrument in the case. He began moving the black object in long sweeps back and forth over the walls, while the attache case emitted a dull, rumbling noise. The rumble rose in pitch as the gadget approached the light switch, but Tepper convinced himself that the change was caused by the metal junction box and conduit buried in the wall. He continued his methodical sweep.

As he swept over the left side of the kitchen door frame the rumble jumped to a piercing shriek. Tepper grunted excitedly, and one of the Negroes went out and came back a few seconds later with a sledge hammer and a pry bar. It took the Negro substantially less than two minutes after that to find my gun.

I was handcuffed without further ado and led outside. Altogether, four of us were arrested in my apartment building. In addition to the couple down the hall, there was an elderly man from the fourth floor. They hadn't found a firearm in his apartment, but they had found four shotgun shells on his closet shelf. Ammunition was also illegal.

Mr Tepper and some of his "deputies" had more searches to carry out, but three large Blacks with baseball bats and knives were left to guard us in front of the apartment building.

The four of us were forced to sit on the cold sidewalk, in various states of undress, for more than an hour until a police van finally came for us.

As other residents of the apartment building left for work, they eyed us curiously. We were all shivering, and the young woman from down the hall was weeping uncontrollably.

One man stopped to ask what it was all about. One of our guards brusquely explained that we were all under arrest for possessing illegal weapons. The man stared at us and shook his head disapprovingly.

Then the Black pointed to me and said: "And that one's a racist." Still shaking his head, the man moved on.

Herb Jones, who used to belong to the Organization and was one of the most outspoken of the "they'll-never-get-my-gun" people before the Cohen Act, walked by quickly with his eyes averted. His apartment had been searched too, but Herb was clean. He had been practically the first man in town to turn his guns over to the police after the passage of the Cohen Act made him liable to ten years imprisonment in a Federal penitentiary if he kept them.

That was the penalty the four of us on the sidewalk were facing. It didn't work out that way, though. The reason it didn't is that the raids which were carried out all over the country that day netted a lot more fish than the System had counted on: more than 800,000 persons were arrested.

At first the news media tried hard to work up enough public sentiment against us so that the arrests would stick. The fact that there weren't enough jail cells in the country to hold us all could be remedied by herding us into barbed-wire enclosures outdoors until new prison facilities could be readied, the newspapers suggested. In freezing weather!

I still remember the *Washington Post* headline the next day: "Fascist-Racist Conspiracy Smashed, Illegal Weapons Seized." But not even the brainwashed American public could fully accept the idea that nearly a million of their fellow citizens had been engaged in a secret, armed conspiracy. . . .

We had made up our minds to have an Organization that would be *ready* the next time the System provided an opportunity to strike. The shame of our failure to act, indeed, our inability to act, in 1989 tormented us and drove us without mercy. It was probably the single most important factor in steeling our wills to whip the Organization into fighting trim, despite all obstacles.

Another thing that helped—at least, with me—was the constant threat of rearrest and prosecution. Even if I had wanted to give it all up and join the TV-and-funnies crowd, I couldn't. I could make no plans for a "normal," civilian future, never knowing when I might be prosecuted under the Cohen Act. (The Constitutional guarantee of a speedy trial, of course, has been "reinterpreted" by the courts until it means no more than our Constitutional guarantee of the right to keep and bear arms.)

So I, and I know this also applies to George and Katherine and Henry, threw myself without reservation into work for the Organization and made only plans for the future of the Organization. My private life had ceased to matter.

Whether the Organization actually *is* ready, I guess we'll find out soon enough. So far, so good, though. Our plan for avoiding another mass roundup, like 1989, seems to have worked.

Early last year we began putting a number of new members, unknown to the political police, into police agencies and various quasi-official organizations, such as the human relations councils. They served as our early-warning network and otherwise kept us generally informed of the System's plans against us.

We were surprised at the ease with which we were able to set up and operate this network. We never would have gotten away with it back in the days of J. Edgar Hoover.

It is ironic that while the Organization has always warned the public against the dangers of racial integration of our police, this has now turned out to be a blessing in disguise for us. The "equal opportunity" boys have really done a wonderful wrecking job on the FBI and other investigative agencies, and their efficiency is way down as a result. Still, we'd better not get over-confident or careless. . . .

XXVIII

November 9, 1993. It's still three hours until first light, and all systems are "go." I'll use the time to write a few pages—my last diary entry. Then it's a one-way trip to the Pentagon for me. The warhead is strapped into the front seat of the old Stearman and rigged to detonate either on impact or when I flip a switch in the back seat. Hopefully, I'll be able to manage a low-level air burst directly over the center of the Pentagon. Failing that, I'll at least try to fly as close as I can before I'm shot down.

It's been more than four years since I've flown, but I've thoroughly familiarized myself with the Stearman cockpit and been briefed on the plane's peculiarities: I don't anticipate any piloting problems. The barn-hangar here is only eight miles from the Pentagon. We'll thoroughly warm up the engine in the barn, and when the door is opened I'll go like a bat out of hell, straight for the Pentagon, at an altitude of about 50 feet.

By the time I hit the defensive perimeter I should be making about 150 miles an hour, and it'll take me just under another 70 seconds to reach the target. Two-thirds of the troops around the Pentagon are niggers, which should greatly boost my chances of getting through.

The sky should still be heavily overcast, and there'll be just enough light for me to make out my landmarks. We've painted the plane to be as nearly invisible as possible under the anticipated flying conditions, and I'll be too low for radar-controlled fire. Considering everything, I believe my chances are excellent.

I regret that I won't be around to participate in the final success of our revolution, but I am happy that I have been allowed to do as much as I have. It is a comforting thought in these last hours of my physical existence that, of all the billions of men and women of my race who have ever lived, I will have been able to play a more vital role than all but a handful of them in determining the ultimate destiny of mankind. What I will do today will be of more weight in the annals of the race than all the conquests of Caesar and Napoleon—if I succeed!

And succeed I must, or the entire revolution will be in the gravest danger. Revolutionary Command estimates that the System will launch its invasion against California within the next 48 hours. Once the order is issued from the Pentagon, we will be unable to halt the invasion. And if my mission today fails, there'll not be enough time for us to try something else.

Monday night, after we had made the final decision on this mission, I underwent the rite of Union. Actually, I have been undergoing the rite for the past 30 hours, and it will not be complete for another three; only in the moment of my death will I achieve full membership in the Order.

To many that may seem a gloomy prospect, I suppose, but not to me. I have known what was ahead of me since my trial last March, and I am grateful that my probationary period has been cut short by five months, partly because of the present crisis and partly because my performance since March has been considered exemplary.

The ceremony Monday was more moving and beautiful than I could have imagined it would be. More than 200 of us assembled in the cellar of the Georgetown gift shop, from which the partitions and stacked crates had been removed to make room for us. Thirty new probationary members were sworn into the Order, and 18 others, including me, participated in the rite of Union. I alone, however, was singled out, because of my unique status.

When Major Williams summoned me, I stepped forward and then turned to face the silent sea of robed figures. What a contrast with the tiny gathering only two years earlier, when seven of us met upstairs for my initiation! The Order, even with its extraordinary standards, is growing with astonishing rapidity.

Knowing fully what was demanded in character and commitment of each man who stood before me, my chest swelled with pride. These were no soft-bellied, conservative businessmen assembled for some Masonic mumbo-jumbo; no loudmouthed, beery red-necks letting off a little ritualized steam about "the goddam niggers"; no pious, frightened churchgoers whining for the guidance or protection of an anthropomorphic deity. These were *real men, White* men, men who were now *one* with me in spirit and consciousness as well as in blood.

As the torchlight flickered over the coarse, gray robes of the motionless throng, I thought to myself: These men are the best my race has produced in this generation—and they are as good as have been produced in any generation. In them are combined fiery passion and icy discipline, deep intelligence and instant readiness for action, a strong sense of self-worth and a total commitment to our common cause. On them hang the hopes of everything that will ever be. They are the vanguard of the coming New Era, the pioneers who will lead our race out of its present depths and toward the unexplored heights above. And I am *one* with them!

Then I made my brief declaration: "Brothers! Two years ago, when I entered your ranks for the first time, I consecrated my life to our Order and to the purpose for which it exists. But then I faltered in the fulfillment of my obligation to you. Now I am ready to meet my obligation fully. I offer you my life. Do you accept it?"

In a rumbling unison their reply came back: "Brother! We accept your life. In return we offer you everlasting life in us. Your deed shall not be in vain, nor shall it be forgotten, until the end of time. To this commitment we pledge our lives."

I know, as certainly as it is possible for a man to know anything, that the Order will not fail me if I do not fail it. The Order has a life which is more than the sum of the lives of its members. When it speaks collectively, as it did Monday, something deeper and older and wiser than any of us speaks—something which cannot die. Of that deeper life I am now about to partake.

Of course, I would have liked to have children by Katherine, so that I could also have immortality of another sort, but that is not to be. I am satisfied.

They've been warming up the engine for about 10 minutes now, and Bill is signalling to me that it's time to go. The rest of the crew has already taken cover in the blast shelter we dug under the barn floor. I will now entrust my diary to Bill, and he will later put it in the hiding place with the other volumes.

Epilog

Thus end Earl Turner's diaries, as unpretentiously as they began.

His final mission was successful, of course, as we all are reminded each year on November 9—our traditional Day of the Martyrs.

With the System's principal military nerve center destroyed, the System's forces poised outside the Organization's California enclave continued to wait for orders which never came. Declining morale, soaring desertions, growing Black indiscipline, and finally, the inability of the System to maintain the integrity of its supply line to its California troops resulted in the gradual erosion of the threat of invasion. Eventually the System began regrouping its forces elsewhere, to meet new challenges in other parts of the country.

And then, just as the Jews had feared, the flow of Organization activists turned exactly 180 degrees from what it had been in the weeks and months immediately prior to July 4, 1993. From scores of training camps in the liberated zone, first hundreds, then thousands of highly motivated guerrilla fighters began slipping through the System's diminishing ring of troops and moving eastward. With these guerrilla forces the Organization followed the example of its Baltimore members and rapidly established dozens of new enclaves, primarily in the nuclear-devastated areas, where System authority was weakest.

The Detroit enclave was initially the most important of these. Bloody anarchy had reigned among the survivors in the Detroit area for several weeks after the nuclear blasts of September 8. Eventually, a semblance of order had been restored, with System troops loosely sharing power with the leaders of a number of Black gangs in the area. Although there were a few isolated White strongholds which kept the roving mobs of Black plunderers and rapists at bay, most of the disorganized and demoralized White survivors in and around Detroit offered no effective resistance to the Blacks, and, just as in other heavily Black areas of the country, they suffered terribly.

Then, in mid-December, the Organization seized the initiative. A number of synchronized lightning raids on the System's military strongpoints in the Detroit area resulted in an easy victory.

The Organization then established certain patterns in Detroit which were soon followed elsewhere. All captured White troops, as soon as they had laid down their weapons, were offered a chance to fight with the Organization against the System. Those who immediately volunteered were taken aside for preliminary screening and then sent to camps for indoctrination and special training. The others were machine-gunned on the spot, without further ado.

The same degree of ruthlessness was used in dealing with the White civilian population. When the Organization's cadres moved into the White strongholds in the Detroit suburbs, the first thing they found it necessary to do was to liquidate most of the local White leaders, in order to establish the unquestioned authority of the Organization. There was no time or patience for trying to reason with shortsighted Whites who insisted that they weren't "racists" or "revolutionaries" and didn't need the help of any "outside agitators" in dealing with their problems, or who had some other conservative or parochial fixation.

The Whites of Detroit and the other new enclaves were organized more along the lines described by Earl Turner for Baltimore than for California, but even more rapidly and roughly. In most areas of the country there was no opportunity for an orderly, large-scale separation of non-Whites, as in California, and consequently a bloody race war raged for months, taking a terrible toll of those Whites who were not in one of the Organization's tightly controlled, all-White enclaves.

Food became critically scarce everywhere during the winter of 1993–1994. The Blacks lapsed into cannibalism, just as they had in California, while hundreds of thousands of starving Whites, who earlier had ignored the Organization's call for a rising against the System, began appearing at the borders of the various liberated zones begging for food. The Organization was only able to feed the White populations already under its control by imposing the severest rationing, and it was necessary to turn many of the latecomers away.

Those who were admitted—and that meant only children, women of child-bearing age, and able-bodied men willing to fight in the Organization's ranks—were subjected to much more severe racial screening than had been used to separate Whites from non-Whites in California. It was no longer sufficient to be merely White; in order to eat one had to be judged the bearer of especially valuable genes.

In Detroit the practice was first established (and it was later adopted elsewhere) of providing any able-bodied White male who sought admittance to the Organization's enclave with one hot meal and a bayonet or other edged weapon. His forehead was then marked with an indelible dye, and he was turned out and could be readmitted permanently only by bringing back the head of a freshly killed Black or other non-White. This practice assured that precious food would not be wasted on those who would not or could not add to the Organization's fighting strength, but it took a terrible toll of the weaker and more decadent White elements.

Tens of millions perished during the first half of 1994, and the total White population of the country reached a low point of approximately 50 million by August of that year. By then, however, nearly half the remaining Whites were in Organization enclaves, and food production and distribution in the enclaves had grown until it was barely sufficient to prevent further losses from starvation.

Although a central government of sorts still existed, the System's military and police forces were, for all practical purposes, reduced to a number of essentially autonomous local commands, whose principal activity became looting for food, liquor, gasoline, and women. Both the Organization and the System avoided large-scale encounters with each other, the Organization confining itself to short, intense raids on System troop concentrations and other facilities, and the System's forces confining themselves to guarding their sources of supply and, in some areas, to attempting to limit the further expansion of the Organization's enclaves.

But the Organization's enclaves continued to expand, nevertheless, both in size and number, all through the five Dark Years preceding the New Era. At one time there were nearly 2,000 separate Organization enclaves in North America. Outside these zones of order and security, the anarchy and savagery grew steadily worse, with the only real authority wielded by marauding bands which preyed on each other and on the unorganized and defenseless masses.

Many of these bands were composed of Blacks, Puerto Ricans, Chicanos, and half-White mongrels. In growing numbers, however, Whites also formed bands along racial lines, even without Organization guidance. As the war of extermination wore on, millions of soft, city-bred, brainwashed Whites gradually began regaining their manhood. The rest died.

The Organization's growing success was not without its setbacks, of course. One of the most notable of these was the terrible Pittsburgh Massacre, of June 1994. The Organization had established an enclave there in May of that year, forcing the retreat of local System forces, but it did not act swiftly enough in identifying and liquidating the local Jewish element.

A number of Jews, in collaboration with White conservatives and liberals, had time to work out a plan of subversion. The consequence was that System troops, aided by their fifth column inside the enclave, recaptured Pittsburgh. The Jews and Blacks then went on a wild rampage of mass murder, reminiscent of the worst excesses of the Jew-instigated Bolshevik Revolution in Russia, 75 years earlier. By the time the blood-orgy ended, virtually every White in the area had either been butchered or forced to flee. The surviving staff members of the Organization's Pittsburgh Field Command, whose hesitation in dealing with the Jews had brought on the catastrophe, were rounded up and shot by a special disciplinary squad acting on orders from Revolutionary Command.

The only time, after November 9, 1993, the Organization was forced to detonate a nuclear weapon on the North American continent was a year later, in Toronto. Hundreds of thousands of Jews had fled the United States to that Canadian city during 1993 and 1994, making almost a second New York of it and using it as their command center for the war raging to the south. So far as both the Jews and the Organization were concerned, the U.S.–Canadian border had no real significance during the later stages of the Great Revolution, and by mid-1994 conditions were only slightly less chaotic north of the border than south of it.

Throughout the Dark Years neither the Organization nor the System could hope for a completely decisive advantage over the other, so long as they both retained the capability for nuclear warfare. During the first part of this period, when the System's conventional military strength greatly exceeded the Organization's, only the Organization's threat of retaliation with its more than 100 nuclear warheads hidden inside the major population centers still under System control kept the System, in most cases, from moving against the Organization's liberated zones.

Later, when Organizational gains, together with growing attrition of the System's forces through desertions, tilted the balance of conventional strength toward the Organization, the System retained control over a number of military units armed with nuclear weapons and, by threatening to use these, forced the Organization to leave certain System strongholds inviolate.

Even the System's elite, pampered nuclear troops were not immune to the processes of attrition which sapped the System's conventional strength, however, and they could postpone the inevitable only temporarily. On January 30, 1999, in the momentous Truce of Omaha, the last group of System generals surrendered their commands to the Organization, in return for a pledge that they and their immediate families would be allowed to live out the remainders of their lives unmolested. The Organization kept its pledge, and a special reservation on an island off the California coast was set aside for the generals.

Then, of course, came the mopping-up period, when the last of the non-White bands were hunted down and exterminated, followed by the final purge of undesirable racial elements among the remaining White population.

From the liberation of North America until the beginning of the New Era for our whole planet, there elapsed the remarkably short time of just under 11 months. Professor Anderson has recorded and analyzed the events of this climactic period in detail in his *History of the Great Revolution*. Here it is sufficient to note that, with the principal centers of world Jewish power annihilated and the nuclear threat of the Soviet Union neutralized, the most important obstacles to the Organization's worldwide victory were out of the way.

From as early as 1993 the Organization had had active cells in Western Europe, and they grew with extraordinary rapidity in the six years preceding the victory in North America. Liberalism had taken its toll in Europe, just as in America, and the old order in most places was a rotted-out shell with only a surface semblance of strength. The disastrous economic collapse in Europe in the spring of 1999, following the demise of the System in North America, greatly helped in preparing the European masses morally for the Organization's final takeover.

That takeover came in a great, Europe-wide rush in the summer and fall of 1999, as a cleansing hurricane of change swept over the continent, clearing away in a few months the refuse of a millennium or more of alien ideology and a century or more of profound moral and material decadence. The blood flowed ankle-deep in the streets of many of Europe's great cities momentarily, as the race traitors, the offspring of generations of dysgenic breeding, and hordes of *Gastarbeiter* met a common fate. Then the great dawn of the New Era broke over the Western world.

The single remaining power center on earth not under Organizational control by early December 1999 was China. The Organization was willing to postpone the solution of the Chinese problem for several years, but the Chinese themselves forced the Organization to take immediate and drastic action. The Chinese, of course, had invaded the Asiatic regions of the Soviet Union immediately after the nuclear strike of September 8, 1993, but until the fall of 1999 they had remained east of the Urals, consolidating the vast, new, conquered territory.

When, during the summer and early fall of 1999, one European nation after another was liberated by the Organization, the Chinese decided to make a grab for European Russia. The Organization countered this move massively, using nuclear missiles to knock out the still-primitive Chinese missile and strategic-bomber capabilities, as well as hitting a number of new Chinese troop concentrations west of the Urals. Unfortunately, this action did not stem the Yellow tide flowing north and west from China.

The Organization still required time to reorganize and reorient the European populations newly under its control before it could hope to deal in a conventional manner with the enormous numbers of Chinese infantry pouring across the Urals into Europe; all its dependable troops at that time were hardly sufficient even for garrison duty in the newly liberated and still not entirely pacified areas of eastern and southern Europe.

Therefore, the Organization resorted to a combination of chemical, biological, and radiological means, on an enormous scale, to deal with the problem. Over a period of four years some 16 million square miles of the earth's surface, from the Ural Mountains to the Pacific and from the Arctic Ocean to the Indian Ocean, were effectively sterilized. Thus was the Great Eastern Waste created.

Only in the last decade have certain areas of the Waste been declared safe for colonization. Even so, they are "safe" only in the sense that the poisons sowed there a century ago have abated to the point that they are no longer a hazard to life. As everyone is aware, the bands of mutants which roam the Waste remain a real threat, and it may be another century before the last of them has been eliminated and White colonization has once again established a human presence throughout this vast area.

But it was in the year 1999, according to the chronology of the Old Era—just 110 years after the birth of the Great One—that the dream of a White world finally became a certainty. And it was the sacrifice of the lives of uncounted thousands of brave men and women of the Organization during the preceding years which had kept that dream alive until its realization could no longer be denied.

Among those uncounted thousands Earl Turner played no small part. He gained immortality for himself on that dark November day 106 years ago when he faithfully fulfilled his obligation to his race, to the Organization, and to the holy Order which had accepted him into its ranks. And in so doing he helped greatly to assure that his race would survive and prosper, that the Organization would achieve its worldwide political and military goals, and that the Order would spread its wise and benevolent rule over the earth for all time to come.

28

Bob Moser

———✦———

"Age of Rage: Young Extremists Find New Targets—and New Recruits" (2004)

The Southern Poverty Law Center was founded in 1971 by Morris Dees and Joe Levin as a small civil rights law firm in Montgomery, Alabama. It has since won Supreme Court cases against white supremacists, compiled extensive information on hate-group activities, and launched programs to promote anti-bias activism and teach tolerance. Bob Moser is a senior writer for Intelligence Report, *a quarterly magazine published by the Center.*

Youth, Hate and Crime

LAST JULY 4, a lesbian couple in Boston took their two children to an Independence Day celebration in a local park—and ran smack into a gang of teenagers who did not appreciate their presence.

After the teens allegedly taunted the family with anti-gay slurs and threats, 15-year-old Anita Santiago allegedly slugged 35-year-old Lisa Craig hard enough to knock her to the ground. According to police reports, Santiago and her fellow gang members then bashed Craig's head against the sidewalk and kicked the woman so brutally that her brain hemorrhaged and she needed more than 200 stitches.

A few hours later, in the blue-collar suburb of Farmingville, N.Y., a Mexican family was startled awake—just in time—by a fire that would tear through their home and reduce it to ashes in minutes. Five boys, ages 15 to 17, had decided to top off their July 4th festivities by torching the house with leftover firecrackers.

Bob Moser, "Age of Rage, Young extremists find new target—and new recruits." From the Southern Poverty Law Center's *Intelligence Report* 114, Summer 2004.

Asked why, one of the teens simply told police that "Mexicans live there"—as if that were reason enough.

Welcome to the harsh new world of young-adult hate. . . . The Independence Day incidents illustrate some major shifts in the ways American kids are learning to hate—and how they act it out.

The Poison Spreads

Hate among kids has probably never been more widespread—and it doesn't stop with racist graffiti, Confederate flag T-shirts, swastika tattoos and homophobic slurs in high-school hallways.

Studies by hate-crime experts like Jack Levin, director of Northeastern University's Brudnick Center and co-author of the new book, *Why We Hate,* show that incidents perpetrated by youngsters, which became more frequent from the mid-1980s to the early 1990s, "plummeted" during the Clinton years.

But since 9/11, the number of hate crimes by kids has risen sharply—and they appear to be more brutal than ever. "What we're seeing," says Eric Ward, a longtime observer of extremist youth who works at Chicago's Center for New Community, "is a more militant, street-fighter culture."

As both the Boston and Farmingville incidents show, the targets of this militance have multiplied—and so have the perpetrators. After 9/11, a disproportionate number of the assaults on Muslim-Americans were committed by teenagers. The same appears true for attacks against sexual and gender minorities, Hispanics and the homeless.

And hate activity is no longer the province of white boys, though they're still the main offenders. Not only are more Hispanic and African-American kids getting involved in hate, but more girls as well.

Social ecologist Ronald Huff, a longtime student of both street and racist youth gangs, estimates that in many cities "anywhere from a third to 50% of gang members are girls."

In another demographic shift, the bulk of hate activity now bubbles up in the suburbs—among reasonably well-off youth.

"Twenty years ago, big cities were hotbeds of hate," says Levin, "But as more and more minority families have moved into suburban areas, the prevalence of hate attacks has also increased there—much of it perpetrated by kids."

Where the classic profile of a young hater in the 1980s was a blue-collar juvenile angered by economic displacement, the more typical picture now is a teenager "raised in a middle-class family in a place where almost everyone is a racial rubber-stamp of himself," Levin says.

"These kids aren't prepared for people who are different. They see them as a threat. They come home in the afternoon to their empty houses, log onto the Internet, visit hate sites, chat rooms, bulletin boards and get ideas."

For kids who've grown up online, there's no longer a need to join large hate groups in order to get those ideas. Neo-Nazi outfits like the National Socialist Movement and Aryan Nations (see Youth Action Corps) still work hard to recruit youngsters into the fold, and concerts featuring adrenaline-fueled "hatecore" music continue to gain popularity and win converts.

But much of the racist activity among kids is springing up from the grassroots, with small groups like the Connecticut White Wolves and Agnostic Neo-Nazis, who draw inspiration from Internet hate sites—and run with it.

"I don't know what's more frightening," says Ward, "kids joining organized hate groups, or the way hate is rising up spontaneously among kids who feel it's OK to terrorize and assault people because of their race or religion or sexual orientation. What does that say about where our society's headed?"

Desperately Seeking Stability

It's an excellent question. Why is juvenile hate spreading in a culture that seems to become more accepting of differences by the day?

There's no shortage of reasons that have been proffered by sociologists and criminologists. Some blame the resegregation of schools and neighborhoods. Some point to the omnipresence of violence in movies, on TV, and in video games.

Some cite misguided "zero tolerance" policies in schools and communities, where kids are increasingly incarcerated for first offenses; on any given day, well over 100,000 U.S. youth are locked up in places that are "not only schools of violence," says Levin, "but crash courses in hatred."

Then there's the lingering death of the American dream: with downward mobility—rather than upward—as their most likely future direction, more middle-class kids are looking to rebel, and looking for somebody to blame.

No single factor is sufficient to explain the spread of youth hatred. But the upsurge in one of its main manifestations—white supremacy—has inspired a theory developed by sociologists like Pamela Perry and Randy Blazak.

In Perry's 2002 book, *Shades of White*, she chronicled the racial attitudes of white kids at two contemporary California high schools—one predominantly white, one minority white. She found what Blazak calls "anomie"—French sociologist Emile Durkheim's term for the sense of confusion brought on by rapid social change.

The confusion, in this case, amounts to a basic question: "[W]hat is the new role of whites in the multicultural chorus?"

As Blazak points out in his forthcoming book, *Ethnic Envy,* "contemporary youth were born in the 1980s and 1990s, long after the frontline civil rights battles." White kids lack a long-term perspective on racial oppression in the U.S.—and end up saying, for instance, that "racism ended in the 1960s" and they're tired of hearing blacks "complaining about it."

They also see Hispanics, lesbians and gay men, Asian-Americans and others embraced and recognized—while straight white culture seems, from their limited vantage points, to be dissed and demonized.

"White kids feel like *their* racial identity is murky nowadays," says Ward. That's been partly responsible for the outbreak of Confederate flag T-shirts in high schools, both North and South, and also in several efforts—usually snuffed out by administrators—to start Caucasian clubs, mostly in California high schools.

"When they bring it up, they get their hands slapped," Ward says, "and they become pariahs. Pariahs can be dangerous."

Hate groups have tailored their recruitment pitches to these frustrated white kids. A perfect example is Jeff Schoep, "commander" of the National Socialist Movement, who says his group "lets our young people know it's all right to be white, and better yet, something to be proud of."

With whites already a minority in some parts of the U.S., it's a pitch that has become very popular among extremist groups—and among bright, middle-class kids like Logan Brown. The 15-year-old lives in California, the first large American state to become minority white, and he's trying to revive the Aryan Nations Youth Action Corps.

Brown insists that he's nothing like "the stereotypical racist," certainly no "redneck." But he yearns for the long-lost days like "the 1920s when everything was white and beautiful. Minorities were few and far between. Gays weren't out of the closet. We were a white civilized nation."

Brown's longing for simplicity and order—two things that seem hopelessly lost in the America of 2004—points up one final, age-old reason why kids turn to hate. They want to know why the world seems so messy, so complicated, so out-of-control.

"Most parents, most teachers don't pretend to have easy answers," notes Ward. "Hate groups do. Hate music does. Hate sites do. The racist Skinhead down the street does, too."

Easy answers can be mighty appealing to young people. But when those answers don't mesh with the complicated realities of contemporary life, the result can be anger, frustration, and violence.

PART SIX

Feminism

ALL THE IDEOLOGIES in this book offer visions of liberation, but, in most cases, it is freedom for the few. Which few is variously defined by class, gender, nation, race, religion, sexuality—the list goes on. Feminism is different, or, at least, it intends to be. According to Catharine Stimpson, feminism offers "a moral vision of women, in all their diversity, and of social justice," and it enables "men and women to re-experience and re-form themselves."[1] Diversity *and* solidarity, equality *and* justice—for men and women, rich and poor, black, brown, red, yellow, and white. Unlike most ideologies, feminism provides a vision of emancipation that, ideally, includes all of humanity.

In America, feminism is often portrayed as the product of the 1960s, but it has a longer, richer history. Indeed, it is difficult to find a time or place when women were not struggling to improve their condition. The birth of feminism as an organized movement coincides with liberal revolutions, as women demanded inclusion in "the rights of man." In 1787 Abigail Adams warned her husband John, a delegate to the American Constitutional Convention, that "if particular care and attention is not paid to the ladies, we are determined to foment a rebellion, and [we] will not hold ourselves bound by any laws in which we have no voice and representation!"[2] In 1789 women petitioned the French National Assembly: "You have destroyed all the prejudices of the past, but you allow the oldest and the most pervasive to remain, which excludes from office, position and honour, and above all from the right of sitting amongst you, half the inhabitants of the kingdom."[3] In 1848 women met for the first equal rights convention at Seneca Falls, New York. Paralleling the Declaration of Independence, they began their "Declaration of Sentiments" with the words, "We hold these truths to be self-evident: that all men and women are created equal."[4] The Seneca Falls delegates demanded equal rights, including the right to vote, but it would be 1920 before women were granted suffrage. In 1983 the Equal Rights Amendment (ERA)—which reads: "Equality of rights under the law shall not be denied or abridged by the United States or by any State on account of sex."—fell short of ratification by three states.[5] Feminists continue to debate the importance of the ERA and its defeat: Was it a necessary step? A symbolic platform? A strategic error? In any case, its failure should remind Americans that sex discrimination persists. The question is: Why? As the following selections suggest, feminists' answers to this question vary.

Equal rights for women and men is the political agenda of liberal feminism, the dominant feminist ideology in the United States and, arguably, throughout the Western world. Mary Wollstonecraft, who is widely regarded as the founding mother of liberal feminism, published her *Vindication of the Rights of Woman* in 1792, shortly after the American and French revolutions. Wollstonecraft attributes the current "follies" and "vices" of women—cunning, ignorance, and vanity—to their unnatural condition; raised as "ladies," taught to please men, women are incapable of exercising their reason and developing their character. However, she insists that if they were given the opportunity, women would demonstrate equal rationality and, hence, deserve equal rights with men: "Let their faculties have room to unfold, and their virtues to gain strength, and then determine where the whole sex must stand in the intellectual scale."

Betty Friedan's writings illustrate more recent arguments for women's rights. In *The Feminine Mystique* (1963), Friedan identified "the problem that has no name"—a vague sense of dissatisfaction shared by many middle-class, stay-at-home mothers and wives. Friedan's book mobilized many women to protest against the underlying inequality it exposed, and, three years later, she founded the National Organization for Women (NOW) to provide a structure for their efforts. Two goals emerge in Friedan's and other liberal feminists' writings: the elimination of sex roles and the extension of equal rights to women. Contemporary liberal feminists echo Wollstonecraft regarding the logic connecting them: natural differences between the sexes do not justify the gender roles society prescribes. Liberal feminists have fought sex discrimination on two related fronts, opposing laws that discriminate against women and, when possible, also using the law to oppose discrimination. The NOW Bill of Rights outlines some of their demands: the ERA, nondiscriminatory employment practices, maternity-leave rights, child-care tax deductions, child-care centers, equal educational opportunities, job training, and reproductive rights.

Recognizing that many women disagree with this liberal feminist agenda, in "Our Revolution Is Unique," Friedan responds to their most frequent criticisms. She insists that liberal feminists do not oppose marriage and children but they do want women to be "free to choose" among these and other options: "We do not speak for every woman in America, but we speak for the *right* of every woman in America to become all she is capable of becoming—on her own and/or in partnership with a man." Nor do liberal feminists hate men. Friedan argues that men who define women as sex objects are often suffering themselves from an image of masculinity—the "macho male"—that prevents them from being fully human. According to Friedan: "The real sexual revolution is the emergence of women from passivity, from thingness, to full self-determination, to full dignity. And insofar as they can do this, men are also emerging from the stage of identification with brutality and masters to full and sensitive complete humanity."

But can women (and men) ever "become all they are capable of becoming" in liberal, capitalist societies? Liberal feminism, with its emphasis on political rights, is often described as "first wave" feminism. "Second wave" feminists, many of them marxists and radicals, regard liberal feminists' emphasis upon legal reform as naïve. They point to deeper sources of women's oppression: capitalism and patriarchy, respectively. For marxist feminists, the traditional family (female homemaker and male breadwinner) is a "convenient" arrangement in which women exchange sexual and domestic services for financial support from men. This is why Marx and Engels call bourgeois marriage legalized prostitution: as an economic unit, the "bourgeois" family is functional for capitalism. According to Engels in *The Origin of the Family, Private Property and the State,* monogamous marriage provides a clear line of descent, facilitating inheritance and, with it, capital accumulation. But the family also has other functions. It is a "haven in a heartless world," a place to act out and/or recover from frustrations at work. It creates artificially high consumption, because each family needs appliances, cars, a home, and so on. It teaches sons to be good providers, and daughters to perform socially necessary labor without monetary compensation. Mothers also form a flexible labor force, available for part-time, temporary, and/or emergency work. Marxist feminists conclude that women's oppression in the family is integral to capitalism.

What, then, is to be done? Orthodox Marxists argue that proletarian women and men must fight together for socialist revolution, which means that women must postpone their personal concerns about the transformation of marriage and family. From this perspective, feminist issues divide the proletariat and thus are counterrevolutionary. Only after the revolution does the real emancipation of women begin. Lenin distinguishes this emancipation from legal reform: "Not withstanding all the laws emancipating woman, she continues to be a domestic slave, because petty housework crushes, strangles, stultifies and degrades her. . . . The real emancipation of women, real communism, will begin only where and when an all-out struggle begins (led by the proletariat wielding the state power) against this petty housekeeping, or rather when its wholesale transformation into a large-scale socialist economy begins."[6] Women must become producers, and to make this possible, familial tasks must be socialized. Unfortunately, "actually existing socialism" has failed to emancipate women, suggesting that sexism both predates and postdates capitalism.

Radical feminists—another second wave group—identify a common problem within marxist and liberal feminism: both perspectives try to be gender-blind and, as a result, they perpetuate gender-biases. How so? Whether through legal reform or economic revolution, liberals and marxists fight to include women in the dominant culture, thus continuing to define liberation in male terms. In contrast to these quests for political and/or economic equality with men, radical feminists celebrate women's differences from men. Indeed, they argue that the oppression of women is a fundamental principle of human society. Historically, women were the first oppressed group, and their oppression remains the broadest, deepest, and hardest to overcome. Radical feminists see every culture as two cultures, a male dominant and a female subordinate one. "Patriarchy" is radical feminists' term for male domination, especially of women's bodies. This domination takes many forms: monogamous heterosexuality reserves women's sexuality for men, while inadequate birth control and social pressure combine to force women to become mothers. Radical feminists seek not merely to invert this male culture but to transform or reconceive it. For example, whereas patriarchy encourages women to nurture husbands and children, radical feminists tell women to nurture themselves.

Radical feminist proposals for social change vary. Many advocate lesbianism. For Charlotte Bunch, "to be a lesbian is to love oneself, woman, in a culture that denigrates and despises women."[7] According to Adrienne Rich, lesbianism may be as much a political statement as a sexual preference. She describes a "lesbian continuum" of "woman-identified experience" that includes many "forms of primary intensity between and among women."[8] Monique Wittig's postmodern vision of lesbianism, included here, is even more radical. Postmoderns argue that Man and Woman are culturally constructed categories based on the presumption that unique individuals share essential features, such as sexual identity. Wittig contends, further, that these categories constitute a sex/gender system that serves specific political purposes: the heterosexist economy of two sexes defined in relation to one another reinforces men's control of women's bodies. It is not enough, she concludes, to replace patriarchy with matriarchy or for women to love women instead of men, since those inversions only perpetuate "the oppressors' definition of us." Lesbianism is better understood as "beyond the categories of sex" altogether. When the Man/Woman dualism disappears, Wittig declares, "we are for the first time in history confronted with the necessity of existing as a person."

For a variety of reasons, many women do not and/or cannot support radical feminist proposals, especially postmodern versions such as Wittig's. Economic inequalities as well as (hetero)sexual orientation keep many women involved in relationships with men. The category Woman also remains problematic for feminists: some think it "essentializes" or universalizes the diverse experiences of different women, while others contend that it remains crucial to emphasize the common features uniting women cross-culturally against global patriarchy. In both cases, it is important to distinguish arguments for a feminist politics based on commonalities among women from conservative defenses of sexual difference, such as those offered by Phyllis Schlafly (see selection 11). According to radical and postmodern feminists, Schlafly's positive woman reinforces the categories of heterosexism and is herself a product of patriarchy.

So, too, are more recent proposals by conservative feminists for what they call "power feminism." Paralleling Schlafly, these conservative theorists argue that radical feminism disempowers women by portraying them as the innocent victims of male sexual violence. Instead, the power feminists insist, women should stop feeling sorry for themselves and take responsibility for the choices they make—for example, women have some power to prevent date rape by making wise decisions about what they wear, how much they drink, where they party and with whom.[9] Some of their contemporaries accuse power feminists of "victim-blaming" and question whether their approach is, in fact, "feminist" at all. As Leslie Heywood and Jennifer Drake put it: "Power feminist tracts often eerily echo my old male coaches, who reacted to expressions of physical pain with 'Don't be a wuss; suck it up!' But after twenty years of 'sucking it up,' a lot of us know the empty frozenness such a philosophy brings, and we know that 'power feminism' is the voice of the father in his latest disguise."[10]

These critics of power feminism are part of a "third wave" of feminist thought that speaks to the experiences of younger women—and men—today. As Heywood and Drake describe it, " 'Third Wave feminism,' feminism in Generation X, is not 'power feminism.' It's not about trying to be men or women either. It's about trying to think through what 'coalition' might mean and on what basis a 'community' might really come into being."[11] For many third wave feminists, the development of global capitalism creates a new context for feminist struggles that raises new questions about what women share cross-culturally. One third waver, Michelle Sidler, focuses on changing economic prospects: "Whereas second wave feminists strove for equality with men, third wave feminists cannot reasonably expect equality from capitalism. But we can fight to preserve basic rights and decent working conditions for people."[12]

On the issue of economic inequalities, some second wave feminists still have valuable insights to offer the next generation. The socialist feminist Heidi Hartmann offers an alternative to radical and marxist feminism that overcomes the mutual limitations of their identity-based politics. Marxist feminism, she explains, focuses on class and neglects patriarchy, whereas radical feminism focuses on patriarchy and minimizes class. For Hartmann, the source of women's continuing oppression is male control over their productive and reproductive labor. She analyzes the intersections of capitalism and patriarchy to find "flashpoints" where different groups of women can join together in coalitions to fight their oppression under both systems. Her goal is one that other socialist feminists share: comprehensive (re)productive freedom, including abortion services, birth control, child care, equal education, freedom of sexual choice, decent housing, good jobs, medical care, social welfare. For socialist feminists, this agenda of (re)productive freedom extends beyond the liberals' "freedom to choose," the marxists' "proletarian revolution," and the radicals' "lesbian separatism" to create political contexts wherein women have genuine choices. And, they insist, those choices "must be available to all people—women, minorities, the disabled and handicapped, medicaid and welfare recipients, teenagers, everyone."[13]

Although socialist feminists continue to offer valuable suggestions for fighting "white supremacist, capitalist, patriarchy," they remain focused on the intersections between multiple aspects of women's identities. For many third wavers, especially multicultural and postcolonial feminists, this bypasses the most serious problem with identity politics, feminist and otherwise. According to Audre Lorde, the very categories of identity politics (e.g., class, gender, race, sexuality) are "the master's tools" for marking, dividing, and conquering women; feminists who use these tools to mobilize women "will never dismantle the master's house." With other multicultural feminists, Lorde resists any definition that categorizes women as a group—for example, as rich or poor, white or black, straight or lesbian—because such categories invariably also define some women in opposition to "other" women. In developing her critique of these dualistic categories, Lorde suggests that feminist struggles require a new form of consciousness, an understanding of human identities as changing, fluid, and multiple.

Gloria Anzaldúa's *mestiza* consciousness" is such an approach to identity, an understanding of oneself in relation to others that develops from living on the borders of many cultures. The perspective she describes does not balance the tensions between different groups of women, reconcile the different aspects within individual women, or compose an essential Woman from the many types of women across the globe. Instead, Anzaldúa urges feminists to expose the exclusionary and oppositional character of traditional identity politics and to work with the "energy" that "comes from a continual creative motion that keeps breaking down the unitary aspect of each new paradigm." For Anzaldúa, the formation of coalitions among women involves a constant movement, back and forth, across the shifting borders of multiple identities. Unlike Hartmann's flashpoints—where fixed identities based on class, gender, and/or race simply intersect—Anzaldúa's *mestiza* consciousness suggests that "unity" within individuals and "solidarity" among groups is always fragile, partial, and temporary.

For Anzaldúa, life in the borderlands challenges communities and individuals to remain continually open to changes in their self-understanding and their relationships with others. Another scholar, Bernice Johnson Reagon, describes the difference between a community and a coalition in similar terms: whereas a community creates a sense of belonging based on a shared identity, coalitions often require people to work with others who profoundly challenge their sense of identity. Of this "real" coalition work, Reagon says, "I feel as if I'm gonna keel over any minute and die. Most of the time you feel threatened to the core and if you don't, you're not really doing no coalescing."[14] Coalition, she argues, is also the only way to be—and stay—alive, especially in an increasingly global world.

In the final selection here, Chandra Mohanty presents a model of feminist solidarity that she would apply to antiglobalization struggles. She presumes that "the local and the global are not defined in terms of physical geography or territory but exist simultaneously and constitute each other." This rejection of geographic and territorial markers allows her to consider where women's lives intersect in international politics and how local and global issues converge within nation-states. Instead of Western/Third World, North/South, or even local/global dimensions, she employs the paradigm One-Third/Two-Thirds World to distinguish between social minorities and majorities "within and between the boundaries of nations" based on their "quality of life." By transforming our sense of inside/outside, distant/close, similar/different, this framework allows her to recognize "historically and culturally specific 'common differences' as the basis for analysis and solidarity." From this perspective, Mohanty makes gender and power relations visible in current discourses on globalization, and she reveals the ways that global capitalism further fragments an already complex reality. This aspect of her approach acknowledges Sidler's (and other third wavers') concerns about economic inequality today: "The condition is so subtle and pervasive that women and men of my generation do not know how to fight it." Yet Mohanty finds new opportunities for "transnational feminist practice" in processes of globalization, including the possibility of "transnational democratic citizenship." In order to see these possibilities, she argues, "our minds must be as ready to move as capital is, to trace its paths and to imagine alternative destinations."

Although many women's lives remain unfree and unequal under global capitalist patriarchy, many women and men today still choke on the sentence, "I am a feminist." This is why Catharine Stimpson labels *feminism* "the 'F' word."[15] That traditional voices choke on it is predictable. That women who have struggled and succeeded also do so is more troubling. Many such women adopt what Betty Friedan calls a three-sex theory: there are men, other women, and me. Some even argue that we live in a postfeminist age. Statistics continue to show, however, that exceptional women are just that—exceptions. Still other women, Stimpson says, choke on the word *feminism* because they are overwhelmed. They say, "I am a feminist," and think, "But I wish I did not have to be." These voices, some of them from the third wave, know that it is not possible to liberate one class, one race, one sex, and that no one can survive alone. Years ago, Pat Parker wrote:

> Black people alone cannot make a revolution in this country. Native American people alone cannot make revolution in this country. Asians alone cannot make revolution in this country. Chicanos alone cannot make revolution in this country. White people alone cannot make revolution in this country. Women alone cannot make revolution in this country. Gay people cannot make revolution in this country. And anyone who tries it will not be successful.[16]

Today only in solidarity across the many borders that divide us can feminists hope to succeed.

NOTES

1. Catharine Stimpson, "The 'F' Word," *Ms.* 16, nos. 1–2 (July–August 1987): 80.

2. Quoted in Jo Freeman, *The Politics of Women's Liberation* (New York: Longman, 1975), 12.

3. Quoted in Sheila Rowbotham, *Women, Resistance, and Revolution: A History of Women and Revolution in the Modern World* (New York: Random House, 1974), 39.

4. Elizabeth Cady Stanton, Susan B. Anthony, and Matilda Josephine Gage, "Declaration and Resolutions of the Seneca Falls Convention," in *Women Leaders in American Politics*, ed. James David Barber and Barbara Kellerman (Englewood Cliffs, N.J.: Prentice Hall, 1986), 201–204.

5. See Jane J. Mansbridge, *Why We Lost the ERA* (Chicago: University of Chicago Press, 1986).

6. V. I. Lenin, "The Emancipation of Women," in *Philosophy of Woman: An Anthology of Classic and Current Concepts*, 2nd ed., ed. Mary Briody Mahowald (Indianapolis: Hackett, 1983), 119.

7. Charlotte Bunch, "Lesbians in Revolt," in *Feminist Frameworks: Alternative Theoretical Accounts of the Relations Between Women and Men*, ed. Alison M. Jaggar and Paula Rothenberg (New York: McGraw-Hill, 1984), 144.

8. Adrienne Rich, "Compulsory Heterosexuality and Lesbian Existence," in Jaggar and Rothenberg, *Feminist Frameworks*, 417.

9. Katie Roiphe, *The Morning After: Sex, Fear, and Feminism* (Boston: Back Bay Books, 1994).

10. Leslie Heywood and Jennifer Drake, "We Learn America Like a Script: Activism in the Third Wave; or, Enough Phantoms of Nothing," in *Third Wave Agenda: Being Feminist, Doing Feminism*, ed. Leslie Heywood and Jennifer Drake (Minneapolis: University of Minnesota Press, 1997), 49–50.

11. Ibid., 50.

12. Michelle Sidler, "Living in McJobdom: Third Wave Feminism and Class Inequity" in Heywood and Drake, *Third Wave Agenda*, 36–37.

13. Quoted in Alison M. Jaggar, *Feminist Politics and Human Nature* (Totowa, N.J.: Rowman and Allanheld, 1983), 318.

14. Bernice Johnson Reagon, "Coalition Politics: Turning the Century," in *Home Girls: A Black Feminist Anthology,* ed. Barbara Smith (New York: Kitchen Table / Women of Color Press, 1983), 356.

15. Stimpson, "The 'F' Word."

16. Pat Parker, "Revolution: It's Not Neat or Pretty or Quick," in *This Bridge Called My Back: Writings by Radical Women of Color,* ed. Cherrie Moraga and Gloria Anzaldúa: foreword by Toni Cade Bambara (Watertown, Mass.: Persephone Press, 1981), 241.

29

Mary Wollstonecraft

Vindication of the Rights of Woman (1792)

Mary Wollstonecraft (1759–1797) supported herself as a teacher, governess, reader, translator, and writer. She belonged to a group of English philosophical radicals that included William Godwin, Tom Paine, Joseph Priestly, and the painter John Henry Fuseli. Shortly before the birth of their daughter, she and Godwin married. Wollstonecraft then died giving birth to Mary Wollstonecraft Godwin, who was the author of Frankenstein *and the wife of the poet Percy Bysshe Shelley. Mary Wollstonecraft is widely regarded as the first liberal feminist; her* Vindication of the Rights of Woman *extended the principles of the American and French revolutions.*

Chapter 13
Some Instances of the Folly which the Ignorance of Women Generates; with Concluding Reflections on the Moral Improvement that a Revolution in Female Manners Might Naturally Be Expected to Produce

THERE ARE MANY follies in some degree peculiar to women—sins against reason of commission as well as of omission—but all flowing from ignorance or prejudice. I shall only point out such as appear to be particularly injurious to their moral character. And in animadverting on them, I wish especially to prove that the weakness of mind and body, which men have endeavoured, impelled by various motives, to perpetuate, prevents their discharging the peculiar duty of their sex; for when weakness of body will not permit them to suckle their children, and weakness of mind makes them spoil their tempers, is woman in a natural state?. . . .

Section III

Ignorance and the mistaken cunning that Nature sharpens in weak heads as a principle of self-preservation, render women very fond of dress, and produce all the vanity which such a fondness may naturally be expected to generate, to the exclusion of emulation and magnanimity.

I agree with Rousseau that the physical part of the art of pleasing consists in ornaments, and for that very reason I should guard girls against the contagious fondness for dress so common to weak women, that they may not rest in the physical part. Yet, weak are the women who imagine that they can long please without the aid of the mind, or, in other words, without the moral art of pleasing. But the moral art, if it be not a profanation to use the word art, when alluding to the grace which is an effect of virtue, and not the motive of action, is never to be found with ignorance; the sportiveness of innocence, so pleasing to refined libertines of both sexes, is widely different in its essence from this superior gracefulness.

A strong inclination for external ornaments ever appears in barbarous states, only the men not the women adorn themselves; for where women are allowed to be so far on a level with men, society has advanced, at least, one step in civilization.

The attention to dress, therefore, which has been thought a sexual propensity, I think natural to mankind. But I ought to express myself with more precision. When the mind is not sufficiently opened to take pleasure in reflection, the body will be adorned with sedulous care; and ambition will appear in tattooing or painting it.

So far is this first inclination carried, that even the hellish yoke of slavery cannot stifle the savage desire of admiration which the black heroes inherit from both their parents, for all the hardly earned savings of a slave are commonly expended in a little tawdry finery. And I have seldom known a good male or female servant that was not particularly fond of dress. Their clothes were their riches; and, I argue from analogy, that the fondness for dress, so extravagant in females, arises from the same cause—want of cultivation of mind. When men meet they converse about business, politics, or literature; but, says Swift, 'how naturally do women apply their hands to each other's lappets and ruffles.' And very natural is it—for they have not any business to interest them, have not a taste for literature, and they find politics dry, because they have not acquired a love for mankind by turning their thoughts to the grand pursuits that exalt the human race, and promote general happiness.

Besides, various are the paths to power and fame which by accident or choice men pursue, and though they jostle against each other, for men of the same profession are seldom friends, yet there is a much greater number of their fellow-creatures with whom they never clash. But women are very differently situated with respect to each other—for they are all rivals.

Before marriage it is their business to please men; and after, with a few exceptions, they follow the same scene with all the persevering pertinacity of instinct. Even virtuous women never forget their sex in company, for they are for ever trying to make themselves *agreeable*. A female beauty, and a male wit, appear to be equally anxious to draw the attention of the company to themselves; and the animosity of contemporary wits is proverbial.

Is it then surprising that when the sole ambition of woman centres in beauty, and interest gives vanity additional force, perpetual rivalships should ensue? They are all running the same race, and would rise above the virtue of morals, if they did not view each other with a suspicious and even envious eye.

An immoderate fondness for dress, for pleasure, and for sway, are the passions of savages; the passions that occupy those uncivilized beings who have not yet extended the dominion of the mind, or even learned to think with the energy necessary to concatenate that abstract train of thought which produces principles. And that women from their education and the present state of civilized life, are in the same condition, cannot, I think, be controverted. To laugh at them then, or satirize the follies of a being who is never to be allowed to act freely from the light of her own reason, is as absurd as cruel; for, that they who are taught blindly to obey authority, will endeavour cunningly to elude it, is most natural and certain.

Yet let it be proved that they ought to obey man implicitly, and I shall immediately agree that it is woman's duty to cultivate a fondness for dress, in order to please, and a propensity to cunning for her own preservation.

The virtues, however, which are supported by ignorance must ever be wavering—the house built on sand could not endure a storm. It is almost unnecessary to draw the inference. If women are to be made virtuous by authority, which is a contradiction in terms, let them be immured in seraglios and watched with a jealous eye. Fear not that the iron will enter into their souls—for the souls that can bear such treatment are made of yielding materials, just animated enough to give life to the body.

> Matter too soft a lasting mark to bear,
> And best distinguish'd by black, brown, or fair.

The most cruel wounds will of course soon heal, and they may still people the world, and dress to please man—all the purposes which certain celebrated writers have allowed that they were created to fulfil. . . .

Section V

As the rearing of children, that is, the laying a foundation of sound health both of body and mind in the rising generation, has justly been insisted on as the peculiar destination of women, the ignorance that incapacitates them must be contrary to the order of things. And I contend that their minds can take in much more, and ought to do so, or they will never become sensible mothers. Many men attend to the breeding of horses, and overlook the management of the stable, who would, strange want of sense and feeling! think themselves degraded by paying any attention to the nursery; yet, how many children are absolutely murdered by the ignorance of women! But when they escape, and are destroyed neither by unnatural negligence nor blind fondness, how few are managed properly with respect to the infant mind! So that to break the spirit, allowed to become vicious at home, a child is sent to school; and the methods taken there, which must be taken to keep a number of children in order, scatter the seeds of almost every vice in the soil thus forcibly torn up.

I have sometimes compared the struggles of these poor children, who ought never to have felt restraint, nor would, had they been always held in with an even hand, to the despairing plunges of a spirited filly, which I have seen breaking on a strand; its feet sinking deeper and deeper in the sand every time it endeavoured to throw its rider, till at last it sullenly submitted.

I have always found horses, animals I am attached to, very tractable when treated with humanity and steadiness, so that I doubt whether the violent methods taken to break them, do not essentially injure them; I am, however, certain that a child should never thus forcibly be tamed after it had injudiciously been allowed to run wild; for every violation of justice and reason, in the treatment of children, weakens their reason. And, so early do they catch a character, that the base of the moral character, experience leads me to infer, is fixed before their seventh year, the period during which women are allowed the sole management of children. Afterwards it too often happens that half the business of education is to correct, and very imperfectly is it done, if done hastily, the faults, which they would never have acquired if their mothers had had more understanding.

One striking instance of the folly of women must not be omitted. The manner in which they treat servants in the presence of children, permitting them to suppose that they ought to wait on them, and bear their humours. A child should always be made to receive assistance from a man or woman as a favour; and, as the first lesson of independence, they should practically be taught, by the example of their mother, not to require that personal attendance, which it is an insult to humanity to require, when in health; and instead of being led to assume airs of consequence, a sense of their own weakness should first make them feel the natural equality of man. Yet, how frequently have I indignantly heard servants imperiously called to put children to bed, and sent away again and again, because master or miss hung about mamma, to stay a little longer. Thus made slavishly to attend the little idol, all those most disgusting humours were exhibited which characterize a spoiled child.

In short, speaking of the majority of mothers, they leave their children entirely to the care of servants; or, because they are their children, treat them as if they were little demi-gods, though I have always observed, that the women who thus idolize their children, seldom show common humanity to servants, or feel the least tenderness for any children but their own.

It is, however, these exclusive affections, and an individual manner of seeing things, produced by ignorance, which keep women for ever at a stand, with respect to improvement, and make many of them dedicate their lives to their children only to weaken their bodies and spoil their tempers, frustrating also any plan of education that a more rational father may adopt; for unless a mother concur, the father who restrains will ever be considered as a tyrant.

But, fulfilling the duties of a mother, a woman with a sound constitution, may still keep her person scrupulously neat, and assist to maintain her family, if necessary, or by reading and conversation with both sexes, indiscriminately, improve her mind. For Nature has so wisely ordered things, that did women suckle their children, they would preserve their own health, and there would be such an interval between the birth of each child, that we should seldom see a houseful of babes. And did they pursue a plan of conduct, and not waste their time in following the fashionable vagaries of dress, the management of their household and children need not shut them out from literature, or prevent their attaching themselves to a science, with that steady eye which strengthens the mind, or practising one of the fine arts that cultivate the taste.

But, visiting to display finery, card-playing, and balls, not to mention the idle bustle of morning trifling, draw women from their duty to render them insignificant, to render them pleasing, according to the present acceptation of the word, to every man, but their husband. For a round of pleasures in which the affections are not exercised, cannot be said to improve the understanding, though it be erroneously called seeing the world; yet the heart is rendered cold and averse to duty, by such a senseless intercourse, which becomes necessary from habit even when it has ceased to amuse.

But, we shall not see women affectionate till more equality be established in society, till ranks are confounded and women freed, neither shall we see that dignified domestic happiness, the simple grandeur of which cannot be relished by ignorant or vitiated minds; nor will the important task of education ever be properly begun till the person of a woman is no longer preferred to her mind. For it would be as wise to expect corn from tares, or figs from thistles, as that a foolish ignorant woman should be a good mother.

Section VI

It is not necessary to inform the sagacious reader, now I enter on my concluding reflections, that the discussion of this subject merely consists in opening a few simple principles, and clearing away the rubbish which obscured them. But, as all readers are not sagacious, I must be allowed to add some explanatory remarks to bring the subject home to reason—to that sluggish reason, which supinely takes opinions on trust, and obstinately supports them to spare itself the labour of thinking.

Moralists have unanimously agreed, that unless virtue be nursed by liberty, it will never attain due strength—and what they say of man I extend to mankind, insisting that in all cases morals must be fixed on immutable principles; and, that the being cannot be termed rational or virtuous, who obeys any authority, but that of reason.

To render women truly useful members of society, I argue that they should be led, by having their understandings cultivated on a large scale, to acquire a rational affection for their country, founded on knowledge, because it is obvious that we are little interested about what we do not understand. And to render this general knowledge of due importance, I have endeavoured to show that private duties are never properly fulfilled unless the understanding enlarges the heart; and that public virtue is only an aggregate of private. But, the distinctions established in society undermine both, by beating out the solid gold of virtue, till it becomes only the tinsel-covering of vice; for whilst wealth renders a man more respectable than virtue, wealth will be sought before virtue; and, whilst women's persons are caressed, when a childish simper shows an absence of mind—the mind will lie fallow. Yet, true voluptuousness must proceed from the mind—for what can equal the sensations produced by mutual affection, supported by mutual respect? What are the cold, or feverish caresses of appetite, but sin embracing death, compared with the modest overflowings of a pure heart and exalted imagination? Yes, let me tell the libertine of fancy when he despises understanding in woman—that the mind, which he disregards, gives life to the enthusiastic affection from which rapture, short-lived as it is, alone can blow! And, that, without virtue, a sexual attachment must expire, like a tallow candle in the socket, creating intolerable disgust. To prove this, I need only observe, that men who have wasted great part of their lives with women, and with whom they have sought for pleasure with eager thirst, entertain the meanest opinion of the sex. Virtue, true refiner of joy!—if foolish men were to fright thee from earth, in order to give loose to all their appetites without a check—some sensual weight of taste would scale the heavens to invite thee back, to give a zest to pleasure!

That women at present are by ignorance rendered foolish or vicious is, I think, not to be disputed; and, that the most salutary effects tending to improve mankind might be expected from a REVOLUTION in female manners, appears, at least, with a face of probability, to rise out of the observation. For as marriage has been termed the parent of those endearing charities which draw man from the brutal herd, the corrupting intercourse that wealth, idleness, and folly, produce between the sexes, is more universally injurious to morality than all the other vices of mankind collectively considered. To adulterous lust the most sacred duties are sacrificed, because before marriage, men, by a promiscuous intimacy with women, learned to consider love as a selfish gratification—learned to separate it not only from esteem, but from the affection merely built on habit, which mixes a little humanity with it. Justice and friendship are also set at defiance, and that purity of taste is vitiated which would naturally lead a man to relish an artless display of affection rather than affected airs. But that noble simplicity of affection, which dares to appear unadorned, has few attractions for the libertine, though it be the charm, which by cementing the matrimonial tie, secures to the pledges of a warmer passion the necessary parental attention; for children will never be properly educated till friendship subsists between parents. Virtue flies from a house divided against itself—and a whole legion of devils take up their residence there.

The affection of husbands and wives cannot be pure when they have so few sentiments in common, and when so little confidence is established at home, as must be the case when their pursuits are so different. That intimacy from which tenderness should flow, will not, cannot subsist between the vicious.

Contending, therefore, that the sexual distinction which men have so warmly insisted upon, is arbitrary, I have dwelt on an observation, that several sensible men, with whom I have conversed on the subject, allowed to be well founded; and it is simply this, that the little chastity to be found amongst men, and consequent disregard of modesty, tend to degrade both sexes; and further, that the modesty of women, characterized as such, will often be only the artful veil of wantonness instead of being the natural reflection of purity, till modesty be universally respected.

From the tyranny of man, I firmly believe, the greater number of female follies proceed; and the cunning, which I allow makes at present a part of their character, I likewise have repeatedly endeavoured to prove, is produced by oppression.

Were not dissenters, for instance, a class of people, with strict truth, characterized as cunning? And may I not lay some stress on this fact to prove, that when any power but reason curbs the free spirit of man, dissimulation is practised, and the various shifts of art are naturally called forth? Great attention to decorum, which was carried to a degree of scrupulosity, and all that puerile bustle about trifles and consequential solemnity, which Butler's caricature of a dissenter brings before the imagination, shaped their persons as well as their minds in the mould of prim littleness. I speak collectively, for I know how many ornaments in human nature have been enrolled amongst sectaries; yet, I assert, that the same narrow prejudice for their sect, which women have for their families, prevailed in the dissenting part of the community, however worthy in other respects; and also that the same timid prudence, or headstrong efforts, often disgraced the exertions of both. Oppression thus formed many of the features of their character perfectly to coincidence with that of the oppressed half of mankind; for is it not notorious that dissenters were, like women, fond of deliberating together, and asking advice of each other, till by a complication of little contrivances, some little end was brought about? A similar attention to preserve their reputation was conspicuous in the dissenting and female world, and was produced by a similar cause.

Asserting the rights which women in common with men ought to contend for, I have not attempted to extenuate their faults; but to prove them to be the natural consequence of their education and station in society. If so, it is reasonable to suppose that they will change their character, and correct their vices and follies, when they are allowed to be free in a physical, moral, and civil sense.[i]

Let woman share the rights, and she will emulate the virtues of man; for she must grow more perfect when emancipated, or justify the authority that chains such a weak being to her duty. If the latter, it will be expedient to open a fresh trade with Russia for whips: a present which a father should always make to his son-in-law on his wedding day, that a husband may keep his whole family in order by the same means; and without any violation of justice reign, wielding this sceptre, sole master of his house, because he is the only thing in it who has reason:— the divine, indefeasible earthly sovereignty breathed into man by the Master of the universe. Allowing this position, women have not any inherent rights to claim; and, by the same rule, their duties vanish, for rights and duties are inseparable.

Be just then, O ye men of understanding; and mark not more severely what women do amiss than the vicious tricks of the horse or the ass for whom ye provide provender—and allow her the privileges of ignorance, to whom ye deny the rights of reason, or ye will be worse than Egyptian task-masters, expecting virtue where Nature has not given understanding.

---

i. I had further enlarged on the advantages which might reasonably be expected to result from an improvement in female manners, towards the general reformation of society; but it appeared to me that such reflections would more properly close the last volume.

30

Betty Friedan

"Our Revolution Is Unique" (1968)

Betty Friedan (b. 1921), author of The Feminine Mystique *(1963), is widely regarded as the founder of modern liberal feminism. A journalist and a psychologist by training, Friedan expressed the sense of dissatisfaction shared by many middle-class, stay-at-home wives and mothers. She founded the National Organization for Women (NOW) in 1966 and then served as its president until 1970. In 1971 she became a founding member of the National Women's Political Caucus and later led the campaign to ratify the Equal Rights Amendment. Her more recent books include* Life So Far *(2000),* The Fountain of Age *(1993), and* The Second Stage *(1981). In this speech she outlines the main tenets of liberal feminism.*

WE NEW FEMINISTS have begun to define ourselves—existentially—through action. We have learned that while we had much to learn from the black civil rights movement and their revolution against economic and racial oppression, our own revolution is unique: it must define its own ideology.

We can cut no corners; we are, in effect, where the black revolution was perhaps fifty years ago; but the speed with which our revolution is moving now is our unearned historical benefit from what has happened in that revolution. Yet there can be no illusion on our part that a separatist ideology copied from black power will work for us. Our tactics and strategy and, above all, our ideology must be firmly based in the historical, biological, economic, and psychological reality of our two-sexed world, which is not the same as the black reality and different also from the reality of the first feminist wave.

Thanks to the early feminists, we who have mounted this second stage of the feminist revolution have grown up with the right to vote, little as we may have used it for our own purposes. We have grown up with the right to higher education and to employment, and with some, not all, of the legal rights of equality. Insofar as we have moved on the periphery of the mainstream of society, with the skills and the knowledge to command its paychecks, even if insufficient, and to make decisions, even if not consulted beyond housework; we begin to have a self-respecting image of ourselves, as women, not just in sexual relation to men, but as full human beings in society. We are able, at least some of us, to see men, in general or in particular, without blind rancor or hostility, and to face oppression as it reveals itself in our concrete experience with politicians, bosses, priests, or husbands. We do not need to suppress our just grievances. We now have enough courage to express them. And yet we are able to conceive the possibility of full affirmation for man. Man is not the enemy, but the fellow victim of the present half-equality. As we speak, act, demonstrate, testify, and appear on television on matters such as sex discrimination in employment, public accommodations, education, divorce-marriage reform, or abortion repeal, we hear from men who feel they can be freed to greater self-fulfillment to the degree that women are released from the binds that now constrain them.

This sense of freeing men as the other half of freeing women has always been there, even in the early writings of Mary Wollstonecraft, Elizabeth Stanton, and the rest; our action-created new awareness has confirmed this.

Another point we are conscious of in the new feminism is that we are a revolution for all, not for an exceptional few. This, above all, distinguishes us from those token spokeswomen of the period since women won the vote, the Aunt Toms who managed to get a place for themselves in society, and who were, I think, inevitably seduced into an accommodating stance, helping to keep the others quiet. We are beginning to know that no woman can achieve a real breakthrough alone, as long as sex discrimination exists in employment, under the law, in education, in mores, and in denigration of the image of women.

Even those of us who have managed to achieve a precarious success in a given field still walk as freaks in "man's world" since every profession—politics, the church, teaching—is still structured as man's world. Walking as a freak makes one continually self-conscious, apologetic, if not defiant, about being a woman. One is made to feel there are three sexes—men, other women, and myself. The successful woman may think, "I am the exception, the 'brilliant' one with the rare ability to be an anthropologist, author, actress, broker, account executive, or television commentator; but you drones out there, you watch the television set.

And what better use can you make of your life than doing the dishes for your loved ones?"

We cannot say that all American women want equality, because we know that women, like all oppressed people, have accepted the traditional denigration by society. Some women have been too much hurt by denigration from others, by self-denigration, by lack of the experiences, education, and training needed to move in society as equal human beings, to have the confidence that they can so move in a competitive society. They say they don't want equality—they have to be happy, adjust to things as they are. Such women find us threatening. They find equality so frightening that they must wish the new feminists did not exist. And yet we see so clearly from younger women and students that to the degree that we push ahead and create opportunities for movement in society, in the process creating the "new women" who are *people first,* to that degree the threat will disappear.

We do not speak for every woman in America, but we speak for the *right* of every woman in America to become all she is capable of becoming—on her own and/or in partnership with a man. And we already know that we speak not for a few, not for hundreds, not for thousands, but for millions—especially for millions in the younger generation who have tasted more equality than their elders. We know this simply from the resonance, if you will, that our actions have aroused in society.

That wave of resonance is world wide. In Canada, they want to have an affiliate of our National Organization for Women, and propose that, ultimately, there will be a World Organization for Women. From Great Britain, France, Italy, the Scandinavian countries, Germany, Japan, New Zealand, women—young, vital new feminists—have asked for guidance.

Women and Sex

As an example of the new feminism in action, consider the matter of abortion law repeal. NOW was the first organization to speak on the basic rights of women on the question of abortion. We said that it is the inalienable human right of every woman to control her own reproductive process. To establish that right would require that all laws penalizing abortion be repealed, removed from the penal code; the state would not be empowered either to force or prevent a woman from having an abortion. Now many groups are working on abortion law repeal, while at the same time California and Washington, D.C., court decisions have spelled out the right of a woman to control her own reproduction.

What right has any man to say to any woman, "You must bear this child"? What right has any state to say it? The child-bearing decision is a woman's right and not a technical question needing the sanction of the state, nor should the state control access to birth control devices.

This question can only really be confronted in terms of the basic personhood and dignity of woman, which is violated forever if she does not have the right to control her own reproductive process. And the heart of this idea goes far beyond abortion and birth control.

Women, almost too visible as sex objects in this country today, are at the same time invisible people. As the Negro was the invisible man, so women are the invisible people in America today. To be taken seriously as people, women have to share in the decisions of government, of politics, of the church—not just to cook the church supper, but to preach the sermon; not just to look up the zip codes and address the envelopes, but to make the political decisions; not just to do the housework of industry, but to make some of the executive decisions. Women, above all, want to say what their own lives are going to be, what their own personalities are going to be, not permitting male experts to define what is "feminine" or isn't or should be.

The essence of the denigration of women is their definition as sex objects. And to confront our inequality, we must confront our own self-denigration and our denigration by society in these terms.

Am I saying therefore, that women must be liberated from sex? No. I am saying that sex will only be liberated, will only cease to be a sniggering dirty joke and an obsession in this society, when women are liberated, self-determining people, liberated to a creativity beyond motherhood, to a full human creativity.

Nor am I saying that women must be liberated from motherhood. I am saying that motherhood will only be liberated to be a joyous and responsible human act, when women are free to make, with full conscious choice and full human responsibility, the decision to be mothers. Then and only then, will they be able to embrace motherhood without conflict. When they are able to define themselves as people, not just as somebody's mother, not just as servants of children, not just as breeding receptacles, but as people for whom motherhood is a freely chosen part of life, and for whom creativity has many dimensions, as it has for men.

The hostility between the sexes has never been worse. The image of woman in avant-garde plays, novels, in the movies, and in the mass image that you can detect behind the family situation comedies on television is that mothers are man-devouring cannibalistic monsters, or else Lolitas, thing-like sex objects: objects not even of heterosexual impulse, objects of a sadistic or masochistic impulse. That impulse is much more a factor in the abortion question than anybody ever admits: the punishment of women.

I maintain that motherhood is a bane and a curse, or at least partly that, as long as women are forced to be mothers—and only mothers—against their will. Women today are forced to live too much through their children and husbands—too dependent on them, and, therefore, forced to take too much varied resentment, vindictiveness, inexpressible resentment, and rage out on their husbands and their children.

Perhaps the least understood fact of American political life is the enormous buried violence of women in this country today. Like all oppressed people, women have been taking their violence out on their own bodies, in all the maladies with which they plague the doctors' offices and the psychoanalysts. They have been taking out their violence inadvertently and in subtle and in insidious ways on their children and on their husbands. And sometimes, they are not so subtle, for the battered child syndrome that we are hearing more and more about in our hospitals is almost always to be found in the instance of unwanted children, and women are doing the battering, as much or more than men.

Man, we have said, is not the enemy. Men will only be truly liberated, to love women and to be fully themselves, when women are liberated to be full people. Until that happens, men are going to bear the burden and the guilt of the destiny they have forced upon women, the suppressed resentment of that passive stage— the sterility of love, when love is not between two fully active, fully participant, fully joyous people, but has in it the element of exploitation. And men will also not be fully free to be all they can be as long as they must live up to an image of masculinity that denies to a man all the tenderness and sensitivity that might be considered feminine. Men have in them enormous capacities that they have to repress and fear in themselves, in living up to this obsolete and brutal man-eating, lion-killing, Ernest Hemingway image of masculinity—the image of all-powerful masculine superiority. All the burdens and responsibilities that men are supposed to shoulder alone, make them, I think, resent women's pedestal, while the burden to women is enforced passivity.

So the real sexual revolution is not cheap headlines in the papers—at what age boys and girls go to bed with each other and whether they do it with or without the benefit of marriage. That's the least of it. The real sexual revolution is the emergence of women from passivity, from thingness, to full self-determination, to full dignity. And insofar as they can do this, men are also emerging from the stage of identification with brutality and masters to full and sensitive complete humanity.

A revolutionary theory that's adequate to the current demand of the sexual revolution must also address itself to the concrete realities of our society. We can only transcend the reality of the institutions that oppress us by confronting them in our actions now; confronting reality, we change it; we begin to create alternatives, not in abstract discussion, but here and now.

Some women who call themselves revolutionaries get into abstractions. They say, "What's really wrong is marriage altogether. What's wrong is having babies altogether; let's have them in test tubes. Man is the oppressor, and women are enslaved. We don't want jobs because who wants to be equal to men who aren't free. All jobs today are just a rat race anyway."

Now we are rationalizing in radical terms of the extremists of the women's liberation ideology. This is a rationalization for inaction, because in the end we're going to weep and go home and yell at our husbands and make life miserable for a while, but we'll eventually conclude that it's hopeless, that nothing can be done.

If we are going to address ourselves to the need for changing the social institutions that will permit women to be free and equal individuals, participating actively in their society and changing that society—with men—then we must talk in terms of what is possible, and not accept what is as what must be. In other words, don't talk to me about test tubes because I am interested in leading a revolution for the foreseeable future of my society. And I have a certain sense of optimism that things can be changed.

Twenty-five years from now test-tube babies may be a reality. But it is my educated guess as an observer of the scene—both from what I know of psychology and what I've observed of actual women and men, old and young, conservative and radical, in this country and other countries—that for the foreseeable future people are going to want to enjoy sexual relationships and control the procreative act and make more responsible, human decisions whether and when to have babies.

We need not accept marriage as it's currently structured with the implicit idea of man, the breadwinner, and woman, the housewife. There are many different ways we could posit marriage. But there seems to be a reasonable guess that men and women are going to want relationships of long-term intimacy tied in with a sexual relationship, although we can certainly posit a larger variety of sex relationships than now seem conventional. And it's not possible, much less conducive to health, happiness, or self-fulfillment, for women or men to completely suppress their sexual needs.

We can change institutions, but it is a fantasy deviation from a really revolutionary approach to say that we want a world in which there will be no sex, no marriage, that in order for women to be free they must have a manless revolution. We have to deal with the world of reality if we are going to have a real revolution.

I don't happen to think that women and men are so completely different that it is impossible for us to see each other as human beings. I think that it is as possible for men to put themselves finally in woman's place by an act of empathy or by guilt or by awareness of human rights as it has been possible for some whites to do for blacks. But it's perhaps not much more possible than that, though there are more bonds between men and women, and really men's stake in this revolution is greater, because a woman can make a man's life hell if it isn't solved. But

I think it would be as much of a mistake to expect men to hand this to women as to consider all men as the enemy, all men as oppressors. This revolution can have the support of men, but women must take the lead in fighting it as any other oppressed group has had to.

I think that it is possible in education to create and disseminate the radical ideology that is needed to influence the great change in expectations and institutions for the revolution of women. In the education of women, I think it is nonsense to keep talking about optional life styles and the freedom of choice that American women have. They do not have them, and we should face this right away. You cannot tell a woman aged eighteen to twenty that she can make a choice to just stay home all her life with her children, her friends, and her husband. This girl is going to live close to a hundred years. There won't be children home to occupy her all her life. If she has intelligence and the opportunity for education it is telling her simply, "Put yourself in a garbage can, except for the years when you have a few little children at home."

The so-called second choice and option—go to school, then have children, stay out for twenty years and then get a job or go back to school—is not satisfactory either. I am not denying the need for occupational therapy for women of my generation who've had to do it this way, but any woman who has run the continuing education gamut knows the limitations of occupational therapy. Women have to do what they can, but they have enormous problems trying to get back after ten or fifteen years. They are mainly just a pool of semi-employable labor and have to be grateful for whatever they can get. Actually only a token few have been involved in these programs.

Some have the idea that there is another choice—and it is immediately implicit that this is a very freakish and exceptional choice—which is to be single-minded about a career like a man. The idea is, don't marry, don't have children, if you really want a demanding profession. Of course, if you do it this way, forget equality for women. I don't want to forget equality for women. I don't accept for most women the necessity of making a choice that no man has to make. This is not to say that women are not to have a free choice to have children or not to have children, to marry or not to marry; but the idea that this choice has to be influenced by professional or political pursuits, that you are going to be sexually frustrated by choosing to be a scientist, is nonsense.

It is a perversion of the new feminism for some to exhort those who would join this revolution to cleanse themselves of sex and the need for love or to refuse to have children. This not only means a revolution with very few followers—but is a copout from the problem of moving in society for the *majority* of women, who do want love and children. To enable *all* women, not just the exceptional few, to participate in society we must confront the fact of life—as a temporary fact of most women's lives today—that women do give birth to children. But we must challenge the idea that a woman is primarily responsible for raising children. Man and society have to be educated to accept their responsibility for that role as well. And this is first of all a challenge to education. . . .

Women as a Political Power

On the question of self-determination, we became painfully aware, in our attempts to get a bill of rights for women into the platforms of both political parties at the last presidential election and as a major issue in the election for all candidates for national office, that we need *political power*. Our only success then was getting the word "sex" added to a rather vague antidiscrimination sentence in the Republican platform.

We must overcome our diversity of varied political beliefs. Our common commitment is to equality for women. And we are not single-issue people; we want a voice for all women, to raise our voices in decision making on all matters from war and peace to the kinds of cities we're going to inhabit. Many large issues concern all of us; on these things we may differ. We will surmount this. Political power is necessary to change the situation of the oppressed 51 per cent, to realize the power potential in the fact that women *are* 51 per cent.

We will do it by getting into city hall ourselves, or by getting into Congress ourselves, regardless of whether our political party is Republican or Democratic or Peace and Freedom. . . .

We must begin to use the power of our actions: to make women finally *visible* as people in America, as conscious political and social power; to change our society *now*, so all women can move freely, as people, in it.

31

Heidi Hartmann

"The Unhappy Marriage of Marxism and Feminism: Towards a More Progressive Union"[1] (1981)

Heidi Hartmann (b. 1945) founded the Institute for Women's Policy Research in Washington, D.C. (1987) and chaired the National Council of Women's Organizations' Task Force on Women and Social Security. An expert on issues involving women and economics, she is the author of Women, Work, and Wages *(1981),* Comparable Worth *(1985), and* Women's Work, Men's Work *(1986), as well as reports on pay equity, sex segregation in the workforce, and women and technology. In 1994 she received a MacArthur Foundation "genius grant" in recognition of her work. The essay reprinted here helped define socialist feminism.*

THE "MARRIAGE" of marxism and feminism has been like the marriage of husband and wife depicted in English common law: marxism and feminism are one, and that one is marxism.[2] Recent attempts to integrate marxism and feminism are unsatisfactory to us as feminists because they subsume the feminist struggle into the "larger" struggle against capital. To continue our simile further, either we need a healthier marriage or we need a divorce.

The inequalities in this marriage, like most social phenomena, are no accident. Many marxists typically argue that feminism is at best less important than class

Source: "The Unhappy Marriage of Marxism and Feminism: Towards a More Progressive Union," in *Women and Revolution* ed. Lydia Sargent (Cambridge, Mass.: South End Press, 1981).

conflict and at worst divisive of the working class. This political stance produces an analysis that absorbs feminism into the class struggle. Moreover, the analytic power of marxism with respect to capital has obscured its limitations with respect to sexism. We will argue here that while marxist analysis provides essential insight into the laws of historical development, and those of capital in particular, the categories of marxism are sex-blind. Only a specifically feminist analysis reveals the systemic character of relations between men and women. Yet feminist analysis by itself is inadequate because it has been blind to history and insufficiently materialist. Both marxist analysis, particularly its historical and materialistic method, and feminist analysis, especially the identification of patriarchy as a social and historical structure, must be drawn upon if we are to understand the development of Western capitalist societies and the predicament of women within them. In this essay we suggest a new direction for marxist feminist analysis. . . .

1.
Marxism and the Woman Question

The woman question has never been the "feminist question." The feminist question is directed at the causes of sexual inequality between women and men, of male dominance over women. Most marxist analyses of women's position take as their question the relationship of women to the economic system, rather than that of women to men, apparently assuming the latter will be explained in their discussion of the former. Marxist analysis of the woman question has taken (several) forms. All see women's oppression in our connection (or lack of it) to production. Defining women as part of the working class, these analyses consistently subsume women's relation to men under workers' relation to capital. . . . All attempt to include women in the category working class and to understand women's oppression as another aspect of class oppression. In doing so all give short shrift to the object of feminist analysis, the relations between women and men. While our "problems" have been elegantly analyzed, they have been misunderstood. The focus of marxist analysis has been class relations; the object of marxist analysis has been understanding the laws of motion of capitalist society. While we believe marxist methodology *can* be used to formulate feminist strategy, these marxist feminist approaches discussed above clearly do not do so; their marxism clearly dominates their feminism.

As we have already suggested, this is due in part to the analytical power of marxism itself. Marxism is a theory of the development of class society, of the accumulation process in capitalist societies, of the reproduction of class dominance, and of the development of contradictions and class struggle. Capitalist societies are driven by the demands of the accumulation process, most succinctly summarized by the fact that production is oriented to exchange, not use. In a capitalist system production is important only insofar as it contributes to the making of profits, and the use value of products is only an incidental consideration. Profits derive from the capitalists' ability to exploit labor power, to pay laborers less than the value of what they produce. The accumulation of profits systematically transforms social structure as it transforms the relations of production. The reserve army of labor, the poverty of great numbers of people and the near-poverty of still more, these human reproaches to capital are byproducts of the accumulation process itself. From the capitalist's point of view, the reproduction of the working class may "safely be left to itself."[3] At the same time, capital creates an ideology, which grows up alongside it, of individualism, competitiveness, domination, and in our time, consumption of a particular kind. Whatever one's theory of the genesis of ideology one must recognize these as the dominant values of capitalist societies.

Marxism enables us to understand many aspects of capitalist societies: the structure of production, the generation of a particular occupational structure, and the nature of the dominant ideology. Marx's theory of the development of capitalism is a theory of the development of "empty places." Marx predicted, for example, the growth of the proletariat and the demise of the petit bourgeoisie. More precisely and in more detail, Braverman among others has explained the creation of the "places" clerical worker and service worker in advanced capitalist societies.[4] Just as capital creates these places indifferent to the individuals who fill them, the categories of marxist analysis, class, reserve army of labor, wage-laborer, do not explain why particular people fill particular places. They give no clues about why *women* are subordinate to *men* inside and outside the family and why it is not the other way around. *Marxist categories, like capital itself, are sex-blind.* The categories of marxism cannot tell us who will fill the empty places. Marxist analysis of the woman question has suffered from this basic problem.

Towards More Useful Marxist Feminism

Marxism is also a *method* of social analysis, historical dialectical materialism. By putting this method to the service of feminist questions, Juliet Mitchell and Shulamith Firestone suggest new directions for marxist feminism. Mitchell says, we think correctly, that

> It is not "our relationship" to socialism that should *ever* be the question—it is the use of scientific socialism [what we call marxist method] as a method of analyzing the specific nature of our oppression and hence our revolutionary

role. Such a method, I believe, needs to understand radical feminism, quite as much as previously developed socialist theories.[5]

As Engels wrote:

> According to the materialistic conception, the determining factor in history is, in the final instance, the production and reproduction of immediate life. This, again, is of a twofold character: on the one side, the production of the means of existence, of food, clothing, and shelter and the tools necessary for that production; on the other side, the production of human beings themselves, the propagation of the species. The social organization under which the people of a particular historical epoch live is determined by both kinds of production.[6]

This is the kind of analysis Mitchell has attempted. In her first essay, "Women: The Longest Revolution," Mitchell examines both market work and the work of reproduction, sexuality, and childrearing.[7]

Mitchell does not entirely succeed, perhaps because not all of women's work counts as production for her. Only market work is identified as production; the other spheres (loosely aggregated as the family) in which women work are identified as ideological. Patriarchy, which largely organizes reproduction, sexuality, and childrearing, has no material base for Mitchell. *Women's Estate,* Mitchell's expansion of this essay, focuses much more on developing the analysis of women's market work than it does on developing the analysis of women's work within the family. The book is much more concerned with women's relation to, and work for, capital than with women's relation to, and work for, men; more influenced by marxism than by radical feminism. . . .

Shulamith Firestone bridges marxism and feminism by bringing materialist analysis to bear on patriarchy.[8] Her use of materialist analysis is not as ambivalent as Mitchell's. The dialectic of sex, she says, is the fundamental historical dialectic, and the material base of patriarchy is the work women do reproducing the species. The importance of Firestone's work in using marxism to analyze women's position, in asserting the existence of a material base to patriarchy, cannot be overestimated. But it suffers from an overemphasis on biology and reproduction. What we need to understand is how sex (a biological fact) becomes gender (a social phenomenon). It is necessary to place all of women's work in its social and historical context, not to focus only on reproduction. Although Firestone's work offers a new and feminist use of marxist methodology, her insistence on the primacy of men's dominance over women as the cornerstone on which all other oppression (class, age, race) rests, suggests that her book is more properly grouped with the radical feminists than with the marxist feminists. Her work remains the most complete statement of the radical feminist position. . . .

2.
Radical Feminism and Patriarchy

The great thrust of radical feminist writing has been directed to the documentation of the slogan "the personal is political." Women's discontent, radical feminists argued, is not the neurotic lament of the maladjusted, but a response to a social structure in which women are systematically dominated, exploited, and oppressed. Women's inferior position in the labor market, the male-centered emotional structure of middle-class marriage, the use of women in advertising, the so-called understanding of women's psyche as neurotic—popularized by academic and clinical psychology—aspect after aspect of women's lives in advanced capitalist society was researched and analyzed. The radical feminist literature is enormous and defies easy summary. At the same time, its focus on psychology is consistent. The New York Radical Feminists' organizing document was "The Politics of the Ego." "The personal is political" means for radical feminists, that the original and basic class division is between the sexes, and that the motive force of history is the striving of men for power and domination over women, the dialectic of sex.[9]

Accordingly, Firestone rewrote Freud to understand the development of boys and girls into men and women in terms of power.[10] Her characterizations of what are "male" and "female" character traits are typical of radical feminist writing. The male seeks power and domination; he is egocentric and individualistic, competitive and pragmatic; the "technological mode," according to Firestone, is male. The female is nurturant, artistic, and philosophical; the "aesthetic mode" is female.

No doubt, the idea that the aesthetic mode is female would have come as quite a shock to the ancient Greeks. Here lies the error of radical feminist analysis: the dialectic of sex as radical feminists present it projects male and female characteristics as they appear in the present back into all of history. Radical feminist analysis has greatest strength in its insights into the present. Its greatest weakness is a focus on the psychological, which blinds it to history.

The reason for this lies not only in radical feminist method, but also in the nature of patriarchy itself, for patriarchy is a strikingly resilient form of social organization. Radical feminists use patriarchy to refer to a social system characterized by male domination over women. Kate Millett's definition is classic:

> Our society . . . is a patriarchy. The fact is evident at once if one recalls that the military, industry, technology, universities, science, political offices, finances—in short, every avenue of power within the society, including the coercive force of the police, is entirely in male hands.[11]

This radical feminist definition of patriarchy applies to most societies we know of and cannot distinguish among them. The use of history by radical feminists is typically limited to providing examples of the existence of patriarchy in all times and places.[12] For both marxist and mainstream social scientists before the women's movement, patriarchy referred to a system of relations between men, which formed the political and economic outlines of feudal and some pre-feudal societies, in which hierarchy followed ascribed characteristics. Capitalist societies are understood as meritocratic, bureaucratic, and impersonal by bourgeois social scientists; marxists see capitalist societies as systems of class domination.[13] For both kinds of social scientists neither the historical patriarchal societies nor today's Western capitalist societies are understood as systems of relations between men that enable them to dominate women.

Towards a Definition of Patriarchy

We can usefully define patriarchy as a set of social relations between men, which have a material base, and which, though hierarchical, establish or create interdependence and solidarity among men that enable them to dominate women. Though patriarchy is hierarchical and men of different classes, races, or ethnic groups have different places in the patriarchy, they also are united in their shared relationship of dominance over their women; they are dependent on each other to maintain that domination. Hierarchies "work" at least in part because they create vested interests in the status quo. Those at the higher levels can "buy off" those at the lower levels by offering them power over those still lower. In the hierarchy of patriarchy, all men, whatever their rank in the patriarchy, are bought off by being able to control at least some women. There is some evidence to suggest that when patriarchy was first institutionalized in state societies, the ascending rulers literally made men the heads of their families (enforcing their control over their wives and children) in exchange for the men's ceding some of their tribal resources to the new rulers.[14] Men are dependent on one another (despite their hierarchical ordering) to maintain their control over women.

The material base upon which patriarchy rests lies most fundamentally in men's control over women's labor power. Men maintain this control by excluding women from access to some essential productive resources (in capitalist societies, for example, jobs that pay living wages) and by restricting women's sexuality.[15] Monogamous heterosexual marriage is one relatively recent and efficient form that seems to allow men to control both these areas. Controlling women's access to resources and their sexuality, in turn, allows men to control women's labor power, both for the purpose of serving men in many personal and sexual ways and for the purpose of rearing children. The services women render men, and which exonerate men from having to perform many unpleasant tasks (like cleaning toilets) occur outside as well as inside the family setting. Examples outside the family include the harassment of women workers and students by male bosses and professors as well as the common use of secretaries to run personal errands, make coffee, and provide "sexy" surroundings. Rearing children, whether or not the children's labor power is of immediate benefit to their fathers, is nevertheless a crucial task in perpetuating patriarchy as a system. Just as class society must be reproduced by schools, work places, consumption norms, etc., so must patriarchal social relations. In our society children are generally reared by women at home, women socially defined and recognized as inferior to men, while men appear in the domestic picture only rarely. Children raised in this way generally learn their places in the gender hierarchy well. Central to this process, however, are the areas outside the home where patriarchal behaviors are taught and the inferior position of women enforced and reinforced: churches, schools, sports, clubs, unions, armies, factories, offices, health centers, the media, etc.

The material base of patriarchy, then, does not rest solely on childrearing in the family, but on all the social structures that enable men to control women's labor. The aspects of social structures that perpetuate patriarchy are theoretically identifiable, hence separable from their other aspects. Gayle Rubin has increased our ability to identify the patriarchal element of these social structures enormously by identifying "sex/gender systems":

> A "sex/gender system" is the set of arrangements by which a society transforms biological sexuality into products of human activity, and in which these transformed sexual needs are satisfied.[16]

We are born female and male, biological sexes, but we are created woman and man, socially recognized genders. *How* we are so created is that second aspect of the *mode* of production of which Engels spoke, "the production of human beings themselves, the propagation of the species."

How people propagate the species is socially determined. If, biologically, people are sexually polymorphous, and society were organized in such a way that all forms of sexual expression were equally permissible, reproduction would result only from some sexual encounters, the heterosexual ones. The strict division of labor by sex, a social invention common to all known societies, creates two very separate genders and a need for men and women to get together for economic reasons. It thus helps to direct their sexual needs toward heterosexual fulfillment, and helps to ensure biological reproduction. In more imaginative societies, biological reproduction might be ensured by other techniques, but the division of labor by sex appears to be the universal solution to date. Although it is theoretically possible that a sexual division of labor not imply inequality between the sexes, in most known societies, the socially acceptable division of labor by sex is one which accords lower status to women's work. The sexual division of labor is also the underpinning of sexual subcultures in which men and women experience life differently; it is the material base of male power which is exercised (in our society) not just in not doing housework and in securing superior employment, but psychologically as well.

How people meet their sexual needs, how they reproduce, how they inculcate social norms in new generations, how they learn gender, how it feels to be a man or a woman—all occur in the realm Rubin labels the sex/gender system. Rubin emphasizes the influence of kinship (which tells you with whom you can satisfy sexual needs) and the development of gender specific personalities via child-rearing and the "oedipal machine." In addition, however, we can use the concept of the sex/gender system to examine all other social institutions for the roles they play in defining and reinforcing gender hierarchies. Rubin notes that theoretically a sex/gender system could be female dominant, male dominant, or egalitarian, but declines to label various known sex/gender systems or to periodize history accordingly. We choose to label our present sex/gender system patriarchy, because it appropriately captures the notion of hierarchy and male dominance which we see as central to the present system.

Economic production (what marxists are used to referring to as *the* mode of production) and the production of people in the sex/gender sphere both determine "the social organization under which the people of a particular historical epoch and a particular country live," according to Engels. The whole of society, then, can be understood by looking at both these types of production and reproduction, people and things.[17] There is no such thing as "pure capitalism," nor does "pure patriarchy" exist, for they must of necessity coexist. What exists is patriarchal capitalism, or patriarchal feudalism, or egalitarian hunting/gathering societies, or matriarchal horticultural societies, or patriarchal horticultural societies, and so on. There appears to be no necessary connection between *changes* in the one aspect of production and changes in the other. A society could undergo transition from capitalism to socialism, for example, and remain patriarchal.[18] Common sense, history, and our experience tell us, however, that these two aspects of production are so closely intertwined, that change in one ordinarily creates movement, tension, or contradiction in the other.

Radical hierarchies can also be understood in this context. Further elaboration may be possible along the lines of defining color/race systems, arenas of social life that take biological color and turn it into a social category, race. Racial hierarchies, like gender hierarchies, are aspects of our social organization, of how people are produced and reproduced. They are not fundamentally ideological; they constitute that second aspect of our mode of production, the production and reproduction of people. I might be most accurate then to refer to our societies not as, for example, simply capitalist, but as patriarchal capitalist white supremacist.

In Part 3 below, we illustrate one case of capitalism adapting to and making use of racial orders and several examples of the interrelations between capitalism and patriarchy.

Capitalist development creates the places for a hierarchy of workers, but traditional marxist categories cannot tell us who will fill which places. Gender and racial hierarchies determine who fills the empty places. *Patriarchy is not simply hierarchical organization,* but hierarchy in which *particular* people fill *particular* places. It is in studying patriarchy that we learn why it is women who are dominated and how. While we believe that most known societies have been patriarchal, we do not view patriarchy as a universal, unchanging phenomenon. Rather patriarchy, the set of interrelations among men that allow men to dominate women, has changed in form and intensity over time. It is crucial that the hierarchy among men, and their differential access to patriarchal benefits, be examined. Surely, class, race, nationality, and even marital status and sexual orientation, as well as the obvious age, come into play here. And women of different class, race, nationality, marital status, or sexual orientation groups are subjected to different degrees of patriarchal power. Women may themselves exercise class, race, or national power, or even patriarchal power (through their family connections) over men lower in the patriarchal hierarchy than their own male kin.

To recapitulate, we define patriarchy as a set of social relations which has a material base and in which there are hierarchical relations between men and solidarity among them which enable them in turn to dominate women. The material base of patriarchy is men's control over women's labor power. That control is maintained by excluding women from access to necessary economically productive resources and by restricting women's sexuality. Men exercise their control in receiving personal service work from women, in not having to do housework or rear children, in having access to women's bodies for sex, and in feeling powerful and being powerful. The crucial elements of patriarchy as we *currently* experience them are: heterosexual marriage (and consequent homophobia), female childrearing and housework, women's economic dependence on men (enforced by arrangements in the labor market), the state and numerous institutions based on social relations among men—clubs, sports, unions, professions, universities, churches, corporations, and armies. All of these elements need to be examined if we are to understand patriarchal capitalism.

Both hierarchy and interdependence among men and the subordination of women are *integral* to the functioning of our society; that is, these relationships are *systemic.* We leave aside the question of the creation of these relations and ask, can we recognize patriarchal relations in capitalist societies? Within capitalist societies we must discover those same bonds between men which both bourgeois and marxist social scientists claim no longer exist, or are, at the most, unimportant leftovers. Can we understand how these relations among men are perpetuated in capitalist societies? Can we identify ways in which patriarchy has shaped the course of capitalist development?

3.
The Partnership of Patriarchy and Capital

How are we to recognize patriarchal social relations in capitalist societies? It appears as if each woman is oppressed by her own man alone; her oppression seems a private affair. Relationships among men and among families seem equally fragmented. It is hard to recognize relationships among men, and between men and women, as *systematically* patriarchal. We argue, however, that patriarchy as a system of relations between men and women exists in capitalism, and that in capitalist societies a healthy and strong partnership exists between patriarchy and capital. Yet if one begins with the concept of patriarchy and an understanding of the capitalist mode of production, one recognizes immediately that the partnership of patriarchy and capital was not inevitable; men and capitalists often have conflicting interests, particularly over the use of women's labor power. Here is one way in which this conflict might manifest itself: the vast majority of men might want their women at home to personally service them. A smaller number of men, who are capitalists, might want most women (not their own) to work in the wage labor market. In examining the tensions of this conflict over women's labor power . . . we will be able to identify the material base of patriarchal relations in capitalist societies, as well as the basis for the partnership between capital and patriarchy.

Industrialization and the Development of Family Wages

. . . Family wages may be understood as a resolution of the conflict over women's labor power which [occurred] between patriarchal and capitalist interests [in the nineteenth century].

Family wages for most adult men imply men's acceptance, and collusion in, lower wages for others, young people, women and socially defined inferior men as well (Irish, blacks, etc., the lowest groups in the patriarchal hierarchy who are denied many of the patriarchal benefits). Lower wages for women and children and inferior men are enforced by job segregation in the labor market, in turn maintained by unions and management as well as by auxiliary institutions like schools, training programs, and even families. Job segregation by sex, by insuring that women have the lower paid jobs, both assures women's economic dependence on men and reinforces notions of appropriate spheres for women and men. For most men, then, the development of family wages secured the material base of male domination in two ways. First, men have the better jobs in the labor market and earn higher wages than women. The lower pay women receive in the labor market both perpetuates men's material advantage over women and encourages women to choose wifery as a career. Second, then women do housework, childcare, and perform other services at home which benefit men directly.[19] Women's home responsibilities in turn reinforce their inferior labor market position.[20]

The resolution that developed in the early twentieth century can be seen to benefit capitalist interests as well as patriarchal interests. Capitalists, it is often argued, recognized that in the extreme conditions which prevailed in the early nineteenth-century industrialization, working-class families could not adequately reproduce themselves. They realized that housewives produced and maintained healthier workers than wage-working wives and that educated children became better workers than noneducated ones. The bargain, paying family wages to men and keeping women home, suited the capitalists at the time as well as the male workers. Although the terms of the bargain have altered over time, it is still true that the family and women's work in the family serve capital by providing a labor force and serve men as the space in which they exercise their privilege. Women, working to serve men and their families, also serve capital as consumers.[21] The family is also the place where dominance and submission are learned, as Firestone, the Frankfurt School, and many others have explained.[22] Obedient children become obedient workers, girls and boys each learn their proper roles.

While the family wage shows that capitalism adjusts to patriarchy, the changing status of children shows that patriarchy adjusts to capital. Children, like women, came to be excluded from wage labor. As children's ability to earn money declined, their legal relationship to their parents changed. At the beginning of the industrial era in the United States, fulfilling children's need for their fathers was thought to be crucial, even primary, to their happy development; fathers had legal priority in cases of contested custody. As children's ability to contribute to the economic well-being of the family declined, mothers came increasingly to be viewed as crucial to the happy development of their children, and gained legal priority in cases of contested custody.[23] Here patriarchy adapted to the changing economic role of children: when children were productive, men claimed them; as children became unproductive, they were given to women. . . .

With respect to capitalism and patriarchy, the adaptation, or mutual accommodation, took the form of the development of the family wage in the early twentieth century. The family wage cemented the partnership between patriarchy and capital. Despite women's increased labor force participation, particularly rapid since World War II, the family wage is still, we argue, the cornerstone of the present sexual division of labor—in which women are primarily responsible for housework and men primarily for wage work. Women's lower wages in the labor market (combined with the need for children to be reared by someone) assure the continued existence of the family as a necessary income pooling unit. The family, supported by the family wage, thus allows the control of women's labor by men both within and without the family.

Though women's increased wage work may cause stress for the family (similar to the stress Kautsky and Engels noted in the nineteenth century), it would be wrong to think that as a consequence, the concepts and the realities of the family and of the sexual division of labor will soon disappear. The sexual division of labor reappears in the labor market, where women work at women's jobs, often the very jobs they used to do only at home—food preparation and service, cleaning of all kinds, caring for people, and so on. As these jobs are low-status and low-paying, patriarchal relations remain intact, though their material base shifts somewhat from the family to the wage differential, from family-based to industrially based patriarchy.[24]

The prediction of nineteenth-century marxists that patriarchy would wither away in the face of capitalism's need to proletarianize everyone has not come true. Not only did marxists underestimate the strength and flexibility of patriarchy, they also overestimated the strength of capital. They envisioned the new social force of capitalism, which had torn feudal relations apart, as virtually all-powerful. . . .

If the first element of our argument about the course of capitalist development is that capital is not all-powerful, the second is that capital is tremendously flexible. Capital accumulation encounters preexisting social forms, and both destroys them and adapts to them. The adaptation of capital can be seen as a reflection of the *strength* of these preexisting forms to persevere in new environments. Yet even as they persevere, they are not unchanged. The ideology with which race and sex are understood today, for example, is strongly shaped by the particular ways racial and sexual divisions are reinforced in the accumulation process. . . .

Industrially based patriarchal relations are enforced in a variety of ways. Union contracts which specify lower wages, lesser benefits, and fewer advancement opportunities for women are not just atavistic hangovers—a case of sexist attitudes or male supremacist ideology—they maintain the material base of the patriarchal system. While some would go so far as to argue that patriarchy is already absent from the family (see, for example, Stewart Ewen, *Captains of Consciousness*),[25] we would not. Although the terms of the compromise between capital and patriarchy are changing as additional tasks formerly located in the family are capitalized, and the location of the deployment of women's labor power shifts,[26] it is nevertheless true, as we have argued above, that the wage differential caused by extreme job segregation in the labor market reinforces the family, and, with it, the domestic division of labor, by encouraging women to marry. The "ideal" of the family wage—that a man can earn enough to support an entire family—may be giving way to a new ideal that both men and women contribute through wage earning to the cash income of the family. The wage differential, then, will become increasingly necessary in perpetuating patriarchy, the male control of women's labor power. The wage differential will aid in *defining* women's work as secondary to men's at the same time it necessitates women's actual continued economic dependence on men. The sexual division of labor in the labor market and elsewhere should be understood as a manifestation of patriarchy which serves to perpetuate it.

Many people have argued that though the partnership between capital and patriarchy exists now, it may *in the long run* prove intolerable to capitalism; capital may eventually destroy both familial relations and patriarchy. The argument proceeds logically that capitalist social relations (of which the family is not an example) tend to become universalized, that women will become increasingly able to earn money and will increasingly refuse to submit to subordination in the family, and that since the family is oppressive particularly to women and children, it will collapse as soon as people can support themselves outside it.

We do not think that the patriarchal relations embodied in the family can be destroyed so easily by capital, and we see little evidence that the family system is presently disintegrating. Although the increasing labor force participation of women has made divorce more feasible, the incentives to divorce are not overwhelming for women. Women's wages allow very few women to support themselves and their children independently and adequately. The evidence for the decay of the traditional family is weak at best. The divorce rate has not so much increased, as it has evened out among classes; moreover, the remarriage rate is also very high. Up until the 1970 census, the first-marriage age was continuing its historic decline. Since 1970, people seem to have been delaying marriage and childbearing, but most recently, the birth rate has begun to increase again. It is true that larger proportions of the population are now living outside traditional families. Young people, especially, are leaving their parents' homes and establishing their own households before they marry and start traditional families. Older people, especially women, are finding themselves alone in their own households, after their children are grown and they experience separation or death of a spouse. Nevertheless, trends indicate that the new generations of young people will form nuclear families at some time in their adult lives in higher proportions than ever before. The cohorts, or groups of people, born since 1930 have much higher rates of eventual marriage and childrearing than previous cohorts. The duration of marriage and childrearing may be shortening, but its incidence is still spreading.[27]

The argument that capital destroys the family also overlooks the social forces which make family life appealing. Despite critiques of nuclear families as psychologically destructive, in a competitive society the family still meets real needs for many people. This is true not only of long-term monogamy, but even more so for raising children. Single parents bear both financial and psychic burdens. For working-class women, in particular, these burdens make the "independence" of labor force participation illusory. Single-parent families have recently been seen by policy analysts as transitional family formations which become two-parent families upon remarriage.[28]

It could be that the effects of women's increasing labor force participation are found in a declining sexual division of labor within the family, rather than in more frequent divorce, but evidence for this is also lacking. Statistics on who does housework, even in families with wage-earning wives, show little change in recent years; women still do most of it.[29] The double day is a reality for wage-working women. This is hardly surprising since the sexual division of labor outside the family, in the labor market, keeps women financially dependent on men—even when they earn a wage themselves. The future of patriarchy does not, however, rest solely on the future of familial relations. For patriarchy, like capital, can be surprisingly flexible and adaptable.

Whether or not the patriarchal division of labor, outside the family and elsewhere, is "ultimately" intolerable to capital, it is shaping capitalism now. As we illustrate below, patriarchy both legitimates capitalist control and delegitimates certain forms of struggle against capital.

Ideology in the Twentieth Century

Patriarchy, by establishing and legitimating hierarchy among men (by allowing men of all groups to control at least some women), reinforces capitalist control, and capitalist values shape the definition of patriarchal good. . . .

If we examine the characteristics of men as radical feminists describe them— competitive, rationalistic, dominating—they are much like our description of the dominant values of capitalist society.

This "coincidence" may be explained in two ways. In the first instance, men, as wage laborers, are absorbed in capitalist social relations at work, driven into the competition these relations prescribe, and absorb the corresponding values.[30] The radical feminist description of men was not altogether out of line for capitalist societies. Secondly, even when men and women do not actually behave in the way sexual norms prescribe, men *claim for themselves* those characteristics which are valued in the dominant ideology. So, for example, the authors of *Crestwood Heights* found that while the men, who were professionals, spent their days manipulating subordinates (often using techniques that appeal to fundamentally irrational motives to elicit the preferred behavior), men and women characterized men as "rational and pragmatic." And while the women devoted great energies to studying scientific methods of childrearing and child development, men and women in Crestwood Heights characterized women as "irrational and emotional."[31]

This helps to account not only for "male" and "female" characteristics in capitalist societies, but for the particular form sexist ideology takes in capitalist societies. Just as women's work serves the dual purpose of perpetuating male domination and capitalist production, so sexist ideology serves the dual purpose of glorifying male characteristics/capitalist values, and denigrating female characteristics/social need. If women were degraded or powerless in other societies, the reasons (rationalizations) men had for this were different. Only in a capitalist society does it make sense to look down on women as emotional or irrational. As epithets, they would not have made sense in the Renaissance. Only in a capitalist society does it make sense to look down on women as "dependent." "Dependent" as an epithet would not make sense in feudal societies. Since the division of labor ensures that women as wives and mothers in the family are largely concerned with the production of use values, the denigration of these activities obscures capital's inability to meet socially determined needs at the same time that it degrades women in the eyes of men, providing a rationale for male dominance. An example of this may be seen in the peculiar ambivalence of television commercials. On one hand, they address themselves to the real obstacles to providing for socially determined needs: detergents that destroy clothes and irritate skin, shoddily made goods of all sorts. On the other hand, concern with these problems must be denigrated; this is accomplished by mocking women, the workers who must deal with these problems.

A parallel argument demonstrating the partnership of patriarchy and capitalism may be made about the sexual division of labor in the work force. The sexual division of labor places women in low-paying jobs, and in tasks thought to be appropriate to women's role. Women are teachers, welfare workers, and the great majority of workers in the health fields. The nurturant roles that women play in these jobs are of low status because capitalism emphasizes personal independence and the ability of private enterprise to meet social needs, emphases contradicted by the need for collectively provided services. As long as the social importance of nurturant tasks can be denigrated because women perform them, the confrontation of capital's priority on exchange value by a demand for use values can be avoided. In this way, it is not feminism but sexism that divides and debilitates the working class.

4.
Towards a More Progressive Union

Many problems remain for us to explore. Patriarchy as we have used it here remains more a descriptive term than an analytic one. If we think marxism alone inadequate, and radical feminism itself insufficient, then we need to develop new categories. What makes our task a difficult one is that the same features, such as the division of labor, often reinforce both patriarchy and capitalism, and in a thoroughly patriarchal capitalist society, it is hard to isolate the mechanisms of patriarchy. Nevertheless, this is what we must do. We have pointed to some starting places: looking at who benefits from women's labor power, uncovering the material base of patriarchy, investigating the mechanisms of hierarchy and solidarity among men. The questions we must ask are endless.

Can we speak of the laws of motion of a patriarchal system? How does patriarchy generate feminist struggle? What kinds of sexual politics and struggle between the sexes can we see in societies other than advanced capitalist ones? What are the contradictions of the patriarchal system and what is their relation to the contradictions of capitalism? . . .

Feminism and the Class Struggle

. . . The struggle against capital and patriarchy cannot be successful if the study and practice of the issues of feminism is abandoned. A struggle aimed only at capitalist relations of oppression will fail, since their underlying supports in patriarchal relations of oppression will be overlooked. And the analysis of patriarchy is essential to a definition of the kind of socialism useful to women. While men and women share a need to overthrow capitalism they retain interests particular to their gender group. It is not clear—from our sketch, from history, or from male socialists—that the socialism being struggled for is the same for both men and women. For a humane socialism would require not only consensus on what the new society should look like and what a healthy person should look like, but more concretely, it would require that men relinquish their privilege.

As women, we must not allow ourselves to be talked out of the urgency and importance of our tasks, as we have so many times in the past. We must fight the attempted coercion, both subtle and not so subtle, to abandon feminist objectives.

This suggests two strategic considerations. First, a struggle to establish socialism must be a struggle in which groups with different interests form an alliance. Women should not trust men to liberate them after the revolution, in part, because there is no reason to think they would know how; in part, because there is no necessity for them to do so. In fact their immediate self-interest lies in our continued oppression. Instead we must have our own organizations and our own power base. Second, we think the sexual division of labor within capitalism has given women a practice in which we have learned to understand what human interdependence and needs are. While men have long struggled *against* capital, women know what to struggle *for*.[32] As a general rule, men's position in patriarchy and capitalism prevents them from recognizing both human needs for nurturance, sharing, and growth, and the potential for meeting those needs in a nonhierarchical, nonpatriarchial society. But even if we raise their consciousness, men might assess the potential gains against the potential losses and choose the status quo. Men have more to lose than their chains.

As feminist socialists, we must organize a practice which addresses both the struggle against patriarchy and the struggle against capitalism. We must insist that the society we want to create is a society in which recognition of interdependence is liberation rather than shame, nurturance is a universal, not an oppressive practice, and in which women do not continue to support the false as well as the concrete freedoms of men.

NOTES

1. Earlier drafts of this essay appeared in 1975 and 1977 co-authored with Amy B. Bridges. Unfortunately, because of the press of current commitments, Amy was unable to continue with this project, joint from its inception and throughout most of its long and controversial history. Over the years many individuals and groups offered us comments, debate, and support. . . . This is a substantially abridged version of the essay as it appeared in *Women and Revolution*, ed. Lydia Sargent (Boston: South End Press, 1981). A more complete version was also published in *Capital and Class* in the summer of 1979. . . .

2. Often paraphrased as "the husband and wife are one and that one is the husband," English law held that "by marriage, the husband and wife are one person in law: that is, the very being or legal existence of the woman is suspended during the marriage, or at least is incorporated and consolidated into that of the Husband." I. Blackstone, *Commentaries*, 1965, 442–445, cited in Kenneth M. Davidson, Ruth B. Ginsburg, and Herma H. Kay, *Sex Based Discrimination* (St. Paul: West, 1974), 117.

3. This is a paraphrase. Karl Marx wrote: "The maintenance and reproduction of the working class is, and must ever be, a necessary condition to the reproduction of capital. But the capitalist may safely leave its fulfillment to the labourer's instincts of self-preservation and propagation." *Capital* (New York: International Publishers, 1967), 1:572.

4. Harry Braverman, *Labor and Monopoly Capital* (New York: Monthly Review Press, 1975).

5. Juliet Mitchell, *Women's Estate* (New York: Vintage Books, 1973), 92.

6. Frederick Engels, *The Origin of the Family, Private Property and the State,* ed. Eleanor Burke Leacock (New York: International Publishers, 1972), "Preface to the First Edition," 71–72. The continuation of this quotation reads, "by the stage of development of labor on the one hand and of the family on the other." It is interesting that, by implication, labor is excluded from occurring within the family; this is precisely the blind spot we want to overcome in this essay.

7. Juliet Mitchell, "Women: The Longest Revolution," *New Left Review,* no. 40 (November–December 1966): 11–37; reprinted by the New England Free Press.

8. Shulamith Firestone, *The Dialectic of Sex: The Case for Feminist Revolution* (New York: [Morrow], 1970).

9. "Politics of Ego: A Manifesto for New York Radical Feminists" can be found in *Rebirth of Feminism,* ed. Judith Hole and Ellen Levine (New York: Quadrangle, 1971), 440–443. "Radical feminists" are those feminists who argue that the most fundamental dynamic of history is men's striving to dominate women. "Radical" in this context does *not* mean anti-capitalist, socialist, counter-cultural, etc., but has the specific meaning of this particular set of feminist beliefs or group of feminists. Additional writings of radical feminists, of whom the New York Radical Feminists are probably the most influential, can be found in Anne Koedt, ed., *Radical Feminism* (New York: Quadrangle, 1973).

10. Focusing on power was an important step forward in the feminist critique of Freud. Firestone argues, for example, that if little girls "envied" penises it was because they recognized that little boys grew up to be members of a powerful class and little girls grew up to be dominated by them. Powerlessness, not neurosis, was the heart of women's situation. More recently, feminists have criticized Firestone for rejecting the usefulness of the concept of the unconscious. In seeking to explain the strength and continuation of male dominance, recent feminist writing has emphasized the fundamental nature of gender-based personality differences, their origins in the unconscious, and the consequent difficulty of their eradication. See Dorothy Dinnerstein, *The Mermaid and the Minotaur* (New York: Harper [and Row], 1976); Nancy Chodorow, *The Reproduction of Mothering* (Berkeley: University of California Press, 1978); and Jane Flax, "The Conflict between Nurturance and Autonomy in Mother-Daughter Relationships and within Feminism," *Feminist Studies* 4, no. 2 (June 1978): 141–189.

11. Kate Millett, *Sexual Politics* (New York: Avon, 1971), 25.

12. One example of this type of radical feminist history is Susan Brownmiller, *Against Our Will: Men, Women, and Rape* (New York: Simon and Schuster, 1975).

13. For the bourgeois social science view of patriarchy, see, for example, Weber's distinction between traditional and legal authority: *Max Weber: The Theories of Social and Economic Organization,* ed. Talcott Parsons (New York: Free Press, 1964), 328–357. These views are also discussed in Elizabeth Fee, "The Sexual Politics of Victorian Social Anthropology," in *Feminist Tradition* (New York: Basic Books, 1966), esp. chap. 3, "Community."

14. See Viana Muller, "The Formation of the State and Oppression of Women: Some Theoretical Considerations and a Case Study in England and Wales," *Review of Radical Political Economics* 9, no. 3 (Fall 1977): 7–21.

15. The particular ways in which men control women's access to important economic resources and restrict their sexuality vary enormously, both from society to society, from subgroup to subgroup, and across time. The examples we use to illustrate patriarchy in this section, however, are drawn primarily from the experience of whites in Western capitalist countries.

The diversity is shown in Rayna Rapp Reiter, ed., *Toward an Anthropology of Women* (New York: Monthly Review Press, 1975); Michelle Rosaldo and Louise Lamphere, eds., *Woman, Culture, and Society* (Stanford, Calif.: Stanford University Press, 1974); and Lia Leibowitz, *Females, Males, Families: A Biosocial Approach* (North Scituate, Mass.: Duxbury, 1978). The control of women's sexuality is tightly linked to the place of children. An understanding of the demand (by men and capitalists) for children is crucial to understanding changes in women's subordination.

Where children are needed for their present or future labor power, women's sexuality will tend to be directed toward reproduction and childrearing. When children are seen as superfluous, women's sexuality for other than reproductive purposes is encouraged, but men will attempt to direct it towards satisfying male needs. The Cosmo girl is a good example of a woman "liberated" from childrearing only to find herself turning all her energies toward attracting and satisfying men. Capitalists can also use female sexuality to their own ends, as the success of Cosmo in advertising consumer products shows.

16. Gayle Rubin, "The Traffic in Women," in Reiter, *Toward an Anthropology of Women*, 159.

17. Himmelweit and Mohun point out that both aspects of production (people and things) are logically necessary to describe a mode of production because by definition a mode of production must be capable of reproducing itself. Either aspect alone is not self-sufficient. To put it simply, the production of things requires people, and the production of people requires things. Marx, though recognizing capitalism's need for people, did not concern himself with how they were produced or what the connections between the two aspects of production were. See Himmelweit and Mohun, "Domestic Labour and Capital," *Cambridge Journal of Economics* 1, no. 1 (March 1977): 15–31.

18. For an excellent discussion of one such transition to socialism, see Batya Weinbaum, "Women in Transition to Socialism: Perspectives on the Chinese Case," *Review of Radical Political Economics*, 8, no. 1 (spring 1976): 34–58.

19. The importance of the fact that women perform labor services for men in the home cannot be overemphasized. As Pat Mainardi said in "The Politics of Housework," "the measure of your oppression is his resistance." See *Sisterhood Is Powerful*, ed. Robin Morgan (New York: Vintage, 1970), 451. Her article, perhaps as important for us as Firestone on love, is an analysis of power relations between women and men as exemplified by housework.

20. Libby Zimmerman has explored the relation of membership in the primary and secondary labor markets to family patterns in New England. See her "Women in the Economy: A Case Study of Lynn, Massachusetts, 1760–1974," Ph.D. dissertation, Heller School, Brandeis, 1977. Batya Weinbaum is currently exploring the relationship between family roles and places in the labor market. See her "Redefining the Question of Revolution," *Review of Radical Political Economics* 9, no. 3 (fall 1977): 54, 78; and *The Curious Courtship of Women's Liberation and Socialism* (Boston: South End Press, 1978). Additional studies of the interaction of capitalism and patriarchy can be found in Zillah Eisenstein, ed., *Capitalist Patriarchy and the Case for Socialist Feminism* (New York: Monthly Review Press, 1978).

21. See Batya Weinbaum and Amy Bridges, "The Other Side of the Paycheck: Monopoly Capital and the Structure of Consumption," *Monthly Review* 28, no. 3 (July–August 1976): 88–103, for a discussion of women's consumption work.

22. For the view of the Frankfurt School, see Max Horkheimer, "Authority and the Family," in *Critical Theory* (New York: Herder and Herder, 1972); and Frankfurt Institute of Social Research, "The Family," in *Aspects of Sociology* (Boston: Beacon, 1972).

23. Carol Brown, "Patriarchal Capitalism and the Female-Headed Family," *Social Scientist* (India), nos. 40–41 (November–December 1975): 28–39.

24. Brown, in "Patriarchal Capitalism," argues, for example, that we are moving from "family based" to "industrially based" patriarchy within capitalism.

25. Stuart Ewen, *Captains of Consciousness* (New York: Random House, 1976).

26. Jean Gardiner, "Women's Domestic Labour," *New Left Review*, no. 89 (January–February 1975): 47–58, clarifies the cause for the shift in location of women's labor, from capital's point of view. She examines what capital needs (in terms of the level of real wages, the supply of labor, and the size of markets) at various stages of growth and of the business cycle. She argues that in times of boom or rapid growth it is likely that socializing housework (or more accurately, capitalizing it) would be the dominant tendency, and that in times of recession, housework will be maintained in its traditional form. In attempting to assess the likely direction of the British economy, however, Gardiner does not assess the economic needs of patriarchy. We argue in this essay that unless one takes patriarchy as well as capital into account one cannot adequately assess the likely direction of the economic system.

27. For the proportion of people in nuclear families, see Peter Uhlenberg, "Cohort Variations in Family Life Cycle Experiences of U.S. Females," *Journal of Marriage and the Family* 36, no. 5 (May 1974): 284–292. For remarriage rates, see Paul C. Glick and Arthur J. Norton, "Perspectives on the Recent Upturn in Divorce and Remarriage," *Demography* 10 (1974): 301–314. For divorce and income levels, see Arthur J. Norton and Paul C. Glick, "Marital Instability: Past, Present, and Future," *Journal of Social Issues* 32, no. 1 (1976): 5–20. Also see Mary Jo Bane, *Here to Stay: American Families in the Twentieth Century* (New York: Basic Books, 1976).

28. Heather L. Ross and Isabel V. Sawhill, *Time of Transition: The Growth of Families Headed by Women* (Washington, D.C.: Urban Institute, 1975).

29. See Kathryn E. Walker and Margaret E. Woods, *Time Use: A Measure of Household Production of Family Goods and Services* (Washington, D.C.: American Home Economics Association, 1976); and Heidi I. Hartmann, "The Family as the Locus of Gender, Class, and Political Struggle: The Example of Housework," *Signs: Journal of Women in Culture and Society* 6, no. 3 (spring 1981).

30. This should provide some clues to class differences in sexism, which we cannot explore here.

31. See John R. Seeley et al., *Crestwood Heights* (Toronto: University of Toronto Press, 1956), 382–394. While men's place may be characterized as "in production," this does not mean that woman's place is simply "not in production"—her tasks, too, are shaped by capital. Her nonwage work is the resolution, on a day-to-day basis, of production for exchange with socially determined need, the provision of use values in a capitalist society (this is the context of consumption). See Weinbaum and Bridges, "The Other Side of the Paycheck," for a more complete discussion of this argument. The fact that women provide "merely" use values in a society dominated by exchange values can be used to denigrate women.

32. Lise Vogel, "The Earthly Family," *Radical America* 7, nos. 4–5 (July–October 1973): 9–50.

Monique Wittig

———•◦•———

"One Is Not Born a Woman" (1981)

The French feminist Monique Wittig (1935–2003) was a novelist, a poet, and a philosopher. The author of L'Opoponax *(1964),* Les Guérillères *(1969),* The Lesbian Body *(1984), and* The Straight Mind and Other Essays *(1992), she was an influential postmodernist who created new meanings for the feminist movement. Wittig taught French and women's studies at the University of Arizona until her unexpected death in 2003.*

A MATERIALIST FEMINIST approach to women's oppression destroys the idea that women are a "natural group": "a social group of a special kind, a group perceived as natural, a group of men considered as materially specific in their bodies." A lesbian society destroys the artificial (social) fact constituting women as a "natural group." A lesbian society pragmatically reveals that the division from men of which women have been the object is a political one and shows how we have been ideologically re-built into a "natural group." In our case, ideology goes far since our bodies as well as our minds are the product of this manipulation. We have been compelled in our bodies and in our minds to correspond, feature by feature, with the *idea* of nature that has been established for us. Distorted to such an extent that our deformed body is what they call "natural," is what is supposed to exist as such before oppression. Distorted to such an extent that at the end oppression seems to be a consequence of this "nature" in ourselves (a nature which is only an *idea*). What a materialist analysis does by reasoning, a lesbian society accomplishes in fact: not only is there no natural group "women" (we lesbians are a living proof of it) but as individuals as well we question "woman," which for us, as for Simone de Beauvoir thirty years ago, is only a myth. She said: "One is not born, but becomes a woman. No biological, psychological, or economic fate determines the figure that the human female presents in society; it is civilization as a whole that produces this creature, intermediate between male and eunuch, which is described as feminine."

However, most of the feminists and lesbian-feminists in America and elsewhere still believe that the basis of women's oppression *is biological as well as* historical. Some of them even claim to find their sources in Simone de Beauvoir. The belief in mother-right and in a "prehistory" when women would have created civilization (because of a biological predisposition), while the coarse and brutal men would have hunted (because of a biological predisposition), does not make the biological approach any better. It is still the same method of finding in women and men a biological explanation of their division, outside of social facts. For me this could never constitute a lesbian approach since it assumes that the basis of society or the beginning of society lies in heterosexuality. Matriarchies are no less heterosexual than patriarchies: it's only the sex of the oppressor that changes. Furthermore, not only is this conception still a prisoner of the categories of sex (woman and man), but it keeps to the idea that the capacity to give birth (biology) is what defines a woman. Although practical facts and ways of living contradict this theory in lesbian society, there are lesbians who affirm that "women and men are different species or races (the words are used interchangeably); men are biologically inferior to women; male violence is a biological inevitability." By doing this, by admitting that there is a "natural" division between women and men, we naturalize history, we assume that men and women have always existed and will always exist. Not only do we naturalize history, but also consequently we naturalize the social phenomena which express our oppression, making change impossible. For example, instead of seeing giving birth as a forced production, we see it as a "natural," "biological" process, forgetting that in our societies births are planned (demography), forgetting that we ourselves are programmed to produce children, while this is the only social activity "short of war" that presents such a great danger of death. Thus, as long as we will be "unable to abandon by will or impulse a lifelong and centuries old commitment to childbearing as *the* female creative act," having control of the production of children will mean much more than the mere control of the material means of this production. Women will have to abstract themselves from the definition "woman" which is imposed upon them.

A materialist feminist approach shows that what we take for the cause or origin of oppression is in fact only the *mark* imposed by the oppressor: the "myth of woman," plus its material effects and manifestations in the appropriated consciousness and bodies of women. Thus, the mark does not preexist oppression. Colette Guillaumin, a French sociologist, has shown that before the socio-economical reality of black slavery, the concept of race did not exist (at least not in its modern meaning: it was applied to the lineage of families). However, now, race, exactly like sex, is taken as an "immediate given," a "sensible given," "physical features." They appear as though they existed prior to reasoning, belonging to a natural order. But what we believe to be a physical and direct perception is only a sophisticated and mythic construction, an "imaginary formation" which reinterprets physical features through the network of relationships in which they are perceived. (They are seen *black*, therefore they *are black*; they are seen *women*, therefore they *are women*. But before being *seen* that way, they first had to be *made* that way.) A lesbian consciousness should always remember how "unnatural," compelling, totally oppressive, and destructive being "woman" was for us in the old days before the women's liberation movement. It was political obligation and those who resisted it were accused of not being "real" women. But then we were proud of it, since in the accusation there was already something like a shadow of victory: the avowal by the oppressor that "woman" is not something that goes without saying, since to be one, one has to be a "real" one (what about the others?). We were also confronted by the accusation of wanting to be men. We still are by certain lesbians and feminists who believe that one has to become more and more of a woman as a political obligation. But to refuse to be a woman does not mean that one has to become a man. And for her who does want to become a man: in what way is her alienation different from wanting to become a woman? At least for a woman, wanting to become a man proves that she escaped her initial programming. But even if she wants to, she cannot become a man. For becoming a man would demand from a woman having not only the outside appearance of a man but his consciousness as well, that is, the consciousness of one who disposes by right of at least two natural "slaves" during his life span. This is impossible since precisely one feature of lesbian oppression consists of making women out of reach for us, since women belong to men. Thus a lesbian *has* to be something else, not woman, not man, a product of society not a product of "nature," for there is no "nature" in society.

The refusal to become heterosexual always meant to refuse to become a man or a woman, consciously or not. For a lesbian this goes further than the refusal of the role "woman." It is the refusal of the economic, ideological and political power of a man. This, we lesbians, and non-lesbians as well, have experienced before the beginning of the lesbian and feminist movement. However, as Andrea Dworkin emphasizes, many lesbians recently "have increasingly tried to transform the very ideology that has enslaved us into a dynamic, religious, psychologically compelling celebration of female biological potential." Thus, some avenues of the feminist and lesbian movement lead us back to the myth of woman which was created by men especially for us, and with it we sink back into a natural group. Thirty years ago Simone de Beauvoir destroyed the myth of woman. Ten years ago we stood up to fight for a sexless society. Now we find ourselves entrapped in the familiar deadlock of "woman is wonderful." Thirty years ago Simone de Beauvoir underlined particularly the false consciousness which consists of selecting among the features of the myth (that women are different from men) those which look good and using them as a definition for women. What the concept of "woman is wonderful" accomplishes is that it retains for defining women the best features which oppression has granted us and it does not radically question the categories "man" and "woman." It puts us in a position of fighting within the class "women" not as the other classes do, for the disappearance of our class, but for the defense of "woman" and its reinforcement. It leads us to develop with complacency "new" theories about our specificity: thus, we call our passivity "non-violence." The ambiguity of the term "feminist" sums up the whole situation. What does "feminist" mean? Feminist is formed with the word "femme," "woman," and means "someone who fights for women." For many of us it means "someone who fights for women as a class and for the disappearance of this class." For many others it means "someone who fights for woman and her defense"—for the myth then and its reinforcement. But why was the word "feminist" chosen? We chose to call ourselves "feminists" ten years ago, not in order to identify ourselves with the oppressor's definition of us, but rather to affirm that our movement had a history and to emphasize the political link with the old feminist movement.

It is, then, this movement that we can question for its meaning of "feminism." It so happens that feminism in the last century could never resolve its contradictions on the subject of nature/culture, woman/society. Women started to fight for themselves as a group and rightly considered that they shared common features. But for them these features were natural and biological rather than social. They went so far as to adopt pseudo-Darwinist theories of evolution. They did not believe like Darwin, however, "that women were less evolved than men, but they did believe that male and female natures had diverged in the course of evolutionary development and that society at large reflected this polarization. . . . The failure of early feminism was that it only attacked the Darwinist charge of female inferiority, while accepting the foundations of this charge—namely, the view of woman as 'unique.' " And finally it was women scholars—and not feminists—who scientifically destroyed this theory. But the early feminists had failed to regard history as a dynamic process which develops from conflicts of interests. Furthermore, they still believed that the cause (origin) of their oppression lay within themselves (among black people only the Uncle Toms believed this). And therefore feminists, after some astonishing victories, found themselves at an impasse for lack of reasons for fighting. They upheld the illogical principle of "equality in difference," an idea now being born again. They fell back into the trap which threatens us once again: the myth of woman.

Thus it remains historically for us to define our oppression in materialist terms, to say that women are a class, which is to say that the category "woman," as well as "man," is a political and economic category, not an eternal one. Our fight aims to suppress men as a class, not through a genocidal, but a political struggle. Once the class "men" disappears, women as a class will disappear as well, for there are no slaves without masters. Our first task, it seems, is to always thoroughly disassociate "women" (the class within which we fight) and "woman," the myth. For "woman" does not exist for us: it is only an imaginary formation, while "women" is the product of social relationship. Furthermore we have to destroy the myth within and outside ourselves. "Woman" is not each one of us, but the political and ideological formation which negates "women" (the product of a relation of exploitation). "Woman" is there to confuse us, to hide the reality "women." In order to become a class and to be aware of it, we have first to kill the myth "woman" even in its most seductive aspects. . . .

To destroy "woman" does not mean to destroy lesbianism, for a lesbian is not a woman and does not love a woman, given that we agree with Christine Delphy that what "makes" woman is a personal dependency on a man (as opposed to an impersonal dependency on a boss). Lesbian is the only concept that I know of which is beyond the categories of sex (woman and man), because lesbian societies are not based upon women's oppression and because the designated subject (lesbian) is *not* a woman either economically or politically or ideologically. Furthermore, what we aim at is not the disappearance of lesbianism, which provides the only social form that we can live in, but the destruction of heterosexuality—the political system based on women's oppression, which produces the body of thought of the difference between the sexes to explain women's oppression.

Beyond or within this class consciousness, this science/experience, while in the separateness of one's ego, do we still have to fight to exist as an autonomous entity? There is no doubt that we have to fight for this entity, since we are left with nothing, once we reject the basic determination "woman" and "man," once we have no more attributes by which to identify ourselves (I am this or that). We are for the first time in history confronted with the necessity of existing as a person.

33

Audre Lorde

"Age, Race, Class, and Sex: Women Redefining Difference" (1980)

Audre Lorde (1934–1992) described herself as "a Black lesbian feminist poet."
Born in Harlem to Grenadan parents, graduate of Hunter College and
Columbia University, librarian by training, mother of two children, inter-
nationally acclaimed poet, and long-term survivor of breast cancer (which
eventually returned and claimed her life), Lorde defies categories. Her writ-
ings challenge any attempt to define an identity by excluding an Other. Her
most famous books include Sister Outsider: Essays and Speeches *(1982),*
Zami: A New Spelling of My Name *(1984), and* A Burst of Light *(1988).*
The following essay was presented at the Copeland Colloquium, Amherst Col-
lege, in April 1980, and later published in Sister Outsider.

MUCH OF WESTERN European history conditions us to see human differences
in simplistic opposition to each other: dominant/subordinate, good/bad, up/
down, superior/inferior. In a society where the good is defined in terms of
profit rather than in terms of human need, there must always be some group of
people who, through systematized oppression, can be made to feel surplus, to
occupy the place of the dehumanized inferior. Within this society, that group is
made up of Black and Third World people, working-class people, older people,
and women.

As a forty-nine-year-old Black lesbian feminist socialist mother of two, including one boy, and a member of an interracial couple, I usually find myself a part of some group defined as other, deviant, inferior or just plain wrong. Traditionally, in american society, it is the members of oppressed, objectified groups who are expected to stretch out and bridge the gap between the actualities of our lives and the consciousness of our oppressor. For in order to survive, those of us for whom oppression is as american as apple pie have always had to be watchers, to become familiar with the language and manners of the oppressor, even sometimes adopting them for some illusion of protection. Whenever the need for some pretense of communication arises, those who profit from our oppression call upon us to share our knowledge with them. In other words, it is the responsibility of the oppressed to teach the oppressors their mistakes. I am responsible for educating teachers who dismiss my children's culture in school. Black and Third World people are expected to educate white people as to our humanity. Women are expected to educate men. Lesbians and gay men are expected to educate the heterosexual world. The oppressors maintain their position and evade responsibility for their own actions. There is a constant drain of energy which might be better used in redefining ourselves and devising realistic scenarios for altering the present and constructing the future.

Institutionalized rejection of difference is an absolute necessity in a profit economy which needs outsiders as surplus people. As members of such an economy, we have *all* been programmed to respond to the human differences between us with fear and loathing and to handle that difference in one of three ways: ignore it, and if that is not possible, copy it if we think it is dominant, or destroy it if we think it is subordinate. But we have no patterns for relating across our human differences as equals. As a result, those differences have been misnamed and misused in the service of separation and confusion.

Certainly there are very real differences between us of race, age, and sex. But it is not those differences between us that are separating us. It is rather our refusal to recognize those differences, and to examine the distortions which result from our misnaming them and their effects upon human behavior and expectation.

Racism, the belief in the inherent superiority of one race over all others and thereby the right to dominance. Sexism, the belief in the inherent superiority of one sex over the other and thereby the right to dominance. Ageism. Heterosexism. Elitism. Classism.

It is a lifetime pursuit for each one of us to extract these distortions from our living at the same time as we recognize, reclaim, and define those differences upon which they are imposed. For we have all been raised in a society where those distortions were endemic within our living. Too often, we pour the energy needed for recognizing and exploring difference into pretending those differences are insurmountable barriers, or that they do not exist at all. This results in a voluntary isolation, or false and treacherous connections. Either way, we do not develop tools for using human difference as a springboard for creative change within our lives. We speak not of human difference, but of human deviance.

Somewhere, on the edge of consciousness, there is what I call a *mythical norm,* which each one of us within our hearts knows "that is not me." In america, this norm is usually defined as white, thin, male, young, heterosexual, christian, and financially secure. It is with this mythical norm that the trappings of power reside within this society. Those of us who stand outside that power often identify one way in which we are different, and we assume that to be the primary cause of all oppression, forgetting other distortions around difference, some of which we ourselves may be practising. By and large within the women's movement today, white women focus upon their oppression as women and ignore differences of race, sexual preference, class, and age. There is a pretense to a homogeneity of experience covered by the word *sisterhood* that does not in fact exist.

Unacknowledged class differences rob women of each other's energy and creative insight. Recently a women's magazine collective made the decision for one issue to print only prose, saying poetry was a less "rigorous" or "serious" art form. Yet even the form our creativity takes is often a class issue. Of all the art forms, poetry is the most economical. It is the one which is the most secret, which requires the least physical labor, the least material, and the one which can be done between shifts, in the hospital pantry, on the subway, and on scraps of surplus paper. Over the last few years, writing a novel on tight finances, I came to appreciate the enormous differences in the material demands between poetry and prose. As we reclaim our literature, poetry has been the major voice of poor, working class, and Colored women. A room of one's own may be a necessity for writing prose, but so are reams of paper, a typewriter, and plenty of time. The actual requirements to produce the visual arts also help determine, along class lines, whose art is whose. In this day of inflated prices for material, who are our sculptors, our painters, our photographers? When we speak of a broadly based women's culture, we need to be aware of the effect of class and economic differences on the supplies available for producing art.

As we move toward creating a society within which we can each flourish, ageism is another distortion of relationship which interferes [with our] vision. By ignoring the past, we are encouraged to repeat its mistakes. The "generation gap" is an important social tool for any repressive society. If the younger members of a community view the older members as contemptible or suspect or excess, they will never be able to join hands and examine the living memories of the community, nor ask the all important question, "Why?" This gives rise to a historical amnesia that keeps us working to invent the wheel every time we have to go to the store for bread.

We find ourselves having to repeat and relearn the same old lessons over and over that our mothers did because we do not pass on what we have learned, or because we are unable to listen. For instance, how many times has this all been said before? For another, who would have believed that once again our daughters are allowing their bodies to be hampered and purgatoried by girdles and high heels and hobble skirts?

Ignoring the differences of race between women and the implications of those differences presents the most serious threat to the mobilization of women's joint power.

As white women ignore their built-in privilege of whiteness and define *woman* in terms of their own experience alone, then women of Color become "other," the outsider whose experience and tradition is too "alien" to comprehend. An example of this is the signal absence of the experience of women of Color as a resource for women's studies courses. The literature of women of Color is seldom included in women's literature courses and almost never in other literature courses, nor in women's studies as a whole. All too often, the excuse given is that the literatures of women of Color can only be taught by Colored women, or that they are too difficult to understand, or that classes cannot "get into" them because they come out of experiences that are "too different." I have heard this argument presented by white women of otherwise quite clear intelligence, women who seem to have no trouble at all teaching and reviewing work that comes out of the vastly different experiences of Shakespeare, Molière, Dostoyevsky, and Aristophanes. Surely there must be some other explanation.

This is a very complex question, but I believe one of the reasons white women have such difficulty reading Black women's work is because of their reluctance to see Black women as women and different from themselves. To examine Black women's literature effectively requires that we be seen as whole people in our actual complexities—as individuals, as women, as human—rather than as one of those problematic but familiar stereotypes provided in this society in place of genuine images of Black women. And I believe this holds true for the literatures of other women of Color who are not Black.

The literatures of all women of Color recreate the textures of our lives, and many white women are heavily invested in ignoring the real differences. For as long as any difference between us means one of us must be inferior, then the recognition of any difference must be fraught with guilt. To allow women of Color to step out of stereotypes is too guilt provoking, for it threatens the complacency of those women who view oppression only in terms of sex.

Refusing to recognize difference makes it impossible to see the different problems and pitfalls facing us as women.

Thus, in a patriarchal power system where whiteskin privilege is a major prop, the entrapments used to neutralize Black women and white women are not the same. For example, it is easy for Black women to be used by the power structure against Black men, not because they are men, but because they are Black. Therefore, for Black women, it is necessary at all times to separate the needs of the oppressor from our own legitimate conflicts within our communities. This same problem does not exist for white women. Black women and men have shared racist oppression and still share it, although in different ways. Out of that shared oppression we have developed joint defenses and joint vulnerabilities to each other that are not duplicated in the white community, with the exception of the relationship between Jewish women and Jewish men.

On the other hand, white women face the pitfall of being seduced into joining the oppressor under the pretense of sharing power. This possibility does not exist in the same way for women of Color. The tokenism that is sometimes extended to us is not an invitation to join power; our racial "otherness" is a visible reality that makes that quite clear. For white women there is a wider range of pretended choices and rewards for identifying with patriarchal power and its tools.

Today, with the defeat of ERA, the tightening economy, and increased conservatism, it is easier once again for white women to believe the dangerous fantasy that if you are good enough, pretty enough, sweet enough, quiet enough, teach the children to behave, hate the right people, and marry the right men, then you will be allowed to co-exist with patriarchy in relative peace, at least until a man needs your job or the neighborhood rapist happens along. And true, unless one lives and loves in the trenches it is difficult to remember that the war against dehumanization is ceaseless.

But Black women and our children know the fabric of our lives is stitched with violence and with hatred, that there is no rest. We do not deal with it only on the picket lines, or in dark midnight alleys, or in the places where we dare to verbalize our resistance. For us, increasingly, violence weaves through the daily tissues of our living—in the supermarket, in the classroom, in the elevator, in the clinic and the schoolyard, from the plumber, the baker, the saleswoman, the bus driver, the bank teller, the waitress who does not serve us.

Some problems we share as women, some we do not. You fear your children will grow up to join the patriarchy and testify against you, we fear our children will be dragged from a car and shot down in the street, and you will turn your backs upon the reasons they are dying.

The threat of difference has been no less blinding to people of Color. Those of us who are Black must see that the reality of our lives and our struggle does not make us immune to the errors of ignoring and misnaming difference. Within Black communities where racism is a living reality, differences among us often seem dangerous and suspect. The need for unity is often misnamed as a need for homogeneity, and a Black feminist vision mistaken for betrayal of our common interests as a people. Because of the continuous battle against racial erasure that Black women and Black men share, some Black women still refuse to recognize that we are also oppressed as women, and that sexual hostility against Black women is practiced not only by the white racist society, but implemented within our Black communities as well. It is a disease striking the heart of Black nationhood, and silence will not make it disappear. Exacerbated by racism and the pressures of powerlessness, violence against Black women and children often becomes a standard within our communities, one by which manliness can be measured. But these woman-hating acts are rarely discussed as crimes against Black women.

As a group, women of Color are the lowest paid wage earners in america. We are the primary targets of abortion and sterilization abuse, here and abroad. In certain parts of Africa, small girls are still being sewed shut between their legs to keep them docile and for men's pleasure. This is known as female circumcision, and it is not a cultural affair as the late Jomo Kenyatta insisted, it is a crime against Black women.

Black women's literature is full of the pain of frequent assault, not only by a racist patriarchy, but also by Black men. Yet the necessity for and history of shared battle have made us, Black women, particularly vulnerable to the false accusation that anti-sexist is anti-Black. Meanwhile, womanhating as a recourse of the powerless is sapping strength from Black communities, and our very lives. Rape is on the increase, reported and unreported, and rape is not aggressive sexuality, it is sexualized aggression. As Kalamu ya Salaam, a Black male writer, points out, "As long as male domination exists, rape will exist. Only women revolting and men made conscious of their responsibility to fight sexism can collectively stop rape."[1]

Differences between ourselves as Black women are also being misnamed and used to separate us from one another. As a Black lesbian feminist comfortable with the many different ingredients of my identity, and a woman committed to racial and sexual freedom from oppression, I find I am constantly being encouraged to pluck out some one aspect of myself and present this as the meaningful whole, eclipsing or denying the other parts of self. But this is a destructive and fragmenting way to live. My fullest concentration of energy is available to me only when I integrate all the parts of who I am, openly, allowing power from particular sources of my living to flow back and forth freely through all my different selves, without the restrictions of externally imposed definition. Only then can I bring myself and my energies as a whole to the service of those struggles which I embrace as part of my living.

A fear of lesbians, or of being accused of being a lesbian, has led many Black women into testifying against themselves. It has led some of us into destructive alliances, and others into despair and isolation. In the white women's communities, heterosexism is sometimes a result of identifying with the white patriarchy, a rejection of that interdependence between women-identified women which allows the self to be, rather than to be used in the service of men. Sometimes it reflects a die-hard belief in the protective coloration of heterosexual relationships, sometimes a self-hate which all women have to fight against, taught us from birth.

Although elements of these attitudes exist for all women, there are particular resonances of heterosexism and homophobia among Black women. Despite the fact that woman-bonding has a long and honorable history in the African and African-american communities, and despite the knowledge and accomplishments of many strong and creative women-identified Black women in the political, social, and cultural fields, heterosexual Black women often tend to ignore or discount the existence and work of Black lesbians. Part of this attitude has come from an understandable terror of Black male attack within the close confines of Black society, where the punishment for any female self-assertion is still to be accused of being a lesbian and therefore unworthy of the attention or support of the scarce Black male. But part of this need to misname and ignore Black lesbians comes from a very real fear that openly women-identified Black women who are no longer dependent upon men for their self-definition may well reorder our whole concept of social relationships.

Black women who once insisted that lesbianism was a white woman's problem now insist that Black lesbians are a threat to Black nationhood, are consorting with the enemy, are basically un-Black. These accusations, coming from the very women to whom we look for deep and real understanding, have served to keep many Black lesbians in hiding, caught between the racism of white women and the homophobia of their sisters. Often, their work has been ignored, trivialized, or misnamed, as with the work of Angelina Grimke, Alice Dunbar-Nelson, Lorraine Hansberry. Yet women-bonded women have always been some part of the power of Black communities, from our unmarried aunts to the amazons of Dahomey.

And it is certainly not Black lesbians who are assaulting women and raping children and grandmothers on the streets of our communities.

Across this country, as in Boston during the spring of 1979 following the unsolved murders of twelve Black women, Black lesbians are spearheading movements against violence against Black women.

What are the particular details within each of our lives that can be scrutinized and altered to help bring about change? How do we redefine difference for all women? It is not our differences which separate women, but our reluctance to recognize those differences and to deal effectively with the distortions which have resulted from the ignoring and misnaming of those differences.

As a tool of social control, women have been encouraged to recognize only one area of human difference as legitimate, those differences which exist between women and men. And we have learned to deal across those differences with the urgency of all oppressed subordinates. All of us have had to learn to live or work or coexist with men, from our fathers on. We have recognized and negotiated these differences, even when this recognition only continued the old dominant/subordinate mode of human relationship, where the oppressed must recognize the masters' difference in order to survive.

But our future survival is predicated upon our ability to relate within equality. As women, we must root out internalized patterns of oppression within ourselves if we are to move beyond the most superficial aspects of social change. Now we must recognize differences among women who are our equals, neither inferior nor superior, and devise ways to use each other's difference to enrich our visions and our joint struggles.

The future of our earth may depend upon the ability of all women to identify and develop new definitions of power and new patterns of relating across difference. The old definitions have not served us, nor the earth that supports us. The old patterns, no matter how cleverly rearranged to imitate progress, still condemn us to cosmetically altered repetitions of the same old exchanges, the same old guilt, hatred, recrimination, lamentation, and suspicion.

For we have, built into all of us, old blueprints of expectation and response, old structures of oppression, and these must be altered at the same time as we alter the living conditions which are a result of those structures. For the master's tools will never dismantle the master's house.

As Paulo Freire shows so well in *The Pedagogy of the Oppressed*,[2] the true focus of revolutionary change is never merely the oppressive situations which we seek to escape, but that piece of the oppressor which is planted deep within each of us, and which knows only the oppressors' tactics, the oppressors' relationships.

Change means growth, and growth can be painful. But we sharpen self-definition by exposing the self in work and struggle together with those whom we define as different from ourselves, although sharing the same goals. For Black and white, old and young, lesbian and heterosexual women alike, this can mean new paths to our survival.

> We have chosen each other
> and the edge of each others' battles
> the war is the same
> if we lose

someday women's blood will congeal
upon a dead planet
if we win
there is no telling
we seek beyond history
for a new and more possible meeting.[3]

NOTES

1. Kalamu ya Salaam, "Rape: A Radical Analysis, An African-American Perspective," in *Black Books Bulletin* 6, no. 4 (1980).

2. New York: Seabury Press, 1970.

3. From "Outlines," unpublished poem.

34

Gloria Anzaldúa

"La Conciencia de la Mestiza: Towards a New Consciousness" (1987)

Gloria Anzaldúa (1942–2004) was a Chicana tejana lesbian-feminist poet and fiction writer. Her complex identity infuses her work: "I am an act of kneading, of uniting and joining that not only has produced both a creature of darkness and a creature of light, but also a creature that questions the definitions of light and dark and gives them new meaning." Anzaldúa is best known for This Bridge Called My Back: Writings by Radical Women of Color *(1981, coedited with Cherrie Moragua),* Borderlands/La Frontera: The New Mestiza *(1987, from which the following essay is excerpted),* Making Face, Making Soul; Haciendo Caras *(1990),* Interviews/Entrevistas *(2000), and* this bridge we call home: radical visions for transformation *(2002, coedited with AnaLouise Keating).*

> *Por la mujer de mi raza*
> *hablará el espíritu.*[1]

JOSÉ VASCONCELOS, MEXICAN philosopher, envisaged *una raza mestiza, una mezcla de razas afines, una raza de color—la primera raza síntesis del globo*. He called it a cosmic race, *la raza cósmica*, a fifth race embracing the four major races of the world.[2] Opposite to the theory of the pure Aryan, and to the policy of racial purity that white America practices, his theory is one of inclusivity. At the confluence of two or more genetic streams, with chromosomes constantly "crossing over," this mixture of races, rather than resulting in an inferior being, provides hybrid progeny, a mutable, more malleable species with a rich gene pool. From this racial, ideological, cultural, and biological cross-pollinization, an "alien" consciousness is presently in the making—a new *mestiza* consciousness, *una conciencia de mujer.* It is a consciousness of the Borderlands.

> *Una lucha de fronteras*/A Struggle of Borders
> Because I, a *mestiza,*
> continually walk out of one culture
> and into another,
> because I am in all cultures at the same time,
> *alma entre dos mundos, tres, cuatro,*
> *me zumba la cabeza con lo contradictorio.*
> *Estoy norteada por todas las voces que me hablan*
> *simultáneamente.*

The ambivalence from the clash of voices results in mental and emotional states of perplexity. Internal strife results in insecurity and indecisiveness. The *mestiza's* dual or multiple personality is plagued by psychic restlessness.

In a constant state of mental nepantilism, an Aztec word meaning torn between ways, *la mestiza* is a product of the transfer of the cultural and spiritual values of one group to another. Being tricultural, monolingual, bilingual or multilingual, speaking a patois, and in a state of perpetual transition, the *mestiza* faces the dilemma of the mixed breed: which collectivity does the daughter of a darkskinned mother listen to?

El choque de un alma atrapado entre el mundo del espíritu y el mundo de la técnica a veces la deja entullada. Cradled in one culture, sandwiched between two cultures, straddling all three cultures and their value systems, *la mestiza* undergoes a struggle of flesh, a struggle of borders, an inner war. Like all people, we perceive the version of reality that our culture communicates. Like others having or living in more than one culture, we get multiple, often opposing messages. The coming together of two self-consistent but habitually incompatible frames of reference[3] causes *un choque,* a cultural collision.

Within us and within *la cultura chicana,* commonly held beliefs of the white culture attack commonly held beliefs of the Mexican culture, and both attack commonly held beliefs of the indigenous culture. Subconsciously, we see an attack on ourselves and our beliefs as a threat and we attempt to block with a counterstance.

But it is not enough to stand on the opposite river bank, shouting questions, challenging patriarchical, white conventions. A counterstance locks one into a duel of oppressor and oppressed; locked in mortal combat, like the cop and the criminal, both are reduced to a common denominator of violence. The counterstance refutes the dominant culture's views and beliefs, and, for this, it is proudly defiant. All reaction is limited by, and dependent on, what it is reacting against. Because the counterstance stems from a problem with authority—outer as well as inner—it's a step towards liberation from cultural domination. But it is not a way of life. At some point, on our way to a new consciousness, we will have to leave the opposite bank, the split between the two mortal combatants somehow healed so that we are on both shores at once and, at once, see through serpent and eagle eyes. Or perhaps we will decide to disengage from the dominant culture, write it off altogether as a lost cause, and cross the border into a wholly new and separate territory. Or we might go another route. The possibilities are numerous once we decide to act and not react.

A Tolerance for Ambiguity

These numerous possibilities leave *la mestiza* floundering in uncharted seas. In perceiving conflicting information and points of view, she is subjected to a swamping of her psychological borders. She has discovered that she can't hold concepts or ideas in rigid boundaries. The borders and walls that are supposed to keep the undesirable ideas out are entrenched habits and patterns of behavior; these habits and patterns are the enemy within. Rigidity means death. Only by remaining flexible is she able to stretch the psyche horizontally and vertically. *La mestiza* constantly has to shift out of habitual formations; from convergent thinking, analytical reasoning that tends to use rationality to move toward a single goal (a Western mode), to divergent thinking,[4] characterized by movement away from set patterns and goals and toward a more whole perspective, one that includes rather than excludes.

The new *mestiza* copes by developing a tolerance for contradictions, a tolerance for ambiguity. She learns to be an Indian in Mexican culture, to be Mexican from an Anglo point of view. She learns to juggle cultures. She has a plural personality, she operates in a pluralistic mode—nothing is thrust out, the good, the bad and the ugly, nothing rejected, nothing abandoned. Not only does she sustain contradictions, she turns the ambivalence into something else.

She can be jarred out of ambivalence by an intense, and often painful, emotional event which inverts or resolves the ambivalence. I'm not sure exactly how. The work takes place underground—subconsciously. It is work that the soul performs. That focal point or fulcrum, that juncture where the *mestiza* stands, is where phenomena tend to collide. It is where the possibility of uniting all that is separate occurs. This assembly is not one where severed or separated pieces merely come together. Nor is it a balancing of opposing powers. In attempting to work out a synthesis, the self has added a third element which is greater than the sum of its severed parts. That third element is a new consciousness—a *mestiza* consciousness—and though it is a source of intense pain, its energy comes from a continual creative motion that keeps breaking down the unitary aspect of each new paradigm.

En unas pocas centurias, the future will belong to the *mestiza.* Because the future depends on the breaking down of paradigms, it depends on the straddling of two or more cultures. By creating a new mythos—that is, a change in the way we perceive reality, the way we see ourselves and the ways we behave—*la mestiza* creates a new consciousness.

The work of *mestiza* consciousness is to break down the subject-object duality that keeps her a prisoner and to show in the flesh and through the images in her work how duality is transcended. The answer to the problem between the white race and the colored, between males and females, lies in healing the split that originates in the very foundation of our lives, our culture, our languages, our thoughts. A massive uprooting of dualistic thinking in the individual and collective consciousness is the beginning of a long struggle, but one that could, in our best hopes, bring us to the end of rape, of violence, of war.

La encrucijada / The Crossroads
A chicken is being sacrificed
    at a crossroads, a simple mound of earth
a mud shrine for *Eshu,*
    Yoruba god of indeterminacy,
who blesses her choice of path.
    She begins her journey.

Su cuerpo es una bocacalle. La mestiza has gone from being the sacrificial goat to becoming the officiating priestess at the crossroads.

As a *mestiza* I have no country, my homeland cast me out; yet all countries are mine because I am every woman's sister or potential lover. (As a lesbian I have no race, my own people disclaim me; but I am all races because there is the queer of me in all races.) I am cultureless because, as a feminist, I challenge the collective cultural/religious male-derived beliefs of Indo-Hispanics and Anglos; yet I am cultured because I am participating in the creation of yet another culture, a new story to explain the world and our participation in it, a new value system with images and symbols that connect us to each other and to the planet. *Soy un amasamiento,* I am an act of kneading, of uniting and joining that not only has produced both a creature of darkness and a creature of light, but also a creature that questions the definitions of light and dark and gives them new meanings.

We are the people who leap in the dark, we are the people on the knees of the gods. In our flesh, (r)evolution works out the clash of cultures. It makes us crazy constantly, but if the center holds, we've made some kind of evolutionary step forward. *Nuestra alma el trabajo,* the opus, the great alchemical work; spiritual *mestizaje,* a "morphogenesis,"[i] an inevitable unfolding. We have become the quickening serpent movement.

Indigenous like corn, like corn, the *mestiza* is a product of crossbreeding, designed for preservation under a variety of conditions. Like an ear of corn—a female seed-bearing organ—the *mestiza* is tenacious, tightly wrapped in the husks of her culture. Like kernels she clings to the cob; with thick stalks and strong brace roots, she holds tight to the earth—she will survive the crossroads.

Lavando y remojando el maíz en agua de cal, despojando el pellejo. Moliendo, mixteando, amasando, haciendo tortillas de masa.[ii] She steeps the corn in lime, it swells, softens. With stone roller on *metate,* she grinds the corn, then grinds again. She kneads and molds the dough, pats the round balls into *tortillas.*

> We are the porous rock in the stone *metate*
> squatting on the ground.
> We are the rolling pin, *el maíz y agua,*
> *la masa harina. Somos el amasijo.*
> *Somos lo molido en el metate.*
> We are the *comal* sizzling hot,
> the hot *tortilla,* the hungry mouth.
> We are the coarse rock.
> We are the grinding motion,
> the mixed potion, *somos el molcajete.*
> We are the pestle, the *comino, ajo, pimienta,*
> We are the *chile colorado,*
> the green shoot that cracks the rock.
> We will abide.

El camino de la mestiza/The Mestiza Way

Caught between the sudden contraction, the breath sucked in and the endless space, the brown woman stands still, looks at the sky. She decides to go down, digging her way along the roots of trees. Sifting through the bones, she shakes them to see if there is any marrow in them. Then, touching the dirt to

---

i. To borrow chemist Ilya Prigogine's theory of "dissipative structures." Prigogine discovered that substances interact not in predictable ways as it was taught in science, but in different and fluctuating ways to produce new and more complex structures, a kind of birth he calls "morphogenesis," which created unpredictable innovations.[5]

ii. *Tortillas de masa harina:* corn tortillas are of two types, the smooth uniform ones made in a tortilla press and usually bought at a tortilla factory or supermarket, and *gorditas,* made by mixing *masa* with lard or shortening or butter (my mother sometimes puts in bits of bacon or *chicarrones*).

her forehead, to her tongue, she takes a few bones, leaves the rest in their burial place.

She goes through her backpack, keeps her journal and address book, throws away the muni-bart metromaps. The coins are heavy and they go next, then the greenbacks flutter through the air. She keeps her knife, can opener and eyebrow pencil. She put bones, pieces of bark, *hierbas*, eagle feather, snakeskin, tape recorder, the rattle and drum in her pack and she sets out to become the complete *tolteca*.

Her first step is to take inventory. *Despojando, desgranando, quitando paja.* Just what did she inherit from her ancestors? This weight on her back—which is the baggage from the Indian mother, which the baggage from the Spanish father, which the baggage from the Anglo?

Pero es difícil differentiating between *lo heredado, lo adquirido, lo impuesto.* She puts history through a sieve, winnows out the lies, looks at the forces that we as a race, as women, have been a part of. *Luego bota lo que no vale, los desmientos, los desencuentros, el embrutecimiento. Aguarda el juicio, hondo y enraizado, de la gente antigua.* This step is a conscious rupture with all oppressive traditions of all cultures and religions. She communicates that rupture, documents the struggle. She reinterprets history and, using new symbols, she shapes new myths. She adopts new perspectives toward the darkskinned, women and queers. She strengthens her tolerance (and intolerance) for ambiguity. She is willing to share, to make herself vulnerable to foreign ways of seeing and thinking. She surrenders all notions of safety, of the familiar. Deconstruct, construct. She becomes a *nahual*, able to transform herself into a tree, a coyote, into another person. She learns to transform the small "I" into the total Self. *Se hace moldeadora de su alma. Según la concepción que tiene de sí misma, así será.*

> *Que no se nos olvide los hombres*
> "*Tú no sirves pa' nada*—
> you're good for nothing.
> *Eres pura vieja.*"

"You're nothing but a woman" means you are defective. Its opposite is to be *un macho*. The modern meaning of the word "machismo," as well as the concept, is actually an Anglo invention. For men like my father, being "macho" meant being strong enough to protect and support my mother and us, yet being able to show love. Today's macho has doubts about his ability to feed and protect his family. His "machismo" is an adaptation to oppression and poverty and low self-esteem. It is the result of hierarchical male dominance. The Anglo, feeling inadequate and inferior and powerless, displaces or transfers these feelings to the Chicano by shaming him. In the Gringo world, the Chicano suffers from excessive humility and self-effacement, shame of self and self-deprecation. Around Latinos he suffers from a sense of language inadequacy and its accompanying discomfort; with Native Americans he suffers from a racial amnesia which ignores our common blood, and from guilt because the Spanish part of him took their land and oppressed them. He has an excessive compensatory hubris when around Mexicans from the other side. It overlays a deep sense of racial shame.

The loss of a sense of dignity and respect in the macho breeds a false machismo which leads him to put down women and even to brutalize them. Co-existing with his sexist behavior is a love for the mother which takes precedence over that of all others. Devoted son, macho pig. To wash down the shame of his acts, of his very being, and to handle the brute in the mirror, he takes to the bottle, the snort, the needle and the fist.

Though we "understand" the root causes of male hatred and fear, and the subsequent wounding of women, we do not excuse, we do not condone and we will no longer put up with it. From the men of our race, we demand the admission/ acknowledgement/disclosure/testimony that they wound us, violate us, are afraid of us and of our power. We need them to say they will begin to eliminate their hurtful put-down ways. But more than the words, we demand acts. We say to them: we will develop equal power with you and those who have shamed us.

It is imperative that *mestizas* support each other in changing the sexist elements in the Mexican-Indian culture. As long as woman is put down, the Indian and the Black in all of us is put down. The struggle of the *mestiza* is above all a feminist one. As long as *los hombres* think they have to *chingar mujeres* and each other to be men, as long as men are taught that they are superior and therefore culturally favored over *la mujer*, as long as to be a *vieja* is a thing of derision, there can be no real healing of our psyches. We're halfway there—we have such love of the Mother, the good mother. The first step is to unlearn the *puta/virgen* dichotomy and to see *Coatlapopeuh—Coatlicue* in the Mother, *Guadalupe*.

Tenderness, a sign of vulnerability, is so feared that it is showered on women with verbal abuse and blows. Men, even more than women, are fettered to gender roles. Women at least have had the guts to break out of bondage. Only gay men have had the courage to expose themselves to the woman inside them and to challenge the current masculinity. I've encountered a few scattered and isolated gentle straight men, the beginnings of a new breed, but they are confused, and entangled with sexist behaviors that they have not been able to eradicate. We need a new masculinity and the new man needs a movement.

Lumping the males who deviate from the general norm with man, the oppressor, is a gross injustice. *Asombra pensar que nos hemos quedado en ese pozo oscuro donde el mundo encierra a las lesbianas. Asombra pensar que hemos, como femenistas y lesbianas, cerrado nuestros corazónes a los hombres, a nuestros hermanos los jotos, desheredados y marginales como nosotros.* Being the supreme crossers of cultures, homosexuals have strong bonds with the queer white, Black, Asian, Native American, Latino, and with the queer in Italy, Australia and the rest of the planet. We come from all colors, all classes, all races, all time periods. Our role is to link people with each other—the Blacks with Jews with Indians with Asians with whites with extraterrestrials. It is to transfer ideas and information from one culture to another. Colored homosexuals have more knowledge of other cultures; have always been at the forefront (although sometimes in the closet) of all liberation struggles in this country; have suffered more injustices and have survived them despite all odds. Chicanos need to acknowledge the political and artistic contribution of their queer. People, listen to what your *jotería* is saying.

The *mestizo* and the queer exist at this time and point on the evolutionary continuum for a purpose. We are a blending that proves that all blood is intricately woven together, and that we are spawned out of similar souls.

> **Somos una genta**
> *Hay tantísimas fronteras*
> que dividen a la gente,
> pero por cada frontera
> existe también un puente.
>
> Gina Valdés[6]

Divided Loyalties. Many women and men of color do not want to have any dealings with white people. It takes too much time and energy to explain to the downwardly mobile, white middle-class women that it's okay for us to want to own "possessions," never having had any nice furniture on our dirt floors or "luxuries" like washing machines. Many feel that whites should help their own people rid themselves of race hatred and fear first. I, for one, choose to use some of my energy to serve as mediator. I think we need to allow whites to be our allies. Through our literature, art, *corridos* and folktales we must share our history with them so when they set up committees to help Big Mountain Navajos or the Chicano farmworkers or *los Nicaragüenses* they won't turn people away because of their racial fears and ignorances. They will come to see that they are not helping us but following our lead.

Individually, but also as a racial entity, we need to voice our needs. We need to say to white society: we need you to accept the fact that Chicanos are different, to acknowledge your rejection and negation of us. We need you to own the fact that you looked upon us as less than human, that you stole our lands, our personhood, our self-respect. We need you to make public restitution: to say that, to compensate for your own sense of defectiveness, you strive for power over us, you erase our history and our experience because it makes you feel guilty—you'd rather forget your brutish acts. To say you've split yourself from minority groups, that you disown us, that your dual consciousness splits off parts of yourself, transferring the "negative" parts onto us. (Where there is persecution of minorities, there is shadow projection. Where there is violence and war, there is repression of shadow.) To say that you are afraid of us, that to put distance between us, you wear the mask of contempt. Admit that Mexico is your double, that she exists in the shadow of this country, that we are irrevocably tied to her. Gringo, accept the doppelganger in your psyche. By taking back your collective shadow the intracultural split will heal. And finally, tell us what you need from us.

By Your True Faces We Will Know You

I am visible—see this Indian face—yet I am invisible. I both blind them with my beak nose and am their blind spot. But I exist, we exist. They'd like to think I have melted in the pot. But I haven't, we haven't.

The dominant white culture is killing us slowly with its ignorance. By taking away our self-determination, it has made us weak and empty. As a people we have resisted and we have taken expedient positions, but we have never been allowed to develop unencumbered—we have never been allowed to be fully ourselves. The whites in power want us people of color to barricade ourselves behind our separate tribal walls so they can pick us off one at a time with their hidden weapons; so they can whitewash and distort history. Ignorance splits people, creates prejudices. A misinformed people is a subjugated people.

Before the Chicano and the undocumented worker and the Mexican from the other side can come together, before the Chicano can have unity with Native Americans and other groups, we need to know the history of their struggle and they need to know ours. Our mothers, our sisters and brothers, the guys who hang out on street corners, the children in the playgrounds, each of us must know our Indian lineage, our afro-*mestisaje*, our history of resistance.

To the immigrant *mexicano* and the recent arrivals we must teach our history. The 80 million *mexicanos* and the Latinos from Central and South America must know of our struggles. Each one of us must know basic facts about Nicaragua, Chile and the rest of Latin America. The Latinoist movement (Chicanos, Puerto Ricans, Cubans and other Spanish-speaking people working together to combat racial discrimination in the market place) is good but it is not enough. Other than a common culture we will have nothing to hold us together. We need to meet on a broader communal ground.

The struggle is inner: Chicano, *indio*, American Indian, *mojado*, *mexicano*, immigrant Latino, Anglo in power, working-class Anglo, Black, Asian—our psyches resemble the bordertowns and are populated by the same people. The struggle has always been inner, and is played out in the outer terrains. Awareness of our situation must come before inner changes, which in turn come before changes in society. Nothing happens in the "real" world unless it first happens in the images in our heads.

> *El día de la Chicana*
> I will not be shamed again
> Nor will I shame myself.

I am possessed by a vision: that we Chicanas and Chicanos have taken back or uncovered our true faces, our dignity and self-respect. It's a validation vision.

Seeing the Chicana anew in light of her history, I seek an exoneration, a seeing through the fictions of white supremacy, a seeing of ourselves in our true guises and not as the false racial personality that has been given to us and that we have given to ourselves. I seek our woman's face, our true features, the positive and the negative seen clearly, free of the tainted biases of male dominance. I seek new images of identity, new beliefs about ourselves, our humanity and worth no longer in question.

Estamos viviendo en la noche de la Raza, un tiempo cuando el trabajo se hace a lo quieto, en el oscuro. El día cuando aceptamos tal y como somos y para en donde vamos y porque—ese día será el día de la Raza. Yo tengo el compromiso de expresar mi visión, mi sensibilidad, mi percepción de la revalidación de la gente mexicana, su mérito, estimación honra, aprecio y validez.

On December 2nd when my sun goes into my first house, I celebrate *el día de la Chicana y el Chicano.* On that day I clean my altars, light my *Coatlalopeuh* candle, burn sage and copal, take *el baño para espantar basura,* sweep my house. On that day I bare my soul, make myself vulnerable to friends and family by expressing my feelings. On that day I affirm who we are.

On that day I look inside our conflicts and our basic introverted racial temperament. I identify our needs, voice them. I acknowledge that the self and the race have been wounded. I recognize the need to take care of our personhood, of our racial self. On that day I gather the splintered and disowned parts of *la gente mexicana* and hold them in my arms. *Todas las partes de nosotros valen.*

On that day I say, "Yes, all you people wound us when you reject us. Rejection strips us of self-worth; our vulnerability exposes us to shame. It is our innate identity you find wanting. We are ashamed that we need your good opinion, that we need your acceptance. We can no longer camouflage our needs, can no longer let defenses and fences sprout around us. We can no longer withdraw. To rage and look upon you with contempt is to rage and be contemptuous of ourselves. We can no longer blame you, nor disown the white parts, the male parts, the pathological parts, the queer parts, the vulnerable parts. Here we are weaponless with open arms, with only our magic. Let's try it our way, the *mestiza*, way, the Chicana way, the woman way.

On that day, I search for our essential dignity as a people, a people with a sense of purpose—to belong and contribute to something greater than our *pueblo*. On that day I seek to recover and reshape my spiritual identity. *¡Anímate! Raza, a celebrar el día de la Chicana.*

> ### El retorno
> All movements are accomplished in six stages,
> and the seventh brings return.
> —*I Ching*[7]
>
> *Tanto tiempo sin verte casa mía,*
> *mi cuna, mi hondo nido de la huerta.*
> —*"Soledad"*[8]

I stand at the river, watch the curving, twisting serpent, a serpent nailed to the fence where the mouth of the Rio Grande empties into the Gulf.

I have come back. *Tanto dolor me costó el alejamiento.* I shade my eyes and look up. The bone beak of a hawk slowly circling over me, checking me out as potential carrion. In its wake a little bird flickering its wings, swimming sporadically like a fish. In the distance the expressway and the slough of traffic like an irritated sow. The sudden pull in my gut, *la tierra, los aguaceros.* My land, *el viento soplando la arena, el lagartijo debajo de un nopalito. Me acuerdo como era antes. Una región desértica de vasta llanuras, costeras de baja altura, de escasa lluvia, de chaparrales formados por mesquites y huizaches.* If I look real hard I can almost see the Spanish fathers who were called "the cavalry of Christ" enter this valley riding their burros, see the clash of cultures commence.

Tierra natal. This is home, the small towns in the Valley, *los pueblitos* with chicken pens and goats picketed to mesquite shrubs. *En las colonias* on the other side of the tracks, junk cars line the front yards of hot pink and lavender-trimmed houses— Chicano architecture we call it, self-consciously. I have missed the TV shows where hosts speak in half and half, and where awards are given in the category of Tex-Mex music. I have missed the Mexican cemeteries blooming with artificial flowers, the fields of aloe vera and red pepper, rows of sugar cane, of corn hanging on the stalks, the cloud of *polvareda* in the dirt roads behind a speeding truck, *el sabor de tamales de rez y venado.* I have missed *la yequa colorada* gnawing the wooden gate of her stall, the smell of horse flesh from Carito's corrals. *He hecho menos las noches calientes sin aire, noches de linternas y lechuzas* making holes in the night.

I still feel the old despair when I look at the unpainted, dilapidated, scrap lumber houses consisting mostly of corrugated aluminum. Some of the poorest people in the U.S. live in the Lower Rio Grande Valley, an arid and semi-arid land of irrigated farming, intense sunlight and heat, citrus groves next to chaparral and cactus. I walk through the elementary school I attended so long ago, that remained segregated until recently. I remember how the white teachers used to punish us for being Mexican.

How I love this tragic valley of South Texas, as Ricardo Sánchez calls it; this borderland between the Nueces and the Rio Grande. This land has survived possession and ill-use by five countries: Spain, Mexico, the Republic of Texas, the Confederacy, and the U.S. again. It has survived Anglo-Mexican blood feuds, lynchings, burning, rapes, pillage.

Today I see the Valley still struggling to survive. Whether it does or not, it will never be as I remember it. The borderlands depression that was set off by the 1982 peso devaluation in Mexico resulted in the closure of hundreds of Valley businesses. Many people lost their homes, cars, land. Prior to 1982, U.S. store owners thrived on retail sales to Mexicans who came across the borders for groceries and clothes and appliances. While goods on the U.S. side have become 10, 100, 1000 times more expensive for Mexican buyers, goods on the Mexican side have become 10, 100, 1000 times cheaper for Americans. Because the Valley is heavily dependent on agriculture and Mexican retail trade, it has the highest unemployment rates along the entire border region; it is the Valley that has been hardest hit.[iii]

"It's been a bad year for corn," my brother, Nune, says. As he talks, I remember my father scanning the sky for a rain that would end the drought, looking up into the sky, day after day, while the corn withered on its stalk. My father has been dead for 29 years, having worked himself to death. The life span of a Mexican farm laborer is 56—he lived to be 38. It shocks me that I am older than he. I, too, search the sky for rain. Like the ancients, I worship the rain god and the maize goddess, but unlike my father I have recovered their names. Now for rain (irrigation) one offers not a sacrifice of blood, but of money.

"Farming is in a bad way," my brother says. "Two to three thousand small and big farmers went bankrupt in this country last year. Six years ago the price of corn was $8.00 per hundred pounds," he goes on. "This year it is $3.90 per hundred pounds." And, I think to myself, after taking inflation into account, not planting anything puts you ahead.

---

iii. Out of the twenty-two border counties in the four border states, Hidalgo County (named for Father Hidalgo, who was shot in 1810 after instigating Mexico's revolt against Spanish rule under the banner of *la Virgen de Guadalupe*) is the most poverty-stricken county in the nation as well as the largest home base (along with Imperial in California) for migrant farmworkers. It was here that I was born and raised; I am amazed that both it and I have survived.

I walk out to the back yard, stare at *los rosales de mamá*. She wants me to help her prune the rose bushes, dig out the carpet grass that is choking them. *Mamagrande Ramona también tenía rosales*. Here every Mexican grows flowers. If they don't have a piece of dirt, they use car tires, jars, cans, shoe boxes. Roses are the Mexican's favorite flower. I think, how symbolic—thorns and all.

Yes, the Chicano and Chicana have always taken care of growing things and the land. Again I see the four of us kids getting off the school bus, changing into our work clothes, walking into the field with Papí and Mamí, all six of us bending to the ground. Below our feet, under the earth lie the watermelon seeds. We cover them with paper plates, putting *terremotes* on top of the plates to keep them from being blown away by the wind. The paper plates keep the freeze away. Next day or the next, we remove the plates, bare the tiny green shoots to the elements. They survive and grow, give fruit hundreds of times the size of the seed. We water them and hoe them. We harvest them. The vines dry, rot, are plowed under. Growth, death, decay, birth. The soil prepared again and again, impregnated, worked on. A constant changing of forms, *renacimientos de la tierra madre*.

> This land was Mexican once
> was Indian always
> and is.
> And will be again.

NOTES

1. This is my own "take-off" on José Vasconcelos's idea. *La Raza Cósmica: Missión de la Raza Ibero-Americana* (México: Aguilar S. A. de Ediciones, 1961).

2. Ibid.

3. Arthur Koestler termed this "bisociation." Albert Rothenberg, *The Creative Process in Art, Science, and Other Fields* (Chicago: University of Chicago Press, 1979), 12.

4. In part, I derive my definitions of "convergent" and "divergent" thinking from Rothenberg, *Creative Process*, 12–13.

5. Harold Gilliam, "Searching for a New World View," *This World*, January 1981, 23.

6. Gina Valdés, *Puentes y Fronteras: Coplas Chicanas* (Los Angeles: Castle Lithograph, 1982), 2.

7. Richard Wilhelm, *The I Ching or Book of Changes*, trans. Cary F. Baynes (Princeton: Princeton University Press, 1950), 98.

8. "Soledad" is sung by the group Haciendo Punta en Otro Son.

35

Chandra Talpade Mohanty

" 'Under Western Eyes' Revisited: Feminist Solidarity through Anticapitalist Struggles" (2003)

Chandra Talpade Mohanty is professor of women's studies at Hamilton College and Core Faculty at the Union Institute Graduate School. Her work has shaped the discourse of transnational feminism, cultural studies, and antiracist pedagogy. She has coedited Third World Women and the Politics of Feminism *(1991) and* Feminist Genealogies, Colonial Legacies, Democratic Futures *(1997). This chapter is from her most recent book,* Feminism Without Borders: Decolonizing Theory, Practicing Solidarity *(2003).*

I WRITE THIS chapter at the urging of a number of friends[1] and with some trepidation, revisiting the themes and arguments of an essay written some sixteen years ago. This is a difficult chapter to write,[2] and I undertake it hesitantly and with humility—yet feeling that I must do so to take fuller responsibility for my ideas, and perhaps to explain whatever influence they have had on debates in feminist theory.

"Under Western Eyes" was not only my very first "feminist studies" publication, it remains the one that marks my presence in the international feminist community. I had barely completed my Ph.D. when I wrote this essay; I am now a professor of women's studies. The "under" of Western eyes is now much more an "inside" in terms of my own location in the U.S. academy.[3] The site from which I wrote the essay consisted of a very vibrant, transnational women's movement, while the site I write from today is quite different. With the increasing privatization and corporatization of public life, it has become much harder to discern such a women's movement from the United States (although women's movements are thriving around the world), and my site of access and struggle has increasingly come to be the U.S. academy. In the United States, women's movements have become increasingly conservative, and much radical, antiracist feminist activism occurs outside the rubric of such movements. Thus, much of what I say here is influenced by the primary site I occupy as an educator and scholar. It is time to revisit "Under Western Eyes," to clarify ideas that remained implicit and unstated in 1986 and to further develop and historicize the theoretical framework I outlined then. I also want to assess how this essay has been read and misread and to respond to the critiques and celebrations. And it is time for me to move explicitly from critique to reconstruction, to identify the urgent issues facing feminists at the beginning of the twenty-first century, to ask the question: How would "Under Western Eyes"—the Third World inside and outside the West—be explored and analyzed almost two decades later? what do I consider to be the urgent theoretical and methodological questions facing a comparative feminist politics at this moment in history? . . .

Revisiting "Under Western Eyes"

. . . .

Under and (Inside) Western Eyes: At the Turn of the Century

There have been a number of shifts in the political and economic landscapes of nations and communities of people in the last two decades. The intellectual maps of disciplines and areas of study in the U.S. academy have shifted as well during this time. The advent and institutional visibility of postcolonial studies for instance is a relatively recent phenomenon—as is the simultaneous rollback of the gains made by race and ethnic studies departments in the 1970s and 1980s. Women's studies is now a well-established field of study with over eight hundred degree-granting programs and departments in the U.S. academy.[4] Feminist theory and feminist movements across national borders have matured substantially since the early 1980s, and there is now a greater visibility of transnational women's struggles and movements, brought on in part by the United Nations world conferences on women held over the last two decades.

Economically and politically, the declining power of self-governance among certain poorer nations is matched by the rising significance of transnational institutions such as the World Trade Organization and governing bodies such as the European Union, not to mention the for-profit corporations. Of the world's largest economies, fifty-one happen to be corporations, not countries, and Amnesty International now reports on corporations as well as nations (Eisenstein 1998b, 1). Also, the hegemony of neoliberalism, alongside the naturalization of capitalist values, influences the ability to make choices on one's own behalf in the daily lives of economically marginalized as well as economically privileged communities around the globe.

The rise of religious fundamentalisms with their deeply masculinist and often racist rhetoric poses a huge challenge for feminist struggles around the world. Finally, the profoundly unequal "information highway" as well as the increasing militarization (and masculinization) of the globe, accompanied by the growth of the prison industrial complex in the United States, poses profound contradictions in the lives of communities of women and men in most parts of the world. I believe these political shifts to the right, accompanied by global capitalist hegemony, privatization, and increased religious, ethnic, and racial hatreds, pose very concrete challenges for feminists. In this context, I ask what would it mean to be attentive to the micropolitics of everyday life as well as to the larger processes that recolonize the culture and identities of people across the globe. How we think of the local in/of the global and vice versa without falling into colonizing or cultural relativist platitudes about difference is crucial in this intellectual and political landscape. And for me, this kind of thinking is tied to a revised race-and-gender-conscious historical materialism.

The politics of feminist cross-cultural scholarship from the vantage point of Third World/South feminist struggles remains a compelling site of analysis for me.[5] Eurocentric analytic paradigms continue to flourish, and I remain committed to reengaging in the struggles to criticize openly the effects of discursive colonization on the lives and struggles of marginalized women. My central commitment is to build connections between feminist scholarship and political organizing. My own present-day analytic framework remains very similar to my earliest critique of Eurocentrism. However, I now see the politics and economics of capitalism as a far more urgent locus of struggle. I continue to hold to an analytic framework that is attentive to the micropolitics of everyday life as well as to the macropolitics of global economic and political processes. The link between political economy and culture remains crucial to any form of feminist theorizing—as it does for my work. It isn't the framework that has changed. It is just that global economic and political processes have become more brutal, exacerbating economic, racial, and gender inequalities, and thus they need to be demystified, reexamined, and theorized.

While my earlier focus was on the distinctions between "Western" and "Third World" feminist practices, and while I downplayed the commonalities between these two positions, my focus now . . . is on what I have chosen to call an anticapitalist transnational feminist practice—and on the possibilities, indeed on the necessities, of cross-national feminist solidarity and organizing against capitalism. While "Under Western Eyes" was located in the context of the critique of Western humanism and Eurocentrism and of white, Western feminism, a similar essay written now would need to be located in the context of the critique of global capitalism (on antiglobalization), the naturalization of the values of capital, and the unacknowledged power of cultural relativism in cross-cultural feminist scholarship and pedagogies.

"Under Western Eyes" sought to make the operations of discursive power visible, to draw attention to what was left out of feminist theorizing, namely, the material complexity, reality, and agency of Third World women's bodies and lives. This is in fact exactly the analytic strategy I now use to draw attention to what is unseen, undertheorized, and left out in the production of knowledge about globalization. While globalization has always been a part of capitalism, and capitalism is not a new phenomenon, at this time I believe the theory, critique, and activism around antiglobalization has to be a key focus for feminists. This does not mean that the patriarchal and racist relations and structures that accompany capitalism are any less problematic at this time, or that antiglobalization is a singular phenomenon. Along with many other scholars and activists, I believe capital as it functions now depends on and exacerbates racist, patriarchal, and heterosexist relations of rule.

Feminist Methodologies: New Directions

What kinds of feminist methodology and analytic strategy are useful in making power (and women's lives) visible in overtly nongendered, nonracialized discourses? The strategy discussed here is an example of how capitalism and its various relations of rule can be analyzed through a transnational, anticapitalist feminist critique, one that draws on historical materialism and centralizes racialized gender. This analysis begins from and is anchored in the place of the most marginalized communities of women—poor women of all colors in affluent and neocolonial nations; women of the Third World/South or the Two-Thirds World.[6] I believe that this experiential and analytic anchor in the lives of marginalized communities of women provides the most inclusive paradigm for thinking about social justice. This particularized viewing allows for a more concrete and expansive vision of universal justice.

This is the very opposite of "special interest" thinking. If we pay attention to and think from the space of some of the most disenfranchised communities of women in the world, we are most likely to envision a just and democratic society capable of treating all its citizens fairly. Conversely, if we begin our analysis from, and limit it to, the space of privileged communities, our visions of justice are more likely to be exclusionary because privilege nurtures blindness to those without the same privileges. Beginning from the lives and interests of marginalized communities of women, I am able to access and make the workings of power visible—to read up the ladder of privilege. It is more necessary to look upward—colonized peoples must know themselves and the colonizer. This particular marginalized location makes the politics of knowledge and the power investments that go along with it visible so that we can then engage in work to transform the use and abuse of power. The analysis draws on the notion of epistemic privilege as it is developed by feminist standpoint theorists (with their roots in the historical materialism of Marx and Lukacs) as well as postpositivist realists, who provide an analysis of experience, identity, and the epistemic effects of social location.[7] My view is thus a materialist and "realist" one and is antithetical to that of postmodernist relativism. I believe there are causal links between marginalized social locations and experiences and the ability of human agents to explain and analyze features of capitalist society. Methodologically, this analytic perspective is grounded in historical materialism. My claim is not that all marginalized locations yield crucial knowledge about power and inequity, but that within a tightly integrated capitalist system, the particular standpoint of poor indigenous and Third World/South women provides the most inclusive viewing of systemic power. In numerous cases of environmental racism, for instance, where the neighborhoods of poor communities of color are targeted as new sites for prisons and toxic dumps, it is no coincidence that poor black, Native American, and Latina women provide the leadership in the fight against corporate pollution. Three out of five Afro-Americans and Latinos live near toxic waste sites, and three of the five largest hazardous waste landfills are in communities with a population that is 80 percent people of color (Pardo 2001, 504–11). Thus, it is precisely their critical reflections on their everyday lives as poor women of color that allow the kind of analysis of the power structure that has led to the many victories in environmental racism struggles.[8] Herein lies a lesson for feminist analysis.

Feminist scientist Vandana Shiva, one of the most visible leaders of the antiglobalization movement, provides a similar and illuminating critique of the patents and intellectual property rights agreements sanctioned by the World Trade Organization (WTO) since 1995.[9] Along with others in the environmental and indigenous rights movements, she argues that the WTO sanctions biopiracy and engages in intellectual piracy by privileging the claims of corporate commercial interests, based on Western systems of knowledge in agriculture and medicine, to products and innovations derived from indigenous knowledge traditions. Thus, through the definition of Western scientific epistemologies as the only legitimate scientific system, the WTO is able to underwrite corporate patents to indigenous knowledge (as to the Neem tree in India) as their own intellectual property, protected through intellectual property rights agreements. As a result, the patenting of drugs derived from indigenous medicinal systems has now reached massive proportions. I quote Shiva:

> [T]hrough patenting, indigenous knowledge is being pirated in the name of protecting knowledge and preventing piracy. The knowledge of our ancestors, of our peasants about seeds is being claimed as an invention of U.S. corporations and U.S. scientists and patented by them. The only reason something like that can work is because underlying it all is a racist framework that says the knowledge of the Third World and the knowledge of people of color is not knowledge. When that knowledge is taken by white men who have capital, suddenly creativity begins. . . . Patents are a replay of colonialism, which is now called globalization and free trade. (2000, 32)

The contrast between Western scientific systems and indigenous epistemologies and systems of medicine is not the only issue here. It is the colonialist and corporate power to define Western science, and the reliance on capitalist values of private property and profit, as the only normative system that results in the exercise of immense power. Thus indigenous knowledges, which are often communally generated and shared among tribal and peasant women for domestic, local, and public use, are subject to the ideologies of a corporate Western scientific paradigm where intellectual property rights can only be understood in possessive or privatized form. All innovations that happen to be collective, to have occurred over time in forests and farms, are appropriated or excluded. The idea of an intellectual commons where knowledge is collectively gathered and passed on for the benefit of all, not owned privately, is the very opposite of the notion of private property and ownership that is the basis for the WTO property rights agreements. Thus this idea of an intellectual commons among tribal and peasant women actually excludes them from ownership and facilitates corporate biopiracy.

Shiva's analysis of intellectual property rights, biopiracy, and globalization is made possible by its very location in the experiences and epistemologies of peasant and tribal women in India. Beginning from the practices and knowledges of indigenous women, she "reads up" the power structure, all the way to the policies and practices sanctioned by the WTO. This is a very clear example then of a transnational, anticapitalist feminist politics.

However, Shiva says less about gender than she could. She is after all talking in particular about women's work and knowledges anchored in the epistemological experiences of one of the most marginalized communities of women in the world—poor, tribal, and peasant women in India. This is a community of women made invisible and written out of national and international economic calculations. An analysis that pays attention to the everyday experiences of tribal women and the micropolitics of their ultimately anticapitalist struggles illuminates the macropolitics of global restructuring. It suggests the thorough embeddedness of the local and particular with the global and universal, and it suggests the need to conceptualize questions of justice and equity in transborder terms. In other words, this mode of reading envisions a feminism without borders, in that it foregrounds the need for an analysis and vision of solidarity across the enforced privatized intellectual property borders of the WTO.

These particular examples offer the most inclusive paradigm for understanding the motivations and effects of globalization as it is crafted by the WTO. Of course, if we were to attempt the same analysis from the epistemological space of Western, corporate interests, it would be impossible to generate an analysis that values indigenous knowledge anchored in communal relationships rather than profit-based hierarchies. Thus, poor tribal and peasant women, their knowledges and interests, would be invisible in this analytic frame because the very idea of an intellectual commons falls outside the purview of privatized property and profit that is a basis for corporate interests. The obvious issue for a transnational feminism pertains to the visions of profit and justice embodied in these opposing analytic perspectives. The focus on profit versus justice illustrates my earlier point about social location and analytically inclusive methodologies. It is the social location of the tribal women as explicated by Shiva that allows this broad and inclusive focus on justice. Similarly, it is the social location and narrow self-interest of corporations that privatizes intellectual property rights in the name of profit for elites.

Shiva essentially offers a critique of the global privatization of indigenous knowledges. This is a story about the rise of transnational institutions such as the WTO, the World Bank, and the International Monetary Fund, of banking and financial institutions and cross-national governing bodies like the MAI (Multinational Agreement on Investments). The effects of these governing bodies on poor people around the world have been devastating. In fundamental ways, it is girls and women around the world, especially in the Third World/South, that bear the brunt of globalization. Poor women and girls are the hardest hit by the degradation of environmental conditions, wars, famines, privatization of services and deregulation of governments, the dismantling of welfare states, the restructuring of paid and unpaid work, increasing surveillance and incarceration in prisons, and so on. And this is why a feminism without and beyond borders is necessary to address the injustices of global capitalism.

Women and girls are still 70 percent of the world's poor and the majority of the world's refugees. Girls and women comprise almost 80 percent of displaced persons of the Third World/South in Africa, Asia and Latin America. Women own less than one-hundredth of the world's property, while they are the hardest hit by the effects of war, domestic violence, and religious persecution. Feminist political theorist Zillah Eisenstein says that women do two-thirds of the world's work and earn less than one-tenth of its income. Global capital in racialized and sexualized guise destroys the public spaces of democracy, and quietly sucks power out of the once social/public spaces of nation-states. Corporate capitalism has redefined citizens as consumers—and global markets replace the commitments to economic, sexual, and racial equality (Eisenstein 1998b, esp. ch. 5).

It is especially on the bodies and lives of women and girls from the Third World/South—the Two-Thirds World—that global capitalism writes its script, and it is by paying attention to and theorizing the experiences of these communities of women and girls that we demystify capitalism as a system of debilitating sexism and racism and envision anticapitalist resistance. Thus any analysis of the effects of globalization needs to centralize the experiences and struggles of these particular communities of women and girls.

Drawing on Arif Dirlik's notion of "place consciousness as the radical other of global capitalism" (Dirlik 1999), Grace Lee Boggs makes an important argument for place-based civic activism that illustrates how centralizing the struggles of marginalized communities connects to larger antiglobalization struggles. Boggs suggests that "[p]lace consciousness . . . encourages us to come together around common, local experiences and organize around our hopes for the future of our communities and cities. While global capitalism doesn't give a damn about the people or the natural environment of any particular place because it can always move on to other people and other places, place-based civic activism is concerned about the health and safety of people and places" (Boggs 2000, 19). Since women are central to the life of neighborhood and communities they assume leadership positions in these struggles. This is evident in the example of women of color in struggles against environmental racism in the United States, as well as in Shiva's example of tribal women in the struggle against deforestation and for an intellectual commons. It is then the lives, experiences, and struggles of girls and women of the Two-Thirds World that demystify capitalism in its racial and sexual dimensions—and that provide productive and necessary avenues of theorizing and enacting anticapitalist resistance.

I do not wish to leave this discussion of capitalism as a generalized site without contextualizing its meaning in and through the lives it structures. Disproportionately, these are girls' and women's lives, although I am committed to the lives of all exploited peoples. However, the specificity of girls' and women's lives encompasses the others through their particularized and contextualized experiences. If these particular gendered, classed, and racialized realities of globalization are unseen and undertheorized, even the most radical critiques of globalization effectively render Third World/South women and girls as absent. Perhaps it is no longer simply an issue of Western eyes, but rather how the West is inside and continually reconfigures globally, racially, and in terms of gender. Without this recognition, a necessary link between feminist scholarship/analytic frames and organizing/activist projects is impossible. Faulty and inadequate analytic frames engender ineffective political action and strategizing for social transformation.

What does the above analysis suggest? That we—feminist scholars and teachers—must respond to the phenomenon of globalization as an urgent site for the recolonization of peoples, especially in the Two-Thirds World. Globalization colonizes women's as well as men's lives around the world, and we need an anti-imperialist, anticapitalist, and contextualized feminist project to expose and make visible the various, overlapping forms of subjugation of women's lives. Activists and scholars must also identify and reenvision forms of collective resistance that women, especially, in their different communities enact in their everyday lives. It is their particular exploitation at this time, their potential epistemic privilege, as well as their particular forms of solidarity that can be the basis for reimagining a liberatory politics for the start of this century.

Antiglobalization Struggles

Although the context for writing "Under Western Eyes" in the mid-1980s was a visible and activist women's movement, this radical movement no longer exists as such. Instead, I draw inspiration from a more distant, but significant, antiglobalization movement in the United States and around the world. Activists in these movements are often women, although the movement is not gender-focused. So I wish to redefine the project of decolonization, not reject it. It appears more complex to me today, given the newer developments of global capitalism. Given the complex interweaving of cultural forms, people of and from the Third World live not only under Western eyes but also within them. This shift in my focus from "under Western eyes" to "under and inside" the hegemonic spaces of the One-Third World necessitates recrafting the project of decolonization.

My focus is thus no longer just the colonizing effects of Western feminist scholarship. This does not mean the problems I identified in the earlier essay do not occur now. But the phenomenon I addressed then has been more than adequately engaged by other feminist scholars. While feminists have been involved in the antiglobalization movement from the start, however, this has not been a major organizing locus for women's movements nationally in the West/North. It has, however, always been a locus of struggle for women of the Third World/ South because of their location. Again, this contextual specificity should constitute the larger vision. Women of the Two-Thirds World have always organized against the devastations of globalized capital, just as they have always historically organized anticolonial and antiracist movements. In this sense they have always spoken for humanity as a whole.

I have tried to chart feminist sites for engaging globalization, rather than providing a comprehensive review of feminist work in this area. I hope this exploration makes my own political choices and decisions transparent and that it provides readers with a productive and provocative space to think and act creatively for feminist struggle. So today my query is slightly different although much the same as in 1986. I wish to better see the processes of corporate globalization and how and why they recolonize women's bodies and labor. We need to know the real and concrete effects of global restructuring on raced, classed, national, sexual bodies of women in the academy, in workplaces, streets, households, cyberspaces, neighborhoods, prisons, and social movements.

What does it mean to make antiglobalization a key factor for feminist theorizing and struggle? To illustrate my thinking about antiglobalization, let me focus on two specific sites where knowledge about globalization is produced. The first site is a pedagogical one and involves an analysis of the various strategies being used to internationalize (or globalize)[10] the women's studies curriculum in U.S. colleges and universities. I argue that this move to internationalize women's studies curricula and the attendant pedagogies that flow from this is one of the main ways we can track a discourse of global feminism in the United States. Other ways of tracking global feminist discourses include analyzing the documents and discussions flowing out of the Beijing United Nations conference on women, and of course popular television and print media discourses on women around the world. The second site of antiglobalization scholarship I focus on is the emerging, notably ungendered and deracialized discourse on activism against globalization.

Antiglobalization Pedagogies

Let me turn to the struggles over the dissemination of a feminist cross-cultural knowledge base through pedagogical strategies "internationalizing" the women's studies curriculum. The problem of "the (gendered) color line" remains, but is more easily seen today as developments of transnational and global capital. While I choose to focus on women's studies curricula, my arguments hold for curricula in any discipline or academic field that seeks to internationalize or globalize its curriculum. I argue that the challenge for "internationalizing" women's studies is no different from the one involved in "racializing" women's studies in the 1980s, for very similar politics of knowledge come into play here.[11]

So the question I want to foreground is the politics of knowledge in bridging the "local" and the "global" in women's studies. How we teach the "new" scholarship in women's studies is at least as important as the scholarship itself in the struggles over knowledge and citizenship in the U.S. academy. After all, the way we construct curricula and the pedagogies we use to put such curricula into practice tell a story—or tell many stories. It is the way we position historical narratives of experience in relation to each other, the way we theorize relationality as both historical and simultaneously singular and collective that determines how and what we learn when we cross cultural and experiential borders.

Drawing on my own work with U.S. feminist academic communities,[12] I describe three pedagogical models used in "internationalizing" the women's studies curriculum and analyze the politics of knowledge at work. Each of these perspectives is grounded in particular conceptions of the local and the global, of women's agency, and of national identity, and each curricular model presents different stories and ways of crossing borders and building bridges. I suggest that a "comparative feminist studies" or "feminist solidarity" model is the most useful and productive pedagogical strategy for feminist cross-cultural work. It is this particular model that provides a way to theorize a complex relational understanding of experience, location, and history such that feminist cross-cultural work moves through the specific context to construct a real notion of universal and of democratization rather than colonization. It is through this model that we can put into practice the idea of "common differences" as the basis for deeper solidarity across differences and unequal power relations.

FEMINIST-AS-TOURIST MODEL. This curricular perspective could also be called the "feminist as international consumer" or, in less charitable terms, the "white women's burden or colonial discourse" model.[13] It involves a pedagogical strategy in which brief forays are made into non-Euro-American cultures, and particular sexist cultural practices addressed from an otherwise Eurocentric women's studies gaze. In other words, the "add women as global victims or powerful women and stir" perspective. This is a perspective in which the primary Euro-American narrative of the syllabus remains untouched, and examples from non-Western or Third World/South cultures are used to supplement and "add" to this narrative.

The story here is quite old. The effects of this strategy are that students and teachers are left with a clear sense of the difference and distance between the local (defined as self, nation, and Western) and the global (defined as other, non-Western, and transnational). Thus the local is always grounded in nationalist assumptions—the United States or Western European nation-state provides a normative context. This strategy leaves power relations and hierarchies untouched since ideas about center and margin are reproduced along Eurocentric lines.

For example, in an introductory feminist studies course, one could include the obligatory day or week on dowry deaths in India, women workers in Nike factories in Indonesia, or precolonial matriarchies in West Africa, while leaving the fundamental identity of the Euro-American feminist on her way to liberation untouched. Thus Indonesian workers in Nike factories or dowry deaths in India stand in for the totality of women in these cultures. These women are not seen in their everyday lives (as Euro-American women are)—just in these stereotypical terms. Difference in the case of non-Euro-American women is thus congealed, not seen contextually with all of its contradictions. This pedagogical strategy for crossing cultural and geographical borders is based on a modernist paradigm, and the bridge between the local and the global becomes in fact a predominantly self-interested chasm. This perspective confirms the sense of the "evolved U.S./Euro feminist." While there is now more consciousness about not using an "add and stir" method in teaching about race and U.S. women of color, this does not appear to be the case in "internationalizing" women's studies. Experience in this context is assumed to be static and frozen into U.S.- or Euro-centered categories. Since in this paradigm feminism is always/already constructed as Euro-American in origin and development, women's lives and struggles outside this geographical context only serve to confirm or contradict this originary feminist (master) narrative. This model is the pedagogical counterpart of the orientalizing and colonizing Western feminist scholarship of the past decades. In fact it may remain the predominant model at this time. Thus implicit in this pedagogical strategy is the crafting of the "Third World difference," the creation of monolithic images of Third World/South women. This contrasts with images of Euro-American women who are vital, changing, complex, and central subjects within such a curricular perspective.

FEMINIST-AS-EXPLORER MODEL. This particular pedagogical perspective originates in area studies, where the "foreign" woman is the object and subject of knowledge and the larger intellectual project is entirely about countries other than the United States. Thus, here the local and the global are both defined as non-Euro-American. The focus on the international implies that it exists outside the U.S. nation-state. Women's, gender, and feminist issues are based on spatial/geographical and temporal/historical categories located elsewhere. Distance from "home" is fundamental to the definition of international in this framework. This strategy can result in students and teachers being left with a notion of difference and separateness, a sort of "us and them" attitude, but unlike the tourist model, the explorer perspective can provide a deeper, more contextual understanding of feminist issues in discretely defined geographical and cultural spaces. However, unless these discrete spaces are taught in relation to one another, the story told is usually a cultural relativist one, meaning that differences between cultures are discrete and relative with no real connection or common basis for evaluation. The local and the global are here collapsed into the international that by definition excludes the United States. If the dominant discourse is the discourse of cultural relativism, questions of power, agency, justice, and common criteria for critique and evaluation are silenced.[14]

In women's studies curricula this pedagogical strategy is often seen as the most culturally sensitive way to "internationalize" the curriculum. For instance, entire courses on "Women in Latin America" or "Third World Women's Literature" or "Postcolonial Feminism" are added on to the predominantly U.S.-based curriculum as a way to "globalize" the feminist knowledge base. These courses can be quite sophisticated and complex studies, but they are viewed as entirely separate from the intellectual project of U.S. race and ethnic studies.[15] The United States is not seen as part of "area studies," as white is not a color when one speaks of people of color. This is probably related to the particular history of institutionalization of area studies in the U.S. academy and its ties to U.S. imperialism. Thus areas to be studied/conquered are "out there," never within the United States. The fact that area studies in U.S. academic settings were federally funded and conceived as having a political project in the service of U.S. geopolitical interests suggests the need to examine the contemporary interests of these fields, especially as they relate to the logic of global capitalism. In addition, as Ella Shohat argues, it is time to "reimagine the study of regions and cultures in a way that transcends the conceptual borders inherent in the global cartography of the cold war" (2001, 1271). The field of American studies is an interesting location to examine here, especially since its more recent focus on U.S. imperialism. However, American studies rarely falls under the purview of "area studies."

The problem with the feminist-as-explorer strategy is that globalization is an economic, political, and ideological phenomenon that actively brings the world and its various communities under connected and interdependent discursive and material regimes. The lives of women are connected and interdependent, albeit not the same, no matter which geographical area we happen to live in.

Separating area studies from race and ethnic studies thus leads to understanding or teaching about the global as a way of not addressing internal racism, capitalist hegemony, colonialism, and heterosexualization as central to processes of global domination, exploitation, and resistance. Global or international is thus understood apart from racism—as if racism were not central to processes of globalization and relations of rule at this time. An example of this pedagogical strategy in the context of the larger curriculum is the usual separation of "world cultures" courses from race and ethnic studies courses. Thus identifying the kinds of representations of (non-Euro-American) women mobilized by this pedagogical strategy, and the relation of these representations to implicit images of First World/North women are important foci for analysis. What kind of power is being exercised in this strategy? What kinds of ideas of agency and struggle are being consolidated? What are the potential effects of a kind of cultural relativism on our understandings of the differences and commonalities among communities of women around the world? Thus the feminist-as-explorer model has its own problems, and I believe this is an inadequate way of building a feminist cross-cultural knowledge base because in the context of an interwoven world with clear directionalities of power and domination, cultural relativism serves as an apology for the exercise of power.

THE FEMINIST SOLIDARITY OR COMPARATIVE FEMINIST STUDIES MODEL. This curricular strategy is based on the premise that the local and the global are not defined in terms of physical geography or territory but exist simultaneously and constitute each other. It is then the links, the relationships, between the local and the global that are foregrounded, and these links are conceptual, material, temporal, contextual, and so on. This framework assumes a comparative focus and analysis of the directionality of power no matter what the subject of the women's studies course is—and it assumes both distance and proximity (specific/universal) as its analytic strategy.

Differences and commonalities thus exist in relation and tension with each other in all contexts. What is emphasized are relations of mutuality, co-responsibility, and common interests, anchoring the idea of feminist solidarity. For example, within this model, one would not teach a U.S. women of color course with additions on Third World/South or white women, but a comparative course that shows the interconnectedness of the histories, experiences, and struggles of U.S. women of color, white women, and women from the Third World/South. By doing this kind of comparative teaching that is attentive to power, each historical experience illuminates the experiences of the others. Thus, the focus is not just on the intersections of race, class, gender, nation, and sexuality in different communities of women but on mutuality and coimplication, which suggests attentiveness to the interweaving of the histories of these communities. In addition the focus is simultaneously on individual and collective experiences of oppression and exploitation and of struggle and resistance.

Students potentially move away from the "add and stir" and the relativist "separate but equal" (or different) perspective to the coimplication/solidarity one. This solidarity perspective requires understanding the historical and experiential specificities and differences of women's lives as well as the historical and experiential connections between women from different national, racial, and cultural communities. Thus it suggests organizing syllabi around social and economic processes and histories of various communities of women in particular substantive areas like sex work, militarization, environmental justice, the prison/industrial complex, and human rights, and looking for points of contact and connection as well as disjunctures. It is important to always foreground not just the connections of domination but those of struggle and resistance as well.

In the feminist solidarity model the One-Third/Two-Thirds paradigm makes sense. Rather than Western/Third World, or North/South, or local/global seen as oppositional and incommensurate categories, the One-Third/Two-Thirds differentiation allows for teaching and learning about points of connection and distance among and between communities of women marginalized and privileged along numerous local and global dimensions. Thus the very notion of inside/outside necessary to the distance between local/global is transformed through the use of a One-Third/Two-Thirds paradigm, as both categories must be understood as containing difference/similarities, inside/outside, and distance/proximity. Thus sex work, militarization, human rights, and so on can be framed in their multiple local and global dimensions using the One-Third/Two-Thirds, social minority/social majority paradigm. I am suggesting then that we look at the women's studies curriculum in its entirety and that we attempt to use a comparative feminist studies model wherever possible.[16]

I refer to this model as the feminist solidarity model because, besides its focus on mutuality and common interests, it requires one to formulate questions about connection and disconnection between activist women's movements around the world. Rather than formulating activism and agency in terms of discrete and disconnected cultures and nations, it allows us to frame agency and resistance across the borders of nation and culture. I think feminist pedagogy should not simply expose students to a particularized academic scholarship but that it should also envision the possibility of activism and struggle outside the academy. Political education through feminist pedagogy should teach active citizenship in such struggles for justice.

My recurring question is how pedagogies can supplement, consolidate, or resist the dominant logic of globalization. How do students learn about the inequities among women and men around the world? For instance, traditional liberal and liberal feminist pedagogies disallow historical and comparative thinking, radical feminist pedagogies often singularize gender, and Marxist pedagogy silences race and gender in its focus on capitalism. I look to create pedagogies that allow students to see the complexities, singularities, and interconnections between communities of women such that power, privilege, agency, and dissent can be made visible and engaged with.

In an instructive critique of postcolonial studies and its institutional location, Arif Dirlik argues that the particular institutional history of postcolonial studies, as well as its conceptual emphases on the historical and local as against the systemic and the global, permit its assimilation into the logic of globalism.[17] While Dirlik somewhat overstates his argument, deradicalization and assimilation should concern those of us involved in the feminist project. Feminist pedagogies of internationalization need an adequate response to globalization. Both Eurocentric and cultural relativist (postmodernist) models of scholarship and teaching are easily assimilated within the logic of late capitalism because this is fundamentally a logic of seeming decentralization and accumulation of differences. What I call the comparative feminist studies/feminist solidarity model on the other hand potentially counters this logic by setting up a paradigm of historically and culturally specific "common differences" as the basis for analysis and solidarity. Feminist pedagogies of antiglobalization can tell alternate stories of difference, culture, power, and agency. They can begin to theorize experience, agency, and justice from a more cross-cultural lens.[18]

After almost two decades of teaching feminist studies in U.S. classrooms, it is clear to me that the way we theorize experience, culture, and subjectivity in relation to histories, institutional practice, and collective struggles determines the kind of stories we tell in the classroom. If these varied stories are to be taught such that students learn to democratize rather than colonize the experiences of different spatially and temporally located communities of women, neither a Eurocentric nor a cultural pluralist curricular practice will do. In fact narratives of historical experience are crucial to political thinking not because they present an unmediated version of the "truth" but because they can destabilize received truths and locate debate in the complexities and contradictions of historical life. It is in this context that postpositivist realist theorizations of experience, identity, and culture become useful in constructing curricular and pedagogical narratives that address as well as combat globalization.[19] These realist theorizations explicitly link a historical materialist understanding of social location to the theorization of epistemic privilege and the construction of social identity, thus suggesting the complexities of the narratives of marginalized peoples in terms of relationality rather than separation. These are the kinds of stories we need to weave into a feminist solidarity pedagogical model.

Antiglobalization Scholarship and Movements

Women's and girls' bodies determine democracy: free from violence and sexual abuse, free from malnutrition and environmental degradation, free to plan their families, free to not have families, free to choose their sexual lives and preferences.—Zillah Eisenstein, *Global Obscenities,* 1998

There is now an increasing and useful feminist scholarship critical of the practices and effects of globalization.[20] Instead of attempting a comprehensive review of this scholarship, I want to draw attention to some of the most useful kinds of issues it raises. Let me turn, then, to a feminist reading of antiglobalization movements and argue for a more intimate, closer alliance between women's movements, feminist pedagogy, cross-cultural feminist theorizing, and these ongoing anticapitalist movements.

I return to an earlier question: What are the concrete effects of global restructuring on the "real" raced, classed, national, sexual bodies of women in the academy, in workplaces, streets, households, cyberspaces, neighborhoods, prisons, and in social movements? And how do we recognize these gendered effects in movements against globalization? Some of the most complex analyses of the centrality of gender in understanding economic globalization attempt to link questions of subjectivity, agency, and identity with those of political economy and the state. This scholarship argues persuasively for a need to rethink patriarchies and hegemonic masculinities in relation to present-day globalization and nationalisms, and it also attempts to retheorize the gendered aspects of the refigured relations of the state, the market, and civil society by focusing on unexpected and unpredictable sites of resistance to the often devastating effects of global restructuring on women.[21] And it draws on a number of disciplinary paradigms and political perspectives in making the case for the centrality of gender in processes of global restructuring, arguing that the reorganization of gender is part of the global strategy of capitalism.

Women workers of particular caste/class, race, and economic status are necessary to the operation of the capitalist global economy. Women are not only the preferred candidates for particular jobs, but particular kinds of women—poor, Third and Two-Thirds World, working-class, and immigrant/migrant women—are the preferred workers in these global, "flexible" temporary job markets. The documented increase in the migration of poor, One-Third/Two-Thirds World women in search of labor across national borders has led to a rise in the international "maid trade" (Parreñas 2001) and in international sex trafficking and tourism.[22] Many global cities now require and completely depend on the service and domestic labor of immigrant and migrant women. The proliferation of structural adjustment policies around the world has reprivatized women's labor by shifting the responsibility for social welfare from the state to the household and to women located there. The rise of religious fundamentalisms in conjunction with conservative nationalisms, which are also in part reactions to global capital and its cultural demands has led to the policing of women's bodies in the streets and in the workplaces.

Global capital also reaffirms the color line in its newly articulated class structure evident in the prisons in the One-Third World. The effects of globalization and deindustrialization on the prison industry in the One-Third World leads to a related policing of the bodies of poor, One-Third/Two-Thirds World, immigrant and migrant women behind the concrete spaces and bars of privatized prisons. Angela Davis and Gina Dent (2001) argue that the political economy of U.S. prisons, and the punishment industry in the West/North, brings the intersection of gender, race, colonialism, and capitalism into sharp focus, just as the factories and workplaces of global corporations seek and discipline the labor of poor, Third World/South, immigrant/migrant women, the prisons of Europe and the United States incarcerate disproportionately large numbers of women of color, immigrants, and noncitizens of African, Asian, and Latin American descent.

Making gender and power visible in the processes of global restructuring demands looking at, naming, and seeing the particular raced, and classed communities of women from poor countries as they are constituted as workers in sexual, domestic, and service industries; as prisoners; and as household managers and nurturers. In contrast to this production of workers, Patricia Fernández-Kelly and Diane Wolf (2001, esp. 1248) focus on communities of black U.S. inner-city youth situated as "redundant" to the global economy. This redundancy is linked to their disproportionate representation in U.S. prisons. They argue that these young men, who are potential workers, are left out of the economic circuit, and this "absence of connections to a structure of opportunity" results in young African American men turning to dangerous and creative survival strategies while struggling to reinvent new forms of masculinity.

There is also increased feminist attention to the way discourses of globalization are themselves gendered and the way hegemonic masculinities are produced and mobilized in the service of global restructuring. Marianne Marchand and Anne Runyan (2000) discuss the gendered metaphors and symbolism in the language of globalization whereby particular actors and sectors are privileged over others: market over state, global over local, finance capital over manufacturing, finance ministries over social welfare, and consumers over citizens. They argue that the latter are feminized and the former masculinized (13) and that this gendering naturalizes the hierarchies required for globalization to succeed. Charlotte Hooper (2000) identifies an emerging hegemonic Anglo-American masculinity through processes of global restructuring—a masculinity that affects men and women workers in the global economy.[23] Hooper argues that this Anglo-American masculinity has dualistic tendencies, retaining the image of the aggressive frontier masculinity on the one hand, while drawing on more benign images of CEOs with (feminized) non-hierarchical management skills associated with teamwork and networking on the other.

While feminist scholarship is moving in important and useful directions in terms of a critique of global restructuring and the culture of globalization, I want to ask some of the same questions I posed in 1986 once again. In spite of the occasional exception, I think that much of present-day scholarship tends to reproduce particular "globalized" representations of women. Just as there is an Anglo-American masculinity produced in and by discourses of globalization,[24] it is important to ask what the corresponding femininities being produced are. Clearly there is the ubiquitous global teenage girl factory worker, the domestic worker, and the sex worker. There is also the migrant/immigrant service worker, the refugee, the victim of war crimes, the woman-of-color prisoner who happens to be a mother and drug user, the consumer-housewife, and so on. There is also the mother-of-the-nation/religious bearer of traditional culture and morality.

Although these representations of women correspond to real people, they also often stand in for the contradictions and complexities of women's lives and roles. Certain images, such as that of the factory or sex worker, are often geographically located in the Third World/South, but many of the representations identified above are dispersed throughout the globe. Most refer to women of the Two-Thirds World and some to women of the One-Third World. And a woman from the Two-Thirds World can live in the One-Third World. The point I am making here is that women are workers, mothers, or consumers in the global economy, but we are also all those things simultaneously. Singular and monolithic categorizations of women in discourses of globalization circumscribe ideas about experience, agency, and struggle. While there are other, relatively new images of women that also emerge in this discourse—the human rights worker or the NGO advocate, the revolutionary militant and the corporate bureaucrat—there is also a divide between false, overstated images of victimized and empowered womanhood, and they negate each other. We need to further explore how this divide plays itself out in terms of a social majority/minority, One-Third/Two-Thirds World characterization. The concern here is with whose agency is being colonized and who is privileged in these pedagogies and scholarship. These then are my new queries for the twenty-first century.[25]

Because social movements are crucial sites for the construction of knowledge, communities, and identities, it is very important for feminists to direct themselves toward them. The antiglobalization movements of the last five years have proven that one does not have to be a multinational corporation, controller of financial capital, or transnational governing institution to cross national borders. These movements form an important site for examining the construction of transborder democratic citizenship. But first a brief characterization of antiglobalization movements is in order.

Unlike the territorial anchors of the anticolonial movements of the early twentieth century, antiglobalization movements have numerous spatial and social origins. These include anticorporate environmental movements such as the Narmada Bachao Andolan in central India and movements against environmental racism in the U.S. Southwest, as well as the antiagribusiness small-farmer movements around the world. The 1960s consumer movements, people's movements against the IMF and World Bank for debt cancelation and against structural adjustment programs, and the antisweatshop student movements in Japan, Europe, and the United States are also a part of the origins of the antiglobalization movements. In addition, the identity-based social movements of the late twentieth century (feminist, civil rights, indigenous rights, etc.) and the transformed U.S. labor movement of the 1990s also play a significant part in terms of the history of antiglobalization movements.[26]

While women are present as leaders and participants in most of these antiglobalization movements, a feminist agenda only emerges in the post-Beijing "women's rights as human rights" movement and in some peace and environmental justice movements. In other words, while girls and women are central to the labor of global capital, antiglobalization work does not seem to draw on feminist analysis or strategies. Thus, while I have argued that feminists need to be anticapitalists, I would now argue that antiglobalization activists and theorists also need to be feminists. Gender is ignored as a category of analysis and a basis for organizing in most of the antiglobalization movements, and antiglobalization (and anticapitalist critique) does not appear to be central to feminist organizing projects, especially in the First World/North. In terms of women's movements, the earlier "sisterhood is global" form of internationalization of the women's movement has now shifted into the "human rights" arena. This shift in language from "feminism" to "women's rights" has been called the mainstreaming of the feminist movement—a successful attempt to raise the issue of violence against women on to the world stage.

If we look carefully at the focus of the antiglobalization movements, it is the bodies and labor of women and girls that constitute the heart of these struggles. For instance, in the environmental and ecological movements such as Chipko in India and indigenous movements against uranium mining and breast-milk contamination in the United States, women are not only among the leadership: their gendered and racialized bodies are the key to demystifying and combating the processes of recolonization put in place by corporate control of the environment. My earlier discussion of Vandana Shiva's analysis of the WTO and biopiracy from the epistemological place of Indian tribal and peasant women illustrates this claim, as does Grace Lee Boggs's notion of "place-based civic activism" (Boggs 2000, 19). Similarly, in the anticorporate consumer movements and in the small farmer movements against agribusiness and the antisweatshop movements, it is women's labor and their bodies that are most affected as workers, farmers, and consumers/household nurturers.

Women have been in leadership roles in some of the cross-border alliances against corporate injustice. Thus, making gender, and women's bodies and labor visible, and theorizing this visibility as a process of articulating a more inclusive politics are crucial aspects of feminist anticapitalist critique. Beginning from the social location of poor women of color of the Two-Thirds World is an important, even crucial, place for feminist analysis; it is precisely the potential epistemic privilege of these communities of women that opens up the space for demystifying capitalism and for envisioning transborder social and economic justice.

The masculinization of the discourses of globalization analyzed by Marchand and Runyan (2000) and Hooper (2000) seems to be matched by the implicit masculinization of the discourses of antiglobalization movements. While much of the literature on antiglobalization movements marks the centrality of class and race and, at times, nation in the critique and fight against global capitalism, racialized gender is still an unmarked category. Racialized gender is significant in this instance because capitalism utilizes the raced and sexed bodies of women in its search for profit globally, and, as I argued earlier, it is often the experiences and struggles of poor women of color that allow the most inclusive analysis as well as politics in antiglobalization struggles.

On the other hand, many of the democratic practices and process-oriented aspects of feminism appear to be institutionalized into the decision-making processes of some of these movements. Thus the principles of nonhierarchy, democratic participation, and the notion of the personal being political all emerge in various ways in this antiglobal politics. Making gender and feminist agendas and projects explicit in such antiglobalization movements thus is a way of tracing a more accurate genealogy, as well as providing potentially more fertile ground for organizing. And of course, to articulate feminism within the framework of antiglobalization work is also to begin to challenge the unstated masculinism of this work. The critique and resistance to global capitalism, and uncovering of the naturalization of its masculinist and racist values, begin to build a transnational feminist practice.

A transnational feminist practice depends on building feminist solidarities across the divisions of place, identity, class, work, belief, and so on. In these very fragmented times it is both very difficult to build these alliances and also never more important to do so. Global capitalism both destroys the possibilities and also offers up new ones.

Feminist activist teachers must struggle with themselves and each other to open the world with all its complexity to their students. Given the new multiethnic racial student bodies, teachers must also learn from their students. The differences and borders of each of our identities connect us to each other, more than they sever. So the enterprise here is to forge informed, self-reflexive solidarities among ourselves.

I no longer live simply under the gaze of Western eyes. I also live inside it and negotiate it every day. I make my home in Ithaca, New York, but always as from Mumbai, India. My cross-race and cross-class work takes me to interconnected places and communities around the world—to a struggle contextualized by women of color and of the Third World, sometimes located in the Two-Thirds World, sometimes in the One-Third. So the borders here are not really fixed. Our minds must be as ready to move as capital is, to trace its paths and to imagine alternative destinations.

NOTES

1. This chapter in its present form owes much to many years of conversation and collaboration with Zillah Eisenstein, Satya Mohanty, Jacqui Alexander, Lisa Lowe, Margo Okazawa-Rey, and Beverly Guy-Sheftall. Thanks also to Sue Kim for her careful and critical reading of "Under Western Eyes." Zillah Eisenstein's friendship has been crucial in my writing this chapter; she was the first person to suggest I do so.

2. "Under Western Eyes" has enjoyed a remarkable life, being reprinted almost every year since 1986 when it first appeared in the left journal *Boundary 2*. The essay has been translated into German, Dutch, Chinese, Russian, Italian, Swedish, French, and Spanish. It has appeared in feminist, postcolonial, Third World, and cultural studies journals and anthologies and maintains a presence in women's studies, cultural studies, anthropology, ethnic studies, political science, education and sociology curricula. It has been widely cited, sometimes seriously engaged with, sometimes misread, and sometimes used as an enabling framework for cross-cultural feminist projects.

3. Thanks to Zillah Eisenstein for this distinction.

4. In fact, we now even have debates about the "future of women's studies" and the "impossibility of women's studies." See the Web site "The Future of Women's Studies," Women's Studies Program, University of Arizona, 2000 at http://info-center.ccit.arizona.edu/~ws/conference; and Brown 1997.

5. See, for instance, the work of Ella Shohat, Lisa Lowe, Aihwa Ong, Uma Narayan, Inderpal Grewal and Caren Kaplan, Chela Sandoval, Avtar Brah, Lila Abu-Lughod, Jacqui Alexander, Kamala Kempadoo, and Saskia Sassen.

6. See the works of Maria Mies, Cynthia Enloe, Zillah Eisenstein, Saskia Sassen, and Dorothy Smith . . . for similar methodological approaches. An early, pioneering example of

this perspective can be found in the "Black Feminist" statement by the Combahee River Collective in the early 1980s.

7. See discussions of epistemic privilege in the essays by Mohanty, Moya, and Macdonald in Moya and Hames-Garcia 2000.

8. Examples of women of color in the fight against environmental racism can be found in the organization Mothers of East Los Angeles (see Pardo 2001), the magazine *ColorLines,* and *Voces Unidas,* the newsletter of the SouthWest Organizing project, Albuquerque, New Mexico.

9. See Shiva, Jafri, Bedi, and Holla-Bhar 1997. For a provocative argument about indigenous knowledges, see Dei and Sefa 2000.

10. In what follows I use the terms "global capitalism," "global restructuring," and "globalization" interchangeably to refer to a process of corporate global economic, ideological, and cultural reorganization across the borders of nation-states.

11. While the initial push for "internationalization" of the curriculum in U.S. higher education came from the federal government's funding of area studies programs during the cold war, in the post–cold war period it is private foundations like the MacArthur, Rockefeller, and Ford foundations that have been instrumental in this endeavor—especially in relation to the women's studies curriculum.

12. This work consists of participating in a number of reviews of women's studies programs, reviewing essays, syllabi, and manuscripts on feminist pedagogy and curricula, and topical workshops and conversations with feminist scholars and teachers over the last ten years.

13. Ella Shohat refers to this as the "sponge/additive" approach that extends U.S.-centered paradigms to "others" and produces a "homogeneous feminist master narrative." See Shohat 2001, 1269–72.

14. For an incisive critique of cultural relativism and its epistemological underpinnings see Mohanty 1997, chapter 5.

15. It is also important to examine and be cautious about the latent nationalism of race and ethnic studies and of women's and gay and lesbian studies in the United States.

16. A new anthology contains some good examples of what I am referring to as a feminist solidarity or comparative feminist studies model. See Lay, Monk, and Rosenfelt 2002.

17. See Dirlik, "Borderlands Radicalism," in Dirlik 1994. See the distinction between "postcolonial studies" and "postcolonial thought": while postcolonial thought has much to say about questions of local and global economies, postcolonial studies has not always taken these questions on board (Loomba 1998–99). I am using Ania Loomba's formulation here, but many progressive critics of postcolonial studies have made this basic point. It is an important distinction, and I think it can be argued in the case of feminist thought and feminist studies (women's studies) as well.

18. While I know no other work that conceptualizes this pedagogical strategy in the ways I am doing here, my work is very similar to that of scholars like Ella Shohat, Jacqui Alexander, Susan Sanchez-Casal, and Amie Macdonald.

19. See especially the work of Satya Mohanty, Paula Moya, Linda Alcoff, and Shari Stone-Mediatore.

20. The epigraph to this section is taken from Eisenstein 1998b, 161. This book remains one of the smartest, most accessible, and complex analyses of the color, class, and gender of globalization.

21. The literature on gender and globalization is vast, and I do not pretend to review it in any comprehensive way. I draw on three particular texts to critically summarize what I consider to be the most useful and provocative analyses of this area; Eisenstein 1998b; Marchand and Runyan 2000; and Basu et al. 1995.

22. See essays in Kempadoo and Doezema 1998; and Puar 2001.

23. For similar arguments, see also Bergeron 2001 and Freeman 2001.

24. Discourses of globalization include the proglobalization narratives of neoliberalism and privatization, but they also include antiglobalization discourses produced by progressives, feminists, and activists in the antiglobalization movement.

25. There is also an emerging feminist scholarship that complicates these monolithic "globalized" representations of women. See Amy Lind's work on Ecuadorian women's organizations (2000), Aili Marie Tripp's work on women's social networks in Tanzania (2002), and Kimberly Chang and L. H. M. Ling's (2000) and Aihwa Ong's work on global restructuring in the Asia Pacific regions (1987 and 1991).

26. This description is drawn from Brecher, Costello, and Smith 2000. Much of my analysis of antiglobalization movements is based on this text, and on material from magazines like *ColorLines, Z Magazine, Monthly Review,* and *SWOP Newsletter.*

References

Basu, Amrita, ed. 1995. *The Challenge of Local Feminisms: Women's Movements in Global Perspective.* Boulder: Westview Press.

Bergeron, Suzanne. 2001. "Political Economy Discourses of Globalization and Feminist Politics." *Signs* 26, no. 4 (summer): 983–1006.

Boggs, Grace Lee. 2000. "A Question of Place." *Monthly Review* 52, no. 2 (June): 18–20.

Brecher, Jeremy, Jim Costello, and Brendan Smith. 2000. *Globalization from Below: The Power of Solidarity.* Boston: South End Press.

Brown, Wendy. 1997. "The Impossibility of Women's Studies." *differences* 9, no. 3: 79–101.

Chang, Kimberly, and L. H. M. Ling. 2000. "Globalization and Its Intimate Other: Filipina Domestic Workers in Hong Kong." In *Gender and Global Restructuring: Sightings, Sites, and Resistances,* edited by Marianne Marchand and Anne Runyan. New York: Routledge.

Davis, Angela, and Gina Dent. 2001. "Prison as a Border: A Conversation on Gender, Globalization, and Punishment." *Signs* 26, no. 4 (summer): 1235–42.

Dei, George, and J. Sefa. 2000. "Rethinking the Role of Indigeneous Knowledges in the Academy." *International Journal of Inclusive Education* 4, no. 2: 111–32.

Dirlik, Arif. 1999. "Place-Based Imagination: Globalism and the Politics of Place." In *Review, A Journal of the Ferdinand Braudel Center for the Study of Economics, Historical Systems, and Civilizations* 22, no. 2 (spring): 151–187.

———. 1994. *After the Revolution: Waking to Global Capitalism.* Hanover, N.H.: Wesleyan University Press.

Eisenstein, Zillah R. 1998b. *Global Obscenities: Patriarchy, Capitalism, and the Lure of Cyberfantasy.* New York: New York University Press.

Fernández-Kelly, Patricia, and Diane Wolf. 2001. "A Dialogue on Globalization." *Signs* 26, no. 4 (summer): 1007–39.

Freeman, Carla. 2001. "Is Local:Global as Feminine:Masculine? Rethinking the Gender of Globalization." *Signs* 26, no. 4 (summer): 1007–38.

Hooper, Charlotte. 2000. "Masculinities in Transition: The Case of Globalization." In *Gender and Global Restructuring: Sightings, Sites and Resistances,* ed. Marianne Marchand and Anne Runyan, 44–58. New York: Routledge.

Kempadoo, Kamala, and Jo Doezema, eds. 1998. *Global Sex Workers, Rights, Resistance, and Redefinition.* London: Routledge.

Lay, Mary M., Janice Monk, and Deborah Silverton Rosenfelt, eds. 2002. *Encompassing Gender: Integrating International Studies and Women's Studies.* New York: Feminist Press of City University of New York.

Lind, Amy. 2000. "Negotiating Boundaries: Women's Organizations and the Politics of Restructuring in Equador." In *Gender and Global Restructuring: Sightings, Sites, and Resistances,* edited by Marianne Marchand and Anne Runyan. New York: Routledge.

Loomba, Ania. 1998–99. "Postcolonialism—or Postcolonial Studies." *Interventions: International Journal of Postcolonial Studies* I, no. 1: 39–42.

Marchand, Marianne, and Anne Runyan, eds. 2000. *Gender and Global Restructuring: Sightings, Sites and Resistances.* New York: Routledge.

Mohanty, Satya. 1997. *Literary Theory and the Claims of History.* Ithaca: Cornell University Press.

Moya, Paula, and Michael R. Hames-Garcia, eds. 2000. *Reclaiming Identity: Realist Theory and the Predicament of Postmodernism.* Berkeley: University of California Press.

Ong, Aihwa. 1991. "The Gender and Labor Politics of Postmodernity." *Annual Review of Anthropology* 20: 279–309.

———. 1987. *Spirits of Resistance and Capitalist Discipline: Factory Women in Malaysia.* Albany: State University of New York Press.

Pardo, Mary. 2001. "Mexican-American Women Grassroots Community Activists: Mothers of East Los Angeles." In *Women's Lives: Multicultural Perspectives,* ed. Margo Okazawa-Rey and Gwyn Kirk, 504–11. Mountain View, CA: Mayfield Publishing Company.

Parreñas, Rachel Salazar. 2001. "Transgressing the Nation-State: The Partial Citizenship and 'Imagined (Global) Community' of Migrant Filipina Domestic Workers." *Signs* 26, no. 4 (summer): 1129–54.

Puar, Jasbir. 2001. "Global Circuits: Transnational Sexualities and Trinidad." *Signs* 26, no. 4 (summer): 1039–66.

Shiva, Vandana, Rebecca Gordon, and Bob Wing. 2000. "Global Brahminism: The Meaning of the WTO Protests: An Interview with Dr. Vandana Shiva," *ColorLines,* 3 (2): 30–32.

Shiva, Vandana, A. H. Jafri, G. Bedi, and R. Holla-Bhar. 1997. *The Enclosure and Recovery of the Commons: Biodiversity, Indigeneous Knowledge and Intellectual Property Rights.* New Delhi: Research Foundation for Science and Technology.

Shohat, Ella. 2001. "Area Studies, Transnationalism, and the Feminist Production of Knowledge." *Signs* 26, no. 4 (summer): 1269–72.

Tripp, Aili Marie. 2002. "Combining Intercontinental Parenting and Research: Dilemmas and Strategies for Women." *Signs* 27, no. 3: 793–811.

PART SEVEN

Environmentalism and Ecology

IN 1983 THE German Greens (*Die Grünen*) won 5.6 percent of the vote and earned twenty-seven seats in the West German National Assembly, or Bundestag. Jonathon Porritt describes how their presence changed the "scenery":

> The main debating chamber of the Bundestag is an austere, somewhat sterile arena; all the men—and the minute sprinkling of women—from the main parties are soberly dressed in black. Die Grünen decided not only to wear their ordinary, everyday clothes, but to bring with them some symbolic token of the Earth itself, a small tree or plant. It sounded to some like one of those typically freaky, offbeat stunts so beloved of Die Grünen—and yet, in the midst of all that moribund formality, to see them coming together in a blaze of colour, of life, of utterly honest political commitment, was an extraordinary inspiration.[1]

Porritt is an obvious partisan, but his words capture the Greens' major concern: because "normal" politics has brought global warming, soil depletion, water pollution, endangered species, toxic chemicals, and nuclear fallout, a new politics is needed to save life on earth. Porritt argues that "Green politics is not only different in *what* it has to say: it is equally different in the *way* it says it."[2]

In "Thinking Green!" Petra Kelly, a spokesperson for *Die Grünen*, explains the ethic practiced by Green activists and politicians: "We must learn to think and act from our hearts, to recognize the interconnectedness of all living creatures, and to respect the value of each thread in the vast web of life." This "holistic" worldview contrasts sharply with "mechanism," the dominant paradigm of industrialized democracies in the Western world. A mechanistic politics "prefers assertion to integration, analysis over synthesis, rational knowledge over intuitive wisdom, competition over cooperation, and expansionism over conservation." Kelly identifies four interrelated principles of Green politics—"nonviolence, ecology, social justice and feminism"—which together constitute a spiritual perspective, a new way of thinking and being that has the power to transform self and society.

Carolyn Merchant calls the ethic espoused by the German Greens and similar groups "ecocentrism" to distinguish it from mainstream environmental politics.[3] The related word *ecology* originates from two Greek terms: *Oekonomie* (household management) and *Oethology* (animal behavior). The concept has deep roots in indigenous cultures that remain committed to living in harmony with natural processes. In 1855 the Native American chief Seattle warned the white man that "his appetite will devour the earth and leave behind a desert. . . . All things are connected. Whatever befalls the Earth, befalls the children of the Earth."[4] Modern ecocentrism began in nineteenth-century Europe, in part, as a reaction against industrialization and urbanization. In Germany, ecology is associated with vitalist philosophy (or *lebensphilosophie*), whose leading theorists—Henri Bergson, Wilhelm Dilthey, Friedrich Nietzsche, and Georges Sorel—emphasize energy flows within and between organisms. An American analogue is the transcendentalist philosophy of Henry David Thoreau and Ralph Waldo Emerson. For Emerson, nature ministers to humanity and disciplines our bodies and souls, teaching us how to live in beauty, harmony, and unity with other creatures on earth. More than a century later, Rachel Carson would reiterate these themes in *Silent Spring,* a founding text of environmental activism. She directed public attention to the potentially disastrous effects of chemical insecticides on the planetary ecosystem. Against arrogant human efforts to alter natural balances that have evolved over eons, she stressed the duty of humanity to live in harmony with other species.

With their emphasis on economic progress, most of the ideologies included in other sections of this book are egocentric or homocentric, rather than ecocentric. Classical liberalism is primarily egocentric: it places man above a natural world, which exists for him to consume and develop. In his famous chapter on property, John Locke declares that "the Earth, and all that is therein, is given to Men for the Support and Comfort of their being." Milton Friedman identifies environmental pollution as a "neighborhood effect" that government should regulate. However, his thinking is based not on ecological concerns but on market principles—that is, those who suffer the effects of pollution should receive just compensation for it.

Utilitarian liberals adopt a more homocentric orientation, portraying humanity as the "steward" of nature, not its master. Their cost-benefit analyses, which seek "the greatest good for the greatest number," can be easily extended to include the environmental impacts of human actions. Al Gore's new accounting methods exemplify their approach. He proposes including "hidden" environmental costs in product prices and imposing productivity standards to give industries an incentive to develop better (i.e., cleaner) technologies. His so-called Global Marshall Plan is also utilitarian in its emphasis on shared management to balance various regional needs. Like John Stuart Mill, Gore argues that active participation by all stakeholders helps coordinate policy and educates people on environmental issues.

Many socialists and anarchists also espouse a homocentric ethic. Although Marx declares that man is a "species-being," placing humanity in nature, he also claims that nature has value only "for man." In praising the wonders of capitalism, he clearly associates industrial development with human progress. Andrew Dobson argues that capitalism and socialism share the same "superideology" of "industrialism."[5] Anarchists, who argue for the simultaneous overthrow of economic, political, and scientific "capital," suggest a more holistic approach to revolution. However, they continue to assume a "dialectic between society (especially economics) and ecology."[6] According to Murray Bookchin, "our ecological problems are fundamentally social problems requiring fundamental social change." Like other species, humanity is the product of natural evolutionary processes. Since the human species has "remarkable powers," we also have "enormous moral responsibility" to create a "social 'second nature' which is ecologically-oriented." For Bookchin and many anarchists, technological developments mediate relationships between humanity and nature: "socially responsible, ecologically sensitive" use of technological resources could produce abundance for all, but a "liberatory eco-technology" cannot be realized without a "new ecological state of mind."

Social and radical anarchists exemplify their eco-consciousness in different political strategies. Bookchin has worked to build a green movement in North America focused on "a new grassroots municipal politics, a new cooperative economics, and a new pattern of science and technology." In his dialogue here with Dave Foreman, the founder of Earth First! an organization dedicated to preserving wilderness and endangered species through "monkeywrenching" (as in throwing a wrench into the works) and other forms of direct action, Bookchin describes their tactics as complementary. Foreman agrees: "We are all engaged in a battle for life against profit," a battle to save humanity from self-extinction. The radical tactics employed by organizations such as Earth First! open up political spaces where other, more conventional, ecologists can continue their work.

The homocentric ethic of utilitarian liberals, socialists, and anarchists shares a focus on species survival. According to Bookchin, however, this " 'species-centered' way of thinking," too easily slides into racist policies, especially regarding overpopulation. He fears that the "we" of environmentalists can contribute to "victim-blaming"—"Let's face it, when you say a black kid in Harlem is as much to blame for the ecological crisis as the President of Exxon, you are letting one off the hook and slandering the other." Bookchin continues, "All this loose talk of 'we' masks the reality of social power and social institutions." Although Bookchin cautions radical ecologists on the issue of racism, he also defends them against charges that they are fascists. Fascists' emphasis on community—local, moral, and/or national—may initially sound holistic, but fascists combine their vision of "blood and soil" with a uniquely modern form of "terroristic coordination." Fascists' monism blurs boundaries between self, society, and nature in order to obliterate all traces of difference. In contrast, ecologists' holism involves the recognition of interdependence between diverse forms of life.[7]

Feminist frameworks that merely augment or reverse traditional ideologies often replicate their egocentric or homocentric ethics. In contrast, ecofeminism stresses "the interrelationship and unity of all life on earth." According to ecofeminists, the domination of nature and the domination of women are closely connected. "Women and nature are the original 'others' in patriarchy—those who are feared, the reminders of mortality, those who must be objectified and dominated."[8] Some feminists criticize ecologists' metaphors, such as "Mother Earth," because they reinforce cultural stereotypes about women as caretakers and nurturers. Ecofeminists argue that this criticism misses the crucial point: even when women are no longer forced to mother, human beings will still be born from women's bodies. Ecofeminists stress that human beings, male and female, are mortal and live and die with the earth.

In *Stolen Harvest: The Hijacking of the Global Food Supply,* Vandana Shiva brings this perspective to the global politics of food production. She begins with seed, "the ultimate symbol of food security," and says that "in giving food to other beings and species, we maintain conditions for our own food security." Seed is a biological, cultural, historical, and spiritual resource, as well as an economic and political one. A few corporations, Shiva argues, increasingly control the "food chain": they aggressively promote hybrid seeds, agricultural monocultures, and production of cash crops for export—all practices that undermine biodiversity and encourage pesticide use and wasteful farming practices. More important, they exploit an economy of scarcity which they, in fact, create. Shiva writes: "In the ecological worldview, when we consume more than we need or exploit nature on principles of greed, we are engaging in theft. In the anti-life view of agribusiness corporations, nature renewing and maintaining herself is a thief. Such a worldview replaces abundance with scarcity, fertility with sterility. It makes theft from nature a market imperative, and hides it in the calculus of efficiency and productivity."

With this insight, we return to the relationship between green and "normal" politics. Andrew Dobson distinguishes between dark green and pale green politics (a distinction that parallels the distinction between ecologists and environmentalists). As he puts it, "Green politics explicitly seeks to decentre the human being, to question mechanistic science and its technological consequences, to refuse to believe that the world was made for human beings—and it does this because it has been led to wonder whether dominant post-industrialism's project of material affluence is either desirable or sustainable."[9] Pale green, or environmental, politics can be assimilated easily by mainstream political parties, since it seeks only "a cleaner service economy, sustained by cleaner technology and producing cleaner affluence." The ideologies discussed above provide numerous examples of this process of assimilation.

Shortly after their 1983 electoral success, *Die Grünen* split into two groups. The *realos* agreed to work within the existing system and formed coalitions with more mainstream parties, especially the socialist left. The *fundis* continued grassroots politics and insisted on more radical changes in political processes. According to Carolyn Merchant, this internal party debate reflects a choice facing the larger environmental movement today. In many Western democracies, green parties now coexist with nonprofit environmental organizations—for example, the Audubon Society and the Sierra Club—and with more radical ecology groups, such as Earth First! and Greenpeace. Green politics has emerged as well in the wake of environmentally destructive socialist policies in the former Soviet Union and its East European satellites. Green protests also often accompany development efforts in the newly industrializing nations of the Third World. Merchant thinks that "the environmental movement has arrived at a crossroads. Environmentalists travel one road, to the right. Ecologists travel another, to the left." However, there is a third way: "At the center of the crossroads, a new road is still in the planning stage." One such "third way" may be an emerging green politics in the United States, which is currently organized through "committees of correspondence," an anarchist model of confederated associations dating back to the Revolutionary War era. Although the activists on this road to the future often support Green Party candidates in state and local elections, they also insist, "we are neither left nor right, we are in front."[10] It is here—at the crossroads—that the greatest challenge to "politics as usual" will emerge. To meet this challenge, human beings must profoundly transform their understanding of life on earth.

NOTES

1. Jonathon Porritt, preface to *Die Grünen: Programme of the German Green Party* (London: Heretic Books, 1983), 3.

2. Ibid.

3. Carolyn Merchant, *Radical Ecology: The Search for a Livable World* (New York: Routledge, 1992).

4. Quoted in Andrew Dobson, *Green Political Thought: An Introduction*, 2nd ed. (New York: Routledge, 1995), 39.

5. Ibid., 30–31.

6. Merchant, *Radical Ecology*, 146.

7. Anna Bramwell, *Ecology in the 20th Century: A History* (New Haven: Yale University Press, 1989), 161.

8. Quoted in Ursula King, *Women and Spirituality: Voices of Protest and Promise*, 2nd ed. (University Park: Pennsylvania State University Press, 1993), 209.

9. Dobson, *Green Political Thought*, 11.

10. Merchant, *Radical Ecology*, 157–158.

36

Ralph Waldo Emerson

Nature (1836)

Ralph Waldo Emerson (1803–1882) was a Harvard-educated preacher, essay-
ist, and poet. From the 1830s to the 1860s he lectured throughout New Eng-
land on political issues, including the Mexican-American War and the Fugi-
tive Slave Law. Nature, *his first book, was followed by two volumes of* Essays
that brought him international renown. A member of the transcendentalist
movement, Emerson was a close friend of Henry David Thoreau.

OUR AGE is retrospective. It builds the sepulchres of the fathers. It writes biogra-
phies, histories, and criticism. The foregoing generations beheld God and nature
face to face; we, through their eyes. Why should not we also enjoy an original
relation to the universe? Why should not we have a poetry and philosophy of
insight and not of tradition, and a religion by revelation to us, and not the history
of theirs? Embosomed for a season in nature, whose floods of life stream around
and through us, and invite us, by the powers they supply, to action proportioned
to nature, why should we grope among the dry bones of the past, or put the living generation into masquerade out of its faded wardrobe? The sun shines to-day
also. There is more wool and flax in the fields. There are new lands, new men,
new thoughts. Let us demand our own works and laws and worship.

Undoubtably we have no questions to ask which are unanswerable. We must
trust the perfection of the creation so far as to believe that whatever curiosity the
order of things has awakened in our minds, the order of things can satisfy. Every
man's condition is a solution in hieroglyphic to those inquiries he would put. He
acts it as life, before he apprehends it as truth. In like manner, nature is already,
in its forms and tendencies, describing its own design. Let us interrogate the

great apparition that shines so peacefully around us. Let us inquire, to what end is nature? . . .

II. Commodity

Whoever considers the final cause of the world will discern a multitude of uses that enter as parts into that result. They all admit of being thrown into one of the following classes: Commodity; Beauty; Language; and Discipline.

Under the general name of commodity, I rank all those advantages which our senses owe to nature. This, of course, is a benefit which is temporary and mediate, not ultimate, like its service to the soul. Yet although low, it is perfect in its kind, and is the only use of nature which all men apprehend. The misery of man appears like childish petulance, when we explore the steady and prodigal provision that has been made for his support and delight on this green ball which floats him through the heavens. What angels invented these splendid ornaments, these rich conveniences, this ocean of air above, this ocean of water beneath, this firmament of earth between? this zodiac of lights, this tent of dropping clouds, this striped coat of climates, this fourfold year? Beasts, fire, water, stones, and corn serve him. The field is at once his floor, his work-yard, his playground, and his bed.

> "More servants wait on man
> Than he'll take notice of."

Nature, in its ministry to man, is not only the material, but is also the process and the result. All the parts incessantly work into each other's hands for the profit of man. The wind sows the seed; the sun evaporates the sea; the wind blows the vapor to the field; the ice, on the other side of the planet, condenses rain on this; the rain feeds the plant; the plant feeds the animal; and thus the endless circulations of the divine charity nourish man.

The useful arts are reproductions or new combinations by the wit of man, of the same natural benefactors. He no longer waits for favoring gales, but by means of steam, he realizes the fable of Aeolus's bag, and carries the two and thirty winds in the boiler of his boat. To diminish friction, he paves the road with iron bars, and, mounting a coach with a ship-load of men, animals, and merchandise behind him, he darts through the country, from town to town, like an eagle or a swallow through the air. By the aggregate of these aids, how is the face of the world changed, from the era of Noah to that of Napoleon! The private poor man hath cities, ships, canal[s], bridges, built for him. He goes to the post-office, and the human race run on his errands; to the book-shop, and the human race read and write of all that happens for him; to the court-house, and nations repair his wrongs. He sets his house upon the road, and the human race go forth every morning, and shovel out the snow, and cut a path for him.

But there is no need of specifying particulars in this class of uses. The catalogue is endless, and the examples so obvious, that I shall leave them to the reader's reflection, with the general remark, that this mercenary benefit is one which has respect to a farther good. A man is fed, not that he may be fed, but that he may work.

III. Beauty

A nobler want of man is served by nature, namely, the love of Beauty. The ancient Greeks call the world . . . beauty. Such is the constitution of all things, or such the plastic power of the human eye, that the primary forms, as the sky, the mountain, the tree, the animal, give us a delight *in and for themselves;* . . .

For better consideration, we may distribute the aspects of Beauty in a threefold manner.

1. First, the simple perception of natural forms is a delight. The influence of the forms and actions in nature is so needful to man, that, in its lowest functions, it seems to lie on the confines of commodity and beauty. To the body and mind which have been cramped by noxious work or company, nature is medicinal and restores their tone. The tradesman, the attorney comes out of the din and craft of the street and sees the sky and the woods, and is a man again. In their eternal calm, he finds himself. The health of the eye seems to demand a horizon. We are never tired, so long as we can see far enough.

But in other hours, Nature satisfies by its loveliness, and without any mixture of corporeal benefit. I see the spectacle of morning from the hilltop over against my house, from daybreak to sunrise, with emotions which an angel might share. The long slender bars of cloud float like fishes in the sea of crimson light. From the earth, as a shore, I look out into that silent sea. I seem to partake its rapid transformations; the active enchantment reaches my dust, and I dilate and conspire with the morning wind. How does nature deify us with a few and cheap elements! Give me health and a day, and I will make the pomp of emperors ridiculous. The dawn is my Assyria; the sunset and moonrise my Paphos, and unimaginable realms of faerie; broad noon shall be my England of the senses and the understanding; the night shall be my Germany of mystic philosophy and dreams. . . .

2. The presence of a higher, namely, of the spiritual element is essential to its perfection. The high and divine beauty which can be loved without

effeminacy, is that which is found in combination with the human will. Beauty is the mark God sets upon virtue. Every natural action is graceful. Every heroic act is also decent, and causes the place and the bystanders to shine. We are taught by great actions that the universe is the property of every individual in it. Every rational creature has all nature for his dowry and estate. It is his, if he will. He may divest himself of it; he may creep into a corner, and abdicate his kingdom, as most men do, but he is entitled to the world by his constitution. In proportion to the energy of his thought and will, he takes up the world into himself. "All those things for which men plough, build, or sail, obey virtue"; said Sallust. . . .

. . . And in common life whosoever has seen a person of powerful character and happy genius will have remarked how easily he took all things along with him,—the persons, the opinions, and the day, and nature became ancillary to a man.

3. There is still another aspect under which the beauty of the world may be viewed, namely, as it becomes an object of the intellect. Beside the relation of things to virtue, they have a relation to thought. The intellect searches out the absolute order of things as they stand in the mind of God, and without the colors of affection. The intellectual and the active powers seem to succeed each other, and the exclusive activity of the one generates the exclusive activity of the other. There is something unfriendly in each to the other, but they are like the alternate periods of feeding and working in animals: each prepares and will be followed by the other. Therefore does beauty, which, in relation to actions, as we have seen, comes unsought, and comes because it is unsought, remain for the apprehension and pursuit of the intellect; and then again, in its turn, of the active power. Nothing divine dies. All good is eternally reproductive. The beauty of nature re-forms itself in the mind, and not for barren contemplation, but for new creation.

All men are in some degree impressed by the face of the world; some men even to delight. This love of beauty is Taste. Others have the same love in such excess, that, not content with admiring, they seek to embody it in new forms. The creation of beauty is Art. . . .

The world thus exists to the soul to satisfy the desire of beauty. This element I call an ultimate end. No reason can be asked or given why the soul seeks beauty. Beauty, in its largest and profoundest sense, is one expression for the universe. God is the all-fair. Truth, and goodness, and beauty, are but different faces of the same All. But beauty in nature is not ultimate. It is the herald of inward and eternal beauty, and is not alone a solid and satisfactory good. It must stand as a part, and not as yet the last or highest expression of the final cause of Nature.

IV. Language

Language is a third use which nature subserves to man. Nature is the vehicle of thought, and in a simple, double, and threefold degree.

1. Words are signs of natural facts.
2. Particular natural facts are symbols of particular spiritual facts.
3. Nature is the symbol of spirit.

1. Words are signs of natural facts. The use of natural history is to give us aid in supernatural history; the use of the outer creation, to give us language for the beings and changes of the inward creation. Every word which is used to express a moral or intellectual fact, if traced to its root, is found to be borrowed from some material appearance. *Right* means *straight; wrong* means *twisted. Spirit* primarily means *wind; transgression,* the crossing of a *line; supercilious,* the *raising of the eyebrow.* We say the *heart* to express emotion, the *head* to denote thought; and *thought* and *emotion* are words borrowed from sensible things, and now appropriated to spiritual nature. Most of the process by which this transformation is made, is hidden from us in the remote time when language was framed; but the same tendency may be daily observed in children. Children and savages use only nouns or names of things, which they convert into verbs, and apply to analogous mental acts.

2. But this origin of all words that convey a spiritual import,—so conspicuous a fact in the history of language,—is our least debt to nature. It is not words only that are emblematic; it is things which are emblematic. Every natural fact is a symbol of some spiritual fact. Every appearance in nature corresponds to some state of the mind, and that state of the mind can only be described by presenting that natural appearance as its picture. An enraged man is a lion, a cunning man is a fox, a firm man is a rock, a learned man is a torch. A lamb is innocence; a snake is subtle spite; flowers express to us the delicate affections. Light and darkness are our familiar expression for knowledge and ignorance; and heat for love. Visible distance behind and before us, is respectively our image of memory and hope. . . .

Because of this radical correspondence between visible things and human thoughts, savages, who have only what is necessary, converse in figures. As we go back in history, language becomes more picturesque, until its infancy, when it is all poetry; or all spiritual facts are represented by natural symbols. The same symbols are found to make the original elements of all languages. It has moreover been observed, that the idioms of all languages approach each other in passages of the greatest eloquence and power. And as this is the first language, so is it the last. This immediate dependence of language upon nature, this conversion of an outward phenomenon into a type of somewhat inhuman life, never loses its power to affect us. It is this which gives that piquancy to the conversation of a strong-natured farmer or backwoodsman, which all men relish.

A man's power to connect his thought with its proper symbol, and so to utter it, depends on the simplicity of his character, that is, upon his love of truth and his desire to communicate it without loss. The corruption of man is followed by the corruption of language. When simplicity of character and the sovereignty of ideas is broken up by the prevalence of secondary desires,—the desire of riches, of pleasure, of power and of praise,—and duplicity and falsehood take place of simplicity and truth, the power over nature as an interpreter of the will is in a degree lost; new imagery ceases to be created, and old words are perverted to stand for things which are not; a paper currency is employed, when there is no bullion in the vaults. In due time the fraud is manifest, and words lose all power to stimulate the understanding or the affections. . . .

3. We are thus assisted by natural objects in the expression of particular meanings. . . . The world is emblematic. Parts of speech are metaphors, because the whole of nature is a metaphor of the human mind. The laws of moral nature answer to those of matter as face to face in a glass. "The visible world and the relation of its parts, is the dial plate of the invisible." The axioms of physics translate the laws of ethics. Thus, "the whole is greater than its part[s]"; "reaction is equal to action"; "the smallest weight may be made to lift the greatest, the difference of weight being compensated by time"; and many the like propositions, which have an ethical as well as physical sense. These propositions have a much more extensive and universal sense when applied to human life, than when confined to technical use.

In like manner, the memorable words of history and the proverbs of nations consist usually of a natural fact, selected as a picture or parable of a moral truth. Thus; A rolling stone gathers no moss; A bird in the hand is worth two in the bush; A cripple in the right way will beat a racer in the wrong; Make hay while the sun shines; 'Tis hard to carry a full cup even; Vinegar is the son of wine; The last ounce broke the camel's back; Long-lived trees make roots first;—and the like. In their primary sense these are trivial facts, but we repeat them for the value of their analogical import. What is true of proverbs, is true of all fables, parables, and allegories.

This relation between the mind and matter is not fancied by some poet, but stands in the will of God, and so is free to be known by all men. . . .

A life in harmony with Nature, the love of truth and of virtue, will purge the eyes to understand her text. By degrees we may come to know the primitive sense of the permanent objects of nature, so that the world shall be to us an open book, and every form significant of its hidden life and final cause.

A new interest surprises us, whilst, under the view now suggested, we contemplate the fearful extent and multitude of objects; since "every object rightly seen, unlocks a new faculty of the soul." That which was unconscious truth, becomes, when interpreted and defined in an object, a part of the domain of knowledge,—a new weapon in the magazine of power.

V. Discipline

In view of the significance of nature, we arrive at once at a new fact, that nature is a discipline. This use of the world includes the preceding uses, as parts of itself.

Space, time, society, labor, climate, food, locomotion, the animals, the mechanical forces, give us sincerest lessons, day by day, whose meaning is unlimited. They educate both the Understanding and the Reason. Every property of matter is a school for the understanding,—its solidity or resistance, its inertia, its extension, its figure, its divisibility. The understanding adds, divides, combines, measures, and finds nutriment and room for its activity in this worthy scene. Meantime, Reason transfers all these lessons into its own world of thought, by perceiving the analogy that marries Matter and Mind.

1. Nature is a discipline of the understanding in intellectual truths. Our dealing with sensible objects is a constant exercise in the necessary lessons of difference, of likeness, of order, of being and seeming, of progressive arrangement; of ascent from particular to general; of combination to one end of manifold forces. Proportioned to the importance of the organ to be formed, is the extreme care with which its tuition is provided,—a care pretermitted in no single case. What tedious training, day after day, year after year, never ending, to form the common sense; what continual reproduction of annoyances, inconveniences, dilemmas; what rejoicing over us of little men; what disputing of prices, what reckonings of interest,—and all to form the Hand of the mind;—to instruct us that "good thoughts are no better than good dreams, unless they be executed!"

The same good office is performed by Property and its filial systems of debt and credit. Debt, grinding debt, whose iron face the widow, the orphan, and the sons of genius fear and hate;—debt, which consumes so much time, which so cripples and disheartens a great spirit with cares that seem so base, is a preceptor whose lessons cannot be foregone, and is needed most by those who suffer from it most. Moreover, property, which has been well compared to snow,—"if it fall level to-day, it will be blown into drifts to-morrow,"—is the surface action of internal machinery, like the index on the face of a clock. Whilst now it is the gymnastics of the understanding, it is hiving, in the foresight of the spirit, experience in profounder laws. . . .

Passing by many particulars of the discipline of nature, we must not omit to specify two.

The exercise of the Will, or the lesson of power, is taught in every event. From the child's successive possession of his several senses up to the hour when he saith, "Thy will be done!" he is learning the secret that he can reduce under his will not only particular events but great classes, nay, the whole series of events, and so conform all facts to his character. Nature is thoroughly mediate. It is made to serve. It receives the dominion of man as meekly as the ass on which the Savior rode. It offers all its kingdoms to man as the raw material which he may mould into what is useful. Man is never weary of working it up. He forges the subtile and delicate air into wise and melodious words, and gives them wing as angels of persuasion and command. One after another his victorious thought comes up with and reduces all things, until the world becomes at last only a realized will,—the double of the man.

2. Sensible objects conform to the premonitions of Reason and reflect the conscience. All things are moral; and in their boundless changes have an unceasing reference to spiritual nature. Therefore is nature glorious with form, color, and motion; that every globe in the remotest heaven, every chemical change from the rudest crystal up to the laws of life, every change of vegetation from the first principle of growth in the eye of a leaf, to the tropical forest and antediluvian coal-mine, every animal function from the sponge up to Hercules, shall hint or thunder to man the laws of right and wrong, and echo the Ten Commandments. . . . Thus the use of commodity, regarded by itself, is mean and squalid. But it is to the mind an education in the doctrine of Use, namely, that a thing is good only so far as it serves; that a conspiring of parts and efforts to the production of an end is essential to any being. The first and gross manifestation of this truth is our inevitable and hated training in values and wants, in corn and meat.

. . . The moral influence of nature upon every individual is that amount of truth which it illustrates to him.

. . . Herein is especially apprehended the unity of Nature,—the unity in variety,—which meets us everywhere. . . . Each creature is only a modification of the other; the likeness in them is more than the difference, and their radical law is one and the same. A rule of one art, or a law of one organization, holds true throughout nature. So intimate is this Unity, that, it is easily seen, it lies under the undermost garment of Nature, and betrays its source in Universal Spirit. For it pervades Thought also. Every universal truth which we express in words, implies or supposes every other truth. *Omne verum vero consonat.* It is like a great circle on a sphere, comprising all possible circles; which, however, may be drawn and comprise it in like manner. Every such truth is the absolute End seen from one side. But it has innumerable sides.

The central Unity is still more conspicuous in actions. Words are finite organs of the infinite mind. They cannot cover the dimensions of what is in truth. They break, chop, and impoverish it. An action is the perfection and publication of thought. A right action seems to fill the eye, and to be related to all nature. "The wise man, in doing one thing, does all; or, in the one thing he does rightly, he sees the likeness of all which is done rightly." . . .

VIII. Prospects

. . . At present, man applies to nature but half his force. He works on the world with his understanding alone. He lives in it and masters it by a penny-wisdom; and he that works most in it is but a half-man, and whilst his arms are strong and his digestion good, his mind is imbruted, and he is a selfish savage. His relation to nature, his power over it, is through the understanding, as by manure; the economic use of fire, wind, water, and the mariner's needle; steam, coal, chemical agriculture; the repairs of the human body by the dentist and the surgeon. This is such a resumption of power as if a banished king should buy his territories inch by inch, instead of vaulting at once into his throne. Meantime, in the thick darkness, there are not wanting gleams of a better light,—occasional examples of the action of man upon nature with his entire force,—with reason as well as understanding. Such examples are, the traditions of miracles in the earliest antiquity of all nations; the history of Jesus Christ; the achievements of a principle, as in religious and political revolutions, and in the abolition of the slave-trade; the miracles of enthusiasm, as those reported of Swedenborg, Hohenlohe, and the Shakers; many obscure and yet contested facts, now arranged under the name of Animal Magnetism; prayer; eloquence; self-healing; and the wisdom of children. These are examples of Reason's momentary grasp of the sceptre; the exertions of a power which exists not in time or space, but an instantaneous in-streaming causing power. The difference between the actual and the ideal force of man is happily figured by the schoolmen, in saying, that the knowledge of man is an evening knowledge, *vespertina cognitio*, but that of god is a morning knowledge, *matutina cognitio.*

The problem of restoring to the world original and eternal beauty is solved by the redemption of the soul. The ruin or the blank that we see when we look at nature, is in our own eye. The axis of vision is not coincident with the axis of things, and so they appear not transparent but opaque. The reason why the world lacks unity, and lies broken and in heaps, is because man is disunited with himself. He cannot be a naturalist until he satisfies all the demands of the spirit. . . .

So shall we come to look at the world with new eyes. It shall answer the endless inquiry of the intellect,—What is truth? and of the affections,—What is good? by yielding itself passive to the educated Will. Then shall come to pass what my poet said: "Nature is not fixed but fluid. Spirit alters, moulds, makes it. The immobility or bruteness of nature is the absence of spirit; to pure spirit it is fluid, it is volatile, it is obedient. Every spirit builds itself a house, and beyond its house a world, and beyond its world a heaven. Know then that the world exists for you. For you is the phenomenon perfect. What we are, that only can we see. All that Adam had, all that Caesar could, you have and can do. Adam called his house, heaven and earth; Caesar called his house, Rome; you perhaps call yours, a cobbler's trade; a hundred acres of ploughed land; or a scholar's garret. Yet line for line and point for point your dominion is as great as theirs, though without fine names. Build therefore your own world. As fast [as] you conform your life to the pure idea in your mind, that will unfold its great proportions. A correspondent revolution in things will attend the influx of the spirit. So fast will disagreeable appearances, swine, spiders, snakes, pests, madhouses, prisons, enemies, vanish; they are temporary and shall be no more seen. The sordor and filths of nature, the sun shall dry up and the wind exhale. As when the summer comes from the south the snow-banks melt and the face of the earth becomes green before it, so shall the advancing spirit create its ornaments along its path, and carry with it the beauty it visits and the song which enchants it; it shall draw beautiful faces, warm hearts, wise discourse, and heroic acts, around its way, until evil is no more seen. The kingdom of man over nature, which cometh not with observation,—a dominion such as now is beyond his dream of God,—he shall enter without more wonder than the blind man feels who is gradually restored to perfect sight."

37

Rachel Carson

———•◦•———

Silent Spring (1962)

Rachel Louise Carson (1907–1964) joined the U.S. Bureau of Fisheries as an aquatic biologist in 1936 after receiving her M.A. from Johns Hopkins University. She later became editor-in-chief for the Fish and Wildlife Services (1940). Her first books, Under the Sea-Wind *(1941) and* The Sea Around Us *(1951), were widely acclaimed. She remarked, "Ever since childhood, I have been fascinated by the sea, and my mind has stored up everything I have ever learned about it." But it is the call to action in* Silent Spring *for which she is best remembered.*

The Obligation to Endure

THE HISTORY OF life on earth has been a history of interaction between living things and their surroundings. To a large extent, the physical form and the habits of the earth's vegetation and its animal life have been molded by the environment. Considering the whole span of earthly time, the opposite effect, in which life actually modifies its surroundings, has been relatively slight. Only within the moment of time represented by the present century has one species—man—acquired significant power to alter the nature of his world.

During the past quarter century this power has not only increased to one of disturbing magnitude but it has changed in character. The most alarming of all man's assaults upon the environment is the contamination of air, earth, rivers, and sea with dangerous and even lethal materials. This pollution is for the most part irrecoverable; the chain of evil it initiates not only in the world that must support life but in living tissues is for the most part irreversible. In this now universal contamination of the environment, chemicals are the sinister and little-recognized partners of radiation in changing the very nature of the world—the very nature of its life. Strontium 90, released through nuclear explosions into the air, comes to earth in rain or drifts down as fallout, lodges in soil, enters into the grass or corn or wheat grown there, and in time takes up its abode in the bones of a human being, there to remain until his death. Similarly, chemicals sprayed on croplands or forests or gardens lie long in soil, entering into living organisms, passing from one to another in a chain of poisoning and death. Or they pass mysteriously by underground streams until they emerge and through the alchemy of air and sunlight, combine into new forms that kill vegetation, sicken cattle, and work unknown harm on those who drink from once pure wells. As Albert Schweitzer has said, "Man can hardly even recognize the devils of his own creation."

It took hundreds of millions of years to produce the life that now inhabits the earth—eons of time in which that developing and evolving and diversifying life reached a state of adjustment and balance with its surroundings. The environment, rigorously shaping and directing the life it supported, contained elements that were hostile as well as supporting. Certain rocks gave out dangerous radiation; even within the light of the sun, from which all life draws its energy, there were short-wave radiations with power to injure. Given time—time not in years but in millennia—life adjusts, and a balance has been reached. For time is the essential ingredient; but in the modern world there is no time.

The rapidity of change and the speed with which new situations are created follow the impetuous and heedless pace of man rather than the deliberate pace of nature. Radiation is no longer merely the background radiation of rocks, the bombardment of cosmic rays, the ultraviolet of the sun that have existed before there was any life on earth; radiation is now the unnatural creation of man's tampering with the atom. The chemicals to which life is asked to make its adjustment are no longer merely the calcium and silica and copper and all the rest of the minerals washed out of the rocks and carried in rivers to the sea; they are the synthetic creations of man's inventive mind, brewed in his laboratories, and having no counterparts in nature.

To adjust to these chemicals would require time on the scale that is nature's; it would require not merely the years of a man's life but the life of generations. And even this, were it by some miracle possible, would be futile, for the new chemicals come from our laboratories in an endless stream; almost five hundred annually find their way into actual use in the United States alone. The figure is staggering and its implications are not easily grasped—500 new chemicals to which the bodies of men and animals are required somehow to adapt each year, chemicals totally outside the limits of biologic experience.

Among them are many that are used in man's war against nature. Since the mid-1940's over 200 basic chemicals have been created for use in killing insects, weeds, rodents, and other organisms described in the modern vernacular as "pests"; and they are sold under several thousand different brand names.

These sprays, dusts, and aerosols are now applied almost universally to farms, gardens, forests, and homes—nonselective chemicals that have the power to kill every insect, the "good" and the "bad," to still the song of birds and the leaping of fish in the streams, to coat the leaves with a deadly film, and to linger on in soil— all this though the intended target may be only a few weeds or insects. Can anyone believe it is possible to lay down such a barrage of poisons on the surface of the earth without making it unfit for all life? They should not be called "insecticides," but "biocides."

The whole process of spraying seems caught up in an endless spiral. Since DDT was released for civilian use, a process of escalation has been going on in which ever more toxic materials must be found. This has happened because insects in a triumphant vindication of Darwin's principle of the survival of the fittest, have evolved super races immune to the particular insecticide used, hence a deadlier one has always to be developed—and then a deadlier one than that. It has happened also because, for reasons to be described later, destructive insects often undergo a "flareback," or resurgence, after spraying, in numbers greater than before. Thus the chemical war is never won, and all life is caught in its violent crossfire.

Along with the possibility of the extinction of mankind by nuclear war, the central problem of our age has therefore become the contamination of man's total environment with such substances of incredible potential for harm—substances that accumulate in the tissues of plants and animals and even penetrate the germ cells to shatter or alter the very material of heredity upon which the shape of the future depends.

Some would-be architects of our future look toward a time when it will be possible to alter the human germ plasm by design. But we may easily be doing so now by inadvertence, for many chemicals, like radiation, bring about gene mutations. It is ironic to think that man might determine his own future by something so seemingly trivial as the choice of an insect spray.

All this has been risked—for what? Future historians may well be amazed by our distorted sense of proportion. How could intelligent beings seek to control a few unwanted species by a method that contaminated the entire environment and brought the threat of disease and death even to their own kind? Yet this is precisely what we have done. We have done it, moreover, for reasons that collapse the moment we examine them. We are told that the enormous and expanding use of pesticides is necessary to maintain farm production. Yet is our real problem not one of *overproduction?* Our farms, despite measures to remove acreages from production and to pay farmers *not* to produce, have yielded such a staggering excess of crops that the American taxpayer in 1962 is paying out more than one billion dollars a year as the total carrying cost of the surplus-food storage program. And is the situation helped when one branch of the Agriculture Department tries to reduce production while another states, as it did in 1958, "It is believed generally that reduction of crop acreages under provisions of the Soil Bank will stimulate interest in use of chemicals to obtain maximum production on the land retained in crops."

All this is not to say there is no insect problem and no need of control. I am saying, rather, that control must be geared to realities, not to mythical situations, and that the methods employed must be such that they do not destroy us along with the insects.

The problem whose attempted solution has brought such a train of disaster in its wake is an accompaniment of our modern way of life. Long before the age of man, insects inhabited the earth—a group of extraordinarily varied and adaptable beings. Over the course of time since man's advent, a small percentage of the more than half a million species of insects have come into conflict with human welfare in two principal ways: as competitors for the food supply and as carriers of human disease.

Disease-carrying insects become important where human beings are crowded together, especially under conditions where sanitation is poor, as in time of natural disaster or war or in situations of extreme poverty and deprivation. Then control of some sort becomes necessary. It is a sobering fact, however, as we shall presently see, that the method of massive chemical control has had only limited success, and also threatens to worsen the very conditions it is intended to curb.

Under primitive agricultural conditions the farmer had few insect problems. These arose with the intensification of agriculture—the devotion of immense acreages to a single crop. Such a system set the stage for explosive increases in specific insect populations. Single-crop farming does not take advantage of the principles by which nature works; it is agriculture as an engineer might conceive it to be. Nature has introduced great variety into the landscape, but man has displayed a passion for simplifying it. Thus he undoes the built-in checks and balances by which nature holds the species within bounds. One important natural check is a limit on the amount of suitable habitat for each species. Obviously then, an insect that lives on wheat can build up its population to much higher levels on a farm devoted to wheat than on one in which wheat is intermingled with other crops to which the insect is not adapted.

The same thing happens in other situations. A generation or more ago, the towns of large areas of the United States lined their streets with the noble elm tree. Now the beauty they hopefully created is threatened with complete destruction as disease sweeps through the elms, carried by a beetle that would have only limited chance to build up large populations and to spread from tree to tree if the elms were only occasional trees in a richly diversified planting.

Another factor in the modern insect problem is one that must be viewed against a background of geologic and human history: the spreading of thousands of different kinds of organisms from their native homes to invade new territories. This worldwide migration has been studied and graphically described by the British ecologist Charles Elton in his recent book *The Ecology of Invasions*. During the Cretaceous Period, some hundred million years ago, flooding seas cut many land bridges between continents and living things found themselves confined in what Elton calls "colossal separate nature reserves." There, isolated from others of their kind, they developed many new species. When some of the land masses were joined again, about 15 million years ago, these species began to move out into new territories—a movement that is not only still in progress but is now receiving considerable assistance from man.

The importation of plants is the primary agent in the modern spread of species, for animals have almost invariably gone along with the plants, quarantine being a comparatively recent and not completely effective innovation. The United States Office of Plant Introduction alone has introduced almost 200,000 species and varieties of plants from all over the world. Nearly half of the 180 or so major insect enemies of plants in the United States are accidental imports from abroad, and most of them have come as hitchhikers on plants.

In new territory, out of reach of the restraining hand of the natural enemies that kept down its numbers in its native land, an invading plant or animal is able to become enormously abundant. Thus it is no accident that our most troublesome insects are introduced species.

These invasions, both the naturally occurring and those dependent on human assistance, are likely to continue indefinitely. Quarantine and massive chemical campaigns are only extremely expensive ways of buying time. We are faced, according to Dr. Elton, "with a life-and-death need not just to find new technological means of suppressing this plant or that animal"; instead we need the basic knowledge of animal populations and their relations to their surroundings that will "promote an even balance and damp down the explosive power of outbreaks and new invasions."

Much of the necessary knowledge is now available but we do not use it. We train ecologists in our universities and even employ them in our governmental agencies but we seldom take their advice. We allow the chemical death rain to fall as though there were no alternative, whereas in fact there are many, and our ingenuity could soon discover many more if given opportunity.

Have we fallen into a mesmerized state that makes us accept as inevitable that which is inferior or detrimental, as though having lost the will or the vision to demand that which is good? Such thinking, in the words of the ecologist Paul Shepard, "idealizes life with only its head out of water, inches above the limits of toleration of the corruption of its own environment . . . Why should we tolerate a diet of weak poisons, a home in insipid surroundings, a circle of acquaintances who are not quite our enemies, the noise of motors with just enough relief to prevent insanity? Who would want to live in a world which is just not quite fatal?"

Yet such a world is pressed upon us. The crusade to create a chemically sterile, insect-free world seems to have engendered a fanatic zeal on the part of many specialists and most of the so-called control agencies. On every hand there is evidence that those engaged in spraying operations exercise a ruthless power. "The regulatory entomologists . . . function as prosecutor, judge and jury, tax assessor and collector and sheriff to enforce their own orders," said Connecticut entomologist Neely Turner. The most flagrant abuses go unchecked in both state and federal agencies.

It is not my contention that chemical insecticides must never be used. I do contend that we have put poisonous and biologically potent chemicals indiscriminately into the hands of persons largely or wholly ignorant of their potentials for harm. We have subjected enormous numbers of people to contact with these poisons, without their consent and often without their knowledge. If the Bill of Rights contains no guarantee that a citizen shall be secure against lethal poisons distributed either by private individuals or by public officials, it is surely only because our forefathers, despite their considerable wisdom and foresight, could conceive of no such problem.

I contend, furthermore, that we have allowed these chemicals to be used with little or no advance investigation of their effect on soil, water, wildlife, and man himself. Future generations are unlikely to condone our lack of prudent concern for the integrity of the natural world that supports all life.

There is still very limited awareness of the nature of the threat. This is an era of specialists, each of whom sees his own problem and is unaware of or intolerant of the larger frame into which it fits. It is also an era dominated by industry, in which the right to make a dollar at whatever cost is seldom challenged. When the public protests, confronted with some obvious evidence of damaging results of pesticide applications, it is fed little tranquilizing pills of half truth. We urgently need an end to these false assurances, to the sugar coating of unpalatable facts. It is the public that is being asked to assume the risks that the insect controllers calculate. The public must decide whether it wishes to continue on the present road, and it can do so only when in full possession of the facts. In the words of Jean Rostand, "The obligation to endure gives us the right to know."

38

Al Gore

Earth in the Balance:
Ecology and the Human Spirit (1992)

Former vice president Al Gore (b. 1948) began to pursue environmental issues when he served as a freshman congressman on the Oversight and Investigations Subcommittee of the House Commerce Committee. Those investigations of hazardous chemical waste dumping led to the Superfund Law, and hearings he later chaired on global warming brought the issue international attention. He was reelected to three terms in the House of Representatives and then to the U.S. Senate. He served as vice president under President Bill Clinton for two terms but failed in his bid for the presidency in the 2000 election. His book Earth in the Balance *is based on political experience, scientific knowledge, and recognition that human survival depends on our relation to nature.*

Eco-nomics: Truth or Consequences

FREE MARKET CAPITALIST economics is arguably the most powerful tool ever used by civilization. As a system for allocating resources, labor, finance, and taxation, for determining the production, distribution, and consumption of wealth, and for directing decisions about virtually every aspect of our lives together, classical economics reigns supreme. Its laws are so pervasive that we take them largely for granted, like the laws of motion and gravity—which, incidentally, were codified by Sir Isaac Newton at the beginning of the Scientific Revolution, only a few decades before Adam Smith codified the major principles that still underlie economics today.

Rival systems, like communism, have been unable to compete in the marketplace of ideas. Although communism failed in large part because it suffocated political freedom, its parallel assault on economic freedom was its real undoing. Indeed, the stunning collapse of the Soviet Union and its empire in Eastern Europe has been due in large part to the perception on both sides of the Iron Curtain that capitalism, because it better incorporates classical economic theory, is simply superior to communism in theory and practice.

And indeed it is. But capitalism's recent triumph over communism should lead those of us who believe in it to do more than merely indulge in self-congratulation. We should instead recognize that the victory of the West—precisely because it means the rest of the world is now more likely to adopt our system—imposes upon us a new and even deeper obligation to address the shortcomings of capitalist economics as it is now practiced.

The hard truth is that our economic system is partially blind. It "sees" some things and not others. It carefully measures and keeps track of the value of those things most important to buyers and sellers, such as food, clothing, manufactured goods, work, and, indeed, money itself. But its intricate calculations often completely ignore the value of other things that are harder to buy and sell: fresh water, clean air, the beauty of the mountains, the rich diversity of life in the forest, just to name a few. In fact, the partial blindness of our current economic system is the single most powerful force behind what seem to be irrational decisions about the global environment.

Fortunately, these shortcomings can be fixed—albeit with great difficulty. The first step is recognizing that economics, like any tool, distorts our relationship to the world even as it gives us impressive new powers. Because we come to rely so completely on the capabilities conferred by our economic system, we adapt our thinking to its contours and begin to assume that our economic theory can provide a comprehensive analysis of whatever we wish it to interpret.

However, just as our eyes fail to see all but a narrow portion of the light spectrum, our economics fails to see—let alone measure—the full value of major parts of our world. Indeed, what we do see and measure is a very thin band within the full spectrum of the costs and benefits from our economic choices. And in both cases, what is out of sight is out of mind.

Much of what we don't see with our economics involves the accelerating destruction of the environment. Many popular textbooks on economic theory fail even to address subjects as basic to our economic choices as pollution or the depletion of natural resources. Although these issues have been studied by many microeconomists in specific business contexts, they have generally not been integrated into economic theory. "There is no point of contact between macroeconomics and the environment," says the World Bank economist Herman Daly, a leading student of the problem.

Consider the most basic measure of a nation's economic performance, gross national product (GNP). In calculating GNP, natural resources are not depreciated as they are used up. Buildings and factories are depreciated; so are machinery and equipment, cars and trucks. So why, for instance, isn't the topsoil in Iowa depreciated when it washes down the Mississippi River after careless agricultural methods have lessened its ability to resist wind and rain? Why isn't that loss measured as an economic cost of the process by which our grain was produced last year? If the rate of topsoil loss is high enough in a given year, the nation may end up poorer, even when the value of the grain produced is taken into account. Meanwhile, our economic reports will assure us that, to the contrary, we are richer for having grown the grain, and richer still because we didn't spend the money required to grow it in an ecologically sound manner and thus keep the topsoil from washing away. This is now more than economic theory: largely because we failed to see the value of growing grain in an ecologically sound manner, we have lost more than half of all the topsoil in Iowa.

There are thousands of other examples. Here is one: the heavy use of pesticides may ensure that the grain we grow achieves the highest possible short-term profits, but the careless and excessive use of pesticides poisons the groundwater reservoirs beneath the field. When we add up the costs and benefits of growing the grain, the loss of that freshwater resource will be ignored. And largely because we have failed to measure the economic value of clean, fresh groundwater, we have contaminated more than half of all the underground reservoirs in the United States with pesticide runoff and other poisonous residues that are virtually impossible to remove.

Or take another situation, one a little farther from home. When an underdeveloped nation cuts down a million acres of tropical rain forest in a single year, the money received from the sale of the logs is counted as part of that country's income for the year. The wear and tear on the chain saws and logging trucks as a result of a year's work in the rain forest will be entered on the expense side of the ledger, but the wear and tear on the forest itself will not. In fact, nowhere in the calculation of that country's GNP will there be an entry reflecting the stark reality that a million acres of rain forest is now gone. This ought to strike anyone as alarming, if not absurd. Yet when the World Bank, the International Monetary Fund, regional development banks, and national lending authorities decide what kinds of loans and monetary assistance to give countries around the world, they base their decisions on how a loan might improve the recipients' economic performance. And for all these institutions, the single most important measure of progress in economic performance is the movement of GNP. For all practical purposes, GNP treats the rapid and reckless destruction of the environment as a good thing!

Robert Repetto, an economist at the World Resources Institute, has led a team that studied the effects of this distortion in national income accounting on the development pattern of Indonesia. That nation's net losses of forest resources now exceed timber harvests: so much topsoil has eroded that the net value of the timber crop has been reduced by approximately 40 percent. Yet while this economic tragedy was unfolding and Indonesia was racing toward the precipice, the official economic reports all showed a rosy picture of steady progress.

Recently I asked the United Nations officials responsible for periodically revising the definition of GNP why this blindness is allowed to remain in our methods of calculation. The definition of GNP and other key yardsticks of economic performance are reviewed by the world community under the aegis of the United Nations every twenty years. And economists like Daly, Repetto, Robert Costanza of the University of Maryland, and others have long urged the changes I was recommending. The officials, who were then beginning their review procedures for this twenty-year cycle, acknowledged the good sense of these changes but claimed it would be difficult and inconvenient to make them now. "Perhaps at the next review," they said—twenty years from now.

What a striking contrast between the awesome power and efficiency our economic system displayed in its philosophical rout of Marxism-Leninism and the abject failure of the very same system to even take note of the poisoning of our water, the fouling of our air, the destruction of tens of thousands of living species every year. We make billions of economic choices every day, and the consequences are bringing us steadily closer to the brink of ecological catastrophe.

Classical economists like to argue that all participants in the struggle between supply and demand have "perfect information"—that everyone who makes an economic choice within this all-powerful, all encompassing framework of calculation can safely be presumed to know all of the facts surrounding and supporting their choices, even if marginal errors of judgment are allowed. The logical extension of "perfect information" is what classical economists call the market-clearing feature of the economic system, which they also assume to be perfect. This notion is best illustrated by the famous story in which an elderly man is walking down the sidewalk with his young granddaughter when she notices a $20 bill and starts to pick it up. "No, no," says the grandfather, stopping the little girl's hand in midair. "If there was a $20 bill there on the sidewalk, it would already be gone. It can't be real."

Such theories border on intellectual arrogance, especially in light of the inability of classical economics to deal with the idea of accounting for lost natural resources. Just as our current system of economics makes absurd and unrealistic assumptions about the information actually available to real people in the real world, it insists upon equally absurd assumptions that natural resources are limitless "free goods."

This assumption stems in part from the fact that the system of national income accounts was established by John Maynard Keynes before the end of the colonial era, during which supplies of natural resources did indeed seem limitless. In fact, it is not entirely coincidental that much of the worst environmental devastation today is taking place in countries that have emerged from their colonial status only in the last generation. Patterns of abusive exploitation of the environment have a momentum that is difficult to reverse—especially if the prevailing economic assumptions were set in place by those who were primarily interested in removing the natural resources from these countries.

Accounting blindness is not limited to the valuation of products alone, however. According to the First Law of Thermodynamics, neither matter nor energy can be either created or destroyed; natural resources, therefore, are transformed into both useful products, called goods, and harmful by-products, including what we sometimes call pollution. Not surprisingly, our economic system measures the efficiency of production, or "productivity," in a way that keeps better track of the good things we produce than the bad. But every production process creates waste; why isn't it accounted for? If a country produces huge amounts of aluminum, for example, why isn't the calcium fluoride sludge, an inevitable by-product, accounted for?

Indeed, improvements in productivity—the single most significant measure of economic "progress"—are currently calculated by a method that embodies yet another absurd assumption: if a new technique has both good and bad consequences, it is permissible, under some circumstances, to measure only the good and simply ignore the bad. When the number of good things produced with each unit of labor, raw materials, and capital go up—usually because somebody has cleverly figured out a "better" way to perform the task at hand—then productivity is said to increase. But what if the clever new process results not only in the increased production of good things but also in an even larger increase in the number of bad things? Shouldn't that count? After all, it may cost a lot of money to deal with the consequences of the extra bad things.

And the absurdity doesn't stop here. Later, when expenditures are required to clean up the pollution, they are usually included in the national accounts as another positive entry on the ledger. In other words, the more pollution we create, the more productive contributions we can make to national output. The *Exxon Valdez* oil spill in Prince William Sound, and efforts to clean it up, to take one example, actually increased our GNP.

Classical economics also fails to account properly for all the costs associated with what we call consumption. Every time we consume something, some sort of waste is created, but this fact is conveniently forgotten by classical economists. When we consume millions of tons of chlorofluorocarbons (CFCs) each year, are they gone? If so, then what is eating the hole in the ozone layer? When we consume 14 million tons of coal each day and 64 million barrels of oil, are they gone? If so, where is all the extra carbon dioxide (CO_2) in the atmosphere coming from?

None of these hidden costs is accounted for properly; indeed, the way our economic system measures productivity doesn't make sense *even within the logic of the system itself.* It is almost as if the ultrarational "economic man" of classical theory actually believes in magic. If our economic goods are produced from natural resources that never have to be depreciated because their supply is limitless, if the production process leaves no unwanted by-products whatsoever, and if our products disappear without a trace when they are consumed, then we are witnessing powerful magic indeed.

I remember as a young child sitting with my father in his office while a man who appeared perfectly rational explained in detail his plans for a machine that would transform lead into gold. I suspected my father of being kinder and more patient than he might otherwise have been in order to give me the opportunity to hear one of the last alchemists on earth. In fact, however, alchemists are anything but an endangered species, because when we pretend to consume goods and resources, we are actually transforming them into a different chemical and physical substance. It is industrial alchemy of a very dangerous form. And at some point, the hidden costs of this alchemy will have to be paid.

Classical economics defines productivity narrowly and encourages us to equate gains in productivity with economic progress. But the Holy Grail of progress is so alluring that economists tend to overlook the bad side effects that often accompany improvements. The problem is, of course, they almost always go together, and wisdom requires balancing the good against the bad to determine whether the overall result is positive or negative. If we measure the value of what we do and consistently ignore important side effects, we will continue to set ourselves up for nasty surprises. When a "new" environmental catastrophe is discovered, for instance, we can often look back and see an accumulation of thousands of seemingly defensible but poorly thought-out decisions, all made according to criteria that do not themselves make any sense when all of the costs and risks are balanced against the benefits. Why weren't the consequences considered ahead of time? The answer lies in our economic system's ability to conceal the ill effects of many choices by resorting to an intellectual device labeled "externalities."

The bad things economists want to ignore while they measure the good things are often said to be too difficult to integrate into their calculations. After all, the bad things usually cannot be sold to anyone, and the responsibility for dealing with their consequences can often be quietly pushed on to someone else. Therefore, since the effort to keep track of the bad things would complicate the valuation of the good things, the bad things are simply defined away as external to the process and called externalities.

This habit of using an arbitrary definition to exclude inconvenient facts from the calculation of what is good and what is bad is a form of dishonesty. Philosophically, it is similar in some ways to the moral blindness implicit in racism and anti-Semitism—which also use arbitrary definitions to justify exclusions from the calculus of right and wrong. A racist, for example, can be seen as a person who draws a circle of value around himself and those of his own race in order to exclude, by definition, those of other races. The racist then often makes choices that artificially inflate the value of those inside the circle at the expense of those outside. Frequently, there is a direct ratio between the increasing value inside the circle and the decreasing value outside. Both slavery and apartheid are examples of this phenomenon at work.

In much the same way, our current system of economics arbitrarily draws a circle of value around those things in our civilization we have decided to keep track of and measure. Then we discover that one of the easiest ways to artificially increase the value of things inside the circle is to do so at the expense of those things left outside the circle. And here too, a direct and perverse ratio emerges: the more pollution dumped into the river, the higher the short-term profits for the polluter and his shareholders; the faster the rain forest is burned, the quicker more pasture becomes available for cattle and the faster they can be turned into hamburgers. Our failure to measure environmental externalities is a kind of economic blindness, and its consequences can be staggering. A mathematician at the University of British Columbia, Colin Clark, has said, "Much of apparent economic growth may in fact be an illusion based on a failure to account for reduction in natural capital."

Robert Repetto and others have suggested a modest change in the way we calculate productivity as a first step toward taking environmental externalities into consideration. He suggests that we carefully measure both beneficial and damaging products from any process and keep track of changes in both categories before measuring changes in productivity. For example, a coal-fired power station produces both kilowatt-hours of electricity and tons of atmospheric pollution. It is easy to evaluate the economic significance of the electricity because it is sold. But it is also possible to evaluate at least some of the economic significance of the atmospheric emissions. Sulfur oxides cause crop losses downwind from the power station, along with materials damage, visibility losses, and medical bills for the treatment of respiratory distress. A great deal of work has gone into calculating the real cost of the effects associated with each additional ton of sulfur dioxide emissions. So far, these valuations are a lot less precise than the values established by the market for electricity. Still, that difficulty ought not to be used as a convenient excuse for asserting that the cost should be placed at zero; there is a well-accepted and agreed-upon range, and some value within that range could and should be used in calculating the costs and benefits of each ton of coal burned.

Coal-burning power stations also provide a good illustration of a related point. When a new law like the Clean Air Act is passed, requiring a reduction in sulfur dioxides, we are told that the productivity of coal-fired power stations will go down—based on a calculation that completely ignores the savings that will result from the lower expenditures to deal with the consequences of pollution every time a ton of coal is burned. Even if we changed the calculation of productivity only enough to include those economic impacts of pollution for which we already have accepted values, we would be that much closer to an accurate definition of true gains or losses.

Past a certain point, however, it is impossible to put a price on the environmental effect of our economic choices. Clean air, fresh water, the sun rising through the mist on a mountain lake, an abundance of life on the land, in the air, and in the sea—the value of these things is incalculable. It would be cynical indeed to conclude that because such treasures have no price, it is reasonable to make decisions based on the assumption that they are worthless. As Oscar Wilde said, "A cynic is one who knows the price of everything and the value of nothing."

In drawing a circle of value around those things we consider important enough to measure in our economic system, we not only exclude a great deal that is important in the environment, we also discriminate against future generations. The accepted formulas of conventional economic analysis contain shortsighted and arguably illogical assumptions about what is valuable in the future as opposed to the present; specifically, the standard "discount rate" that assesses cost and benefit flows resulting from the use or development of natural resources routinely assumes that all resources belong totally to the present generation. As a result, any value that they may have to future generations is heavily "discounted" when compared to the value of using them up now or destroying them to make way for something else. The effect is to magnify the power of one generation to compromise all future generations. In the words of Herman Daly, "There is something fundamentally wrong in treating the earth as if it were a business in liquidation."

In 1972 the Bruntland Commission, established by the United Nations to examine the connection between economic development and protection of the environment, focused our attention on the need for "intergenerational equity"—an insistence that decisions by the present generation be made with an awareness of their impact on future generations. Although this phrase has become a fixture in the rhetoric about the environment, it is not yet reflected in the way our economic system measures the effect of our decisions in the real world. As a result, we continue to act as if it is perfectly all right to use up as many natural resources in our own lifetime as we possibly can.

The current debate over sustainable development is based on the widespread recognition that many investments by major financial institutions, such as the World Bank, have stimulated economic development in the Third World by encouraging the short-term exploitation of natural resources, thus emphasizing short-term cash flow at the expense of longer-term, sustainable growth. This pattern has prevailed both because of a tendency to discount the future value of natural resources and because of a failure to properly depreciate their value as they are used up in the present.

This partial blindness in the way we account for the impact of our decisions on the natural world is also a major obstacle to our efforts to formulate sensible responses to the strategic threats now facing the environment. Typically, we cite hugely inflated estimates of the expense involved in changing our current policies, with no analysis whatsoever of the expense associated with the impact of the changes that will occur if we do nothing.

For example, the loss of 75 percent of California's annual moisture has long been predicted by some climatologists as a consequence of global warming. Yet because the scale of the problem is so large, no one seems to even consider including the cost of the water shortage in California in our calculation of the benefits of an aggressive program to counter global warming. We should also calculate the costs of doing nothing, because the consequences of the seven-year drought are already staggering and may get worse. One of the lesser costs came to my attention as chairman of the Senate subcommittee that oversees NASA, and it illustrates my point perfectly. Early in 1991, NASA announced that the drought in California had dried up deepwater reservoirs far below the dry lake bed on which the space shuttle lands when it returns from orbit. The six-foot fissures unexpectedly appearing in the surface of the lake bed may eventually pose a threat to the landing strip. If a new landing facility becomes necessary, it will cost a lot of money. It seems only fair that this new landing strip be included on the expense side of the ledger in calculating the costs of doing nothing to counter global warming. (When I suggested that this new expense be added to the Office

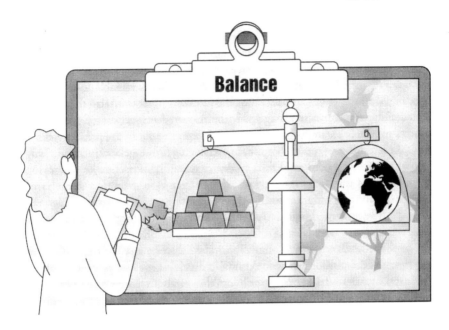

of Management and Budget's analysis, they said, "You've got to be kidding." "Only partly," I responded.)

But the problem goes far beyond our response to the drought in California. In many ways, the Bush administration's entire cost-benefit analysis is misguided and reflects an apparent inability to see the magnitude of the environmental crisis. Thus far, the administration has been blind to the true value of preserving the environment while keenly aware—like Oscar Wilde's cynic—of the price. When President Bush welcomed an international conference on the global environment in the spring of 1990, his staff prepared materials for the visiting negotiators that contained a graphic illustration of the administration's approach to balancing short-term monetary gains against long-term environmental destruction. In the illustration, several bars of gold rested on one tray of a scale; on the other tray perched the entire earth and all its natural systems, seemingly with a weight and value roughly equivalent to the six bars of gold. A scientist, or perhaps an economist, is noting the careful balance on her clipboard. Although several delegates from other countries commented privately that it seemed to be an ironic symbol of Bush's approach to the crisis, the president and his staff seemed wholly oblivious of the absurdity of their willingness to place the entire earth in the balance.

Some of America's best corporations are doing a much better job of responding creatively to the crisis. Those that have made a strong commitment to environmental responsibility have found, to their surprise, that when they start to "see" their pollution and look for ways to minimize it, they begin to "see" new ways to cut down on their use of expensive raw materials and new ways to improve efficiency in virtually every part of the production process. Some of these companies have also reported that this new attentiveness to each stage of production has also resulted in a sharp reduction in product defects. For example, the 3M company credits its Pollution Prevention Pays program with major improvements in profits; Xerox and several other companies have reported the same experience.

Some companies are trying to guess whether the new public awareness of the environment is temporary or permanent. Major paper mills, for example, facing a round of investment in new capacity, must decide whether the current interest in recycled paper is here to stay. If so, then large investments in recycling plants will be profitable; if not, they may face serious risks in making such investments. Such prophecies often tend to be self-fulfilling, of course. But here is where the government can play an important role—and too often has failed to do. The Bush administration talks loudly about the tendency of a free marketplace to solve all problems. But many of our markets are highly regulated, often in hidden ways. In the case of the paper industry, for instance, taxpayers currently subsidize the manufacture of paper products made from virgin timber, both as the largest single purchaser and by further subsidizing the construction of logging roads into national forests. In addition, the federal government pays the entire cost of managing the forest system, including many activities that exclusively benefit the timber industry. All of these policies encourage further destruction of a critical natural resource.

The Bush administration and the entire U.S. government ought to understand the economic significance of a healthy environment as a kind of infrastructure supporting future productivity. If it is destroyed, many jobs now at risk will be lost. A case in point is the heated dispute between the timber industry in the Pacific Northwest and conservationists eager to protect the endangered spotted owl. This issue has been billed as a conflict between jobs and the environment. But if the remaining 10 percent of old-growth forest is logged out, as the timber industry prefers, the jobs will be lost anyway. The only question is whether the effort to create new jobs will begin now or later, after the forest is completely gone.

The current administration also ought to do a much better job of encouraging appropriate technologies, since they can be an important benefit to set against all the costs of environmental degradation. Japan, for example, is already implementing an ambitious plan to cultivate what it believes will be a massive global market for new technologies for renewable energy and environmentally benign processes. Tragically, however, after having developed the first products using wind and solar energy, the United States is now a net importer of both technologies.

There is an Alice-in-Wonderland quality to much of our current approach to economic analysis. Even as we have ignored the consequences for the environment of our present economic decisions, attention has been focused on increasingly frenetic speculation, merger mania, asset shuffling, and a range of other activities largely unrelated to the creation of competitive goods and services. The result is not only a diminished competitive position for the United States in the world economy, but also an acceleration of the trend toward the kind of short-term thinking that will make it harder to formulate a creative and effective response to the environmental crisis.

But it is not yet too late to avert the worst effects of this crisis, and the United States ought to lead the way. Victory in our epic struggle with communism, whose features were infinitely worse—for individuals and for the environment—than anything our economic system has produced, should give us confidence, as well as a sense of obligation, to address the challenges now before us. We must correct the shortcomings in the rules and procedures that guide the millions of daily decisions that are the nerves and sinews of Adam Smith's invisible hand: we must address the deficiencies of our current methods for defining what is progress and what is absurdity.

Some of the changes needed will be relatively simple to implement. Others will be more difficult. But all will require the courage to see things as they are, to avoid deceiving ourselves, to train ourselves to recognize when sophisticated imbecilities are substituted for serious analysis. In 1989, for example, the president's Council of Economic Advisers concluded in its annual report that "there is no justification for imposing major costs on the economy in order to slow the growth of greenhouse gas emissions." Part of the reasoning used to support this conclusion was that "the average temperature differential between New York City and Atlanta is as large as the most extreme predictions of warming yet there is no evidence that Atlanta's warmer climate produces a greater health risk than New York's." But if New York will be as hot as Atlanta, what will Atlanta be like? What will southern California be like? What will the midwestern droughts be like? What changes will occur in the global climate pattern? These questions and others were of course ignored as the political equivalent of externalities.

Years from now, if their policies are followed and global warming causes terrible destruction to the global environment with no serious effort having been made to stop it, members of the Bush administration will no doubt be properly humble and contrite. And it will hardly be the first time that devotion to the convenience of the present has blinded decision-makers to their obligation to prepare for the future. But the time for action is now, and for inspiration we might look back to one of history's most visionary leaders.

On November 12, 1936, Winston Churchill grew so exasperated with the continuing failure of Britain to prepare for Hitler's onslaught that he charged in a speech to the House of Commons: "The Government simply cannot make up their minds, or they cannot get the Prime Minister to make up his mind. So they go on in strange paradox, decided only to be undecided, resolved to be irresolute, adamant for drift, solid for fluidity, all-powerful to be impotent. . . . The era of procrastination, of half-measures, of soothing and baffling expedients, of delays, is coming to its close. In its place we are entering a period of consequences. . . ."

39

Petra Kelly

"Thinking Green!" (1994)

Petra Kelly (1947–1992) was a founder of the West German Green Party (Die Grünen), whose 1983 electoral success brought Green politics international attention. Kelly was speaker for the Green Parliamentary Group, the twenty-eight Green MPs seated in the German Parliament. A supporter of direct action, she participated in civil disobedience for many causes across the globe. Her central political commitments were to peace and nonviolence, ecology, feminism, and human rights. She also founded and chaired an organization to fight childhood cancer, the disease that claimed the life of her ten-year-old sister. "Thinking Green!" articulates her vision of "a movement in which politics means the power to love and the power to feel united. . . ."

"Never doubt that a small group of thoughtful, committed citizens can change the world. Indeed, it's the only thing that ever has."

—Margaret Mead

WHEN WE FOUNDED the West German Green Party, we used the term "anti-party party" to describe our approach to politics based on a new understanding of power, a "counter-power" that is natural and common to all, to be shared by all, and used by all for all. This is the power of transformation, rooted in the discovery of our own strength and ability to be active participants in society. This kind of power stands in stark contrast to the power of domination, terror, and oppression, and is the best remedy for powerlessness.

Reprinted from *Thinking Green! Essays on Environmentalism, Feminism, and Nonviolence* (1994) by Petra K. Kelly with permission of Parallax Press, Berkeley, California, www.parallax.org

Using power to dominate humans and nature has brought us to an impasse and can never take us beyond it. We must learn to think and act from our hearts, to recognize the interconnectedness of all living creatures, and to respect the value of each thread in the vast web of life. This is a spiritual perspective, and it is the foundation of all Green politics. It entails the radical, nonviolent transformation of the structures of society and of our way of thinking, so that domination is no longer the primary *modus operandi*. At the root of all Green political action is nonviolence, starting with how we live our lives, taking small, unilateral steps towards peace in everything we do. Green politics requires us to be both tender and subversive. Affirming tenderness as a political value is already subversive. In Green politics, we practice tenderness in relations with others; in caring for ideas, art, language, and culture; and in cherishing and protecting the Earth.

To think Green is to build solidarity with those working for social justice and human rights everywhere, not bound by ideologies. The problems that threaten life on Earth were produced collectively, they affect us collectively, and we must act collectively to change them. We cannot retreat into isolation. The Green vision of a just society is one in which economic, social, and individual rights are guaranteed and protected, and everyone is free from exploitation, violence, and oppression.

Politicians give speeches about these values while working to undermine them. The benefits of the current political and economic systems are reserved for the privileged; therefore, any meaningful movement for social justice must focus on systemic change, on transforming both the oppressive state and economic structures that concentrate wealth and power in the hands of a few. The Green methodology is not to work from the top down, but to begin at the grassroots, empowering ourselves to direct our own destinies through the cultivation of civil space and democratic social forms.

First and foremost, Green politics is grassroots politics. Politics from the top is almost always corrupt and compromised. To bring about change from below is to challenge the moral authority of those who make decisions on our behalf. Through grassroots organization, education, and empowerment, we work to reverse the state-orientation of politics and instead open up a civil space in which we are active subjects, not passive objects of those in power. Substantive change in politics at the top will come only when there is enough pressure from below. The essence of Green politics is to live our values. We in the West German Green Party hurt ourselves over and over again by failing to maintain tenderness with each other as we gained power. We need to rededicate ourselves to our values, respect each other, be tolerant of differences, and stop trying to coerce and control one another.

Nonviolence, ecology, social justice, and feminism are the key principles of Green politics, and they are inseparably linked. We know, for example, that the wasteful patterns of production and consumption in the industrial North deplete and ravage the environment and furnish the motive and means for the violent appropriation of materials from the weaker nations in the South and for the wasteful process of militarization throughout the world. In both capitalist and state socialist countries, human beings are reduced to economic entities, with little or no regard for the human or ecological costs. Politics from the top, the pattern of hierarchical domination, is the characteristic of patriarchy. It is not a coincidence that power rests in the hands of men, benefits accrue first and foremost to men, and that women are exploited at all levels of society.

The Green approach to politics is a kind of celebration. We recognize that each of us is part of the world's problems, and we are also part of the solution. The dangers and the potentials for healing are not just outside us. We begin to work exactly where we are. There is no need to wait until conditions become ideal. We can simplify our lives and live in ways that affirm ecological and humane values. Better conditions will come because we have begun.

We have found so many ways to think each other to death—neutron warheads, nuclear reactors, Star Wars defense systems, and many other methods of mass destruction. We are killing each other with our euphemisms and abstractions. In warfare, we accept the deaths of thousands and millions of people we call our "enemy." When we dehumanize people, devalue nature, and exalt narrowly defined self-interests, destruction is sure to follow. The healing of our planet requires a new way of thinking about politics and about life. At the heart of this is the understanding that all things are intimately interconnected in the complex web of life. It can therefore be said that the primary goal of Green politics is an inner revolution. Joanna Macy calls this "the greening of the self."[1]

Politics needs spirituality. The profound political changes we need in order to heal our planet will not come about through fragmented problem solving or intellectual analyses that overlook the deepest yearnings and intuitions of the heart. Some of my fellow Greens have maintained their dogmatic leftist perspectives and remain suspicious of spirituality, confusing it with organized religion. I share many of their criticisms of religious institutions, but I firmly disagree with their dismissing spiritual concerns and wisdom. The long work of bringing harmony to the Earth requires a holistic vision based on mature values and deep intuitions.

Today's politics are based on the mechanistic worldview that prefers assertion to integration, analysis over synthesis, rational knowledge over intuitive wisdom, competition over cooperation, and expansionism over conservation. A few new ideas are not enough. We need an entirely new way of thinking. As we begin to cultivate a rich inner life and experience our connection with all of life, we realize how little of what society tells us we need is actually important for our well-being. We must reduce consumption and not cooperate with any practices that harm the natural world or other humans. This is not a sacrifice. It is the way to sustain ourselves.

Green politics must address the spiritual vacuum of industrial society, the alienation that is pervasive in a society where people have grown isolated from nature and from themselves. We in the Greens must also address our own alienation. Our social structures shape this alienation, and they themselves are shaped by it. It is a vicious cycle, and our work of healing must address the whole process. We have forgotten our historical rootedness in an integrated way of life. We must learn from those cultures that have maintained their traditions of wisdom and harmony with nature—Australian Aborigines, American Indians, and others. Tragically, many of these societies are threatened by the same forces that threaten the environment. We must join them in their struggles to preserve their values and traditions.

One such endangered society, Tibet, has been ruthlessly exploited and its people violently oppressed. The exiled leader of the Tibetan people, His Holiness the Dalai Lama, is, for me, a living example of how spiritual vision can influence politics:

> Peace starts within each one of us. When we have inner peace, we can be at peace with those around us. When our community is in a state of peace, it can share that peace with neighboring communities. . . . What is important is that we each make a sincere effort to take seriously our responsibility for each other and for the natural environment.[2]

We have little reason to place our hope in governments or established political parties, for their primary interest is always in extending their own power. But we can find hope in the strength and imagination of people working at the grassroots to create positive change. We Greens work within the political system solely for the benefit and empowerment of those at the grassroots. Our efforts within the halls of government are not to replace work at the grassroots. Our commitments are, first and foremost, to those who elected us. We must work with them, nonviolently, for life-affirming solutions to the problems of our day.

Green politics is based on direct democracy—our effort is to redefine and reorganize power so that it flows from the bottom up. We seek to decentralize power and maximize the freedom and self-determination of individuals, communities, and societies. This means moving power out of the hands of centralized bureaucracies—above all, the military-industrial complex—and empowering people on the local level. It also means reaching across national borders and ideologies to build alliances with others also working for peace and ecology. It means moving government power away from the state towards smaller and smaller units of organization. In economics, grassroots democracy means a production system that maximizes workers' self-management and minimizes corporate or government control. It means units of production scaled to a comprehensible human dimension and that are locally responsive and globally responsible. The day may come when the Greens find a truly democratic and ecological partner among the established political parties, but until then, we must work in government as an anti-party party, an experiment in radical parliamentary opposition unwilling to compromise fundamental values for the sake of expediency.

Thinking green—to think with the heart—is the solution to many if not all of our political dead-ends. To continue increasing production, consumption, and the depletion of our natural resources will only lead us further down the path of suffering. Albert Einstein said that with the splitting of the atom everything changed except the way people think. A new way of thinking must come soon, or the damage will be irreparable. Means and ends cannot be separated. "There is no way to peace. Peace is the way."[3]

NOTES

1. Joanna Macy, *World as Lover, World as Self* (Berkeley: Parallax Press, 1991), p. 183.

2. The Dalai Lama, "The Nobel Peace Prize Lecture," in *A Policy of Kindness* (Ithaca: Snow Lion Publications, 1990), p. 19.

3. A. J. Muste, *The Essays of A. J. Muste,* edited by Nat Hentoff (New York: Simon & Schuster, 1970).

40

Murray Bookchin and Dave Foreman

Defending the Earth: A Dialogue Between Murray Bookchin and Dave Foreman (1991)

Murray Bookchin (b. 1921), the American-born child of Russian immigrants active in the Bolshevik revolution, began his political organizing in the 1930s with the Spanish Civil War. His politics has evolved from orthodox Marxist to left-libertarian. He is the founder of the Vermont-based Institute for Social Ecology, author of numerous books on anarchism, ecology, and technology. His ideas have influenced the international green movement and the American Green Party. He is currently semiretired, and lives in Burlington, Vermont.

Dave Foreman (b. 1947) is a founder of Earth First!—a radical environmental group known for its "monkeywrenching" tactics, including "spiking" trees to protect them from logging. Foreman has published Ecodefense: A Field Guide to Monkeywrenching *(1985) and* Confessions of an Eco-Warrior *(1991), both defenses of ecotage, a form of sabotage, on behalf of the environment. Arrested on felony charges in 1989 and accused of tactics that risk injuring people, he pleaded guilty, received a suspended sentence, and continues to organize for Mother Earth.*

Murray Bookchin and Dave Foreman, "Looking for Common Ground," in *Defending the Earth, A Dialogue Between Murray Bookchin and Dave Foreman,* ed., Steve Chase (Boston, MA: South End Press, 1991).

Chapter 1 Looking for Common Ground

Murray Bookchin:

I HAVE BEEN a social activist for over 55 years. I was a radical labor union organizer in the 1930s and 1940s, and I was deeply involved in the civil rights movement, the New Left, and the countercultural movement of the 1960s and 1970s. I have also been a longtime activist in the ecology movement. I am pleased, for example, that Roderick Nash set the record straight in his book *The Rights of Nature* by pointing out that I was on the ecological battlefront a long time ago, well before the word "ecology" was even widely used.

Most people do not know that I was on the ecological frontlines as far back as 1952. At that time, I opposed the use of pesticides and additives in food. In 1954, I campaigned against nuclear testing and fallout. I protested the radioactive pollution problems of the "peaceful atom" that became public with the Windscale nuclear reactor incident in Great Britain in 1956 and then later when Con Edison attempted to construct the world's largest nuclear reactor in the very heart of New York City in 1963. Since then, I have been active in anti-nuke alliances such as Clamshell and Shad and their predecessors such as Ecology Action East. More recently, I've done what I can as a member of the Burlington Greens in Vermont and I have helped start a continental Left Green Network that works within the Green Committees of Correspondence. My goal has long been to help build a genuinely radical North American green movement that will harmonize the relationships among human beings and between society and the biosphere.

However, I have never limited my efforts to activism and organizing. I have had a long and vital concern with ecological philosophy and social theory. I do not think it is possible to overestimate the value of thinking insightfully and creatively about defending the Earth. We need ideas, good ideas, to guide our activist work. That is what we have always emphasized at the Institute for Social Ecology which I cofounded in 1974 with Dan Chodorkoff, and which is still going strong today.

In the book by Roderick Nash I just mentioned, Nash maintains that I have "few equals" when it comes to "time spent laboring in the trenches of radical environmental theory."[1] I like to think that this is true. Without sounding too immodest, I have been on the "frontline" of green political thought. Since 1952, I have written over thirteen books on social/ecological theory, including *Our Synthetic Environment*, which came out six months before Rachel Carson's *Silent Spring, Toward An Ecological Society, The Ecology of Freedom, The Modern Crisis,* and, most recently, *Remaking Society: Pathways to a Green Future.* I have also taught over 2,000 students at the Institute and have traveled and lectured widely.

So I urge people: when you feel that you want to be critical of my ideas, and I think that you should, please be good enough to read my writings and listen to what I have to say. I'm getting a lot of critical stuff right now from the academic professorial crowd in which people are criticizing me on the basis of only one or two articles and sometimes even hearsay. I am not asking you to read *all* of my stuff, just enough to make a responsible assessment and criticism.

If people do read my work, they will discover that besides having been a labor organizer in foundries and auto plants in a number of big industrial cities, besides having been a revolutionary leftist for over 55 years, I share a good deal of the ecological state of mind of my conservation friends in Earth First!. Does that surprise people? Frankly, I see eye to eye with the activists of Earth First! on a large number of things. In many ways, I think they and Dave Foreman are doing a wonderful job. I feel a very keen sympathy for their many direct-action campaigns to protect wilderness. They are not terrorists as the FBI would have you believe. They are doing important work, work I strongly support.

While support for wilderness preservation is peppered throughout my writings, people may not realize that I am a "wilderness freak." I have not spent all my time on picket lines, in meetings, in my office, or in libraries. My passion for wilderness areas, for wildlife, is a lifelong passion. From my childhood onward, when the Bronx still had some stands of original forest, I loved exploring the wild world. I've been to almost every national forest and every national park in the United States and many in Europe, from the Olympics and the Smokeys to the Black Forest in Germany. I've picked up the Appalachian Trail as far north as Vermont, and as far south as Tennessee. I've hiked it everywhere in between. I couldn't stop heading for the Ramapo Mountains every single weekend for the greater part of two years when I taught in New Jersey. I love those mountains dearly.

Some of the greatest moments in my life have been hiking deep into forest areas in winter alone, where if I so much as sprained my ankle I would freeze to death. My greatest regret now that I am 70 and suffer from a severe case of osteoarthritis is that I can no longer hike in the wilderness. Today, I have to be a more distant admirer. I would physically stand shoulder to shoulder with everyone in Earth First! to defend wild areas if I could. On this score, there is no opposition between Dave Foreman and myself, none whatsoever!

Our society has got to learn to live in peace with the planet, with the rest of the biosphere. We are in complete agreement on this fundamental point. We now live under the constant threat that the world of life will be irrevocably undermined by a society gone mad in its need to grow—replacing the organic by the inorganic, soil by concrete, forest by barren earth, and the diversity of life-forms by simplified ecosystems; in short, by turning back the evolutionary clock to an earlier, more inorganic, mineralized world that is incapable of supporting complex life-forms of any kind, including the human species. The entire world of life, including those few but wonderful wild places that remain, must be protected. Indeed, wild areas must be expanded. Dave and I have no disagreement on this.

I also agree that we need to promote a rational solution to the human population problem. The world's human population needs to be brought into a workable equilibrium with the "carrying capacity" of the planet. Sooner or later, the mindless proliferation of human beings will have to be dealt with. It is absolutely essential, however, that we first clearly identify what we mean by terms like "overpopulation" and "carrying capacity."

This is where the thinking of some deep ecologists frightens me. We need an understanding of the problem that has nothing to do with gas chambers and racism. I know what it means to face the brunt of a "population control" program. All my relatives in Europe are dead. They were murdered in the Nazi Holocaust. They were slaughtered in the name of a "population problem." For Hitler, the world would be overpopulated if just one Jew was left alive.

I've never believed that people in Earth First! are fascists. I am afraid, however, of certain positions and statements, the tendency of which remind me of things I heard fifty years ago when there was a world-wide fascist movement that used "naturalistic" Malthusian arguments to justify racist population control policies. This abuse of the "overpopulation" issue is not just a distant historical issue, either. The abuse of the population issue is ongoing. Just look at what the Rockefeller crowd is trying to do in the Third World. It is a remarkably dangerous question which has to be carefully and rationally discussed if we are to resist racism, sexism, and genocide. Even deep ecologists like Warwick Fox agree that it is "monstrous" to talk of AIDS as a population control measure or, in the name of "letting nature seek its balance," refusing to aid starving children in Ethiopia.[2]

So I ask all of you, everyone in the ecology movement, to please be careful about the population problem. This is a hot issue; a very hot issue. Don't kid yourselves about the objectives of many of those who talk of population control. I went through the 1930s. We paid the price of sixty million lives back then as the result of a racist, imperialist war and mass extermination policy. This sort of thing is not radical ecology. We have to explore this matter carefully and respect the very reasonable fears of women and people of color who have been victimized by population control programs in the past. We have to explore what a humane and ecologically sound solution is. It is important that we unscramble what constitutes the social aspects of the problem from the purely biological ones and to understand how these two aspects of the problem interact with each other. Please, let us be careful. Can we agree on this?

Let me move on to another concern. The ultimate moral appeal of Earth First! is that it urges us to safeguard the natural world from our ecologically destructive societies, that is, in some sense, from ourselves. But, I have to ask, who is this "us" from which the living world has to be protected? This, too, is an important question. Is it "humanity?" Is it the human "species" *per se*? Is it people, as such? Or is it our particular society, our particular civilization, with its hierarchical social relations which pit men against women, privileged whites against people of color, elites against masses, employers against workers, the First World against the Third World, and, ultimately, a cancer-like, "grow or die" industrial capitalist economic system against the natural world and other life-forms? Is this not the social root of the popular belief that nature is a mere object of social domination, valuable only as a "resource?"

All too often we are told by liberal environmentalists, and not a few deep ecologists, that it is "we" as a species or, at least, "we" as an amalgam of "anthropocentric" individuals that are responsible for the breakdown of the web of life. I remember an "environmental" presentation staged by the Museum of Natural History in New York during the 1970s in which the public was exposed to a long series of exhibits, each depicting examples of pollution and ecological disruption. The exhibit which closed the presentation carried a startling sign, "The Most Dangerous Animal on Earth." It consisted simply of a huge mirror which reflected back the person who stood in front of it. I remember a black child standing in front of that mirror while a white school teacher tried to explain the message which this arrogant exhibit tried to convey. Mind you, there was no exhibit of corporate boards of directors planning to deforest a mountainside or of government officials acting in collusion with them.

One of the problems with this asocial, "species-centered" way of thinking, of course, is that it blames the victim. Let's face it, when you say a black kid in Harlem is as much to blame for the ecological crisis as the President of Exxon, you are letting one off the hook and slandering the other. Such talk by environmentalists makes grassroots coalition-building next to impossible. Oppressed people know that humanity is hierarchically organized around complicated divisions that are ignored only at their peril. Black people know this well when they confront whites. The poor know this well when they confront the wealthy. The Third World knows it well when it confronts the First World. Women know it well when they confront patriarchal males. The radical ecology movement needs to know it too.

All this loose talk of "we" masks the reality of social power and social institutions. It masks the fact that the social forces that are tearing down the planet are the same social forces which threaten to degrade women, people of color, workers, and ordinary citizens. It masks the fact that there is a historical connection between the way people deal with each other as social beings and the way they treat the rest of nature. It masks the fact that our ecological problems are fundamentally social problems requiring fundamental social change. That is what I mean by *social* ecology. It makes a big difference in how societies relate to the natural world whether people live in cooperative, non-hierarchical, and decentralized communities or in hierarchical, class-ridden, and authoritarian mass societies. Similarly, the ecological impact of human reason, science, and technology depends enormously on the type of society in which these forces are shaped and employed.

Perhaps the biggest question that all wings of the radical ecology movement must satisfactorily answer is just what do we mean by "nature." If we are committed to defending nature, it is important to clearly understand what we mean by this. Is nature, the real world, essentially the remnants of the Earth's pre-human and pristine biosphere that has now been vastly reduced and poisoned by the "alien" presence of the human species? Is nature what we see when we look out on an unpeopled vista from a mountain? Is it a cosmic arrangement of beings frozen in a moment of eternity to be abjectly revered, adored, and untouched by human intervention? Or is nature much broader in meaning? Is nature an evolutionary process which is cumulative and which *includes* human beings?

The ecology movement will get nowhere unless it understands that the human species is no less a product of natural evolution than blue-green algae, whales, and bears. To conceptually separate human beings and society from nature by viewing humanity as an inherently unnatural force in the world leads, philosophically, either to an anti-nature "anthropocentrism" or a misanthropic aversion to the human species. Let's face it, such misanthropy does surface within certain ecological circles. Even Arne Naess admits that many deep ecologists "talk as if they look upon humans as intruders in wonderful nature."[3]

We are part of nature, a product of a long evolutionary journey. To some degree, we carry the ancient oceans in our blood. To a very large degree we go through a kind of biological evolution as fetuses. It is not alien to natural evolution that a species called human beings has emerged over billions of years which is capable of thinking in sophisticated ways. Our brains and nervous systems did not suddenly spring into existence without long antecedents in natural history. That which we most prize as integral to our humanity—our extraordinary capacity to think on complex conceptual levels—can be traced back to the nerve network of primitive invertebrates, the ganglia of a mollusk, the spinal cord of a fish, the brain of an amphibian, and the cerebral cortex of a primate.

We need to understand that the human species has evolved as a remarkably creative and social life-form that is organized to create a place for itself in the natural world, not only to adapt to the rest of nature. The human species, its different societies, and its enormous powers to alter the environment were not invented by a group of ideologues called "humanists" who decided that nature was "made" to serve humanity and its needs. Humanity's distinct powers have emerged out of eons of evolutionary development and out of centuries of cultural development. These remarkable powers present us, however, with an enormous moral responsibility. We can contribute to the diversity, fecundity, and richness of the natural world—what I call "first nature"—more consciously, perhaps, than any other animal. Or, our societies—"second nature"—can exploit the whole web of life and tear down the planet in a rapacious, cancerous manner.

The future that awaits the world of life ultimately depends upon what kind of society or "second nature" we create. This probably affects, more than any other single factor, how we interact with and intervene in biological or "first nature." And make no mistake about it, the future of "first nature," the primary concern of conservationists, is dependent on the results of this interaction. The central problem we face today is that the social evolution of "second nature" has taken a wrong turn. Society is poisoned. It has been poisoned for thousands of years, from before the Bronze Age. It has been warped by rule by elders, by patriarchy, by warriors, by hierarchies of all sorts which have led now to the current situation of a world threatened by competitive, nuclear-armed, nation-states and a phenomenally destructive corporate capitalist system in the West and an equally ecologically destructive, though now crumbling, bureaucratic state capitalist system in the East.

We need to create an ecologically oriented society out of the present anti-ecological one. If we can change the direction of our civilization's social evolution, human beings can assist in the creation of a truly "free nature," where all of our human traits—intellectual, communicative, and social—are placed at the service of natural evolution to consciously increase biotic diversity, diminish suffering, foster the further evolution of new and ecologically valuable life-forms, and reduce the impact of disastrous accidents or the harsh effects of harmful change. Our species, gifted by the creativity of natural evolution itself, could play the role of nature rendered self-conscious.

Audience Member:

Excuse me, I want to know what you have to say about the technological fix called genetic engineering? I'm hearing other species, other animals, being spoken about by you as subordinate moments in the evolution of human consciousness, the self-consciousness which you call "second nature." It seems to me that if we choose to believe this about other organisms then there is no reason to resist genetically engineering other organisms to suit our wishes. What kind of spiritual perspective does this represent?

Murray Bookchin:

I have some surprising news for you. I don't believe that human beings are lords over nature and that animals and other forms of life are subordinates. I beg you again, please, read what I have written and listen with care to what I have to say. For years, I have advocated an ethics of complementarity. Complementarity, as distinguished from domination, presupposes a new sensibility that respects other forms of life for their own sake and that responds actively in the form of a creative, loving, and supportive symbiosis.

Let me make it very plain. I don't trust the current scientific establishment to invent a toothpick, let alone tinker with bio-engineering. I believe that we have to bring all of this garbage to an end right now. The current social setup means that the scientific establishment is not *morally* capable of dealing with bio-technology. The truth is, given the current structure of technological innovation, it will put almost anything it creates to some kind of malicious and vicious purpose.

I am not advancing a view that approves of "natural engineering." The natural world, as I have stressed repeatedly in my writings, is much too complex to be "controlled" by human ingenuity, science, and technology. My own anarchist proclivities have fostered in my thinking a love of spontaneity, be it in human behavior or in natural development. Natural evolution cannot be denied its own spontaneity and fecundity. That is why one part of our struggle should always be to protect and expand wilderness areas.

Furthermore, let's completely put an end to the claims that I approve of cruelty to animals. Admittedly, I'd like to see a cure, if possible, to cancer, to diseases that cause pain and so on, but believe me, torturing animals in the name of research is monstrous. It has to be stopped. I just saw a documentary about what they do to research animals. It is unspeakable what a man preparing an MA thesis will do to an animal in order to merely prove that the animal feels pain. Do they have to "discover" that? These are great minds at work indeed! The power to torment living beings has to be taken away from researchers. The current state of affairs is horrible.

So understand that at this moment, where things stand right now, I am practically a Luddite. I should make that plain. Our society is so immoral that it can't be entrusted to invent anything until we are able to sit down and decide, as a socially responsible, ecologically sensitive community, how we're going to design and use our technology. This is not to say that I oppose research or technology, but this society is not morally fit to decide what is necessary or not.

Another way is possible, of course. Eco-technologies can and should be developed. There has been some interesting work in this area during the last twenty-five years. I have personally experimented with various eco-technologies since 1974 at the Institute for Social Ecology. There we put up solar collectors, windmills, ecologically designed buildings; we worked with aquaculture and organic agriculture assisted by a variety of tools and techniques. Other groups such as the New Alchemy Institute have been working on these things even more intensely than we have. I am convinced a liberatory eco-technology is possible. Hopefully, we can all agree on that.

If people do read my work, we can also put to rest the supposition that my outlook is anti-spiritual. This claim is utter nonsense. Anyone who reads *The Ecology of Freedom* will find that it repeatedly calls for a new ecological sensibility, for a new spirituality. There is full agreement on the need for a spiritual connection to the natural world. The only possible disagreement is whether or not this ecological spiritual sensibility will be naturalist or supernaturalist in orientation.

Since spirituality can mean a decent, indeed, a wholesome sensitivity to nature and its subtle interconnections, it is very important that we keep the ecology movement from degrading this concept into a required or expected belief in an atavistic, simple-minded form of nature worship peopled by gods, goddesses, and eventually by a new hierarchy of priests and priestesses. People who believe that the solution to the ecological crisis is to create a new "green religion" or to revive beliefs in ancient gods, goddesses, or wood-sprites are mystically obscuring the need for social change. The tendency to do just this among many deep ecologists, eco-feminists, and "New Age" greens concerns me. The distinction I make between a needed naturalistic spirituality and an unnecessary, and potentially harmful, supernaturalistic "green religion" is a valuable contribution, I think.

Let me close by saying I believe that there is much common ground between Dave Foreman and myself. As I said before, we should give our support to Earth First! and their direct-action campaigns to preserve what is left of wild nature. Dave is on the frontline on this question and deserves, together with the rest of Earth First!, our full support, especially now when Earth First! is under attack by the FBI.

We cannot let the FBI get away with painting the radical ecology movement as "terrorist." I've been involved in radical direct-action politics all my life. I know what it is like to be attacked by the FBI. I know what a bunch of lunatics they are. People seriously working to defend the Earth will soon find themselves going up against powerful utilities, large corporations, private detective agencies, local police departments, and the FBI. I only wish I still had the physical ability to directly take part in daring nonviolent direct-action campaigns such as Redwood Summer.

I also want to say that I think that many of the political differences between Dave and myself are complementary. Dave and Earth First! work on preserving the wilderness; I and others are trying to create a new grassroots municipal politics, a new cooperative economics, a new pattern of science and technology to go along with their direct action, demonstrations, rallies, and protests to protect wilderness. We need to learn that we are different aspects of a single movement. We also need to try to amicably deal with those principled political differences that do exist between us. There are probably still some major problems between us that have to be explored. Yet, even if we can't straighten them all out, we must at least learn how to better work together on what we can agree on. Our future depends on it.

Dave Foreman:

I agree with everything Murray just said, and I feel like I should just sit down. I'm not sure I have a whole lot more to add. Agreeing with Murray might seem a little strange for someone who started his political career as a college freshman campaigning for Barry Goldwater in 1964. Yet, I really do.

Let me begin my remarks by giving you a little background on my own work and perspective within the ecology movement. I'll leave out, for now, the story of my getting over my brief infatuation with Goldwaterism. All I can say in my defense is that I didn't know at the time that Goldwater stood for paranoid anti-communism and subservience to big business. I thought he was talking about a return to libertarian, Jeffersonian democracy.

Anyway, by the early 1970s I was working as a mule-packer and horse-shoer up in northern New Mexico and getting more and more concerned about what was happening to the national forests up there. Finally, I decided to go back to Albuquerque and try to get a graduate degree in biology and get involved in the conservation movement. I immediately got involved in the U.S. Forest Services's first Roadless Area Review and Evaluation (RARE) program, which turned out to be a horrible farce. I was also studying herpetology at the time and we were supposed to go out and pickle 50 snakes and lizards before the end of the semester. Well, I was studying herpetology because I liked snakes and lizards, so I ended up dropping out of grad school by the middle of the first semester and I have been a professional rabble-rousing conservationist ever since.

I first went to work for The Wilderness Society early in 1973 for $250 a month as their New Mexico representative and I slowly worked my way up until I went to Washington, D.C. in the late 1970s as their chief lobbyist. After going through the Carter administration process, where we got lobbied more than we lobbied them, and where it seemed like the more influence and access we had, the more we compromised, a number of us began to ask what had happened to the environmental movement. At that time, newspapers and TV news were reassigning all their environmental reporters, because the environmental movement was dull. We were also concerned that environmental groups were becoming indistinguishable from the corporations they were supposedly fighting. I guess if you organize yourself like a corporation, you begin to think like a corporation. People who had once gotten a job in the movement by being active volunteers now were more concerned with improving their individual careers. They did not want to rock the boat because they didn't want to spoil their chances of being administrative aide to a senator, or an assistant secretary of the interior at some point in the future.

Given our frustration with the conventional conservation movement, several of us who worked for The Wilderness Society, the Sierra Club, and Friends of the Earth began talking about sparking a fundamentalist revival within the environmental movement. We wanted to get back to the basics of John Muir and Aldo Leopold. So on a camping trip in the desert in Mexico, we decided it was time to quit talking about how bad things had gotten and actually do something about it.

We started Earth First!. Maybe we were all just going through an early midlife crisis. I don't know. We sure had fun lowering banners down the front of the Glen Canyon Dam, making it look like it had cracked. That was one of our first actions. We were kicking up our heels a bit and playing the Coyote of the environmental movement. We tried to do things with a sense of humor. Lord knows most of the social change movement in this country lacks a sense of humor. This was one of the things we very much wanted to bring to our work. Perhaps because of it, Earth First! caught on a lot better than we ever dreamed it would.

As we developed Earth First!, we began to explore some techniques of radical organizing. Earth First! originally came out of the mainstream conservation movement, and that is still where my roots are, and that is still the audience that I feel most comfortable speaking to and trying to influence. I think the greatest strength and accomplishment of Earth First! has been our ability to redefine the parameters of the national environmental debate. Back at the beginning of the Reagan administration, the Sierra Club was being called a bunch of environmental extremists. Well, we in Earth First! put an end to all that.

Back in those days, there was a spectrum of debate with the rape-the-land artists over at one end and the "Big Ten" environmental organizations over at the other. Yet, in an attempt to be credible, proper, and respectable, the conservationists kept moving over towards the rape-the-land-artists before we ever even opened our mouths. The eventual result, of course, was a narrowing of the spectrum of debate, a narrowing that favored the big industry developers. So, we in Earth First! tried to create some space on the far end of the spectrum for a radical environmentalist perspective. And, as a result of our staking out the position of unapologetic, uncompromising wilderness lovers with a bent for monkey-wrenching and direct action, I think we have allowed the Sierra Club and other groups to actually take stronger positions than they would have before and yet appear to be more moderate than ever. What's different now is that they are compared to us.

I think that the role of an avant garde group is to throw out ideas that are objected to as absurd or ridiculous at first, but which end up trickling into the mainstream and becoming more accepted over time. We were the first people to talk about the preservation of all old-growth forests. Before us, no mainstream conservation groups were even talking about old growth. Now we've got the Audubon Society and The Wildlife Federation coming in on this issue. We were the first people to really bring direct action to rainforest campaigns. And now that's become very much a mainstream activity.

We were pretty clear from the beginning, however, that we were not *the* radical environmental movement. We only saw ourselves as one slice of the radical environmental movement. I know I have no absolute, total, and complete answer to the worldwide ecological crisis we are in. My path is not the right path; it's the path that works for me. I think there are dozens and dozens of other approaches and ideas that we will need in order to solve the crisis we're in right now. We need that kind of diversity within our movement. In Earth First!, we have tended to specialize in what we're good at: wilderness preservation and endangered species. That doesn't mean the other issues aren't important; it just means that we mostly talk about what we know most about. We work on what moves us most particularly. It doesn't mean that we're the whole operation, or that we're covering all the bases. We need all the approaches and angles.

I need to emphasize, too, that while I work on those things I know best, on those issues which touch me the most deeply, it doesn't mean that the social problems that Murray mentioned are irrelevant, or that I'm not sympathetic to them. Hell, I've been arrested six times standing in front of bulldozers, or logging trucks, or otherwise fighting giant corporations that are trying to destroy our national parks and our national forests. I think my book *Ecodefense: A Field Guide to Monkey-wrenching* is probably one of the most effective little anti-capitalist tracts ever written. I know we are talking radical, anti-capitalist social change here.

One problem I've had in getting the fullness of my message out comes from my impatience at seeing eco-catastrophe going on all around me while so many of those on the left who are always talking about social justice don't seem to even see the problem or care about other species. Let's face it: right now we're in the greatest extinction crisis in the entire three and one half billion year history of life on this planet. Raymond Dasmann has said that World War III has already begun and that it is being waged by the multinational corporations against the Earth.[4] We may lose one-third of all species in the next 20 years because of multinational greed.

I am deeply concerned about what is happening to people all over the world. Yet, unlike much of the left, I'm also very concerned with what's happening to a million other species on the planet who haven't asked for this eco-catastrophe to happen to them. And I have a connection that is very fundamental and very passionate with those other species. I feel a real kinship with them, as well as with members of my own species. And I think, as Murray pointed out, it's very difficult to separate the two concerns. Or, at least, it should be. Regardless of what our emphasis is, regardless of whether it's goose music that plays a symphony to us, or the diversity of people in a vibrant place like New York City that plays a symphony to us, I think we have to recognize that we are on the same side.

Unfortunately for me, when you see this kind of eco-crisis all around you and you react to it, and you begin to suggest some of the things that may happen if we don't wise up and change our way of living on this planet, your ideas may come out as though you're welcoming some of those things. It may come out as though you're saying "ought" instead of "is." I think the problem of the Cassandra is to try to make it very clear that you're predicting certain things because you don't want them to happen, because you want people to wake up. It's not that you're chortling over any suffering. You are compassionate. You are concerned. You're on the side of all the people who are the victims of multinational imperialism around the world. That probably hasn't come out as clearly as it should have in my discussions to date of ecological problems. But it is very real to me, and I'm very concerned about it.

Audience Member:

Mr. Foreman, if you have the slightest commitment to linking issues of social justice with questions of ecological degradation and to trying to find common ground here, how do you reconcile this new tone with your repeated statements in the Earth First! journal that in order to save the ecology of the United States we need to militarily close the U.S.-Mexican border and keep what you call the Latin American hordes from overwhelming us?

Dave Foreman:

I don't think you've ever read anything I've written! I've seen comments circulating like you've described. Ed Abbey has said things somewhat like that, but I've never written anything about militarily sealing the border.[5] Listen, I live in the Southwest. All my relatives on my sister's side are Hispanic. I spend a lot of time in Mexico and have a lot of concern for Central America's problems. I support bi-lingual education and legislation. I have also actively supported the Sandinista revolution in Nicaragua and opposed U.S. foreign policy in the region.

I think, however, that there comes a time when we have to ask some tough questions about whether standard political solutions are going to work. I've looked at what happens to people from south of the border and Arizona, how they're exploited by large corporations. I look at how an open border serves as an overflow safety valve to get rid of dissidents in Latin America and to provide a source of cheap, nonunion labor for corporations here at home. And I ask myself, what is being solved by that? I think we delude ourselves when we pretend that somehow by having an open border we're solving any problems in Latin America.

I'm not saying seal the border. I don't think that works. Hell, I'm in complete sympathy with the Central American sanctuary movement. I see the repression and the police state that the border patrol is creating in California. But I think that we delude ourselves when we come up with simple solutions to complex problems. It's not sealing the border and it's not opening the border. I think that we will have to solve the deeper problem on a much more multi-pronged basis.

For one thing, it is probably going to require changing U.S. foreign policy. I think if we're going to help solve the social and ecological problems of Latin America we've got to get the CIA out of there; we've got to get United Fruit Company out of there; we've got to get the United States government backed into the position where it can't go in and prop up dictators when their own people throw them out. Our government has done that in Guatemala, in Chile, and it keeps trying in Nicaragua. That is at the heart of most of the problems. As I said before, I'd be happy to join all of you sitting in front of military disembarkation points when they start to invade Nicaragua, which is certainly the most progressive and the most ecological country in Latin America right now, despite the concessions that the U.S. government keeps forcing the Sandinistas to make.

We are all engaged in a battle for life against profit. We are engaged in a struggle for a life of egalitarianism instead of a life of greed and imperialism. We have the same enemies. We are fighting the same battle, regardless of what we emphasize. Gifford Pinchot, the first Director of the United States Forest Service, said there are only two things on Earth, people and natural resources. I think Donald Trump and George Bush would amend that by saying there's only one thing on

Earth, natural resources. Ordinary people become just another "natural resource" to the big imperial man. Murray is right. It's one fight.

I must say, however, that for all my intellectual understanding of imperialism, it was directly encountering the repressive power of the FBI and doing a little time in federal custody that really brought home to me the reality of peoples' suffering throughout the world. Personally experiencing a little of the repressive power of the state has a tendency, I think, to create a lot more sympathy for oppressed groups around the world. I certainly have a more visceral appreciation for peoples' suffering these days since the FBI visited me.

From my viewpoint, the FBI effort against me began at about five in the morning on May 30, 1989. A Doberman down the street started barking, so I put my ear plugs in. About two hours later, my wife went to answer the door as it was about to be broken down and opened it up to six men standing there with drawn .357 Magnums and wearing bulletproof vests. They flashed badges at her and pushed her out of the way. They then started running down the hall to our bedroom—they somehow already knew right where it was.

At this point, I vaguely began to come awake as I heard an unfamiliar but authoritative voice yelling my name. I opened up my eyes, still with my ear plugs in, disoriented. May in Tucson is very hot, and I didn't have anything on. And I woke up and there were three guys with bulletproof vests and drawn .357 Magnums standing around the bed. That kind of alarm clock doesn't have a snooze button; you can't go back to sleep for another five minutes. At first I thought, am I on *Candid Camera?* But I realized very quickly that these guys were serious.

I then started thinking about some of the FBI attacks on the Black Panthers, like the FBI/Chicago Police murder of Fred Hampton, who was shot in his apartment while he lay asleep in bed. I fully expected bullets to start coming my way. But being a nice, middle-class honky male, they can't get away with that stuff quite as easily as they could with Fred, or with all the native people on the Pine Ridge Reservation back in the early 70s. So they just dragged me out of bed. They let me put on a pair of shorts, and they hauled me outside.

I did not know what I was being arrested for until six hours later, when I saw a magistrate. Essentially what had happened, we found out, was that the FBI had spent three years and two million dollars trying to frame a bunch of people in Earth First! for trying to create a conspiracy to damage government property. We now know for a fact that the FBI infiltrated Earth First! groups across the country with informers and agent-provocateurs seeking to entrap people into illegal activities. They have amassed 500 hours of tape recordings of our meetings, our personal conversations, and our phone calls. They have also broken into our houses and offices and tried to intimidate numerous ecology activists in several states by agent interrogations and grand jury investigations.

My supposed co-conspirators, three unarmed activists who were arrested by some 50 armed FBI agents on foot, on horseback, and in two helicopters while standing at the base of a power line tower in the desert, were arrested the day before me. Mind you, these three environmentalists were driven to the site by an undercover FBI agent who had infiltrated Earth First!. The whole escapade was largely his idea. He was the only one talking about explosives. I, of course, was nowhere near the "scene" but I was still described by the FBI as "the financier, the leader, the guru to get all this going." I was likened to a "mafia boss" and the other three defendants were described as my "munchkins."

I had only met the FBI infiltrator a couple of times before and very briefly. I couldn't even remember his last name. We had never planned to do anything together. But that doesn't matter to the FBI. Back in the 1970s, the FBI issued a memo to all their field offices telling them that when you are trying to break up a dissident group, don't worry if you have any evidence or facts. Just go in, make a big arrest, make wild charges, have a press conference, and that's what the media's going to pick up. That's the news story. The damage to the group is done. You can always drop the charges against them later. That's no problem. It almost invariably gets less attention in the press. The big lie that the FBI pushed at their press conference the day after the arrests was that we were a bunch of terrorists conspiring to cut the power lines into the Palo Verde and Diablo Canyon nuclear facilities in order to cause a nuclear meltdown and threaten public health and safety.

Essentially what we need to understand is that the Federal Bureau of Investigation, which was formed just after the Palmer raids in 1921, was set up from the very beginning to inhibit internal political dissent. They rarely go after criminals. They're a thought police. And let's face it, that's what the whole government is. Foreman's first law of government reads that the purpose of the state, and all its constituent elements, is the defense of an entrenched economic elite and philosophic orthodoxy. Thankfully, there's a corollary to that law—they aren't always very smart and competent in carrying out their plans.

In this case, I think the U.S. government has made a major tactical mistake, because even the usually compliant mass media are not buying its story. We have gotten some remarkably even-handed press coverage. I also recently spoke to the Sierra Club international assembly and had a terrific response. People just aren't buying it. So I'm very hopeful we're going to overcome this, though we will undoubtedly be hearing more from the FBI in the future.

Before I close, let me just say that I agree with Murray that the warped social evolution of our civilization has left us with a very weird way of looking at reality. I agree a lot with Dave Ehrenfeld, who characterizes the dominant philosophy of the modern world as being one where human beings are the measure of all value; where we think that we can solve all problems, either through techno-logical means or through sociological means; where we believe that all resources are either infinite or have infinite substitutes; and where we believe that human civilization will continue to progress and will exist forever. And to me, that is stark, raving insanity.[6]

I think there is no reason, divine or otherwise, why human beings, unless they wake up, will not make themselves extinct. There is a great deal of madness around us. Julian Simon, for example, is a Republican economist who said recently that there really are no limits to economic growth because, after all, we'll soon be able to change any element into any other element.[7] Therefore, the supply of cop-per is restrained only by the entire weight of the universe. I can't even begin to talk to somebody like that. I mean, we aren't only speaking a different language, we're living on different planets in different dimensions.

And it's that kind of common madness that I think is profoundly irrational. I talk a lot about being non-rational, about using all sides of my brain, including the good old reptilian cortex back here. But I think there is nothing more rational, nothing more sensible than trying to keep in mind what Aldo Leopold called the first rule of intelligent tinkering: *save all the pieces.* We aren't saving all the pieces. Species and whole habitats are being destroyed at a rate unparalleled in the Earth's history. It is as if we are going through a complicated Swiss watch with a bulldozer right now.

My own response to this situation is a sort of weird, cowboy twist on Zen Bud-dhism. I don't believe in reforming the system any more. I believe in monkey-wrenching it, thwarting it, and helping it to fall on its face by using its own stored energy against itself. When people talk to me about the destruction of property, about the evils of destroying bulldozers, all I can say is that a bulldozer is made out of iron ore. It's part of the Earth. A bulldozer is the Earth, transmogrified into a monster destroying itself. By monkeywrenching it, you liberate a bull-dozer's dharma nature and return it to the Earth.

As I see it, Murray and I, atheists that we both probably are, are trying in var-ious ways to help industrial civilization find its own dharma nature, and become an egalitarian, more tribal society that respects people and respects the Earth once again.

NOTES

1. Roderick Nash, *The Rights of Nature: A History of Environmental Ethics,* 164.

2. Warwick Fox, "The Deep Ecology-Ecofeminism Debate and its Parallels," *Environmental Ethics,* No. 11, 1989, n38.

3. Arne Naess, "Finding Common Ground," *Green Synthesis,* no. 30, March 1989, 9.

4. Raymond Dasmann works with bioregionalist Peter Berg at the Planet Drum Foundation which publishes the *Raise the Stakes* newspaper and helped organize the North American bioregional movement.

5. For a look at Foreman's initial position on immigration, see Dave Foreman, "Is Sanctuary the Answer?" *Earth First!* November 1, 1987, 21–22.

6. For a full presentation of Ehrenfeld's critical view of humanism, see David Ehrenfeld, *The Arrogance of Humanism* (New York: Oxford University Press, 1978).

7. For a full presentation of Simon's critical view of ecological limit to growth theories, see Julian Simon, *The Ultimate Resource* (Princeton: Princeton University Press, 1981).

41

Vandana Shiva

⎯⎯⎯⎯⎯

Stolen Harvest: The Hijacking of the Global Food Supply (2000)

Vandana Shiva (b. 1952), a physicist by training, conducts and supports inter-disciplinary research on ecological, gender, and social issues. Her work has challenged current perceptions of agricultural production, food consumption, and Third World women. She has founded the Research Foundation for Science, Technology and Ecology (1982), an academic/activist partnership; Navdanya (1991), a movement to protect living resources, especially native seeds; and Diverse Women for Diversity (1998), an organization bringing together women in food, agriculture, patents and biotechnology. Her recent books include Water Wars *(2001),* Patents, Myths, and Reality *(2001), and* Tomorrow's Biodiversity *(2000).*

FOOD IS OUR most basic need, the very stuff of life.

According to an ancient Indian Upanishad, "All that is born is born of *anna* [food]. Whatever exists on earth is born of *anna*, lives on *anna*, and in the end merges into *anna*. *Anna* indeed is the first born amongst all beings."[1]

More than 3.5 million people starved to death in the Bengal famine of 1943. Twenty million were directly affected. Food grains were appropriated forcefully from the peasants under a colonial system of rent collection. Export of food grains continued in spite of the fact that people were going hungry. As the Bengali writer Kali Charan Ghosh reports, 80,000 tons of food grain were exported from

Vandana Shiva, *Stolen Harvest: The Hijacking of the Global Food Supply* (Cambridge, MA: South End Press, 2000). Reprinted by permission of South End Press and Zed Books Ltd.

Bengal in 1943, just before the famine. At the time, India was being used as a supply base for the British military. "Huge exports were allowed to feed the people of other lands, while the shadow of famine was hourly lengthening on the Indian horizon."[2]

More than one-fifth of India's national output was appropriated for war supplies. The starving Bengal peasants gave up over two-thirds of the food they produced, leading their debt to double. This, coupled with speculation, hoarding, and profiteering by traders, led to skyrocketing prices. The poor of Bengal paid for the empire's war through hunger and starvation—and the "funeral march of the Bengal peasants, fishermen, and Artisans."[3]

Dispossessed peasants moved to Calcutta. Thousands of female destitutes were turned into prostitutes. Parents started to sell their children. "In the villages jackals and dogs engaged in a tug-of-war for the bodies of the half-dead."[4]

As the crisis began, thousands of women organized in Bengal in defense of their food rights. "Open more ration shops" and "Bring down the price of food" were the calls of women's groups throughout Bengal.[5]

After the famine, the peasants also started to organize around the central demand of keeping a two-thirds, or *tebhaga*, share of the crops. At its peak the Tebhaga movement, as it was called, covered 19 districts and involved 6 million people. Peasants refused to let their harvest be stolen by the landlords and the revenue collectors of the British Empire. Everywhere peasants declared, *"Jan debo tabu dhan debo ne"*—"We will give up our lives, but we will not give up our rice." In the village of Thumniya, the police arrested some peasants who resisted the theft of their harvest. They were charged with "stealing paddy."[6]

A half-century after the Bengal famine, a new and clever system has been put in place, which is once again making the theft of the harvest a right and the keeping of the harvest a crime. Hidden behind complex free-trade treaties are innovative ways to steal nature's harvest, the harvest of the seed, and the harvest of nutrition.

The Corporate Hijacking of Food and Agriculture

I focus on India to tell the story of how corporate control of food and globalization of agriculture are robbing millions of their livelihoods and their right to food both because I am an Indian and because Indian agriculture is being especially targeted by global corporations. Since 75 percent of the Indian population derives its livelihood from agriculture, and every fourth farmer in the world is an Indian, the impact of globalization on Indian agriculture is of global significance.

However, this phenomenon of the stolen harvest is not unique to India. It is being experienced in every society, as small farms and small farmers are pushed to extinction, as monocultures replace biodiverse crops, as farming is transformed from the production of nourishing and diverse foods into the creation of markets for genetically engineered seeds, herbicides, and pesticides. As farmers are transformed from producers into consumers of corporate-patented agricultural products, as markets are destroyed locally and nationally but expanded globally, the myth of "free trade" and the global economy becomes a means for the rich to rob the poor of their right to food and even their right to life. For the vast majority of the world's people—70 percent—earn their livelihoods by producing food. The majority of these farmers are women. In contrast, in the industrialized countries, only 2 percent of the population are farmers.

Food Security Is in the Seed

For centuries Third World farmers have evolved crops and given us the diversity of plants that provide us nutrition. Indian farmers evolved 200,000 varieties of rice through their innovation and breeding. They bred rice varieties such as Basmati. They bred red rice and brown rice and black rice. They bred rice that grew 18 feet tall in the Gangetic floodwaters, and saline-resistant rice that could be grown in the coastal water. And this innovation by farmers has not stopped. Farmers involved in our movement, Navdanya, dedicated to conserving native seed diversity, are still breeding new varieties.

The seed, for the farmer, is not merely the source of future plants and food; it is the storage place of culture and history. Seed is the first link in the food chain. Seed is the ultimate symbol of food security.

Free exchange of seed among farmers has been the basis of maintaining biodiversity as well as food security. This exchange is based on cooperation and reciprocity. A farmer who wants to exchange seed generally gives an equal quantity of seed from his field in return for the seed he gets.

Free exchange among farmers goes beyond mere exchange of seeds; it involves exchanges of ideas and knowledge, of culture and heritage. It is an accumulation of tradition, of knowledge of how to work the seed. Farmers learn about the plants they want to grow in the future by watching them grow in other farmers' fields.

Paddy, or rice, has religious significance in most parts of the country and is an essential component of most religious festivals. The *Akti* festival in Chattisgarh, where a diversity of *indica* rices are grown, reinforces the many principles of biodiversity conservation. In Southern India, rice grain is considered auspicious, or *akshanta*. It is mixed with *kumkum* and turmeric and given as a blessing. The priest is given rice, often along with coconut, as an indication of religious regard. Other agricultural varieties whose seeds, leaves, or flowers form an essential component of religious ceremonies include coconut, betel, arecanut, wheat, finger and little millets, horsegram, blackgram, chickpea, pigeon pea, sesame, sugarcane, jackfruit seed, cardamom, ginger, bananas, and gooseberry.

New seeds are first worshipped, and only then are they planted. New crops are worshipped before being consumed. Festivals held before sowing seeds as well as harvest festivals, celebrated in the fields, symbolize people's intimacy with nature.[7] For the farmer, the field is the mother; worshipping the field is a sign of gratitude toward the earth, which, as mother, feeds the millions of life forms that are her children.

But new intellectual-property-rights regimes, which are being universalized through the Trade Related Intellectual Property Rights Agreement of the World Trade Organization (WTO), allow corporations to usurp the knowledge of the seed and monopolize it by claiming it as their private property. Over time, this results in corporate monopolies over the seed itself.

Corporations like RiceTec of the United States are claiming patents on Basmati rice. Soybean, which evolved in East Asia, has been patented by Calgene, which is now owned by Monsanto. Calgene also owns patents on mustard, a crop of Indian origin. Centuries of collective innovation by farmers and peasants are being hijacked as corporations claim intellectual-property rights on these and other seeds and plants.[8]

"Free Trade" or "Forced Trade"

Today, ten corporations control 32 percent of the commercial-seed market, valued at $23 billion, and 100 percent of the market for genetically engineered, or transgenic, seeds.[9] These corporations also control the global agrochemical and pesticide market. Just five corporations control the global trade in grain. In late 1998, Cargill, the largest of these five companies, bought Continental, the second largest, making it the single biggest factor in the grain trade. Monoliths such as Cargill and Monsanto were both actively involved in shaping international trade agreements, in particular the Uruguay Round of the General Agreement on Trade and Tarriffs [sic], which led to the establishment of the WTO.

This monopolistic control over agricultural production, along with structural adjustment policies that brutally favor exports, results in floods of exports of foods from the United States and Europe to the Third World. As a result of the North American Free Trade Agreement (NAFTA), the proportion of Mexico's food supply that is imported has increased from 20 percent in 1992 to 43 percent in 1996. After 18 months of NAFTA, 2.2. million Mexicans have lost their jobs, and 40 million have fallen into extreme poverty. One out of two peasants is not getting enough to eat. As Victor Suares has stated, "Eating more cheaply on imports is not eating at all for the poor in Mexico."[10]

In the Philippines, sugar imports have destroyed the economy. In Kerala, India, the prosperous rubber plantations were rendered unviable due to rubber imports. The local $350 million rubber economy was wiped out, with a multiplier effect of $3.5 billion on the economy of Kerala. In Kenya, maize imports brought prices crashing for local farmers who could not even recover their costs of production.

Trade liberalization of agriculture was introduced in India in 1991 as part of a World Bank/International Monetary Fund (IMF) structural adjustment package. While the hectares of land under cotton cultivation had been decreasing in the 1970s and 1980s, in the first six years of World Bank/IMF-mandated reforms, the land under cotton cultivation increased by 1.7 million hectares. Cotton started to displace food crops. Aggressive corporate advertising campaigns, including promotional films shown in villages on "video vans," were launched to sell new, hybrid seeds to farmers. Even gods, goddesses, and saints were not spared: in Punjab, Monsanto sells its products using the image of Guru Nanak, the founder of the Sikh religion. Corporate, hybrid seeds began to replace local farmers' varieties.

The new hybrid seeds, being vulnerable to pests, required more pesticides. Extremely poor farmers bought both seeds and chemicals on credit from the same company. When the crops failed due to heavy pest incidence or large-scale seed failure, many peasants committed suicide by consuming the same pesticides that had gotten them into debt in the first place. In the district of Warangal, nearly 400 cotton farmers committed suicide due to crop failure in 1997, and dozens more committed suicide in 1998.

Under this pressure to cultivate cash crops, many states in India have allowed private corporations to acquire hundreds of acres of land. The state of Maharashtra has exempted horticulture projects from its land-ceiling legislation. Madhya Pradesh is offering land to private industry on long-term leases, which, according to industry, should last for at least 40 years. In Andhra Pradesh and Tamil Nadu, private corporations are today allowed to acquire over 300 acres of land for raising shrimp for exports. A large percentage of agricultural production on these lands will go toward supplying the burgeoning food-processing industry, in which mainly transnational corporations are involved. Meanwhile, the United States has taken India to the WTO dispute panel to contest its restrictions on food imports.

In certain instances, markets are captured by other means. In August 1998, the mustard-oil supply in Delhi was mysteriously adulterated. The adulteration was restricted to Delhi but not to any specific brand, indicating that it was not the work of a particular trader or business house. More than 50 people died. The government banned all local processing of oil and announced free imports of soybean oil. Millions of people extracting oil on tiny, ecological, cold-press mills lost their livelihoods. Prices of indigenous oilseed collapsed to less than one-third their previous levels. In Sira, in the state of Karnataka, police officers shot farmers protesting the fall in prices of oilseeds.

Imported soybeans' takeover of the Indian market is a clear example of the imperialism on which globalization is built. One crop exported from a single country by one or two corporations replaced hundreds of foods and food producers, destroying biological and cultural diversity, and economic and political democracy. Small mills are now unable to serve small farmers and poor consumers with low-cost, healthy, and culturally appropriate edible oils. Farmers are robbed of their freedom to choose what they grow, and consumers are being robbed of their freedom to choose what they eat.

Creating Hunger with Monocultures

Global chemical corporations, recently reshaped into "life sciences" corporations, declare that without them and their patented products, the world cannot be fed.

As Monsanto advertised in its $1.6 million European advertising campaign:

> Worrying about starving future generations won't feed them. Food biotechnology will. The world's population is growing rapidly, adding the equivalent of a China to the globe every ten years. To feed these billion more mouths, we can try extending our farming land or squeezing greater harvests out of existing cultivation. With the planet set to double in numbers around 2030, this heavy dependency on land can only become heavier. Soil erosion and mineral depletion will exhaust the ground. Lands such as rainforests will be forced into cultivation. Fertilizer, insecticide, and herbicide use will increase globally. At Monsanto, we now believe food biotechnology is a better way forward.[11]

But food is necessary for all living species. That is why the *Taittreya Upanishad* calls on humans to feed all beings in their zone of influence.

Industrial agriculture has not produced more food. It has destroyed diverse sources of food, and it has stolen food from other species to bring larger quantities of specific commodities to the market, using huge quantities of fossil fuels and water and toxic chemicals in the process.

It is often said that the so-called miracle varieties of the Green Revolution in modern industrial agriculture prevented famine because they had higher yields. However, these higher yields disappear in the context of total yields of crops on farms. Green Revolution varieties produced more grain by diverting production away from straw. This "partitioning" was achieved through dwarfing the plants, which also enabled them to withstand high doses of chemical fertilizer.

However, less straw means less fodder for cattle and less organic matter for the soil to feed the millions of soil organisms that make and rejuvenate soil. The higher yields of wheat or maize were thus achieved by stealing food from farm animals and soil organisms. Since cattle and earthworms are our partners in food production, stealing food from them makes it impossible to maintain food production over time, and means that the partial yield increases were not sustainable.

The increase in yields of wheat and maize under industrial agriculture were also achieved at the cost of yields of other foods a small farm provides. Beans, legumes, fruits, and vegetables all disappeared both from farms and from the calculus of yields. More grain from two or three commodities arrived on national and international markets, but less food was eaten by farm families in the Third World.

The gain in "yields" of industrially produced crops is thus based on a theft of food from other species and the rural poor in the Third World. That is why, as more grain is produced and traded globally, more people go hungry in the Third World. Global markets have more commodities for trading because food has been robbed from nature and the poor.

Productivity in traditional farming practices has always been high if it is remembered that very few external inputs are required. While the Green Revolution has been promoted as having increased productivity in the absolute sense, when resource use is taken into account, it has been found to be counterproductive and inefficient.

Perhaps one of the most fallacious myths propagated by Green Revolution advocates is the assertion that high-yielding varieties have reduced the acreage under cultivation, therefore preserving millions of hectares of biodiversity. But in India, instead of more land being released for conservation, industrial breeding actually increases pressure on the land, since each acre of a monoculture provides a single output, and the displaced outputs have to be grown on additional acres, or "shadow" acres.[12]

A study comparing traditional polycultures with industrial monocultures shows that a polyculture system can produce 100 units of food from 5 units of inputs, whereas an industrial system requires 300 units of input to produce the same 100 units. The 295 units of wasted inputs could have provided 5,900 units of additional food. Thus the industrial system leads to a decline of 5,900 units of food. This is a recipe for starving people, not for feeding them.[13]

Wasting resources creates hunger. By wasting resources through one-dimensional monocultures maintained with intensive external inputs, the new biotechnologies create food insecurity and starvation.

The Insecurity of Imports

As cash crops such as cotton increase, staple-food production goes down, leading to rising prices of staples and declining consumption by the poor. The hungry starve as scarce land and water are diverted to provide luxuries for rich consumers in Northern countries. Flowers, fruits, shrimp, and meat are among the export commodities being promoted in all Third World countries.

When trade liberalization policies were introduced in 1991 in India, the agriculture secretary stated that "food security is not food in the *go-downs* but dollars in the pocket." It is repeatedly argued that food security does not depend on food "self-sufficiency" (food grown locally for local consumption), but on food "self-reliance" (buying your food from international markets). According to the received ideology of free trade, the earnings from exports of farmed shrimp, flowers, and meat will finance imports of food. Hence any shortfall created by the diversion of productive capacity from growing food for domestic consumption to growing luxury items for consumption by rich Northern consumers would be more than made up.

However, it is neither efficient nor sustainable to grow shrimp, flowers, and meat for export in countries such as India. In the case of flower exports, India spent Rs. 1.4 billion as foreign exchange for promoting floriculture exports and earned a mere Rs. 320 million.[14] In other words, India can buy only one-fourth of the food it could have grown with export earnings from floriculture.[15] Our food security has therefore declined by 75 percent, and our foreign exchange drain increased by more than Rs. 1 billion.

In the case of meat exports, for every dollar earned, India is destroying 15 dollars' worth of ecological functions performed by farm animals for sustainable agriculture. Before the Green Revolution, the byproducts of India's culturally sophisticated and ecologically sound livestock economy, such as the hides of cattle, were exported, rather than the ecological capital, that is, the cattle themselves. Today, the domination of the export logic in agriculture is leading to the export of our ecological capital, which we have conserved over centuries. Giant slaughterhouses and factory farming are replacing India's traditional livestock economy. When cows are slaughtered and their meat is exported, with it are exported the renewable energy and fertilizer that cattle provide to the small farms of small peasants. These multiple functions of cattle in farming systems have been protected in India through the metaphor of the sacred cow. Government agencies cleverly disguise the slaughter of cows, which would outrage many Indians, by calling it "buffalo meat."

In the case of shrimp exports, for every acre of an industrial shrimp farm, 200 acres of productive ecosystems are destroyed. For every dollar earned as foreign exchange from exports, six to ten dollars' worth of destruction takes place in the local economy. The harvest of shrimp from aquaculture farms is a harvest stolen from fishing and farming communities in the coastal regions of the Third World. The profits from exports of shrimp to U.S., Japanese, and European markets show up in national and global economic growth figures. However, the destruction of local food consumption, ground-water resources, fisheries, agriculture, and livelihoods associated with traditional occupations in each of these sectors does not alter the global economic value of shrimp exports; such destruction is only experienced locally.

In India, intensive shrimp cultivation has turned fertile coastal tracts into graveyards, destroying both fisheries and agriculture. In Tamil Nadu and Andhra Pradesh, women from fishing and farming communities are resisting shrimp cultivation through *satyagraha*. Shrimp cultivation destroys 15 jobs for each job it creates. It destroys $5 of ecological and economic capital for every dollar earned through exports. Even these profits flow for only three to five years, after which the industry must move on to new sites. Intensive shrimp farming is a non-sustainable activity, described by United Nations agencies as a "rape and run" industry.

Since the World Bank is advising all countries to shift from "food first" to "export first" policies, these countries all compete with each other, and the prices of these luxury commodities collapse. Trade liberalization and economic reform also include devaluation of currencies. Thus exports earn less, and imports cost more. Since the Third World is being told to stop growing food and instead to buy food in international markets by exporting cash crops, the process of globalization leads to a situation in which agricultural societies of the South become increasingly dependent on food imports, but do not have the foreign exchange to pay for imported food. Indonesia and Russia provide examples of countries that have moved rapidly from food-sufficiency to hunger because of the creation of dependency on imports and the devaluation of their currencies.

Stealing Nature's Harvest

Global corporations are not just stealing the harvest of farmers. They are stealing nature's harvest through genetic engineering and patents on life forms.

Genetically engineered crops manufactured by corporations pose serious ecological risks. Crops such as Monsanto's Roundup Ready soybeans, designed to be resistant to herbicides, lead to the destruction of biodiversity and increased use of agrochemicals. They can also create highly invasive "superweeds" by transferring the genes for herbicide resistance to weeds. Crops designed to be pesticide factories, genetically engineered to produce toxins and venom with genes from bacteria, scorpions, snakes, and wasps, can threaten non-pest species and can contribute to the emergence of resistance in pests and hence the creation of "superpests." In every application of genetic engineering, food is being stolen from other species for the maximization of corporate profits.

To secure patents on life forms and living resources, corporations must claim seeds and plants to be their "inventions" and hence their property. Thus corporations like Cargill and Monsanto see nature's web of life and cycles of renewal as "theft" of their property. During the debate about the entry of Cargill into India in 1992, the Cargill chief executive stated, "We bring Indian farmers smart technologies, which prevent bees from usurping the pollen."[16] During the United Nations Biosafety Negotiations, Monsanto circulated literature that claimed that "weeds steal the sunshine."[17] A worldview that defines pollination as "theft by bees" and claims that diverse plants "steal" sunshine is one aimed at stealing nature's harvest, by replacing open, pollinated varieties with hybrids and sterile seeds, and destroying biodiverse flora with herbicides such as Monsanto's Roundup.

This is a worldview based on scarcity. A worldview of abundance is the worldview of women in India who leave food for ants on their doorstep, even as they create the most beautiful art in *kolams, mandalas,* and *rangoli* with rice flour. Abundance is the worldview of peasant women who weave beautiful designs of paddy to hang up for birds when the birds do not find grain in the fields. This view of abundance recognizes that, in giving food to other beings and species, we maintain conditions for our own food security. It is the recognition in the *Isho Upanishad* that the universe is the creation of the Supreme Power meant for the benefits of (all) creation. Each individual life form must learn to enjoy its benefits by farming a part of the system in close relation with other species. Let not any one species encroach upon others' rights.[18] The *Isho Upanishad* also says,

> a selfish man over-utilizing the resources of nature to satisfy his own ever-increasing needs is nothing but a thief, because using resources beyond one's needs would result in the utilization of resources over which others have a right.[19]

In the ecological worldview, when we consume more than we need or exploit nature on principles of greed, we are engaging in theft. In the anti-life view of agribusiness corporations, nature renewing and maintaining herself is a thief. Such a worldview replaces abundance with scarcity, fertility with sterility. It makes theft from nature a market imperative, and hides it in the calculus of efficiency and productivity.

Food Democracy

What we are seeing is the emergence of food totalitarianism, in which a handful of corporations control the entire food chain and destroy alternatives so that people do not have access to diverse, safe foods produced ecologically. Local markets are being deliberately destroyed to establish monopolies over seed and food systems. The destruction of the edible-oil market in India and the many ways through which farmers are prevented from having their own seed supply are small instances of an overall trend in which trade rules, property rights, and new technologies are used to destroy people-friendly and environment-friendly alternatives and to impose anti-people, anti-nature food systems globally.

The notion of rights has been turned on its head under globalization and free trade. The right to produce for oneself or consume according to cultural priorities and safety concerns has been rendered illegal according to the new trade rules. The right of corporations to force-feed citizens of the world with culturally inappropriate and hazardous foods has been made absolute. The right to food, the right to safety, the right to culture are all being treated as trade barriers that need to be dismantled.

This food totalitarianism can only be stopped through major citizen mobilization for democratization of the food system. This mobilization is starting to gain momentum in Europe, Japan, India, Brazil, and other parts of the world.

We have to reclaim our right to save seed and to biodiversity. We have to reclaim our right to nutrition and food safety. We have to reclaim our right to protect the earth and her diverse species. We have to stop this corporate theft from the poor and from nature. Food democracy is the new agenda for democracy and human rights. It is the new agenda for ecological sustainability and social justice.

NOTES

1. *Taittreya Upanishad,* Gorakhpur: Gita Press, p. 124.

2. Kali Charan Ghosh, *Famines in Bengal, 1770–1943,* Calcutta: Indian Associated Publishing Company, 1944.

3. Bondhayan Chattopadhyay, "Notes Towards an Understanding of the Bengal Famine of 1943," *Transaction,* June 1981.

4. MARS (Mahila Atma Raksha Samiti, or Women's Self Defense League), Political Report prepared for Second Annual Conference, New Delhi: Research Foundation for Science, Technology, and Ecology (RFSTE), 1944.

5. Peter Custers, *Women in the Tebhaga Uprising,* Calcutta: Naya prokash, 1987, p. 52.

6. Peter Custers, p. 78.

7. Festivals like *Uganda, Ramanavami, Akshay Trateeya, Ekadashi Aluyana Amavase, Naga Panchami, Noolu Hunime, Ganesh Chaturthi, Rishi Panchami, Navartri, Deepavali, Rathasaptami, Tulsi Vivaha Campasrusti,* and *Bhoomi Puja* all include religious ceremonies around the seed.

8. Vandana Shiva, Vanaja Ramprasad, Pandurang Hegde, Omkar Krishnan, and Radha Holla-Bhar, "The Seed Keepers," New Delhi: Navdanya, 1995.

9. These companies are DuPont/Pioneer (U.S.), Monsanto (U.S.), Novartis (Switzerland), Groupe Limagrain (France), Advanta (U.K. and Netherlands), Guipo Pulsar/Semins/ELM (Mexico), Sakata (Japan), KWS HG (Germany), and Taki (Japan).

10. Victor Suares, Paper presented at International Conference on Globalization, Food Security, and Sustainable Agriculture, July 30–31, 1996.

11. "Monsanto: Peddling 'Life Sciences' or 'Death Sciences'?" New Delhi: RFSTE, 1998.

12. ASSINSEL (International Association of Plant Breeders), "Feeding the 8 Billion and Preserving the Planet," Nyon, Switzerland: ASSINSEL.

13. Francesca Bray, "Agriculture for Developing Nations," *Scientific American,* July 1994, pp. 33–35.

14. *Business India,* March 1998.

15. T. N. Prakash and Tejaswini, "Floriculture and Food Security Issues: The Case of Rose Cultivation in Bangalore," in *Globalization and Food Security: Proceedings of Conference on Globalization and Agriculture,* ed. Vandana Shiva, New Delhi, August 1996.

16. Interview with John Hamilton, *Sunday Observer,* May 9, 1993.

17. Hendrik Verfaillie, speech delivered at the Forum on Nature and Human Society, National Academy of Sciences, Washington, DC, October 30, 1997.

18. Vandana Shiva, "Globalization, Gandhi, and Swadeshi: What is Economic Freedom? Whose Economic Freedom?" New Delhi: RFSTE, 1998.

19. Vandana Shiva, "Globalization, Gandhi, and Swadeshi."

PART EIGHT

Nationalism and Globalization

LIKE FEMINISM and environmentalism, nationalism and globalization function both as additions to mainstream ideologies and as challenges to traditional concepts of ideology. The result is considerable scholarly disagreement about how to characterize them. Some critics portray nationalism as a "thin" ideology because it concentrates on the "exceptional worth of the nation" and little else,[1] while others argue that it—like terrorism—is not an ideology but a "strategy that some ideologues use to try to advance their causes."[2] Similarly, some analysts claim that globalization is merely an ideology of "liberal capitalism" and/or "state security."[3] The history of the nation-state sheds new light on the roles nationalism and globalization play in the changing meaning of the word "ideology."

The nation-state itself is a relatively recent phenomenon whose future is increasingly uncertain. The notion that nationalities should be organized as states arose only in the late eighteenth century.[4] Before that time, communities based in heredity, language, custom, tradition, religion, even territory—the marks of a nation—were organized not as states but as other social and political entities—for example, cities, clans, guilds, kingdoms, manors, or sects. The very term "nation-state" is an interesting amalgam of two different concepts. In Max Weber's famous definition, a *"state* is a governing body with a *"monopoly of the legitimate use of physical* force within a given territory."[5] As a military and police power, the state can be further distinguished from the government, which is a legislative and administrative (policymaking) body—although anarchists note the common root of the words *policy* and *police.* Both state and government are distinct from the nation. The Latin root of *nation* is *nasci,* which means "to be born of"; its connotation of "common blood ties" suggests that the term should be reserved for a "self-aware ethnic group"—with or without a state. What scholars frequently refer to as "nation-building" would be better described as "state-building," while "nationalism" more properly refers to citizens' sense of identity with "their" polyethnic state and loyalty toward it.[6]

Only since the late-eighteenth-century development of liberal democracies have nations been closely associated with states. Joseph Mazzini, an Italian nationalist who fought for a united Italy, provides one of the first descriptions of this combination, declaring that the Italian nation-state "is the sentiment of love, the sense of fellowship which binds together all the sons of that territory." Mazzini regards the nation-state as an organic whole—a moral and political unity, greater than the sum of its parts, to which individuals owe a sacred duty. He argues that to be worthy of the name, a nation must represent all of its people; it must be a republic, which he defines as "the Country of all and for all." A supporter of "liberal nationalism," Mazzini thought that independent national states would co-exist in international harmony: "The universal recognition of the right of national self-determination would bring universal peace."

Unlike Mazzini's Italy, whose territory was geographically defined by the Italian peninsula, most nation-states are what Benedict Anderson calls "imagined communities." They are created by a variety of phenomena, which include educational, immigration, and linguistic policies as well as religious and cultural traditions. According to Anderson, capitalism and print technology played major roles in the development of the modern European nation-state. Early book markets were limited to readers of Latin, an elite language associated with the Catholic Church and the Roman Empire. Following the Protestant Reformation, the Lutheran Bible became the first best seller and revolutionized information exchange. Political elites had long communicated in vernacular "state" languages; now a Protestant mass readership needed Bibles in a variety of print languages. While meeting this demand, capitalists simultaneously mobilized new middle-class and female readers and created new markets for political as well as religious texts.

Anderson describes the process of "choosing" national languages as "a gradual, unselfconscious, pragmatic, not to say haphazard development." The result was that print-capitalism created a "unified field of exchange and communication below Latin and above the spoken vernaculars." Distinct markets gradually emerged among consumers reading French, English, Dutch, German, and so on. Print-language also fixed meanings and created a sense of "antiquity"—of spatial and temporal permanence—for newly created nations. Last, the print medium increased the status of state languages by distinguishing them from subnational oral dialects. Where territorial borders were arbitrary, nation-states now could form as linguistic communities.

Ironically, capitalism, which thus contributed to the formation of nation-states, is today a force that erodes their boundaries and creates a new international order. Kenichi Ohmae argues that national borders are no longer meaningful economically. Instead, to identify boundaries that make sense in a borderless world, he examines the "four 'I's": investment, industry, information technology, and individual consumers.[7] The first, investment capital, flows easily across national borders when economic opportunities arise; that flow increasingly involves the assets of private corporations rather than government funds. Second, industrial corporations also move between nations, bringing capital, jobs, managers, and technology, while seeking markets, materials, and workers. Third, information technology now allows companies to operate in multiple locations via long-distance communications networks. Fourth, individual consumers are increasingly focused on buying the best product for the best price regardless of where it is produced.

In this borderless world, Ohmae argues, the "natural economic zones" are "regional states," which, unlike nation-states, are primarily oriented toward opportunities in the global economy. To varying extents, these regional states are free from the "baggage" of nation-states: "The implicit goal of their policies and their actions is not to defer to some outdated insistence on self-sufficiency, to buy off some well-wired constituency, to satisfy some emotional craving for the trappings of sovereignty, to tie up some bloc of votes, to feed some vocal demand for protection, or to keep some current government in power." When organized well, regional states function as "loose political federations" and serve as global "ports of entry" for their member countries. Composed of 5–20 million people, an efficient size for sales and service markets, they develop policies to "help companies to learn and to respond quickly to changing conditions—rather than policies that either protect or isolate them from competition or external change." Their main purpose is to improve the quality of life for their residents. Ohmae sums it up: "People came first; borders came afterwards. It is time for economic policy to remember this simple fact."

In Ohmae's neoliberal analysis, economic markets are the major factor in globalization. Other scholars disagree, emphasizing the inability of markets adequately to address global inequities and injustices.[8] Like capitalism, terrorism is a global phenomenon today—one fueled by desperate poverty and cultural differences. In his "Origins of Terrorism," Edward Said traces the origins of the 9/11 terrorist attacks to the history of twentieth-century U.S. foreign policy. "Aimed at symbols: the World Trade Center, the heart of American capitalism, and the Pentagon, the headquarters of the American military establishment," the terrorists' actions reflected the "enormous distance" between the world of U.S. politics and Islam. According to Said, the United States presents Arabs and Muslims with a "schizophrenic picture" of political principles—democracy, freedom, justice, and law—at odds with self-interested economic and security policies. Meanwhile, Western "fantasies about the Other with a capital O"—a phenomenon Said calls "orientalism"—only reinforce the mutual misunderstanding. As Said puts it, "the Muslim is thought of as being what we are not: fanatical, violent, lustful, irrational, and so on." This oppositional construct works to legitimate Western dominance in the Middle East, but it misses the shared roots of Judaism, Christianity, and Islam. Said is critical of all oppositional binaries: a politics of "us" vs. "them," he argues, often backfires. Many Arabs and Muslims believe that Islamic civilization is fighting for survival against Western barbarians, he warns, while in the United States, " 'terrorism' has become synonymous now with anti-Americanism, which in turn has become synonymous with being critical of the U.S., which in turn has become synonymous with being unpatriotic." This "series of equations" conveniently bypasses the concept of state terrorism—the "structure of terror," created by hegemonic liberal capitalism, that was the symbolic target of the 9/11 attacks. It also precludes "real engagement" of U.S. citizens and policymakers with the Islamic world.

Like Said, Sulayman Nyang calls into question the stereotyping of all Muslims as fundamentalists. Instead of Said's view from the West, however, Nyang offers a view of Islam from inside. Islam is first defined by a "geography of the mind," by public declarations of faith among members of a community. Within that community, further distinctions are drawn on the basis of property ownership, whose purpose is to serve higher goals of family and community. Although Islam is not socialist, members of society do have mutual obligations and, to varying degrees, the state may pursue distributive justice. Islam regards all human beings as God's children, descendants of Adam and Eve, created to live together in peace. As Nyang puts it, "This commonwealth consists of the Islamic *umma* and those members of the human race who are called *ahl al-kitah* (peoples of the book)—a category including Jews and Christians . . ." and, at various times, Zoroastrians, Hindus, and Buddhists. Even in its more expansionist moments, Nyang argues, Islamic universalism recognizes the mental and physical borders of distinct peoples. "This is to say that the Muslims in their quest for a just order among human beings saw the relationship between the geography of religion and the theology of space." Unlike Muslim fundamentalism, Islamic universalism pursues global justice through peace, not terror.

Muslim fundamentalism is, of course, only one of the new fundamentalisms shaping global politics.[9] The last three readings in this section offer different ways of characterizing the relationship between fundamentalism and globalization. Samuel Huntington asserts that the relevant conflicts in contemporary world politics arise at the level of civilization, which he defines as "the highest cultural grouping of people and the broadest level of cultural identity people have short of that which distinguishes humans from other species." Post–Cold War international relations, he argues, will be shaped more by civilizations than by nation-states or even by regional economies. Major clashes will occur between Western and non-Western civilizations—more specifically, between the West and Islam—over economic resources, especially oil, as well as cultural values. Regarding the latter, Huntington argues that "Western civilization is both Western and modern. Non-Western civilizations have attempted to become modern without becoming Western." Unlike Said and Nyang, Huntington recognizes only the West as supportive of universal principles such as human rights—not Islam or Judaism or, for that matter, socialism. He concludes that "For the relevant future, there will be no universal civilization, but instead a world of different civilizations, each of which will have to learn to coexist with the others."

According to Benjamin Barber, two opposed tendencies are shaping global politics today: "The planet is falling precipitantly apart *and* coming reluctantly together at the very same moment." These two tendencies—which he designates Jihad and McWorld—"operate with equal strength in opposite directions, the one driven by parochial hatreds, the other by universalizing markets, the one re-creating ancient subnational and ethnic borders from within, the other making national borders porous from without." Moving beyond Ohmae's portrait of globalization, Barber's McWorld adds ecological, information-technology, and resource concerns to market forces; he presents each aspect as "transnational, transideological, and transcultural" in its implications. Barber's overriding concern is that McWorld is "commercialized, homogenized, depoliticized, bureaucratized," but not democratized. Jihad, the tendency toward subnational, factional politics, is no more democratic, however. Of its "players," Barber writes: "they are cultures, not countries; parts, not wholes; sects, not religions, rebellious factions and dissenting minorities at war not just with globalism but with the traditional nation state." Barber fears that Jihad replaces civil discourse with identity politics, creating an international scene that resembles gang warfare, but he expects globalization eventually to trump such "retribalization." The relevant question, then, is what form this global politics will take. Like Ohmae, Barber envisions a confederation, although his emphasis is on the creation of democratic institutions that can combine local participation with global representation.

Barber regards these global democratic impulses as the legacy of the European Enlightenment. Of the authors included here, it is Fred Dallmayr who envisions a process of globalization that moves farthest beyond oppositional binaries—"us vs. them," "the West vs. the Rest," Jihad vs. McWorld—and integrates local/national/global politics. Drawing on the work of Richard Falk, Dallmayr proposes "an alternative global path leading between and beyond culture clashes and global domination." It is a path of dialogue and "globalization from below," a path supported by grassroots movements, world religions and cultures, as well as by scholars and politicians. Here democratic universalism is no longer the province of the European Enlightenment or Western civilization or the Christian religion. Indeed, Dallmayr's "intercivilizational dialogue" begins with a question: "Who is universal?" To illustrate the difference between the nationalism conveyed by Mazzini's love of country and more dangerous fundamentalisms, Dallmayr tells the following *hadith:* "As reported by Ibn Majah: 'A man once asked the Prophet [Muhammad] if bigotry is to love one's tribe. 'No," replied the Prophet. 'Bigotry is to help your tribe to tyrannize others.' "

With this precept in mind, we might ask another question: What if the tension between universal rights and particular identities begins and ends with the nation-state?[10] If so, the decoupling of nations from states may yet reveal global and local alternatives to terrorism, in its many forms. This process also suggests a need to rethink the meaning of ideology, a concept closely associated with the rise of European nation-states. Mainstream ideologies persist, but they are now accompanied by tendencies toward "global or universal ideologies" and "more diverse, unstructured, and temporary combinations."[11] Like that of the nation-state, the future of ideologies is uncertain. As one scholar sums it up: "What is clear is that ideologies cannot come to an end, nor is there a winning ideology. . . . For that to happen history would have to have a finishing post, and human imagination would have to grind to a halt."[12]

NOTES

1. Michael Freeden, *Ideology: A Very Short Introduction* (Oxford: Oxford University Press, 2003), 98.

2. Terence Ball and Richard Dagger, *Political Ideologies and the Democratic Ideal,* 5th ed. (New York: Pearson Longman, 2004), 7.

3. Andrew Heywood, *Political Ideologies: An Introduction,* 3rd ed. (New York: Palgrave Macmillan, 2003), 325.

4. Hans Kohn, *Nationalism: Its Meaning and History* (Princeton, N.J.: Van Nostrand, 1965), 9. Kohn provides an excellent, though brief, history of nationalism.

5. Max Weber, "Politics as a Vocation," in *From Max Weber: Essays in Sociology,* ed. Hans Gerth and C. Wright Mills (New York: Oxford University Press, 1958), 78.

6. Walker Connor, "A Nation Is a Nation, Is a State, Is an Ethnic Group, Is a . . . ," in *Nationalism,* ed. John Hutchinson and Anthony D. Smith (New York: Oxford University Press, 1994), 36–46.

7. Kenichi Ohmae, *The End of the Nation State: The Rise of Regional Economies* (New York: Free Press, 1995), 2–5.

8. Joseph E. Stiglitz, *Globalization and Its Discontents* (New York: Norton, 2002), ch. 9.

9. Andrew Heywood, in *Political Ideologies,* offers one of the more insightful and inclusive definitions of fundamentalism: "Fundamentalism is a style of thought in which certain principles are recognized as essential 'truths' that have unchallengeable and overriding authority, regardless of their content" (p. 299). By this definition, some liberal democrats' commitment to global human rights is a secular fundamentalism.

10. For an early discussion of this question, see: Yael Tamir, *Liberal Nationalism* (Princeton: Princeton University Press, 1993).

11. Freeden, 94.

12. Ibid., 102.

42

Joseph Mazzini

———◆———

The Duties of Man (1858)

Joseph Mazzini (1805–1872) was an ardent Italian nationalist and republican, whose life is a tale of insurrection, imprisonment, and exile. He founded Young Italy, an organization dedicated to liberating and uniting the Italian city-states. Mazzini lived to see Italian unification, although it occurred under a monarchical, not a republican, government. He continued to work to educate his countrymen, especially the working class, until his death. In The Duties of Man *he describes man's desire for unity expressed in love of country.*

5
Duties to Country

YOUR FIRST DUTIES—first, at least, in importance—are, as I have told you, to Humanity. You are *men* before you are *citizens* or *fathers*. If you do not embrace the whole human family in your love, if you do not confess your faith in its unity—consequent on the unity of God—and in the brotherhood of the Peoples who are appointed to reduce that unity to fact—if wherever one of your fellow men groans, wherever the dignity of human nature is violated by falsehood or tyranny, you are not prompt, being able, to succour that wretched one, or do not feel yourself called, being able, to fight for the purpose of relieving the deceived or oppressed—you disobey your law of life, or do not comprehend the religion which will bless the future.

Reprinted from Joseph Mazzini, *The Duties of Man and Other Essays*, by permission of the publishers, J. M. Dent and Everyman's Library.

But what can *each* of you, with his isolated powers, *do* for the moral improvement, for the progress of Humanity? You can, from time to time, give sterile expression to your belief; you may, on some rare occasion, perform an act of *charity* to a brother not belonging to your own land, no more. Now, *charity* is not the watchword of the future faith. The watchword of the future faith is *association,* fraternal cooperation towards a common aim, and this is as much superior to *charity* as the work of many uniting to raise with one accord a building for the habitation of all together would be superior to that which you would accomplish by raising a separate hut each for himself, and only helping one another by exchanging stones and bricks and mortar. But divided as you are in language tendencies, habits, and capacities, you cannot attempt this common work. The *individual* is too weak, and Humanity too vast. *My God,* prays the Breton mariner as he puts out to sea, *protect me, my ship is so little, and Thy ocean so great!* And this prayer sums up the condition of each of you, if no means is found of multiplying your forces and your powers of action indefinitely. But God gave you this means when he gave you a Country, when, like a wise overseer of labour, who distributes the different parts of the work according to the capacity of the workmen, he divided Humanity into distinct groups upon the face of our globe, and thus planted the seeds of nations. Bad governments have disfigured the design of God, which you may see clearly marked out, as far, at least, as regards Europe, by the courses of the great rivers, by the lines of the lofty mountains, and by other geographical conditions; they have disfigured it by conquest, by greed, by jealousy of the just sovereignty of others; disfigured it so much that to-day there is perhaps no nation except England and France whose confines correspond to this design. They did not, and they do not, recognise any country except their own families and dynasties, the egoism of caste. But the divine design will infallibly be fulfilled. Natural divisions, the innate spontaneous tendencies of the peoples will replace the arbitrary divisions sanctioned by bad governments. The map of Europe will be remade. The Countries of the People will rise, defined by the voice of the free, upon the ruins of the Countries of Kings and privileged castes. Between these Countries there will be harmony and brotherhood. And then the work of Humanity for the general amelioration, for the discovery and application of the real law of life, carried on in association and distributed according to local capacities, will be accomplished by peaceful and progressive development; then each of you, strong in the affections and in the aid of many millions of men speaking the same language, endowed with the same tendencies, and educated by the same historic tradition, may hope by your personal effort to benefit the whole of Humanity.

To you, who have been born in Italy, God has allotted, as if favouring you specially, the best-defined country in Europe. In other lands, marked by more uncertain or more interrupted limits, questions may arise which the pacific vote of all will one day solve, but which have cost, and will yet perhaps cost, tears and blood; in yours, no. God has stretched round you sublime and indisputable boundaries; on one side the highest mountains of Europe, the Alps; on the other the sea, the immeasurable sea. Take a map of Europe and place one point of a pair of compasses in the north of Italy on Parma; point the other to the mouth of the Var, and describe a semicircle with it in the direction of the Alps; this point, which will fall, when the semicircle is completed, upon the mouth of the Isonzo, will have marked the frontier which God has given you. As far as this frontier your language is spoken and understood; beyond this you have no rights. Sicily, Sardinia, Corsica, and the smaller islands between them and the mainland of Italy belong undeniably to you. Brute force may for a little while contest these frontiers with you, but they have been recognised from of old by the tacit general consent of the peoples; and the day when, rising with one accord for the final trial, you plant your tricoloured flag upon that frontier, the whole of Europe will acclaim re-risen Italy, and receive her into the community of the nations. To this final trial all your efforts must be directed.

Without Country you have neither name, token, voice, nor rights, no admission as brothers into the fellowship of the Peoples. You are the bastards of Humanity. Soldiers without a banner, Israelites among the nations, you will find neither faith nor protection; none will be sureties for you. Do not beguile yourselves with the hope of emancipation from unjust social conditions if you do not first conquer a Country for yourselves; where there is no Country there is no common agreement to which you can appeal; the egoism of self-interest rules alone, and he who has the upper hand keeps it, since there is no common safeguard for the interests of all. Do not be led away by the idea of improving your material conditions without first solving the national question. You cannot do it. Your industrial associations and mutual help societies are useful as a means of educating and disciplining yourselves; as an economic fact they will remain barren until you have an Italy. The economic problem demands, first and foremost, an increase of capital and production; and while your Country is dismembered into separate fragments—while shut off by the barrier of customs and artificial difficulties of every sort, you have only restricted markets open to you—you cannot hope for this increase. Today—do not delude yourselves—you are not the working-class of Italy; you are only fractions of that class; powerless, unequal to the great task which you propose to yourselves. Your emancipation can have no practical beginning until a National Government, understanding the signs of the times, shall, seated in Rome, formulate a Declaration of Principles to be the guide for Italian progress, and shall insert into it these words, *Labour is sacred, and is the source of the wealth of Italy.*

Do not be led astray, then, by hopes of material progress which in your present conditions can only be illusions. Your Country alone, the vast and rich Italian Country, which stretches from the Alps to the farthest limit of Sicily, can fulfil these hopes. You cannot obtain your *rights* except by obeying the commands of *Duty*. Be worthy of them, and you will have them. O my Brothers! love your Country. Our Country is our home, the home which God has given us, placing therein a numerous family which we love and are loved by, and with which we have a more intimate and quicker communion of feeling and thought than with others; a family which by its concentration upon a given spot, and by the homogeneous nature of its elements, is destined for a special kind of activity. Our Country is our field of labour; the products of our activity must go forth from it for the benefit of the whole earth; but the instruments of labour which we can use best and most effectively exist in it, and we may not reject them without being unfaithful to God's purpose and diminishing our own strength. In labouring according to true principles for our Country we are labouring for Humanity; our Country is the fulcrum of the lever which we have to wield for the common good. If we give up this fulcrum we run the risk of becoming useless to our Country and to Humanity. Before *associating* ourselves with the Nations which compose Humanity we must exist as a Nation. There can be no association except among equals; and you have no recognised collective existence.

Humanity is a great army moving to the conquest of unknown lands, against powerful and wary enemies. The Peoples are the different corps and divisions of that army. Each has a post entrusted to it; each a special operation to perform; and the common victory depends on the exactness with which the different operations are carried out. Do not disturb the order of the battle. Do not abandon the banner which God has given you. Wherever you may be, into the midst of whatever people circumstances may have driven you, fight for the liberty of that people if the moment calls for it; but fight as Italians, so that the blood which you shed may win honour and love, not for you only, but for your Country. And may the constant thought of your soul be for Italy, may all the acts of your life be worthy of her, and may the standard beneath which you range yourselves to work for Humanity be Italy's. Do not say *I;* say *we*. Be every one of you an incarnation of your Country, and feel himself and make himself responsible for his fellow-countrymen; let each one of you learn to act in such a way that in him men shall respect and love his Country.

Your Country is one and indivisible. As the members of a family cannot rejoice at the common table if one of their number is far away, snatched from the affection of his brothers, so you should have no joy or repose as long as a portion of the territory upon which your language is spoken is separated from the Nation.

Your Country is the token of the mission which God has given you to fulfil in Humanity. The faculties, the strength of *all* its sons should be united for the accomplishment of this mission. A certain number of common duties and rights belong to every man who answers to the *Who are you?* or the other peoples, *I am an Italian.* Those duties and those rights cannot be represented except by one *single* authority resulting from your votes. A Country must have, then, a single government. The politicians who call themselves federalists, and who would make Italy into a brotherhood of different states, would dismember the Country, not understanding the idea of Unity. The States into which Italy is divided to-day are not the creation of our own people; they are the result of the ambitions and calculations of princes or of foreign conquerors, and serve no purpose but to flatter the vanity of local aristocracies for which a narrower sphere than a great Country is necessary. What you, the people, have created, beautified, and consecrated with your affections, with your joys, with your sorrows, and with your blood, is the City and the Commune, not the Province or the State. In the City, in the Commune, where your fathers sleep and where your children will live, where you exercise your faculties and your personal rights, you live out your lives as *individuals.* It is of your City that each of you can say what the Venetians say of theirs: *Venezia la xe nostra: l'avemo fatta nu* (Venice is our own: we have made her). In your City you have need of *liberty* as in your Country you have need of *association.* The Liberty of the Commune and the Unity of the Country—let that, then, be your faith. Do not say Rome and Tuscany, Rome and Lombardy, Rome and Sicily; say Rome and Florence, Rome and Siena, Rome and Leghorn, and so through all the Communes of Italy. Rome for all that represents Italian life; your commune for whatever represents the *individual* life. All the other divisions are artificial, and are not confirmed by your national tradition.

A Country is a fellowship of free and equal men bound together in a brotherly concord of labour towards a single end. You must make it and maintain it such. A Country is not an aggregation, it is an *association.* There is no true Country without a uniform right. There is no true Country where the uniformity of that right is violated by the existence of caste, privilege, and inequality—where the powers and faculties of a large number of individuals are suppressed or dormant—where there is no common principle accepted, recognised, and developed by all. In such a state of things there can be no Nation, no People, but only a multitude, a fortuitous agglomeration of men whom circumstances have brought together and different circumstances will separate. In the name of your love for your Country you must combat without truce the existence of every privilege, every inequality, upon the soil which has given you birth. One privilege only is lawful—the privilege of Genius when Genius reveals itself in brotherhood with Virtue; but it is a privilege conceded by God and not by men, and when you acknowledge it and follow its inspirations, you acknowledge it freely by the exercise of your own reason and your own choice. Whatever privilege claims your submission in virtue of force or heredity, or any right which is not a common right, is a usurpation and a tyranny, and you ought to combat it and annihilate it. Your Country should be your Temple. God at the summit, a People of equals at the base. Do not accept any other formula, any other moral law, if you do not want to dishonour your Country and yourselves. Let the secondary laws for the gradual regulation of your existence be the progressive application of this supreme law.

And in order that they should be so, it is necessary that *all* should contribute to the making of them. The laws made by one fraction of the citizens only can never by the nature of things and men do otherwise than reflect the thoughts and aspirations and desires of that fraction; they represent, not the whole country, but a third, a fourth part, a class, a zone of the country. The law must express the general aspiration, promote the good of all, respond to a beat of the nation's heart. The whole nation therefore should be, directly or indirectly, the legislator. By yielding this mission to a few men, you put the egoism of one class in the place of the Country, which is the union of *all* the classes.

A Country is not a mere territory; the particular territory is only its foundation. The Country is the idea which rises upon that foundation; it is the sentiment of love, the sense of fellowship which binds together all the sons of that territory. So long as a single one of your brothers is not represented by his own vote in the development of the national life—so long as a single one vegetates uneducated among the educated—so long as a single one able and willing to work languishes in poverty for want of work—you have not got a Country such as it ought to be, the Country of all and for all. *Votes, education, work* are the three main pillars of the nation; do not rest until your hands have solidly erected them.

And when they have been erected—when you have secured for every one of you food for both body and soul—when freely united, entwining your right hands like brothers round a beloved mother, you advance in beautiful and holy concord towards the development of your faculties and the fulfilment of the Italian mission—remember that that mission is the moral unity of Europe; remember the immense duties which it imposes upon you. Italy is the only land that has twice uttered the great word of unification to the disjoined nations. Twice Rome has been the metropolis, the temple, of the European world; the first time when our conquering eagles traversed the known world from end to end and prepared it for union by introducing civilised institutions; the second time when, after the Northern conquerors had themselves been subdued by the potency of Nature, of great memories and of religious inspiration, the genius of Italy incarnated itself in the Papacy and undertook the solemn mission—abandoned four centuries ago—of preaching the union of souls to the peoples of the Christian world. Today a third mission is dawning for our Italy; as much vaster than those of old as the Italian People, the free and united Country which you are going to found, will be greater and more powerful than Caesars or Popes. The presentiment of this mission agitates Europe and keeps the eye and the thought of the nations chained to Italy.

Your duties to your Country are proportioned to the loftiness of this mission. You have to keep it pure from egoism, uncontaminated by falsehood and by the arts of that political Jesuitism which they call diplomacy.

The government of the country will be based through your labours upon the worship of principles, not upon the idolatrous worship of interests and of opportunity. There are countries in Europe where Liberty is sacred within, but is systematically violated without; peoples who say, *Truth is one thing, utility another: theory is one thing, practice another.* Those countries will have inevitably to expiate their guilt in long isolation, oppression, and anarchy. But you know the mission of our Country, and will pursue another path. Through you Italy will have, with one only God in the heavens, one only truth, one only faith, one only rule of political life upon earth. Upon the edifice, sublimer than Capitol or Vatican, which the people of Italy will raise, you will plant the banner of Liberty and of Association, so that it shines in the sight of all the nations, nor will you lower it ever for terror of despots or lust for the gains of a day. You will have boldness as you have faith. You will speak out aloud to the world, and to those who call themselves the lords of the world, the thought which thrills in the heart of Italy. You will never deny the sister nations. The life of the Country shall grow through you in beauty and in strength, free from servile fears and the hesitations of doubt, keeping as its *foundation* the people, as its *rule* the consequences of its principles logically deduced and energetically applied, as its *strength* the strength of all, as its *outcome* the amelioration of all, as its *end* the fulfilment of the mission which God has given it. And because you will be ready to die for Humanity, the life of your Country will be immortal.

43

Benedict Anderson

Imagined Communities: Reflections on the Origin and Spread of Nationalism (1983)

Benedict Richard O'Gorman Anderson (b. 1936) was born in China. His father was an Imperial Maritime Officer, and an active supporter of Irish nationalist movements. Anderson received a B.A. in classics from Cambridge University and a Ph.D. in government at Cornell University, where he later directed the Modern Indonesia Program. After he authored the "Cornell Paper" of 1966, which attributed the 1965 Indonesian coup to discontented army officers rather than to communist insurgents, Anderson was banned from further research in Indonesia. This excerpt from his best-known work traces the origins of nationalism.

3
The Origins of National Consciousness

IF THE DEVELOPMENT of print-as-commodity is the key to the generation of wholly new ideas of simultaneity, still, we are simply at the point where communities of the type "horizontal-secular, transverse-time" become possible. Why, within that type, did the nation become so popular? The factors involved are obviously complex and various. But a strong case can be made for the primacy of capitalism.

As already noted, at least 20,000,000 books had already been printed by 1500,[1] signalling the onset of Benjamin's "age of mechanical reproduction." If manuscript

Source: Benedict Anderson, *Imagined Communities, Reflections on the Origin and Spread of Nationalism* (New York: Verso, 1991).

knowledge was scarce and arcane lore, print knowledge lived by reproducibility and dissemination.[2] If, as Febvre and Martin believe, possibly as many as 200,000,000 volumes had been manufactured by 1600, it is no wonder that Francis Bacon believed that print had changed "the appearance and state of the world."[3]

One of the earlier forms of capitalist enterprise, book-publishing felt all of capitalism's restless search for markets. The early printers established branches all over Europe: "in this way a veritable 'international' of publishing houses, which ignored national [*sic*] frontiers, was created."[4] And since the years 1500–1550 were a period of exceptional European prosperity, publishing shared in the general boom. "More than at any other time" it was "a great industry under the control of wealthy capitalists."[5] Naturally, "book-sellers were primarily concerned to make a profit and to sell their products, and consequently they sought out first and foremost those works which were of interest to the largest possible number of their contemporaries."[6]

The initial market was literate Europe, a wide but thin stratum of Latin-readers. Saturation of this market took about a hundred and fifty years. The determinative fact about Latin—aside from its sacrality—was that it was a language of bilinguals. Relatively few were born to speak it and even fewer, one imagines, dreamed in it. In the sixteenth century the proportion of bilinguals within the total population of Europe was quite small; very likely no larger than the proportion in the world's population today, and—proletarian internationalism notwithstanding— in the centuries to come. Then and now the bulk of mankind is monoglot. The logic of capitalism thus meant that once the elite Latin market was saturated, the potentially huge markets represented by the monoglot masses would beckon. To be sure, the Counter-Reformation encouraged a temporary resurgence of Latin-publishing, but by the mid-seventeenth century the movement was in decay, and fervently Catholic libraries replete. Meantime, a Europe-wide shortage of money made printers think more and more of peddling cheap editions in the vernaculars.[7]

The revolutionary vernacularizing thrust of capitalism was given further impetus by three extraneous factors, two of which contributed directly to the rise of national consciousness. The first, and ultimately the least important, was a change in the character of Latin itself. Thanks to the labours of the Humanists in reviving the broad literature of pre-Christian antiquity and spreading it through the print-market, a new appreciation of the sophisticated stylistic achievements of the ancients was apparent among the trans-European intelligentsia. The Latin they now aspired to write became more and more Ciceronian, and, by the same token, increasingly removed from ecclesiastical and everyday life. In this way it acquired an esoteric quality quite different from that of Church Latin in mediaeval times. For the older Latin was not arcane because of its subject matter or style, but simply because it was written at all, i.e. because of its status as *text*. Now it became arcane because of what was written, because of the language-in-itself.

Second was the impact of the Reformation, which, at the same time, owed much of its success to print-capitalism. Before the age of print, Rome easily won every war against heresy in Western Europe because it always had better internal lines of communication than its challengers. But when in 1517 Martin Luther nailed his theses to the chapel-door in Wittenberg, they were printed up in German translation, and "within 15 days [had been] seen in every part of the country."[8] In the two decades 1520–1540 three times as many books were published in German as in the period 1500–1520, an astonishing transformation to which Luther was absolutely central. His works represented no less than one third of *all* German-language books sold between 1518 and 1525. Between 1522 and 1546, a total of 430 editions (whole or partial) of his Biblical translations appeared. "We have here for the first time a truly mass readership and a popular literature within everybody's reach."[9] In effect, Luther became the first best-selling author *so known*. Or, to put it another way, the first writer who could "sell" his *new* books on the basis of his name.[10]

Where Luther led, others quickly followed, opening the colossal religious propaganda war that raged across Europe for the next century. In this titanic "battle for men's minds," Protestantism was always fundamentally on the offensive, precisely because it knew how to make use of the expanding vernacular print-market being created by capitalism, while the Counter-Reformation defended the citadel of Latin. The emblem for this is the Vatican's *Index Librorum Prohibitorum*— to which there was no Protestant counterpart—a novel catalogue made necessary by the sheer volume of printed subversion. Nothing gives a better sense of this siege mentality than François I's panicked 1535 ban on the printing of *any* books in his realm—on pain of death by hanging! The reason for both the ban and its unenforceability was that by then his realm's eastern borders were ringed with Protestant states and cities producing a massive stream of smugglable print. To take Calvin's Geneva alone: between 1533 and 1540 only 42 editions were published there, but the numbers swelled to 527 between 1550 and 1564, by which latter date no less than 40 separate printing-presses were working overtime.[11]

The coalition between Protestantism and print-capitalism, exploiting cheap popular editions, quickly created large new reading publics—not least among merchants and women, who typically knew little or no Latin—and simultaneously mobilized them for politico-religious purposes. Inevitably, it was not merely the Church that was shaken to its core. The same earthquake produced Europe's first important non-dynastic, non-city states in the Dutch Republic and the Commonwealth of the Puritans. (François I's panic was as much political as religious.)

Third was the slow, geographically uneven, spread of particular vernaculars as instruments of administrative centralization by certain well-positioned would-be absolutist monarchs. Here it is useful to remember that the universality of Latin in mediaeval Western Europe never corresponded to a universal political system. The contrast with Imperial China, where the reach of the mandarinal bureaucracy and of painted characters largely coincided, is instructive. In effect, the political fragmentation of Western Europe after the collapse of the Western Empire meant that no sovereign could monopolize Latin and make it his-and-only-his language-of-state, and thus Latin's religious authority never had a true political analogue.

The birth of administrative vernaculars predated both print and the religious upheaval of the sixteenth century, and must therefore be regarded (at least initially) as an independent factor in the erosion of the sacred imagined community. At the same time, nothing suggests that any deep-seated ideological, let alone proto-national, impulses underlay this vernacularization where it occurred. The case of "England"—on the northwestern periphery of Latin Europe—is here especially enlightening. Prior to the Norman Conquest, the language of the court, literary and administrative, was Anglo-Saxon. For the next century and a half virtually all royal documents were composed in Latin. Between about 1200 and 1350 this state-Latin was superseded by Norman French. In the meantime, a slow fusion between this language of a foreign ruling class and the Anglo-Saxon of the subject population produced Early English. The fusion made it possible for the new language to take its turn, after 1362, as the language of the courts—and for the opening of Parliament. Wycliffe's vernacular *manuscript* Bible followed in 1382.[12] It is essential to bear in mind that this sequence was a series of "state," not "national," languages; and that the state concerned covered at various times not only today's England and Wales, but also portions of Ireland, Scotland *and France*. Obviously, huge elements of the subject populations knew little or nothing of Latin, Norman French, or Early English.[13] Not till almost a century *after* Early English's political enthronement was London's power swept out of "France."

On the Seine, a similar movement took place, if at a slower pace. As Bloch wrily puts it, "French, that is to say a language which, since it was regarded as merely a corrupt form of Latin, took several centuries to raise itself to literary dignity,"[14] only became the official language of the courts of justice in 1539, when François I issued the Edict of Villers-Cotterêts.[15] In other dynastic realms Latin survived much longer—under the Habsburgs well into the nineteenth century. In still others, "foreign" vernaculars took over: in the eighteenth century the languages of the Romanov court were French and German.[16]

In every instance, the "choice" of language appears as a gradual, unselfconscious, pragmatic, not to say haphazard development. As such, it was utterly different from the selfconscious language policies pursued by nineteenth-century dynasts confronted with the rise of hostile popular linguistic-nationalisms. . . . One clear sign of the difference is that the old administrative languages were *just that:* languages used by and for officialdoms for their own inner convenience. There was no idea of systematically imposing the language on the dynasts' various subject populations.[17] Nonetheless, the elevation of these vernaculars to the status of languages-of-power, where, in one sense, they were competitors with Latin (French in Paris, [Early] English in London), made its own contribution to the decline of the imagined community of Christendom.

At bottom, it is likely that the esotericization of Latin, the Reformation, and the haphazard development of administrative vernaculars are significant, in the present context, primarily in a negative sense—in their contributions to the dethronement of Latin. It is quite possible to conceive of the emergence of the new imagined national communities without any one, perhaps all, of them being present. What, in a positive sense, made the new communities imaginable was a half-fortuitous, but explosive, interaction between a system of production and productive relations (capitalism), a technology of communications (print), and the fatality of human linguistic diversity.[18]

The element of fatality is essential. For whatever superhuman feats capitalism was capable of, it found in death and languages two tenacious adversaries.[19] Particular languages can die or be wiped out, but there was and is no possibility of humankind's general linguistic unification. Yet this mutual incomprehensibility was historically of only slight importance until capitalism and print created monoglot mass reading publics.

While it is essential to keep in mind an idea of fatality, in the sense of a *general* condition of irremediable linguistic diversity, it would be a mistake to equate this fatality with that common element in nationalist ideologies which stresses the primordial fatality of *particular* languages and their association with *particular* territorial units. The essential thing is the *interplay* between fatality, technology, and capitalism. In pre-print Europe, and, of course, elsewhere in the world, the diversity of spoken languages, those languages that for their speakers were (and are) the warp and woof of their lives, was immense; so immense, indeed, that had print-capitalism sought to exploit each potential oral vernacular market, it would have remained a capitalism of petty proportions. But these varied idiolects were capable of being assembled, within definite limits, into print-languages far fewer in number. The very arbitrariness of any system of signs for sounds facilitated the assembling process.[20] (At the same time, the more ideographic the signs, the vaster the potential assembling zone. One can detect a sort of descending hierarchy here from algebra through Chinese and English, to the regular syllabaries of French or Indonesian.) Nothing served to "assemble" related vernaculars more than capitalism, which, within the limits imposed by grammars and syntaxes, created mechanically reproduced print-languages capable of dissemination through the market.[21]

These print-languages laid the bases for national consciousnesses in three distinct ways. First and foremost, they created unified fields of exchange and communication below Latin and above the spoken vernaculars. Speakers of the huge variety of Frenches, Englishes, or Spanishes, who might find it difficult or even impossible to understand one another in conversation, became capable of comprehending one another via print and paper. In the process, they gradually became aware of the hundreds of thousands, even millions, of people in their particular language-field, and at the same time that *only those* hundreds of thousands, or millions, so belonged. These fellow-readers, to whom they were connected through print, formed, in their secular, particular, visible invisibility, the embryo of the nationally imagined community.

Second, print-capitalism gave a new fixity to language, which in the long run helped to build that image of antiquity so central to the subjective idea of the nation. As Febvre and Martin remind us, the printed book kept a permanent form, capable of virtually infinite reproduction, temporally and spatially. It was no longer subject to the individualizing and "unconsciously modernizing" habits of monastic scribes. Thus, while twelfth-century French differed markedly from that written by Villon in the fifteenth, the rate of change slowed decisively in the sixteenth. "By the 17th century languages in Europe had generally assumed their modern forms."[22] To put it another way, for three centuries now these stabilized print-languages have been gathering a darkening varnish; the words of our seventeenth-century forebears are accessible to us in a way that to Villon his twelfth-century ancestors were not.

Third, print-capitalism created languages-of-power of a kind different from the older administrative vernaculars. Certain dialects inevitably were "closer" to each print-language and dominated their final forms. Their disadvantaged cousins, still assimilable to the emerging print-language, lost caste, above all because they were unsuccessful (or only relatively successful) in insisting on their own print-form. "Northwestern German" became Platt Deutsch, a largely spoken, thus sub-standard, German, because it was assimilable to print-German in a way that Bohemian spoken-Czech was not. High German, the King's English, and, later, Central Thai, were correspondingly elevated to a new politico-cultural eminence. (Hence the struggles in late-twentieth-century Europe by certain "sub-" nationalities to change their subordinate status by breaking firmly into print—and radio.)

It remains only to emphasize that in their origins, the fixing of print-languages and the differentiation of status between them were largely unselfconscious processes resulting from the explosive interaction between capitalism, technology and human linguistic diversity. But as with so much else in the history of nationalism, once "there," they could become formal models to be imitated, and, where expedient, consciously exploited in a Machiavellian spirit. Today, the Thai government actively discourages attempts by foreign missionaries to provide its hill-tribe minorities with their own transcription-systems and to develop publications in their own languages: the same government is largely indifferent to what these minorities *speak*. The fate of the Turkic-speaking peoples in the zones incorporated into today's Turkey, Iran, Iraq, and the USSR is especially exemplary. A family of spoken languages, once everywhere assemblable, thus comprehensible, within an Arabic orthography, has lost that unity as a result of conscious manipulations. To heighten Turkish-Turkey's national consciousness at the expense of any wider Islamic identification, Atatürk imposed compulsory romanization.[23] The Soviet authorities followed suit, first with an anti-Islamic, anti-Persian compulsory romanization, then, in Stalin's 1930s, with a Russifying compulsory Cyrillicization.[24]

We can summarize the conclusions to be drawn from the argument thus far by saying that the convergence of capitalism and print technology on the fatal diversity of human language created the possibility of a new form of imagined community, which in its basic morphology set the stage for the modern nation. The potential stretch of these communities was inherently limited, and, at the same time, bore none but the most fortuitous relationship to existing political boundaries (which were, on the whole, the highwater marks of dynastic expansionisms).

Yet it is obvious that while today almost all modern self-conceived nations—and also nation-states—have "national print-languages," many of them have these languages in common, and in others only a tiny fraction of the population "uses" the national language in conversation or on paper. The nation-states of Spanish America or those of the "Anglo-Saxon family" are conspicuous examples of the first outcome; many ex-colonial states, particularly in Africa, of the second. In other words, the concrete formation of contemporary nation-states is by no means isomorphic with the determinate reach of particular print-languages. To account for the discontinuity-in-connectedness between print-languages, national consciousness, and nation-states, it is necessary to turn to the large cluster of new political entities that sprang up in the Western hemisphere between 1776 and 1838, all of which self-consciously defined themselves as nations, and, with the interesting exception of Brazil, as (non-dynastic) republics. For not only were they historically the first such states to emerge on the world stage, and therefore inevitably provided the first real models of what such states should "look like," but their numbers and contemporary births offer fruitful ground for comparative enquiry.

NOTES

1. The population of that Europe where print was then known was about 100,000,000. Febvre and Martin, *The Coming of the Book*, pp. 248–49.

2. Emblematic is Marco Polo's *Travels*, which remained largely unknown till its first printing in 1559. Polo, *Travels*, p. xiii.

3. Quoted in Eisenstein, "Some Conjectures," p. 56.

4. Febvre and Martin, *The Coming of the Book*, p. 122. (The original text, however, speaks simply of "par-dessus les frontières." *L'Apparition*, p. 184.)

5. Ibid., p. 187. The original text speaks of "puissants" (powerful) rather than "wealthy" capitalists. *L'Apparition*, p. 281.

6. "Hence the introduction of printing was in this respect a stage on the road to our present society of mass consumption and standardisation." Ibid., pp. 259–60. (The original text has "une civilisation de masse et de standardisation," which may be better rendered "standardised, mass civilization." *L'Apparition*, p. 394).

7. Ibid., p. 195.

8. Ibid., pp. 289–90.

9. Ibid., pp. 291–95.

10. From this point it was only a step to the situation in seventeenth-century France where Corneille, Molière, and La Fontaine could sell their manuscript tragedies and comedies directly to publishers, who bought them as excellent investments in view of their authors' market reputations. Ibid., p. 161.

11. Ibid., pp. 310–15.

12. Seton-Watson, *Nations and States*, pp. 28–29; Bloch, *Feudal Society*, I, p. 75.

13. We should not assume that administrative vernacular unification was immediately or fully achieved. It is unlikely that the Guyenne ruled from London was ever primarily administered in Early English.

14. Bloch, *Feudal Society*, I, p. 98.

15. Seton-Watson, *Nations and States*, p. 48.

16. Ibid., p. 83.

17. An agreeable confirmation of this point is provided by François I, who, as we have seen, banned all printing of books in 1535 and made French the language of his courts four years later!

18. It was not the first "accident" of its kind. Febvre and Martin note that while a visible bourgeoisie already existed in Europe by the late thirteenth century, paper did not come into general use until the end of the fourteenth. Only paper's smooth plane surface made the mass reproduction of texts and pictures possible—and this did not occur for still another seventy-five years. But paper was not a European invention. It floated in from another history—China's—through the Islamic world. *The Coming of the Book*, pp. 22, 30, and 45.

19. We still have no giant multinationals in the world of publishing.

20. For a useful discussion of this point, see S. H. Steinberg, *Five Hundred Years of Printing*, chapter 5. That the sign *ough* is pronounced differently in the words although, bough, lough, rough, cough, and hiccough, shows both the idiolectic variety out of which the now-standard spelling of English emerged, and the ideographic quality of the final product.

21. I say "nothing served . . . more than capitalism" advisedly. Both Steinberg and Eisenstein come close to theomorphizing 'print' *qua* print as the genius of modern history. Febvre and

Martin never forget that behind print stand printers and publishing firms. It is worth remembering in this context that although printing was invented first in China, possibly 500 years before its appearance in Europe, it had no major, let alone revolutionary impact—precisely because of the absence of capitalism there.

22. *The Coming of the Book*, p. 319. Cf. *L'Apparition*, p. 477: "Au XVIIe siècle, les langues nationales apparaissent un peu partout cristallisées."

23. Hans Kohn, *The Age of Nationalism*, p. 108. It is probably only fair to add that Kemal also hoped thereby to align Turkish nationalism with the modern, romanized civilization of Western Europe.

24. Seton-Watson, *Nations and States*, p. 317.

References

Bloch, Marc. *Feudal Society.* Trans. I. A. Manyon. Chicago: University of Chicago Press. 1961. 2 vols.

Eisenstein, Elizabeth L. "Some Conjectures about the Impact of Printing on Western Society and Thought: A Preliminary Report." *Journal of Modern History,* 40:1 (March 1968). pp. 1–56.

Febvre, Lucian, and Henri-Jean Martin. *The Coming of the Book. The Impact of Printing, 1450–1800.* London: New Left Books. 1976. [Translation of *L'Apparition du Livre.* Paris: AlbinMichel. 1958]

Kohn, Hans. *The Age of Nationalism.* New York: Harper. 1962.

Polo, Marco. *The Travels of Marco Polo.* Trans. and ed. William Marsden. London and New York: Everyman's Library. 1946.

Seton-Watson, Hugh. *Nations and States. An Enquiry into the Origins of Nations and the Politics of Nationalism.* Boulder, Colo: Westview Press. 1977.

Steinberg, S. H. *Five Hundred Years of Printing.* Rev. ed. Harmondsworth: Penguin. 1966.

44

Kenichi Ohmae

The End of the Nation State: The Rise of Regional Economies

*Kenichi Ohmae (b. 1943), professor of public policy, international manage-
ment consultant, public speaker, and founder of "Reform of Heisei," a citizen
movement for political and administrative reform in Japan, is widely known
as "Mr. Strategy." Dr. Ohmae was a director of McKinsey & Company, Inc.,
an international management consulting firm, for twenty-three years. He
continues to advise some of Japan's most internationally successful companies as well as other Asian, European, and North American multinational
corporations. The author of more than one hundred books, he assists businesses and governments in developing regional economic strategies.*

Chapter Seven
The Emergence of Region States

. . . THE GLUE HOLDING traditional nation states together, at least in economic
terms, has begun to dissolve. Buffeted by sudden changes in industry dynamics,
available information, consumer preferences, and flows of capital; burdened by
demands for the civil minimum and for open-ended subsidies in the name of the
national interest; and hog-tied by political systems that prove ever-less responsive
to new challenges, these political aggregations no longer make compelling sense

as discrete, meaningful units on an up-to-date map of economic activity. They are still there, of course, still major players on the world stage. But they have, for the most part, lost the ability to put global logic first in the decisions they make.

For nation states and especially for their leaders, the primary issue remains protection—of territory, of resources, of jobs, of industries, even of ideology. In Guangzhou, however, the capital of the state of Guangdong, young Chinese ladies have something else on their minds: Avon lipstick. Some time back, Avon ran a TV commercial that implied that Cantonese girls, if they managed to get a hold of Avon products, could easily be as attractive as Hong Kong girls. With the right makeup and, perhaps, the right (suitably short) outfit, a happy world of clubs and music and dancing and romance was theirs for the taking.

The result: there are now more than 30,000 Avon ladies selling products door-to-door in Guangdong alone; in Shanghai, where operations have just started, there are another 6,000. These salespeople, no less than the girls eagerly snatching up their wares, probably do not remember how to spell "communism" any more. Their minds are on the possibilities suddenly open to them through the global market, not on the backward-looking concerns of the nation state to which they belong.

By contrast, the territorial dividing lines that do make sense belong to what I call "region states"—geographical units like northern Italy; Baden-Würtemberg (or the upper Rhine);[1] Wales; San Diego / Tijuana; Hong Kong/southern China; the Silicon Valley/Bay Area in California; and Pusan (at the southern tip of the Korean peninsula) and the cities of Fukuoka and Kitakyushu in the north of the Japanese island of Kyushu. Other such areas include the Growth Triangle of Singapore, Johore (the southernmost state of Malaysia), and the neighboring Riau Islands of Indonesia (including Batam, a large tax-free zone); Research Triangle Park in North Carolina; the Rhône-Alps region of France, centered on Lyons, with its tight business and cultural ties to Italy; the Languedoc-Roussillon region, centered on Toulouse, with its tight linkages with Catalonia; Tokyo and its outlying areas; Osaka and the Kansai region; the Malaysian island of Penang . . . and even the newly emerging Greater Growth Triangle, unveiled in 1992 across the Strait of Malacca, connecting Penang, Medan (an Indonesian city in Sumatra), and Phuket in Thailand.

In a borderless world, these are the natural economic zones. Though limited in geographical size, they are often huge in their economic influence. . . . For example, Japan's Shutoken region—Tokyo and the three immediately neighboring prefectures—has a cumulative GNP that, were it a full-blown nation state, would rank it third worldwide after the United States and Germany. Similarly, Japan's Kansai region—Osaka, Kobe, and Kyoto—would rank sixth, just after the U.K. Instead of being able to join the G-7, however, Kansai's mayors and governors must commute weekly to Tokyo, hat in hand, to get approval and permission and resources for whatever they want to do. Not only do regional leaders in

Japan not get to take the seat at the global table to which their economies ought to entitle them, they do not even enjoy the same regional freedoms that leaders of the states in the United States and of the *Länder* in Germany do.

These region states may or may not fall within the borders of a particular nation. Whether they do is purely an accident of history. In practical terms, it really does not matter. Like Singapore, many are, in effect, city states, which have willingly—and explicitly—given up some of the trappings of nation states in return for the (relatively) unfettered ability to tap extensively into the four I's of the global economy.

Region states are not, however, the same thing—although they may be the same size—as a megacity like Calcutta or Mexico City. Unlike region states, these immense human aggregations either do not or cannot look to the global economy for solutions to their problems or for the resources to make those solutions work. They look, instead, to the central governments of the nation states in which they reside.

By virtue of their political subordination, megacities are immune to global logic, neither seeking it out nor able to harness it when available. Absent these global linkages, however, they are, as a rule, unable to bootstrap themselves back onto a healthy trajectory of growth. In effect, deference to sovereignty isolates them and robs them of the only workable means for improvement. At the same time, deference to sovereignty imposes a huge, often unsupportable burden on their central governments, which—consistent with the civil minimum—must pour endless resources into their bottomless pits of need. Thus, as with declining industries, the economic dynamics of megacities graph a downward spiral from which there is no self-contained escape. Region states are different in that they gladly sidestep the bunting and hoopla of sovereignty in return for the ability to harness the global I's to their own needs.

Population, then, is not the key issue. What matters most is that each region state possesses, in one or another combination, the essential ingredients for successful participation in the global economy. With only 2.5 million people (70 percent Chinese, 20 percent Malay, and 10 percent Indian) and virtually no natural resources, Singapore—by natural endowment, a kind of Costa Rica in Asia—simply could not have prospered without inviting in the global economy. Its sister island of Penang has learned the lesson well. . . . Both have had the wisdom and the will—and the determination—to put global logic first. . . .

Ports of Entry

"All politics," as Tip O'Neill, former Speaker of the U.S. House of Representatives, was wont to say, "is local." Region states, however, are economic not political units, and they are anything but local in focus. They may lie within the borders of an established nation state, but they are such powerful engines of development because their primary orientation is toward—and their primary linkage is with—the global economy. They are, in fact, among its most reliable ports of entry.

Region states welcome foreign investment. They welcome foreign ownership. They welcome foreign products. In fact, they welcome whatever will help employ their people productively, improve their quality of life, and give them access to the best and cheapest products from anywhere in the world. And they have learned that such access is often best and easiest when the products are not produced at home. (Singaporeans, for example, enjoy better and cheaper agricultural products than do the Japanese, although Singapore has no farmers—and no farms—of its own.) Region states also welcome the chance to use whatever surplus these activities generate to ratchet up their people's quality of life still further, not to fund the civil minimum or subsidize outmoded industries. Their leaders do not show up somewhere in the world trying to attract factories and investment and then appear on TV back home vowing to protect local companies no matter what. In a word, they consistently put global logic first.

Region states make such effective ports of entry to the global economy because the very characteristics that define them are shaped by the demands of that economy. They must, for example, be large enough to provide an attractive market for the brand development of leading consumer products. Hence, they tend to be between 5 and 20 million people in size. The range is broad, but the extremes are clear: not half a million, not 50 or 100 million. That is because they must be small enough for their citizens to share interests as consumers, but still of sufficient size to justify economies not of scale (which, after all, can be leveraged from a base of any size through exports to the rest of the world), but of service—that is, the infrastructure of communications, transportation, and professional services essential to participation in the global economy. (They must have, for example, at least one international airport and, more than likely, one good harbor with international-class freight-handling facilities.)

As the reach of TV expands, advertising becomes efficient. Although trying to achieve penetration of a consumer brand throughout all of Japan or Indonesia may be prohibitively expensive, establishing it firmly in the Osaka[2] or Jakarta regions is far more affordable—and far more likely to generate handsome returns. Much the same is true with sales and service networks, customer satisfaction programs, market surveys, and management information systems: efficient scale is to be found at the regional, not the national, level. This matters because, on balance, it is modern marketing techniques that shape the economies of region states. For individual companies, political borders are little more than an artificial, externally imposed source of inefficiency. What counts, instead, is the geographical clustering of broad similarities in taste and preference.

In order to sell branded consumer goods, for example, TV advertising is essential. Something like 100,000 gross rating points (GRP) are needed to establish a reasonable level of brand recognition. But the cost of such advertising is sufficiently high that it can be justified only when it reaches a large enough audience—say, several million potential consumers. After the brand is established, the next step is to get all the other essential pieces in place: shelf control in retail outlets, just-in-time delivery, after-sales service, cooperative promotions with local retailers, and the like. This means setting up a logistics and marketing operation dedicated to the region—again an expensive undertaking justified only by the potential size of the market. Thus, if the market is too small, it cannot get over the threshold to qualify as a stand-alone region state. Conversely, if it is so large—either in population or geographical extent—that several parallel operations systems are required to service it, it lacks the focused coherence to qualify as a region state.

Where true economies of service exist, religious, ethnic, and racial distinctions are not important—or at least, they are of as little importance as human nature allows. Singapore is 70 percent ethnic Chinese, but its 30 percent minority is no problem because commercial prosperity creates sufficient affluence to keep them contented. Nor are ethnic differences a source of concern for potential investors. In Indonesia, however, with its 250 or so different tribal groups, 18,000 islands, and 188 million people, no organization theory known to man can define a mode of political order secure or stable enough to calm all investors' fears.

Still, Indonesia has traditionally attempted to impose a single form of political order from the center by applying fictional averages. They do not work.[3] But if the country's leaders allowed economies of service to define, within Indonesia, two or three Singapore-sized region states, they *could* be managed. A recent (1991) effort to make Batam Island an open economy linked with Singapore has already attracted more than 50 foreign corporations, mostly from Japan. A comparable effort in Medan is now under way. If successful, these initiatives spearheaded by President Suharto, would work against, rather than exacerbate, the country's manifold social divisions.

Indeed, because the orientation of region states is toward the global economy, not toward their host nations, they help breed an internationalism of outlook that defuses many of the usual kinds of social tensions. In the United States, for example, the Japanese have already established about 120 "transplant" auto industry-related factories throughout the Mississippi Valley. More are on the way. As their share of the domestic industry's production grows, people in the region, who look to these plants for their livelihoods and for the tax revenues to support their local communities, will stop caring whether the plants belong to U.S.- or Japan-headquartered companies. All they will care about are the economic benefits of having them there—in the Valley Region State.

The mere existence of relevant service economies does not, of course, mean that a region will always act—or even aspire to act—as a local outpost of the global economy. . . . Annalee Saxenian has shown that,[4] for much of its history, Silicon Valley in California, that great engine of much of the microelectronics industry in the United States, prospered—especially by comparison with that other regional center of microelectronics, Route 128 in Massachusetts—because its laid-back, freewheeling style attracted topflight people, ideas, and venture capitalists and allowed them to combine and recombine in a "networked" industrial model. By providing an open, local point of connection to the fast-moving, worldwide universe of technology and technologists, it quickly outpaced its Massachusetts rival. . . .

By contrast, Route 128 went to Washington as it were, turned lobbyist, studied "competitiveness" as a way to get more federal funding for R&D, and grew protectionist. It has also begun to discourage, even fear, foreign investments as well as foreign takeovers. The inevitable result: Japan is now developing a Silicon Island on Kyushu; Taiwan is trying to create a Silicon Island of its own; and Korea is nurturing a Silicon Peninsula. This is the worst of all possible outcomes: less new money in Massachusetts and a host of newly energized and well-funded competitive areas.

Such defensiveness is the detritus of old suspicions. It very much gets in the way. But it does not have to. When, for example, Hollywood recognized that it was about to face a severe capital shortage, it did not throw up protectionist barriers against foreign money. Instead, it invited Rupert Murdoch into 20th-Century-Fox, C. Itoh and Toshiba into Time-Warner, Sony into Columbia, and Matsushita into MCA. The result: a $15 billion infusion of new capital—and, equally important, $15 billion less for Japan or anyone else to set up a competing Hollywood of its own.

These experiences do not argue for entrusting all efforts to forge productive linkages with the global economy to the fragmented, idiosyncratic choices of individual companies. They certainly do not argue for getting government, at any level, involved in picking those industries or technologies that should be so linked. Between the extremes of centrally directed industrial policy and hands-off free markets, however, there is room for regional policy. Done well, this can easily make the difference between local prosperity and local versions of nation state–type paralysis. The trick, as Saxenian notes, is to develop policies that "help companies to learn and respond quickly to changing conditions—rather than policies that either protect or isolate them from competition or external change."

The goal, in other words, is to foster the development of flexible communities of interest through local networks. These networks provide multiple forums for collaboration and the exchange of opinions. But, in aggregate, they also make possible the economies of service that legitimize region-based infrastructure for communicating with—and connecting to—the global economy.

The heart of the challenge, remember, is not to solve all problems locally, but rather to make it possible to solve them by harnessing global resources. The effectiveness of region states depends on their ability to tap global solutions. When nation states were the dominant actors in economic affairs, a potential infusion of new resources or new talent was not always welcome: there might be vested interests to protect or suspicions of foreign influence to gratify for political ends. Region states, by contrast, carry virtually none of this baggage. The implicit goal of their policies and their actions is not to defer to some outdated insistence on self-sufficiency, to buy off some well-wired constituency, to satisfy some emotional craving for the trappings of sovereignty, to tie up some bloc of votes, to feed some vocal demand for protection, or to keep some current government in power. It is to improve the quality of their people's lives by attracting and harnessing the talents and resources of the global economy, not by warding that economy off so that special interests can flourish.

No wonder, then, that when the people in Guangzhou tell their leaders in Beijing that they need to be joined with Hong Kong economically, if not politically, the latter's response is to say, Let's not get too carried away here. Let's not move too fast. Let's not create a model we might not want other regions to emulate. We want to control this. Greater openness may be necessary, but we want to decide when and how fast and how far. More to the point, we want to be sure that whatever new revenue such openness generates can be identified, captured, and put to use funding the civil minimums of less advanced areas. We have all of China to worry about, and we do worry. It is politically intolerable for us to let the economic fortunes of different regions get—and, worse, be seen to get—too far out of balance.

To which, naturally, the people in Guangzhou respond, You still don't get it. *You* may be worried about providing civil minimums, but *we* have to worry about how to become more like—as well as how to compete with—the Hong Kongs and Singapores and Taiwans of this world. We have to convince foreign investors that we are preferable to these other regions as a subject for their energies. They don't have to come here. They don't have to bring their money or their technology or their skills here. They can easily take them elsewhere. Press these golden geese too hard or make their laying house too unattractive, and they will work their magic in a competitor's backyard.

At the same time, of course, the people of Guangzhou know that they cannot deny a significant, ongoing relationship with the rest of mainland China. That connection is real—and is part of their strength and appeal. What they cannot afford is to be victims of tight, centralized control. But they can productively be—in fact, they would do well to be—part of a loose grouping of Chinese regional states, a kind of Chinese federation or commonwealth. This would well serve both sets of interests. The ironic lesson of history, however, is that when strong, centrally controlled nation states—the former Soviet Union, for example—prove unwilling to give up the illusion of power in order to enhance the quality of life of their people, the reality of that power erodes.

Old habits die hard, and the habits of power die hardest of all. Even—perhaps especially—when there has been a history of loose federation, as in the United States under the Articles of Confederation, there is often great reluctance to re-embrace either its logic or its ideals. All too often, what is remembered of those troubled years between the Treaty of Paris and the Constitution is the image of a feeble central government unable to do much of anything, let alone intervene effectively on the economic front. But it is precisely those protection-minded interventions that a return to federation is designed to prevent.

However soothing the illusion of control or of the beneficial effects of top-down intervention, the record shows that pitifully few such actions have ever restored hard-hit industries or regions to health. There are, of course, many kinds of policy actions by governments that *are* both useful and necessary. Just think, for example, of the financial regulation established during the early days of the New Deal in the U.S. But these are usually not the kinds of things that rabid defenders of central power have in mind.

Nation states, for the most part, opt for solutions that, however wasteful or inefficient, maintain at least the illusion of control. During the past ten years, for example, the United States has demanded more and more loudly that Japan open up its domestic market to rice.[5] The Rice Millers Association of America has played an influential lobbying role in Washington. After frustrating bilateral talks, the issue was brought into the Uruguay Round and, by extension, under the auspices of the new World Trade Organization. Japan has finally—and grudgingly—agreed to a gradual opening of its market, starting with 300,000 tons in 1993 and increasing by annual increments of 100,000 tons. In return, Japan will initially be able to assess a very stiff tariff, which will slowly decrease over time. This—as such nation state–based negotiations go—is a resounding victory.

However, what if Japan's 11 regional *do-shu* or natural business areas had been charged with handling the issue in place of the central government in Tokyo? The negotiators would have been the same people who have to compete with other *do-shus* for their economic survival, rather than those who face demands from local farmers and prefectural officials for more than US $10 billion a year in subsidies (*just to import rice worth only $300 million!*). Representatives from Tohoku-do, then, at the northeastern end of Honshu, might have chosen to visit rice-growing areas along the Mississippi in the United States and offer local farmers a deal: let us invest in your operations to produce high-quality and low-cost rice and then let us sell some percentage of it in Japan. U.S. farmers would then have had access to Japanese money and markets, and Tohoku-do farmers would have had access to a good business deal and to cheap rice for their people.

No one would fight to keep markets closed. Moreover, if all the *do-shus* behaved in a similar way and structured comparable deals with a variety of partners in Thailand, Australia, or wherever, Japanese consumers would stand to save more than US $40 billion annually from the grossly inflated prices they now have to pay. Everybody would win—except the lobbyists, who might find themselves out of a job. By contrast, leaving the issue to central governments means that Japanese farmers scream out against opening up the market and extort an additional US $72 billion from Tokyo to "permit" it, Japanese consumers have no access to inexpensive rice, and U.S. farmers have no access to Japanese money and only a tiny bit of access to their market. Everybody loses—except the lobbyists, who now enjoy even greater job security.

Because of the pressures operating on them, the predictable focus of nation states is on mechanisms for propping up troubled industries. This goes nowhere. The endless trade negotiations,[6] for example, between Japan and the United States, may have played well to voters back home, but the actions to which they led have rescued no industry, revived no sector of the economy, and been of advantage to no consumers. Textiles, semiconductors, automobiles, consumer electronics—these industries do not develop according to the whims of policymakers, but only in response to the defining logic of the competitive marketplace. If U.S. share in an industry has fallen, it is not because policy failed but because individual consumers decided to buy from other suppliers. But even when government policy succeeds—as, for example, did Japan's reluctant agreement to allow domestic sales of U.S.-made mobile phones—the home country does not benefit; the company does. In this case, the chips for the "U.S." handsets sold in Japan were made—and the handsets assembled—in Malaysia.

This, certainly, is not welcome news in established seats of power. Centrists shudder at the implications of region states or federations of region states because they have come to look upon the system of control they know best as if it were given in the very nature of things. But it is not. It is just an accident of history, nothing more, that modern economic theory crystallized at about the same time as the modern nation state. Had Adam Smith written one century earlier, it might be much easier for us now to view the connections between economic activity and nation states in quite a different light. So, too, if John Maynard Keynes had written half a century later. Indeed, for much of history, as Jane Jacobs reminds us in *Cities and the Wealth of Nations*, the meaningful units of economic life were—in fact, still are—urban aggregations and their respective hinterlands. It is centralized power over economic affairs that is the latecomer here. For a limited historical moment, it best suited the needs of development. That moment has now passed.

Where prosperity exists, it is region-based. And when a region prospers, its good fortune spills over into adjacent territories inside and outside the political federation of which it is a part. Economic progress in and around Bangkok, for example, has prompted investors to explore options elsewhere in Thailand. Much the same is true of Kuala Lumpur in Malaysia, of Jakarta in Indonesia, and, of course, of Singapore, which is rapidly becoming the unofficial capital of ASEAN [Association of Southeast-Asian States]. It could also be true of São Paulo in Brazil—if, that is, the central Brazilian government learns to treat it as a genuine region state and permits it to join the global economy. If it does, at least one region in Brazil could well join the OECD within ten years or so. If it does not—because of concerns for the civil minimum or fears that fairness among regions would be sacrificed—then the country as a whole may well fall off the roster of NIEs [National Intelligence Estimates].

Region states are not—and need not be—the enemies of central government. Handled gently, by federation, these ports of entry to the global economy may well prove to be their very best friends.

NOTES

1. Kenichi Ohmae, "Forum: If they fall, so will our stock markets—Tokyo's soaring property prices," *New York Times*, October 11, 1987.

2. Kenichi Ohmae, " 'Unfair' trade?" *Business Tokyo*, January 1987.

3. Kenichi Ohmae, "Per favore confermere di avere ricevut bene," *L'Espresso*, May 27, 1987.

4. Annalee Saxenian, *Regional Advantage: Culture and Competition in Silicon Valley and Route 128* (Cambridge, Mass.: Harvard University Press, 1994).

5. Kenichi Ohmae, "A special report on Japan: Some foreign firms too busy making profit to complain," *International Herald Tribune*, March 19, 1986.

6. Kenichi Ohmae, "Special report: The myth and reality of the Japanese corporation," *Chief Executive*, Summer 1981.

45

Sulayman Nyang

"Religion and the Maintenance of Boundaries: An Islamic View" (2002)

Sulayman Nyang (b. 1944) is professor of African studies at Howard University. Writing on Islamic, African, and Middle Eastern affairs, he is best known for Islam, Christianity, and African Identity *(1984) and* A Line in the Sand: Saudi Arabia's Role in the Gulf War *(1995, with Evan Heindricks). From 1975 to 1978, he served as deputy ambassador and head of chancery at the Gambia Embassy in Jeddah, Saudi Arabia.*

RELIGION IS ONE of the oldest sources of boundaries among human beings. It remains one of the most important means of demarcating and maintaining boundaries in our time. The necessity of taking account of religious values is particularly acute for men and women living in states and societies where notions of boundaries—geographical and metaphysical—are related to notions of divine will, expressed through revelation of a sacred law, as is the case in Islam. M. Raquibuz Zaman's review of the Islamic tradition in the preceding chapter[1] highlights this way of thinking, for he cites several Qur'anic verses and Prophetic statements to justify the right of ownership and the sanctity of private property. This treatment is certainly warranted, for the *shari'a* prescriptions for ordering human relations remain perhaps the first and most essential consideration that most Muslims employ. I want to approach the topic in a slightly different manner, however, focusing on both the metaphysical and physical aspects of boundary formation and maintenance from an Islamic point of view.

Religion as a Source of Boundaries

Religions claim transcendence beyond time and place. But the historical fact is that in most human societies religions arose from and responded to the conditions of specific human groups. These ethnic or geographic origins of religious beliefs have been well documented by anthropologists, historians, and social scientists.[2] Boundary lines in the early human communities were erected and maintained through some ritualistic expression of shared faith. Since one human being cannot read the mind of another, the only way to determine belief is by some explicit profession and affirmation of membership in a belief system.

Some religious systems have erected elaborate means of admission to their community. Others make fewer demands on those who would enter their fold. Nevertheless, all religious systems create boundaries between their believers and outsiders by requiring some overt demonstration of conviction. In Islam, the means of crossing the boundary from non-Islam to Islam is relatively straightforward: through the *shahada* or the profession of faith that "There is no god but God, and Muhammad is the messenger of God." This first pillar of the Islamic faith is the moral equivalent of a public declaration delimiting the borders of one's mind. A non-Muslim who decides voluntarily to embrace Islam is making both a mental and a social/physical decision. By declaring his faith as a Muslim, he is telling members of his immediate family and the rest of society that the mental borders defining his family and the culture with which he identifies have been redrawn in accordance with the teachings of his newly adopted faith.

This geography of the mind has a number of social consequences. The new believer must now be trusted by all members of his new religion. His faithfulness to Islam cannot be challenged within the community because no other believer can directly probe his mind and know absolutely whether he is a true believer or not. From the point of view of external verification of his faith, the only means by which the border guard of the faith can attest to his fidelity and sincerity is through his compliance with the rituals of the new faith. This is why rituals are crucial for the maintenance of boundaries and in the perpetuation of social solidarity among the members of a particular religion. We will return to the role of ritual in maintaining boundaries shortly.

Religions not only establish boundaries between believers and unbelievers, they also frequently create or legitimate boundaries among believers. I am referring now not to spiritual boundaries, which shared conviction is supposed to tear down, but to physical boundaries such as the rights of property ownership. As Zaman's elaboration of the Islamic laws on property demonstrates, Islam has been closely aligned through the centuries with private property. Under the shari'a, property may be acquired in three ways: by *iktisab* (earning), *wiratha* (inheritance), and *hiba* (gift). Maulana Muhammad 'Ali, a leading Indo-Pakistani intellectual of the twentieth century, describes the right of an individual to acquire property as "one of the basic laws regulating human society."[3] The Qur'an makes clear that this right is enjoyed by both men and women: "Men shall have the benefit of what they earn and women shall have the benefit of what they earn" (4:32). Both sexes also have a right to inherit property: "Men shall have a portion of what the parents and the near relatives leave and women shall have a portion of what the parents and the near relatives leave" (4:7). While no formal legal limitations are placed upon the property or wealth that an individual may acquire or dispose of, moral injunctions certainly circumscribe the behavior of the faithful in this area.

The Qur'an warns Muslims not to seek wealth through immoral means, such as through deceit (e.g., 4:29), bribery (2:188), usury (2:275–76), and the misappropriation of wealth held in trust (4:58)—for example, the property of orphans (4:6). Moreover, a number of other proscriptions in Islam may be seen as related to honest dealing in property acquisition. For example, the strong condemnation of gambling is coupled with a rebuke against consumption of alcoholic beverages in Q. 2:219. The connection between gambling and obtaining or losing property is obvious, but the connection with intoxicants is perhaps not so straightforward. Certainly, consumption of alcohol may be condemned for other reasons as well. In Q. 4:43 Muslims are told not to approach their daily prayers in a state of intoxication. But finally when the Qur'an proscribes intoxicants altogether in a later revelation (5:90), alcohol is once again linked with gambling because "they excite enmity and hatred among you." Producing, selling, and imbibing liquor and other forms of intoxicants are all condemned, like gambling, because they promote, among other things, fraudulent and harmful exchanges of wealth, potentially threatening the stability of society.

The Qur'an gives full rights of disposal of property to its legitimate owners, whether male or female, but at the same time it requires that the owners be most careful in spending the resulting wealth.[4] There are many injunctions of a general nature to this effect. Thus, the Qur'an describes the righteous servants of Allah (*'ibad al-Rahman*) as "they who, when they spend, are neither extravagant, nor parsimonious, and keep between these the just mean" (25:67). And elsewhere: "And do not make your hand to be shackled to your neck [in miserliness], nor stretch it forth to the utmost limit of its stretching forth, lest you should [afterwards] become blameworthy and destitute" (17:29). These restrictions on the exercise of rights of property by individual owners is described as *hajr* in a number of *hadiths* from the prophet Muhammad. One widely cited report from Imam Bukhari's collection of hadith reads as follows: "There is no charity unless a man has sufficient to give, and whoever spends in charity and he is himself in want or his family is in want or he has a debt to pay, it is more in the fitness of things that the debt should be paid than that he should spend in charity or free a slave or make a gift, and such a gift or charity shall be annulled, for he has no right to waste the wealth of the people *(amwal al-nas)*."[5] The reference to the "wealth of the people" in this hadith is a clear example of the Islamic view that though an individual owns property, that ownership *in the moral sense* is not exclusive to him or her. Spending one's wealth in even the worthiest of causes, as in charity, may be objectionable if the prior claims of one's dependents are not met.

In short, we can conclude that the owner of movable or immovable property, whether male or female, has the right to sell, barter, or bequeath it in any fashion deemed moral in light of Islamic teachings. Overarching all such transactions is the fundamental Qur'anic injunction: "Woe to the defrauders, who, when they take the measure from men, take it fully; but when they measure out to others or weigh out for them, they are deficient" (83:1–3).

The preceding discussion of private property rights is fundamental to our discussion of territorial boundaries, not only because individual owners are the building blocks of any national economy, but because the legal rulings and the general moral precepts we have outlined above apply equally to the state in its own business transactions. What is permitted the individual is permitted the state; what is prohibited the individual is prohibited the state. On the basis of the Qur'anic statements discussed above, general agreement has existed among Muslim scholars that in light of Islam's protection of individual property rights, governments have no right to deprive citizens of such ownership. This is not to say, of course, that the moral purview of the state is not broader than that of the individual. Whereas the individual is responsible to family and perhaps immediate neighbors, the state must take account of the welfare of all those residing within its jurisdiction. This obligation was historically fulfilled through the collection and distribution of the alms tax *(zakat)*, which has already been discussed in the previous chapter. During the past two centuries, under the influence of socialist ideologies from Europe, a few Muslim intellectuals have sought to portray the Qur'anic vision of mutual obligations in society as a form of proto-socialism, while rejecting some of the more extreme aspects of Marxism. As Maulana Muhammad 'Ali argues: "Islam is thus opposed to Bolshevism, which recognizes no individual rights of property; but it is at the same time socialistic in its tendencies, inasmuch as it tries to bring about a more or less equal distribution of wealth."[6] The question is, how far does Islamic ethics permit the state to move down the path of distributive justice?

The debate among Muslims on this issue is rich and ranges along the spectrum from total rejection to acceptance of various degrees of state intervention. Much of the controversy centers around the right of modern nation-states to nationalize private property in the name of social welfare and economic development. All modern Muslim states have to various degrees pursued such policies, and, in the face of religious opposition, have mobilized religious supporters to provide Islamic sanction for their policies. Thus, when Nasser undertook his Arab socialist schemes in Egypt, Mahmud Shaltut, the shaykh of al-Azhar, the leading religious functionary of the state, produced a treatise arguing that Islam and Arab socialism were compatible. Other, "independent" Muslim intellectuals, such as Mustafa Siba'i, a leader of the Syrian Muslim Brotherhood, and the Indo-Pakistani scholar Khalifa 'Abd al-Hakim, have also promoted the idea of "Islamic socialism." In their view, the goal of state intervention should be to alleviate poverty and class differences, not eradicate them as the Communists wanted to do, because such goals are contrary to the natural order described in the Qur'an.[7]

Such arguments have been strongly challenged by other Muslim thinkers, and in some cases of state intervention, the *'ulama,* the guardians of the religious law, have led a conservative backlash. Particularly susceptible to challenge from the 'ulama have been land reforms, which represent an obviously dramatic claim on the part of the state to reinterpret shari'a laws for the sake of the national good. When the shah of Iran undertook land reforms as part of his White Revolution in the mid-1960s, the Iranian 'ulama, including Ayatollah Khomeini, were almost unanimous in their opposition to the redistribution of private property.[8] Such reactions have been evident in other major instances of land reform, including in Pakistan and Egypt. In the case of Iran, the 'ulama's mobilization against the shah during the White Revolution (which incidentally did little to improve the condition of the nation's peasant farmers) proved a harbinger of the revolution that came fifteen years later.

Religion as a Maintainer of Boundaries

Linking religion to private property, as most Muslims have done over the centuries, produces significant social and political consequences. The right to enjoy private property is meaningless without the existence of law and order. Hence, Islamic political thought has historically emphasized the need for law and order, leading even some of the greatest Muslim thinkers to accept tyrannical or, in modern parlance, authoritarian rule. "For," as al-Ghazali (d. 1111) famously put it, "if we were to decide that all wilayat [political authority] are now null and void, all institutions of public welfare would also be absolutely null and void. How should the capital be dissipated in straining after the profit?"[9] The "capital" al-Ghazali refers to here is the shari'a, which establishes and regulates all institutions of public welfare.[10] These institutions allow men and women in society, both individually and collectively, to carry out the primary purpose of life, the worship of the Most High God. But they also promote social peace and harmony through the regulation of human institutions, including the right to own and dispose of one's property. Surely, the preservation of such physical boundaries would be among the chief "profits" al-Ghazali had in mind.

All religions, no matter how universalistic their claims, are in the final analysis boundary maintainers, not just in the physical domain as discussed with regard to property, but also in the metaphysical realm.[11] This is largely because of their doctrine and their definition of reality. In the particular case of Islam, though Muslims claim that all human beings are the creatures of Allah and descendants of Adam and Eve, they strongly emphasize the line demarcating believers from unbelievers. Hence the juristic terms discussed by Zaman, dar al-Islam and dar al-harb. The first realm is that which harbors the men and women who embrace the belief in one God (tawhid), and the other is inhabited by the unbelievers (kafirun). Dar al-Islam and dar al-harb are as much metaphysical as physical constructs. We see clearly in these concepts how boundary lines are drawn not on geographical or biological differences, but on matters of faith. These concepts require us to distinguish between mental and physical boundaries among humans.[12]

Mental boundaries are those boundaries that are visible only to the perceiving agent. One can never know with certainty who else shares one's mental boundaries. This raises some acute problems for ideologically based human groupings whose physical and metaphysical integrity rests on trusting others who claim to hold the same convictions.

Hypocrisy and dissimulation have been the two most formidable threats to the integrity and security of social formations in human history. All religions as social groups have historically tried to maintain and protect their boundaries from penetration and infiltration. We know, for example, that the ancient Israelites were very much aware of the dangers posed by infiltration. According to linguists familiar with the Israelites' language, the Hebrew word shibboleth was used to distinguish aggressors and hypocrites from the devout; although the word simply meant "stream," its special use, as a test of pronunciation, gave it a special function (as can be seen in its English meaning). The very creation of a word like this reveals the strategic and social consciousness of the Israelites that the preservation of their community required both physical and mental tests.

In the case of Islam, inner acceptance of the faith has entailed the public performance of various ritual obligations, such as the pilgrimage, alms-giving, fasting, and most conspicuously, prayer. Yet from its very origins as a social phenomenon, Islam has grappled with the problems of false expressions of faith. The Qur'an repeatedly warns the faithful to beware the deceptions of hyp-ocrites, who may give physical indications of their sincerity, but have not fully crossed the mental boundary separating believers and unbelievers: "Woe to the worshippers, those who are neglectful of their prayers, those who [want but] to be seen [as Muslims], but refuse [even] the small kindnesses" (107:4–7).

In more extreme cases, that of the renegade apostate *(murtadd)* who re-nounces his religion, the penalty adduced by most medieval jurists was execu-tion. The legal rationale for this penalty was that his apostasy signified that he was either a hypocrite or an unbeliever disguised as a believer. In either event, he was a spy who posed a danger to the physical integrity of the Muslim commu-nity rather than to its spiritual integrity. This danger was considerable in the early days of Islam—from which the punishment is derived—because the community was constantly threatened by enemies from within and without.[13]

Cases like this one illustrate how the ethical questions are virtually indistin-guishable from the legal and political ones. Since membership in an ethnic, nation-al, or religious community confers social, political, and psychological protection and benefits upon those who are eligible and certified, it becomes problematic if someone who was at one time deemed worthy of privileges turns out to be an outsider posing as an insider. This is why words become an important means by which Muslims hold one another accountable for their deeds in this life. Histor-ically, under Muslim rule, those who converted to the faith by declaring the shahada immediately became eligible for all the rights and prerogatives of the community, including ownership of land, just as those who were born Muslim. Conversely, those who recanted became subject to sanctions.

The problem of dealing with hypocrites and renegades was not confined to legal disputations. The early history of Islam witnessed philosophical and theo-logical controversies among Muslim intellectuals trying to demarcate the mental boundaries, especially as these boundaries influenced the social and physical realms of human belief and action.[14] The question was: What actions signify an absence of faith? How can the community discern the true believer from the hyp-ocrite? The intellectual contests between the Mu'tazilites and other schools of thought during the ninth and tenth centuries is perhaps the best-known case of such philosophical wrangling. The Mu'tazilites believed that human beings are responsible for their actions within the human realm, producing a view of human agency and hence responsibility that is not contingent on external factors. The Ash'arites took the view that a combination of human will and divine sanction underlie all human activity, that no result in the physical or metaphysical universe is the product simply of human intent. This view leads logically to a predeter-ministic view of one's own place in the universe. The Murji'ites sought to chart a middle course on the question of human agency. Their leaders preferred to defer judgment to the end of time, when the Truth will be known only through divine revelation. This metaphysical "fence-sitting"—eventually adopted as a sort of compromise position among Muslim theologians—could well be construed as a sanction for the politics of indifference. Such a theological attitude of course yields a variety of outcomes. On the one hand, it promotes an ethic of toleration by removing judgment on matters of faith from human hands. But on the other hand, this position can easily become the basis for the acceptance of the status quo and the unenthusiastic conformity with changes brought about by revolutionary means. It may yield as fatalistic a view of human life as some of the predestinarian principles of the Ash'arites, making the maintenance of mental and physical boundaries not a human activity, but a divine will.

Regardless of how one feels about the different strategies developed by religious communities to maintain their boundaries, the fact remains that social and political order can only become a reality when men and women live in peace. This is where Islam provided the ancient world with a new paradigm of social definition and identification. Using what we might term "Adamic" and "Abrahamic" criteria to determine who belongs where and why, Islam holds all human beings to be essentially the same because they are all the children of Adam. This universal category confers upon all human beings the attributes of a creature deemed as God's representative on earth through genetic links to Adam and Eve.

However, a being devoid of faith in the Creator is considered *kafir*, a word which conveys both the sense of lack of belief and lack of gratitude. For this and other related reasons, he or she is excluded from the Abrahamic commonwealth. This commonwealth consists of the Islamic *umma* and those members of the human race who are called *ahl al-kitab* (peoples of the book)—a category including Jews and Christians, who also began with the Abrahamic ethic, but in one crucial way or another departed from it in the course of their evolution. As Zaman points out in the preceding chapter, the category was extended to include Zoroastrians, Hindus, and Buddhists when Islam expanded east of the Arabian peninsula. In describing the Islamic view of boundaries, therefore, we can argue that Muslims at the height of their power—when they might have succumbed to the temptations of exclusivism—recognized the utility and reality of both mental and physical boundaries, and they tried to defend and protect the rights of members of the various groups under their rule by formulating a public policy which allowed mental space to determine physical space. This is to say that the Muslims in their quest for a just order among human beings saw the relationship between the geography of religion and the theology of space.

The Islamic geography of religion made it impossible for the Islamic conquerors of the Middle East to uproot and relocate the vanquished as other conquerors had done in the ages before them. It also enabled them to articulate a policy of accommodation which respects the property rights of the defeated through the assessment of a special kind of tax *(kharaj)*. The theology of space, it must be emphasized, allowed the Muslims to recognize and protect the rights of all property owners, Muslim and non-Muslim.[15]

Two points made by Zaman bear repeating in our discussion of the Muslim approach to property rights. The first issue relates to the belief that the universe is a created *entity,* with humans as temporary custodians of this world. Unlike many Western exponents of the principle that a piece of land belongs to the person who mixes his labor with it, the Islamic view categorically states that private ownership is justifiable, but it is and must be seen always as holding property in trust. In his exposition, Zaman has shed ample light on the different schools of jurisprudence and their rulings on ownership.

What needs to be emphasized here is the second point, that the ethics of ownership in this case is so religiously bound that the believer's acts can be read ethically and legally simultaneously. In other words, ownership cannot in itself be the goal of a righteous individual; it is always merely a means to the pursuit of higher goals, and Islam always enjoins the promotion of family and communal well-being as among the highest. The Qur'an and the hadith literature identified with the prophet Muhammad convey to Muslims that this life is temporary and human beings should not be too fixated upon it. However, Islam does not teach its followers that this life is an illusion, as some creeds maintain. Rather, it teaches that compared to the next life *(al-akhira),* this life is insignificant. This is why Muslims pray for success in this life and success in the next life.

No strand of Muslim thought has grappled so deeply with the moral importance of physical and mental boundaries as has that of the Sufis, who came to the understanding that ownership is socially acceptable but mentally unnecessary. To most Sufi masters the idea of owning a thing is acceptable, but one must not forget that ownership brings only temporary utility. Investing too much emotional and psychic energy in such items of passing value can be spiritually counterproductive. In the logic of the Sufi master, material things, which are seen by many human beings as extensions of their egos, erect unwarranted boundaries among people. To the Sufi master, the only boundary worth preserving is that which separates the believer from the unbeliever. Though unbelievers share with believers common ancestry from Adam and Eve, their lack of faith in the Creator disqualifies them as reliable associates in this world. Again we return to the ingratitude implied in the term *kafir:* The unbeliever does not give credit to the very one who gives his life and ultimately takes his life in death. By being an unbeliever the neighbor who shares physical space with the Muslim in a human society is a traveling partner on the highway of life, but one fated sooner or later to part ways with the believer. The Muslim's destination is heavenward, whereas that of her unbelieving neighbor is earthbound.

NOTES

1. M. Raquibuz Zaman, "Islamic Perspectives on Territorial Boundaries and Autonomy," in *Islamic Political Ethics: Civil Society, Pluralism, and Conflict*, ed. Sohail H. Hashmi (Princeton, N.J.: Princeton University Press, 2002), 79–101.—Ed.

2. For a discussion of the variety of human religious thought and the impact of ethnocultural history on human societies, see Ninian Smart, *World-views: Crosscultural Explorations of Human Beliefs* (New York: Charles Scribner's Sons, 1983).

3. Maulana Muhammad 'Ali, *The Religion of Islam* (Columbus, Ohio: Ahmadiyya Anjuman Isha'at Islam, 1990), 509.

4. Ibid., 510.

5. *Sahih al-Bukhari*, bk. 24 (*kitab al-zakat*), chap. 17, cited ibid., 511.

6. Ibid., 509.

7. For a convenient anthology of Muslim arguments on socialism, see John J. Donohue and John L. Esposito, *Islam in Transition: Muslim Perspectives* (New York: Oxford University Press, 1982), 98–139.

8. See Ervand Abrahamian, *Khomeinism: Essays on the Islamic Republic* (Berkeley: University of California Press, 1993), 10, 55.

9. Quoted in H. A. R. Gibb, "Constitutional Organization," in *Law in the Middle East*, ed. Majid Khadduri and Herbert Liebesny (Washington, D.C.: Middle East Institute, 1955), 19.

10. Ibid., 20.

11. Almost all students of religion will agree that, though the world religions claim to be universal, their distinctiveness demarcates them from others making similar claims. For some recent discussions on this phenomenon and the challenge of pluralism, see Harold Coward, *Pluralism: Challenge to World Religions* (Maryknoll, N.Y.: Orbis Books, 1985).

12. For a discussion by modern Muslims of the relevance of these terms, see Hasan Moinuddin, *Charter of the Islamic Conference* (New York: Oxford University Press, 1987), 42–53; and Mohammad Talaat al-Ghunaimi, *The Muslim Conception of International Law and the Western Approach* (The Hague: Martinus Nijhoff, 1968), 184.

13. Al-Mawardi summarizes some of the opinions regarding the treatment of renegades who departed from the Islamic fold but later recanted. Abu al-Hasan al-Mawardi, *al-Ahkam al-Sultaniyya: The Laws of Islamic Governance*, trans. Asadullah Yate (London: Ta-Ha Publishers, 1996), chap. 5.

14. For details on these medieval theological disputes, see Fazlur Rahman, *Islam* (Chicago: University of Chicago Press, 1979), chap. 5.

15. For a balanced discussion on the treatment of religious minorities by both Muslims and Christians in the medieval period, see Mark R. Cohen, *Under Crescent and Cross: The Jews in the Middle Ages* (Princeton: Princeton University Press, 1994).

46

Edward W. Said

"Origins of Terrorism" (2001)

Edward Said (1935–2003) was born in Jerusalem and dispossessed from Palestine in 1948. Spending the rest of his life advocating Palestinian self-determination, he regarded the Oslo peace agreement between Israel and the P.L.O. as "an instrument of Palestinian surrender," and the U.S. as a "dishonest broker" in the peace process. Said was professor of English and comparative literature at Columbia University. Many of his writings examine Western perceptions of the Islamic world; his most famous book is Orientalism *(1978). The following article is based on a radio conversation with David Barsamian, in which Said reflects on the meaning of the 9/11 terrorist attacks in their immediate aftermath.*

KGNU, Boulder, Colorado, September 24, 2001

THE EVENTS OF SEPTEMBER 11, 2001, *have bewildered and confused many Americans. What might be a good place to start, to give people some understanding as to the context and background that would motivate terrorist hijackers?*

Speaking as a New Yorker, it was a shocking and terrifying event, I mean, particularly the scale of it. It was designed to shock and terrify and paralyze and do a whole lot of terrible and, in my opinion, inexcusable things.

Edward W. Said, "Origins of Terrorism," in *Culture and Resistance, Conversations with Edward W. Said*, ed. David Barsamanian and Edward W. Said (Cambridge, Mass.: South End Press, 2003), 103–115, 121–131. © 2003 by Edward Said, reprinted with the permission of the Wylie Agency, Inc.

But it was obviously the result of a great deal of planning, as well as very auda-cious—some might even say brilliant—execution. And, at the bottom of it, an implacable desire to do harm. Not quite indiscriminate, I would say, because it was aimed at symbols: the World Trade Center, the heart of American capitalism, and the Pentagon, the headquarters of the American military establishment. But it was not meant to be argued with. It wasn't part of any negotiation and obvi-ously no message was intended with it. It spoke for itself, which is unusual.

I think that it comes out of a long dialectic of U.S. involvement abroad that spans the entire past century. Involvement in the affairs of the Islamic world, the oil-producing world, the Arab world, the Middle East. All those areas of the world that are considered to be essential to U.S. interests and security that include oil and strategic power; the control and positioning of the United States in the Persian Gulf; the protection of allies like Israel, Saudi Arabia, and others. And through this dialectic, and a relentlessly unfolding series of interactions, the United States has played, to the residents of this area, a very distinctive role, which most Amer-icans, I think, have been either shielded from or are simply unaware of.

It's important to understand first of all that there are two worlds here—there's the world of people who live in that environment and the world of people who live in the United States. And there really is very little in common between them. There never has been much direct contact as there had been, for example, between Great Britain and the Islamic world, including Afghanistan, and cer-tainly the Gulf and India and, for example, Iraq. The United States has been pro-tected by its enormous distance from the place, including the Atlantic Ocean, the Mediterranean, and the sheer difficulty of getting there. But there's also been another barrier—and that is, of course, language and religion.

This is an area of the world, starting, let's say, in Bosnia and moving East, all across Central Asia and then down into the Middle East, Pakistan, Bangladesh, Indonesia to the East and then the Arab countries in the middle, all across north Africa, which is largely Muslim, where 1.2 billion Muslims live, where the United States is seen in two quite different ways. One, the official United States, the United States of armies and interventions, such as in 1953 when it overthrew the nation-alist government of Mohammad Mossadegh in Iran and brought back the shah. The United States that has been involved first in the Gulf War and then in the tremendously damaging—damaging to civilians, that is—sanctions, against Iraq. The United States is the supporter of Israel against the Palestinians, first in the establishment of the state in 1948, then in the occupation of 1967, the Lebanese war, the invasion of Lebanon by Israel in 1982, the Intifadas of 1987 and 2000. The United States supplies Israel with enormous amounts of weapons. So if you live in the area, you see these things as part of a continuing drive for dominance and with it, a kind of obduracy to the wishes and desires and aspirations of the people there.

I think that most Arabs and Muslims feel that the United States hasn't really been paying much attention to their desires, but has been pursuing its policies for its own sake, without much in the way of explanation or attempts to somehow justify them. And above all, pursuing these policies not according to many of the principles that the United States proclaims are its own: democracy, self-determination, freedom of speech, freedom of assembly, and its commitment to international law. It's very hard, for example, to justify the thirty-four-year-old occupation of the West Bank and Gaza—140 Israeli settlements and roughly 400,000 settlers brought with the support and financing of the United States—and say this is part of U.S. adherence to international law and UN resolutions.

So all of this is a record that keeps building up in an area in which—and here we come now to the really sad part—the rulers have been supported by the United States against the wishes of the people. And there is a general sense in which the United States is flouting its own principles in order to maintain such governments and regimes in power and really have very little to do with the large number of people who are dominated by these regimes.

The result is a kind of schizophrenic picture of the United States. Every Arab or Muslim that I know is tremendously interested in the United States. Many of them send their children here for education. Many of them come here for vacations. Some do business here or come for training. They are perfectly aware of what an extraordinary country this is on the one hand. And on the other, there's the other view which is that the U.S. government is a different thing and is quite impervious to the appeals of conscience and decency and international law. Now, in this rather heady mixture of violence and, how shall I say it, policies that are remarkably unpopular right down to the last iota, it's not hard for demagogues, especially people who claim to speak in the name of religion, in this case Islam, to raise a crusade against the United States, to raise a banner and say that we must defend against this policy and somehow bring America down; we have to first of all resist and second we have to fight them.

And don't forget, ironically, and this is the last point to be made here, that many of these people, including Osama bin Laden and the Afghan Taliban as well as the mujahideen, the fighters with them, were in fact supported and nourished by the United States in the early 1980s during the Soviet invasion of Afghanistan, when it was thought that to rally Islam against godless communism would be doing the Soviet Union a very bad turn indeed and that in fact transpired. I remember in 1986 a group of mujahideen came to Washington and were greeted by President Reagan, who called them "freedom fighters."[1]

This was the going mantra for a long time. And then there was the sense of betrayal that many ordinary Muslims feel, living, as I say, in poverty and desperation. Above all, I think, in desperation—desperation and ignorance. It's not difficult to start rallying people in the name of Islam. These preachers, by the way, are completely self-appointed spokespeople of Islam. They don't represent Islam in any formal sense. They're not imams, they're not sheiks. They are self-appointed warriors for Islam, and in the case of Osama bin Laden in particular, who is a Saudi, a man who feels himself to be a patriot because U.S. forces are in Saudi Arabia, which is sacred because of the prophet Mohammed, and who feels it is his duty to start fulminating against the United States, and turning against the people who brought them there. There is also this great sense of triumphalism, that just as we defeated the Soviet Union, we can do this. And out of this, this sense of desperation and pathological religion, there develops an all-encompassing drive to harm and hurt, without regard for the innocent and the uninvolved, which was the case in New York.

Now to understand all of this is of course not at all to condone it. What terrifies me is that we're entering a phase here where speaking about this, as something that can be understood historically, without any sympathy or condoning of it, is going to be forbidden, and thought of as unpatriotic. It's very dangerous. It is precisely incumbent on every citizen to quite understand the world we're living in and the history, of which we are not only a part, but in many ways forming as a superpower.

In your article in the London Observer *entitled "Islam and the West Are Inadequate Banners," you say the U.S. drive for war "uncannily resembles Captain Ahab in pursuit of Moby Dick."[2] Tell me what you have in mind there.*

Captain Ahab in Melville's great novel *Moby Dick* was a man possessed with an obsessional drive to pursue the white whale which had harmed him, which had torn his leg out, to the ends of the earth, no matter what happened.[3] In the final scene of the novel, Captain Ahab is being borne out to sea, wrapped around the white whale with the rope of his own harpoon and going obviously to his death. It was a scene of almost suicidal finality. I think that in this whipping up of the American people, the government has indulged in a similar drive for retribution, for perfectly understandable reasons—that is to say, this is a tremendous blow inflicted on the United States. There's no question that a great deal of harm and terrible loss was inflicted on us as a people and as a society. That anything goes—the rising tide of war and retribution and bringing to justice and wanted dead or alive, all the words that George Bush has used in public—suggests not so much an orderly and considered progress towards bringing the man to justice according to international norms, but rather something apocalyptic, something of the order of the criminal atrocity itself.

I feel that that is simply making matters a lot, lot worse, because there are always consequences. And it would seem to me that to give Osama bin Laden, who has been demonized—he has in fact been turned into Moby Dick, made a symbol of all that's evil in the world—to give him a kind of mythological proportion is really playing his game. I think we need to secularize the man, we need to bring him down to the realm of reality, treat him as a criminal, as a man who is a demagogue, who has unlawfully unleashed violence against innocent people, and punish him accordingly. Not to bring down the world around him and ourselves, if necessary. But to deal with him as one deals with people who committed horrible crimes. It's inevitable that Americans feel now that they are at war with Islam. Despite the calls of the president and Mayor Giuliani and others to say we are not at war with Islam, the fact is that everywhere you look in this society there've been dozens, if not hundreds, of incidents against Muslims and people who look like Muslims to the people attacking them.[4] There was the case of a Sikh killed in Arizona and others whose properties have been defaced.[5]

A Pakistani was murdered in Texas.[6]

Yes, and many people in New York have felt the brunt of this. People have been visited by the police and the FBI because they have Middle Eastern names and so on. So there's an atmosphere not only of mobilization but of a descending fear, and a kind of paranoia which befits a country at war against a disembodied kind of super enemy called Osama bin Laden and Islam. I really think that the media has played a very important role in all of this by insisting on the same images over and over again, by demonizing, by repeating and not permitting what in effect is reflection. In this desire to report what's happening, the media has simply fallen into the prevailing mood and has rushed it to further judgement and to further action which I think is terribly hasty and in my opinion probably going to produce more problems than it solves.

There seems to be a certain pattern at work here, as you suggest. First, in the 1970s, the demonization of Arafat and the PLO, followed by Ayatollah Khomeini, Muammar Qaddafi, Saddam Hussein, and now Osama bin Laden.

There's certainly that and also, at least in the case of Saddam and Osama bin Laden, there's been an unwillingness to state the complicity of the United States in the rise of these figures to power. Certainly as I mentioned about bin Laden, but also in case of Saddam, who was nurtured by the United States as an enemy of Iran. He was given a lot of arms and support by the United States in the period preceding his occupation of Kuwait.

But you know, what is quite worrisome in all of this is the absence of attempts at analysis and reflection rather than attempts to differentiate and define. I mean take the word "terrorism." "Terrorism" has become synonymous now with anti-Americanism, which in turn has become synonymous with being critical of the United States, which in turn has become synonymous with being unpatriotic. That's an unacceptable series of equations. And I think what we need is to go back, for example, to the debates in the United Nations during the 1970s as to what terrorism is. I mean you can't say about mujahideen in Afghanistan in 1980 fighting the Soviets that they were "freedom fighters," and then say that now that they are trying to defend against the incursion of other countries into Afghanistan they are terrorists. Particularly in that there seems to be an undeclared or semi-declared war against the Taliban, who you know are not an attractive bunch by any means. I think the definition of terror and terrorism has to be more precise, so that we are able, since we have this great power as a nation, to discriminate between, for example, what it is that the Palestinians are doing to fight the Israeli military occupation, which has been there for almost thirty-five years now and terrorism of the sort that resulted in the World Trade Center bombing. Besides, there is also state terrorism.

Eqbal Ahmad of Pakistan, a noted scholar and activist once told me that terrorism is the poor man's B-52.[7]

On one level I think that's certainly true, that is to say, the weapons of the weak are likely to be this kind, speaking now not of course on the level of what took place at the World Trade Center. I'd like to make a distinction between that and the kind of terror that involves, for example, a young man from Gaza living in the most horrendous conditions—of overpopulation, poverty, ignorance, hunger, most of it, in fact I would say 90 percent of it, imposed by Israel as part of its occupation and its siege policies against Palestinians—strapping dynamite around himself and then throwing himself into a crowd of Israelis. I've never condoned or agreed with it, but at least it is understandable as a result of a desperate human being who feels himself being crowded out of life and all of his surroundings, his fellow citizens, other Palestinians, his parents, sisters, and brothers, all of them dying or being hurt, wanting to do something, to strike back. That can be understood as the act of a desperate person trying to free herself or himself from what he thinks are unjustly imposed conditions. It's not something I agree with but at least you could understand it.

Now, here we're talking about something different, because these people are obviously not desperate and poor refugee camp dwellers. The people who perpetrated the terror of the World Trade Center and Pentagon attacks were obviously middle-class, educated enough to be able to go to flight school in Florida, and could speak English. This is now transcending the political and moving into the metaphysical. And it's a leap that I think is very important to keep one's eye on, because it suggests the kind of cosmic quality—and, I would also say, the demagogical quality—of the minds at work here. They refuse to engage in or have no interest in dialogue or political organization or persuasion of the sort that makes political change and improves one's situation versus this kind of thing which is bloody-minded destruction for no other reason than to do it. Note that there was no claim for this terror bombing. There was no political message behind it. There were no demands. There were no statements. It was a silent piece of terror imposed on a population without discrimination or negotiation. I can't say that this is the poor person's B-52 bombing.

But I would also want to add that some of the things that powers like Britain, the United States, and France have done against lesser people, like bombing them from the air, where the bomber cannot be reached by essentially defenseless people, are also inexcusable. This is what the Israelis are doing in the West Bank and Gaza, using F-16s to attack Palestinian homes, which are completely undefended—there is no Palestinian army, or air force, or anti-aircraft capability—I think that too has the structure of terror. It's meant to impose fear, it's indiscriminate, and there is no chance for any response. It is pure destruction for the sake of destruction and terrorizing people. So, we're in an area where a lot of unpleasant things done by them and done by us, whoever them and us are, resemble each other rather too closely.

Again, Eqbal Ahmad commented that "revolutionary terror if ever engaged in must be sociologically and psychologically selective." He said, "Don't hijack a plane. . . . Don't kill children." And then he points out that "the great revolutions, the Chinese, the Vietnamese, the Algerian, and the Cuban, never engaged in hijacking type of terrorism." [8]

They didn't and it's important to remember that they were somewhat earlier than the period of the great hijackings of the late 1960s and early 1970s, when jet travel had become more prevalent and much more symbolic of national communication across borders.

But did you see any revolutionary component to these actions?

No, of course not. That's what I was saying earlier. There was no message in it, no attempt to change people's minds. It's not part of anything. The Algerians, in fact, did use terror. They put bombs in restaurants and cafes in Algiers, killing French people. It's not something I myself approve of or would advocate in any way, but it was part of a political movement to rid Algeria of the French occupation, which had been there for 130 years. The September 11 attack is part of nothing. It's a vague, and unstated, and unclear mass attack, involving exclusively innocent people as its victims and with no conceivable end in sight except terror for its own sake. In that respect, it's a kind of metaphysical leap into another realm—the realm of crazy abstraction and mythological generalities, involving people who in my opinion have hijacked Islam for purposes of their own. It's very important not to fall into that trap and try to respond by a metaphysical retaliation of some sort.

. . .

In your introduction to the updated version of Covering Islam: How the Media and the Experts Determine How We See the Rest of the World, *you say that "Malicious generalizations about Islam have become the last acceptable form of denigration of foreign culture in the West."*[9] *Talk about the role of popular culture in shaping views on Arabs, Muslims, and Islam. Jack Shaheen has a new book out, called* Reel Bad Arabs, *about how Hollywood has vilified Arabs, Muslims, and Islam.*[10] *Do you think that's an important area to examine?*

Very much so. I've thought so from the beginning, and I started to write about this subject in my book *Orientalism.* There is an age-old structure of Islam and I suppose the Arabs along with it—by the way, many people think Afghanistan is part of the Arab world—where discriminations are not made, and where it's assumed that we're talking about a quintessential core of attributes, most of them fantasies about the Other with a capital O. So that the Muslim is thought of as being what we are not: fanatical, violent, lustful, irrational, and so on. That idea has persisted because it's based very deeply in religious roots where Islam is thought of as a kind of competitor of Christianity. Islam arises out of the same soil as Christianity, the religion of Abraham, first in Judaism, then Christianity, then in Islam. There was also a long period of approximately 800 years, where Islam dominated Europe, when the Muslim conquests, the Arab conquests, begin in the middle of the seventh century and continue until the fifteenth century.

That sense of Islam as a threatening Other has continued. Plus, of course, the polemical quality of the knowledge about Islam and the Arabs that develops during the colonial period in what I called orientalism, where the study of the Other has a lot to do with the control and dominance of Europe and the West generally in the Islamic world. I must say that very little has changed. If you look at the curricula of most universities and schools in this country, considering our long encounter with the Islamic world, there is very little there that you can get hold of that is really informative about Islam. And if you look at the popular media you'll see that the stereotype that begins with Rudolph Valentino in *The Sheik* has really remained and developed into the transnational villain of television and film and popular culture in general.[11]

It is very easy to make wild generalizations about Islam. All you have to do is read almost any issue of the *New Republic* and you'll see Islam associated with radical evil, and the idea that the Arabs have a depraved culture, and so forth. These are impossible generalizations to make virtually about any other religion or ethnic group in the world today in the United States, where there is a great sensitivity, as there should be, to African Americans, Asian Americans, Latin Americans, and so on. But here this thing persists, and one of the main reasons for its persistence has been the absence of a real engagement on the part of Muslims and Arabs in this debate.

The reasons for that are complicated, too long to examine here, but there has been remarkable unawareness in the Islamic and Arab world of what the West and residents of Western countries—now one shouldn't generalize—for the most part see as the Muslim or the Arab. There isn't a cultural policy, there isn't a sense of engaging in a debate or dialogue. A dialogue of cultures is absent so far as Islam is concerned, so far as the Arabs are concerned. Israel plays a great role in all of this. People feel that if you, and I've had this in my own experience, try to talk about the Arab world, if you try to bring an Arab writer to America, there's always an outcry as to why isn't there balance? Why didn't you bring an Israeli writer? Or in some ways, if you talk about Arab culture and Arab civilization, you are somehow being anti-Israel. That's a very constant structure with which one has to deal. The ground is not easy to negotiate because it is full of political traps and pitfalls.

I want to add something about the role of higher education. If you look at Columbia University, which has a Middle East languages department, which has a religion department, we don't regularly offer a course on the Koran. Studying the Koran is necessary to an understanding of Islam. It's as simple as that. It's like studying Christianity without looking at the Bible, without looking at the New Testament. It's like studying Judaism without looking at the Old Testament. This is, alas, the case of studying Islam, where you look at summaries in books and accounts by Western scholars of what Islam is rather than looking at the main text itself which, in Islam, plays a much greater role than either the gospels in Christianity or the Torah in Judaism.

Returning to Covering Islam, *in your introduction you say that "A core of 'experts' on the Islamic world has grown to prominence, and during a crisis they are brought out to pontificate on formulaic ideas about Islam on news programs or talk shows."[12] A prestigious talk program on PBS is the nightly one hour* Charlie Rose Show. *I have the guest list from the first week after the September 11th attacks. Let me read you some of the names: Wesley Clark, Sandy Berger, Anthony Lewis, Frank Rich, David Halberstam, Jim Hoagland, Mort Zuckerman, and three times Fouad Ajami, who is a regular CBS pundit who moves seamlessly onto PBS.*

It shows you the emphasis, which is to treat things such as this, which is, in effect, a terrible event not just in the United States but one having vast international consequences, ramifications, and roots, as essentially a matter of security and military strategy. Not every one of these guests that you mentioned is in the same boat, but I would say that the emphasis is largely on those sorts of things and none of them with the exception of Ajami can be considered somebody who knows anything at all, even in an educated way, about the Islamic or Arab worlds. None of them. Ajami is an expert who has made it quite plain that he has cast his lot with the American right-wing, the neo-conservative movement. He takes very conciliatory positions vis-à-vis Israel, and because he is an Arab and a Muslim, he is seen as an ideal informant for talk shows. Whereas in fact, on the basis of what he has published and the things that he has said, he has revealed himself to be a man of no particular intellectual interest, who nobody that I know of in the field and in the Islamic and Arab world even knows, much less takes seriously. It's a remarkable case of cognitive dissonance. Experts are treated as such without either the competence or the stature, or the work and the knowledge that such a deference implies. It's really quite striking. Whereas I can think quite easily of half a dozen people in this country who would do a much better and much more informed job on matters having to do with the Islamic and Arab world than Ajami.

Talk about two wings of the Islamic world that are going to be affected by military action—Egypt in the West and Pakistan in the East.

These are very large issues to consider but the Egyptian government has been beset by Islamic movements that began basically as a part of the nationalist community in Egypt, say in the 1930s with the rise of the Muslim Brotherhood, which was anti-British, anti-imperialist, anti-monarchical. Of course, always with the aim of establishing an Islamic state in what is predominantly an Islamic country, although Egypt isn't entirely Islamic. There is an important minority of Coptic Christians who feel themselves to be just as Egyptian as the Muslim Egyptians. In any case, that community of Muslim nationalists has shifted to one that has become highly, in my terms anyway, reactionary, that sees itself as bearing the burden of originary, primitive Islam, to try to return Egypt to the Sharia, to try to return Egypt to seventh century Mecca, to destroy the intrusions of modern civilization. They, of course, have grabbed public attention because they're armed, they're relatively well-organized, and some of their offshoots are capable of suicide missions of the sort that would involve the killing of tourists and the assassination of Anwar Sadat. They are a disruptive and insurrectionary force.

This doesn't mean that all the pious people, the women who wear hejabs and the men who wear the robes and grow beards, are all part of this. There is also a large protest group inside Egypt that has split against the government in its policies, mainly economic and foreign policies that have created a class of impoverished university graduates who appear by the hundreds of thousands every year with no jobs, no opportunities, no easy place to live, no way to earn a living and take care of a family. Islam groups them all together.

The government has played a very dangerous game with them. It has sometimes submitted to their demands, for example, to censor and ban books that are considered pornographic and anti-Islamic; to file cases against professors and writers and public personalities; to go after communities thought of as deviant, whether gay or religious. Every so often the government leans over and throws them a sop and bans programs on television and bans novels and so on rather than taking a line that is quite clear because they find it difficult to do this.

In Pakistan, on the other hand, there is a tradition of Islamic insurrection which has been quite unsuccessful. Whenever there has been an opportunity for elections to determine whether an Islamic government is wanted or not, they inevitably lose. But they, too, are capable of disruptions, assassinations, and so on. They also express the dissatisfactions with what is a skewed economy. This is a nuclear power that can't resolve problems of poverty and famine and unemployment in the large cities like Karachi. We're dealing with very unstable mixes here. Now, to have imposed upon them the burden of a massive military action of the United States can unsettle them profoundly. In places like Pakistan, the idea of this military government of Pervez Musharraf being destabilized by an Islamic or a pro-Taliban movement is more threatening because of the nuclear capability, which any government that comes to power will have. It's not a pleasant thing to contemplate.

A front-page photograph in the September 22nd New York Times *shows two Pakistani policemen beating and kicking an unarmed demonstrator. Four Pakistanis were killed in Karachi.*[13]

Of course, it is a military government and the idea is that we're mobilizing and we are going to do this with the United States. Obviously there are economic rewards, some of their debt is going to be forgiven.[14] There's going to be more economic aid and the stature of Pervez Musharraf's government will be enhanced by the United States. But as with all of these interventions, the results are going to be, in the long run, more negative than they're going to be positive.

But the situation is rich with ironies, particularly in Pakistan, which nurtured the mujahideen during the 1980s and actually created the Taliban and helped install them into power.

Yes, and still does. The Pakistani intelligence services are really—how should I put it—the controllers of the Taliban. There's a healthy back and forth in trade and support, and drug trafficking between Afghanistan and Pakistan that is quasi-official. It's not just one or two people. It involves whole branches of the Pakistani secret services. That's not so easily controlled once the violence begins.

Finally, what are some good sources of information?

There's a whole series of writings about Afghanistan. I would start with the works of the man you mentioned, Eqbal Ahmad, who died two years ago, a dear friend.[15] I would say he is the one essential figure that we ought to have with us because he knew Afghanistan. He himself was Pakistani. He knew the West. He knew the Arab world. He was a Muslim. He was a man of modern sensibility and vast historical information. I'd begin with the writings of Eqbal Ahmad. A whole series of essays, interviews with you, are available. I would say that on questions having to do with Arabs or Islam, there's a whole library of material. Certainly the works of Albert Hourani and Philip Hitti.[16] On contemporary Egypt, there's a vast library, as there is on Pakistan and Afghanistan. I think what we ought to try to get at are authoritative sources that are not polemical and are not Defense Department manuals for conquest and war.

NOTES

1. Eqbal Ahmad, *Confronting Empire,* p. 134. See also Eqbal Ahmad, *Terrorism: Theirs and Ours* (New York: Seven Stories Press/Open Media, 2001), p. 4.

2. Edward W. Said, "Islam and the West Are Inadequate Banners," *The Observer* (London), September 16, 2001, p. 27.

3. Herman Melville, *Moby Dick, or the Whale* (New York: Modern Library, 1992).

4. Darryl Fears, "Hate Crimes Against Arabs Surge, FBI Finds," *Washington Post,* November 26, 2002, p. A2.

5. See Phuong Ly and Petula Dvora, "Japanese Americans Recall '40s Bias, Understand Arab Counterparts' Fear," *Washington Post,* September 20, 2001, p. B1.

6. Somini Sengupta, "Torn Between Silence and Open Discussion," *New York Times,* September 19, 2001, p. B10.

7. Eqbal Ahmad, personal conversation with the author.

8. Eqbal Ahmad, "Terrorism: Theirs and Ours," presentation at the University of Colorado, Boulder, October 12, 1998. Transcript available from Alternative Radio.

9. Edward W. Said, *Covering Islam: How the Media and the Experts Determine How We See the Rest of the World.* Updated and revised ed. (New York: Vintage, 1997), p. xii.

10. Jack G. Shaheen, *Reel Bad Arabs: How Hollywood Vilifies a People* (Northampton, Massachusetts: Interlink, 2001).

11. The *Sheik,* directed by George Melford (1921) and *Son of the Sheik,* directed by George Fitzmaurice (1926).

12. Said, *Covering Islam,* p. xi.

13. See David Rohde, "Militants in Kashmir Deny Pakistani Support," *New York Times,* September 22, 2002, p. 1:27, and photograph on p. 1:1.

14. Edward Alden, "Bush Offers Fresh Help to Pakistan," *Financial Times* (London), February 14, 2002, p. 10.

15. See Ahmad and Barsamian, *Eqbal Ahmad: Confronting Empire.*

16. See, among others, Philip Hitti, *History of the Arabs,* 10th rev. ed. (New York: Palgrave Macmillan, 2002). Albert Hourani, *A History of the Arab Peoples* (New York: Warner Books, 1992).

47

Samuel P. Huntington

"The Clash of Civilizations?" (1993)

Samuel P. Huntington (b. 1927) served as White House coordinator of security planning for the National Security Council from 1977 to 1978. The author of numerous books on national security, democratization and development, cultural politics, and American national identity, he is presently Albert J. Weatherhead III University Professor and chairman of the Harvard Academy of International and Area Studies. The Clash of Civilizations and the Re-making of World Order (1996) presents an extended version of his argument here.

The Next Pattern of Conflict

WORLD POLITICS is entering a new phase, and intellectuals have not hesitated to proliferate visions of what it will be—the end of history, the return of traditional rivalries between nation states, and the decline of the nation state from the conflicting pulls of tribalism and globalism, among others. Each of these visions catches aspects of the emerging reality. Yet they all miss a crucial, indeed a central, aspect of what global politics is likely to be in the coming years.

It is my hypothesis that the fundamental source of conflict in this new world will not be primarily ideological or primarily economic. The great divisions among humankind and the dominating source of conflict will be cultural. Nation states will remain the most powerful actors in world affairs, but the principal conflicts of

Reprinted by permission of *Foreign Affairs*, (Vol. 72, No. 3, Summer 1993). Copyright 2003 by the Council on Foreign Relations, Inc.

global politics will occur between nations and groups of different civilizations. The clash of civilizations will dominate global politics. The fault lines between civilizations will be the battle lines of the future.

Conflict between civilizations will be the latest phase in the evolution of conflict in the modern world. For a century and a half after the emergence of the modern international system with the Peace of Westphalia, the conflicts of the Western world were largely among princes—emperors, absolute monarchs and constitutional monarchs attempting to expand their bureaucracies, their armies, their mercantilist economic strength and, most important, the territory they ruled. In the process they created nation states, and beginning with the French Revolution the principal lines of conflict were between nations rather than princes. In 1793, as R. R. Palmer put it, "The wars of kings were over; the wars of peoples had begun." This nineteenth-century pattern lasted until the end of World War I. Then, as a result of the Russian Revolution and the reaction against it, the conflict of nations yielded to the conflict of ideologies, first among communism, fascism-Nazism and liberal democracy, and then between communism and liberal democracy. During the Cold War, this latter conflict became embodied in the struggle between the two superpowers, neither of which was a nation state in the classical European sense and each of which defined its identity in terms of its ideology.

These conflicts between princes, nation states and ideologies were primarily conflicts within Western civilization, "Western civil wars," as William Lind has labeled them. This was as true of the Cold War as it was of the world wars and the earlier wars of the seventeenth, eighteenth and nineteenth centuries. With the end of the Cold War, international politics moves out of its Western phase, and its centerpiece becomes the interaction between the West and non-Western civilizations and among non-Western civilizations. In the politics of civilizations, the peoples and governments of non-Western civilizations no longer remain the objects of history as targets of Western colonialism but join the West as movers and shapers of history.

The Nature of Civilizations

During the Cold War the world was divided into the First, Second and Third Worlds. Those divisions are no longer relevant. It is far more meaningful now to group countries not in terms of their political or economic systems or in terms of their level of economic development but rather in terms of their culture and civilization.

What do we mean when we talk of a civilization? A civilization is a cultural entity. Villages, regions, ethnic groups, nationalities, religious groups, all have distinct cultures at different levels of cultural heterogeneity. The culture of a village in southern Italy may be different from that of a village in northern Italy, but both will share in a common Italian culture that distinguishes them from German villages. European communities, in turn, will share cultural features that distinguish them from Arab or Chinese communities. Arabs, Chinese and Westerners, however, are not part of any broader cultural entity. They constitute civilizations. A civilization is thus the highest cultural grouping of people and the broadest level of cultural identity people have short of that which distinguishes humans from other species. It is defined both by common objective elements, such as language, history, religion, customs, institutions, and by the subjective self-identification of people. People have levels of identity: a resident of Rome may define himself with varying degrees of intensity as a Roman, an Italian, a Catholic, a Christian, a European, a Westerner. The civilization to which he belongs is the broadest level of identification with which he intensely identifies. People can and do redefine their identities and, as a result, the composition and boundaries of civilizations change.

Civilizations may involve a large number of people, as with China ("a civilization pretending to be a state," as Lucian Pye put it), or a very small number of people, such as the Anglophone Caribbean. A civilization may include several nation states, as is the case with Western, Latin American and Arab civilizations, or only one, as is the case with Japanese civilization. Civilizations obviously blend and overlap, and may include subcivilizations. Western civilization has two major variants, European and North American, and Islam has its Arab, Turkic and Malay subdivisions. Civilizations are nonetheless meaningful entities, and while the lines between them are seldom sharp, they are real. Civilizations are dynamic; they rise and fall; they divide and merge. And, as any student of history knows, civilizations disappear and are buried in the sands of time.

Westerners tend to think of nation states as the principal actors in global affairs. They have been that, however, for only a few centuries. The broader reaches of human history have been the history of civilizations. In *A Study of History*, Arnold Toynbee identified 21 major civilizations; only six of them exist in the contemporary world.

Why Civilizations Will Clash

Civilization identity will be increasingly important in the future, and the world will be shaped in large measure by the interactions among seven or eight major civilizations. These include Western, Confucian, Japanese, Islamic, Hindu, Slavic-Orthodox, Latin American and possibly African civilization. The most important conflicts of the future will occur along the cultural fault lines separating these civilizations from one another.

Why will this be the case?

First, differences among civilizations are not only real; they are basic. Civilizations are differentiated from each other by history, language, culture, tradition and, most important, religion. The people of different civilizations have different views on the relations between God and man, the individual and the group, the citizen and the state, parents and children, husband and wife, as well as differing views of the relative importance of rights and responsibilities, liberty and authority, equality and hierarchy. These differences are the product of centuries. They will not soon disappear. They are far more fundamental than differences among political ideologies and political regimes. Differences do not necessarily mean conflict, and conflict does not necessarily mean violence. Over the centuries, however, differences among civilizations have generated the most prolonged and the most violent conflicts.

Second, the world is becoming a smaller place. The interactions between peoples of different civilizations are increasing; these increasing interactions intensify civilization consciousness and awareness of differences between civilizations and commonalities within civilizations. North African immigration to France generates hostility among Frenchmen and at the same time increased receptivity to immigration by "good" European Catholic Poles. Americans react far more negatively to Japanese investment than to larger investments from Canada and European countries. Similarly, as Donald Horowitz has pointed out, "An Ibo may be . . . an Owerri Ibo or an Onitsha Ibo in what was the Eastern region of Nigeria. In Lagos, he is simply an Ibo. In London, he is a Nigerian. In New York, he is an African." The interactions among peoples of different civilizations enhance the civilization-consciousness of people that, in turn, invigorates differences and animosities stretching or thought to stretch back deep into history.

Third, the processes of economic modernization and social change throughout the world are separating people from longstanding local identities. They also weaken the nation state as a source of identity. In much of the world religion has moved in to fill this gap, often in the form of movements that are labeled "fundamentalist." Such movements are found in Western Christianity, Judaism, Buddhism and Hinduism, as well as in Islam. In most countries and most religions the people active in fundamentalist movements are young, college-educated, middle-class technicians, professionals and business persons. The "unsecularization of the world," George Weigel has remarked, "is one of the dominant social facts of life in the late twentieth century." The revival of religion, "la revanche de Dieu," as Gilles Kepel labeled it, provides a basis for identity and commitment that transcends national boundaries and unites civilizations.

Fourth, the growth of civilization-consciousness is enhanced by the dual role of the West. On the one hand, the West is at a peak of power. At the same time, however, and perhaps as a result, a return to the roots phenomenon is occurring among non-Western civilizations. Increasingly one hears references to trends toward a turning inward and "Asianization" in Japan, the end of the Nehru legacy and the "Hinduization" of India, the failure of Western ideas of socialism and nationalism and hence "re-Islamization" of the Middle East, and now a debate over Westernization versus Russianization in Boris Yeltsin's country. A West at the peak of its power confronts non-Wests that increasingly have the desire, the will and the resources to shape the world in non-Western ways.

In the past, the elites of non-Western societies were usually the people who were most involved with the West, had been educated at Oxford, the Sorbonne or Sandhurst, and had absorbed Western attitudes and values. At the same time, the populace in non-Western countries often remained deeply imbued with the indigenous culture. Now, however, these relationships are being reversed. A de-Westernization and indigenization of elites is occurring in many non-Western countries at the same time that Western, usually American, cultures, styles and habits become more popular among the mass of the people.

Fifth, cultural characteristics and differences are less mutable and hence less easily compromised and resolved than political and economic ones. In the former Soviet Union, communists can become democrats, the rich can become poor and the poor rich, but Russians cannot become Estonians and Azeris cannot become Armenians. In class and ideological conflicts, the key question was "Which side are you on?" and people could and did choose sides and change sides. In conflicts between civilizations, the question is "What are you?" That is a given that cannot be changed. And as we know, from Bosnia to the Caucasus to the Sudan, the wrong answer to that question can mean a bullet in the head. Even more than ethnicity, religion discriminates sharply and exclusively among people. A person can be half-French and half-Arab and simultaneously even a citizen of two countries. It is more difficult to be half-Catholic and half-Muslim.

Finally, economic regionalism is increasing. The proportions of total trade that were intraregional rose between 1980 and 1989 from 51 percent to 59 percent in Europe, 33 percent to 37 percent in East Asia, and 32 percent to 36 percent in North America. The importance of regional economic blocs is likely to continue to increase in the future. On the one hand, successful economic regionalism will reinforce civilization-consciousness. On the other hand, economic regionalism may succeed only when it is rooted in a common civilization. The European Community rests on the shared foundation of European culture and Western Christianity. The success of the North American Free Trade Area depends on the convergence now underway of Mexican, Canadian and American cultures. Japan, in contrast, faces difficulties in creating a comparable economic entity in East Asia because Japan is a society and civilization unique to itself. However strong the trade and investment links Japan may develop with other East Asian countries, its cultural differences with those countries inhibit and perhaps preclude its promoting regional economic integration like that in Europe and North America.

Common culture, in contrast, is clearly facilitating the rapid expansion of the economic relations between the People's Republic of China and Hong Kong, Taiwan, Singapore and the overseas Chinese communities in other Asian countries. With the Cold War over, cultural commonalities increasingly overcome ideological differences, and mainland China and Taiwan move closer together. If cultural commonality is a prerequisite for economic integration, the principal East Asian economic bloc of the future is likely to be centered on China. This bloc is, in fact, already coming into existence. As Murray Weidenbaum has observed,

> Despite the current Japanese dominance of the region, the Chinese-based economy of Asia is rapidly emerging as a new epicenter for industry, commerce and finance. This strategic area contains substantial amounts of technology and manufacturing capability (Taiwan), outstanding entrepreneurial, marketing and services acumen (Hong Kong), a fine communications network (Singapore), a tremendous pool of financial capital (all three), and very large endowments of land, resources and labor (mainland China). . . . From Guangzhou to Singapore, from Kuala Lumpur to Manila, this influential network—often based on extensions of the traditional clans—has been described as the backbone of the East Asian economy.[1]

Culture and religion also form the basis of the Economic Cooperation Organization, which brings together ten non-Arab Muslim countries: Iran, Pakistan, Turkey, Azerbaijan, Kazakhstan, Kyrgyzstan, Turkmenistan, Tadjikistan, Uzbekistan and Afghanistan. One impetus to the revival and expansion of this organization, founded originally in the 1960s by Turkey, Pakistan and Iran, is the realization by the leaders of several of these countries that they had no chance of admission to the European Community. Similarly, Caricom, the Central American Common Market and Mercosur rest on common cultural foundations. Efforts to build a broader Caribbean–Central American economic entity bridging the Anglo-Latin divide, however, have to date failed.

As people define their identity in ethnic and religious terms, they are likely to see an "us" versus "them" relation existing between themselves and people of different ethnicity or religion. The end of ideologically defined states in Eastern Europe and the former Soviet Union permits traditional ethnic identities and animosities to come to the fore. Differences in culture and religion create differences over policy issues, ranging from human rights to immigration to trade and commerce to the environment. Geographical propinquity gives rise to conflicting territorial claims from Bosnia to Mindanao. Most important, the efforts of the West to promote its values of democracy and liberalism as universal values, to maintain its military predominance and to advance its economic interests engender countering responses from other civilizations. Decreasingly able to mobilize support and form coalitions on the basis of ideology, governments and groups will increasingly attempt to mobilize support by appealing to common religion and civilization identity.

The clash of civilizations thus occurs at two levels. At the micro-level, adjacent groups along the fault lines between civilizations struggle, often violently, over the control of territory and each other. At the macro-level, states from different civilizations compete for relative military and economic power, struggle over the control of international institutions and third parties, and competitively promote their particular political and religious values.

The Fault Lines between Civilizations

The fault lines between civilizations are replacing the political and ideological boundaries of the Cold War as the flash points for crisis and bloodshed. The Cold War began when the Iron Curtain divided Europe politically and ideologically. The Cold War ended with the end of the Iron Curtain. As the ideological division of Europe has disappeared, the cultural division of Europe between Western Christianity, on the one hand, and Orthodox Christianity and Islam, on the other, has reemerged. The most significant dividing line in Europe, as William Wallace has suggested, may well be the eastern boundary of Western Christianity in the year 1500. This line runs along what are now the boundaries between Finland and Russia and between the Baltic states and Russia, cuts through Belarus and Ukraine separating the more Catholic western Ukraine from Orthodox eastern Ukraine, swings westward separating Transylvania from the rest of Romania, and then goes through Yugoslavia almost exactly along the line now separating Croatia and Slovenia from the rest of Yugoslavia. In the Balkans this line, of course, coincides with the historic boundary between the Hapsburg and Ottoman empires. The peoples to the north and west of this line are Protestant or Catholic; they shared the common experiences of European history—feudalism, the Renaissance, the Reformation, the Enlightenment, the French Revolution, the Industrial Revolution; they are generally economically better off than the peoples to the east; and they may now look forward to increasing involvement in a common European economy and to the consolidation of democratic political systems. The peoples to the east and south of this

Western
Christianity
circa 1500

Orthodox
Christianity
and Islam

RUSSIA

FINLAND

SWEDEN

ESTONIA

LATVIA

LITHUANIA

BELA-
RUSSIA

POLAND

CZECH
REP.

SLOVAKIA

UKRAINE

SLOVENIA
HUNG.

MOLD.

CROATIA

ROMANIA

BOSNIA

SERBIA

MONTE-
NEGRO

MACEDONIA

BULGARIA

ALB.

ITALY

GREECE

Black Sea

TURKEY

N

0 ⊢———⊣ 200
MILES

Source: W. Wallace, THE TRANSFORMATION OF
WESTERN EUROPE, London: Pinter, 1990.
Map by Ib Ohlsson for FOREIGN AFFAIRS.

line are Orthodox or Muslim; they historically belonged to the Ottoman or Tsarist empires and were only lightly touched by the shaping events in the rest of Europe; they are generally less advanced economically; they seem much less likely to develop stable democratic political systems. The Velvet Curtain of culture has replaced the Iron Curtain of ideology as the most significant dividing line in Europe. As the events in Yugoslavia show, it is not only a line of difference; it is also at times a line of bloody conflict.

Conflict along the fault line between Western and Islamic civilizations has been going on for 1,300 years. . . .

The interactions between civilizations vary greatly in the extent to which they are likely to be characterized by violence. Economic competition clearly predominates between the American and European subcivilizations of the West and between both of them and Japan. On the Eurasian continent, however, the proliferation of ethnic conflict, epitomized at the extreme in "ethnic cleansing," has not been totally random. It has been most frequent and most violent between groups belonging to different civilizations. In Eurasia the great historic fault lines between civilizations are once more aflame. This is particularly true along the boundaries of the crescent-shaped Islamic bloc of nations from the bulge of Africa to central Asia.

Violence also occurs between Muslims, on the one hand, and Orthodox Serbs in the Balkans, Jews in Israel, Hindus in India, Buddhists in Burma and Catholics in the Philippines. Islam has bloody borders. . . .

The West versus the Rest

The West is now at an extraordinary peak of power in relation to other civilizations. Its superpower opponent has disappeared from the map. Military conflict among Western states is unthinkable, and Western military power is unrivaled. Apart from Japan, the West faces no economic challenge. It dominates international political and security institutions and with Japan international economic institutions. Global political and security issues are effectively settled by a directorate of the United States, Britain and France, world economic issues by a directorate of the United States, Germany and Japan, all of which maintain extraordinarily close relations with each other to the exclusion of lesser and largely non-Western countries. Decisions made at the U.N. Security Council or in the International Monetary Fund that reflect the interests of the West are presented to the world as reflecting the desires of the world community. The very phrase "the world community" has become the euphemistic collective noun (replacing "the Free World") to give global legitimacy to actions reflecting the interests of the United States and other Western powers.[2] Through the IMF and other international economic institutions, the West promotes its economic interests and imposes on other nations the economic policies it thinks appropriate. In any poll of non-Western peoples, the IMF undoubtedly would win the support of finance ministers and a few others, but get an overwhelmingly unfavorable rating from just about everyone else, who would agree with Georgy Arbatov's characterization of IMF officials as "neo-Bolsheviks who love expropriating other people's money, imposing undemocratic and alien rules of economic and political conduct and stifling economic freedom."

Western domination of the U.N. Security Council and its decisions, tempered only by occasional abstention by China, produced U.N. legitimation of the West's use of force to drive Iraq out of Kuwait and its elimination of Iraq's sophisticated weapons and capacity to produce such weapons. It also produced the quite unprecedented action by the United States, Britain and France in getting the Security Council to demand that Libya hand over the Pan Am 103 bombing suspects and then to impose sanctions when Libya refused. After defeating the largest Arab army, the West did not hesitate to throw its weight around in the Arab world. The West in effect is using international institutions, military power and economic resources to run the world in ways that will maintain Western pre-

dominance, protect Western interests and promote Western political and economic values.

That at least is the way in which non-Westerners see the new world, and there
is a significant element of truth in their view. Differences in power and struggles
for military, economic and institutional power are thus one source of conflict
between the West and other civilizations. Differences in culture, that is basic values and beliefs, are a second source of conflict. V. S. Naipaul has argued that
Western civilization is the "universal civilization" that "fits all men." At a superficial level much of Western culture has indeed permeated the rest of the world.
At a more basic level, however, Western concepts differ fundamentally from
those prevalent in other civilizations. Western ideas of individualism, liberalism,
constitutionalism, human rights, equality, liberty, the rule of law, democracy,
free markets, the separation of church and state, often have little resonance in
Islamic, Confucian, Japanese, Hindu, Buddhist or Orthodox cultures. Western
efforts to propagate such ideas produce instead a reaction against "human rights
imperialism" and a reaffirmation of indigenous values, as can be seen in the support for religious fundamentalism by the younger generation in non-Western
cultures. The very notion that there could be a "universal civilization" is a Western idea, directly at odds with the particularism of most Asian societies and their
emphasis on what distinguishes one people from another. Indeed, the author of
a review of 100 comparative studies of values in different societies concluded
that "the values that are most important in the West are least important worldwide."[3] In the political realm, of course, these differences are most manifest in
the efforts of the United States and other Western powers to induce other peoples to adopt Western ideas concerning democracy and human rights. Modern
democratic government originated in the West. When it has developed in non-
Western societies it has usually been the product of Western colonialism or
imposition.

The central axis of world politics in the future is likely to be, in Kishore Mahbubani's phrase, the conflict between "the West and the Rest" and the responses
of non-Western civilizations to Western power and values.[4] Those responses generally take one or a combination of three forms. At one extreme, non-Western
states can, like Burma and North Korea, attempt to pursue a course of isolation,
to insulate their societies from penetration or "corruption" by the West, and, in
effect, to opt out of participation in the Western-dominated global community.
The costs of this course, however, are high, and few states have pursued it exclusively. A second alternative, the equivalent of "band-wagoning" in international
relations theory, is to attempt to join the West and accept its values and institutions. The third alternative is to attempt to "balance" the West by developing
economic and military power and cooperating with other non-Western societies

against the West, while preserving indigenous values and institutions; in short, to modernize but not to Westernize. . . .

The Confucian-Islamic Connection

The obstacles to non-Western countries joining the West vary considerably. They are least for Latin American and East European countries. They are greater for the Orthodox countries of the former Soviet Union. They are still greater for Muslim, Confucian, Hindu and Buddhist societies. Japan has established a unique position for itself as an associate member of the West: it is in the West in some respects but clearly not of the West in important dimensions. Those countries that for reason of culture and power do not wish to, or cannot, join the West compete with the West by developing their own economic, military and political power. They do this by promoting their internal development and by cooperating with other non-Western countries. The most prominent form of this cooperation is the Confucian-Islamic connection that has emerged to challenge Western interests, values and power.

Almost without exception, Western countries are reducing their military power; under Yeltsin's leadership so also is Russia. China, North Korea and several Middle Eastern states, however, are significantly expanding their military capabilities. They are doing this by the import of arms from Western and non-Western sources and by the development of indigenous arms industries. One result is the emergence of what Charles Krauthammer has called "Weapon States," and the Weapon States are not Western states. Another result is the redefinition of arms control, which is a Western concept and a Western goal. During the Cold War the primary purpose of arms control was to establish a stable military balance between the United States and its allies and the Soviet Union and its allies. In the post–Cold War world the primary objective of arms control is to prevent the development by non-Western societies of military capabilities that could threaten Western interests. The West attempts to do this through international agreements, economic pressure and controls on the transfer of arms and weapons technologies.

The conflict between the West and the Confucian-Islamic states focuses largely, although not exclusively, on nuclear, chemical and biological weapons, ballistic missiles and other sophisticated means for delivering them, and the guidance, intelligence and other electronic capabilities for achieving that goal. The West promotes nonproliferation as a universal norm and nonproliferation treaties and inspections as means of realizing that norm. It also threatens a variety of sanctions against those who promote the spread of sophisticated weapons and proposes some benefits for those who do not. The attention of the West focuses, naturally, on nations that are actually or potentially hostile to the West.

The non-Western nations, on the other hand, assert their right to acquire and to deploy whatever weapons they think necessary for their security. They also have absorbed, to the full, the truth of the response of the Indian defense minister when asked what lesson he learned from the Gulf War: "Don't fight the United States unless you have nuclear weapons." Nuclear weapons, chemical weapons and missiles are viewed, probably erroneously, as the potential equalizer of superior Western conventional power. China, of course, already has nuclear weapons; Pakistan and India have the capability to deploy them. North Korea, Iran, Iraq, Libya and Algeria appear to be attempting to acquire them. A top Iranian official has declared that all Muslim states should acquire nuclear weapons, and in 1988 the president of Iran reportedly issued a directive calling for development of "offensive and defensive chemical, biological and radiological weapons."

Centrally important to the development of counter-West military capabilities is the sustained expansion of China's military power and its means to create military power. Buoyed by spectacular economic development, China is rapidly increasing its military spending and vigorously moving forward with the modernization of its armed forces. It is purchasing weapons from the former Soviet states; it is developing long-range missiles; in 1992 it tested a one-megaton nuclear device. It is developing power-projection capabilities, acquiring aerial refueling technology, and trying to purchase an aircraft carrier. Its military buildup and assertion of sovereignty over the South China Sea are provoking a multilateral regional arms race in East Asia. China is also a major exporter of arms and weapons technology. It has exported materials to Libya and Iraq that could be used to manufacture nuclear weapons and nerve gas. It has helped Algeria build a reactor suitable for nuclear weapons research and production. China has sold to Iran nuclear technology that American officials believe could only be used to create weapons and apparently has shipped components of 300-mile-range missiles to Pakistan. North Korea has had a nuclear weapons program under way for some while and has sold advanced missiles and missile technology to Syria and Iran. The flow of weapons and weapons technology is generally from East Asia to the Middle East. There is, however, some movement in the reverse direction; China has received Stinger missiles from Pakistan.

A Confucian-Islamic military connection has thus come into being, designed to promote acquisition by its members of the weapons and weapons technologies needed to counter the military power of the West. It may or may not last. At present, however, it is, as Dave McCurdy has said, "a renegades' mutual support pact, run by the proliferators and their backers." A new form of arms competition is thus occurring between Islamic-Confucian states and the West. In an old-fashioned arms race, each side developed its own arms to balance or to achieve superiority against the other side. In this new form of arms competition, one side is developing its arms and the other side is attempting not to balance but to limit and prevent that arms build-up while at the same time reducing its own military capabilities.

Implications for the West

This article does not argue that civilization identities will replace all other identities, that nation states will disappear, that each civilization will become a single coherent political entity, that groups within a civilization will not conflict with and even fight each other. This paper does set forth the hypotheses that differences between civilizations are real and important; civilization-consciousness is increasing; conflict between civilizations will supplant ideological and other forms of conflict as the dominant global form of conflict; international relations, historically a game played out within Western civilization, will increasingly be de-Westernized and become a game in which non-Western civilizations are actors and not simply objects; successful political, security and economic international institutions are more likely to develop within civilizations than across civilizations; conflicts between groups in different civilizations will be more frequent, more sustained and more violent than conflicts between groups in the same civilization; violent conflicts between groups in different civilizations are the most likely and most dangerous source of escalation that could lead to global wars; the paramount axis of world politics will be the relations between "the West and the Rest"; the elites in some torn non-Western countries will try to make their countries part of the West, but in most cases face major obstacles to accomplishing this; a central focus of conflict for the immediate future will be between the West and several Islamic-Confucian states.

This is not to advocate the desirability of conflicts between civilizations. It is to set forth descriptive hypotheses as to what the future may be like. If these are plausible hypotheses, however, it is necessary to consider their implications for Western policy. These implications should be divided between short-term advantage and long-term accommodation. In the short term it is clearly in the interest of the West to promote greater cooperation and unity within its own civilization, particularly between its European and North American components; to incorporate into the West societies in Eastern Europe and Latin America whose cultures are close to those of the West; to promote and maintain cooperative relations with Russia and Japan; to prevent escalation of local inter-civilization conflicts into major inter-civilization wars; to limit the expansion of the military strength of Confucian and Islamic states; to moderate the reduction of Western military capabilities and maintain military superiority in East and Southwest Asia; to exploit differences and conflicts among Confucian and Islamic states; to support in other civilizations groups sympathetic to Western values and interests; to strengthen international institutions that reflect and legitimate Western interests and values and to promote the involvement of non-Western states in those institutions.

In the longer term other measures would be called for. Western civilization is both Western and modern. Non-Western civilizations have attempted to become modern without becoming Western. To date only Japan has fully succeeded in this quest. Non-Western civilizations will continue to attempt to acquire the wealth, technology, skills, machines and weapons that are part of being modern. They will also attempt to reconcile this modernity with their traditional culture and values. Their economic and military strength relative to the West will increase. Hence the West will increasingly have to accommodate these non-Western modern civilizations whose power approaches that of the West but whose values and interests differ significantly from those of the West. This will require the West to maintain the economic and military power necessary to protect its interests in relation to these civilizations. It will also, however, require the West to develop a more profound understanding of the basic religious and philosophical assumptions underlying other civilizations and the ways in which people in those civilizations see their interests. It will require an effort to identify elements of commonality between Western and other civilizations. For the relevant future, there will be no universal civilization, but instead a world of different civilizations, each of which will have to learn to coexist with the others.

NOTES

1. Murray Weidenbaum, *Greater China: The Next Economic Superpower?* St. Louis: Washington University Center for the Study of American Business, Contemporary Issues, Series 57, February 1993, pp. 2–3.

2. Almost invariably Western leaders claim they are acting on behalf of "the world community." One minor lapse occurred during the run-up to the Gulf War. In an interview on "Good Morning America," Dec. 21, 1990, British Prime Minister John Major referred to the actions "the West" was taking against Saddam Hussein. He quickly corrected himself and subsequently referred to "the world community." He was, however, right when he erred.

3. Harry C. Triandis, *The New York Times,* Dec. 25, 1990, p. 41, and "Cross-Cultural Studies of Individualism and Collectivism," Nebraska Symposium on Motivation, vol. 37, 1989, pp. 41–133.

4. Kishore Mahbubani, "The West and the Rest," *The National Interest,* Summer 1992, pp. 3–13.

48

Benjamin R. Barber

———◆◆◆———

"Jihad Vs. McWorld" (1992)

Benjamin R. Barber (b. 1939) is Kekst Professor of Civil Society at the University of Maryland, Director, New York office, The Democracy Collaborative, and the author of many books including Strong Democracy *(1984),* Jihad vs. McWorld *(1995),* A Place for Us *(1998),* A Passion For Democracy: American Essays *(1998), and* The Truth of Power: Intellectual Affairs In the Clinton White House *(2001). Barber's work bridges the gaps between political theory and practice. He served as informal adviser to President Bill Clinton and is best-known for his defense of "strong democracy," a participatory politics requiring civic education and responsible citizens. "Jihad Vs. McWorld" outlines the threats to democracy posed by fundamentalism and globalization.*

JUST BEYOND the horizon of current events lie two possible political futures—both bleak, neither democratic. The first is a retribalization of large swaths of humankind by war and bloodshed: a threatened Lebanonization of national states in which culture is pitted against culture, people against people, tribe against tribe—a Jihad in the name of a hundred narrowly conceived faiths against every kind of interdependence, every kind of artificial social cooperation and civic mutuality. The second is being borne in on us by the onrush of economic and ecological forces that demand integration and uniformity and that mesmerize

Benjamin R. Barber, "Jihad Vs. McWorld." Published originally in The *Atlantic Monthly* March 1992 as an introduction to *Jihad vs. McWorld* (Ballatine paperback, 1996), a volume that discusses and extends the themes of the original article.

the world with fast music, fast computers, and fast food—with MTV, Macintosh, and McDonald's, pressing nations into one commercially homogenous global network: one McWorld tied together by technology, ecology, communications, and commerce. The planet is falling precipitantly apart *and* coming reluctantly together at the very same moment.

These two tendencies are sometimes visible in the same countries at the same instant: thus Yugoslavia, clamoring just recently to join the New Europe, is exploding into fragments; India is trying to live up to its reputation as the world's largest integral democracy while powerful new fundamentalist parties like the Hindu nationalist Bharatiya Janata Party, along with nationalist assassins, are imperiling its hard-won unity. States are breaking up or joining up: the Soviet Union has disappeared almost overnight, its parts forming new unions with one another or with like-minded nationalities in neighboring states. The old interwar national state based on territory and political sovereignty looks to be a mere transitional development.

The tendencies of what I am here calling the forces of Jihad and the forces of McWorld operate with equal strength in opposite directions, the one driven by parochial hatreds, the other by universalizing markets, the one re-creating ancient subnational and ethnic borders from within, the other making national borders porous from without. They have one thing in common: neither offers much hope to citizens looking for practical ways to govern themselves democratically. If the global future is to pit Jihad's centrifugal whirlwind against McWorld's centripetal black hole, the outcome is unlikely to be democratic—or so I will argue.

McWorld, or the Globalization of Politics

Four imperatives make up the dynamic of McWorld: a market imperative, a resource imperative, an information-technology imperative, and an ecological imperative. By shrinking the world and diminishing the salience of national borders, these imperatives have in combination achieved a considerable victory over factiousness and particularism, and not least of all over their most virulent traditional form—nationalism. It is the realists who are now Europeans, the utopians who dream nostalgically of a resurgent England or Germany, perhaps even a resurgent Wales or Saxony. Yesterday's wishful cry for one world has yielded to the reality of McWorld.

THE MARKET IMPERATIVE.   Marxist and Leninist theories of imperialism assumed that the quest for ever-expanding markets would in time compel nation-based capitalist economies to push against national boundaries in search of an international economic imperium. Whatever else has happened to the scientistic predictions of Marxism, in this domain they have proved farsighted. All national economies are now vulnerable to the inroads of larger, transnational markets within which trade is free, currencies are convertible, access to banking is open, and contracts are enforceable under law. In Europe, Asia, Africa, the South Pacific, and the Americas such markets are eroding national sovereignty and giving rise to entities—international banks, trade associations, transnational lobbies like OPEC and Greenpeace, world news services like CNN and the BBC, and multinational corporations that increasingly lack a meaningful national identity—that neither reflect nor respect nationhood as an organizing or regulative principle.

The market imperative has also reinforced the quest for international peace and stability, requisites of an efficient international economy. Markets are enemies of parochialism, isolation, fractiousness, war. Market psychology attenuates the psychology of ideological and religious cleavages and assumes a concord among producers and consumers—categories that ill fit narrowly conceived national or religious cultures. Shopping has little tolerance for blue laws, whether dictated by pub-closing British paternalism, Sabbath-observing Jewish Orthodox fundamentalism, or no-Sunday-liquor-sales Massachusetts puritanism. In the context of common markets, international law ceases to be a vision of justice and becomes a workaday framework for getting things done—enforcing contracts, ensuring that governments abide by deals, regulating trade and currency relations, and so forth.

Common markets demand a common language, as well as a common currency, and they produce common behaviors of the kind bred by cosmopolitan city life everywhere. Commercial pilots, computer programmers, international bankers, media specialists, oil riggers, entertainment celebrities, ecology experts, demographers, accountants, professors, athletes—these compose a new breed of men and women for whom religion, culture, and nationality can seem only marginal elements in a working identity. Although sociologists of everyday life will no doubt continue to distinguish a Japanese from an American mode, shopping has a common signature throughout the world. Cynics might even say that some of the recent revolutions in Eastern Europe have had as their true goal not liberty and the right to vote but well-paying jobs and the right to shop (although the vote is proving easier to acquire than consumer goods). The market imperative is, then, plenty powerful; but, notwithstanding some of the claims made for "democratic capitalism," it is not identical with the democratic imperative.

THE RESOURCE IMPERATIVE.   Democrats once dreamed of societies whose political autonomy rested firmly on economic independence. The Athenians idealized what they called autarky, and tried for a while to create a way of life simple and austere enough to make the polis genuinely self-sufficient. To be free meant to be independent of any other community or polis. Not even the Athenians were able to achieve autarky, however: human nature, it turns out, is dependency. By the time of Pericles, Athenian politics was inextricably bound up with a flowering empire held together by naval power and commerce—an empire that, even as it appeared to enhance Athenian might, ate away at Athenian independence and autarky. Master and slave, it turned out, were bound together by mutual insufficiency.

The dream of autarky briefly engrossed nineteenth-century America as well, for the underpopulated, endlessly bountiful land, the cornucopia of natural resources, and the natural barriers of a continent walled in by two great seas led many to believe that America could be a world unto itself. Given this past, it has been harder for Americans than for most to accept the inevitability of inter-dependence. But the rapid depletion of resources even in a country like ours, where they once seemed inexhaustible, and the maldistribution of arable soil and mineral resources on the planet, leave even the wealthiest societies ever more resource-dependent and many other nations in permanently desperate straits.

Every nation, it turns out, needs something another nation has; some nations have almost nothing they need.

THE INFORMATION-TECHNOLOGY IMPERATIVE.   Enlightenment science and the technologies derived from it are inherently universalizing. They entail a quest for descriptive principles of general application, a search for universal solutions to particular problems, and an unswerving embrace of objectivity and impartiality.

Scientific progress embodies and depends on open communication, a common discourse rooted in rationality, collaboration, and an easy and regular flow and exchange of information. Such ideals can be hypocritical covers for power-mongering by elites, and they may be shown to be wanting in many other ways, but they are entailed by the very idea of science and they make science and globalization practical allies.

Business, banking, and commerce all depend on information flow and are facilitated by new communication technologies. The hardware of these technologies tends to be systemic and integrated—computer, television, cable, satellite, laser, fiber-optic, and microchip technologies combining to create a vast interactive communications and information network that can potentially give every person on earth access to every other person, and make every datum, every byte, available to every set of eyes. If the automobile was, as George Ball once said (when he gave his blessing to a Fiat factory in the Soviet Union during the Cold War), "an ideology on four wheels," then electronic telecommunication and information systems are an ideology at 186,000 miles per second—which makes for a very small planet in a very big hurry. Individual cultures speak particular languages;

commerce and science increasingly speak English; the whole world speaks logarithms and binary mathematics.

Moreover, the pursuit of science and technology asks for, even compels, open societies. Satellite footprints do not respect national borders; telephone wires penetrate the most closed societies. With photocopying and then fax machines having infiltrated Soviet universities and *samizdat* literary circles in the eighties, and computer modems having multiplied like rabbits in communism's bureaucratic warrens thereafter, *glasnost* could not be far behind. In their social requisites, secrecy and science are enemies.

The new technology's software is perhaps even more globalizing than its hardware. The information arm of international commerce's sprawling body reaches out and touches distinct nations and parochial cultures, and gives them a common face chiseled in Hollywood, on Madison Avenue, and in Silicon Valley. Throughout the 1980s one of the most-watched television programs in South Africa was *The Cosby Show*. The demise of apartheid was already in production. Exhibitors at the 1991 Cannes film festival expressed growing anxiety over the "homogenization" and "Americanization" of the global film industry when, for the third year running, American films dominated the awards ceremonies. America has dominated the world's popular culture for much longer, and much more decisively. In November of 1991 Switzerland's once insular culture boasted best-seller lists featuring *Terminator 2* as the No. 1 movie, *Scarlett* as the No. 1 book, and Prince's *Diamonds and Pearls* as the No. 1 record album. No wonder the Japanese are buying Hollywood film studios even faster than Americans are buying Japanese television sets. This kind of software supremacy may in the long term be far more important than hardware superiority, because culture has become more potent than armaments. What is the power of the Pentagon compared with Disneyland? Can the Sixth Fleet keep up with CNN? McDonald's in Moscow and Coke in China will do more to create a global culture than military colonization ever could. It is less the goods than the brand names that do the work, for they convey life-style images that alter perception and challenge behavior. They make up the seductive software of McWorld's common (at times much too common) soul.

Yet in all this high-tech commercial world there is nothing that looks particularly democratic. It lends itself to surveillance as well as liberty, to new forms of manipulation and covert control as well as new kinds of participation, to skewed, unjust market outcomes as well as greater productivity. The consumer society and the open society are not quite synonymous. Capitalism and democracy have a relationship, but it is something less than a marriage. An efficient free market after all requires that consumers be free to vote their dollars on competing goods, not that citizens be free to vote their values and beliefs on competing political candidates and programs. The free market flourished in junta-run Chile, in military-governed Taiwan and Korea, and, earlier, in a variety of autocratic European empires as well as their colonial possessions.

The ecological imperative.   The impact of globalization on ecology is a cliché even to world leaders who ignore it. We know well enough that the German forests can be destroyed by Swiss and Italians driving gas-guzzlers fueled by leaded gas. We also know that the planet can be asphyxiated by greenhouse gases because Brazilian farmers want to be part of the twentieth century and are burning down tropical rain forests to clear a little land to plough, and because Indonesians make a living out of converting their lush jungle into toothpicks for fastidious Japanese diners, upsetting the delicate oxygen balance and in effect puncturing our global lungs. Yet this ecological consciousness has meant not only greater awareness but also greater inequality, as modernized nations try to slam the door behind them, saying to developing nations, "The world cannot afford *your* modernization; ours has wrung it dry!"

Each of the four imperatives just cited is transnational, transideological, and transcultural. Each applies impartially to Catholics, Jews, Muslims, Hindus, and Buddhists; to democrats and totalitarians; to capitalists and socialists. The Enlightenment dream of a universal rational society has to a remarkable degree been realized—but in a form that is commercialized, homogenized, depoliticized, bureaucratized, and, of course, radically incomplete, for the movement toward McWorld is in competition with forces of global breakdown, national dissolution, and centrifugal corruption. These forces, working in the opposite direction, are the essence of what I call Jihad.

Jihad, or the Lebanonization of the World

OPEC, the World Bank, the United Nations, the International Red Cross, the multinational corporation . . . there are scores of institutions that reflect globalization. But they often appear as ineffective reactors to the world's real actors: national states and, to an ever greater degree, subnational factions in permanent rebellion against uniformity and integration—even the kind represented by universal law and justice. The headlines feature these players regularly: they are cultures, not countries; parts, not wholes; sects, not religions; rebellious factions and dissenting minorities at war not just with globalism but with the traditional nation-state. Kurds, Basques, Puerto Ricans, Ossetians, East Timoreans, Quebecois, the Catholics of Northern Ireland, Abkhasians, Kurile Islander Japanese, the Zulus of Inkatha, Catalonians, Tamils, and, of course, Palestinians—people without countries, inhabiting nations not their own, seeking smaller worlds within borders that will seal them off from modernity.

A powerful irony is at work here. Nationalism was once a force of integration and unification, a movement aimed at bringing together disparate clans, tribes, and cultural fragments under new, assimilationist flags. But as Ortega y Gasset noted more than sixty years ago, having won its victories, nationalism changed its strategy. In the 1920s, and again today, it is more often a reactionary and divisive force, pulverizing the very nations it once helped cement together. The force that creates nations is "inclusive," Ortega wrote in *The Revolt of the Masses*. "In periods of consolidation, nationalism has a positive value, and is a lofty standard. But in Europe everything is more than consolidated, and nationalism is nothing but a mania. . . ."

This mania has left the post–Cold War world smoldering with hot wars; the international scene is little more unified than it was at the end of the Great War, in Ortega's own time. There were more than thirty wars in progress last year, most of them ethnic, racial, tribal, or religious in character, and the list of unsafe regions doesn't seem to be getting any shorter. Some new world order!

The aim of many of these small-scale wars is to redraw boundaries, to implode states and resecure parochial identities: to escape McWorld's dully insistent imperatives. The mood is that of Jihad: war not as an instrument of policy but as an emblem of identity, an expression of community, an end in itself. Even where there is no shooting war, there is fractiousness, secession, and the quest for ever smaller communities. Add to the list of dangerous countries those at risk: In Switzerland and Spain, Jurassian and Basque separatists still argue the virtues of ancient identities, sometimes in the language of bombs. Hyperdisintegration in the former Soviet Union may well continue unabated—not just a Ukraine independent from the Soviet Union but a Bessarabian Ukraine independent from the Ukrainian republic; not just Russia severed from the defunct union but Tatarstan severed from Russia. Yugoslavia makes even the disunited, ex-Soviet, nonsocialist republics that were once the Soviet Union look integrated, its sectarian fatherlands springing up within factional motherlands like weeds within weeds within weeds. Kurdish independence would threaten the territorial integrity of four Middle Eastern nations. Well before the current cataclysm Soviet Georgia made a claim for autonomy from the Soviet Union, only to be faced with its Ossetians (164,000 in a republic of 5.5 million) demanding their own self-determination within Georgia. The Abkhasian minority in Georgia has followed suit. Even the good will established by Canada's once promising Meech Lake protocols is in danger, with Francophone Quebec again threatening the dissolution of the federation. In South Africa the emergence from apartheid was hardly achieved when friction between Inkatha's Zulus and the African National Congress's tribally identified members threatened to replace Europeans' racism with an indigenous tribal war. After thirty years of attempted integration using the colonial language (English) as a unifier, Nigeria is now playing with the idea of linguistic multiculturalism—which could mean the cultural breakup of the nation into hundreds of tribal fragments. Even Saddam Hussein has benefited from the threat of internal Jihad, having used renewed tribal and religious warfare to turn last season's mortal enemies into reluctant allies of an Iraqi nationhood that he nearly destroyed.

The passing of communism has torn away the thin veneer of internationalism (workers of the world unite!) to reveal ethnic prejudices that are not only ugly and deep-seated but increasingly murderous. Europe's old scourge, anti-Semitism, is back with a vengeance, but it is only one of many antagonisms. It appears all too easy to throw the historical gears into reverse and pass from a Communist dictatorship back into a tribal state.

Among the tribes, religion is also a battlefield. ("Jihad" is a rich word whose generic meaning is "struggle"—usually the struggle of the soul to avert evil. Strictly applied to religious war, it is used only in reference to battles where the faith is under assault, or battles against a government that denies the practice of Islam. My use here is rhetorical, but does follow both journalistic practice and history.) Remember the Thirty Years War? Whatever forms of Enlightenment universalism might once have come to grace such historically related forms of monotheism as Judaism, Christianity, and Islam, in many of their modern incarnations they are parochial rather than cosmopolitan, angry rather than loving, proselytizing rather than ecumenical, zealous rather than rationalist, sectarian rather than deistic, ethnocentric rather than universalizing. As a result, like the new forms of hypernationalism, the new expressions of religious fundamentalism are fractious and pulverizing, never integrating. This is religion as the Crusaders knew it: a battle to the death for souls that if not saved will be forever lost.

The atmospherics of Jihad have resulted in a breakdown of civility in the name of identity, of comity in the name of community. International relations have sometimes taken on the aspect of gang war—cultural turf battles featuring tribal factions that were supposed to be sublimated as integral parts of large national, economic, postcolonial, and constitutional entities.

The Darkening Future of Democracy

These rather melodramatic tableaux vivants do not tell the whole story, however. For all their defects, Jihad and McWorld have their attractions. Yet, to repeat and insist, the attractions are unrelated to democracy. Neither McWorld nor Jihad is remotely democratic in impulse. Neither needs democracy; neither promotes democracy.

McWorld does manage to look pretty seductive in a world obsessed with Jihad. It delivers peace, prosperity, and relative unity—if at the cost of independence, community, and identity (which is generally based on difference). The primary political values required by the global market are order and tranquillity, and freedom—as in the phrases "free trade," "free press," and "free love." Human rights are needed to a degree, but not citizenship or participation—and no more social justice and equality than are necessary to promote efficient economic production and consumption. Multinational corporations sometimes seem to prefer doing business with local oligarchs, inasmuch as they can take confidence from dealing with the boss on all crucial matters. Despots who slaughter their own populations are no problem, so long as they leave markets in place and refrain from making war on their neighbors (Saddam Hussein's fatal mistake). In trading partners, predictability is of more value than justice.

The Eastern European revolutions that seemed to arise out of concern for global democratic values quickly deteriorated into a stampede in the general direction of free markets and their ubiquitous, television-promoted shopping malls. East Germany's Neues Forum, that courageous gathering of intellectuals, students, and workers which overturned the Stalinist regime in Berlin in 1989, lasted only six months in Germany's mini-version of McWorld. Then it gave way to money and markets and monopolies from the West. By the time of the first all-German elections, it could scarcely manage to secure three percent of the vote. Elsewhere there is growing evidence that *glasnost* will go and *perestroika*—defined as privatization and an opening of markets to Western bidders—will stay. So understandably anxious are the new rulers of Eastern Europe and whatever entities are forged from the residues of the Soviet Union to gain access to credit and markets and technology—McWorld's flourishing new currencies—that they have shown themselves willing to trade away democratic prospects in pursuit of them: not just old totalitarian ideologies and command-economy production models but some possible indigenous experiments with a third way between capitalism and socialism, such as economic cooperatives and employee stock-ownership plans, both of which have their ardent supporters in the East.

Jihad delivers a different set of virtues: a vibrant local identity, a sense of community, solidarity among kinsmen, neighbors, and countrymen, narrowly conceived. But it also guarantees parochialism and is grounded in exclusion. Solidarity is secured through war against outsiders. And solidarity often means obedience to a hierarchy in governance, fanaticism in beliefs, and the obliteration of individual selves in the name of the group. Deference to leaders and intolerance toward outsiders (and toward "enemies within") are hallmarks of tribalism—hardly the attitudes required for the cultivation of new democratic women and men capable of governing themselves. Where new democratic experiments have been conducted in retribalizing societies, in both Europe and the Third World, the result has often been anarchy, repression, persecution, and the coming of new, noncommunist forms of very old kinds of despotism. During the past year, Havel's velvet revolution in Czechoslovakia was imperiled by partisans of "Czechland" and of Slovakia as independent entities. India seemed little less rent by Sikh, Hindu, Muslim, and Tamil infighting than it was immediately after the British pulled out, more than forty years ago.

To the extent that either McWorld or Jihad has a *natural* politics, it has turned out to be more of an antipolitics. For McWorld, it is the antipolitics of globalism: bureaucratic, technocratic, and meritocratic, focused (as Marx predicted it would be) on the administration of things—with people, however, among the chief things to be administered. In its politico-economic imperatives McWorld has been guided by laissez-faire market principles that privilege efficiency, productivity, and beneficence at the expense of civic liberty and self-government.

For Jihad, the antipolitics of tribalization has been explicitly antidemocratic: one-party dictatorship, government by military junta, theocratic fundamentalism—often associated with a version of the *Führerprinzip* that empowers an individual to rule on behalf of a people. Even the government of India, struggling for decades to model democracy for a people who will soon number a billion, longs for great leaders; and for every Mahatma Gandhi, Indira Gandhi, or Rajiv Gandhi taken from them by zealous assassins, the Indians appear to seek a replacement who will deliver them from the lengthy travail of their freedom.

The Confederal Option

How can democracy be secured and spread in a world whose primary tendencies are at best indifferent to it (McWorld) and at worst deeply antithetical to it (Jihad)? My guess is that globalization will eventually vanquish retribalization. The ethos of material "civilization" has not yet encountered an obstacle it has been unable to thrust aside. Ortega may have grasped in the 1920s a clue to our own future in the coming millennium.

> Everyone sees the need of a new principle of life. But as always happens in similar crises—some people attempt to save the situation by an artificial intensification of the very principle which has led to decay. This is the meaning of the "nationalist" outburst of recent years. . . . things have always gone that way. The last flare, the longest; the last sigh, the deepest. On the very eve of their disappearance there is an intensification of frontiers—military and economic.

Jihad may be a last deep sigh before the eternal yawn of McWorld. On the other hand, Ortega was not exactly prescient; his prophecy of peace and internationalism came just before blitzkrieg, world war, and the Holocaust tore the old order to bits. Yet democracy is how we remonstrate with reality, the rebuke our aspirations offer to history. And if retribalization is inhospitable to democracy, there is nonetheless a form of democratic government that can accommodate parochialism and communitarianism, one that can even save them from their defects and make them more tolerant and participatory: decentralized participatory democracy. And if McWorld is indifferent to democracy, there is nonetheless a form of democratic government that suits global markets passably well—representative government in its federal or, better still, confederal variation.

With its concern for accountability, the protection of minorities, and the universal rule of law, a confederalized representative system would serve the political needs of McWorld as well as oligarchic bureaucratism or meritocratic elitism is currently doing. As we are already beginning to see, many nations may survive in the long term only as confederations that afford local regions smaller than "nations" extensive jurisdiction. Recommended reading for democrats of the twenty-first century is not the U.S. Constitution or the French Declaration of Rights of Man and Citizen but the Articles of Confederation, that suddenly pertinent document that stitched together the thirteen American colonies into what then seemed a too loose confederation of independent states but now appears a new form of political realism, as veterans of Yeltsin's new Russia and the new Europe created at Maastricht will attest.

By the same token, the participatory and direct form of democracy that engages citizens in civic activity and civic judgment and goes well beyond just voting and accountability—the system I have called "strong democracy"—suits the political needs of decentralized communities as well as theocratic and nationalist party dictatorships have done. Local neighborhoods need not be democratic, but they can be. Real democracy has flourished in diminutive settings: the spirit of liberty, Tocqueville said, is local. Participatory democracy, if not naturally apposite to tribalism, has an undeniable attractiveness under conditions of parochialism.

Democracy in any of these variations will, however, continue to be obstructed by the undemocratic and antidemocratic trends toward uniformitarian globalism and intolerant retribalization which I have portrayed here. For democracy to persist in our brave new McWorld, we will have to commit acts of conscious political will—a possibility, but hardly a probability, under these conditions. Political will requires much more than the quick fix of the transfer of institutions. Like technology transfer, institution transfer rests on foolish assumptions about a uniform world of the kind that once fired the imagination of colonial administrators. Spread English justice to the colonies by exporting wigs. Let an East Indian trading company act as the vanguard to Britain's free parliamentary institutions. Today's well-intentioned quick-fixers in the National Endowment for Democracy and the Kennedy School of Government, in the unions and foundations and universities zealously nurturing contacts in Eastern Europe and the Third World, are hoping to democratize by long distance. Post Bulgaria a parliament by first-class mail. Fed Ex the Bill of Rights to Sri Lanka. Cable Cambodia some common law.

Yet Eastern Europe has already demonstrated that importing free political parties, parliaments, and presses cannot establish a democratic civil society; imposing a free market may even have the opposite effect. Democracy grows from the bottom up and cannot be imposed from the top down. Civil society has to be built from the inside out. The institutional superstructure comes last. Poland may become democratic, but then again it may heed the Pope, and prefer to found its politics on its Catholicism, with uncertain consequences for democracy. Bulgaria may become democratic, but it may prefer tribal war. The former Soviet Union may become a democratic confederation, or it may just grow into an anarchic and weak conglomeration of markets for other nations' goods and services.

Democrats need to seek out indigenous democratic impulses. There is always a desire for self-government, always some expression of participation, accountability, consent, and representation, even in traditional hierarchical societies. These need to be identified, tapped, modified, and incorporated into new democratic practices with an indigenous flavor. The tortoises among the democratizers may ultimately outlive or outpace the hares, for they will have the time and patience to explore conditions along the way, and to adapt their gait to changing circumstances. Tragically, democracy in a hurry often looks something like France in 1794 or China in 1989.

It certainly seems possible that the most attractive democratic ideal in the face of the brutal realities of Jihad and the dull realities of McWorld will be a confederal union of semi-autonomous communities smaller than nation-states, tied together into regional economic associations and markets larger than nation-states—participatory and self-determining in local matters at the bottom, representative and accountable at the top. The nation-state would play a diminished role, and sovereignty would lose some of its political potency. The Green movement adage "Think globally, act locally" would actually come to describe the conduct of politics.

This vision reflects only an ideal, however—one that is not terribly likely to be realized. Freedom, Jean-Jacques Rousseau once wrote, is a food easy to eat but hard to digest. Still, democracy has always played itself out against the odds. And democracy remains both a form of coherence as binding as McWorld and a secular faith potentially as inspiriting as Jihad.

49

Fred R. Dallmayr

"Globalization: Curse or Promise?" (2001)

Fred R. Dallmayr (b. 1929) is Packey Dee Professor at the University of Notre Dame. His work exemplifies the cross-cultural dialogue he espouses, bringing together the insights of contemporary European and non-Western political thought. His recent books—including Beyond Orientalism: Essays on Cross-cultural Encounter *(1996),* Alternative Visions: Paths in the Global Village *(1998), and* Achieving Our World: Toward a Global and Plural Democracy *(2001), which includes this essay—develop the concept of "cosmopolitan democracy" suggested here.*

IN MAY 1996, Czech President Václav Havel delivered a lecture at Harvard University with the title "A Challenge to Nourish Spiritual Roots Buried Under Our Thin Global Skin." In that lecture, Havel pointed to prominent signs of our time, but above all to what he called "an almost banal truth: that we now live in a single global civilization." Although factually, to be sure, humankind has always inhabited a single globe, it is only in our time that this factual cohabitation is coalescing into, or taking the shape of, a common civilization. Among the factors contributing to this development, Havel accentuated the "modern idea of constant progress," the rapid "evolution of science" closely linked with this idea, and finally the so-called information revolution happening before our eyes—a revolution that has enmeshed (and continues to enmesh) our world in "webs of telecommunication networks" that not only transmit information of all kinds at lightning

Source: Fred R. Dallmayr, *Achieving Our World, Toward a Global and Plural Democracy* (New York: Rowman and Littlefield Publishers, 2001).

speed but also convey "integrated models of social, political and economic behavior." As a result of this battery of factors, he observed, our time is in the grip of a triumphant globalism or globalization—a process whereby, "for the first time in the long history of the human race," our planet is transformed in a few short decades into "a single civilization, one that is essentially technological."[1]

Havel's assessment of the signs of our time seems on the mark. Despite a rich welter of diverse, often conflicting, strands and tendencies, our age does indeed seem pervaded by a relentless and near-providential force or momentum, a momentum carrying humankind forward toward a kind of global destiny or cosmopolis. Yet, despite the undeniable strength of this force, globalization is by no means beyond controversy. Although widely acknowledged as a factual occurrence, intense dispute rages over the meaning or significance of globalization as well as its deeper (political and cultural) implications. This chapter attempts to explore or unravel this controversy by proceeding in three steps:

1. The first section looks at the process of globalization as seen and interpreted by prominent Western intellectuals and social scientists. The emphasis here will be mainly on empirical-descriptive accounts, while moral-evaluative criteria are held in abeyance.

2. The second section shifts the focus of attention to evaluative assessments proceeding from a deeper experiential level—especially the experience of people in "developing" societies who have been in large measure the passive targets or victims of Western-style globalization in our century.

3. To conclude, the third part explores the possibility of a new and different kind of globalization—what Richard Falk has called "globalization from below"—as an antidote or counterweight to strategies of global domination.

What Is Globalization?

Given its dramatic effects, globalization could not and did not escape the attention of Western social scientists. As one may recall, it was the communications analyst Marshall McLuhan who first coined the phrase "the global village"— although his comments were limited to somewhat aphoristic impressions. In the meantime, the process supporting McLuhan's phrase has become the target of a vast academic literature seeking to determine its basic causes and characteristic features.[2] Among Western scholars pursuing this line of inquiry, probably the most prominent is the sociologist Roland Robertson, well known for a string of writings devoted to the topic. In articles of 1987, Robertson basically followed McLuhan's intuitive lead by arguing that globalization might best be understood as "the crystallization of the entire world as a single place" or as the emergence of a "global human condition." The more concrete features of this conception were spelled out in greater detail in subsequent writings. In his book *Globalization: Social Theory and Global Culture* (1992), Robertson distinguished between the objective-empirical and the subjective-experiential dimensions of the process. As a concept, he wrote, globalization refers "both to the compression of the world and the intensification of the consciousness of the world as a whole." Amplifying this statement in the light of recent sociological theory, he added that globalization is "best understood as indicating the problem of the form in terms of which the world becomes 'united,' but by no means integrated in a naive functionalist mode." The term hence might be seen as "a conceptual entry to the problem of 'world order' in the most general sense."[3]

In the same book, although acknowledging the recently gathering momentum, Robertson also reflected on the more recessed origins and historical unfolding of globalization. In terms of this broader historical trajectory, the book passed in review various stages of global evolution, extending basically from the (Western) Renaissance to the present time. This evolutionary sketch moved from the rise of the modern European nation-state and the dissemination of European culture (through the vehicle of colonialism) to the formation of the League of Nations and the United Nations in our century, and finally to the Cold War of superpowers and the ensuing post–Cold War period characterized (in Robertson's view) by the rise of "multiculturality and polyethnicity." Given this evolutionary background in Western modernity, Robertson perceptively views globalism or global politics as intimately linked with the issue of "the interpretation of and the response to modernity." In recent times, this linkage has been complicated by a certain intellectual questioning of modernity itself. To this extent, Robertson emphasizes, globalization must be seen as closely related "to modernity and modernization, as well as to postmodernity and 'postmodernization.' " In its acute and presently most relevant sense, the concept appears to him "most clearly applicable to a particular series of relatively recent developments concerning the *concrete structuration of the world as a whole*" (where "structuration" is a term borrowed from the conceptual arsenal of Anthony Giddens).[4]

A slightly different account of the historical trajectory of globalization has been advanced by political economists who view the entire process as basically rooted in the cycles of growth and stagnation of the unfolding capitalist world economy. In this account, globalization—whose roots again are traced to the Renaissance or "Age of Discovery"—is not so much a smoothly continuous growth but rather a process punctuated by upward and downward movements, that is, by periods of expansion and decline or stagnation. Some economic analysts apply to these movements the theory of the "Kondratieff cycles," which are said to last roughly half a century and to be subdivided into roughly equal periods of accelerated and decelerated or shrinking growth. Most political economists place the real "take-off" phase of globalization in the nineteenth century, an era marked by the stability of the gold standard and international high finance and, in Karl Polanyi's famous formulation, by the economically spurring effects of "a hundred years' peace." According to Angus Maddison, globalization in the sense of capitalist expansion prior to World War I was supported and guaranteed by the continuing economic presence of Great Britain as well as the rising economic power of the United States. Although interrupted or decelerated during the interbellum period, the process of globalizing growth resumed after World War II at a rapid pace, ushering in the "golden age of capitalism" (Maddison's phrase) underpinned by the undisputed economic hegemony of the United States. More recently this golden age has not so much come to an end, but been muted or blurred by the end of the Cold War, the rise of new quasihegemonic actors, and the unstable conjunctures of the world economy.[5]

Despite the stronger accent on cycles of growth, most political economists agree with Robertson regarding the linkage between globalization and modernization or the unfolding and dissemination of Western modernity. In fact, this linkage is a widely shared assumption of social scientists across disciplinary boundaries. In the words of international relations specialist Raimo Väyrynen, the dominant interpretation of globalization in the social sciences today is "moored in the theory of modernization," with the result that globalization is viewed basically as "but a part of the larger social movement towards modernity, and, ultimately, reflexive modernization or postmodernity." Among contemporary social theorists, this interpretation is prominently endorsed by Anthony Giddens who views globalization as one of the intrinsic "consequences of modernity," an assessment based on the premise that the gist of modernity consists in the process of distantiation, dislocation, or "disembedding" whereby traditional symbol systems are lifted out of their local contexts and redistributed across new dimensions of time and space. Elaborating on this premise, Giddens defines globalization as "interaction across distance" or as "the intensification of worldwide social relations which link distant localities in such a way that local happenings are shaped by events many miles away and vice versa." This account is not far removed from the argument of James Rosenau, who presents globalization as a "boundary-eroding" process, and especially as a movement jeopardizing the "domestic-foreign frontier." Elements of the same account can also be found in the writings of sociologist Mike Featherstone, who postulates the emergence of something like a global or transnational culture, that is, a synthetic system of symbolic meanings transcending local contexts at least in the field of legal and commercial rules and procedures.[6]

Although innovative and informative in many ways, contemporary social science literature exhibits a notable shortcoming (which, perhaps, is the result of a *"déformation professionnelle"*). Despite a wealth of empirical data and explanatory schemes, contemporary studies of globalization—with some exceptions—tend to be marked by a kind of bland descriptivism, that is, by a tendency to observe and meticulously analyze empirical occurrences while studiously endeavoring to remain ethically neutral and politically disengaged. Yet, in this particular field of inquiry, the option of neutral disengagement appears to be unavailable—except at the price of naiveté or complicity. As most observes will agree, globalization is not simply an accident or fortuitous happening. Although fueled by a powerful momentum, its trajectory is neither automatic nor akin to a natural *force majeure:* overtly or covertly, its movement is backed up by hegemonic political stratagems as well as by intellectual preferences of a distinct cultural provenance. Here again, most social scientists will not simply ignore such strategies or preferences, but report them in a seemingly matter-of-fact way. An instructive case in point is the work of Lucian Pye, a spokesman of mainstream American political science and an expert on "development" (an earlier stand-in for globalization). Writing in 1966, in his book *Aspects of Political Development,* Pye noted, without further commentary, that the process of development or modernization

> might also be called Westernization, or simply advancement and progress; it might, however, be more accurately termed the diffusion of a world culture— a world culture based on advanced technology and the spirit of science, on a rational view of life, a secular approach to social relations. . . . At an accelerating rate, the direction and the volume of cross-cultural influences has become nearly a uniform pattern of the Western industrial world imposing its practices, standards, techniques, and values upon the non-Western world.[7]

Judged by the usual canons of academic neutrality (or circumlocution), Pye's comments are surprisingly candid and revealing—notwithstanding his failure to elaborate on their implications. It would be quite misleading and unfair, of course, to suggest that Western social scientists have been uniformly bland or noncommittal on the globalization issue. Both during the Cold War and in more recent years, a number of social analysts and intellectuals in the United States have been troubled by and openly critical of the asymmetry of global relations and the reality of Western hegemony in the postcolonial world. An important example is Immanuel Wallerstein, whose "world-system theory" has for several decades exposed and critiqued the inequities besetting global economic and cultural relations.[8] The persistence of Western hegemony in the postcolonial era is also the central theme of Edward Said's *Culture and Imperialism,* published in the aftermath of the Cold War. As Said observes in that study, imperialism did not become a thing of the past with the dismantling of the "classical [European] empires"; on the contrary, the emergence of the United States as the last superpower suggests "that a new set of force lines will structure the world." Traditional empires have always been characterized by a "twinning of power and legitimacy," that is, the juncture of domination in the political and cultural spheres. This juncture, Said notes, has not changed in our time. What is different in the "American century" is the "quantum leap in the reach of cultural authority," due in large measure to "the unprecedented growth in the apparatus for the diffusion and control of information." He adds, "Rarely before in human history has there been so massive an intervention of force and ideas from one culture to another as there is today from America to the rest of the world."[9]

As it happens, postcolonial hegemony is not only the topic of intellectuals critical of Western domination but also—more surprisingly—of U.S. policy analysts and strategic global theorists like Samuel Huntington. Huntington's work is often cited and attacked for his provocative thesis of an impending "clash of civilizations," first formulated in essay-form in 1993—a thesis that transfers the traditional rivalry or enmity between states into the arena of cross-cultural relations. Although dubious in many respects, passages in his work can also be invoked as providing a candid exposé of strategic realities in the "American century." Here are a few lines from his famous essay of 1993, titled "The Clash of Civilizations?"—lines that hardly require elaborate commentary:

> The West is now at an extraordinary peak of power in relation to other civilizations. Its superpower opponent has disappeared from the map. . . . It dominates international political and security institutions and with Japan international economic institutions. Global political and security issues are effectively settled by a directorate of the United States, Britain and France, world economic issues by a directorate of the United States, Germany and Japan, all of which maintain extraordinarily close relations with each other to the exclusion of lesser and largely non-Western countries. Decisions made at the U.N. Security Council or in the International Monetary Fund that reflect the interests of the West are presented to the world as reflecting the desires of the world community. The very phrase "the world community" has become the euphemistic collective noun (replacing "the Free World") to give global legitimacy to actions reflecting the interests of the United States and other Western powers.[10]

Given his indisputable expertise and academic prestige, Huntington's observations carry considerable evidential weight; they can surely not be dismissed as the ramblings of a marginalized dissenter.

Divergent Assessments

In its overall effects, globalization or the emergence of a "one-world" scenario is a gripping historical drama saturated with promises and risks. Moral as well as practical-political assessments of this drama vary greatly—depending in large measure on the observer's respective position or location in the globalizing process. In the eyes of many—though surely not all—Western observers, globalization is almost entirely synonymous with progress or civilizational advance. The spreading of industry, science, and technology, coupled with the expanding reach of media and market forces, tends to be greeted as a glorious panacea, perhaps even as the dawn of a worldwide "enlightenment" liberating people everywhere from the shackles of ignorance, oppression, and economic backwardness. It is hard to deny a certain kernel of truth in this acclaim of liberal modernity, especially when the accent is placed on such features as democratization and the dissemination of human rights. Although hardly an uncritical modernizer, Václav Havel finds it important to acknowledge the positive or life-enhancing and enriching aspects of globalization. In his assessment, the global networks and "capillaries" that are integrating humankind also "convey information about certain modes of human coexistence that have proven their worth, like democracy, respect for human rights, the rule of law, the laws of the marketplace." These features of liberal modernity, he notes, give people "not only the capacity for worldwide communication, but also a coordinated means of defending themselves against many common dangers," thus making "life on this earth easier" and open to "hitherto unexplored horizons."[11]

Havel's nuanced assessment stands in stark contrast with a fashionable kind of liberal euphoria or triumphalism that, disdainful of subtleties, erects Western modernity into an ideological blueprint. In the eyes of some Western observers, the collapse of the Soviet Union and of East European Communism has ushered in the prospect of a near-eschatological dénouement: the prospect of the culmination and perhaps even "end" of history (in the sense of the resolution of historical antagonisms). While political theorists and intellectuals find evidence for this prospect in the spreading of individual rights and freedoms, neoliberal economists focus their attention on the unleashing of capitalist production and initiative. A brief glance at neoliberal literature corroborates this focus. Thus Kenichi Ohmae celebrates in his writings the emergence of a "borderless world"—more specifically of a borderless world economy transcending and even erasing traditional political boundaries. In Ohmae's view, the true engines of globalization today are giant businesses and transnational corporations that increasingly dictate the pace of economic production and trade; under the impact of these steamrolling engines, traditional nation-states as well as local forms of management and production are progressively dwarfed and swept aside. In a similar vein, Lowell Bryan and Diana Farrell speak explicitly of the "unleashing" of global capitalism where market forces are finally "unbound." In their account, economic globalization is closely linked with cultural transformation, in the sense that global capital-

ism is paralleled and undergirded by the rise of transnational media and communications networks effectively bent on standardizing global consumer tastes.[12]

Needless to say, (neo)liberal euphoria has not gone unchallenged or unop-
posed; given the deep traumas and agonies afflicting the contemporary global
scene, heady celebrations of capitalism "unbound" are empirically dubious as
well as morally and politically inappropriate and offensive. The dubious and lop-
sided character of economic triumphalism has been exposed by numerous political economists and other global experts. Thus, pointing to the convergence or
complicity of market practices with political and military forms of hegemony,
economists Andrew Hurrell and Ngaire Woods have critiqued the persistent and
even deepening strains of "inequality" fostered, as well as covered up, by the
process of globalization. Likewise, using in part Foucauldian language, Stephen
Gill speaks of a "disciplinary neoliberalism," meaning by that phrase a grand ideology seeking to legitimate the unchecked sway of transnational capital around
the world. Pushing the critical edge of his analysis, Gill perceives this ideology
also as the engine of global cultural streamlining and adaptation, that is, as the
harbinger of a "market civilization" coercively instilling habits of consumerism,
political apathy, and dependence (especially in nonhegemonic societies). Although
attempting to steer a middle course, Raimo Väyrynen's study on *Global Transformation* is equally explicit about global disparities. In his view, economic globalization has a "dual character" in terms of its consequences; while mobilizing new
resources, opening up new markets, and fueling economic growth, its pursuit
also diminishes the "social and political control of capital," thereby increasing
"inequalities" both within and between societies and thus contributing to "social
marginalization within nations and economic gaps between them." Relying on a
large set of economic indicators, Väyrynen draws this conclusion:

> The present world is characterized by the growing polarization between rich
> and poor countries. Empirical evidence on the world income distribution by
> countries shows that it is becoming increasingly bimodal or "twin-peaked." . . .
> In other words, the international middle class has been shrinking at the expense
> of the upper class or, alternatively, the upper class has disappeared and all well-
> off countries belong to the middle class.[13]

This emergence of an international class structure—the division between
middle-class and underclass societies—is paralleled and intensified by a cultural
divide: that between hegemonic and nonhegemonic cultural frameworks and traditions. While the former are largely compatible and aligned with globalization,
the latter undergo a process of dislocation and marginalization—an experience
that is prone to lead to resentment and perhaps countercultural resistance. In his
address at Harvard, Havel clearly perceived this cultural division or asymmetry

(though without in any way endorsing Huntington's scenario). As he noted at the time, the much belabored rise of the "global village" actually harbors an internal fissure, in the sense that so-called global civilization is today no more than "a thin veneer over the sum total of human awareness, if I may put it that way." To a considerable extent, this veneer or "single epidermis" of globalism is deceptive, because it "merely covers or conceals the immense variety of cultures, of peoples, of religious worlds, of historical traditions and historically formed attitudes, all of which, in a sense, lie 'beneath' it." Havel speaks in this context of the "underside of humanity" overshadowed by globalization, a "hidden dimension" of humankind that "demands more and more clearly to be heard and to be granted a right to life." Seen in this light, our age appears inhabited by a dual and even "contradictory" process. In the same measure as the world at large increasingly accepts the "new habits" of globalism, a countermovement or resurgence of localism is occurring: "Ancient traditions are reviving, different religions and cultures are awakening to new ways of being, seeking new room to exist, and struggling with growing fervor to realize what is unique to them and what makes them different from others."[14]

Assessments of this cultural (or countercultural) revival vary, depending again in large measure on the observer's location. From the vantage of many Western "development" experts and policy analysts, local or indigenous cultural traditions appear mainly as roadblocks or obstacles hampering the path of modernization and global progress. In his 1993 essay, Huntington offered a culture-dependent gradation of obstacles to globalism. As he pointed out, "the obstacles to non-Western countries joining the West vary considerably"; they are "least for Latin American and East European countries," somewhat "greater for the Orthodox countries of the former Soviet Union" and "still greater for Muslim, Confucian, Hindu and Buddhist societies."[15] More philosophically trained Western observers are prone to detect in cultural revival a theoretical (perhaps even metaphysical) problem: the danger of the upsurge of cultural "relativism" in opposition to the yardsticks of global "universalism" (embodied in science and progress). Inhabitants of non-Western or nonhegemonic societies are less likely to share this view; for most of them, globalization is not so much a theoretical as a social, economic, and existential problem, accompanied often by marginalization, economic misery, and social and cultural alienation. This does not necessarily mean a wholesale opposition to Western modernity. Open- and fair-minded intellectuals in non-Western countries will often be ready to grant the benefits of modernization. The fact that the latter *can* generate a new dynamism in traditional societies, which, in turn, may release untapped social energies, especially among previously silenced or oppressed strata. Yet, as long as they have not yet completely "joined" or been assimilated into the West, the same intellectuals cannot fail to be attentive to prevailing political and economic disparities in the global arena. They can hardly forget that, in large measure, the benefits of globalizing modernity have come—and continue to come—to non-Western societies through the vehicle of colonialism or else postcolonial forms of Western hegemony. To this extent and from that angle, globalization is liable to be experienced as a mode of foreign intervention and manipulation, that is, as a "globalization from above" promoted (in subtle and not-so-subtle ways) by colonial and neocolonial masters.

Sometimes, under circumstances of extreme provocation, reaction to Western globalism or universalism may take the form of a radical self-enclosure or self-encapsulation, a retreat into an indigenous life-form coupled with a complete rejection of foreign (especially Western) influence. In such situations, leaders of indigenous movements may brand Western globalism as a curse, perhaps even as a Satanic plot designed to undermine or destroy cultural autonomy, including traditional religious beliefs and practices. This, in a nutshell, is what one means today by such terms as *fundamentalism* or *communalism,* especially their militant and xenophobic varieties.[16] Given their often destructive or devastating effects—sometimes culminating in "ethnic cleansing"—no one can be indifferent to the grave dangers signaled by these terms. To be sure, condemnation of these movements comes easily from the lips of neoliberal globalizers, especially those unperturbed by the implications of Western (economic, technological, and military) hegemony. However, global ideologues are not, and should not be, the only critics of a reactionary fundamentalism. More compelling and persuasive in this domain are critical voices otherwise friendly or sympathetic to nonhegemonic peoples. One of these voices is again that of Edward Said, hardly suspect of neoliberal euphoria. In his *Culture and Imperialism,* Said has eloquently castigated contemporary tendencies toward self-enclosure:

> All those nationalist appeals to pure or authentic Islam, or to Afrocentrism, *négritude,* or Arabism had a strong response, without sufficient consciousness that those ethnicities and spiritual essences would come back to exact a very high prize [*sic*] from their successful adherents. [Frantz] Fanon was one of the few to remark on the dangers posed to a great sociopolitical movement like decolonization by an untutored national consciousness. Much the same could be said about the dangers of an untutored religious consciousness. . . . National security and a separatist identity are the watchwords.[17]

Whither Globalization? A Promising Path

While it is relatively easy—though no less necessary—to criticize reactionary or fundamentalist movements, it is much more difficult to chart a course able to avoid the pitfalls of both nativist localism or separatism and neocolonial hegemony or domination. The perils of the former are readily apparent to globalizers—who prefer to turn a blind eye to the second danger. The reverse situation obtains in the case of the marginalized or oppressed. Yet, the drawbacks of self-enclosure should be evident even to its fervent devotees. For one thing, retreatism is clearly only a reactive or negative mode of behavior, with stifling effects even on what it seeks to affirm. Moreover, even if stubbornly pursued, fundamentalist retreat can hardly fully succeed in our time—given that it is only the flip-side of, and hence largely parasitic on, what it rejects. As Havel observed, many groups or movements today are struggling against modern Western civilization and its pro-ponents by "using weapons provided by the very civilization they oppose"; thus, they sometimes employ "radar, computers, lasers, nerve gases, and perhaps, in the future, even nuclear weapons—all products of the world they challenge—to help defend their ancient heritage." Apart from noting internal contradictions, these comments also point to the most ominous and perilous corollaries of self-enclosure: the bent toward destruction in the form of both domestic violence and external aggression.[18]

So, how can one find another way, an alternative global path leading between and beyond culture clashes and global domination? A shorthand formula for this path might be "grassroots globalization" or (with Richard Falk) "globalization from below," meaning the attempt to forge or build up the global city through the interaction of cultures and peoples around the world. In many ways, this seems to be the only fruitful and promising path today, that is, a path preserving the promise contained in the movement of globalization. Here again, Havel can serve as an insightful mentor. In terms of his address, world civilization should not blithely be equated with European or Western civilization, which in any case forms only a thin veneer or epidermis covering the globe. The real challenge fac-ing humankind today, he stated, is to "start understanding itself as a multicul-tural and multipolar civilization," as a complex and densely textured fabric whose meaning lies "not in undermining the individuality of different spheres of culture and civilization but in allowing them to be more completely themselves." What this understanding brings into view is a global city bent neither on inter-necine warfare nor on uniformity or unilateral domination. In Havel's words, the global city

> must be an expression of the authentic will of everyone, growing out of the genuine spiritual roots hidden beneath the skin of our common, global civi-lization. If it is merely disseminated through the capillaries of this skin, the way Coca-Cola ads are—as a commodity offered by some to others—such a code can hardly be expected to take hold in any profound or universal way.[19]

Once universalism is seen no longer as a hegemonic tool nor as a target of abuse, it becomes clear that the path to the global city can proceed only from the ground up, that is, through the labor of cross-cultural interaction, critical engagement, and reciprocal learning. This travail necessarily has to start from local traditions and historically sedimented practices and beliefs; by moving from this core and opening themselves up to cross-cultural interrogation and testing, local traditions are likely to shed their dogmatic crust and become available again as rich resources of human and social transformation. As it happens, there are grassroots movements today operating across boundaries and pointing in the direction of a global civil society: movements such as interfaith alliances, ecological and feminist networks, and intersocietal labor coalitions. These movements are corroborated by developments in contemporary philosophy and literature. While traditional Western philosophy has tended to posture as blandly universal or absolute, recent philosophical initiatives have contributed to a fuller appreciation of the role of interhuman and cross-cultural dialogue. Most prominent among contemporary writings in this domain are the works of Hans-Georg Gadamer, Raimundo Panikkar, Mikhail Bakhtin, and Tzvetan Todorov. As is well known, Gadamer has portrayed both textual reading and intersubjective encounter as forms of dialogical exchange where initial assumptions first serve as launching pads of questioning, only to be called into question in turn by the demands of the encounter.[20] In the writings of Panikkar, what is particularly intriguing is the notion of an "imparative philosophy" (from Latin *imparare*, to learn) seen as a philosophy dedicated to learning through dialogue. What Panikkar has in mind is not simply a "comparative" approach or procedure—if the latter denotes the collection of comparative data by a neutral observer or spectator. This view closely resonates with the perspective of Todorov, who often draws on insights garnered from Bakhtin. In his epilogue to *The Conquest of America* (recounting one of the cruelest episodes of genocide), Todorov discloses his own normative stance or commitment—a commitment to "communication" or "dialogue," specifically a "dialogue of (or between) cultures." As he writes, somewhat hopefully, it is this dialogue of cultures that "characterizes our age" and that is "incarnated by ethnology, at once the child of colonialism and the proof of its death throes."[21]

As one should realize, however, the path of dialogue and "globalization from below" is charted not only by academic philosophers and scholars; it is also the course recommended by all or most of the great world religions and cultural traditions around the globe. This aspect can readily be documented. As Muslims surely will acknowledge, Islam cannot be tied to a particular country or locality but is linked with the *"umma"*—which is potentially global in character. This nonlocal character of Islam is repeatedly stressed in the Qur'an, including the first surah where God is called *"rabbi alamin,"* which means lord and sustainer of the entire universe. In a similar way, Buddhists and Confucians cannot limit their concerns to a narrow region or ethnic nationality without forfeiting the depth dimension of their beliefs—just as little as Christians can afford to remain ethno- or Eurocentric. Devoid of empirical identity, the notion of buddhahood resists any attempt at parochial or status-related fixation. Although taking its bearings from circumscribed "relationships," Confucianism ruptures or transcends confining boundaries through its emphasis on *"ren"* (humaneness) which is not regionally nor ethnically specific. Even Hinduism—which seems so closely rooted in the Indian soil—confounds and transgresses national borders in many ways, especially through its core notion of *"brahman,"* which (as articulated by Advaita Vedanta) links or integrates human beings everywhere with the divine. To this extent, Havel seems to be on firm ground when he speaks of an "archetypal spirituality" pervading humankind (even beyond the limits of organized faiths), adding that "lying dormant in the deepest roots of most, if not all, cultures" there is a common bond that is not so much jeopardized by, but rather "anchored in the great diversity of human traditions."[22]

To be sure, great care must be taken in this domain to avoid every kind of triumphalism, that is, to screen "globalization from below" from the temptation of global hegemony and imperialism. One way to guard against this temptation is to distinguish between globalization and a doctrinaire globalism treating the global village as a *fait accompli*. From the vantage of grassroots globalization, universality and global unity can only be seen as a pledge or promise, not as anyone's privilege or secure possession. Although it is important to affirm and not to relinquish universal hopes, prudence dictates attention to critical questions like these: Who or which human agency genuinely embodies universalism, or who can legitimately speak "in the name of" the universal (that is, Who is universal)?[23] For the sake of their own integrity, world religions (and cultural traditions) might do well to be mindful of these questions, and thus avoid the confusion of *umma* or catholicity with global-imperial ambitions. In sacred scripture, Christians (for example) are exhorted to spread the "good news" around the world— but that news is one of grace and charity and not of empire. This distinction clearly requires that one also differentiates between teaching and hegemonically sanctioned conversion. In this context, members of all faiths—especially missionaries— might usefully recall a passage in the Qur'an that states "No coercion in matters of faith" (*la ikhra fid-din*), a saying not too far from the Buddhist principle of nonviolence and the Confucian emphasis on humaneness. A saying of the prophet Muhammad is worth remembering here. As reported by Ibn Majah: "A man once asked the Prophet if bigotry is to love one's tribe. 'No,' replied the Prophet. 'Bigotry is to help your tribe to tyrannize others.'"[24] This *hadith*, in my view, can serve as the motto of intercivilizational dialogue today, illustrating the meaning of "globalization from below."

NOTES

1. Havel's address was presented at Harvard at a convocation during which he received an honorary doctoral degree. The text is cited from *Just Commentary*, no. 28 (July 1996): 1.

2. See Marshall McLuhan, *The Gutenberg Galaxy: The Making of Typographic Man* (Toronto: University of Toronto Press, 1962); also his *The Global Village: Transformation in World Life and Media in the 21st Century* (New York: Oxford University Press, 1989). According to Jan Aart Scholte, globalization has in recent decades become a "buzzword, a term as ambiguous as it is popular." See Scholte, "Beyond the Buzzword: Toward a Critical Theory of Globalization," in *Globalization: Theory and Practice*, ed. Eleonore Kofman and Gillian Youngs (London: Pinter, 1996), 44–45.

3. Roland Robertson, *Globalization: Social Theory and Global Culture* (Newbury Park, Calif.: Sage, 1992), 8, 51. See also Robertson, "Globalization and Societal Modernization: A Note on Japan and Japanese Religion," *Sociological Analysis* 47 (1987): 38; "Globalization Theory and Civilization Analysis," *Comparative Civilizations Review* 17 (1987): 23; also Marshall McLuhan, *Explorations in Communication*, ed. E. S. Carpenter (Boston: Beacon Press, 1960).

4. Robertson, *Globalization*, 8, 50, 53, 105. See also Anthony Giddens, *The Constitution of Society: Outline of the Theory of Structuration* (Berkeley: University of California Press, 1984).

5. Angus Maddison, *Phases of Capitalist Development* (Oxford: Oxford University Press, 1982), 85–95, 248–53. See also Karl Polanyi, *The Great Transformation: The Political and Economic Origins of Our Time* (Boston: Beacon Press, 1957); and Raimo Väyrynen, "Economic Cycles, Power Transitions, Political Management and Wars between Major Powers," *International Studies Quarterly* 27 (1983): 389–418.

6. See Väyrynen, *Global Transformation: Economics, Politics, and Culture* (Helsinki: Sitra, 1997), 32; Giddens, *The Consequences of Modernity* (Stanford, Calif.: Stanford University Press, 1990), 21–29, 64; James N. Rosenau, *Along the Domestic/Foreign Frontier: Exploring Governance in a Turbulent World* (Cambridge: Cambridge University Press, 1997), 81–82; Mike Featherstone, "Localism, Globalism, and Cultural Identity," in *Global/Local: Cultural Production and the Transnational Imaginary*, ed. Rob Wilson and Wimal Dissanayake (Durham, N.C.: Duke University Press, 1996), 60–65. Compare also Featherstone, ed., *Global Culture: Nationalism, Globalization and Modernity* (Newbury Park, Calif.: Sage, 1990), and Featherstone, *Undoing Culture: Globalization, Postmodernism and Identity* (Newbury Park, Calif.: Sage, 1995).

7. Lucian Pye, *Aspects of Political Development* (Boston: Little, Brown, 1966), 44–45.

8. See Immanuel Wallerstein, *The Modern World-System*, 2 vols. (New York: Academic Press, 1974); *The Capitalist World-Economy* (Cambridge: Cambridge University Press, 1979); and *Geopolitics and Geoculture: Essays on the Changing World-System* (Cambridge: Cambridge University Press, 1991).

9. Edward W. Said, *Culture and Imperialism* (New York: Knopf, 1993), 282, 291, 319.

10. Samuel Huntington, "The Clash of Civilizations?" *Foreign Affairs* 72 (Summer 1993): 39. In the meantime, Huntington has fleshed out and greatly expanded his argument in book form (whose title omits the question mark of the earlier essay). See *The Clash of Civilizations and the Remaking of World Order* (New York: Simon & Schuster, 1996).

11. Havel, "A Challenge," *Just Commentary*, 1–2.

12. See Kenichi Ohmae, *The Borderless World: Power and Strategy in the Interlinked Economy* (New York: Harper, 1990); Lowell Bryan and Diana Farrell, *Market Unbound: Unleashing Global*

Capitalism (New York: John Wiley, 1996). Compare also John H. Dunning, *The Globalization of Business: The Challenge of the 1990s* (London: Routledge, 1993); Saskia Sassen, "The Spatial Organization of Information Industries: Implications for the Role of the State," in *Globalization: Critical Reflections*, ed. James Mittelman (Boulder, Colo.: Lynne Rienner, 1996), 33–52; and Chris Farrand, "The Globalization of Knowledge and the Politics of Global Intellectual Property: Power, Governance and Technology," in *Globalization: Theory and Practice*, ed. Eleonore Kofman and Gillian Youngs (London: Pinter, 1996), 175–87. The eschatological reference is to Francis Fukuyama, *The End of History and the Last Man* (New York: Free Press, 1992).

13. Väyrynen, *Global Transformation*, 3, 15. See also Saskia Sassen, *Globalization and Its Discontents* (New York: New Press, 1999); Richard Falk, *Predatory Globalization: A Critique* (Cambridge, UK: Polity Press, 1999); Andrew Hurrell and Ngaire Woods, "Globalization and Inequality," *Millennium* 24 (1995): 447–70; Stephen Gill, "Globalization, Market Civilization, and Disciplinary Neoliberalism," *Millennium* 24 (1995): 399–442; further David Loy, "The Religion of the Market," *Just Commentary*, no. 30 (August 1996): 1–10. (I am indebted to Väyrynen for alerting me to some of these texts).

14. Havel, "A Challenge," *Just Commentary*, 2.

15. Huntington, "The Clash of Civilizations?" *Foreign Affairs*, 45. As an astute policy analyst, Huntington quickly added that countries that for some reason "do not wish to, or cannot join the West compete with the West by developing their own economic, military and political power" and "by cooperating with other non-Western countries." The most ominous cooperation, in Huntington's view, is the "Confucian–Islamic connection."

16. In their book titled *Fundamentalism Observed*, Martin Marty and R. Scott Appleby state that "religious fundamentalism has appeared as a tendency, a habit of mind, found within religious communities and paradigmatically embodied in certain representative individuals and movements, which manifests itself as a strategy or set of strategies by which beleaguered believers attempt to preserve their distinct identity as a people or group. Feeling this identity to be at risk in the contemporary era, they fortify it by a selective retrieval of doctrines, beliefs and practices from a sacred past." See *Fundamentalism Observed* (Chicago: University of Chicago Press, 1990), 8. Compare also Abdel Salam Sidahmed and Anoushiravan Ehteshami, eds., *Islamic Fundamentalism* (Boulder, Colo.: Westview Press, 1996).

17. Said, *Culture and Imperialism*, 307.

18. Havel, "A Challenge," *Just Commentary*, 2. In fairness one should grant that not all forms of self-enclosure are violence-prone; counter-examples would be Amish and Mennonite communities.

19. Havel, "A Challenge," *Just Commentary*, 2. For the notion of "globalization from below" see Richard Falk, "The World Order between Inter-State Law and the Law of Humanity: The Role of Civil Society Institutions," in *Cosmopolitan Democracy: An Agenda for a New World Order*, ed. Daniele Archibugi and David Held (Cambridge, UK: Polity Press, 1995), 163–79; and "Cultural Foundations for the International Protection of Human Rights," *Human Rights in Cross-Cultural Perspectives: A Quest for Consensus*, ed. Abdullahi Ahmed An-Na'im (Philadelphia: University of Pennsylvania Press, 1992), 44–64.

20. See Hans-Georg Gadamer, *Truth and Method*, 2nd ed., trans. Joel Weinsheimer and Donald G. Marshall (New York: Crossroad, 1989); and *Dialogue and Dialectic*, trans. P. Christopher Smith (New Haven: Yale University Press, 1980). Relying in part on Gadamer's writings I have articulated a perspective termed *differential hermeneutics* or *hermeneutics of difference*, applicable

especially to cross-cultural encounters. See my *Beyond Orientalism: Essays on Cross-Cultural Encounter* (Albany, N.Y.: State University of New York Press, 1996), 39–62.

21. See Tzvetan Todorov, *The Conquest of America: The Question of the Other,* trans. Richard Howard (New York: Harper & Row, 1984), 250; Mikhail M. Bakhtin, *The Dialogical Imagination,* ed. Michael Holquist (Austin: University of Texas Press, 1981); Raimundo Panikkar, "What Is Comparative Philosophy Comparing?" in *Interpreting Across Cultures: New Essays in Comparative Philosophy,* ed. Gerald J. Larson and Eliot Deutsch (Princeton: Princeton University Press, 1988), 116–36. Compare also my "Toward a Comparative Political Theory," in *Border Crossings: Toward a Comparative Political Theory,* ed. Dallmayr (Lanham, Md.: Lexington Books, 1999), 1–10.

22. Havel, "A Challenge," 3. Regarding the universalizing tendency in Confucianism see "'The 'Moral Universal' from the Perspectives of East Asian Thought," in *Confucian Thought: Selfhood as Creative Transformation,* ed. Tu Weiming (Albany, N.Y.: State University of New York Press, 1985), 19–34. Compare also Lionel M. Jensen, *Manufacturing Confucianism: Chinese Traditions and Universal Civilization* (Durham, N.C.: Duke University Press, 1997).

23. In this connection, one would do well to remember the words of Michel Foucault: "Nothing is more inconsistent than a political regime that is indifferent to truth; but nothing is more dangerous than a political system that claims to lay down the truth. The function of 'telling the truth' must not take the form of law, just as it would be pointless to believe that it resides by right in the spontaneous interplay of communication. The task of telling the truth is an endless labor: to respect it in all its complexity is an obligation which no power can do without—except by imposing the silence of slavery." See Lawrence D. Kritzman, ed., *Michel Foucault: Politics, Philosophy, Culture; Interviews and Other Writings 1977–1984* (New York: Routledge, 1988), 267.

24. See *Words of the Prophet Muhammad: Selections from the Hadith,* compiled by Maulana Wahiduddin Khan (New Delhi: Al-Risala Books, 1996), 95.

CREDITS